Enemies Near and Far

Columbia Studies in Terrorism and Irregular Warfare

Columbia Studies in Terrorism and Irregular Warfare

BRUCE HOFFMAN, SERIES EDITOR

This series seeks to fill a conspicuous gap in the burgeoning literature on terrorism, guerrilla warfare, and insurgency. The series adheres to the highest standards of scholarship and discourse and publishes books that elucidate the strategy, operations, means, motivations, and effects posed by terrorist, guerrilla, and insurgent organizations and movements. It thereby provides a solid and increasingly expanding foundation of knowledge on these subjects for students, established scholars, and informed reading audiences alike.

For a complete list of books in this series, see page 505.

Enemies Near and Far

How Jihadist Groups
Strategize, Plot, and Learn

DAVEED GARTENSTEIN-ROSS
AND THOMAS JOSCELYN

Columbia
University
Press

New York

Columbia University Press
Publishers Since 1893
New York   Chichester, West Sussex
cup.columbia.edu

Library of Congress Cataloging-in-Publication Data
Names: Gartenstein-Ross, Daveed, 1976– author. | Joscelyn, Thomas,
    1976- author.
Title: Enemies near and far : how Jihadist groups strategize, plot, and learn /
    Daveed Gartenstein-Ross and Thomas Joscelyn.
Description: New York : Columbia University Press, [2021] | Series:
    Columbia studies in terrorism and irregular warfare | Includes
    bibliographical references and index.
Identifiers: LCCN 2021027099 (print) | LCCN 2021027100 (ebook) |
    ISBN 9780231195256 (trade paperback) | ISBN 9780231195249 (hardback) |
    ISBN 9780231551267 (ebook)
Subjects: LCSH: Terrorism—Middle East—History—21st century. |
    Organizational learning—Middle East—History—21st century. |
    Qaida (Organization)—History—21st century. | IS (Organization)—
    History—21st century. | Jihad—History—21st century. | Insurgency—
    Religious aspects—Islam.
Classification: LCC HV6433.M5 G38 2021 (print) | LCC HV6433.M5 (ebook) |
    DDC 363.3250956—dc23
LC record available at https://lccn.loc.gov/2021027099
LC ebook record available at https://lccn.loc.gov/2021027100

Columbia University Press books are printed on permanent and durable
acid-free paper.
Printed in the United States of America

Cover design: Lisa Hamm

Contents

1 The Fire Next Time 1

2 Learning to Win 16

3 The Far-Enemy Strategy 41

4 The Unfriendly Skies: Plots Against Aviation 70

5 The Early Adopter: Anwar al-Awlaki in the Digital Space 107

6 Strategic Learning: Al-Qaeda and Jihadism in the Arab Spring 165

7 The Islamic State's Rise and Rule 217

8 The *Fitna*: ISIS Versus al-Qaeda 255

9 How al-Qaeda Survived the War in Afghanistan 314

10 ISIS's External Operations: A Study in Innovation 355

11 The Past and Future of Jihadist Organizational Learning 380

Acknowledgments 401
Abbreviations 405
Notes 407
Index 481

1

The Fire Next Time

Shortly after noon on January 3, 2014, police in Orestiada, a Greek town of twenty thousand located about four miles from the Turkish border, pulled over a taxi that had just entered the country. The passenger was a slender, dark-skinned twenty-three-year-old named Ibrahim Boudina, a French citizen of Algerian descent whose journey to Greece had begun in Syria. Authorities' search turned up a large amount of cash and a document titled "How to Make Artisanal Bombs in the Name of Allah." The police nonetheless let Boudina go, as no arrest warrant had been issued for him.[1]

Of course, even the Keystone Kops would have been suspicious. Greek officials shared information about Boudina and his belongings with their French colleagues. The French, in turn, began surveilling the home of Boudina's father in Mandelieu-la-Napoule, a picturesque town on the French Riviera. Suspecting that Boudina and an accomplice were preparing an attack, agents of the Direction Générale de la Sécurité Intérieure, France's domestic counterterrorism agency, raided the house and arrested Boudina on February 11. They found a handgun, bomb-making instructions, and three Red Bull cans filled with explosives.[2]

Boudina's plan to launch an attack in France marked the culmination of about five years of involvement in the jihadist movement. As a simple definition, modern jihadism is an ideological trend that seeks violent overthrow of the existing political order in favor of a transnational theocratic entity, with the creation of a caliphate being the most common objective. The term *jihadist* is an organic term, the way those within the movement refer to themselves, which is why we employ it in this book. It should be understood, though, that the Arabic word *jihad*, which translates to *struggle*, is an established Islamic religious concept with many connotations, and most Muslims interpret the term in significantly different ways than do the self-proclaimed jihadists. Boudina first immersed himself in a jihadist milieu in 2009, when he began attending a mosque in Cannes with a notable presence of hardline Salafists.[3] Boudina became part of a group of militants associated with the mosque who gained notoriety as "the Cannes-Torcy cell." In September 2012 two cell members threw a grenade into a Jewish grocery in the Paris suburb of Sarcelles, prompting French law enforcement to arrest eleven people in a multicity raid that also killed the cell's leader.[4] But the raids failed to catch Boudina, who fled to Syria. Little is known about his time there. Although he may have initially fought under the banner of Jabhat al-Nusra, al-Qaeda's Syrian affiliate, Boudina eventually joined the notorious Islamic State militant group (better known as ISIS), which in turn dispatched him to carry out an attack in Europe in its name.[5]

Boudina's rudimentary skill set contributed to his plot's failure. To begin with, Greek authorities found enough evidence on Boudina when he entered Europe to expose him. Further, Boudina's attempts to evade electronic surveillance were lacking. He tried but failed to wipe his computer's search history and change his IP address, allowing French officials to retrieve key digital evidence. Boudina's Facebook chat history revealed his allegiance to ISIS, as he communicated with known ISIS figures over that unsecure platform. Even Boudina's knowledge of explosives fell short. He managed to prepare triacetone triperoxide but didn't know how to detonate it and frantically engaged in a series of incriminating online searches.[6]

Boudina's mission was one of a number of failed ISIS plots targeting Europe in the run-up to, and just after, the organization's seismic June 2014 announcement that it had created a caliphate. Some of the failed plots were darkly humorous, like a less funny version of *Four Lions*, the 2010 British comedy about amateur terrorists. One operative was French university student Sid Ahmed Ghlam, who authorities caught because he called them after shooting himself in the leg. But the ironic way Ghlam was caught doesn't negate the danger he posed. This became clear when police found the corpse of dance instructor Aurélie Châtelain close to where they apprehended Ghlam.[7] Châtelain had been shot in the head three times. French authorities concluded that Ghlam had likely shot himself while trying to carjack her. Subsequent searches of Ghlam's car and home turned up four Kalashnikovs, a stolen police-issue pistol, bulletproof vests, and handwritten notes about potential targets.[8]

Four months later a plot designed to terrorize Europe ended with a jammed gun and American passengers becoming international heroes. On August 21, 2015, on the Thalys express train from Amsterdam to Paris, twenty-five-year-old Moroccan national Ayoub El Khazzani emerged from the bathroom shirtless, wielding a pistol and assault rifle. Khazzani's first shot hit a passenger's neck. But then his rifle jammed. Three Americans, two of them servicemembers, rushed Khazzani and subdued him.[9] Even the passenger who Khazzani shot in the neck survived.

After the failures of Boudina, Ghlam, and Khazzani, ISIS's efforts to strike the West appeared nascent at best. But less than three months after Khazzani's attempt—on November 13, 2015—ISIS launched a devastating attack that brought urban warfare to the streets of Paris. ISIS fighters shot up restaurants and cafés. They attacked the Bataclan theater during a concert, held dozens of hostages for more than two hours, and tortured their captives until stopped by a French police raid. Three suicide bombers detonated triacetone triperoxide bombs outside the Stade de France. In total, 130 civilians lost their lives.

ISIS launched another devastating attack in Europe four months later. On March 22, 2016, coordinated suicide bombings ripped through a terminal in the Brussels airport and the city's Maelbeek train station, killing thirty-two people and wounding over one hundred. Never before had a single jihadist network perpetrated a mass casualty attack in Europe, then bore the full weight of law enforcement and intelligence descending upon it, only to regroup and carry out a second mass casualty attack on the Continent.

After the Brussels bombings, a wave of assaults inspired or directed by ISIS continued to batter Europe. France was struck again in July 2016 during Nice's Bastille Day celebrations. Following fireworks and an air show, Mohamed Lahouaiej-Bouhlel plowed a large truck into a crowd on the Promenade des Anglais. He drove more than a mile, running down as many people as he could, then leaped from the vehicle and opened fire. The attack claimed eight-six lives. Four days later a seventeen-year-old Afghan migrant seeking asylum in Germany attacked passengers on a train in Würzburg with an ax and knife, wounding four. Two other European attacks were claimed in ISIS's name before the end of the month: A suicide bombing injured fifteen restaurant patrons outside a concert in the German city of Ansbach, and two attackers stormed a church in the French city of Rouen, slit an eighty-four-year-old priest's throat, and took hostages.

In December 2016 an ISIS-inspired Tunisian rammed a truck into a Berlin Christmas market, killing twelve. Just hours into 2017 an ISIS-inspired gunman opened fire in Istanbul's Reina nightclub, killing thirty-nine. In March 2017 Khalid Masood drove his car into pedestrians on London's Westminster Bridge before hopping out and stabbing a policeman. Five people lost their lives and another fifty were injured. On May 22, in an attack that was grisly even by ISIS's standards, a suicide bomber struck at the end of an Ariana Grande concert in Britain's Manchester Arena, leaving twenty-two people dead and fifty-nine wounded. As the *New York Times* noted, the target, "a concert spilling over with girls in their teens or younger, with their lives ahead of them, out for a fun night," felt even more personal than most.[10] In June three more ISIS "soldiers"—the term the group used for those who carried out attacks in its name—rammed a van into a crowd on London Bridge, then attacked Borough Market with knives. They killed eight and injured forty-eight. In August 2017 Younes Abouyaaqoub drove a van onto the packed Las Ramblas boulevard in Barcelona. He drove over 1,600 feet and left carnage in his wake, killing thirteen people and injuring more than a hundred.

ISIS also directed or inspired many other attacks across the globe, including an airplane blown up midflight in Egypt, hundreds of worshippers slain in a Sufi mosque in the Sinai, forty-nine people killed in a gay nightclub in Orlando, hundreds killed in Easter Sunday attacks in Sri Lanka, and cities and towns overrun by ISIS-affiliated militants in Libya, Mozambique, Nigeria, the Philippines, and Tunisia.

How had ISIS perpetrated one of history's bloodiest urban terrorist assaults after so many failures, then maintained an unprecedented attack tempo? The group's breakthrough is partly attributable to improvement in its operatives' tradecraft. Further, ISIS developed an innovation that would bolster its terrorist plots by exploiting the combination of social media's growing prevalence and improvements in end-to-end encryption. European officials coined the term *remote-controlled terrorism* to describe how ISIS began connecting with aspiring terrorists online through its multilingual base of operatives—a phenomenon that we call the virtual plotter model (see chapter 10). The "virtual plotters" in ISIS's external operations network used the online space to identify potential recruits, radicalize them, select attack targets and timing, and even provide technical assistance. In short, ISIS figured out how to offer operatives essentially all the same services digitally that were once provided by physical networks.

ISIS's ability to strike Europe thus improved markedly in a short time. Analysts underestimated its capabilities even when the group stood on the threshold of launching some of the most significant terrorist attacks ever to strike the West. In addition to being underestimated, ISIS's capabilities were misunderstood. Authorities' response to each unsuccessful plot prior to the Paris attacks followed the same pattern: Investigators quickly labeled each failed attack the work of "lone wolves," individual attackers with no relationship to broader networks, then seemingly stopped looking for further connections.

But it became clear soon after the Paris attacks that these failed plots had not been the work of isolated lone wolves. Abdelhamid Abaaoud, the ground commander of the Paris attacks, had directed the attempts of Ghlam, Khazzani, and several others.[11] The early efforts' lack of success deflected attention from ISIS's more sophisticated operational planning, serving as an unintentional smokescreen that helped the group "calmly prepare" its coming Paris operation, in the words of one French official.[12] Because Ghlam, Khazzani, and other attackers were seen as unrelated to one another, officials did not identify the infrastructure coordinating ISIS's Europe attacks. Put more bluntly, the last best chance to stop ISIS's devastating attacks in Paris was missed.

This failure can be attributed in part to consensus errors, which occur when it is not just a few scholars or analysts who misread critical developments but virtually an entire field of experts (80 percent or more) who agree on conclusions that prove incorrect. We introduce this concept not to disparage anyone. Rather, we are compelled to point out the existence of consensus errors because at key junctures over the past two decades, something important was missing from prevailing interpretations of jihadist groups and their activities. This book's theoretical framework describes how jihadist groups engage in organizational learning. Such a framework should not only provide insight into the enemy but should also serve as a critical mirror that empowers us to better understand our own weaknesses and vulnerabilities. If militants are engaging in effective organizational learning, those who are seeking to understand or stop them should be doing so as well. The existence of consensus errors points to blind spots where our own field's learning processes have proved deficient.

Three Tales of Consensus Errors

Militant groups can be difficult to interpret due to their clandestine nature. They disguise their activities and organizational structure and often spread disinformation about themselves. These interpretive challenges are compounded by observers' tendency to view militant groups as static rather than as learning organizations. This section briefly outlines three relatively recent consensus errors: the impact of the "Arab Spring" revolutions on the jihadist movement; the competition between al-Qaeda and its offspring, ISIS; and the myth of lone-wolf terrorism.

THE ARAB SPRING REVOLUTIONS

In early 2011 the Middle East and North Africa was gripped by revolutionary fervor. Uprisings forced Tunisia's Zine El Abidine Ben Ali and Egypt's Hosni Mubarak from power. Libya's Muammar al-Qaddafi lost power, and his life, after a popular uprising and controversial NATO intervention. The governments of Syria and Yemen were fatally weakened, and within a few years both countries would be embroiled in deadly, tragic, and seemingly intractable conflicts that played to the advantage of jihadist groups.

But when these revolutions first struck the Middle East and North Africa (MENA) region, observers were heartened by the sight of long-standing dictators being forced from power by their own people. In early 2011 a consensus emerged among terrorism experts and regional security analysts, none of whom were immune from the prevailing optimism, that the Arab uprisings were devastating to jihadism in general and to al-Qaeda specifically. This view was embraced not least within the U.S. government. Former CIA deputy director Michael Morell explains the intelligence community's early assessment of the revolutions in his memoir *The Great War of Our Time*, regretfully recalling that his agency "thought and told policy-makers that this outburst of popular revolt would damage al Qa'ida by undermining the group's narrative. Our analysts figured that the protests would send a signal throughout the region that political change was possible without al Qa'ida's leading the way and without the violence that al Qa'ida said was necessary."[13] John Brennan, who served as President Barack Obama's senior counterterrorism adviser and later as CIA director, declared in a June 2011 speech that the uprisings were "the most profound change in the modern history of the Arab world" and that al-Qaeda and like-minded militants had "been left on the sidelines, watching history pass them by." Brennan said their ideology had been rejected and their calls to violence "thoroughly repudiated" by the protesters.[14]

Pundits echoed this view. Fareed Zakaria wrote that the Arab uprisings were "a total repudiation of al-Qaeda's founding ideology" and, in words he would regret in three years' time, stated that we should "stop cowering in fear of an impending caliphate."[15] Ian Black noted in the *Guardian* shortly after al-Qaeda's longtime leader Osama bin Laden was killed that "none of the uprisings that have shaken the region . . . has involved significant Islamist activity—let alone the violent, extremist jihadi ideas promoted by bin Laden, Ayman al Zawahiri and their ilk." Black argued that the uprisings had rendered al-Qaeda "irrelevant" even before bin Laden's death and that the idea that the group "poses a serious challenge to the Arab regimes is dead."[16]

The vast majority of prominent analysts and scholars agreed. London School of Economics scholar Fawaz Gerges proclaimed that the Arab Spring uprisings not only shook "the foundation of the authoritarian order in the Middle East, but they have also hammered a deadly nail in the coffin of a terrorism narrative which has painted al-Qaeda as the West's greatest threat."[17] Omar Ashour wrote that "the Arab Spring delivered a heavy blow to jihadism and significantly undermined its rationale."[18] After interviewing several prominent terrorism analysts for a February 2011 *New York Times* report, Scott Shane wrote that, for most analysts, "the past few weeks have the makings of an epochal disaster for Al Qaeda, making the jihadists look like ineffectual bystanders to history while offering young Muslims an appealing alternative to terrorism."[19]

These views were not just wrong: They were a 180-degree misreading of what was about to transpire. Reflecting years later on the analytic climate during this period, respected terrorism scholar Bruce Hoffman noted that "the triumphalism of Osama bin Laden's death coinciding with the ending of the first phase of the Arab Spring created a concatenation of judgment where anyone who stood in the way was kind of bowled over or knocked aside."[20] This description of analysts who disagreed with the prevailing triumphalism—that is, those who turned out to be *right* about the impact of the revolutions—being knocked aside is correct. Analytic disagreements during this period were deeply felt and frequently personalized. While the question of whether the regional revolutions would increase or decrease the standing of militant groups should have been a technical question, in practice analysts who held dissenting views found themselves deprived of opportunities (conferences, speaking opportunities, consulting projects, etc.). Their social standing took a hit. The incentives to side with the majority were clear.

This is one way groupthink can emerge. When majorities actively marginalize dissenting opinions, it creates incentives for others to adhere to the prevailing view. Such incentives to side with the majority have nothing to do with the substantive merits of a position. The majority perspective may then appear more powerful than it is: The numbers favoring a consensus may be overwhelming, but they are less impressive if one understands the professional incentives to adopt that view. The tendency toward groupthink is likely accelerated in the social media age, where our every thought or opinion can be instantly quantified, its popularity or unpopularity measured.

The Arab Spring did not turn out how the consensus of analysts promised. There has likely been no series of events as energizing to the jihadist movement as the regional revolutions and their aftermath. We explain in detail later in this book how jihadist organizations adapted to the revolutions and used the turmoil to their advantage.

THE COMPETITION BETWEEN AL-QAEDA AND ISIS

A second set of errors concerns the competition between al-Qaeda and ISIS following the latter organization's rise in 2013–2014. For several years, al-Qaeda had engaged in low-key growth in the post–Arab Spring MENA region, often having new affiliates use names other than al-Qaeda and explicitly disclaim being a part of the global jihadist outfit. Following its expulsion from al-Qaeda, ISIS adopted the opposite approach. While al-Qaeda wanted the world to think it was nowhere, which helped it to stay off states' counterterrorism and counterinsurgency radar, ISIS wanted the world to think it was everywhere, a strategy designed to produce rapid growth. ISIS loudly proclaimed its presence over social media, launching a messaging campaign that would be the envy of Fortune 500 companies, and at one point even fabricated its control over the Libyan city of Derna. Although the group's capture of Derna was fictitious, it was widely reported by major media outlets, including CNN, *Time*, and the Associated Press, as well as by many analysts.

The brash ISIS openly wooed al-Qaeda's affiliates, trying to absorb its parent's global network. Most analysts believed that ISIS decidedly possessed the upper hand in this intra-jihadist competition.[21] Observers routinely suggested that al-Qaeda faced "a growing risk of irrelevance," and that major al-Qaeda branches were likely to defect to its competitor.[22] This reading of the competition between al-Qaeda and ISIS did not reflect the actual strength of the two organizations. Rather than understanding these militant groups as learning organizations and searching for subtleties, omissions, and misrepresentations in their messaging, analysts often took the organizations' messaging at something like face value. It is thus unsurprising that a group emphasizing its strength at every opportunity appeared to be on the verge of rendering irrelevant another group that disguised its successes.

Largely due to this surface-level reading of the competition, analysts widely assumed that al-Qaeda's only road to maintaining influence was replicating ISIS's model of conspicuous growth—for example, by carrying out spectacular attacks in the West.[23] But al-Qaeda defied conventional wisdom. Rather than trying to replicate ISIS's model, the group continued to downplay its successes rather than publicizing them and embed further within local populations. In this way al-Qaeda presented itself to the world as less threatening than its bloodthirsty rival. In this book we argue that al-Qaeda's efforts in this regard were a qualified strategic success. Our point is not that al-Qaeda *won* its competition with its upstart competitor. Rather, it is that misreading al-Qaeda's actual strategy hindered America's ability to forge an effective response.

THE MYTH OF LONE-WOLF TERRORISM

A third set of consensus errors involved the over-labeling of terrorism as the work of "lone wolves." As we have explained, this tendency caused authorities to squander some of the best opportunities they had to uncover the November 2015 Paris attackers before they struck. So ingrained was the over-labeling of lone-wolf attackers that it continued even after the Paris assaults.

This chapter has outlined the wave of European attacks claimed in ISIS's name in the summer of 2016, including Mohamed Lahouaiej-Bouhlel's slaughter of Bastille Day revelers, the attack on a Würzburg train, and the Ansbach suicide bombing. Analysts, journalists, and scholars quickly described the perpetrators of each of these attacks as lone wolves.[24] The designation was generally applied within twenty-four hours of each attack, before any real information about its planning and execution emerged, and long before authorities had concluded their investigation. For instance, within a day of the Nice attack, observers had already described Lahouaiej-Bouhlel as a lone wolf who was not actually linked to ISIS.[25]

The labeling of these attacks as the work of lone wolves proved either erroneous or at least premature. When ISIS claimed responsibility for the Würzburg train attack, the group released a video featuring the perpetrator, which showed that the group had advance knowledge of what he would do. The German press ultimately published transcripts showing that the Würzburg and Ansbach attackers had been in touch with virtual plotters. Further, although it is not conclusive, some evidence suggests that a virtual plotter may have assisted Lahouaiej-Bouhlel in his attack.

The over-labeling of attacks as the work of lone-wolf terrorists has, fortunately, declined.[26] Consensus errors can be corrected. But absent changes in the way we interpret jihadist groups, other consensus errors will likely produce costly misunderstandings in the future.

An Antidote: The Organizational Learning Paradigm

Deficits in our understanding of jihadist groups can be costly. They have contributed to strategic mistakes and tactical errors. There are numerous reasons for such misreadings. The clandestine nature of militant groups is surely significant. The analytic climate can also color interpretations. But a more fundamental problem is that analytic conceptions of these organizations are often static when the groups themselves are dynamic, devoting significant resources to organizational learning. Organizational learning is, put simply, a necessity for jihadist groups.

All three consensus errors that this chapter explores are in important ways rooted in a static conception of jihadist groups. Analysts saw the Arab Spring revolutions as devastating to the movement in part because they viewed al-Qaeda as possessing a single narrative holding that the region's regimes could only be overthrown by violent means, and they thus underestimated the militants' ability to adapt their messaging and positioning to the new geopolitical realities. With respect to the competition between al-Qaeda and ISIS, analytic readings of the two organizations tended to take claims they made at face value, when both organizations were actively disseminating disinformation about their strength and standing. A more dynamic conception of these groups could have focused more attention on the subtleties, omissions, and misrepresentations in their messaging. The third consensus error we identified, the tendency to over-read lone-actor attacks as the work of lone wolves who lacked organizational connections, is also linked to overlooking jihadist groups' learning, including development of the virtual plotter model. Appreciation of how jihadist groups might learn to leverage technological advances to influence attacks abroad could have called into question the over-labeling of lone-wolf attacks.

How can we better anticipate jihadist groups' plots, strategies, and trajectories? This book contends that jihadist groups' organizational learning processes are critical to understanding them. Primary source materials allow us to trace the history of jihadist networks in a way that could not be accomplished before, as we draw from a wealth of newly available information about al-Qaeda, ISIS, and other groups. The organizational learning lens illuminates how internal and external dynamics— such as the emergence of pioneering strategists or the outbreak of regional instability—influence jihadists' preferences and decisions.

This book's second chapter outlines the scholarly literature's understanding of organizational learning. A rich body of scholarship provides a foundation for some critical questions this book addresses. What is organizational learning, and what distinguishes it from individual learning? When and why do organizations pursue learning? How do they overcome natural inertia to engage in organization-wide learning processes? What kinds of organizational learning might a group pursue, ranging from incremental change to sweeping reforms, and what are their advantages and drawbacks? What factors influence the outcome of organizational learning efforts? Since future organizational learning by jihadist groups will likely be intertwined with new technologies, the second chapter also introduces our primary theoretical contribution: the violent non-state-actor technology adoption curve. This four-phase curve shows how militant groups adopting new technologies move from early adoption and iteration to a (non-inevitable) breakthrough stage before entering a phase of intensified technological competition with their foes.

The third chapter shows how al-Qaeda made the far-enemy strategy, of focusing its militant activities against the West, into the dominant paradigm for jihadist groups for a period. The decision to prioritize the far enemy over the near one was a strategic calculation: There was no compelling ideological reason to prioritize the fight against one foe over the other. Long before instability wracked the MENA region's governments in early 2011, the far-enemy strategy emerged from al-Qaeda's assessment of the setbacks that other militant Islamist groups faced, including how the campaigns of the Armed Islamic Group of Algeria, Islamic Jihad and Gama'a al-Islamiyya in Egypt, and the Libyan Islamic Fighting Group floundered in the 1990s. Some assessments of the post–Arab Spring al-Qaeda misread the group in part because they viewed it exclusively through the lens of the far-enemy strategy without contemplating how regional turmoil might shift the group's strategic preferences. To understand al-Qaeda's later shift away from a far-enemy-focused strategy, it is first necessary to understand how that strategy initially emerged.

After embracing the far-enemy strategy, al-Qaeda launched the attacks of September 11, 2001, that claimed around three thousand lives on American soil. The fourth chapter explores jihadists' ongoing attempts to target aviation. Aviation attacks serve as an important case study in how jihadists adapt and innovate their external operations strategies in response to counterterrorism challenges. The aviation industry was a primary target of jihadist operations even before the 9/11 attacks and has remained in the crosshairs since. Far from being a juvenile obsession, a strategic purpose underlies this focus, as aviation plays a central role in global commerce and the world economy. States have responded to every aviation plot by developing costly new security measures. In this cat-and-mouse game, jihadists have designed new methods to circumvent these measures, such as hiding bombs in underwear or printer cartridges.

The fifth chapter explores a new generation of jihadists who set the stage for the later virtual plotter innovation. On November 5, 2009, Maj. Nidal Malik Hasan shot and killed thirteen of his fellow Americans at Fort Hood, Texas. He was influenced by the teachings of the ideologue Anwar al-Awlaki, a high-ranking member of al-Qaeda in the Arabian Peninsula. While the concept of "individual jihad" had been advanced by previous theorists, Awlaki did the most to lay the groundwork for a dramatic growth in this kind of threat. Awlaki also represented a step forward in jihadist groups' learning about galvanizing followers to action through new communication technologies. Awlaki kept a blog and posted his sermons to YouTube. His use of social media allowed him to reach audiences in new ways, and ISIS would later build on Awlaki's trailblazing efforts.

The sixth chapter explores jihadism in the Arab Spring. It draws on new materials that provide an important look into the adaptations and internal processes that helped jihadists exploit the revolutions. Despite prominent revolutionaries' democratic sentiments, jihadist leaders were quick to figure out how they could fill regional power vacuums.

The seventh chapter examines ISIS's rise from an insurgent organization in Iraq to a self-declared caliphate. The world was stunned by ISIS's surge across Iraq and Syria in 2014. The United States' 2003 invasion of Iraq not only made it easier for jihadists to target Americans in the region, it also created an opportunity for al-Qaeda and its allies to lay the groundwork for a state in the heart of the Middle East. Ultimately, al-Qaeda lost control of its Iraqi arm. ISIS's rise exposed weaknesses in al-Qaeda's management structure and demonstrated that jihadists could make significant gains even while defying al-Qaeda's approach, which had grown more careful and image-conscious.

The eighth chapter digs deeper into this last point, exploring the competing models of al-Qaeda and ISIS. The two groups adopted strategies that were, in many respects, diametrically opposed to one another. ISIS wanted to supercharge its global growth while al-Qaeda wanted to stay off the counterterrorism radar even as it made regional advances. In both cases, the groups' claims about ISIS's strength and al-Qaeda's weakness were misleading. In the case of the Libyan city of Derna, al-Qaeda-aligned militias dominated the city, yet ISIS's propaganda and al-Qaeda's silence convinced analysts that ISIS had seized control. Al-Qaeda also adopted a more pragmatic and gradualist approach than ISIS, which employed more brutal, uncompromising tactics. Al-Qaeda, in contrast, focused more on winning local support and building coalitions with like-minded armed groups. As ISIS's territorial caliphate crumbled, al-Qaeda maintained the upper hand in areas like Africa's Sahel region, the Horn of Africa, and Afghanistan. That being said, ISIS has been able to maintain growth in multiple theaters even as its caliphate fell, including some spaces that have not been regarded as jihadist battlegrounds previously, such as Mozambique.

Turning to one geographic space where al-Qaeda's more patient approach paid dividends, the ninth chapter shows how al-Qaeda reorganized its operations in Afghanistan and Pakistan, an outgrowth of its organizational processes designed to foster resilience. Although America's drone campaign took a toll on the group, al-Qaeda relocated key personnel out of the drones' "kill box" in northern Pakistan to safe havens in Afghanistan and Iran. Al-Qaeda also built relationships with Central Asian and Pakistani militant groups. As airstrikes and counterterrorism raids killed its fighters, al-Qaeda turned to those partners to replenish its ranks. In September 2014 al-Qaeda announced the creation of al-Qaeda in the Indian Subcontinent, which solidified the organization's enduring presence in South Asia. Despite this announcement, al-Qaeda rarely advertises the extent of its presence in the region due to its adoption of a policy known as "not standing out." As intended, this policy has clouded analytic assessments of the group.

Although al-Qaeda's strategic patience—a product of its learning processes—strengthened the group, ISIS also engaged in highly innovative learning in multiple spheres, including in terrorist attacks abroad. Thus, the tenth chapter outlines a new era of external operations that emerged after ISIS's rise, as exemplified in operations like the November 2015 Paris attacks and March 2016 Brussels suicide bombings. Through the Amniyat al-Kharji, the group's external operations wing, ISIS built a global terrorist network capable of executing sophisticated attacks in far-flung locations. Picking up where Awlaki left off, ISIS exploited technological developments to create the virtual plotter model, which fostered a wave of lone-actor jihadist attacks that was unprecedented in its reach and impact.

How will jihadists continue to evolve strategically and tactically in the years ahead? In our concluding chapter, we anticipate that they will refine their tactics based on their evaluation of their own past performance as well as new government countermeasures. Many new tactics will also stem from the pattern that the violent non-state-actor technology adoption curve describes: As a consumer technology becomes widely available, terrorists will look for ways to adapt it, as they did with social media and drones. This chapter concludes by outlining how governments can more effectively counter jihadist groups' adaptations. We emphasize the importance of countering these groups' capacity for organizational learning.

Substate violence is, of course, about far more than jihadism. There have been many other devastating ideologically driven attacks in recent years. To name just a few prominent terrorist attacks, Anders Breivik claimed seventy-seven lives in Norway in 2011, Dylann Roof slaughtered nine congregants at the Emanuel African Methodist Episcopal Church in 2015, a white supremacist shooter claimed eleven lives at Pittsburgh's Tree of Life synagogue in 2018, a ferocious March 2019 attack in New Zealand killed fifty mosque-goers, and a white supremacist gunman killed twenty-three people at a Walmart in El Paso, Texas, in August 2019. The dramatic January 6, 2021, attack on the U.S. Capitol placed a deserved spotlight on the growing phenomenon of domestic violent extremism in the United States. Nor are terrorists the only violent non-state actors that can cause large-scale loss of life. Powerful cartels and gangs have killed tens of thousands in Mexico and Latin America, bringing entire states to the brink of ruin.

The urgency of understanding how various violent non-state actors learn is apparent. The technology tsunami that we are experiencing will give these groups unprecedented capabilities. While this book focuses on jihadism, the underlying theory it advances about how militant groups engage in organizational learning is more broadly applicable. It is vital that we learn the key lessons of the past two decades because this problem set is growing more diverse and challenging. We hope we can help to reduce the intensity of the fire that will burn next time.

2

Learning to Win

We began this book with the tale of Ibrahim Boudina, the first operative that ISIS dispatched to attack Europe. The amateurish Boudina was unable to wipe his computer's search history or change his IP address. He resorted to incriminating online searches when he couldn't figure out how to detonate triacetone triperoxide explosives. Other operatives in the first wave of would-be ISIS attackers in Europe displayed similar incompetence, such as when Sid Ahmed Ghlam shot himself in the leg.

Then ISIS struck Paris, and 130 lives were lost. The idea that ISIS was incapable of launching attacks in Europe was put to rest. And the group managed to keep drawing blood through a wave of further attacks. ISIS had managed to learn quickly, with deadly results. The group's ability to improve the operational security and bomb-making capabilities of its Europe-based terrorists, along with other aspects of their tradecraft, is a microcosm of jihadist groups' broader capacity for learning. How are some militant groups able to drastically improve in short periods? Why are other groups seemingly doomed to fail? The answer can be found, in part, in a group's capacity for organizational learning. We believe that applying an organizational learning perspective to these groups is critical to assessing their future patterns of recruitment, violence, and many other activities. An organizational learning perspective will help observers understand jihadist groups as dynamic and better anticipate their adaptations.

This chapter reviews the scholarly literature on organizational learning and makes two primary contributions. First, it provides a framework for understanding organizational learning in jihadist groups. Second, this chapter introduces the violent non-state-actor technology adoption curve, which provides a model for how violent non-state actors—and jihadist groups in particular—seek to adopt and adapt new technological capabilities.

Reviewing the Literature: Violent Non-State Actors and Organizational Learning

For jihadist groups, the ability to innovate is a necessity rather than a luxury. Bruce Hoffman notes that terrorist groups have a "fundamental organizational imperative" to learn.[1] Facing an array of internal and external challenges, jihadist groups must adapt quickly and creatively or suffer the consequences. For jihadist groups to survive their array of adversaries, from state actors to rival militants, they must build resilience and develop strong learning processes.[2] Hoffman thus describes the imperative for terrorist organizational learning as "an almost Darwinian principle of natural selection," where "every new terrorist generation learns from its predecessors, becoming smarter, tougher and more difficult to capture or eliminate."[3] Three primary environmental triggers push jihadists and other violent non-state actors to learn: states, rival organizations, and technology.

State actors pose an existential threat to jihadist groups. Jihadist groups that fail to shore up their vulnerabilities and develop coherent responses to counterterrorism policies designed to kill or capture their members will eventually be degraded to the point of irrelevance. Similarly, terrorist groups that cannot overcome defensive counterterrorism measures may be rendered obsolete. Militant organizations that can overcome the challenges posed by state actors can typically identify gaps in their own capabilities, institutionalize best practices, and become effective innovators.

Competition among militant groups is another driver of organizational learning. Competing militant groups vie for the same pool of operatives and supporters. Those that innovate in messaging, recruitment, and military operations will prosper. Those incapable of adapting will see their support base wither.

Technology should also be understood as an environmental factor exogenous to violent non-state actors that creates pressure to innovate and opportunities to do so. Hoffman describes a "technology treadmill" in which terrorist groups must engage in a constant process of innovation.[4] For-profit companies also engage in a similar process of constant innovation: In the commercial sphere, rapid and often unpredictable technological change places a premium on sound learning capabilities and mechanisms.[5] Businesses compete with rivals to maintain a competitive advantage. Firms must be responsive to consumers' changing needs, just as violent non-state actors must be attuned to the demands of their support base. Given the impetus shared by violent non-state actors and for-profit firms to engage in organizational learning, the rich literature on organizational learning in the business world provides valuable insight into the drivers, obstacles, processes, and dynamics that shape how militant groups learn. Gary Ackerman made a similar point in the context of innovation (a concept fundamentally connected to organizational learning), noting that the literature on innovation that exists in "disciplines as diverse as business management, public policy and sociology" manages to provides "a treasure trove of insights . . . but has remained largely untapped by terrorism researchers."[6]

It is worth acknowledging several notable exceptions in the terrorism studies literature to the relative neglect of theories and concepts from the organizational learning literature. *Aptitude for Destruction*, a 2005 report by the RAND Corporation's Brian Jackson and colleagues, reviews organizational learning principles that the authors find applicable to terrorist groups and illustrates them through several case studies.[7] Michael Kenney's 2007 book *From Pablo to Osama* examines the successes of cartels and jihadist groups through the lens of their ability to learn and store information as well as adapt to changes in their environment.[8] The same year, Adam Dolnik published *Understanding Terrorist Innovation*, which explores technological and tactical progression in terrorist operations.[9] Dolnik enumerates factors that explain why terrorists innovate in the face of costly hurdles and how they do so.

There was a further surge of scholarly interest in terrorist learning and innovation almost a decade after the publication of Kenney and Dolnik's books. *Understanding Terrorism Innovation and Learning* is a 2015 volume coedited by Magnus Ranstorp and Magnus Normark that, like RAND's report, reviews the academic literature on learning and innovation and provides a series of case studies on innovation and learning in the context of terrorist groups.[10] A special issue of the journal *Studies in Conflict & Terrorism* published in late 2017 was devoted to organizational learning in terrorist groups.[11] Yannick Veilleux-Lepage's 2020 book *How Terror Evolves* uses a framework derived from evolutionary theory to examine how innovation occurs in the context of airline hijackings.[12] While this volume seeks to understand the inner workings of *groups*, Veilleux-Lepage examines the *tactic* of airline hijacking from an evolutionary perspective. More recently, the International Centre for the Study of Radicalisation and Political Violence, based in the Department of War Studies at King's College London, has published a couple of monographs examining aspects of militant groups' innovation and creativity.[13]

But even these valuable studies leave much to be discerned about the organizational learning of violent non-state actors in general and jihadist groups in particular. This book is designed to make two distinct contributions to this conversation. First, jihadist groups are highly opaque, and much of the previous scholarship exploring jihadist organizational learning has by necessity been based on inference. But over the past decade important troves of new documents have become available, enabling us to take a more detailed look "under the hood" through documents that provide direct insight into jihadist groups' organizational learning. Second, much scholarship on jihadist organizational learning has been segmented topically—for example, examining how groups innovate in the realm of improvised explosive devices or social media. We aim to take a more sweeping look at these groups' learning processes. The decisions these groups have made about organizational learning contributed to several innovations simultaneously, while other strategic decisions precluded certain kinds of innovation. Essentially, this book endeavors to examine multiple processes and products of learning over an extended period instead of focusing on individual case studies.

The remainder of this chapter explores the process of organizational learning in violent non-state actors. We draw from scholarship related to terrorism, organizational design, organizational psychology, and business. We begin by defining organizational learning and distinguishing it from individual learning. The chapter then examines the conditions—catalysts and inhibitors—under which violent non-state actors begin or avoid organizational learning. We then outline the multistage process by which organizational learning in violent non-state actors occurs. The chapter then explores factors influencing the type of organizational learning a violent non-state actor will undertake before introducing the violent non-state-actor technology adoption curve.

Defining Organizational Learning

What distinguishes organizational from individual learning? While the concept of individual learning is relatively clear, the notion of learning at the organizational level is more challenging. The conceptual difficulty can be understood by posing the following question: If an individual in an organization gains new knowledge, then the organization necessarily has more knowledge than it did before; so does learning by an individual within an organization constitute organizational learning?

The answer is no. The reason for this can be discerned if we hypothesize that the individual learner leaves the firm a month later. If the individual's learning has not been transferred to the organization, any firm investment in the individual's learning has not resulted in organizational learning. This pinpoints the difference between individual and organizational learning: For organizational learning to occur, a transference of learning between the individual and organization is necessary. Organizational learning requires that the organization acquire new or updated knowledge that it can distribute and store internally. Although distinct, individual learning and organizational learning influence one another. Organizations are composed of individuals, and organizations also create and enforce norms, traditions, and models that influence individuals.[14]

Various scholarly definitions of organizational learning exist, but the literature identifies two overarching requirements. First, processes must be in place to translate knowledge gained at the individual level into organizational knowledge, such that the organization is "no longer dependent upon the original learner."[15] Second, organizational learning is greater than the sum of the organization's parts. Organizational learning should not be viewed simply as an aggregation of the knowledge of various members: Through absorbing, distributing, and institutionalizing knowledge across multiple levels of the organization, the initial information gathered at the individual level is amplified. Organizational learning is a force multiplier.

While scholars of organizational learning have arrived at a rough consensus on the factors differentiating organizational from individual learning, there is no consensus definition of organizational learning. Some scholars define organizational learning narrowly. For instance, Jackson and colleagues hold that organizational learning must be intentional and used by the group "to make better strategic decisions, improve its ability to develop and apply specific tactics, and increase its chance of success in its operations."[16] In other words, only beneficial changes constitute learning. A similar definition is provided by innovation scholars David O'Sullivan and Lawrence Dooley, who define commercial innovation as "the process of making changes, large and small, radical and incremental, to products, processes, and services that results in the production of something new for the organization that adds value to customers and contributes to the knowledge store of the organization."[17] Both definitions' requirements of intentionality and positive change are unduly restrictive. Requiring intentionality erases organizational learning that may be unintentional yet real. Such learning occurs, for example, during the constant experimentation that accompanies the initial establishment of an organization's culture. Second, it is problematic to require that organizational learning result in changes. It may, in fact, result in a firmer commitment to current structures and processes that are working as intended. Third, the notion that only beneficial changes result from organizational learning is inaccurate. As just one example, organizational learning can produce tactical innovations that appear beneficial but are ultimately strategically harmful.

Louise Kettle and Andrew Mumford provide an alternative definition of organizational learning for terrorist groups that we find satisfactory. They define terrorist learning as "the acquisition of knowledge to inform terrorist related activities in the future."[18] This definition clarifies that knowledge acquisition is not synonymous with learning but, rather, is a potential starting point for the learning process. Moreover, it proposes that learning need not necessarily result in change but can result in any form of impact. Indeed, they note that the result of learning may be to "reinforce existing ideas and actions."[19] Kettle and Mumford's definition also has the advantage of clarifying that learning need not result in beneficial outcomes. Another definition of organizational learning, in this case formulated outside the context of violent non-state actors, that we find insightful is economist George P. Huber's, which holds that "an entity learns if, through its processing of information, the range of its potential behaviors is changed."[20] Like Kettle and Mumford, Huber holds that learning need not result in "observable changes in behavior."[21] Change stemming from organizational learning can be cognitive rather than behavioral: It can produce modifications to an organization's worldview that are not immediately evident to an outside observer. Huber also clarifies that organizational learning need not produce beneficial results. Learning occurs even when organizations "incorrectly learn" or else "correctly learn that which is incorrect."[22] Adapting the insights of these two scholarly definitions, we define organizational learning in the jihadist context as the acquisition and subsequent processing of information or knowledge that changes the range of potential behaviors related to the group's activities.

Obstacles and Drivers: Why Do Organizations Learn?

Why, when, and how do jihadist groups learn? Organizational learning can be uncomfortable, and intentional learning can be costly. The factors catalyzing or inhibiting violent non-state actors' organizational learning may generally be organized into two groups: exogenous and endogenous.

EXOGENOUS FACTORS

The most visible driver of learning is a shift in an organization's exogenous environment that leaves little choice but to innovate. Organizations usually possess strategies and tactics rooted in existing conditions. When conditions evolve, they may be forced to engage in organizational learning.

Sudden political, social, and economic shifts may serve as an exogenous factor that drives or inhibits organizational learning. Consider the aftermath of a natural disaster in a rural area of a country where the recognized government lacks the capacity to respond effectively. A community is left without electricity, food, water, and shelter. A violent non-state actor may be able to fill the vacuum. If the violent non-state actor has never controlled a geographic area or provided services, the political, social, and economic shifts wrought by the disaster may trigger the actor to quickly learn how to provide assistance in order to co-opt the community. Similarly, the political changes wrought by the 2011 Arab Spring revolutions presented jihadist organizations with opportunities and challenges and triggered organizational learning.

Technological changes can serve as another catalyst for organizational learning.[23] New technologies can render old practices obsolete. Innovations in social media, communications, end-to-end encryption, and other spheres have reshaped—and continue to reshape—militants' tactics and strategies.

Rival organizations can be a driver of organizational learning. Competition forces organizations to modify policies and procedures to keep pace with or surpass other actors in the same space that are vying for the same resources.

ENDOGENOUS FACTORS

Although organizations are most likely to be dramatically catalyzed by exogenous shifts, endogenous factors are also important drivers of, and obstacles to, learning. Endogenous shifts may occur at the organizational or individual level. We first explore organization-level factors, then turn to individual-level factors.

Organizational culture is often the greatest obstacle to organizational learning, particularly learning likely to produce sweeping changes. Definitions of organizational culture differ, but at its core scholars understand it as the norms, values, and boundaries deemed appropriate by the organization and its members.[24] As organizations become more successful, they typically become increasingly committed to their norms and practices. The institutionalization of norms is beneficial in many ways. Creation of an organizational culture is an "effective way of controlling and coordinating people without elaborate and rigid formal control systems."[25] But organizational culture can also create impediments to learning. Cultural inertia can foster complacency or even arrogance, thus preventing organizations from recognizing the gap between their capabilities and their objectives.[26]

While organizational culture often acts as an obstacle to learning, in some organizations it is a major catalyst. If an organization develops a culture where norms encourage learning, change, and evolution, organizational culture may stimulate organizational learning. Google's institutionalization of "20 percent time" is one powerful example of how learning and innovation might be ingrained in an organization's culture.[27]

Organizational size also has an impact on organizational learning. As organizations expand, they typically create new layers of procedures and bureaucracy. Such modifications improve an organization's ability to implement policies and strengthen intraorganizational communication, but they also serve as a hindrance to organizational learning, particularly learning that disrupts the status quo.[28] To modify policies and procedures, bureaucratized organizations must implement changes across multiple departments, a complex undertaking. Organizational size can thus raise the costs of organizational learning and can make large organizations resistant to sweeping change. Business professors Michael Tushman and Charles O'Reilly III describe the challenges large entities face in incorporating new knowledge as "rooted in the size, complexity, and interdependence in the organization's structures, systems, procedures, and processes."[29]

Cultural and structural inertia are in part consequences of the tradeoff between exploration and exploitation in organizational learning. In 1991 Stanford sociologist James March published a seminal article explaining the exploration/exploitation dynamic, observing that exploration involved "experimentation with new alternatives" while exploitation seeks to improve an organization's efficiency through "refinement and extension of existing competencies, technologies and paradigms."[30] Although organizations should pursue both kinds of learning, March discerned a general preference for exploitation. Other scholars have noted that this preference can result in short-term improvements but "diminishing returns to the organization" in the long term.[31] Similarly, in *The Innovator's Dilemma*, Harvard Business School professor Clayton Christensen examines how even the most well-run companies decline. Christensen argues that in doing everything "right," such as being attentive to short-term market trends, adjusting to customer feedback, and investing in innovations that "promised the best returns," titans who concentrate on incremental improvements can be felled by rivals that invest in disruptive innovations.[32]

Individual-level factors in an organization can have disproportionate influence on its willingness and capacity to engage in learning. Ackerman highlights the role of "guardians of the status quo" in inhibiting learning. These guardians are beneficiaries of an organization's current policies and procedures and could lose power or influence if the organization changes tack. They thus directly or indirectly deter systemic adaptations but do not inhibit incremental learning.[33] In contrast, highly entrepreneurial individuals, whether at the top echelons or lower levels of an organization, may drive organizational learning on their own. One example in the jihadist context is Khalid Sheikh Mohammed, who spearheaded considerable innovation in al-Qaeda's external operations, including those that resulted in the 9/11 attacks. Identifying and eliminating entrepreneurs of violence like Mohammed is essential for state actors seeking to undermine jihadist groups' organizational learning capabilities.

Competition within an organization can also be an obstacle to learning. Executives or commanders may try to stymie intraorganizational rivals' efforts to engage in exploration. Even organizations that recognize the need for learning may be subverted by insiders trying to advance their own self-interest. But while sometimes a hindrance to innovation, competition between midlevel officials can also spur organizational learning as rivals engage in one-upmanship. In such cases, organizational learning may be internally fragmented if rivals won't share knowledge with one another.

Now that we have explored how exogenous and endogenous factors influence an organization's willingness to learn, we turn to the processes by which organizational learning occurs.

Processes of Organizational Learning

One of the more comprehensive frameworks explaining organizational learning processes is Huber's "Organizational Learning: The Contributing Processes and the Literatures," which identifies four stages of organizational learning: knowledge acquisition, information interpretation, information distribution, and organizational memory.[34] While all four stages must be fulfilled for learning to be assimilated and adopted across an organization, the stages don't necessarily occur in a specific order. Kettle and Mumford assert a slight variant of the four stages: identification, distribution, retention, and implementation. Unlike Huber's model, Kettle and Mumford position identification as the required first step, followed by the other three in any order.[35] The differences between the two models are subtle, and a key takeaway from both Huber's and Kettle and Mumford's frameworks is that organizational learning rarely follows a linear path. Organizations often alternate between acquiring new knowledge and analyzing and incorporating it. We adopt Huber's model of organizational learning processes with a significant adaptation borrowed from Kettle and Mumford: We hold that knowledge acquisition is the necessary first stage of the process, followed by the other three stages in any order (see figure 2.1).

Interpretation

Distribution

Knowledge
Acquisition

Organizational
Memory

FIG. 2.1 The process of organizational learning

ACQUISITION

Acquisition involves collection of information relevant to a learning objective. Organizations can draw from many sources, both internal and external. When seeking knowledge externally, an organization may engage in vicarious learning by watching the behavior of others.[36] Vicarious learning allows organizations "to acquire large, integrated patterns of behavior without having to form them gradually by tedious trial and error."[37] But the depth of vicarious learning may be limited. Generally only the public-facing behavior of other organizations can be observed, although direct cooperation with other groups can address some limitations of vicarious learning.

Organizations may also find knowledge through grafting, or recruiting "new members who possess knowledge not previously available within the organization."[38] Data repositories serve as another critical source of external information for organizations engaged in learning. But while data repositories provide explicit knowledge, information that can be codified and transmitted through written documents, results have been mixed with respect to their effectiveness in conveying tacit knowledge, information difficult to express in written or verbal form that relates to the implementation of an activity.[39] That being said, rapid developments in communication technology suggest that the internet may become increasingly capable of conveying tacit knowledge.[40]

Another way of thinking about the acquisition phase relates to the scope of an organization's learning. Organizations may either cast a broad net to search for new opportunities and knowledge or they may pursue a specific kind of information related to a perceived weakness or capabilities gap. Huber identifies four typologies for categorizing the scope of organizational learning. Organizations may engage in scanning, the "wide-ranging sensing" of developments, both internal and external, that could affect an organization's activities.[41] Scanning is often preemptive, aiming to identify issues before they directly impact an organization, and is likely directed by an organization's leadership. In contrast, focused search involves targeted examination of a defined issue. Noticing involves knowledge obtained unintentionally, through an organization's routine behaviors, often by individuals at the lower levels. Finally, performance monitoring involves assessment of an organization's own behavior.

Organizations can also draw on the existing knowledge of their members. One of the most influential sources of information is congenital knowledge, the inherited and institutionalized knowledge of an organization's founding members.[42] Initial decisions about an organization's structure, aims, and strategy are largely based on the decisions, knowledge, and outlook of the founders.[43] These inherited practices and procedures often prove formative in determining why, when, and how organizations learn.

But perhaps the most effective source of knowledge is experiential learning, which allows organizations to use trial and error to identify best practices. The effectiveness of experiential learning often depends on an organization's tolerance for risk and failure, as mistakes are "a rich breeding ground" for experiential learning.[44]

INTERPRETATION

Interpretation is the process by which meaning is imposed upon information that an organization has obtained. Information will be largely meaningless unless organizations can analyze and interpret it. Interpretation can be highly subjective and thus susceptible to organizational and individual biases. Numerous factors determine how organizations interpret information. An organization resistant to change or riven by internal schisms may be incapable of accurate interpretation. Organizational culture is often a crucial determinant. Ideological flexibility or rigidity influences how an organization interprets information. An organization wedded to a certain doctrine may be susceptible to biases, a factor germane for groups that subscribe to Salafi jihadist beliefs, which are in many ways inflexible. Additionally, rivals in an organization may interpret information to serve their own purposes even if it comes at the expense of the organization.

DISTRIBUTION

The distribution phase facilitates the transmission of knowledge from individuals and small groups to the organization as a whole. Distribution "significantly lowers the risk that an organization's learning will deteriorate" and ensures that knowledge obtained by an individual or small group will be retained even if the individual or group leaves.[45] However, the distribution process stands in tension with specialization of labor in a bureaucratic organization. Organizations in a growth state often pursue specialization to maximize efficiency. Specialization and its counterpart, compartmentalization, may reduce the likelihood that information is shared across an organization. This is especially salient in violent non-state actors, for whom information silos may be integral to operational security. When separate departments have information silos, they may be unaware when information they obtain would be valuable to other departments, resulting in inefficiencies and redundancy. Organizations intent on diffusing and institutionalizing knowledge must thus develop information-sharing policies.

Other impediments to distribution may be unique to violent non-state actors. For instance, the process of distributing knowledge may expose violent non-state actors' clandestine activities. Distribution requires coordination between different parts of the organization, which is generally not problematic for regular firms but may increase violent non-state actors' physical signature and reveal the scope and shape of their networks to adversaries.

ORGANIZATIONAL MEMORY

The organizational memory phase ensures that knowledge that is acquired, interpreted, and distributed throughout the organization is conserved and packaged so that individuals far from the original source of information can benefit from it. Storage often involves conversion of information from one type of knowledge to another. Business professors Mick Beeby and Charles Booth identify three types of knowledge conversion or transfer relevant to organizational memory: socialization, externalization, and internalization.[46] Socialization refers to the sharing of tacit knowledge within an organization, which in some cases can be conveyed through organizational culture. Externalization involves the "conversion of tacit into explicit knowledge through a process of codification."[47] This kind of knowledge conversion is likely to be incomplete, as some information will be lost in the conversion because of the sticky and intransigent nature of tacit knowledge. Finally, internalization concerns the transfer of explicit into tacit knowledge through routinization. Although this process may appear counterintuitive, as organizations typically seek to codify knowledge so it is easily transferable to new members, this step would ingrain explicit knowledge into an organization's cultural DNA.

Types of Organizational Learning

The type of learning an organization pursues depends on factors that include its appetite for learning and change, its capacity for risk, its ability to learn, and its needs. Several scholarly frameworks explain the distinctions among kinds of organizational learning. We highlight three that we find particularly valuable for understanding how violent non-state actors learn.

One framework distinguishes continuous improvement from discontinuous learning. Jackson and colleagues explain this distinction as "a question of the degree of change involved, not of how fast the change occurs."[48] Continuous learning aims to improve the activities an organization is already undertaking. This kind of learning is minimally disruptive yet can still produce significant outcomes. For example, even minor improvements in bomb construction can produce a higher body count. In contrast, discontinuous learning occurs when an organization seeks to fundamentally alter its behavior or introduce new capabilities. Although discontinuous learning is often associated with shifts at the strategic level, it can also affect an organization's tactical and operational capabilities. Through discontinuous learning, an organization can adopt novel tools, services, or activities that do not necessarily result in an immediate change in strategic course.

A second framework is offered by organizational learning theorists Chris Argyris and Donald Schön, who divide learning into single-loop, double-loop, and deutero-learning.[49] Single-loop learning, similar to continuous learning, involves correcting an organization's operating procedures within existing norms, policies, and objectives, while double-loop learning involves changing the organization's underlying policies and activities. Double-loop learning is thus analogous to discontinuous learning. Deutero-learning focuses on the learning process itself, evaluating previous instances of learning and identifying best practices. Deutero-learning represents potentially the most valuable type of learning.

A third framework considers the scope of change and accounts for the drivers of change. This framework, developed by organizational theorists David Nadler and Michael Tushman, identifies two spectrums of organizational learning: strategic/incremental and anticipatory/ reactive.[50] The strategic/incremental spectrum assesses the scope of orga- nizational learning, closely resembling the continuous/discontinuous binary, where incremental changes correspond to continuous learning and strategic changes to discontinuous learning. (While our definition of organizational learning rejects the idea that learning necessarily entails change, we employ the terminology of *changes* here to faithfully repre- sent Nadler and Tushman's work.) The anticipatory/reactive spectrum examines when an organization pursues learning. Anticipatory learning occurs when an entity seeks to gain an advantage preemptively, absent a precipitating event, while reactive learning is triggered by an external incident or change.

Based on these two spectrums, Nadler and Tushman identify four learning typologies (see figure 2.2): tuning, adaptation, reorientation, and re-creation. They describe change that is incremental and anticipatory as tuning, where organizations fine-tune their skills and capabilities. Nadler and Tushman define incremental and reactive learning as adaptation, pro- viding a solution to short-term obstacles but unlikely to resolve deeper issues. If jihadist groups over-rely on it, they may fall into an adaptation trap, wherein overdependence on adaptation may inhibit strategic learning. Nadler and Tushman's other two typologies focus on strategic learning aimed at fostering fundamental organizational change. They categorize learning that is strategic and anticipatory as reorientation and learning that is strategic and reactive as re-creation. Both kinds of learn- ing carry benefits and risks. Because reorientation occurs in a relatively low-pressure environment with no triggering event, organizations have

	Strategic	Incremental
Anticipatory	Reorientation	Tuning
Reactive	Re-creation	Adaptation

FIG. 2.2 Nadler and Tushman's organizational learning typologies

greater flexibility to explore various forms of knowledge. However, they may not accurately predict what kind of knowledge will be best suited to future challenges. Indeed, while an organization may engage in intentional anticipatory learning aimed at forestalling emerging challenges, certain factors—including flawed assumptions about the future—could produce ineffective learning outcomes. Organizations involved in re-creation face their own challenges. Such organizations are responding to a triggering event and can thus identify, generally with a high degree of accuracy, the kind of knowledge they need to obtain. But the obstacles associated with adopting sweeping change are greater, as re-creation occurs in an environment that is not conducive to learning.

These three frameworks constitute a comprehensive set of insights that this book draws upon in its consideration of organizational learning. The frameworks highlight two important ways to distinguish types of organizational learning: the scope and objective of the learning and the precipitating cause. With respect to scope, organizations can adjust their current procedures (hereafter called *continuous learning*) or adopt radical changes designed to upend the organizational status quo (hereafter called *discontinuous learning*). The causes of learning can be broadly described as either proactive or reactive. Proactive learning is when an organization perceives an opportunity to gain an advantage over competitors, while reactive learning is triggered by something that forces an organization to modify its behavior.

Factors Influencing the Outcome of Violent Non-State-Actor Organizational Learning

Many factors can influence the outcome of organizational learning, including internal dynamics (organizational structure, intragroup communications, membership, and culture) and external factors, such as the political and social environment.

ORGANIZATIONAL STRUCTURE

The degree of centralization and bureaucratization in an organization will affect its ability to explore new knowledge and exploit and disseminate that knowledge internally. A complex relationship exists between centralization and organizational learning. We discuss three degrees of organizational centralization: decentralized, centralized, and ambidextrous organizations.

Decentralized organizations are generally well equipped to engage in exploration. Cells in a decentralized structure do not have to coordinate their behavior across a hierarchy and have more autonomy to pursue new knowledge. Unconstrained by bureaucracy, decentralized organizations generally adapt more quickly than do centralized networks.[51] Decentralized organizations can respond in an agile manner as problems grow in complexity, as these organizations can "overcome the slowness of sequential decision processes."[52] However, lack of coordination among an organization's cells can create inefficiencies in the exploration process. Decentralization also presents obstacles to the exploitation of information as decentralized entities have trouble disseminating and storing knowledge internally. As political scientist Calvert Jones notes, "a decentralized, improvised pattern of learning could result in a fragmented, unstable source of organizational memory that impedes exploitation."[53] Because decentralized organizations struggle to commit knowledge to their institutional memory, they may lose information when key learners depart. Moreover, it is difficult for decentralized groups to implement strategic-level changes across the organization.[54] In cases of extreme decentralization, disparate cells may not communicate with one another at all, thus confining organizational learning to the cellular level.[55]

Centralized organizations often face obstacles to engaging in robust exploration activities because of the amount of bureaucracy involved in decision-making. The bureaucracy of most centralized organizations inhibits the "experimentation, search, risk-taking and innovation" involved in exploration.[56] Such centralized organizations may "plod along slowly and relentlessly" and are often unprepared to respond rapidly to developments.[57] But centralization is conducive to exploitation of existing knowledge. Centralization improves internal coordination, which facilitates dissemination of information throughout the organization, reduces redundancy in the exploration process, and reduces "competition and deception" between cells involved in exploration.[58] Despite this advantage, centralized organizations are not always perfectly situated to exploit information, which must pass through multiple layers of bureaucracy before it can be fully assimilated. Information may become distorted, condensed, or lost during the process of transmission.

Although the centralization/decentralization dichotomy offers a helpful framework for analyzing the relationship between organizational structure and learning, jihadist groups are generally not fully centralized or decentralized. Instead, these groups tend to maintain a dynamic balance between the two models. Typically, cells further from the organization's core (both geographically and hierarchically) are given autonomy to innovate and explore but are still responsive to the group leadership's strategic guidance.[59]

A third organizational model, the ambidextrous organization, excels at both exploration and exploitation.[60] These entities have decentralized decision-making systems that enable robust search activities but also include centralized subunits that focus on coordinating activities and strategy across the organization.[61] Tushman and O'Reilly explain that ambidextrous organizations "are simultaneously tight and loose. They are tight in that the corporate culture in each is broadly shared and emphasizes norms critical for innovation such as openness, autonomy, initiative, and risk taking. The culture is loose in that the manner in which these common values are expressed varies according to the type of innovation required."[62]

The ability of a group's leadership to instill core values crucial to learning allows the organization to retain its creativity even as it synthesizes and institutionalizes new knowledge.

INTRAGROUP COMMUNICATION

Another key determinant of learning is an organization's capacity to communicate. Organizational learning depends on the ability to disseminate information internally. Efficient exploration cannot occur unless units responsible for gathering new knowledge are aware of the knowledge that other units and members already possess. Exploitation requires that organizations disseminate knowledge acquired by exploratory units. If knowledge is not disseminated, or if it is distorted in the process of dissemination, the learning process will be imperfect.

Security threats influence how information is disseminated. Jihadist groups must balance information sharing with internal security, which often takes precedence. These groups regularly prioritize measures that will reduce their vulnerability to threats, even when these measures limit their ability to share knowledge and coordinate the collection of new information. One such measure is compartmentalization.

MEMBERSHIP OF AN ORGANIZATION

The makeup of an organization's personnel has a profound effect on learning. Three variables related to an organization's membership have a particularly important impact on learning: congenital knowledge, the ability of an organization to absorb new knowledge, and stability of membership.

With respect to congenital knowledge, jihadist groups often form around a small cadre of individuals who play an outsize role in shaping the organization's strategy, direction, and approach to learning. For instance, bin Laden's emphasis on entrepreneurship and providing autonomy to junior-level individuals continues to define al-Qaeda's innovation doctrine.[63] The characteristics, principles, and assumptions of a jihadist group's founders will be instructive in anticipating how that group will learn throughout its life cycle.

An organization's absorptive capacity depends on its learning processes and the kind of knowledge being absorbed. New knowledge that is similar to an organization's congenital knowledge, or to knowledge it has already assimilated, will be easier to absorb. Organizations may take longer, and struggle more, to assimilate "foreign" knowledge or information unrelated to their existing knowledge base.[64] An organization's culture, including its willingness to assimilate knowledge that conflicts with existing assumptions, is another determinant of absorptive capacity.

Another factor salient to the outcome of jihadist learning is the stability of a group's membership. High levels of attrition or personnel turnover can have a deleterious effect on organizational learning. This is especially true when information is concentrated in a few select members or when organizations are decentralized and lack bureaucratic controls. Hierarchies and centralized organizations are more resilient to turnover because they are less dependent on any single individual and because they commit information to institutional memory more effectively.[65] Organizations involved in complex tasks that require critical thinking and intra-organization coordination are also more susceptible to turnover because newcomers will experience a steep learning curve and will potentially make errors. But there is also a positive, if unintended, learning consequence to personnel turnover. "Old-timers" who have been with an organization for extended periods thrive at exploitation, in large part because they are attuned to an organization's procedures, but they are often ineffective explorers and can even be a source of resistance to new approaches.[66] Newcomers are less aware of, and less constrained by, institutional processes, making them well equipped to engage in exploration, although not in exploitation.[67]

Applying these scholarly observations about membership and organizational learning to jihadist groups, they experience disproportionately high levels of attrition due to leadership decapitation, conflict with counterinsurgent forces, and defections, among other causes. Such turnover is disruptive. The death or capture of a leader will result in the loss of a certain amount of organizational knowledge and memory. The elimination of highly connected individuals in compartmentalized jihadist organizations is also likely to hamper intragroup communication and coordination and hinder the group's efforts to exploit knowledge it has acquired. But high levels of personnel turnover and attrition may also drive jihadist innovation. The fluidity of membership ensures that new ideas and concepts are constantly introduced, and the risk of death provides further incentive for newcomers to innovate.

ORGANIZATIONAL CULTURE AND LEARNING MECHANISMS

As we noted, bin Laden's early efforts to encourage al-Qaeda's rank and file to innovate instilled an entrepreneurial spirit in the organization. An organization that encourages exploration through risk taking can inspire members to innovate. An organization that prefers stability and continuity can discourage members from pursuing new learning opportunities.

The preferences of a group's founders and leaders heavily influence the culture it adopts. Leaders play an outsize role in setting the tone of an organization. They dictate goals and strategy, establish procedures, and shape organizational direction. Although the influence of any single individual diminishes as the organization ages, leaders retain considerable authority. A group's leadership has a pronounced impact on the outcomes of organizational learning.[68]

A group's tolerance for risk also has an impact on the outcomes of organizational learning. To facilitate successful learning outcomes, organizations must be willing to tolerate risk and even encourage personnel to make mistakes as they experiment.[69] Organizations that exhibit aversion to risk will discourage members from testing new ideas.

Some private firms, aware of the relationship between risk tolerance and innovation, have gone to lengths to foster environments where employees are encouraged to experiment. The payroll services company SurePayroll offers an annual $400 award, known as the Best New Mistake Award, to employees who take risks and learn from their mistakes. SurePayroll's president said, "If you don't encourage people to take risks, then you end up with incrementalism forever. Mistakes are the tuition you pay for success."[70]

But the factors that jihadist groups consider when determining their tolerance for risk differ from those weighed by for-profit companies. Employees of for-profit firms who make errors typically aren't killed or arrested as a result. This fact may push jihadist groups toward a more conservative approach to innovation. Conversely, jihadist groups must constantly adapt to state actors and other rivals. They must balance the perils of failure with the grave consequences of stagnation.

Ideology also plays a role in determining jihadist groups' appetite for risk and broader view of organizational learning. Jihadist groups are heavily influenced by their religiopolitical worldview, generally referred to as Salafi jihadism.[71] Although this worldview allows for tactical and even strategic flexibility, ideological considerations still influence and constrain jihadist groups' organizational learning processes. Jihadist organizations may choose to pursue knowledge that aligns with their worldview while eschewing needed changes that are incongruent with their ideology.

EXTERNAL ENVIRONMENT

In the years leading up to 9/11, al-Qaeda's base in Afghanistan served as an ideal location for training recruits and formulating new plots. Facing extremely limited counterterrorism pressure, the group methodically planned 9/11 and deployed cells to Western Europe and the United States to lay the groundwork for the attack. By September 2001, al-Qaeda was well positioned to carry out its mission.

The preparation for the 9/11 plot illustrates how an organization's external environment can influence the way it learns. Jihadist groups in high-threat environments must prioritize their security, which often has a detrimental impact on learning processes. Groups operating in a low-threat environment can engage in robust exploration and exploitation. Al-Qaeda's experience in Afghanistan before 9/11 and ISIS's while it enjoyed a monopoly of violence in its caliphate territory demonstrate the possibilities for learning available to violent non-state actors in permissive locations. Al-Qaeda's training camps played a particularly crucial role in facilitating learning and the transfer of implicit knowledge.[72]

The Violent Non-State-Actor Technology Adoption Curve

In the current dynamic technological environment, jihadist groups' organizational learning processes and outcomes are highly connected to new and emerging technologies. To elucidate this, we propose a theoretical model, the violent non-state-actor technology adoption curve. This curve consists of four phases. Early adoption is marked by a violent non-state actor attempting to adopt a new technology and then disproportionately underperforming or failing. The second phase is iteration, during which the consumer technology the violent non-state actor is attempting to repurpose undergoes improvements. These improvements are designed to benefit consumers, but the violent non-state actor benefits too, honing its uses of the same technology. The third phase is breakthrough, where the violent non-state actor's success rate with the technology significantly improves. The final phase is competition, where adversaries adapt to counter this breakthrough. Following the violent non-state actor's seemingly sudden success in the breakthrough phase, technology companies, state actors, and other stakeholders develop countermeasures. The contours of this phase are the most difficult to anticipate, as both the violent non-state actor and its adversaries enter uncharted territory while technology plunges forward apace. The violent non-state actor technology adoption curve is shown in figure 2.3.

It is not inevitable that a violent non-state actor's attempts to adopt a technology will ultimately succeed after initial efforts fall short. Nor is it inevitable that a violent non-state actor will fail in the earliest stages of adopting a new technology. Sometimes its very first effort will be a stunning success—often followed by a series of disappointing second acts, as the actor moves into the iteration phase. Our adoption curve should not

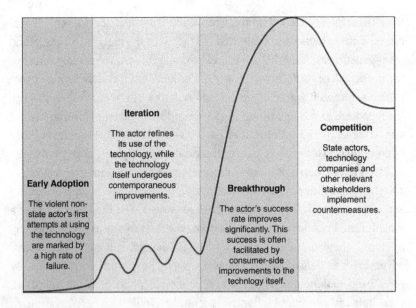

Early Adoption

The violent non-state actor's first attempts at using the technology are marked by a high rate of failure.

Iteration

The actor refines its use of the technology, while the technology itself undergoes contemporaneous improvements.

Breakthrough

The actor's success rate improves significantly. This success is often facilitated by consumer-side improvements to the technlogy itself.

Competition

State actors, technology companies and other relevant stakeholders implement countermeasures.

FIG. 2.3 The violent non-state-actor technology adoption curve

be understood as deterministic but rather as a frequently repeated pattern that holds explanatory power. The adoption curve is intended to help practitioners and scholars avoid misdiagnosing a violent non-state actor's actions early in the adoption process.

Specifically, it is at best overly simplistic, and perhaps outright inaccurate, to see the violent non-state actor's early attempts as "failures" and its later third-phase attempts as "successes" in a binary fashion. In understanding the problems with this binary, it is useful to consider improvements made by tech companies. Scholars of entrepreneurship understand that it may take companies time to iterate before they find success. For instance, Rovio Entertainment Corporation designed fifty-one unsuccessful games before producing the wildly popular Angry Birds.[73] Many for-profit firms now perceive a need to bring less-than-perfect products to market, which are generally known as the minimum viable product (MVP).[74] In contrast to businesses in earlier technological generations, where a poor initial product could doom a firm's reputation, in the digital space, firms can rapidly improve products even while they are in customers' hands.

MVP principles allow a firm to disseminate a product soon after it is viable, take advantage of initial limited contact with the market to understand what consumers like and dislike, and leverage this data to rapidly improve the product. The initial attempts are not failures but rather learning opportunities. Just as it would be inaccurate to think of the early stages in the MVP process as a firm failing, so too should early attempts in the violent non-state actor adoption curve be viewed outside the success/failure binary. Early attempts are part of the process of learning and iterating.

The violent non-state-actor technology adoption curve should help counter the tendency to discount a violent non-state actor's efforts to employ a new technology during its early stages. The inclination to see a violent non-state actor's failures with a new technology as static and permanent is flawed and dangerous. It often leads violent non-state actors' adversaries to delay countermeasures until the breakthrough stage. By reframing violent non-state actors' processes of technology adoption, stakeholders can more effectively counter malicious exploitation of technologies.

This chapter's discussion of the factors influencing learning processes and outcomes and its violent non-state-actor technology adoption curve will shape the book's discussion of how jihadist groups' organizational learning influences their operations. These groups must engage in a perpetual process of adaptation. We now turn to jihadist groups' learning in practice, beginning with an examination of a strategic shift that proved highly consequential: al-Qaeda's refocusing of its militant activities against the "far enemy." The shift toward prioritizing the fight against the far enemy was itself the product of organizational learning—specifically, of al-Qaeda's examination of the disastrous results for the movement that three failed regional jihads produced in the 1990s.

3

The Far-Enemy Strategy

Osama bin Laden's first declaration of war against America came in an eight-thousand-word fax sent to the London-based newspaper *Al-Quds Al-Arabi* in September 1996. "There is no greater duty after faith," read the eloquent Arabic-language statement, than "warding off the Israeli-American alliance occupying the land of the two holy mosques and the land of the ascension of the Prophet."[1]

Bin Laden was then a relatively obscure Saudi dissident newly arrived in eastern Afghanistan, one of the more remote corners of the planet. Bin Laden's statement argued against conclusions long ago embraced by his own movement's theoreticians. As international relations scholar Sohail Hashmi notes, there was then "a consensus among radical Islamist groups" that "the United States, though an enemy, was too powerful to attack directly, at least in the foreseeable future."[2] Despite the odds stacked against him, it soon became clear that bin Laden's ambition of striking a faraway superpower was anything but delusional.

Motivating these efforts was the al-Qaeda's founder's view that the U.S.-led West and Israel were conquering the world's Muslims by dividing them. Bin Laden's declaration outlined his reasons for treating the "Israeli-American alliance" as the jihadist movement's main enemy rather than the "near enemy" of nominally Islamic regimes (which his movement held to be composed of apostates and heretics) that ruled the world's

Muslim-majority countries. The 9/11 attacks may create the misleading perception that al-Qaeda and the jihadist movement always saw the West as its primary foe. Although bin Laden long despised the United States and the West, there is a more complex story to be told about how the far enemy became al-Qaeda's strategic priority by the mid-1990s, at least for a fleeting moment.

At the core of how al-Qaeda came to prioritize its fight against the far enemy is organizational learning the group undertook at the strategic level. As the son of a well-connected Saudi construction magnate who refurbished Islam's holiest sites in Mecca and Medina, bin Laden was intimately familiar with Saudi Arabia's royal family. When bin Laden definitively turned against the Saudi monarchy, its king was Fahd bin Abdul Aziz al-Saud, who became the crown prince in 1975 and the king in 1982. Despite suffering a stroke in 1995, he remained Saudi Arabia's nominal ruler until his death in 2005.

As crown prince, Fahd dedicated hundreds of millions of dollars to the anti-Soviet war effort in 1980s-era Afghanistan, which this chapter discusses in detail. Under Fahd, Saudi Arabia and Pakistan coordinated anti-Soviet efforts, creating a network of fighters, guns, and money stretching from the Gulf into South Asia. Bin Laden began his jihadist career in this milieu, working alongside the Saudi and Pakistani intelligence services.[3] Bin Laden first traveled to Pakistan in the early 1980s, soon after the Afghan–Soviet war began. Upon arrival, bin Laden became "a major financier of the mujahedin, providing cash to the relatives of wounded or martyred fighters, building hospitals, and helping the millions of Afghan refugees fleeing to the border region of Pakistan."[4] But it was his first trip to the front lines in 1984 that left a lasting impression on bin Laden and left him with a thirst for action.

Although there is no evidence that bin Laden ever worked directly with the Americans, the CIA backed the broader Saudi-Pakistani war in the hope of dealing a strategic blow to the Soviet Union.[5] While bin Laden and the United States were on the same side of the Afghan–Soviet war, the rich young Saudi despised the United States even then.

Al-Qaeda was founded in the final days of the Afghan–Soviet war. The minutes from al-Qaeda's first meetings in August 1988 were ambiguous as to the group's objectives. Although these minutes explained that al-Qaeda's goal was to make Islam "victorious," they lacked explanation of what victory meant or how it might be achieved. The minutes revealed, though, that considerable attention was devoted to al-Qaeda's organizational structure, attesting to the importance its founders placed on developing bureaucratic practices and procedures.[6]

The first Gulf War prompted the group's objectives to become more specific. Whatever bin Laden's view of the Saudi regime before Saddam Hussein's August 1990 invasion of Kuwait, he remained willing to accept its help during the Afghan–Soviet war. But the Iraqi dictator's advance into Kuwait uprooted bin Laden's relationship with the Saudi regime, which justifiably feared that Saddam would extend his military campaign into its territory. Bin Laden approached the Saudi royals. He proposed that he and his men could protect the kingdom on their own, claiming that he could raise an "Islamic army" of sixty thousand men.[7]

Bin Laden's offer was delusional. He didn't have nearly that many fighters, let alone the capability to repel Saddam Hussein's powerful military. Riyadh declined his offer, and defense of the land of the two holy mosques fell to an American-led coalition that used Saudi Arabia as a staging area for the campaign to liberate Kuwait in early 1991. Much of the world celebrated the American-led victory, but bin Laden did not. For him, the presence of American forces in the Islamic holy land was a sacrilege, far worse than Iraq's occupation of Kuwait.

Al-Qaeda was involved in some attacks abroad beginning in these early days. In November 1991 Paulo José de Almeida Santos, a Portuguese al-Qaeda recruit, was arrested in Rome after he tried to assassinate Mohammed Zahir Shah, the former Afghan king.[8] In December 1992 the group bombed two hotels in Yemen that housed U.S. soldiers heading to the Horn of Africa to support Operation Restore Hope, a UN-sanctioned humanitarian mission to Somalia. Al-Qaeda played an indeterminate role in the October 1993 downing of a U.S. helicopter in Mogadishu, the infamous "Black Hawk Down" incident.[9]

These early steps were a prelude to bin Laden's 1996 declaration of war. Bin Laden saw America's presence in Saudi Arabia not as a defensive force against Saddam Hussein's continuing provocations but as occupiers. In his declaration, bin Laden described "the occupation of the land of the two holy mosques" as "one of the worst catastrophes to befall the Muslims since the death of the Prophet."[10] Much of bin Laden's declaration of war was in fact a condemnation of the Saudi government, which he criticized for suppressing a fundamentalist Islamic reform movement and for replacing sharia laws with "temporal laws." Bin Laden said the typical Saudi suffered under poor economic conditions while the ruling clique ransacked the country's oil wealth.

Still, bin Laden stopped short of calling for a rebellion against the Saudi royals. Indeed, in an interview he gave around that time, he held "open the possibility of reconciliation between the Saudi government and its people, but only after it effects 'essential changes, the most important of which is to bring back Islamic law.' "[11] Instead of calling for violent overthrow of the Saudi regime in his 1996 statement, bin Laden focused his call to violence on the "Israeli-American alliance," at whose behest he saw the Saudi government acting—and who, in turn, he viewed as critical to propping up the House of Saud. The good news, in bin Laden's view, was that America could be defeated. This was shown by the U.S.'s flight from Somalia after the aforementioned October 1993 bloodshed. Addressing the Americans, bin Laden said: "You left the country, defeated and carrying your dead. . . . Your impotence and weakness were evident."[12]

While bin Laden didn't call for violent overthrow of the Saudi regime in his 1996 statement, his stance toward the kingdom progressively hardened. By the spring of 2003 an al-Qaeda-linked insurgency took root in Saudi Arabia. The al-Qaeda-initiated fight "would be the longest and most violent sustained internal struggle against the Saudi monarchy and establishment since the founding of the modern Saudi state."[13] Bin Laden's loyalists targeted Westerners and Saudi officials, engaging in near-daily skirmishes with security forces for several months in 2003. This violent campaign only began to subside in 2006.[14] But the Saudis ultimately crushed the uprising, forcing al-Qaeda to regroup in Yemen.

This chapter tells the story of how al-Qaeda, through its organizational learning processes, came to prioritize the fight against the far enemy. As we noted, at the time of bin Laden's 1996 declaration there was a consensus in the jihadist movement that the near enemy should be militants' priority. Jihadists were engaged in three major conflicts in the Middle East and North Africa region, none of them against the far enemy. The Armed Islamic Group (GIA) waged a bloody war against the Algerian government that would claim around 150,000 lives. Gama'a al-Islamiyya and Tanzim al-Jihad regularly conducted attacks designed to weaken Hosni Mubarak's grip on Egypt, while Muammar al-Qaddafi's regime faced the Libyan Islamic

Fighting Group (LIFG).[15] Al-Qaeda's occasional attacks against American targets aside, essentially all the major jihadist battles were against regional governments, and al-Qaeda itself sponsored or conducted attacks on near-enemy targets throughout the 1990s.

Bin Laden's 1996 statement thus suggested a new path. When al-Qaeda executed its deadly bombings against two American embassies in East Africa in August 1998, it galvanized the jihadist movement in a way that a faxed document could not. Disagreements remained, but they were largely resolved—at least temporarily—by the 9/11 attacks. Put simply, the scale of the violence in New York, Washington, and Pennsylvania captured the jihadist imagination, and the American response further encouraged jihadist groups, in investigative journalist Camille Tawil's words, "to unite behind bin Laden, despite their grave reservations about his agenda."[16]

Ideological Antecedents and the Early Fights Against the Near Enemy

Understanding the conception of the 9/11 attacks requires an examination of the ideological forebears who helped blaze the path to striking the towers. In chapter 2, we note that ideological rigidity or flexibility plays a role in determining organizations' appetite for learning. Jihadist groups possess rigid ideologies that inform their worldview, but they can be quite flexible and willing to engage in organizational learning on matters of strategy or tactics. One mistake that observers frequently make is viewing al-Qaeda's far-enemy focus that emerged in the 1990s as an ideological rather than a strategic decision. To be clear, there were ideological reasons that al-Qaeda and other jihadists viewed the United States and the West as an enemy. Our point is that the decision to prioritize the fight against the far enemy over the near one was strategic rather than ideological. The fact that the movement's enemy prioritization was dictated by pragmatic rather than ideological concerns later allowed a deprioritization of the far enemy when regional opportunities grew in the post–Arab Spring environment.

We now turn to the intellectual history critical to discussion of how the far enemy came to dominate al-Qaeda's strategic outlook during an important period. From Sayyid Qutb to Muhammad Abd al-Salam Faraj to

Abdullah Azzam and Jalaluddin Haqqani, the movement's military strategy underwent several important iterations before bin Laden's rise to prominence.

SAYYID QUTB

Sayyid Qutb (1906–1966), originally a literary critic, is a theorist whose contributions proved to be a lasting influence, including on jihadist groups active today. Numerous factors contributed to his radicalization, including Britain's occupation of Egypt and American support for Israel's establishment. But Qutb also spent a formative period in the United States, which deeply influenced him. During his two years studying in America in the late 1940s, Qutb grew disgusted by what he saw as the country's licentiousness. The shocked Qutb saw sex and sexuality everywhere he turned, from the hotels of New York City to even church dances in Greeley, Colorado.

To Qutb, America's dominant position in the postwar world made the country's moral degeneration all the more threatening. Qutb's experiences in America didn't just stoke his hatred for the country but also shaped the themes in his theoretical work, which addressed the decline of the "Muslim world." Qutb's secularist contemporaries believed Islamic societies had declined because they gave religion too privileged a position. Qutb instead blamed deviation from the original values in the Qur'an and the Prophet Muhammad's example, the Sunna.[17]

Qutb's ideal society would abide by the tenets of Islam's original sources and live in submission to God's absolute authority over rule and law. He argued that deviation from this ideal constituted *jahiliya*, a term that literally means *ignorance* but has specific theological connotations.[18] For Qutb, a political system that fails to make God sovereign and implement Islamic law is *jahiliya*. This definition encompassed both sides of the Cold War but didn't just describe the two superpowers. Qutb wrote that "all the societies existing in the world today are of *jahiliya*," including "all the existing so-called 'Muslim' societies."[19] Even nominally Islamic countries governed and organized their societies in ways that were "not based on submission to God alone."[20] The major themes in Qutb's work—including the importance of implementing God's law and reviving the glory of the global

Muslim community, or the Ummah—are now common refrains in jihadist groups' discourse.

Another aspect of Qutb's writing that had a powerful impact on later militant movements was his discussion of the need for a dedicated vanguard, a core of believers who could begin laying the conditions for Qutb's envisioned theocracy. Qutb reflected on how the task of reviving Islam could begin:

> It is necessary that there should be a vanguard which sets out with this determination and then keeps walking on the path, marching through the vast ocean of *jahiliya* which has encompassed the entire world. . . . They ought to be aware of their position vis-à-vis this *jahiliya*, which has struck its stakes throughout the earth: when to cooperate with others and when to separate from them: what characteristics and qualities they should cultivate, and with what characteristics and qualities the *jahiliya* immediately surrounding them is armed; how to address the people of *jahiliya* in the language of Islam, and what topics and problems ought to be discussed; and where and how to obtain guidance in all these matters.[21]

The vanguard was so central to Qutb's vision that he dedicated his signature work *Milestones* (*Ma'alim fi-l-tariq*) to this group.[22] Qutb did not live long enough to operationalize what this vanguard would mean in practice, as Egyptian president Gamal Abdel Nasser executed him in 1966. It would be up to later militant thinkers to articulate what Qutb's program meant in practice.

MUHAMMAD ABD AL-SALAM FARAJ

Egyptian militant Muhammad Abd al-Salam Faraj's core contribution to jihadist thought was concretizing the strategy of violently confronting impious governments that were nominally Muslim. He led a branch of Tanzim al-Jihad, known in English as Egyptian Islamic Jihad (EIJ). Faraj wrote an internally distributed tract titled *Jihad: The Neglected Duty* in which he argued that Muslims were obligated to revive the caliphate, which had ended with the Ottoman Empire's dissolution. Faraj wrote that "the tyrants [*tawagheet*] of this world will not disappear except by the force of the sword."[23]

His reference to tyrants seems to denote all non-Islamic forms of authority. Faraj, like Qutb, imagined an eventual world order in which sovereignty belonged to God. Faraj argued that what is commonly considered the abode of Islam (*dar al-Islam*) had actually become the abode of unbelief (*dar al-kufr*) because secular laws and rulings now governed Muslim lands. If Muslims are forced to submit to an authority that has fallen into *kufr*, Faraj reasoned, that authority loses the right to govern, and the Muslims must replace it through violent revolution.

One notable section of Faraj's tract is titled "the near enemy and the far enemy." In it, Faraj argues that while "liberating the holy lands is a *sharia* obligation"—a reference to the fight against Israel—the jihadists' struggle against Egypt's government should take precedence because "fighting the near enemy is of more importance than fighting the far enemy."[24] Faraj's militant career accordingly focused on the near-enemy government of Egypt. He described the destruction of Israel as "useless" unless Muslim societies were first transformed.[25]

Faraj served as a key leader in the EIJ cell that assassinated Egyptian president Anwar Sadat on October 6, 1981, then launched a hasty insurrection. Sadat's murder failed to galvanize a large-scale revolt against the regime, although violent clashes shook the southern city of Asyut, with dozens of police killed. Faraj was executed for his role in the plot to assassinate Sadat.

Hashmi notes the relative lack of theological argument in Faraj's tract.[26] Faraj rooted his prioritization of the near enemy in the fact that the Prophet Muhammad "described the believer as 'sagacious and prudent,' and this means that the Muslim knows what is useful and what is harmful."[27] Faraj thus relied on the words of the Prophet to allow the believer to pragmatically consider whether to prioritize the near or far enemy. Under Faraj's calculus, which enemy should be prioritized by militants would be a proper subject of organizational learning.

EARLY FIGHTS AGAINST THE NEAR ENEMY

Around the time of Sadat's assassination, Islamists were taking aim at some of the Middle East's most powerful states. In 1979 Juhayman al-Otaybi and his followers seized Mecca's Grand Mosque. Syrian Islamists sustained an uprising against Hafez al-Assad's government from 1976 until the regime brutally suppressed them in 1982. But none of the early campaigns seriously challenged the near-enemy regimes.

Otaybi held views that are either eccentric or outright heretical from a Salafi perspective. For example, he declared that his colleague Muhammad al-Qahtani was the Mahdi.[28] Nonetheless, Otaybi's story constituted one of the rebellions against the region's regimes that would inform jihadist groups' strategic learning. Further, despite his theological eccentricities, Otaybi adhered to some ideas that would become central to jihadist ideology. For example, one of Otaybi's pamphlets reveals such themes as the argument that Muslim rulers had deviated from implementing God's law.[29]

Otaybi and four hundred to five hundred of his armed followers slipped into the tens of thousands of worshippers visiting the Grand Mosque on the morning of November 20, 1979. Before the morning (*fajr*) prayer, the attackers killed several police officers, locked the mosque's outer doors, and took control of the holy sites. From the pulpit, Otaybi declared that the Mahdi had arrived. The worshippers had become his hostages (though many were later freed by the militants).

Violence is thought to be religiously proscribed within the Grand Mosque's walls, so Saudi authorities had to obtain a fatwa from Sheikh Abdul Aziz bin Baz, the country's highest religious authority, before they felt comfortable launching a counteroffensive.[30] The Saudis tried several times to retake the mosque, with some spectacular failures. For example, Saudi defense minister Prince Sultan "directed a suicidal helicopter assault in which troops were lowered on ropes into the vast courtyard in the center of the mosque. They were slaughtered."[31] The king promptly replaced Prince Sultan with Prince Turki al-Faisal as the operation's head.

Prince Turki asked France for assistance. Although the Saudis conducted much of the combat in the final assault—the French dispatched only three commandos—jihadist groups came to see France's involvement as emblematic of how the far enemy would step in to prop up the near one.

The takeover of the Grand Mosque was audacious, but the Syrian revolt was the bloodiest of the early near-enemy-focused campaigns. The Syrian Muslim Brotherhood had participated in parliamentary politics until Assad's Ba'athist regime seized power and banned the Islamist group's political participation. The Brotherhood waged an increasingly aggressive military campaign in response.

Isolated incidents of Islamist violence through the 1960s and early 1970s built into a wider revolt beginning in 1976, when several Brotherhood-affiliated groups launched attacks against the regime. The violence escalated in 1979–1980, when militants killed thirty-two cadets in an assault on an Aleppo military academy and tried to assassinate Assad. The regime's crackdown corralled the rebels into Hama in western Syria. In February 1982 Assad's army leveled parts of the city, killing thousands of rebels and civilians.[32] As in Saudi Arabia a few years earlier, the state crushed a militant Islamic movement.

Jihadists grappled with the implications of these battles with the near enemy. Killing an Egyptian president, capturing Islam's holiest site, and warring against Assad's regime were not minor feats. But they hadn't brought jihadists measurably closer to their objectives. One noteworthy attempt to make sense of these events was Abu Musab al-Suri's nine-hundred-page *The Syrian Experience*, which blamed the Syrian revolt's failure on the Muslim Brotherhood and an associated militant group, the Fighting Vanguard. In addition to tactical critiques, Suri attacked the Brotherhood's lack of a "considered strategic program" and its failure to establish a central administration for military operations.[33] These mistakes, in his estimation, guaranteed that any victories the rebellion experienced would be short-lived. Suri did not fault the strategy of fighting the near enemy, but in blaming the Brotherhood for the uprising's failure, he advanced a key theme that appeared in the work of other jihadist theoreticians. Ayman al-Zawahiri's *Bitter Harvest*, which first appeared in 1988 when Zawahiri was an EIJ leader, heaped scorn on the Brotherhood's influential Egyptian branch. Zawahiri delivered a harsh verdict on sixty years of Brotherhood activism in Egypt.[34]

Brotherhood-linked ideologues like Qutb might have influenced the course of jihadism, but in the wake of the early jihadist campaigns, Salafi jihadist thinkers increasingly defined themselves against the Brotherhood, which was viewed as the province of incompetents and sellouts. Suri's screed and Zawahiri's *Bitter Harvest* set the tone for the coming jihadist wave that rejected the Brotherhood's poorly organized militancy and some of its branches' pragmatic approach to electoral politics.

The Afghan Jihad

As the near-enemy campaigns fizzled, events more than 1,500 miles to the east changed the course of jihadism. The Soviet invasion of Afghanistan in December 1979 and Moscow's futile decade-long military campaign in the country sparked the first global Muslim militant mobilization of modern times.[35] It came at an opportune time for Islamist militants. With their movement floundering, the Afghan jihad was a chance to regroup and perhaps to reassess their approach.

The Soviets invaded Afghanistan for numerous reasons, including an Islamist insurgency that threatened the country's pro-Soviet regime, concerns that America might meddle there as a hedge against a hostile new revolutionary government in Iran, and infighting among Afghanistan's communists that culminated in the assassination of the country's president.[36] The invasion generated widespread outrage in Muslim-majority countries. Foreign volunteers poured into the region to assist the anti-Soviet war effort, including "humanitarian aid workers, cooks, drivers, accountants, teachers, doctors, engineers and religious preachers."[37] There was also a sizable contingent of foreign fighters.

THE THEORETICIAN: ABDULLAH AZZAM

Several participants in the Afghan–Soviet conflict emerged as important theorists explaining why foreign Muslims were obligated to contribute to the anti-Soviet struggle. Much of this thinking centered on the necessity of waging a defensive jihad against an invading force. Steven Brooke notes that foreign fighters drawn to South Asia "were not motivated by a desire to confront the far enemy" but rather by the fact that the Soviet Union had "invaded Muslim lands."[38] One participant who powerfully articulated this view was Abdullah Azzam, a Palestinian-born cleric who held a doctorate in Islamic studies from Cairo's Al-Azhar University.

After the Soviet invasion, Azzam traveled to Pakistan, where he established the Maktab al-Khidamat (Services Bureau), one of the better-known organizations supporting the anti-Soviet mobilization. Assassinated under mysterious circumstances in 1989, Azzam remains highly regarded in jihadist circles today.[39] In 1984 Azzam issued a consequential fatwa titled "Defending Muslim Lands: The Most Important of the Obligations on Every

Muslim." In it, Azzam distinguished between offensive jihad as a collective obligation (*fard kifaya*) and defensive jihad as an individual obligation (*fard 'ayn*). Azzam argued that the defense of Afghanistan was *fard 'ayn* because of the non-Muslim invasion. In such a situation, he explained, the obligation to wage defensive jihad first falls on the Muslims who dwell there. If they cannot defend the lands, the religious imperative broadens, encompassing any Muslim in a position to help repel the invasion. When an obligation is *fard 'ayn*, there is no need to seek parental or spousal permission to fulfill it. (Although Azzam's ruling has gained the most notoriety, Jalaluddin Haqqani actually made this argument several years before Azzam did.[40])

Azzam envisioned the rise of an Islamic state in Afghanistan.[41] But his fatwa does not clarify what agenda Azzam had beyond Afghanistan. He was silent on whether militants should overthrow nominally Muslim regimes. Azzam built on Qutb and Faraj in articulating a rationale for obligatory jihad but didn't offer a comprehensive program for global jihad or any solution to the recent setbacks that Salafi jihadists had faced.

AFGHANISTAN'S JIHADIST MILIEU

During this period, Afghanistan was crawling with jihadists obsessed with the questions Azzam seemed to ignore. Why hadn't they been able to defeat the so-called Muslim regimes? What should they be doing differently? The anti-Soviet jihad attracted Egyptian hardliners, adventurous Gulf Salafists, and Muslim Brothers, many of whom had experienced persecution or defeat in their home countries. When the Soviet Union withdrew from Afghanistan, these global jihadist factions began considering their future direction.

Bin Laden was the war's most famous foreign fighter. The future al-Qaeda leader first traveled to Pakistan in the early 1980s and, as detailed earlier, soon became a major financier of the mujahedin. Bin Laden and Abdullah Azzam grew close, just one relationship among many forged during the conflict that would have lasting ramifications.

The Egyptian hardliners were especially influential in the Afghan milieu. Ayman al-Zawahiri and Sayyid Imam al-Sharif (better known as Dr. Fadl) of EIJ had both lived relatively privileged lives before devoting themselves to religious militancy. Zawahiri was born in 1951 to an upper-class family in Cairo. He completed medical school at Cairo University, then earned a master's degree in surgery. Zawahiri and his younger brother, Mohammed, immersed themselves in Egypt's burgeoning militant scene, and the Zawahiri brothers became key figures in EIJ. Ayman famously served as the group's spokesman during the hastily organized trials that followed Sadat's assassination and eventually became the group's emir. Sharif, who was born in 1950, also studied medicine at Cairo University and first met Zawahiri at the school. Sharif was renowned for his brilliance and piety, and he and Zawahiri bonded over their shared commitment to Islamist causes. Although Sharif initially declined Zawahiri's invitation to join EIJ, his friendship with Zawahiri and involvement in the Afghan jihad forged his path to a key leadership position in the group.[42]

Many Egyptian Islamists who went to Afghanistan had already endured the crackdown that followed Sadat's assassination and viewed the Afghan-Soviet war as a training ground for a renewed campaign to overthrow Egypt's near-enemy government. Indeed, Zawahiri's *Bitter Harvest* may have been written in part to persuade Afghanistan's foreign fighters to go to war against near-enemy regimes in their native lands rather than participate in political processes. Like Zawahiri, Sharif wrote an influential essay designed to guide the post-Afghanistan jihadist movement. Sharif's *The Essential Guide for Preparation* demonstrates how deeply ingrained the near-enemy strategy was, as it assumed that the need to prioritize the fight against nominally Muslim regimes was self-evident. "It is necessary to begin by fighting the near enemy," Sharif wrote, as "the rulers who don't rule by Islam's *sharia* in many of the Muslim lands, these people are *kuffar* . . . and most of these people claim affiliation [with Islam] so they in their *kufr* have become apostates."[43] Since the apostate is deemed more dangerous than the disbeliever, fighting the former over the latter naturally takes precedence.

But for all the focus on the near enemy during this period, the jihadist movement also grew increasingly anti-American and anti-Western. There were tensions between Azzam and members of EIJ—disagreements that ultimately contributed to al-Qaeda's birth—but anti-Americanism was a point of agreement. Although EIJ theorists favored fighting the near enemy, they still perceived the hands of the West as driving their country's problems. Fawaz Gerges notes a document produced by the group in the 1980s titled *America, Egypt and the Islamist Movement* that identified the United

States as its main enemy.[44] Similarly, in his 1988 article "al-Qaeda al-Sulbah" (the solid base), Azzam warned of "global plans against Islam" and portrayed America as "trying to steal the fruits of this great jihad."[45] For the jihadists, even the United States' role in defeating the Soviet invasion was evidence of the far enemy's evil schemes.

The Battle of Jaji and the Birth of al-Qaeda

The Battle of Jaji, a campaign fought against Soviet forces in April to May 1987, was a euphoric moment for bin Laden. He had established a base for Arab fighters near Khost in eastern Afghanistan in 1986. It was a divisive move, with one former comrade contending that it would result in young Arabs dying needlessly.[46] Azzam also thought Arab fighters should be embedded with Afghan units to teach the latter about "true Islam" and thus opposed the creation of a separate Arab force.

Bin Laden forged ahead anyway. His fighters called their Khost base al-Masada, Arabic for *the lion's den*. Al-Masada was close to a Soviet garrison, and the enemy moved against bin Laden's outpost in the spring of 1987. Bin Laden and his comrades unexpectedly held their ground against Russian special forces (*spetsnaz*). There are varying accounts of the battle, with some mujahedin claiming they routed the Soviets through superior tactics.[47] Even if some of their tales are hyperbolic, the Arab fighters clearly fought better than the Soviets expected. The battle launched bin Laden to prominence in the Arabic-language media.

Although the Battle of Jaji was insignificant to the outcome of the Afghan–Soviet war, it is historically important because of the impact it had on bin Laden. The battle was his biggest success as a militant to that point. The Battle of Jaji and bin Laden's other exploits in the Afghan–Soviet war convinced bin Laden that fighting secular superpowers wasn't desperate or suicidal. Further, his growing confidence contributed to his break from his mentor. Abdullah Azzam's son Hutaifa observed that the post-Jaji bin Laden possessed greater self-assurance, which Hutaifa saw as partially responsible for bin Laden eventually separating himself from Azzam.[48] While al-Qaeda continued to publicly laud Azzam in the decades to come, bin Laden's organization was founded not to praise Azzam but to bury him. Al-Qaeda was specifically designed to supersede Azzam's Maktab al-Khidamat (MaK). *Tareekh Osama* (Osama's history), a computer file seized from Benevolence International Foundation's Sarajevo offices that contains al-Qaeda's founding minutes, reveals how al-Qaeda's founders saw their organization as addressing MaK's flaws. Al-Qaeda's first generation of leaders faulted MaK for "mismanagement and bad treatment," with bin Laden saying al-Qaeda would be "making a change" from MaK's methods of finance and administration.[49]

From the outset, al-Qaeda's leadership envisioned a hierarchical, rules-based organization. The minutes from al-Qaeda's first meetings decreed that all members would have to obey the group's "statutes and instructions." One founding document, which the Combating Terrorism Center at West Point identifies as al-Qaeda's original bylaws, goes into depth about the group's decision-making processes and command structure.[50] Al-Qaeda's emir was to be the ultimate authority on strategic decisions, with a final say on appointment of the group's leadership. One of the emir's responsibilities would be to "discuss and implement" annual plans, along with al-Qaeda's budget and internal structure. The emir appointed all members of the leadership council, al-Qaeda's most senior decision-making body. While the document states that the emir has what amounts to an irrefutable final say on strategic matters, it limits his involvement in day-to-day operations. The emir should take a largely hands-off approach at the operational and tactical level, with his involvement limited to participating in "periodic meetings" and reviewing the performance of subordinates and committees. Responsibility for day-to-day matters fell to the chairs of various committees (military, security, political, economic, etc.) and their deputies. Although the group's structure would not remain static over time, it is evident that even from its earliest days al-Qaeda embraced an ambidextrous approach to learning. Its emir was primarily overseeing al-Qaeda's strategic discussion while operational and tactical matters were delegated. The group would increasingly devolve tactical responsibilities, creating multiple parallel laboratories for refining its deadly craft.

In its early days, al-Qaeda lacked a clear, long-term vision, particularly with respect to the near-enemy / far-enemy question. Despite a *Rashomon*-like divergence in the various insider accounts purporting to explain what the group's leaders originally wanted, it is clear that al-Qaeda always had a purpose that extended beyond Afghanistan. Internal documents produced in the late 1980s articulated such goals as supporting "the Jihad movement in the world" and coordinating between jihadist movements in various theaters.[51]

Jamal al-Fadl is a former associate of bin Laden's who fell out with the jihadist icon after Fadl embezzled funds. After fleeing from the group, Fadl emerged as a key prosecution witness in the East Africa Embassy bombings trial, where he provided an account of al-Qaeda's founding ambitions. Despite Fadl's broken English and lingering questions about his credibility, his account is consistent with others in suggesting that al-Qaeda had goals extending beyond Afghanistan. Fadl said bin Laden and his associates wanted to "make Khalifa," an Arabic word for the caliphate, after the Afghan–Soviet war ended.[52] Other accounts of al-Qaeda's early days confirm that the group took a broad view of its purpose. Bin Laden's associate Abu Obaida al-Banshiri reportedly said that al-Qaeda would function as a body "ready to uphold Islam and defend Muslims in any part of the world."[53] Jamal Khashoggi, a Saudi journalist who reported on the Afghan jihad and knew bin Laden, says that al-Qaeda's founder believed "the flame of jihad should continue elsewhere."[54]

While al-Qaeda was established with a purpose ranging beyond Afghanistan, it is at best debatable whether the group had a meaningful strategic vision from the beginning. At al-Qaeda's founding, the group had not yet definitively prioritized the fight against the far enemy. The outlook of one key jihadist leader prefigured bin Laden's own agenda, and with it al-Qaeda's eventual focus on the far enemy.

Jalaluddin Haqqani's Crucial Role

Azzam's impact on the ideological and strategic evolution of the jihadist movement cannot be overstated. But another figure, a close friend of Azzam's, might have been more important still.

The present-day Haqqani network is named after the Dar al-Ulum Haqqaniyya madrassa in Pakistan's North-West Frontier province, a Deobandi seminary from which Jalaluddin Haqqani (b. 1939) graduated "with the equivalent of a doctoral degree" in 1970.[55] After spending a short time in Pakistan teaching at the Haqqaniyya madrassa and campaigning on behalf of an Islamist candidate for Pakistan's National Assembly, Jalaluddin returned to Afghanistan and established a madrassa. Under normal circumstances, "Jalaluddin might have gone on to a successful and non-violent career in Pak-Afghan Islamist politics."[56] But in the turbulent 1970s-era South Asia, this was not to be. Armed conflict, primarily between Soviet-backed Afghan communists and Islamists, reshaped Jalaluddin's career.

Jalaluddin Haqqani led an unsuccessful uprising against the pro-Soviet regime of Sardar Mohammed Daoud Khan in Paktika province, which resulted in "most of its leaders either fleeing to Pakistan or in jail."[57] Undeterred, Jalaluddin joined the executive committee of the Hizb-i-Islami Afghanistan party, which was designed to merge "all of the factions of anti-Daoud Sunni Islamist activism into one organization."[58] When Hizb-i-Islami split into two factions—one led by Muhammad Khalis and another by Gulbuddin Hekmatyar—Jalaluddin's Haqqani network joined the Khalis-led faction. As a part of that group, the Haqqani network fought the Soviets in the Afghan–Soviet War.

Jalaluddin Haqqani was closely allied with the Saudi and Pakistani intelligence services, and his outfit became their preferred conduit for weapons and supplies.[59] Haqqani was also the CIA's man for a time, receiving shoulder-fired missiles, cash, and other assistance.[60] Rep. Charlie Wilson, an early advocate of the mujahedin's cause, glorified Haqqani as "goodness personified."[61] The Haqqani network became an ever more potent force during the Afghan–Soviet conflict.

While Jalaluddin wasn't the only militant leader to host Arab foreign fighters during the Afghan–Soviet war, he was the most welcoming. Mujahedin commanders tended to view the presence of Arab fighters as a nuisance, but Haqqani incorporated them directly into his battle plans.[62] In their seminal work *Fountainhead of Jihad*, Vahid Brown and Don Rassler explore Haqqani's role in helping al-Qaeda establish a foothold in the region and beyond. The summary that follows is largely derived from their work.

Azzam and Haqqani likely influenced one another, as the two were close. Azzam even authored his will in Haqqani's home. Haqqani hosted other key members of bin Laden's initial cadre too, and al-Qaeda's first two military leaders, Abu Hafs al-Masri and Abu Obaida al-Banshiri, gained fighting experience under Haqqani's auspices before joining bin Laden.[63] The first major battle involving Arab volunteers took place in 1986 in Zhawar, a rugged area on Haqqani's home turf in Afghanistan's Paktia province. Some of al-Qaeda's first training camps were built nearby.[64]

As early as 1988 Haqqani spoke of expanding the militants' efforts beyond Afghanistan, to Central Asia, Palestine, and Kashmir.[65] In May 1990 Haqqani established the National Commanders Shura to coordinate military efforts in Afghanistan after the Soviet withdrawal. During a speech before a National Commanders Shura–sponsored conference of Afghan commanders and scholars in 1991, Haqqani explained that, while "in the past, we had one enemy, Russia . . . our enemies are numerous and stronger because now America, Britain, China and all non-Muslim countries have backed the Russians in an attempt to weaken the Muslim community." Thus, Haqqani surmised, "the premise that made jihad a sacred duty of all Muslims in the past still holds and backing the jihad and helping in its path is a duty of all Muslims."[66]

The speech foreshadowed in important ways bin Laden's later rationale for war against the far enemy. From 1992 to 1995, the Haqqanis worked with al-Qaeda to export jihad throughout the former Soviet states in Central Asia and the Caucasus region.[67] The Haqqanis and al-Qaeda collaborated on an initiative dubbed the Furqaan Project, in which they jointly trained recruits who would return to their home countries to fight. Even after bin Laden relocated to Sudan, Jalaluddin Haqqani's territory continued to serve as a hub for al-Qaeda camps.

The Haqqanis' loyalty to al-Qaeda helps explain why the latter has proven so resilient. Jalaluddin, along with his sons and brothers, controlled a vital piece of turf straddling the Afghanistan–Pakistan border, territory that became the epicenter of events in the jihadist world for more than three decades. The Taliban announced Jalaluddin's death in September 2018, but by then his legacy was secure. His son Sirajuddin had risen to become the Taliban's deputy emir, charged with overseeing militant operations throughout Afghanistan.

The Failure of the Religio-Nationalist Jihads

More persuasive than words in shifting the jihadist movement's orientation was the stark contrast of the mujahedin's success in Afghanistan with the regimes of the Middle East and North Africa crushing the near-enemy-focused religio-nationalist jihads.

The Soviet Union's withdrawal from Afghanistan in February 1989 did not end the country's armed conflict. A rebranded communist government led by Mohammad Najibullah clung to nominal power. Indeed, through a combination of hard and soft power, Najibullah's government managed to survive longer than outside observers expected.[68] But this only worked while the Soviet Union bankrolled him. After the Soviet government collapsed, the mujahedin overran Kabul in April 1992. Many "Afghan Arabs," as Arab foreign fighters were known, fought in the war against Afghanistan's government until Najibullah fell.

Jihadists who returned from Afghanistan launched protracted campaigns against the governments of Algeria, Egypt, and Libya. These campaigns were definitive failures that spurred al-Qaeda's organizational learning and its development of a far enemy strategy.

The civil war in Algeria was the era's most severe conflict with a near-enemy regime. The country descended into chaos after a military junta canceled the 1992 elections, in which the government feared the Islamic Salvation Front would win. Algeria had been spiraling toward a crisis even before the election debacle. There had already been signs of Islamist insurgency in the 1980s, led by Mustafa Bouyali.[69] The remnants of Bouyali's followers joined forces with Algerian returnees from Afghanistan. The Afghan Arab veterans introduced truly brutal tactics. Beheadings, first inflicted on Algerian army conscripts in Guemar in November 1991, became disturbingly commonplace.[70]

The Algerian military contributed its own atrocities to the protracted war while the jihadist-led GIA grew increasingly brutal. GIA's use of grotesque violence proved to be a grave error, as the jihadists themselves came to understand. Abu Musab al-Suri later commented that loss of popular support contributed to the jihadists' defeat because "cohesion between the mujahedin, their people and their Ummah is the first support for them in the world of reasons—after God's guaranteeing of success—in these confrontations, and they will usually lose confrontations when they lose that support."[71]

In 1995 Zawahiri tried to orient the Algerian militants' efforts away from the local regime, in part to win back public support. Zawahiri urged GIA leader Djamel Zitouni to target Israel and the United States, which he argued would build the jihadists' popularity.[72] Zitouni rejected Zawahiri's argument, explaining that when GIA targeted France, it did so out of near-enemy logic because of France's close connection to the Algerian government. In contrast, Zitouni explained, Israel and the United States did not factor into GIA's military strategy. "Since we have been commanded to fight the nearest, as they pose the greatest danger to us, we fight France," Zitouni reasoned, "while you fight Israel or America, because they are the nearest threat to you."[73]

GIA splintered as the Algerian military gained the upper hand. The Salafist Group for Preaching and Combat tried to salvage the jihad, but the Algerian battlefront closed by 2002. By then more than one hundred thousand people had died in the war.

Neither the Egyptian nor Libyan jihads lasted nearly so long. The Egyptian jihadist campaign was already faltering by 1997, the year the militant group Gama'a al-Islamiyya slaughtered more than sixty people, mainly foreign tourists, at a historical site in Luxor. The ensuing public backlash empowered Hosni Mubarak's regime to mount a comprehensive crackdown.[74] This clampdown consisted of intelligence collection, military strikes against Gama'a and EIJ, and efforts to counter their funding. The government purged religious extremists from state institutions. Egyptian officials also focused on controlling the country's borders to prevent Islamist militant groups from receiving outside assistance. These policies eliminated, at least temporarily, the threat posed by Egypt's jihadists.

The Libyan Islamic Fighting Group (LIFG), which was founded by Libyan Afghan jihad veterans, also failed in its campaign to overthrow a near-enemy regime. A crackdown following the group's attempted assassination of Qaddafi all but ended the country's jihad. LIFG's military chief advised the group to halt operations in Libya in 1998.[75]

By the late 1990s every national jihad campaign had failed or was faltering. Bin Laden and al-Qaeda concluded that the movement's problem was the near-enemy strategy.

Al-Qaeda's Years in Sudan

Even before the national jihad campaigns burned out, intelligence community experts discerned growing transnationalism in the jihadist movement. A 1993 State Department intelligence assessment noted that the "melting pot" of the Afghan jihad "gave the militant Islamists numerous ideological and logistical ties with fighters from other countries," and stated that "the victory over the Soviet Union has inspired many of them to continue their jihad against other infidels."[76] The assessment correctly predicted that jihadists would soon view the United States as one of their leading enemies.

Al-Qaeda's Afghanistan–Pakistan safe haven diminished for several reasons in the early 1990s, including infighting among mujahedin factions and the Pakistani government's 1993 decision to start expelling Arabs in response to accusations that it was harboring terrorists.[77] Bin Laden decided to move his militant outfit's operations to Sudan. He made al-Qaeda a key investor in the country's agricultural and construction industries. Al-Qaeda also solidified its relationship with other jihadist groups that Sudan's Islamist government was harboring or supporting, including LIFG and EIJ. But the most important part of al-Qaeda's expansion during its Sudan years was its international outreach. Working through small reconnaissance teams and front organizations like the Benevolence International Foundation and Al Haramain Islamic Foundation, al-Qaeda forged ties with like-minded militant groups and took part in campaigns across the globe. As the 9/11 Commission Report explained, bin Laden raised al-Qaeda's profile through an entity he dubbed the Islamic Army Shura, through which "he enlisted groups from Saudi Arabia, Egypt, Jordan, Lebanon, Iraq, Oman, Algeria, Libya, Tunisia, Morocco, Somalia, and Eritrea," while establishing "cooperative but less formal relationships with other extremist groups from these same countries; from the African states of Chad, Mali, Niger, Nigeria, and Uganda; and from the Southeast Asian states of Burma, Thailand, Malaysia, and Indonesia."[78]

Some of al-Qaeda's best-known terrorist attacks during this period departed from the near-enemy strategy. Consistent with Brooke's observation that foreign fighters drawn to Afghanistan were not there to fight the far enemy per se, al-Qaeda's attacks on American targets prior to bin Laden's 1996 declaration could be justified by the fact that American troops were on Muslim soil. Indeed, one of al-Qaeda's more robust efforts during this time took place in the Horn of Africa. Bin Laden deployed operatives, led by Abu Obaida al-Banshiri, to create a new safe haven for al-Qaeda in the region.[79] Al-Qaeda grew interested in the Horn before the United States deployed troops to Somalia, although Abdel Bari Atwan, a journalist who knew bin Laden, claims the operatives were sent in anticipation of the U.S. military's arrival.[80] Al-Qaeda sent trainers to Somalia and, as Peter Bergen notes, Arab veterans of the Afghan–Soviet war taught their Somali trainees "that the most effective way to shoot down a helicopter with a rocket-propelled grenade was to hit the vulnerable tail rotor."[81] Once U.S. troops were on the ground in Somalia, al-Qaeda's stated focus shifted to expelling them.[82] It isn't clear if the same fighters whom al-Qaeda operatives had trained were involved in the October 1993 downing of a U.S. helicopter in Mogadishu.[83] But bin Laden seemingly believed this to be the case. Further, the networks and relationships that al-Qaeda built in East Africa in the early 1990s would prove useful years later, culminating in the 1998 bombings of U.S. embassies in Kenya and Tanzania. Another of al-Qaeda's efforts focused on the Caucasus.[84]

According to Fadl, Sudan's government grew leery of allowing al-Qaeda to conduct training in the country, likely due to the political fallout from an unsuccessful assassination attempt against Hosni Mubarak in June 1995, which was linked to Sudan-based Egyptian militants whom bin Laden supported.[85] Nevertheless, al-Qaeda was able to establish several training facilities in Sudan, in tandem with other militant groups sheltering there.

But al-Qaeda's multicontinent reach and growing profile drew unwanted attention to the group's presence in Sudan. In 1996 Sudan's government, facing pressure from the United States and others, demanded that al-Qaeda leave and seized the construction equipment that formed the backbone of bin Laden's business in the country.[86] Al-Qaeda returned to Afghanistan.

Several fatwas issued by scholars associated with al-Qaeda during this period dealt with striking the United States. Fadl mentioned two fatwas mandating that the group fight the U.S. presence in the Gulf, one issued in 1991/1992 and another at the end of 1992.[87] According to Fadl, a third fatwa was issued in late 1992 or early 1993 condemning the American presence in Somalia.[88] Although Fadl's testimony can be difficult to follow at times, the first fatwa seems to have focused on America allegedly stealing Muslim oil and money, with the second based on a tradition, attributed to the Prophet Muhammad, that Islam should be the only religion present and observed in the Arabian Peninsula.[89] The third fatwa invoked the precedent of medieval jurist Ibn Taymiyya's fatwa on fighting the Tartars who invaded Syria.[90] Bin Laden referenced this same fatwa of Ibn Taymiyya in his 1996 declaration of war against America. Partially corroborating Fadl's assertions, a 1997 CIA analysis mentions fatwas issued by al-Qaeda in early 1992.[91]

Although in hindsight al-Qaeda was clearly taking steps toward adopting a far-enemy strategy, at this point the group's strategy could be described as the product of continuous rather than discontinuous learning. The fatwas regarding the United States could be seen as an extension of the rationale for the anti-Soviet jihad of the 1980s, as the United States was on Islamic lands. But discontinuous change was in the works.

The First Waves

Al-Qaeda in the early to mid-1990s fought in southern Sudan, took aim at the American military in Yemen and Somalia, and supported jihadists in Bosnia, Chechnya, and Egypt. But the group started looking further afield, to targets in the United States.

A first wave of operations focusing on the continental United States and nonmilitary U.S. targets gathered momentum in the early 1990s. These plots had a complex relationship with al-Qaeda that cannot be described as hierarchical command-and-control and were the work of various linked extremists, including Ramzi Yousef, Khalid Sheikh Mohammed (Yousef's uncle), and Omar Abdel Rahman (best known as the Blind Sheikh). Yousef, a Kuwaiti-born man of Pakistani origin, studied in Britain in the late 1980s. He traveled to the Philippines in 1991, where he made contact with the Abu Sayyaf militant group. In September 1992 he arrived in the United States, falsely claiming asylum as an Iraqi refugee. The Egyptian-born Omar Abdel Rahman was a well-regarded cleric in jihadist circles and one of bin Laden's most important theological allies during the 1990s. Sheikh Omar was initially involved with the Gama'a al-Islamiyya and EIJ militant groups, issuing judgments of apostasy against secular-leaning rulers like Anwar Sadat. Sheikh Omar traveled to South Asia during the Afghan jihad before coming to the United States in 1990. He preached and wrote in favor of global jihadism from his perch on American soil.

Sheikh Omar, Khalid Sheikh Mohammed, and Yousef were part of a network responsible for the February 1993 bombing of the World Trade Center, an ambitious plot targeting New York City landmarks, and the 1995

"Bojinka" plot, which aimed to blow up multiple airliners.[92] Although it was not yet widely embraced within the movement, these jihadists used a far-enemy logic to justify the 1993 World Trade Center plot. Still, the links to al-Qaeda remain murky.

Jihadist activity proliferated in Europe in the 1990s. Many Afghan Arab veterans went there in part because they could not return to their home countries. Senior militant leaders who settled in Europe included Hani al-Sibai, Abu Qatada, Abu Musab al-Suri, Rachid Ramda (a GIA spokesman), and Khalid al-Fawwaz (who served as bin Laden's London-based representative). Europe became a funding and propaganda base to support jihadist activity against near-enemy regimes. London in particular provided a jihadist refuge. Abu Musab al-Suri, who came to London in 1994, said that "being in London during that period would place you at the center of events."[93]

The British government took a mainly lenient approach toward jihadist veterans on its soil. These militants were a diverse group that included former Afghan Arabs and, according to Suri, an Algerian cell supporting the GIA's insurgency. Most observers believe the British government adopted this approach because it did not see jihadists as a direct threat. Another explanation—held by some informed observers and not fully inconsistent with the first—holds that letting the militants work in plain sight made them easier to surveil. The jihadists knew there were lines they could not cross if they were to continue enjoying relative freedom in London. Plotting against British targets was out of the question, and the militants sometimes displayed pragmatism in their dealings with authorities.[94] For instance, Britain reached out to jihadists when it perceived a possible security threat over its extradition to France of Rachid Ramda, who was accused of masterminding a series of bombings against the French public transit system. In 1996–1997, Abu Qatada took three meetings with members of the security services. Despite proclaiming his desire for Islam to conquer the world, the cleric gave assurances that he would use his influence to prevent attacks on British soil.[95]

Suri was deeply involved in developing the jihadist network in Spain. When Spanish authorities disrupted logistics cells supporting GIA's campaign in the late 1990s, none of these cells were found to be plotting attacks against Spain.[96] Suri was allegedly involved in the 1984 attack against the El Descanso restaurant in Madrid that was frequented by U.S. personnel, although nothing definitive has come to light about his role.[97] In 1994 Suri and his colleague Abu Dahdah founded the group Soldados de Alá (Soldiers of God).[98] Both Suri and Abu Dahdah recruited in Spain for jihadist struggles abroad, including in Bosnia, Chechnya, and Afghanistan.[99] Abu Khalid al-Suri, who later emerged in the Syrian civil war as Zawahiri's mediator between Jabhat al-Nusra and ISIS, also helped direct the Spanish network. While in Spain, Abu Khaled maintained contact with Khaled al-Fawwaz.[100]

Although al-Qaeda had, at this point, made no organizational decision to prioritize the far enemy, elements were in place that could produce a strategic shift driven by organizational learning. Associates of the organization had attempted attacks against the West, including on U.S. soil, and the presence of jihadists in the West was growing. Coupled with the failure of the regional jihads, there was much that al-Qaeda could draw upon to engage in discontinuous learning at the strategic level.

Al-Qaeda's Campaign Against the West

Instrumental to al-Qaeda's post-Sudan activities was an Afghanistan-based militant group known as the Taliban. When Najibullah's government fell, Kabul fell not to Pashtun mujahedin factions but to the better-organized Tajik forces. "It was a devastating psychological blow because for the first time in 300 years the Pashtuns had lost control of the capital," Ahmed Rashid wrote. "An internal civil war began almost immediately."[101]

During the Afghan–Soviet war, a network of madrassas funded by Saudi Arabia had sprung up near Pakistan's border with Afghanistan. These schools—which often resembled the aforementioned Dar al-Ulum Haqqaniyya—served a purpose related to the war: students were indoctrinated with the kind of militant religious ideas that Pakistani and Saudi planners believed would provide them an ideological impetus to fight the Soviets with fanatical zeal. This network of schools gave birth to the Taliban: The group derives its name from the madrasa network, as the word *Taliban* is the plural form of *talib*, or student.

The Taliban emerged from Afghanistan's chaos in 1994. There are different accounts of how the group formed, but Rashid finds one to be the most plausible. In this recounting, two neighbors approached Taliban leader Mullah Mohammed Omar to inform him that a warlord "had abducted two teenage girls, their heads had been shaved and they had been taken to a military camp and repeatedly raped." In response, Omar and thirty *talibs* "attacked the base, freeing the girls and hanging the commander from the barrel of a tank."[102]

The Taliban's founding leader, Mullah Omar, was born into a Pashtun tribe in 1959 and became a village mullah in Kandahar province. His studies were interrupted by the Soviet invasion, and he was wounded four times in the fighting. The most notable injury was to his right eye, which was permanently blinded.

The Taliban were effective fighters. They promised an alternative to Afghanistan's prevailing lawlessness by ruthlessly imposing order in areas they controlled through the extremely harsh version of Islamic law that the group brought with it. The Taliban's advance was rapid. Within two years of the Taliban's founding, it captured Kandahar and Kabul. The group's rapid advances were helped by the support it received from Pakistan's Inter-Services Intelligence agency.[103]

After becoming Afghanistan's de facto rulers, the Taliban allowed al-Qaeda to shelter in the country following the latter's expulsion from Sudan. From its new perch in Afghanistan, al-Qaeda rebuilt its finances and became an appealing organization for aspiring militants thanks to its infrastructure for training operatives and planning attacks. Al-Qaeda was not the only militant group in Taliban-run Afghanistan, but it had the most to offer foreign jihadists.

From his new Afghanistan safe haven, bin Laden issued two declarations of war against America. In the first pronouncement, described at the beginning of this chapter, bin Laden's overarching grievance was America's military presence in Saudi Arabia, but he also cited American support for Israel and U.S.-led sanctions against Saddam Hussein's Iraq as justifications for his fight.[104] Bin Laden framed his anti-American terrorism as an act of self-defense.

Bin Laden's second declaration of war, issued in February 1998, had four other signatories: Zawahiri, who then led EIJ; Rifa'i Ahmad Taha, chief of Gama'a al-Islamiyya; Jamiat Ulema-e-Pakistan secretary Mir Hamza; and Fazlur Rahman, emir of the Jihad Movement of Bangladesh. This fatwa, which announced a "Global Islamic Front," asserted that "the ruling to kill the Americans and their allies, civilian and military, is an individual duty for every Muslim who can do it in any country in which it is possible to do it, in order to liberate the al-Aqsa Mosque and the holy mosque [Mecca] from their grip, and in order for their armies to move out of the lands of Islam." The declaration proved divisive. The announcement and the terrorist attacks that followed it were meant to galvanize the jihadist movement. But some jihadists, including prominent LIFG figures, openly denounced it. There was also some opposition within EIJ.[105] But several key EIJ figures joined their leader, Zawahiri, in the new Global Islamic Front, while various LIFG leaders also remained on good terms with al-Qaeda and rose to senior positions in the organization.

EIJ worked closely with bin Laden's enterprise throughout the 1990s, although some accounts claim the groups did not officially merge until the summer of 2001. It seems clear that bin Laden was more committed to fighting the far enemy than was Zawahiri, who for years viewed the Egyptian government as his priority.[106] On May 26, 1998, bin Laden and Zawahiri held a press conference of sorts to promote the new Global Islamic Front. Bin Laden described Zawahiri's EIJ as "one of the main organizing groups" behind the new anti-American initiative. Two of Sheikh Omar's sons also attended, handing out copies of their father's will. Bin Laden repeatedly portrayed the Blind Sheikh as a victim of American aggression.

Sheikh Omar's last testament would become an influential fatwa. The Egyptian cleric, who was imprisoned in the United States on terrorism charges related to the landmarks plot, authorized a campaign of terrorism against America and its allies. "Cut off all relations with [the Americans, Christians, and Jews], tear them to pieces, destroy their economies, burn their corporations, destroy their peace, sink their ships, shoot down their planes and kill them on air, sea, and land," the imprisoned Sheikh wrote. "And kill them wherever you may find them, ambush them, take them hostage, and destroy their observatories." In case anyone missed the point, Sheikh Omar added: "Kill these infidels."[107] Sheikh Omar was a trained cleric, unlike bin Laden and Zawahiri. One of the jihadist movement's leading theological lights had provided unequivocal endorsement of both fighting against the United States and striking a full range of targets.

Less than three months later, the Global Islamic Front struck. On August 7, 1998, suicide truck bombs exploded within minutes of one another at the U.S. embassies in Nairobi, Kenya, and in Dar es-Salaam, Tanzania. The Nairobi attack killed 213 people and wounded around 4,000. The scale of the carnage was smaller yet considerable in Dar es-Salaam, with 11 dead and 85 wounded.

The East Africa plot dated back to the early 1990s, when bin Laden and his men were headquartered in Sudan. Bin Laden found inspiration in the success of Hizballah's 1983 bombings in Lebanon, which pushed the U.S. military from part of the Middle East. On October 23, 1983, a pair of suicide bombers had simultaneously driven explosives-laden trucks into the U.S. Marine barracks and the quarters of French paratroopers, forces in the country to try to stabilize Lebanon's multisided civil war. More than 300 people died, including 241 U.S. servicemembers and 58 French peacekeepers. President Ronald Reagan subsequently withdrew U.S. forces from the country.

The 9/11 Commission concluded that bin Laden had asked Iran and Hizballah for assistance in replicating the deadly Lebanese bombings. Bin Laden met with Iranian representatives and had a face-to-face meeting with Hizballah's master terrorist, Imad Mughniyah, a man who bedeviled American and Israeli counterterrorism officials for decades.[108] Hizballah agreed to provide al-Qaeda with the "tactical expertise" necessary to carry out similar bombings.[109] The knowledge that needed to be transferred from Hizballah to al-Qaeda was both explicit and tacit, and particularly in this era where the internet remained nascent, tacit knowledge was best transferred in person. An al-Qaeda delegation trained in Hizballah's Lebanese stronghold, the Bekaa Valley.[110]

Two former al-Qaeda operatives later told American authorities that they witnessed this close cooperation between the militant groups. During the embassy bombings trial, Jamal al-Fadl told the court that one al-Qaeda operative who attended the training returned to Sudan with tapes showing how to blow up "big buildings."[111] The second operative is Ali Mohamed, an EIJ member who personally conducted surveillance on potential targets, including the American embassy in Nairobi, in the early 1990s.[112] During his plea deal proceedings, Mohamed told a New York court that he oversaw the security for bin Laden's meeting with Mughniyah. Mohamed testified that Hizballah had trained bin Laden's men. Why would al-Qaeda's founder, a strict Sunni with a negative opinion of the Shia, cooperate with Shia militants as he prepared for this operation? Mohamed's answer was simple and related to al-Qaeda's prioritization of organizational learning. Bin Laden, Mohamed said, wanted to employ the "same method" used on the Marines in Beirut, "to force the United States to pull out from Saudi Arabia."[113]

Al-Qaeda's strikes did not shatter American resolve, as bin Laden may have hoped. Still, the U.S. response to the attacks suggested to the jihadist movement that al-Qaeda could operate with relative impunity. America undertook limited strikes in Afghanistan and Sudan that did little damage to the militant outfit. The combination of the successful terrorist attacks and the perceived weakness of the U.S. response strengthened al-Qaeda. America hadn't left the Middle East, but it didn't seem up to fighting.

Bin Laden saw the attacks as a turning point. He said in a September 2000 speech that they "succeeded in mobilizing the masses," thus moving al-Qaeda "from the phase of potentiality to the phase of expansion and preparedness and large responsibilities."[114] The attacks and U.S. response drew new waves of jihadist volunteers to al-Qaeda, which built several additional training camps in Logar province.[115]

At the turn of the new millennium, al-Qaeda was the world's strongest jihadist brand. Its rise was directly attributable to its embrace of the far-enemy strategy. Other militant groups had simply failed to show that their strategies could succeed. As al-Qaeda prepared for the 9/11 hijackings, Zawahiri penned a tract, *Knights Under the Prophet's Banner*, which outlined his reasons for striking at the far enemy. He wrote that attacks on America would deal a blow to the "master" that is protecting its "lackey," Israel, and would also curry favor across the broader Ummah. He anticipated that various Muslim regimes would enter the ensuing war on the side of the "Crusaders and Jews," thus revealing their true face to the Muslims. All of this, Zawahiri reasoned, served al-Qaeda's ultimate goal of "restoration of the caliphate."[116]

From the perspective of bin Laden and Zawahiri, the near and far enemy were allies in the same global war against Muslims. Bin Laden would continue to espouse this theory of world politics until his dying day. While regional opportunities that the Arab Spring revolutions created for the movement have caused some deprioritization of the far enemy compared to the near one, Zawahiri continues to view the near and far enemies as connected and believes that attacks against one can damage the other.

4

The Unfriendly Skies

Plots Against Aviation

Sixteen days after the 9/11 attacks, President George W. Bush stood between two airplanes at O'Hare International Airport, one from United and the other from American. The president reassured a crowd of airline employees and citizens clutching American flags that keeping planes in the air would be a crucial early victory over the terrorists. "When they struck, they wanted to create an atmosphere of fear," President Bush said. "And one of the great goals of this nation's war is to restore public confidence in the airline industry. It's to tell the traveling public: Get on board."[1]

The 9/11 attacks were a watershed moment for aviation security. The nineteen operatives hadn't raised alarms on any watch lists. They waltzed through airport security with box cutters and utility knives, then easily seized the cockpits of four large passenger jets. As the 9/11 Commission Report noted, each security layer that was "relevant to hijackings—intelligence, passenger prescreening, checkpoint screening, and onboard security—was seriously flawed prior to 9/11. Taken together, they did not stop any of the 9/11 hijackers from getting on board four different aircraft at three different airports."[2]

The aviation sector instituted drastic changes after the attacks. The Aviation and Transportation Act became law in November 2001.

Responsibility for airport security was stripped from private firms and federalized under the new Transportation Security Administration (TSA). The federal government invested billions of dollars in new aviation security measures, including mandatory training for airport employees, stronger watch lists, bans on potentially dangerous passenger items, enhanced baggage and passenger screening, fortified cockpit doors, and more air marshals. These measures were enough to reassure civilians to get on board, as the president put it, but they weren't enough to stop terrorists from trying to get back on board too. Jihadist plots against aviation only increased after 9/11. In the face of mounting security efforts, al-Qaeda and other jihadist groups engaged in organizational learning about the new defenses and launched new attacks.

Brian Michael Jenkins likened accumulating aviation security measures to an archaeological dig. "I can point to every machine and every procedure and say, that came about because of that incident in 1988, that came about because of that incident in 2001," he said. "We take off our shoes because there was a shoe bomber, we have restrictions on liquids because there was a plot involving liquid explosives."[3] If the past is any guide, we are now creating new fossils for future digs to unearth.

The Strategy Behind Attacks Against Aviation

The jihadist focus on aviation is far from arbitrary. Aircraft are attractive targets for numerous reasons, beginning with the sheer vulnerability of passengers—concentrated groups of people trapped in a closed environment.[4] There is no opportunity for help from below and no way for passengers to escape. People can die instantly and with no warning, while in the midst of a completely mundane activity. Psychologist Robert Bor, an aviophobia expert, noted that after the 9/11 attacks "we can see in our minds the fact that the people on the planes were alive one second and dead the next."[5] Aviation terrorism generally results in dramatic publicity and terrorizes the public.[6] An examination of aviation terrorism in the pre-jihadist era makes this motivation clear. The secular nationalist group Popular Front for the Liberation of Palestine, for example, expressly favored air hijackings for this reason. After the group carried out a spate of nonlethal hijackings in the late 1960s, its founder, George Habash, said that "when we hijack a plane it has more effect than if we kill a hundred Israelis in battle. For decades, world public opinion has been neither for nor against the Palestinians. It simply ignored us. At least the world is talking about us now."[7] A similar dynamic holds true for jihadist terrorism: Aviation attacks demand attention.

Aviation is also a symbolic target. Flag carriers like Air France and Egypt Air, and even large private companies like American Airlines and British Air, are seen as stand-ins for states.[8] As Yannick Veilleux-Lepage notes, "flag carriers acted, and continue to act, as highly visible global ambassadors of the home country and as the government's 'chosen instruments' for promoting national identities on an international level."[9] Aviation attacks can thus be seen as declarations of war.

Perhaps most significantly, aviation terrorism creates financial and economic burdens for state actors at little expense to the jihadists. This imbalance has been explicated in jihadist literature. In 2010, for example, Anwar al-Awlaki explained the rationale for targeting cargo planes in al-Qaeda in the Arabian Peninsula's (AQAP) online English-language magazine *Inspire*. This special issue of *Inspire* was published just after the group attempted what became known as the parcels plot, which this chapter discusses in detail. Although AQAP's bombs were defused, the organization considered the plot a success. Despite killing no one and destroying nothing, the plot's success, Awlaki reasoned, was getting bombs on board two planes.

Awlaki gloated that in the wake of such a plot "you either spend billions of dollars to inspect each and every package, or you do nothing and we keep trying again."[10] Awlaki's assessment of billions in new financial burdens was not unreasonable, if high in this particular case. Still, the measures implemented in response to AQAP's earlier Christmas Day bomb plot in 2009, also discussed in this chapter, cost around $1.2 billion per year.[11] In contrast, jihadist aviation plots typically cost a mere few thousand dollars to execute.

A single operative who strikes the aviation sector can have an enormous impact. After an attack, flights are typically cut back, customer demand drops temporarily, and updated security measures may be implemented. And that's even if the attack is an apparent failure. The cost of a plot is shouldered beyond the target country's borders. The aviation industry accounts for around 3.5 percent of the global economy, with an estimated impact of $2.7 trillion.[12] Aviation plots disrupt a globally interconnected industry, upon which numerous other industries depend.

A similar strategic logic applies to attacks on other modes of transportation that are also frequent jihadist targets. Plots against buses and trains are terrifying, symbolic, and economically damaging. Such attacks are also easier to execute than those targeting aircraft, as buses and trains have less stringent security measures.[13] Yet jihadists' obsession with aviation makes strategic sense despite the existence of other more vulnerable targets. Aviation is thus an ideal case study in jihadist organizational learning. The first section in this chapter examines the 9/11 attacks, the preeminent example of jihadists targeting aviation. We then put those attacks into context by exploring several jihadist attempts against aviation prior to 9/11 that should be understood as precursors. Finally, the chapter turns to subsequent attempts against aviation that demonstrate organizational learning in jihadist external operations.

9/11: A Success of the Jihadist Imagination

Osama bin Laden and his men wanted to strike locations that held symbolic meaning for their enemies. The World Trade Center symbolized America's economic dominance. The Pentagon, its military might. The terrorists also intended to strike another target, likely either the White House or U.S. Capitol, the two main seats of America's political power. Fortunately, the final intended target was spared when passengers on United Flight 93 revolted against the hijackers. The plane plunged into an open field near Shanksville, Pennsylvania. The 9/11 attack was the most devastating terrorist attack in history and an era-defining world event.

Al-Qaeda developed its plans for 9/11 by learning from past operations, combining concepts that had been tried in previous hijackings, and adapting them for this unprecedentedly ambitious assault. The resulting attack caught the U.S. intelligence community off guard. No terrorist organization had ever simultaneously hijacked multiple planes and turned them into human-piloted cruise missiles. The 2002 Joint Congressional Inquiry into 9/11 found that U.S. intelligence "did not produce any specific assessments of the likelihood that terrorists would use airplanes as weapons, and U.S. policymakers apparently remained unaware of this kind of potential threat."[14] Indeed, in a classified report submitted to Congress in 2000, the FBI and Federal Aviation Administration (FAA) determined that the overall threat to "domestic civil aviation in the United States" was "relatively low." The FBI confirmed that terrorist organizations were "operating within the U.S.," but did not find "evidence of plans to target domestic civil aviation." The FBI concluded that domestic terrorist activity was "focused primarily on fundraising, recruiting new members, and disseminating propaganda" while foreign terrorists principally focused "on U.S. interests overseas."[15]

The closest the U.S. intelligence community came to warning that an operation at the scale of 9/11 could be in the works was a Presidential Daily Brief (PDB) delivered to George W. Bush on August 6, 2001.[16] Even that document gave little indication of the imminent assault. The CIA-compiled brief was titled "Bin Ladin Determined to Strike in US." The CIA reported that al-Qaeda's founder had wanted to attack inside the United States since at least 1997 and that "patterns of suspicious activity" in America were "consistent with preparations for hijackings or other types of attacks." The PDB cited other reports of possible al-Qaeda planning inside the United States but stopped well short of envisioning the 9/11 mission. If anything, the brief cautioned against alarmism: the CIA stated that it could not "corroborate some of the more sensational threat reporting," including a 1998 analysis suggesting that bin Laden "wanted to hijack a US aircraft to gain the release of" Sheikh Omar Abdel Rahman and other imprisoned militants.

The idea of hijacking a plane to force a hostage exchange was hardly new. Terrorist groups of various ideological stripes had attempted this kind of operation many times. Al-Qaeda's own jihadist allies had conducted such a hijacking in December 1999, when five militants overtook Indian Airlines Flight 814. After three stops, the commandeered aircraft landed in Kandahar, where Taliban fighters surrounded the plane. The hijackers negotiated with Indian authorities to free three jihadists: Maulana Masood Azhar, who went on to found the al-Qaeda-linked Jaish-e-Mohammed;

Omar Saeed Sheikh, who later conspired with al-Qaeda to kidnap and behead *Wall Street Journal* reporter Daniel Pearl; and the Kashmiri militant Mushtaq Ahmed Zargar. All three militants were released in exchange for Flight 814's passengers. Given this recent success, there was good reason to suspect that al-Qaeda might attempt a similar operation to free Sheikh Omar.

That being said, a potential plot to force an exchange for the Blind Sheikh was the only specific type of hijacking that the August 2001 PDB mentioned. But al-Qaeda had a very different idea in mind. Writing with the benefit of hindsight, both the 9/11 Commission and 2002 Congressional Joint Inquiry into the hijackings found there was good reason to suspect al-Qaeda would repurpose airplanes as flying bombs. The Joint Inquiry found that the U.S. intelligence community "produced at least twelve reports" between December 1994 and August 2001 "suggesting that terrorists might use airplanes as weapons."[17] Some of these reports described seemingly far-fetched ideas, such as one al-Qaeda member's desire to fly an explosives-laden hang glider into Egypt's presidential palace. The would-be terrorist, an unnamed U.S. citizen, even practiced hang gliding and then brought a glider to Afghanistan. But he had problems with his glider, then was arrested before he could attempt an attack.[18] At least two of the twelve intelligence reports did not involve plots with any known links to al-Qaeda or Salafi jihadism, while others were dubiously sourced or ill-defined.

But several of the twelve reports in fact prefigured the 9/11 hijackings. In August 1998 U.S. intelligence learned that an al-Qaeda-linked group "planned to fly an explosive-laden plane from a foreign country into the World Trade Center." The FAA concluded that this plot was "highly unlikely" because any "flight originating outside the United States would be detected" well in advance of reaching its target.[19] Still another report, generated in August 2001, indicated that al-Qaeda may have considered crashing a hijacked plane into the U.S. embassy in Nairobi.[20]

There is no reason to think that the 9/11 plot would have been stopped if U.S. intelligence had scrutinized these reports more carefully. Then, as now, American intelligence suffered from a deluge of threat reporting. Twelve reports were an insignificant fraction of the total collection on terrorist threats. Still, two of the twelve reports that the Joint Inquiry cited included evidence of advanced plotting by al-Qaeda-linked actors. One plot unfolded in December 1994, when a small team of hijackers took control of an airliner flying from Algiers to Paris. The second involved several planned attacks that were foiled in the Philippines in 1995. In both cases jihadists considered flying hijacked airliners into targets. These two incidents are important, and we now consider them in detail.

Air France Flight 8969

On Christmas Eve of 1994 a team of four hijackers overtook Air France Flight 8969, which was set to fly from Algiers to Paris. The terrorists had disguised themselves as Algerian policemen. They initially entered the plane to check passengers' travel paperwork but quickly dropped the pretense of being police and commandeered the plane. The jihadists belonged to Algeria's Armed Islamic Group (GIA). In 1993 GIA had begun systematically attacking foreigners, especially French citizens, due to France's support for Algeria's military junta.[21]

After taking over the plane, the hijackers first tried to barter for the freedom of two imprisoned Islamic Salvation Front leaders.[22] The jihadists wasted little time before they shot and killed two passengers. The first was an Algerian policeman, whom they called to the front of the plane and shot in the head. The attackers tossed his body into a baggage cart.[23] The second victim was a Vietnamese diplomat serving as the commercial attaché at the embassy in Algiers.[24] After dropping their initial demand, the hijackers insisted that they be allowed to fly to Paris. When authorities refused, the attackers murdered French passenger Yannick Beugnet, who worked as a cook at the ambassador's residence in Algiers.[25] With the threat of more bloodshed, authorities quickly acceded to the terrorists' demands and cleared the plane for takeoff after Beugnet's body was thrown onto the tarmac.

As events progressed, the hijackers settled on their endgame: slamming the plane into the Eiffel Tower.[26] It's unclear if this was one of their objectives from the outset or if the Eiffel Tower option was improvised during the course of events. It's clear, though, that the attackers considered multiple outcomes before Paris's iconic wrought-iron tower became their focus.

The terrorists failed to destroy the French capital's tallest building. While en route to Paris, the plane's captain informed his captors that the auxiliary power had been running during the time spent on the tarmac in Algiers, and the plane had burned through so much fuel that the aircraft would be unable to reach its destination.[27] The plane landed at Marseille to refuel.

Whether or not the captain's claim about the need for refueling was subterfuge, French authorities outmaneuvered the hijackers after the plane touched down around 3 a.m. on December 26. The jihadists agreed to allow food and water to be brought on board, unaware that the ostensible airport employees delivering these provisions were actually officers in France's elite National Gendarmes Intervention Group, and that their real purpose was conducting reconnaissance for an assault on the plane.[28] Soon a squad of Gendarmes troops stormed the cabin and neutralized all four hijackers. The rescue operation lasted seventeen minutes. All hostages on board the plane in Marseille were freed.

The hijacking of Air France Flight 8969 marks the first known instance where jihadists considered flying a plane into a high-profile landmark. When the CIA later tried to determine when jihadists had first thought of using hijacked jets as kamikaze weapons, this plot loomed large. In a November 2001 paper, CIA analysts wrote that the "idea of hijacking planes for suicide attacks had long been current in jihadist circles." The first example cited was Air France Flight 8969.[29]

While open sources do not reveal what al-Qaeda thought of this operation, the group's leaders were certainly aware of it. They could conceivably have discerned a key flaw in the GIA's plan: none of the hijackers were pilots. This allowed the plane's captain to potentially dupe the terrorists by claiming that the jet was running out of fuel. And the hijackers might not have known how to hit their target even if they had made it to Paris.

Project Bojinka

Less than two weeks before Air France Flight 8969, jihadists attempted another spectacular airborne attack that likely influenced the 9/11 plot. On December 11, 1994, thirteen days before the hijacking in Algiers, a bomb detonated on board Philippine Airlines Flight 434, killing a Japanese passenger and damaging the aircraft.

The flight was scheduled to have multiple legs, from Manila to Cebu, then on to Tokyo.[30] Ramzi Yousef had personally placed the bomb aboard Flight 434 during the Manila–Cebu leg. Yousef wasn't a member of al-Qaeda but had numerous ties to the organization. His uncle and co-plotter in the Philippine attacks, Khalid Sheikh Mohammed (KSM), would later become the chief planner of 9/11. Osama bin Laden's brother-in-law reportedly funded Yousef's activities.[31]

Yousef boarded Philippine Airlines Flight 434 for its Manila–Cebu leg with the materials to build a bomb hidden on him. It was the kind of assemblage that MI6's fictional quartermaster Q might have prepared for James Bond: Yousef had stashed explosives in a bottle of contact lens solution, his shoes contained metal wires, and his Casio wristwatch was to serve as the bomb's timer.[32] When the flight took off, Yousef went into the bathroom to assemble the bomb, then placed it under a seat. The bomb exploded hours later, after Yousef had disembarked.

The attack was part of a larger plot, "Project Bojinka," which derived its name from a gibberish word that KSM had heard tossed about among the mujahedin in Afghanistan.[33] The bombing of Philippine Airlines Flight 434 was intended as a test run for a multiphase assault on targets in the Philippines and beyond. The intended carnage included the assassination of U.S. president William J. Clinton and Pope John Paul II during their scheduled visits to the Philippines, the bombing of twelve planes over the Pacific Ocean, and the hijacking of a plane that would be flown into the CIA's Langley headquarters. Other than the "test" bombing of Flight 434, none of this was ever carried out. In early 1995 Philippine authorities uncovered Yousef's bomb-making facility in Manila, forcing him to flee to Pakistan, where he was arrested later that year at one of bin Laden's safe houses in Islamabad. Yet, despite its operational failure, Project Bojinka became a wellspring of plots against aviation in the years to come.

Outlandishly grandiose as such a plot might have seemed at the time, the Bojinka plotters took some concrete steps toward their envisioned attack on CIA headquarters. One of Yousef and KSM's co-conspirators was a Pakistani pilot named Abdul Hakim Murad. He was one of three men who were supposed to plant explosives on planes.[34] Airplane bombings weren't

Murad's only task. Under Yousef and KSM's direction, he intended to hijack a plane in the United States. In a foreshadowing of the 9/11 plot, Murad confessed to the FBI in 1996 that he had "received flight training at schools in New York, North Carolina, California and Texas."[35] Murad told the Bureau that he planned "to fly a plane into C.I.A. headquarters in Langley, Va., or another federal building."[36]

In mid-1996 KSM traveled to Afghanistan where he briefed bin Laden on Project Bojinka.[37] Around the same time, Abu Hafs al-Masri (a.k.a. Mohammed Atef), al-Qaeda's military chief, commissioned a study to determine the feasibility of hijacking operations like the planned assault on CIA headquarters.[38] KSM also told bin Laden that he and Yousef had come up with still another idea: shipping nitrocellulose-filled jackets on U.S.-bound cargo planes and detonating them midair.[39]

Project Bojinka generated at least three separate ideas that al-Qaeda would pursue in the years that followed. The 9/11 attacks used suicide hijackers who received flight training in the United States, as Murad had. A 2006 al-Qaeda plot to blow up several planes flying from Heathrow Airport to the United States was another Bojinka by-product. And AQAP tried to destroy cargo planes bound for the United States in 2010, replacing KSM's explosives-filled jackets with bombs disguised as computer printers. Project Bojinka's progeny thus illustrate aspects of the violent non-state-actor technology adoption curve that this book introduces. At the heart of the operation stood technical breakthroughs that KSM and Yousef thought would enable attacks on aviation. The initial plot (the early adoption) failed when it was broken up by authorities, but al-Qaeda continued to iterate on the plot's basic ideas for at least a decade and a half thereafter. Whether the organization was able to reach the breakthrough phase of the curve is debatable, although AQAP thought they did: That is why the organization released a special issue of *Inspire* to celebrate the parcels plot. On the other hand, the argument against considering the parcels plot a breakthrough is the simple fact that it killed no one.

Beyond 9/11: The Early Years

Al-Qaeda drew upon past plots as it developed its plans for 9/11. In the runup to history's deadliest terrorist attack, al-Qaeda demonstrated its ability to learn on both a tactical and design level. Al-Qaeda personnel closely studied flight protocols and other security measures, and the hijackers took flights over New York and Washington to scope out their targets. They watched how flight teams behaved, gauging their movements to determine the optimal time to make a run at the cockpit.[40] Such learning is tactical.

Another form of organizational learning related to al-Qaeda's organizational design—specifically, where inside the organization initiative could be taken to propose plots. The group recognized the utility of "terrorist entrepreneurs"—although such an idea was not wholly new to al-Qaeda, as terrorist entrepreneurship can be glimpsed even in some of the group's earliest plots.[41] KSM's precise relationship with al-Qaeda before the late 1990s is murky. He clearly knew bin Laden years before planning for 9/11 began in earnest and had consorted with various al-Qaeda figures throughout the 1990s. KSM later told his American interrogators that he had first brought up the idea of weaponizing hijacked planes at a 1996 meeting with bin Laden.[42] Al-Qaeda's sinister opus may not have happened were it not for the group's willingness to work with entrepreneurial-minded jihadists from outside the organization.

KSM told U.S. officials that he didn't become a formal al-Qaeda member until 1998 or 1999, after bin Laden endorsed his plan to hijack commercial planes.[43] Bin Laden tried to temper KSM's grandiose ideas into something that stood a reasonable chance of success. This meant identifying the most impactful targets and nixing far-fetched plans, like KSM's aspiration to land one hijacked plane, kill the passengers, and broadcast a message lambasting U.S. foreign policy.[44] Bin Laden also took control of staffing the operation, settling on people who were largely outside al-Qaeda's direct orbit. The men, from Hamburg, were Ramzi Binalshibh, Marwan al-Shehhi, Ziad Jarrah, and Mohammed Atta. With funding from al-Qaeda and guidance from KSM, Shehhi, Jarrah, and Atta went on to become pilots for the 9/11 hijackings, while Binalshibh, unable to obtain a U.S. visa, became a point of contact between KSM and the other three.[45] The fourth pilot was Hani Hanjour, a Saudi citizen whom al-Qaeda's leadership selected for the job due to his prior flight experience.[46]

The other fifteen operatives came to be known as the "muscle hijackers," although the 9/11 Commission took care to note that they were hardly physically imposing. Two of them, Nawaf al-Hazmi and Khalid al-Mihdhar, were among the first to take part in the preparations for 9/11, while the remaining thirteen were selected during the latter half of 2000.[47] While a willingness to achieve martyrdom was reportedly foremost among the selection criteria, "demonstrable patience" was the second most important attribute. Such operations could take years to plan, and al-Qaeda had to trust its operatives to remain disciplined.[48] By July 2001 all fifteen muscle hijackers and all four pilots were in the United States.

The final two months leading up to the attack were filled with surveillance flights, gym workouts, and other last-minute preparations. Mohammed Atta, who served as the attack's operational leader, traveled to Spain on July 8 to inform Binalshibh that all the pieces were in place. The men discussed target selection and tactics, as well as bin Laden's insistence that the attack take place as soon as possible.[49] Through the rest of July and August, Atta and the other hijackers took a flurry of flights across America to conduct surveillance and meet with one another.[50] All the tickets for the hijacked flights had been purchased by September 5, and the hijackers checked in to lodgings near their departure airports a few days before the attack.[51]

For al-Qaeda, the devastation wrought on 9/11 was a spectacular success. The organizational learning that al-Qaeda exhibited in orchestrating 9/11 propelled jihadist aviation attacks for years to come, sharply escalating the battle between aviation security and jihadist groups that continues until today.

The Shoe Bomber

Despite heightened security measures and hyperawareness across the globe, it didn't take long for jihadists to try another aviation attack. On December 22, 2001, an al-Qaeda recruit named Richard Reid boarded Miami-bound American Airlines Flight 63 in Paris with a bomb hidden in his shoe. The bomb contained two kinds of explosives: the accelerant triacetone triperoxide and pentaerythritol tetranitrate (PETN).[52] A vigilant flight attendant caught Reid trying to light a fuse in his shoe. Attendants and passengers sprang into action, dumping water on Reid and restraining him using anything they could find, including plastic cuffs, seat-belt extensions, and headphone cords. Doctors who were on board administered a dose of Valium from the plane's medical kit.[53] The aircraft safely made an emergency landing in Boston.

The shoe bombing attempt revealed an alarming degree of organizational foresight. Even as al-Qaeda was finalizing its preparations for 9/11, it was in the middle stages of a second complex aviation plot that also required months of planning. The origins of Reid's attack can be traced to the summer of 2001, when two of bin Laden's top lieutenants, Sayf al-Adl and Abu Muhammad al-Masri, approached Egyptian explosives expert Tariq Mahmoud Ahmed al-Sawah with an urgent request.[54] Adl and Masri knew that if the upcoming "planes operation" succeeded, the United States and its European allies would tighten aviation security. Al-Qaeda's leadership reasoned that a follow-on attack on aviation would compound the economic and psychological impact of the New York and Washington "raids." The group correctly determined that there would still be exploitable gaps in aviation security. Adl and Masri tasked Sawah with developing "a shoe-bomb prototype that could be used to bring down a commercial airliner in flight."[55]

Reid was an established al-Qaeda operative prior to 9/11. After receiving his assignment from Adl and Masri, he traveled through Europe and the Middle East to scout targets. The timing of his reconnaissance missions and eventual attempted bombing establishes that al-Qaeda had the organizational capacity to direct complex operations both before *and after* 9/11.

Al-Qaeda provided Reid direct tactical assistance in addition to strategic guidance. Reid and would-be co-conspirator Saajid Mohammed Badat traveled to Afghanistan to collect their explosive devices, according to Badat.[56] Although Badat backed out at the last minute, he confirmed that senior al-Qaeda leadership was aware of the operation.[57] "The American economy is like a chain," bin Laden explained, according to Badat. "So after the September 11 attacks the [shoe-bomb] operation will ruin the American aviation industry and in turn the whole economy will come down."[58]

Reid's behavior at the Paris airport was suspicious. He paid for a one-way ticket in cash and didn't check any bags for a transatlantic flight. Authorities even suspected that Reid might be dangerous: French police pulled him aside for questioning and spoke to him so long that he missed the flight he was initially scheduled to take on December 21.[59] But they were unable to uncover Reid's ties to al-Qaeda or an impending plot. He emerged from his interrogation with a ticket for a flight the next day.

Al-Qaeda had built Reid what was, at the time, an undetectable bomb. Footwear did not have to go through X-ray screening, and a standard walk-through metal detector would not pick up nonmetallic explosives. Al-Qaeda had preemptively identified a hole in security and exploited it.

It was not post-9/11 security enhancements that prevented Reid from downing a packed plane. Instead, he was foiled by the situational awareness of flight attendants and passengers, with an assist from basic chemistry: Tests on the explosives later revealed that the fuse in Reid's shoe was too damp to ignite, either because of his perspiration or the rainy weather he had walked through on the way to the airport.[60]

The FAA announced the next day that all U.S. airports would adopt random shoe checks of passengers. Eventually authorities would screen all shoes at U.S. airports (although this practice would later be scaled back with the advent of TSA PreCheck). Global airports followed suit, and shoe removal has become a commonplace, though not universal, procedure around the world—a seemingly permanent legacy of a single al-Qaeda plot from more than two decades ago.

Chechnya's Female Suicide Attackers

America and its allies have not been the only targets of jihadist attacks on aviation. The first successful post-9/11 jihadist attack on passenger aircraft took place in Russia.

On August 24, 2004, two female Chechen suicide bombers, Satsita Dzhbirkhanova and Amanat Nagayeva, blew up two passenger planes departing from Domodedovo International Airport in Moscow, killing all ninety people on board the flights. The bombings were described as "Russia's 9/11," the deadliest terrorist attack on Russian aviation to that point.[61] These women, and other Chechen female suicide bombers, would come to be popularly known as the "black widows," a controversial term portraying them as vindictive extremists bent on exacting revenge for husbands, brothers, or sons lost at the hands of Russian forces.

As was the case for the shoe-bomb plot, the female Chechen bombers struck during a period of enhanced aviation security. Security at rail stations and airports had tightened after the bombing of a Moscow metro train killed forty-one people in February 2004. The two Domodedovo bombers were nonetheless able to pass through security, although not without drawing attention. The women were likely profiled upon entering the airport, and security officers briefly detained them before handing the women over to a police captain with counterterrorism responsibilities. Curiously, the captain let them go without further examination. The bombers then bought last-minute tickets from a scalper who, among other things, bribed officials to get one of the women on board a plane.[62]

They then followed Reid's footsteps in using nonmetallic explosives to evade X-ray screening and beat the metal detector. The women passed the luggage and passenger checks despite carrying hexogen, a powerful military-grade explosive, in their bras and around their waists.[63] While Reid's plan required a cleverly hidden explosive, the militants who planned the August 2004 attack adopted a brazenly simple technique. Instead of wasting time and resources building a complex device, they recruited women. Given the "positive security bias" that sees women as less threatening than men, female bombers were—and remain—less likely to attract suspicion.[64] Although Russian security agencies were aware of the potential for female attackers, authorities still apparently applied insufficient scrutiny to the two women.

Organizational learning is possible when a group conducts a tailored analysis of its unique operating environments. As chapter 2 discusses, this intake of new knowledge is called exploration. The Chechen terrorists exploited a vulnerability specific to Russia, making Russia's endemic corruption work to their advantage. The fact that the operatives entrusted their plot's success to a dubious ticket scalper emphasizes their confidence that Russia's corrupt atmosphere would aid the attack's success. Although Russia had erected a vast security apparatus, the jihadists knew that low levels of professionalism could compromise its capabilities.

After the bombings, Russian security underwent a reconstruction not unlike the United States' reforms in the wake of 9/11. At Domodedovo, airport personnel were screened and monitored more closely. Passenger registration, as well as luggage and passenger checks, were revamped. In 2007 Domodedovo became one of the first airports to install full-body scanners.[65]

The Liquid Bomb Plot

Through late 2006, post-9/11 aviation plots had featured a few individual attackers, rather than the dozens who conducted the multiple hijackings in 2001. Bruce Hoffman notes that by 2003 the "prevailing paradigm" viewed aviation terrorism as a threat of the past since security measures had become stricter across the world.[66] The Domodedovo incident seemed like an anomaly.

The British liquid bomb plot refuted this view. On August 10, 2006, authorities announced the apprehension of more than twenty suspects who were part of a plot to blow up seven transatlantic flights bound for North America from Britain. The plotters planned on exploiting another security vulnerability. Airport security was oriented toward detecting solid explosives. The attackers realized they could sneak liquid explosives through security checkpoints by hiding them in sport drink bottles. The plotters decided to inject a false bottom section of each bottle with explosives dyed the same color as the beverage. To the naked eye, the bomb components would seem like normal sealed bottles. The attackers could even drink from them.

Defense Intelligence Agency director Lt. Gen. Michael D. Maples described the plotters as "an al-Qaeda cell, directed by al-Qaeda leadership in Pakistan." Rashid Rauf, the plot's primary facilitator, was an experienced al-Qaeda operative who coordinated between the plotters in Britain and al-Qaeda's leadership in Pakistan.[67]

An official al-Qaeda document that German authorities later discovered reveals the processes of knowledge intake and experimentation that undergirded this plot. In it, Rauf wrote that he and others had analyzed "the various machines that were used for checking baggage and persons at airports," and "found it was very difficult to detect liquids [sic] explosives."[68] The plotters decided to smuggle hydrogen peroxide onto planes. They tested different methods of disguising the chemical and discovered what Rauf described as a "major breakthrough": hydrogen peroxide could be colored without compromising its explosive properties, meaning it could be disguised inside seemingly unopened containers.

British intelligence apprehended the would-be bombers before they could launch the plot. Department of Homeland Security Secretary Michael Chertoff commented that if the plot had not been stopped, the attack could have been on par with 9/11. "If they had succeeded in bringing liquid explosives on seven or eight aircraft," he said, "there could have been thousands of lives lost and an enormous economic impact with devastating consequences for international air travel."[69]

The liquid bomb plot transformed aviation security across the world. TSA and British authorities banned liquids and gels from flights, with few exceptions. Requirements have loosened somewhat over the past decade— restrictions now prevent passengers from bringing liquid containers larger than 100 milliliters through security and require that these containers be placed in transparent bags for screening. There are no signs of such rules being eliminated well over a decade after the liquid bomb plot was stopped.

The Entrepreneur of Bomb Design: Ibrahim al-Asiri

We explained (chapter 2) that highly entrepreneurial individuals can have a disproportionate impact on organizational learning. Before his demise in an August 2018 U.S. airstrike, Ibrahim al-Asiri had the greatest impact of anyone in the history of terrorism on jihadist bomb-making innovation.

Asiri was the master bombmaker for AQAP, al-Qaeda's formidable affiliate in Yemen. Numerous devices used in aviation plots over the course of a decade were traced to him, many reflecting striking creativity. Asiri's own brother, Abdullah, carried out a suicide bombing in 2009 against Saudi Arabia's security chief, Prince Mohammed bin Nayef. To gain the meeting, Abdullah claimed he was ready to leave the jihadist movement. He passed through aviation-style security before meeting with the prince. Abdullah detonated a bomb hidden in his rectal cavity, killing himself and injuring his target.

Ibrahim al-Asiri was a critical internal driver of organizational learning in al-Qaeda, achieving breakthroughs in bomb design and transferring his technical knowledge to the organization by educating "a cadre of bomb-makers."[70] When knowledge is disseminated through an organization's institutional memory, the group no longer depends on a single innovator. We now examine several major plots that Asiri's abilities made possible.

THE UNDERWEAR BOMBER

On Christmas Day 2009, Northwest Airlines Flight 253 was in for an unpleasant holiday surprise. Twenty-three-year-old Nigerian Umar Farouk Abdulmutallab boarded the Detroit-bound flight in Amsterdam with a PETN-based bomb sewn into his underpants. The bomb evaded detection because the explosive material, stored in a plastic container, did not set off metal detectors. The weapon was hidden in the crotch of his underwear, and Abdulmutallab correctly assumed that routine searches wouldn't find the explosive. As the plane prepared to land, Abdulmutallab stuck a syringe into the six-inch-long container in his underwear that held the PETN. Although the substance in the syringe was designed to detonate the bomb, Abdulmutallab only succeeded in starting a small but painful fire rather than igniting a catastrophic explosion.

A fast-acting passenger seated next to Abdulmutallab named Jasper Schuringa pulled the syringe out of the terrorist's hands. Other passengers leaped into action, with some pouring water on Abdulmutallab and others using their hands to smother the flames. Schuringa held Abdulmutallab in a headlock until a flight attendant arrived with a fire extinguisher. Once again, it was alert passengers and not security measures that foiled a potentially deadly aviation plot.

Abdulmutallab's operation faced, and evaded, more daunting security barriers than did Reid's. Abdulmutallab's underwear bomb passed through checkpoints in three countries before he boarded the U.S.-bound plane: in Ghana, Nigeria, and the Netherlands.[71] Each leg of the journey brought him up against increasingly advanced security measures. Carry-on screenings, shoe removal, and liquid restrictions had all been put in place after previous threats, and the underwear bomb plot adjusted to all of them. The location of the bomb ensured that nothing short of a highly intimate search would uncover the explosive.

The son of a former Nigerian banker and a recent graduate of a London university, Abdulmutallab was well-traveled, refined, clean-cut.[72] After radicalizing during his time in London, Abdulmutallab traveled to Yemen in August 2009, four months before the attack, focusing on, as Abdulmutallab later told the FBI, finding one man: Anwar al-Awlaki. Abdulmutallab told FBI investigators that "lectures of the great and rightly guided mujahideen who is alive, Sheikh Anwar al-Awlaki," had inspired him to become a jihadist militant.[73] The young Nigerian eventually met his hero, and Awlaki groomed him for the mission. Before the attack, the al-Qaeda ideologue hosted Abdulmutallab at an AQAP training camp, where the group's leadership hatched a plan to have the new volunteer use novel explosive devices. Abdulmutallab received training in "shooting skills and tactical scenarios."[74] The bomber was also given the explosive device at the camp, which Asiri had skillfully crafted.[75]

Governments once again adjusted their security procedures in response to this plot, either expanding their use of full-body scanners or beginning to use them for the first time. Body scanners have now become a seemingly permanent feature of the aviation security landscape.

THE PARCELS PLOT

AQAP struck again in October 2010. The group hid explosive devices in desktop printer cartridges bound from Yemen to synagogues in Chicago via Federal Express and UPS. Airport security officials waved the packages through checkpoints in multiple countries. As in the underwear bomb plot, Asiri reportedly built the devices.[76] The explosives were shipped by international air cargo, and officials believe the bombs were meant to detonate midair instead of at their ostensible destinations.[77] The bombs carried hallmarks of the underwear bomber's device but were about "four times as powerful," containing three hundred to four hundred grams of PETN.[78]

The plot may have succeeded if not for a jihadist defector, Jabir al-Fayfi. While it is unlikely that Fayfi provided specific details about the plot, his warnings alerted Riyadh to the possibility of an aviation attack.[79] Saudi intelligence was then able to uncover almost every major detail of the plot, including the routing numbers of the two explosives-laden packages.[80]

Using this information, investigators seized the first explosive device in Dubai. It contained three hundred grams of PETN hidden in a desktop printer cartridge. Although the package had never left the Middle East, the device had flown on board two different passenger jets.

But finding the device on the UPS plane proved disturbingly difficult. With the explosive package having already left Dubai, the Americans notified German federal police that the bomb-carrying plane was to make its next stop at Germany's Cologne-Bonn airport, a UPS hub, before continuing to Britain. But by the time German police learned of the potentially deadly package, it was too late. The plane had taken off again.[81]

When the plane landed at Britain's East Midlands Airport, officials cordoned off the cargo area and conducted a thorough search of its cargo but found nothing out of the ordinary. Bomb experts even cleared the printer cartridge hiding four hundred grams of PETN. The object had failed to arouse suspicion even after passing through an X-ray scanner and being examined by trained dogs.[82] Authorities decided to clear the plane for takeoff.

But officials then called from Dubai. They had just discovered PETN in the Hewlett-Packard cartridge routed through their country. These officials instructed their British colleagues on how to locate the explosives, which were carefully disguised to avoid X-ray detection. British authorities again cordoned off the area and found the bomb during this second search.[83]

Al-Qaeda had been able to smuggle bombs onto several planes and even to disguise them so cleverly that British bomb experts couldn't detect them. The parcel plot revealed al-Qaeda's propensity for continuous learning in a manner consistent with our violent non-state-actor technology adoption curve: The group's tacticians and bomb-makers did not suddenly pursue a different type of attack but instead improved upon past plots.

Although the parcel plot was foiled, AQAP released a special issue of its English-language digital magazine *Inspire* celebrating the seemingly failed effort. In it, Anwar al-Awlaki explained that "after the operation of brother Umar Farouk [the underwear bomber] we have been experimenting with ways to bring down airplanes. We have researched the various security systems employed by airports. We looked into X-Ray scanners, full-body scanners, sniffing dogs and other aspects of security. The resulting bomb was a device that we were confident that, with the will of

Allah, it would pass through the most stringent and up-to-date security equipment."[84]

The process of organizational learning and iteration thus stands at the center of AQAP's account of its own operation. Awlaki's explanation links the parcels plot to the underwear bomb plot, explaining that the aftermath of the underwear bomb plot set off a significant amount of research into aviation security systems. That learning bore fruit. X-rays detect explosives through identifying objects that have a different density or mass compared to what is expected in their normal form. Armed with this knowledge, Asiri created a powder-based PETN that mimicked the normal toner material in ink cartridges, resulting in a similar X-ray cross section. "The toner cartridge contains the toner which is carbon based and that is an organic material. The carbon's molecular number is close to that of PETN," AQAP explained.[85]

Still, AQAP's real accomplishment in the parcel plot was decidedly low-tech. The militants realized they could exploit the less stringent screening process for air cargo. Awlaki explained the group's thinking: "Since 9-11 the West has been stepping up defenses for its commercial aircrafts. . . . But what about cargo planes?"[86] AQAP discerned that air cargo was not subjected to the same level of screening as passenger luggage. There were several reasons for this disparity. For one, the air cargo industry relies on speed and affordability of delivery, and subjecting every package to screening equivalent to that of passenger air baggage would significantly add to delivery time and cost. Moreover, freight planes were thought to be less appealing terrorist targets than passenger aircraft, where a successful attack could kill hundreds.

AQAP recognized that cargo bombs could be highly destructive even if they were not as lethal as those detonated aboard passenger aircraft. As Awlaki explained in *Inspire*,

the air freight is a multi-billion dollar industry. . . . For the trade between North America and Europe, air cargo is indispensable and to be able to force the West to install stringent security measures sufficient enough to stop our explosive devices would add a heavy economic burden. . . . We knew that cargo planes are staffed by only a pilot and a co-pilot so our objective was not to cause maximum casualties but to cause maximum losses to the American economy.[87]

The idea of economic jihad articulated in *Inspire* related to organizational learning that al-Qaeda as a whole was undertaking at the strategic level. One letter recovered during the raid on Osama bin Laden's Abbottabad compound and apparently authored in early 2010 sets forth a similar rationale for launching attacks inside the United States.[88] The author of the letter, presumably bin Laden, explained that while the jihadists would continue their fight against the United States and its allies in Iraq and Afghanistan, it was preferable to strike inside America based on a strict cost–benefit analysis. He complained that the American people, despite high unemployment rates and the expenses incurred fighting overseas, hadn't really felt the impact of the 9/11 wars. "One large operation inside the U.S. will affect the security and the nerves of 300 million Americans, while killing 1,000 Americans in eight years [the death toll from the war in Afghanistan at the time] has very little impact on their nerves," bin Laden wrote. He advised that striking economic targets, including the oil supply, would make the average American feel the pinch. Bin Laden pointed to Abdulmutallab's failed 2009 bombing to support his point, stating that the attack "made them incur direct and indirect expenses, about 40 billion dollars, which is double what the administration has spent on the war each year for the last eight years." The basis for bin Laden's math isn't clear, but his argument was straightforward.

As for the parcel plot, even being loaded on board cargo planes, the bombs still had the potential to kill large numbers of people. The bomb that FedEx carried ended up traveling on two different passenger flights, a reflection of the fact that the distinction between cargo and passenger travel was fairly blurry at the time of the parcel plot. The Department of Transportation found that over a third of air cargo that entered the United States in 2010 was shipped on passenger jets.[89]

Following this scare, aviation security services around the world once again modified their practices, enhancing screening procedures for incoming flights from high-risk countries like Yemen and Somalia. Many countries also implemented tighter cargo screening. Britain and the United States also moved to ensure that the parcel plot's specific bomb delivery method could never again be used on board a passenger flight, prohibiting toner and ink cartridges weighing over five hundred grams and sixteen ounces, respectively, in passenger hand luggage.[90]

UNDERWEAR BOMBER 2.0

The new regulations did little to dim Asiri and AQAP's ambitions. In May 2012, two years after the parcels plot, AQAP introduced an improved version of the underwear bomb. American officials concluded that Asiri was the engineer behind this newest plot as well.

Asiri's new device was more advanced than the one Abdulmutallab nearly detonated in 2009. TSA chief John Pistole later explained the bomb-maker's enhancements, saying the bomb Asiri prepared in 2012 was "a next generation device" that was "new and improved in many respects" compared to Abdulmutallab's.[91] *Time* quoted at length Pistole's description of how Asiri had devised a deadly new device:

> The device featured "a new type of explosive that we had never seen," Pistole said. "All of our explosive detection equipment . . . wasn't calibrated to detect that. And all of our 800 bomb-sniffing dogs had not been trained for that specific type."
>
> The use of a new explosive has been previously reported, but Pistole continued with less familiar details about Underwear 2 that reflect the growing sophistication of Asiri's sinister craftsmanship. He said the device included redundancy, by means of two different syringes to mix liquid explosive compounds—"a double initiation system," apparently a response to a failure of Abdulmutallab's initiation process. In essence, Pistole said, "they made two devices."
>
> Finally, Pistole said, the new bomb was encased in simple household caulk in an effort to trap vapors that might alert any bomb-sniffing machines or dogs that did happen to be capable of identifying the explosive.[92]

Fortunately, the man selected to carry out the operation was in fact a "double agent" working for Saudi and British intelligence.[93] The agent absconded with the device after it had been given to him, thwarting the plot. Absent this intelligence operation, there is a strong chance the bomb would have made it through security undetected.

As the second underwear plot shows, Asiri remained confident that there would always be exploitable vulnerabilities in airport security. In 2012 Asiri was reportedly working with medical professionals to create "body bombs," or surgically implanted improvised explosive devices. These complex explosives would be virtually undetectable to full-body scanners.[94] Asiri's innovations in bomb design reaffirmed AQAP's organizational dynamism even in the face of counterterrorism pressure.

Post–Arab Spring Attacks on African Aviation

The Arab Spring sparked a significant increase in jihadist activity in Africa. A number of post-2011 aviation-related plots in Africa are instructive examples of jihadist organizational learning. The plots discussed in this section were innovative in their own right, incorporating techniques such as concealed explosives in electronic devices and the use of complicit airport employees. The plots also exhibited a greater degree of technical ability than many observers expected from Africa's jihadists.

These plots unfolded in countries where airport security is comparatively lax. The state-of-the-art detection systems and tight employee regulations in place throughout the West do not exist in places like Egypt or Somalia. But even if African aviation presents a softer target, learning organizations will seek to strike at their enemies' key vulnerabilities, wherever they might lie. This chapter now examines the two most notable aviation-related attacks in Africa after the Arab Spring's onset.

METROJET FLIGHT 9268

On October 31, 2015, Metrojet Flight 9268 left the Sharm El Sheikh International Airport in Egypt's Sinai Peninsula around 6 a.m., bound for Saint Petersburg, Russia. A two-pound bomb placed near the pressure bulkhead exploded, downing the plane and killing all 224 people on board.

Three hours after the explosion, ISIS's Egyptian affiliate, Wilayat Sinai, claimed responsibility, praising the "fighters of the Islamic State" who downed the plane, which was "carrying over 220 Russian crusaders." ISIS subsequently boasted about the attack in its English-language *Dabiq* magazine, publishing photographs of a Schweppes soda can in which the group claimed to have concealed the bomb. Russian investigators concluded that a complicit airport baggage handler had placed the bomb in the plane's luggage hold.[95]

Wilayat Sinai pledged *bayah* (an oath of allegiance) to ISIS on November 10, 2014, heralding a period of more frequent and complex attacks for the Egyptian jihadist group. Although the group had targeted the tourism sector before, most of the militants' focus had been dedicated to Egyptian security forces.[96] In contrast, the Metrojet bombing struck an international target and was designed to punish Russia for its recent entry into the Syrian civil war on the side of Bashar al-Assad's regime. At the time, the bombing was the deadliest attack ISIS had carried out beyond its caliphate's borders.

The Metrojet attack employed a unique explosive, causing instant decompression.[97] The bomb was both effective and inventively hidden, but the attack wouldn't have succeeded without airport staff working on the terrorists' behalf. Although the 2004 plot involving Chechen widows took advantage of Russia's endemic corruption, the ticket agents and others who helped the bombers make it on board believed they were facilitating nonterrorist illicit activity. In contrast, the Metrojet attack recruited employees who willingly advanced Wilayat Sinai's plot.

Airport employees can be dangerous insiders. It is difficult to fully eliminate the insider threat at international airports, where a wide variety of employees and contractors enjoy access to sensitive locations. Security personnel, immigration officers, and flight crew members have all been involved in various illicit insider schemes. An insider does not need a security officer's level of access to spy, sabotage, or otherwise advance a conspiracy. Sometimes there is unique value in the innocuous-seeming insider: Baggage handlers, concession and restaurant employees, taxi and shuttle drivers, and cleaning or construction crew members have all provided valuable insider assistance to illicit schemes.

Adding to the difficulty of detecting insiders is the tendency for background checks to clear employees who prove dangerous. As Mike Vivian, a veteran civil aviation pilot and security consultant, said: "Security is only as good as the weakest link—and that weakest link may well be the airport staff member, who whilst passing all appropriate checks and screening is secretively becoming radicalized."[98] Meanwhile, obscure pieces of knowledge can become deadly in the wrong hands. For instance, Vivian suggested that having an insider place the bomb in the Metrojet attack likely enhanced the explosive power of the device, as compared to placement by an outside terrorist who lacked specialized knowledge about the plane. Vivian noted that the bomb "was adjacent to a pressure bulkhead, and this would have a devastating effect. Clearly, someone had to have some knowledge of air-side working and the inside of an Airbus and the relevant place where to put the device."[99]

After the crash, Egypt spent millions of dollars upgrading its airport security. Many of the employee gates at the country's airports were sealed, and those that remain open were equipped with X-ray machines, fingerprint-based access, and police dogs. Egypt also introduced explosives-detection machines at arrival halls, with a new policy of sealing off luggage after it went through screening.[100]

DAALLO AIRLINES FLIGHT 159

Just a few months later, on February 2, 2016, suicide bomber Abdullahi Abdisalam Borleh, a member of the Somali militant group al-Shabaab, blasted a hole in the fuselage of Daallo Airlines Flight 159 shortly after it took off from Mogadishu's airport. Although the explosion created a gap large enough to suck Borleh out of the plane, the pilot was able to make an emergency landing because the aircraft hadn't reached cruising altitude when the bomb detonated.

Authorities believe the attacker used an explosive hidden in a laptop. The bomb had a timer programmed to detonate midflight, but a delay at the airport meant the weapon exploded at an earlier flight stage than intended. The attacker likely wanted to strike at a major international airline rather than an obscure Somali company: The bomber and other passengers were "scheduled to fly with Turkish Airlines" but were moved to the Daallo flight because of bad weather.[101] Similar to the Metrojet attack, the device was positioned to maximize the damage it caused. Had the bomb detonated at cruising altitude, the blast may have set off a secondary explosion in the fuel tank.[102]

As in Wilayat Sinai's Metrojet attack, Shabaab exploited insider vulnerabilities. Surveillance footage showed two airport workers putting the laptop on an X-ray belt, then later giving the computer to Borleh in the departure lounge. One of these workers, security official Abdiweli Maow, had in fact sneaked the laptop through an employee gate the day before. Borleh's flight that day was canceled, so the computer had to be brought back on February 2. A bomb with the potential to kill scores of people thus made it past screening for a second time.[103]

The Daallo attack represented Shabaab's most threatening penetration of airport security and highlighted the group's adaptations in executing aviation plots. The device was relatively advanced, leading officials to conclude that a senior commander in Shabaab's explosives wing had built it. Col. Hassan Ali Nur Shute, the chief prosecutor in the criminal case, said Shabaab "fitted the explosives in the laptop with sophistication. It was difficult for the staff to detect; they have not seen that kind of technique used before."[104]

Shabaab didn't wait long before trying to replicate this method. Just one month later, on March 7, another laptop bomb exploded in the screening area of Somalia's Beledweyne Airport. Authorities discovered and defused two additional bombs in the airport, one hidden in a printer.[105] These bomb designs were reminiscent of Asiri's printer cartridge plot. In light of AQAP's geographic proximity and close relationship to Shabaab, it is likely that the two groups shared ways to build and use hard-to-detect bombs.

The Somali government enhanced security at Mogadishu's airport in the aftermath of the Daallo Airlines attack. In April 2017, a little over a year after the bombing, the general manager of the airport showcased its updated security system, which included three layers of scanner-based screening, sniffer dogs, and procedures for examining laptops to differentiate between normally functioning computers and explosive devices.[106] As usual, jihadists got to work finding a way around the new measures. In April 2017, U.S. intelligence determined that jihadist bomb-makers had started crafting laptop-based explosive devices that did not rely on the computer's battery to serve as a detonator, meaning they could pass through the screening process with the power turned on. This led the U.S. government to issue a temporary ban on electronic devices larger than a cellphone for passengers on U.S.-bound flights from airports in the Middle East and Africa with high terrorist threats.[107]

The Sydney Plot

A recent plot targeting Australia provides a glimpse into the potential future of aviation terrorism. The planned attack employed the "virtual plotter" model of supporting terrorist attacks from abroad (see chapter 10). In July 2017 Syria-based ISIS commander Tarek Khayat directed his

Sydney-based brothers, Khaled and Mahmoud, to bomb an Etihad flight that was heading to Abu Dhabi with four hundred passengers and crew. Tarek Khayat put Khaled and Mahmoud in contact with a senior ISIS member who guided them in constructing the explosive device. This virtual plotter then had another ISIS operative in Turkey mail the Khayat brothers a partially assembled PETN-based device through international air cargo.[108]

The bomb components made it to Australia, where the Khayat brothers assembled them into a functioning device that they hid in a meat mincer and a Barbie doll. On July 15 they placed the explosive device in the carry-on luggage of a fourth brother, Amer Khayat, who was traveling to Lebanon via Abu Dhabi for a family visit. This made Amer an unwitting accomplice as well as a would-be unwilling victim of his brothers' plot.

The explosive device was thwarted by a chance carry-on baggage check by Etihad that found Amer Khayat's bag to be overweight. At that point "the bombs were removed from the hand luggage" by Amer's brothers, who were concerned that their plot might be uncovered by authorities following the baggage check.[109] Australian security wasn't aware the plot until eleven days later, when they received a tip from Israeli intelligence.[110] The Australians arrested the plotters as they were in the midst of organizing a new, nonaviation attack.

Although the Sydney plot was unsuccessful, Australian officials described it as one of "the most sophisticated plots that has ever been attempted on Australian soil."[111] ISIS was continuing to engage in organizational learning, formulating multicontinent terrorist plots employing new methods.

One such idea introduced in the Sydney plot was "hybridization" of the planning process. Previously, virtual plotters who wanted remote operatives to carry out a bomb attack had to either provide the attacker a ready-made device or give them step-by-step directions for making the bomb from scratch. Both options are fraught with risk. By sending an explosive in ready-to-assemble parts, ISIS created an innovative third possibility, reducing the amount of "do-it-yourself" expertise required for its model of terrorism. Hybridization expedited the bomb assembly process and minimized the possibility of error while bolstering the quality of the explosive.[112]

A second innovation was that the plot was designed to minimize opportunities for interdiction. Even if the Khayats were on a watch list, their use of a mule as the actual bomber would have helped the conspirators circumvent aviation security. By using an uninvolved third party, the plotters neutralized many psychological and emotional factors that can compromise a plot. Behavioral detection, which is frequently employed at security checkpoints, would not have identified Amer Khayat as a threat, as he had no idea that he had been conscripted as his brothers' bomber.

The use of a third-party attacker also meant that ISIS wouldn't lose skilled operatives. In the past, terrorists guided by virtual plotters had conducted attacks themselves. In Sydney, neither of the major conspirators planned on carrying out the attack, instead deciding to sacrifice a relative for their mission. This allowed ISIS to retain two loyal operatives. The use of unwitting terrorists therefore increases the potential for follow-on attacks.

Australia announced increased aviation security measures after the foiled attack, many of which were already common elsewhere. For example, Australia began using improved screening processes that would better align with the European Union's stricter protocols.[113] The government also ramped up border security, particularly for international air cargo.

Attacks on Airports

Airports are softer targets than are aircraft, and another attractive focus for jihadists. Although there is security in and around airports, terrorists can enter most Western airports without being subjected to background or identity checks, or even a security screening, which is usually only required of ticketed passengers.[114] Even someone who is on a watch list or no-fly list, or who security services have flagged as a potential terrorist, can strike an airport.

Large numbers of people gather in several highly accessible areas of airports. Many airports have waiting lounges, restaurants, and shops outside the security screening area. Nearly all airports contain predictable bottlenecks, such as the waiting line for security, lines for taxis or other ground transportation, and the baggage claim area. Terrorists can conceal themselves in the crowd, then strike.

In addition to the immediate loss of life and damage to facilities, operations targeting airports can cause airlines to reroute planes or delay flights.

Airports across the globe are also typically filled with tourists, including Westerners. In this section we review a number of instances where jihadists plotted against or attacked airports. The instances we examine are telling yet not comprehensive. Al-Qaeda-aligned terrorists have targeted airports since the late 1990s while ISIS and its predecessor, al-Qaeda in Iraq, have struck airports on several occasions as well.

THE LAX PLOT

On December 14, 1999, a suspicious customs officer in Port Angeles, Washington, noticed that the last passenger off a ferry from Victoria, British Columbia, seemed especially nervous. The passenger, Ahmed Ressam, was referred for a secondary inspection along with his rented Chrysler sedan. Ressam tried to run away as inspectors began to pat him down. Officers then found explosives in his car's spare tire well. Ressam, a native of Algeria, later told a U.S. court that he intended to pack the explosives into suitcases that he would detonate at Los Angeles International Airport (LAX).[115]

Ressam had relocated from France to Montreal in 1994, falsely claiming asylum. For the next four years he lived a life of petty crime, robbing tourists and trafficking in stolen passports.[116] In early 1998 he traveled to Pakistan, then to Afghanistan. Ressam met with Abu Zubaydah, a veteran jihadist facilitator, who arranged for Ressam to train in the Khalden camp in April 1998. Although some observers have argued that Zubaydah wasn't technically a member of al-Qaeda, he nonetheless had extensive connections to the most senior levels of the organization. Bin Laden trusted Zubaydah to handle some of al-Qaeda's most sensitive missions, including the group's relocation from Sudan to Afghanistan in 1996. Zubaydah also learned details of al-Qaeda's inner workings that only the most trusted comrades could know about, including the alias and true identity of 9/11 planner Khalid Sheikh Mohammed.[117]

Ressam later told an American court that Khalden housed recruits of diverse nationality, including Algerians, Chechens, Frenchmen, Germans, Jordanians, Saudis, Swedes, Turks, and Yemenis.[118] Ressam received extensive training, later saying that he had learned how to "blow up the infrastructure of a country," including "electric plants, gas plants, airports, railroads, large corporations."[119]

Ressam's thwarted plot against LAX is not usually thought of as an al-Qaeda plot. For example, the 9/11 Commission describes Ressam's plans as "essentially independent" of the group.[120] Several facts indicate, though, that the story is more complicated than this. As the 9/11 Commission itself noted, Ressam "had been recruited, trained, and prepared in a network affiliated with" al-Qaeda and its allies.[121]

During the trial of one of his co-conspirators, Ressam testified that he did not intend to conduct the plot on his own. Instead, a group at the Khalden camp made plans to relocate to Canada and carry out a larger operation from there. Ressam explained that a group of around thirty jihadists composed the Algerian group at Khalden.[122] This cohort was further divided into cells, with five or six men in each cell responsible for attacking a specific region after leaving the camp. While Ressam's cell was tasked with striking the United States, other cells were assigned to other geographies.[123]

Ressam said that he and other members of his cell discussed attacking an airport or consulate. Their planned strike inside the United States was intended to be part of a worldwide campaign, with other operations slated to occur "in Europe, in the Gulf, against U.S. and Israel."[124] Indeed, several planned attacks that were in some way traceable to al-Qaeda were foiled during this period, including an operation in Jordan that Abu Zubaydah and at least one other man who had sworn allegiance to bin Laden orchestrated. In November 1999 Jordanian authorities intercepted a call between Abu Zubaydah and Khadr Abu Hoshar. "The time for training is over," Zubaydah said.[125] Jordanian intelligence quickly deciphered his meaning: Abu Hoshar and a team of fifteen others planned to strike Western and Jewish targets. One of Abu Hoshar's co-conspirators, an American named Raed Hijazi, had sworn allegiance to bin Laden earlier that month, with Zubaydah reportedly accepting Hijazi's oath on bin Laden's behalf.[126] The plots in Jordan were stopped, but the jihadists had set multiple plans in motion at once, including that of Ressam and his comrades.

Two individuals coordinated Ressam's plot: a man based in Pakistan known as Abu Jaffar, who was the chief overseer, and a second remote conspirator named Abu Doha. The prosecution in Ressam's case described Abu Doha as a "high-ranking al-Qaeda member with close ties to Osama Bin Laden."[127] Abu Doha informed Ressam in the summer of 1999 that "the other members of the Montreal cell would not be joining him to carry out the attack against the United States."[128] At that point, Ressam decided to carry out an attack on his own.

Ressam nevertheless received assistance from various al-Qaeda operatives or al-Qaeda-affiliated actors during his planning process, including from Abu Zubaydah and individuals in Montreal with their own ties to the al-Qaeda network. Ressam claimed to his FBI interrogators that bin Laden "was aware of the Los Angeles operation."[129] The Algerian even "called an Afghanistan-based facilitator to inquire into whether Bin Laden wanted to take credit for the attack," although "he did not get a reply."[130] Under questioning by U.S. officials, Ressam accurately identified Zacarias Moussaoui and Richard Reid as Khalden attendees.

The sum of evidence thus suggests that Ressam should be considered an al-Qaeda actor even though he was granted a significant degree of autonomy. This is consistent with al-Qaeda's "terrorist entrepreneur" model. Once the larger plot was called off, Ressam took matters into his own hands, deciding to conduct a more limited bombing.

THE SWISS AIRPORT PLOTS

In December 2005 a group of men linked to the Algeria-based Salafist Group for Preaching and Combat (GSPC) conspired to down an El Al plane taking off from Geneva, Switzerland, using rockets or a surface-to-air missile. After the plot was detected, the Israelis rerouted El Al's Switzerland-bound flights from Geneva to Zurich for a full week.[131] Both the target and intended mode of attack bore similarities to al-Qaeda's unsuccessful attempt to destroy an El Al jet in Mombasa, Kenya, in 2002.

After the GSPC loyalists failed to acquire the arms necessary to shoot down the jet, the plotters set their eyes on the airports in Zurich and Geneva. The seven men intended to attack the airports with improvised explosive devices hidden in backpacks.[132] Swiss authorities detained the group and announced that the men were tied to a broader GSPC-linked network in Europe. "Those who were arrested in Switzerland maintained contact with similar cells in France and Spain, which were likewise smashed," the Swiss Federal Prosecutor's Office said in a statement.[133] The French and Spanish governments detained other suspects allegedly tied to the Swiss cell.

QUEEN ALIA INTERNATIONAL AIRPORT PLOT

In March 2006 Jordanian officials disrupted a plot targeting passengers at the Queen Alia International Airport south of Amman. According to a Department of Homeland Security assessment, the jihadists wanted to attack "Western and Jewish passengers" as "they exited the customs arrival area and walked through the foyer of the terminal."[134]

There is evidence connecting the airport plot to al-Qaeda's regional affiliate. Four months earlier, on November 9, 2005, bombers dispatched by al-Qaeda in Iraq had struck three Amman hotels, killing sixty people and wounding more than one hundred in the deadliest terrorist attack in the country's history. The Jordanian government found that the airport plotters planned to use the same type of explosives as the suicide bombers in that earlier attack.[135] One of the detained terrorists said that "al-Qaeda [in Iraq] would claim responsibility," had the cell succeeded.[136]

THE GLASGOW INTERNATIONAL AIRPORT ATTACK

More than a year later, two aspiring terrorists tied to al-Qaeda in Iraq, the Indian-born aeronautical engineer Bilal Abdulla and the British-born Kafeel Ahmed, tried to kill travelers at Glasgow International Airport in Scotland as part of a broader multicity attack. On the evening of June 29, 2007, British authorities discovered two car bombs in London and neutralized both of them.

The following day Abdulla and Ahmed launched the second part of their plan. The pair attempted to drive a Jeep Cherokee filled with gas canisters through the glass doors of the Glasgow Airport's main terminal. Instead, they crashed the Jeep into a concrete pillar.[137] That security barrier likely saved many lives. It was one of the busiest days of the year at the airport, as summer break in Scotland had just begun and families were setting off on vacation. Around four thousand people were in or near the main terminal. After the initial assault failed, Abdulla jumped from the car and began hurling homemade petrol explosives. He then bathed himself in gasoline and set himself on fire, running to the back of the Jeep to try to detonate the petrol containers inside. Nearby civilians and police officers stopped both terrorists before they could do more harm. The only person to die was Ahmed, who succumbed to his burns a little over a month later.

Abdulla survived the Cherokee's blaze and was later convicted on terrorism charges.

Authorities discovered that the two men had ties to al-Qaeda in Iraq, although the strength of this connection remains ambiguous. A U.S. intelligence official told the *New York Times* that Abdulla and Ahmed's cell phones contained the numbers of al-Qaeda in Iraq members.[138] Authorities also found al-Qaeda propaganda, including bin Laden's lectures, on Ahmed's computer.[139] Authorities also saw similarities between the bombs in London and Glasgow and those deployed by al-Qaeda in Iraq. Their vehicle-borne improvised explosive devices were packed with shrapnel and nails that would have flown outward from the blast.[140]

DOMODEDOVO INTERNATIONAL AIRPORT ATTACK

On January 24, 2011, a suicide bomber from the North Caucasus blew himself up in the arrival area of Moscow's Domodedovo International Airport, killing three dozen people and wounding nearly two hundred.

Russian authorities were already on alert that Domodedovo was a target. After all, nearly seven years earlier two female Chechen suicide bombers had detonated bombs on a pair of jets departing from Domodedovo. Suicide bombers had carried out several attacks in Russia since then, including March 29, 2010, bombings at Moscow metro stations by a pair of female terrorists.[141] New body scanners and other security measures had already been introduced at the airport after the 2004 bombings. With the 2014 Sochi Winter Olympics three years away, Russia's government had further incentive to prevent attacks. But the January 2011 attack proved how easy it could be for terrorists to cause mayhem at a major aviation hub. The bomber struck the densely packed international arrivals hall. As a spokeswoman for the airport explained, security allowed "free access" to this area.[142] This gave the terrorist easy entry into an area filled with hundreds of people without having to pass through the screening applied to ticketed passengers. Two weeks later the al-Qaeda-linked Islamic Caucasus Emirate released a video of its emir, Doku Umarov, claiming responsibility for the attack.

The Domodedovo bomber was sent by the Caucasus Emirate's suicide squad, the Riyad-us Saliheen ("Garden of Paradise") Martyrs' Brigade. That unit was responsible for a string of attacks, including the aforementioned

March 2010 suicide bombing at Moscow metro stations.[143] Prior to the Domodedovo bombing, Umarov had recorded a video in which he appeared alongside two figures: a jihadist known as Khamzat, who headed the Riyad-us Saliheen Martyrs' Brigade, and the bomber responsible for the airport strike, a young man known as Saifullah. Umarov boasted that Saifullah was preparing for a "special operation," a warning that was anything but empty.[144] The Caucasus Emirate and its Riyad-us Saliheen Martyrs' Brigade had multiple ties to al-Qaeda.[145]

THE BRUSSELS AIRPORT ATTACK

Like its predecessor, al-Qaeda in Iraq, Abu Bakr al-Baghdadi's ISIS has targeted airports. On March 22, 2016, Ibrahim El Bakraoui and Najim Laachraoui blew themselves up at Brussels Airport in Belgium. A third suicide bomber, Khalid El Bakraoui (Ibrahim's younger brother), detonated his device at the Maelbeek metro station. Thirty-two people died and dozens more were wounded. The terrorist trio responsible for this first ISIS operation against an airport was part of a larger European network that orchestrated the November 2015 ISIS assault on Paris.

THE ATATÜRK AIRPORT ATTACK

Three months after the attack in Brussels, on June 28, 2016, another team of three suspected ISIS members struck Istanbul's Atatürk Airport. No group claimed responsibility for the shootings and bombings, which killed forty-five people and wounded more than two hundred. At the time, ISIS was hesitant to claim operations in Turkey, which had long been the key gateway for foreign fighters traveling to Syria.

The three attackers first opened fire on civilians and security personnel, then detonated their explosive vests. Two of the attackers were identified as Russians, Rahim Bulgarov and Vadim Osmanov.[146] Turkish officials said the chief planner of the operation was a Chechen ISIS member named Akhmed Chatayev.[147]

Abu Bakr al-Baghdadi's caliphate had attracted many fighters from the Caucasus region, including Chatayev. Chatayev was a well-known jihadist who had lost an arm battling Russian forces in 2000, along with a foot after a separate clash in 2012. These setbacks didn't halt the double amputee's militant career. In 2015 the U.S. Treasury Department designated Chatayev as a terrorist, noting that he "was part of a group of militants that was planning attacks against U.S. and Turkish facilities."[148] The massacre at Atatürk Airport spurred Turkish officials to launch a series of counterterrorism raids, reportedly arresting two dozen people in Istanbul (although it isn't clear how many were ISIS members).[149]

Organizational Learning in External Operations

In a special issue of *Inspire* dedicated to the 2010 parcels plot, which al-Qaeda dubbed "Operation Hemorrhage," the militant group pithily summarized the adaptation cycle that was the crux of its aviation operations: "If your opponent covers his right cheek, slap him on his left."[150] Throughout this chapter, we have seen governments and the aviation industry cover their metaphorical right cheek with bolstered security, only for jihadist groups to come back and slap them on the left cheek with innovative new plots. Terrorist groups have proven remarkably adept at beating new security measures. Even when plots were not fully executed, this was typically due to external factors like intelligence work or last-minute technical mishaps rather than effective aviation security.

Jihadist groups and the aviation industry are engaged in organizational learning designed to gain an advantage over the other. They both actively work to acquire knowledge that informs their future decisions. The learning on both sides stems from a zero-sum competition between the two. The success of a militant group's external operations means the defeat of existing airport security protocols, and vice versa. Because both sides must overcome the other in order to succeed, the impetus for organizational learning is frequently situated on the reactive end of the anticipatory/reactive spectrum. To "win," one side must be responsive to the adaptations of the other. But jihadist groups have proven capable of anticipating their enemies' actions and reacting to them when they do occur. The shoe-bomb plot is an example of jihadists functioning on the anticipatory end of the spectrum (but what they anticipated was the aviation security reaction to the 9/11 attacks). The failure of the shoe-bomb plot, and the subsequent requirement that passenger footwear undergo screening, did not stop al-Qaeda from nearly pulling off successful aviation attacks using ever more sophisticated and subtly concealed devices.

The terrorists have somewhat of an advantage. Jihadist external operations are offensive while security is inherently defensive. Thus, a lack of anticipatory changes is not always due to a failure of imagination on the part of airport security. Instead, it is often difficult to preemptively implement complicated and expensive security changes without some basis for believing that the threat they are designed to counteract actually exists.

Both aviation security and jihadists are constantly refining their existing structures. The airline industry does this in part through tacking on additional security procedures and working to streamline existing ones, and jihadists often do it through tinkering with their earlier innovations. In light of the fact that a zero-sum competition of this kind tends to favor the actor on the offense, former TSA chief Kip Hawley has advocated for what is known as complexity-based security, which calls for a shift from a linear, homogenous checklist of procedures to an unpredictable, flexible, and heterogeneous process across airports.[151]

These differences in organizational learning between terrorists and their adversaries tend to highlight the strengths of the jihadists' model. As we have demonstrated, jihadists have created versatile organizations with the ability to shape-shift according to want and need. This model has allowed jihadists to remain adaptive adversaries in their aviation plots, a dynamic likely to remain in place for a long time.

5

The Early Adopter

Anwar al-Awlaki in the Digital Space

It was a beautiful day. A warm Texas breeze wafted down with no rain in sight. The sign outside Fort Hood welcomed all to "The Great Place." Within its barbed wire-lined confines, the Soldier Readiness Processing Center was unremarkable. The squat, beige structure was largely indistinguishable from the surrounding buildings to an unfamiliar eye.

U.S. Army major Nidal Malik Hasan was not an unfamiliar eye. He knew exactly where to go. At around 1:30 p.m. on November 5, 2009, the thirty-nine-year-old psychiatrist entered the processing center and opened fire with a .45-caliber Smith & Wesson pistol, carrying out the worst mass shooting on a military base in American history. By the time his rampage was over, thirteen Americans were dead and over forty wounded.

The shooting was not the desperate act of a deranged man who had snapped. The system should have been blinking red with respect to Hasan for years. He had openly displayed his growing extremism and had been in contact with one of the world's most dangerous jihadist ideologues. Yet, at the time of the atrocity, U.S. officials struggled to explain why the officer had massacred his putative comrades-in-arms. A Pentagon investigation, released two months after the murders, did not make a single direct mention of jihadist motivations, a baffling yet revealing omission.[1]

Hasan had left a trail of breadcrumbs pointing to his radicalization that was largely missed even after the massacre. In June 2007, more than two years before his attack, Hasan delivered a presentation to colleagues at the Walter Reed Army Medical Center in Washington, D.C., titled "The Koranic World View as It Relates to Muslims in the U.S. Military." The lecture was ostensibly a warning of the possible effects of the wars in Iraq and Afghan- istan on the psychology of Muslim servicemembers. But in retrospect, it is clear that Hasan was describing the gradual unsettling of his own mind and worldview. One coworker later remarked on the bizarre nature of Hasan's talk.[2] Indeed, Hasan's slides reflected a violent, fundamentalist interpretation of Islam. On one page, Hasan listed a series of bullet points: *Osama Bin Laden, Taliban, Suicide bombers,* and *Iran*. He then explained these actors' intentions and goals: "If Muslim groups can convince Muslims that they are fighting for God against injustices of the 'infidels;' ie: enemies of Islam, then Muslims can become a potent adversary ie: suicide bombing, etc." Hasan then summed up a central aspect of the jihadist worldview: "We love death more then [*sic*] you love life!"

The remainder of the presentation adopts a similarly sinister tone. It appears that Hasan was describing his own extreme views as if they were how any Muslim properly following Islamic doctrines would under- stand the issues. "Muslims may be seen as moderate (compromising) but God is not," read another slide. "Fighting to establish an Islamic State to please God, even by force, is condoned by the [*sic*] Islam," Hasan claimed. Other lines revealed Hasan's own darkening views. "It's getting harder and harder for Muslims in the service to morally justify being in a military that seems constantly engaged against fellow Muslims," he wrote. The second-to-last line in the presentation read: "Muslims [*sic*] Soldiers should not serve in any capacity that renders them at risk to hurting/killing believers unjustly."

On the final page of the fifty-slide deck, Hasan advised that the Defense Department "should allow Muslims [*sic*] Soldiers the option of being released as 'Conscientious objectors' to increase troop morale and decrease adverse events." In retrospect, these words read like either a veiled threat or a des- perate cry for help.

On December 17, 2008, Hasan tripped a FBI surveillance wire when he emailed an American-born cleric who had built an extensive and occasion- ally murderous audience throughout the English-speaking world: Anwar al-Awlaki.[3] Hasan sent an email from his personal account to Awlaki through the "Contact the Sheikh" button on Awlaki's website.[4] Hasan wrote (typos and misspellings preserved from the original):

> There are many soldiers in the us armed forces that have converted to Islam while in the service. There are also many Muslims who join the armed forces for a myriad of different reasons. Some appear to have internal conflicts and have even killed or tried to kill other us soldiers in the name of Islam i.e. Hasan Akbar, etc. Others feel that there is no conflict.
>
> Previous Fatwas seem vague and not very definitive. Can you make some general comments about Muslims in the u.s. military. Would you consider someone like Hasan Akbar or other soldiers that have committed such acts with the goal of helping Muslims/Islam (Lets just assume this for now) fighting Jihad and if they did die would you consider them shaheeds. I realize that these are difficult questions but you seem to be one of the only ones that has lived in the u.s. has a good understadning of the the Qur'an and Sunna and is not afraid of being direct.[5]

Hasan Akbar was a U.S. Army sergeant who killed two fellow soldiers and wounded fourteen at Camp Pennsylvania in Kuwait at the beginning of the Iraq War in March 2003. Thus, Hasan was asking Awlaki whether he should view men like Akbar, who attack fellow Americans in uniform, as martyrs whose actions will place them in Paradise.

Awlaki didn't respond to Hasan's initial query. But the Army major didn't give up. Hasan sent at least sixteen messages to the American-born ideologue. Awlaki replied only twice, giving cursory answers that were notable for their lack of substance. After Hasan's atrocity at Fort Hood, U.S. officials seized on the narrow fact that Awlaki didn't explicitly condone the mass shooting in order to downplay the massacre's relationship to jihadism.[6] In his short replies, Awlaki simply accepted Hasan's praise and promised to keep an eye out for any prospective brides, as Hasan had requested. Remarkably, the FBI released a statement saying that Joint Terrorism Task Force (JTTF) investigators "assessed that the content of those communications was consistent with research being conducted by Major Hasan in his position as a psychiatrist at the Walter Reed Medical Center."[7] The FBI added: "Because the content of the communications was explainable by his research and nothing else derogatory was found, the JTTF concluded that Major Hasan was not involved in terrorist activities or terrorist planning."

That reading is absurd. It misses the fact that Hasan's correspondence with Awlaki began by asking whether someone *in his exact position* should be regarded as a martyr for killing fellow members of the U.S. military. It misses the fawning nature of Hasan's emails. In one message Hasan said he wanted to hold an essay contest in Awlaki's honor, the topic being "Why is Anwar Al Awlaki a great activist and leader." Hasan wanted to award a $5,000 scholarship to the winner. Hasan also inquired about different ways to donate money via Awlaki's website, even offering to pay its domain fee. It is impossible to believe that sponsoring essay contests in Awlaki's honor or inquiring about sending him money fell within the purview of Hasan's research.

Throughout this mostly one-sided correspondence, Hasan consistently referred to Awlaki as a respected religious authority and asked for his counsel on various hot-button issues. In his second-to-last email to Awlaki, written in May 2009, Hasan explained he had "heard a speaker defending suicide bombings as permissible" and added that he had been using the unnamed speaker's "logic in debates to see how effective it really is." By the most innocent interpretation, Hasan's emails to Awlaki are a fanboy's cry for his idol's attention. Since the recipient was an influential jihadist, it is impossible to justify the JTTF's strange conclusion that the correspondence was explainable by his research.

The argument that Awlaki didn't directly sanction Hasan's attack at Fort Hood rested on similarly flimsy premises. As noted, Hasan's very first email to Awlaki specifically asked whether Hasan Akbar should be seen as a role model. Hasan also referred to Akbar's actions in his presentation at Walter Reed. It is easy, in hindsight, to see the parallel between the slayings in Texas and those in Kuwait more than six years earlier. As Awlaki himself subsequently noted, the point of Hasan's emails was to receive clerical approval for a deed like Akbar's: The Army psychiatrist was seeking advice about the permissibility of killing fellow soldiers. It is true that Awlaki didn't specifically address Hasan's question in their private correspondence, but the cleric did sanction the violence in later public statements, even referring to Hasan as one of his "students."[8]

More to the point, a reading of Awlaki's public statements before the Fort Hood attack would clearly reveal his answer to Hasan's question. On December 11, 2008, six days before Hasan's first email, Awlaki posted a blog entry titled "A Muslim for the Sake of the Disbelievers."[9] The blog harshly criticized a Muslim who had emailed to ask why the cleric preached violent jihad when Islam was a religion of peace. Awlaki couldn't conceal his contempt. For Muslims like the unnamed inquisitor, Awlaki wrote, "fighting for Islam, and for the ummah is terrorism, but he manages to shop for a fatwa that would allow him to serve in the armies of the disbelievers and fight against his brothers." Awlaki wrote that "being a Muslim for the sake of the disbelievers permeates his every action," and he imagined that if the unnamed inquisitor "meets a Muslim he frowns and if he meets a disbeliever his face beams with a smile."

If Hasan read Awlaki's post, he would have been aware of what Awlaki thought of Muslims who served in the U.S. military. Awlaki reiterated his disdain for Muslims who fought against their co-religionists in a message sent to his email list, including Hasan, on July 14, 2009.[10] The cleric blasted any Muslim soldier who fought for America and its allies in the war on terror as "a heartless beast, bent on evil, who sells his religion for a few dollars." Concerning any Muslims "fighting on behalf of America against the mujahideen in Pakistan, Somalia and the Maghrib," Awlaki asked: "What kind of twisted figh[t] is this?" Any army allied with the United States was "the worst of creation. Blessed are those who fight against them and blessed are those *shuhada* [martyrs] who are killed by them." Hasan doubtless understood these messages as applying to himself personally.

This chapter begins by contextualizing the distinctive contribution Awlaki made to the jihadist movement as a radicalizer. We then turn to what is unique about the online space, where Awlaki made such a contribution to the jihadist cause, and how this space can facilitate radicalization. Awlaki was instrumental in moving jihadists past the in-person, peer-to-peer model of radicalization, and devising mechanisms that helped jihadist ideology to proliferate at scale. We then provide a short biography of Awlaki's life before turning to the output of his lectures, videos, and writings. This content helped trigger a new wave of terrorism across the world.

Awlaki as a Radicalizer

Hasan wasn't the first terrorist Awlaki inspired, nor would he be the last. Awlaki's legacy continues to bedevil law enforcement and counterterrorism officials, and the scholarly literature confirms Awlaki's unique power as a radicalizing figure.[11] We begin by exploring the concept of radicalization before turning to how the online environment has altered radicalization dynamics.

It is worth noting at the outset that there is no consensus definition of *radicalization*, nor is there a consensus model describing how it occurs. The lack of a consensus definition is unsurprising and does not call into question the validity of the concept. There is similarly no consensus definition of *terrorism*, nor is there a consensus definition of *war*, *civil war*, or *insurgency*.[12] The fact that these concepts lack consensus definitions does not call them into question. Despite the lack of a consensus definition of *radicalization*, common threads can be discerned in the scholarship. As Peter Neumann notes, most definitions of radicalization can be distinguished through their emphasis on the progression to either extremist *views* or extremist *behaviors*.[13] While some scholars may adopt exaggerated views about the distinction between *belief* and *action*, this distinction does exist. Awlaki and other jihadist radicalizers have attempted to promote the adoption of both extremist views and behaviors. We can see that in Nidal Hasan's case, for example, he displayed his extremist views publicly and reached out to Awlaki to assist in the formation of these views prior to taking action (i.e., the Fort Hood shooting). This book thus defines *radicalization* as Neumann does, as "the process whereby people become extremists."[14] While much academic debate focuses on defining *extremism* in relationship to either views or behaviors, Neumann advocates a sensibly holistic definition that incorporates both.

Mohammed Hafez and Creighton Mullins make the important observation that, despite sometimes heated debates in the field of radicalization studies, there is "some consensus on the key variables that produce radicalization and violent extremism."[15] They highlight grievances, networks, ideologies, and enabling environments and support structures as variables about which there is agreement. But Hafez and Mullins note that despite this agreement on variables that may drive extremism, the field is far from a scholarly consensus on the models tracing an individual's transformation to the embrace of extremism.[16] In many ways, radicalization models can be seen as metaphors for how the adoption of extremist views or behaviors comes about. Is there an orderly, relatively linear process? Are there multiple distinct pathways? Or is the best model something completely different?

One influential metaphor for radicalization has been that of a process. Some scholarship has criticized this conception for overemphasizing the role of ideology.[17] Thus, subsequent scholarship has tended to reject the process metaphor, instead describing variegated "pathways" to terrorist violence. This work rejects the idea that radicalization is the culmination of "linear development," and instead sees the phenomenon "as part of an 'activist career,' understood as 'a long-lasting social activity articulated by phases of joining, commitment, and defection.' "[18] Other academic work counsels against process or pathway metaphors. Hafez and Mullins argue instead for the use of *puzzle* because there is no "orderly sequence of steps or procedures that produce an output."[19]

In this book, we are agnostic about the best overarching model for conceptualizing radicalization. Debates over which model is most powerful will continue for years. It is just as clear that jihadist groups, and figures like Awlaki and his successors, are experiencing an alarming degree of success in radicalizing others to their cause. Their successes stem, in part, from new opportunities presented by the digital space.

The Social Science of Online Radicalization

Why was Awlaki so effective as a radicalizer? An important starting point is understanding the unique power of the internet, and social media in particular, in identity formation. It is a highly consequential space for extremist groups.

THE EVOLUTION OF THE INTERNET

Before turning to social science to illuminate the dynamics of radicalization in the online space, it is worth briefly exploring the internet's evolution. The shift from Web 1.0 to Web 2.0 to the social web had a profound impact on violent non-state actors. The first iteration of the internet, Web 1.0—the "read-only" Web—was characterized by static web pages that could be read but offered little to no interactivity. Around the turn of the century, Web 2.0, the "read-write" Web, emerged. It allowed users to create blogs, post multimedia content (e.g., audio recordings or videos), and engage more easily with content on web pages. Web 2.0 offered greater interactivity but did not change the average Web user into a content producer.

The social web turned this dynamic on its head. On the social web—including Facebook, MySpace, Twitter, and YouTube—users were no longer primarily consumers of someone else's material but became content producers.[20] Awlaki rose to prominence as Web 2.0 was giving way to the social web, which positioned him to be an early adopter of this new means of disseminating the jihadist message.

THE SOCIAL SCIENCE OF ONLINE IDENTITY FORMATION

Research produced by psychologists, sociologists, and communication scholars stretching back to before the advent of social media, or even the internet, helps explain radicalization dynamics in the age of Twitter. Academics have studied the impact of computer-mediated communication on human behavior since the 1960s. Literature on the subject, especially three concepts from the field of social psychology—identity demarginalization, group polarization, and the social identity model of deindividuation effects—has strong explanatory power regarding the impact of the online space for violent non-state actors that depend on radicalizing others.

Identity demarginalization theory, as articulated by Katelyn McKenna and John Bargh in a 1998 study, explores why some social groups are more drawn to online communication than others. McKenna and Bargh found that individuals with "concealable and culturally devalued identities" were more likely to participate in and value online communities than individuals with mainstream identities.[21] They found that people who posted in online forums dedicated to concealable identities—for example, those dedicated to minority sexual identities—valued the feedback and opinions of other group members more strongly than did members of forums focused on marginalized identities that are easier to perceive, such as obesity and stuttering. "For the first time," the authors write, individuals exploring their marginalized identities online "can reap the benefits of joining a group of similar others: feeling less isolated and different, disclosing a long secret part of oneself, sharing one's own experiences and learning from those of others, and gaining emotional and motivational support."[22]

Online communities may be uniquely powerful among groups with concealable identities because of the internet's anonymity, reach, and in-group reinforcement. Relative anonymity can embolden individuals with concealable marginalized identities to discuss issues that may be taboo in a mainstream social setting.[23] For example, in a study of lesbian, gay, and bisexual online groups, one participant in these groups commented: "I think it's much easier to talk about certain things online such as relationships, sexual things and compliments and insults. It's easier to talk to someone when you don't have to see the physical reaction and think of a response right away."[24]

In a study examining the website Stormfront and the white nationalist movement, Neal Caren and colleagues note that the absence of spatial boundaries allows online communities "to draw in otherwise isolated movement participants."[25] The same phenomenon has been observed in online interactions between Salafi jihadists.[26]

Participation in online communities can also reinforce what McKenna and Bargh dub demarginalization. They found that people who actively took part in online discussions not only came to "consider the group identity more important than did those who did not actively participate" but also intensified marginalized behaviors based on positive reinforcement from group members.[27] Joining and receiving positive feedback from a like-minded group online can help members come to view their concealed identities more positively, sometimes to the point of incorporating them into their public personas.

Group polarization theory expands on some of the themes highlighted in identity demarginalization. Group polarization refers to the propensity for groups to become more extreme in outlook through mutual reinforcement. Numerous studies conclude that groups that interact online experience a greater degree of group polarization than groups that interact face-to-face.[28] A key reason may be the general absence of visual and verbal cues in online communication. People interacting online can speak freely without having to worry about the physical expressions of their peers. This reduces inhibitions, and participants become willing to "contribute more novel arguments and engage in more one-upmanship behavior," which may drive group polarization.[29]

The social identity model of deindividuation effects (SIDE) provides a framework for understanding processes like group polarization and demarginalization in an online setting. SIDE is a revision of classic deindividuation theory, which suggests that group immersion and anonymity within a group result in a loss of self-awareness and an increase in anti-normative behavior.[30] SIDE, in contrast, concludes that in an online context, anonymity and group immersion do not foster antinormative behavior. Rather, they cause participants to ignore differences between in-group members and to more closely embrace a group identity. The SIDE model found that individuals who adopt a group identity are receptive to group cues and are thus more susceptible to adopting the behavior of that group, regardless of whether such behavior is normative or antinormative in society as a whole.[31]

The SIDE model has significant implications for online communications. Several studies suggest that the internet reduces the importance of personal characteristics and interpersonal differences and increases the salience of group identity and group norms.[32] Anonymity in interactions may also accentuate distinctions between members of the group and nonmembers and intensify intergroup hostility.

Other factors besides anonymity may also facilitate the shift from individual to group identity online. Information technology and decision sciences scholar Russell Haines and Joan Ellen Cheney Mann conclude that group identity becomes more salient in online interactions when a group identifier (for example, avatars distinguishing in- and out-group members) is visible.[33] They found that individuals with some (even limited) awareness of other group members' opinions were more likely to conform to group norms than were individuals who had no awareness of group members' opinions. The scholars concluded that group influence decreases in completely anonymous online situations—for example, where "no labels are attached to comments"—due to lack of awareness of others' opinions.[34] But group influence increases when common group identifiers exist. This finding is particularly relevant for platforms like Twitter and Facebook, where group identifiers can be reflected in avatars and other symbols attached to a user's profile.

Identity demarginalization, group polarization, and SIDE all have considerable explanatory power in explaining online radicalization. All three theories demonstrate that certain characteristics of online communications, including reduced social cues and anonymity, strengthen group influence at the expense of individual identity. Extremist violent non-state actors recognize the value of the online space. Social media affords them a unique level of peer-to-peer interaction between like-minded individuals, irrespective of their proximity to each other. Those with criminal or extremist interests may have previously struggled to find communities that share these interests, but those communities and their members are increasingly accessible through social media. Community members often establish personal relationships.

These dynamics bring us back to Awlaki.

A Portrait of the Ideologue

Awlaki is perhaps the most prolific jihadist ideologue of all time, producing hundreds of hours of audio and video lectures, along with written essays, blog posts, and other content. The internet gave him an outlet for unleashing his prolific works. Awlaki was well known for adopting various mediums that only became available after 2000.

EARLY LIFE

Awlaki's career has fueled numerous debates about how people radicalize. The pre-AQAP Awlaki seemingly held polar opposite views within short spans of time. Early perceptions of Awlaki in America were shaped by his work immediately after the 9/11 hijackings, when he appeared to be outspoken in rejecting violence and serving as a bridge-builder between Muslims and non-Muslims inside the United States.[35] According to one interpretation of his life, it was only the U.S. government's heavy-handed reaction to 9/11 that set Awlaki down his radical path.[36] Yet it should be noted that some U.S. government organs went out of their way to embrace him in the aftermath of those attacks. Awlaki attended a luncheon at the Pentagon as part of a Muslim outreach effort and led prayers during a meeting on Capitol Hill.[37] Further, moving beyond the polemicism that often accompanies public-sphere interpretations of Awlaki, evidence points to a strong likelihood that Awlaki harbored some jihadist beliefs well before 9/11. In fact, one of the enduring mysteries surrounding Awlaki concerns his relationships with several of the 9/11 hijackers.

Awlaki was born to Yemeni immigrants in New Mexico in 1971. His father, Nasser al-Awlaki, earned a master's degree in agricultural economics but the family was eventually drawn back to Yemen by the elder

Awlaki's career in academia and politics. Nasser al-Awlaki became president of Sana'a University in 2001 and served as agricultural minister and then as an economic adviser to president Ali Abdullah Saleh's government.[38] Although Saleh was at times tolerant of al-Qaeda and affiliated militants in his country's territory for essentially pragmatic reasons, the Yemeni president became a firm American counterterrorism ally in the post-9/11 world.

Anwar al-Awlaki returned to the United States in 1991 and attended Colorado State University on a Yemeni government scholarship. In 1993 he visited Afghanistan shortly before graduating with a bachelor's degree in civil engineering. Local and foreign mujahedin had evicted Soviet forces from Afghanistan a few years earlier, but the country had never stabilized. A fellow Colorado State student who knew Awlaki later claimed that he wasn't extreme enough to have joined al-Qaeda at the time, but the journey halfway around the world clearly influenced him.[39] Upon returning to Fort Collins for his studies, Awlaki began wearing an Afghan hat and citing the works of jihadist thinker Abdullah Azzam (see chapter 3).[40]

After returning from Afghanistan, Awlaki began his career as a preacher on the Colorado State campus. He started serving as an imam at the Denver Islamic Society around 1995. According to an unnamed leader of the society who spoke with local media, Awlaki "gave a series of sermons on jihad struggles around the world" not long after he started.[41] Awlaki was already contributing to those struggles in more ways than just sermonizing. He convinced a student from Saudi Arabia to join the fight in Bosnia. That same student later migrated to fight in the conflict in Chechnya, where he was killed in 1999. Drawing on one of Azzam's most important ideas, Awlaki believed these conflicts were *fard 'ayn*, which means they created an individual obligation to participate. Muslims didn't need permission from their parents or their governments—or anyone else—before joining these jihads.[42]

In 1996 Awlaki relocated to California, where he pursued a master's degree in education at San Diego State University while working as an imam at Al-Ribat Mosque in San Diego. The FBI first became suspicious of Awlaki during his stint in San Diego. Awlaki served as vice president of the Charitable Society for Social Welfare, an ostensibly benign organization that was in reality a front for al-Qaeda and other jihadist causes.[43] The charity had been founded by Shaykh Abd al-Majid al-Zindani, a key Yemeni backer of bin Laden and al-Qaeda. The U.S. government designated Zindani as a terrorist in 2004, with the Treasury Department describing him as a bin Laden "loyalist" who had "a long history" with the al-Qaeda emir, "notably serving as one of his spiritual leaders."[44] Zindani's al-Iman University in Sanaa has been an incubator for al-Qaeda and associated groups. One of its prominent graduates is John Walker Lindh, an American who joined al-Qaeda in Afghanistan prior to 9/11 and fought side by side with the Taliban.[45] Awlaki admired Zindani, writing on his personal blog that he had "benefited" from the jihadist thinker's teachings and had been "given permission from the administration of the University of Eman in Yemen to attend any class at any level."[46] Awlaki wrote that he "took advantage of" the offer and studied Islamic jurisprudence at al-Iman. Zindani was clearly fond of Awklaki, putting himself at risk to protect the American cleric.

Zindani was hardly the only suspicious character in Awlaki's life when he was in San Diego. The FBI opened its first formal counterterrorism inquiry into Awlaki in June 1999 after agents learned that he "was in contact with a number of persons of investigative interest," including someone implicated in a separate investigation into Sheikh Omar Abdel Rahman's terrorist network.[47] But the most suspicious of his contacts during this period were future 9/11 hijackers Nawaf al-Hazmi and Khalid al-Mihdhar.

AWLAKI AND THE 9/11 PLOT

In 2000 Awlaki met two of the future 9/11 hijackers, both of whom clearly respected the cleric. American investigators failed to discover irrefutable proof that Awlaki knew of their designs, but this hardly settles the question of Awlaki's potential role in the attacks. He never admitted to any role in the 9/11 plot, but the FBI, the Congressional Joint Inquiry into the 9/11 attacks, and the 9/11 Commission's final report all document noteworthy behavior on the cleric's part.

Indeed, American officials missed a major lead in the 9/11 plot in January 2000 when Hazmi and Mihdhar arrived in California, where the two became close with Awlaki.[48] The CIA failed to alert the FBI when Hazmi and Mihdhar traveled to the United States shortly after attending an al-Qaeda summit in Malaysia. After a stint in Los Angeles, Hazmi and Mihdhar made their way to Awlaki's mosque in San Diego. Khalid Sheikh Mohammed later told U.S. officials that he was concerned about the duo's ability to navigate American society since neither of them spoke English well.[49] KSM generally prohibited members of the hijacker team from visiting mosques in the United States, but he made an exception for Hazmi and Mihdhar. They chose to seek out Awlaki in San Diego.

Under questioning after his capture, KSM denied that al-Qaeda had a support network in Southern California. But the 9/11 Commission did not buy KSM's story. "We do not credit this denial," the commissioners wrote. "We believe it is unlikely that Hazmi and Mihdhar—neither of whom, in contrast to the Hamburg group [of hijackers], had any prior exposure to life in the West—would have come to the United States without arranging to receive assistance from one or more individuals informed in advance of their arrival."[50] The Commission had difficulty retracing Hazmi and Mihdhar's movements during their initial two weeks in California, which "may reflect al Qaeda tradecraft designed to protect the identity of anyone who may have assisted them during that period."[51] The Congressional Joint Inquiry into the 9/11 hijackings concluded, based on FBI reports, that Awlaki became the "spiritual advisor" for Hazmi and Mihdhar and held "closed-door meetings" with the two men.[52] Aspects of the pair's biography make it unlikely that they met Awlaki by pure chance. Mihdhar had ties to the al-Qaeda-linked Islamic Army of Aden, which was responsible for conducting some of bin Laden's earliest attacks in Yemen, where Awlaki had deep ties and had spent several years of his life.[53] Both Hazmi and Mihdhar were also veterans of the jihad in Bosnia, the same conflict in which Awlaki had once convinced a member of his community to participate.[54]

Hazmi then chose Awlaki to be his imam on a second occasion, underscoring his respect for the cleric. Awlaki relocated to Falls Church, Virginia, in 2001 and became an imam at the Dar Al-Hijrah Islamic Center. Hazmi left San Diego and joined Awlaki at Dar Al-Hijrah.[55] A third 9/11 hijacker, Hani Hanjour, also made his way to Awlaki's new mosque. A member of the mosque assisted Hazmi and Hanjour by helping "them find an apartment in the area," according to the joint inquiry.[56] This same congregant also drove them, "along with two other hijackers, to Connecticut and then to Paterson, New Jersey," a trip that proved critical to the 9/11 plot. During their two-night stay in Connecticut, the terrorists made a "total of 75 calls ... to locate [an] apartment, flight schools, and car rental agencies," all of which would be used to advance the plot. After 9/11, a phone number for Dar Al-Hijrah was found during a search of the home of Ramzi Binalshibh, the Germany-based point man for the hijackers.[57] While this history of meetings and relationships does not add up to smoking-gun evidence of Awlaki's role in the 9/11 plot, it would amount to a remarkable series of coincidences.

Naturally, some investigators concluded that all of this *was* more than just coincidence. In his interviews with the FBI, Awlaki claimed ignorance about Hazmi, the 9/11 hijacker who seems to have followed him from San Diego to Virginia. According to the 9/11 Commission, Awlaki "admitted meeting with Hazmi several times" but claimed he didn't recall what was discussed.[58]

In the spring of 2001, as the hijackers began their final preparations for the 9/11 attacks, Awlaki delivered a sermon at the funeral for a Muslim woman whose son served in the U.S. Army. The short encounter with the cleric left a deep impression on the son of the deceased, Nidal Malik Hasan. Months before the massacre at Fort Hood, Hasan reminded Awlaki in an email that the two "met briefly a very long time ago" at Dar Al-Hijrah, adding "I doubt if you remember me."[59]

Awlaki was allowed to leave the United States for London in March 2002. Once in the United Kingdom, he penned an online essay titled "Why Muslims Love Death," in which he praised Palestinian suicide bombers. Awlaki also lauded suicide bombers in a lecture he delivered during the trip to London. He returned to the United States that fall and met with Ali al-Timimi, another extremist ideologue who was convicted on terrorism-related charges in 2005 and sentenced to life in prison.[60] Timimi had met with a small group of men who played paintball in preparation for jihad and exhorted them to travel to South Asia to prepare to fight U.S. soldiers. He affirmed that the Pakistan-based militant group Lashkar-e-Taiba "was on the correct path," thus sanctioning the young men's scheme to obtain training at Pakistan-based camps run by the group.[61] During his encounter with Timimi in 2002, Awlaki reportedly discussed recruiting youth in the United States for jihad.[62] Despite this, authorities let Awlaki leave the United States once again. London would be one of his first stops.

THE LONDON YEARS

Awlaki had already developed a fan base in the United Kingdom during his earlier travels to the country. His early network in Britain was first uncovered by scholar Alexander Meleagrou-Hitchens, who has undertaken extensive research into Awlaki's life.[63] One of Meleagrou-Hitchens's sources was an Afghan jihadist veteran known as Abu Muntasir, who had known Awlaki in Britain. Muntasir said that Awlaki had "always supported jihad" in Afghanistan, Bosnia, Chechnya, and similar battlefields. While this alone does not peg Awlaki as an al-Qaeda supporter in the late 1990s, it shows he had already adopted some tellingly hardline views. Awlaki's late-career "ideological worldview" was "essentially the same as it was then, but his answers to our problems have changed," Abu Muntasir claimed. But the same progression could be glimpsed within al-Qaeda itself. The jihadist group only definitively prioritized attacking the United States after first devoting resources to various battlefields in other parts of the world. As we discuss at length in chapter 3, al-Qaeda supported jihadist efforts in Afghanistan, Bosnia, and Chechnya throughout the 1990s.

Whatever his outlook at the time, Awlaki became something of a rock star in Britain's fundamentalist scene. Islamist groups organized a speaking tour for Awlaki from 2002 to 2004, during which Awlaki raged against America's alleged war on Islam.

Awlaki returned to his native Yemen in 2004. Before his return to Yemen, Awlaki may have been unlikely to receive another invitation to the Pentagon, but he was still able to move through the West, even if he might attract suspicion along the way. In Yemen he began to unambiguously use his talents to advance the jihadist movement. Awlaki was arrested by Yemeni security services and detained for around eighteen months. Once released, he moved to the remote province of Shabwah in eastern Yemen, where he became known as an AQAP spokesman and official. In that role he became perhaps history's most successful jihadist propagandist and was also directly involved in terrorist plots.

Awlaki was eventually killed in a controversial drone strike on September 30, 2011. Another American, Samir Khan, also died in the strike.

Awlaki as Early Adopter: The Messages and Their Distribution

Awlaki's sermonizing began well before his return to Yemen. In fact, Awlaki's fame began to grow in the 1990s through lengthy lectures that he recorded on CDs, which were sold in box sets to listeners across the United States and Britain.[64] Awlaki's showmanship and oratorical gifts were apparent even from the early days. While he was still based in the United States, the cleric's lectures often dealt with themes from Islam's early history, with titles like the "The Life of Mohammed" and "The Lives of the Prophets." These recordings remain widely available, as Awlaki's devoted followers ensured they migrated from CDs to the online space.

Ever the early adopter, Awlaki switched formats just as MP3 players replaced CDs, uploading lectures to the internet. His work was reposted on platforms like YouTube, with repackaged Awlaki videos continuing to proliferate on the site years after his death. YouTube eventually removed tens of thousands of Awlaki-related videos from its platform, some of which included direct incitement to violence.[65] Awlaki also joined the blogging wave, creating an eponymous site in 2008. Among other things, this blog allowed Awlaki to connect more directly with his supporters, a number of whom, like Nidal Hasan, understood his words as a call to action. As a review of his work demonstrates, their interpretation was correct.

"CONSTANTS ON THE PATH OF JIHAD" (2005)

In 2005 Awlaki recorded one of the seminal lectures of his jihadist career, "Constants on the Path of Jihad." The work was inspired by a treatise of Yusuf al-Ayeri, the first head of AQAP. The six "constants" that the lecture title references all stress that Muslims should consider themselves in a perpetual state of war. Illustrating this, the lecture's subsections were titled "Jihad will continue until the Day of Judgment," "Jihad does not depend on an individual or individuals," "Jihad is not dependent on a particular land," "Jihad is not dependent on a battle," "Victory is not limited to military victory," and "The definition of defeat." Awlaki's lecture gained a wide audience online and remains popular to this day, as his fans continue to produce and share various English-language transcriptions of the six-hour talk.[66]

As Awaki explained, jihad was not merely one part of the Islamic religious doctrine but the "peak of Islam." Although he held that jihad was needed to restore the caliphate, religious warfare wouldn't end with the rise of a new pan-Islamic empire. Instead, jihad "would be necessary for all times . . . just like fasting in Ramadan." To be sure, the lecture recognized some nonviolent meanings of jihad. But their existence did not make the lecture shy away from endorsing military meanings of the term, proclaiming that suicide attacks offered Muslims the opportunity to dispel the popular misconception that their violence was merely an expression of socioeconomic frustrations. "When you have a Muslim who has a chance of success from the worldly point of view, and searches for martyrdom, it completely destroys the theories of the *kuffar* (i.e., suicide, poor, oppression etc.) and forces them to look at the true reason as to why someone would give up his life," Awlaki stated.

Territorial success in the form of a worldwide Islamic government was a chief goal of jihad, Awlaki said, and would remain so. "Indeed, in the end, the Ummah will achieve victory in the battlefield and gain hold of the entire world," Awlaki claimed.

Just as victory wasn't limited to battlefield success, defeat could also come in multiple forms. For Awlaki, Muslims could only be truly defeated if they gave up their fervor for jihad. "The conflict in its reality is a conflict of ideas that is translated into physical battles," Awlaki explained. "But its essence is a conflict of ideas. So if a person gives up his ideas, that is defeat." Muslims would taste defeat if they submitted to *kaffir* (infidel) ideas, such as Western-style democracy. "If one is a Muslim and follows another way of life such as Modernism, Secularism, Communism etc., even if it may be partial, he has been defeated," Awlaki pronounced.

In Awlaki's vision, the conflict between true Islam and democracy precluded Muslims from cooperating with secular states. The American-born ideologue railed against any Muslim who claimed he could perform *dawa* (evangelism) and slowly transform Western society from within. Such an attitude, he argued, was an illegitimate compromise. "Constants" ended with a tribute to the Taliban, which had lost its Islamic Emirate in Afghanistan in the aftermath of the 9/11 hijackings. Ayeri originally penned his treatise after the Taliban and al-Qaeda experienced catastrophic losses in

Afghanistan in the early 2000s. Curiously, Awlaki seemingly removed some of Ayeri's direct references to Mullah Omar and Osama bin Laden, but he retained Ayeri's praise of the Taliban.[67]

The significance of "Constants on the Path of Jihad" for Awlaki's career cannot be overstated. And the video influenced its intended audience. Members of the "Toronto 18," who plotted to terrorize the Canadian government and behead the prime minister in 2006, listened to the lecture on a laptop. The six-hour discourse also served as an inspiration for the "Fort Dix Six," a group that planned to kill American servicemembers at a military base in New Jersey in 2007. "You gotta hear this lecture," Shain Duka, one of the suspects, said while under surveillance.[68] Duka told his coconspirators that Awlaki spoke "the truth, no holds barred, straight how it is!" The lecture also helped shape the views of other terrorists for years to come.[69] Umar Farouk Abdulmutallab evoked "Constants" as a key influence while in American custody.[70]

Awlaki, it seems, had carefully chosen which of his jihadist forebears to evoke in "Constants." Like Awlaki, Ayeri had been one of al-Qaeda's online innovators. A veteran of the jihad in Afghanistan, Ayeri went on to lead bin Laden's forces in Saudi Arabia. During the course of a short-lived insurgency inside the kingdom, security forces killed Ayeri in May 2003, then disposed of a string of his successors. But Ayeri had already showcased how to embrace the increasingly internet-based information environment and find new ways to deliver the jihadist message.

Ayeri was al-Qaeda's first webmaster. He ran alNeda.com (The Call), which spread the organization's message just after 9/11. Although jihadist groups had used the internet to attract new followers since the mid-1990s, Ayeri's creation was unique because it became a central clearinghouse for al-Qaeda's leaders, who regularly posted messages and attack claims. Al-Qaeda took credit for the April 2002 Ghriba synagogue bombing in Tunisia and October 2002 Bali bombings on alNeda. Throughout 2002 and 2003, Ayeri and his men played a cat-and-mouse game with counterterrorism professionals and amateur hackers who tried to take down al-Qaeda's site. The al-Qaeda men often stayed one step ahead of their digital pursuers by hiding source files and content on sports sites and other unrelated domains. Eventually, an American hacker took alNeda.com down for good in April 2003, weeks after Saudi security forces killed Ayeri.

Ayeri's successors were also innovators. In 2003 the *Encyclopedia of Jihad*, a constantly edited and rewritten work, started to spread online.[71] The first generation of AQAP's leadership saw great value in the *Encyclopedia of Jihad*, a do-it-yourself guide to conducting terrorist attacks that offered readers advice on a wide range of jihad-related topics, from physical fitness to manufacturing explosives to conducting surveillance. The encyclopedia's online success helped inspire AQAP to launch two online magazines in 2003: *Sawt al-Jihad* (Voice of Jihad) and *Mu'askar al-Battar*. These publications promoted the works of Ayeri and other extremists. Both online magazines provided do-it-yourself tips similar to the encyclopedia, including insights into hostage-taking and poisoning.

THE HEREAFTER (2006)

In his lecture series The Hereafter, Awlaki discusses the afterlife. *New York Times* reporter Scott Shane has described The Hereafter series as some of Awlaki's "most insidious material" due to its content, and the manner in which it serves as a bridge for his audience from his earlier, seemingly more innocuous lectures to his explicitly extremist content. "For those who fall under al-Awlaki's spell," Shane wrote, " 'The Hereafter' is a crucial way-station along the path from 'The Life of the Prophet' to [Awlaki's] explicit endorsement of attacks on American civilians."[72]

The most inflammatory content in The Hereafter appears in a segment on past and future clashes between the Muslim world and "the Romans," a broad term Awlaki uses to encompass "the Europeans, which extends to Latin America, Canada, the U.S., etc.—the Caucasians." He refers to these groups as "Romans" to situate current world politics within the framework of Islamic prophesy. Awlaki described a future where "Islam will rule the world . . . *Kuffar* will be stamped out [and] the choice will be 'either Islam or death.' " Awlaki continued: "There will be big battles in the future between Muslims and the ones who are called Romans. That's number one. And it also mentions, or indicates, that there will be a lot of them who are Muslim. There will be a political entity which the Muslims are fighting with. But at the same time, there will be many of them, Romans, who are fighting with the Muslims. They are Muslims. And this shows that Islam will spread in the West."[73]

Elsewhere in the series, Awlaki claims that Islamic prophesy condemns the West for its excesses. In one lecture he says the AIDS epidemic is Allah's punishment against Western society for its lenient sexual norms: "AIDS was a disease that did not exist before. Allah sent it on the people because *zina* [unlawful sexual intercourse] is public and it is advertised for in movies, on billboards, etc. Even advertisement of cigarettes or cars, there is nudity—this is also advertisement of zina. People should not think that if they find the cure for AIDS, it'll be ok, because Allah will send another disease that didn't exist before."[74]

Awlaki's Hereafter lectures have been specifically referenced in criminal cases. For example, these sermons were cited as evidence against Adel Daoud, who was indicted in 2012 for attempting to detonate a car bomb in Chicago. Daoud had distributed these lectures as part of his effort to encourage violent jihad.[75] Court documents pertaining to the 2015 San Bernardino shooting in which jihadists killed fourteen people linked these lectures to shooter Syed Farook and his neighbor Enrique Marquez, who was charged with material support for terrorism. An affidavit submitted by an FBI agent in that case noted that "Farook introduced Marquez to radical Islamic ideology, which included expressing disdain towards Muslims in the U.S. military that killed other Muslims, and discussing the extremist views of the now-deceased imam and Islamic lecturer Anwar al-Aulaqi."[76] The affidavit noted that in 2010 "Marquez listened to 'The Hereafter.'"[77] Nicholas Young, the first member of U.S. law enforcement to be convicted of material support for ISIS, also had a copy of The Hereafter in his possession when his residence was searched.[78]

THE EXTREMIST BLOGGER

A stint in Yemeni detention, from 2006 through December 2007, put a moratorium on Awlaki's work. But by June 2008 Awlaki had launched his eponymous blog and was publishing some of his most important writings and speeches. After "Constants on the Path of Jihad," Awlaki's next-biggest online hit was "44 Ways of Supporting Jihad," which he posted to his blog in January 2009. As the title suggests, Awlaki outlined to supporters various ways they could get involved in jihad, from sheltering mujahedin and supporting their families to more active measures, such as carrying out martyrdom operations. Awlaki echoed the work of Abdullah Azzam when he wrote that jihad was obligatory on every Muslim because "Muslim lands are occupied by the *kuffar*" and the "rule of the law of

Allah" was "absent from this world." Every "Muslim who wants to please Allah" should make it his or her "duty to find ways to practice it [jihad] and support it." Awlaki had advice for readers who might not be willing to move to Yemen or Afghanistan. Writing that "Jihad is in need of money," Awlaki wrote that using one's wealth to support the mujahedin was "probably the most important contribution the Muslims of the West could do for Jihad."

From Awlaki's perspective, AQAP's early efforts at instigating individual jihad had a defect: They were written almost entirely in Arabic, limiting their ability to reach a Western audience. Awlaki addressed this problem head on in "44 Ways," where he noted that "most of the Jihad literature is available only in Arabic and publishers are not willing to take the risk of translating it. The only ones who are spending the money and time translating Jihad literature are the Western intelligence services . . . and too bad, they would not be willing to share it with you." Awlaki wrote that one way for aspiring jihadists to support the cause was embracing what he called "WWW Jihad." The internet provided opportunities for readers to establish "discussion forums that offer a free, uncensored medium for posting information relating to Jihad," set up email lists, or build "websites to cover" issues such as "mujahideen news, Muslim POWs, and Jihad literature." Such activity would turn "brothers and sisters" into "internet mujahideen." Interestingly, it seems Awlaki plagiarized much of "44 Ways" from a 2003 work, Muhammad bin Ahmad al-Salim's "39 Ways to Serve and Participate in Jihad," a copy of which was found in Osama bin Laden's compound.[79]

Awlaki published dozens of other works on his blog. Another entry of note, posted in 2008, was titled "A Question About the Method of Establishing Khilafa." In it, Awlaki rejected any nonviolent program for resurrecting the caliphate. He thus found organizations like the Muslim Brotherhood and Hizb ut-Tahrir to be ideologically weak. "It is a deception and a lie to use democracy and claim to be adherents to the democratic system but not believe in it," he wrote. Muslims simply "do not try to infiltrate the system and work from within." Only violent jihad would lead to "re-establishing khilafa," Awlaki maintained. Echoing Azzam, Awlaki concluded that violent jihad was obligatory. "Today the Muslim world is under occupation and the statements of our scholars are clear that it becomes [*fard 'ayn*] on every able Muslim to fight to free the Muslim land,"

Awlaki wrote. Awlaki ended his post with a call for "total war," evoking the concept advanced by the Prussian general Carl von Clausewitz, "but with the Islamic rules of engagement."

Inspire Magazine

In July 2010 Awlaki and Samir Khan produced the first issue of *Inspire*, AQAP's English-language online magazine that disseminated jihadist ideas and tactics in a snarky, almost hipster tone. The magazine became the pair's principal effort to win over Westerners during the last year and a half of the two propagandists' lives. The idea of a web magazine for aspiring jihadists was not original to Awlaki and Khan: As we discussed, AQAP had experimented with do-it-yourself online publications as early as 2003, although not in English. But *Inspire* proved to be so instrumental to Awlaki's career, and to jihadist organizational learning about propaganda, that we dedicate a full section to exploring its significance.

AQAP published seventeen issues of *Inspire* starting in July 2010. More than half of these were compiled after Awlaki and Khan were killed in a September 2011 drone strike. The e-zine has been tied to terrorists responsible for a number of high-profile plots in the United States and Europe, including the April 2013 Boston Marathon bombings (which employed a bomb design straight from *Inspire*) and the December 2015 mass shooting in San Bernardino, California.

ABDULLAH AZZAM'S CONTINUING INFLUENCE

In *Inspire*, Abdullah Azzam's teachings that Muslims were obligated to wage holy war were repeatedly cited as a justification for individual terrorism in the West. *Inspire*'s staff built off Azzam's argument. Although it is debatable whether Awlaki's arguments were true to the spirit or intent of Azzam's ideas, in *Inspire* Awlaki and Khan walked readers through their interpretation of Azzam's call to arms, which the pair presented as a justification for individual acts of terrorism against American and European civilians.

To understand Awlaki's ideological contributions, it is necessary to recall what Azzam actually taught. In his fatwa "Defending Muslim Lands," Azzam declared that jihad was necessary until all occupied Muslim territory was liberated from its conquerors.[80] Azzam's edict was not limited to defensive wars or restricted to the Soviet invasion of Afghanistan. If the infidels "infringe upon a hand span of Muslim land, jihad becomes *fard 'ayn* for its people and for those nearby," Azzam ruled. If those Muslims failed to defeat the infidels, then the obligation "spreads to those behind, and carries on spreading in this process, until the jihad is *fard 'ayn* upon the whole earth from the East to the West." Azzam stated that his fatwa covered not just Afghanistan and Palestine but also "the Philippines, Kashmir, Lebanon, Chad, Eritrea," and elsewhere, since all this ground had "previously fallen into the possession of the infidel."

Azzam did not aim his ire at the Arab regimes. *Inspire* correctly credited Egyptian jihadists with focusing on Muslim-majority countries throughout the Middle East and North Africa.[81] As we have shown, the Egyptian jihadists believed that regimes in countries such as their native Egypt, Libya, and Tunisia were legitimate targets because the Arab tyrants who ruled them did not adhere to sharia. But the Egyptian extremists did not strictly limit their fight to these "near enemy" governments. Nor, of course, did Osama bin Laden. Al-Qaeda ultimately concluded that America and its "New World Order," as Awlaki put it, were the primary reason for the Arab regimes that allegedly occupied Muslim land enduring.

The far-enemy strategy could claim some basis in Azzam's writings, which were deeply anti-American. He ruled that cooperating with the United States against the Soviets in Afghanistan was *haram* (prohibited by Islamic law) and inveighed against Islamic scholars who allowed their pupils to study in the United States. *Inspire* even credited Azzam, rightly or wrongly, with being "among the first to call for jihad against America."[82]

INSPIRE AND THE QUESTION OF A CALIPHATE

The publication drew a connection between American weakness and a future Islamic revival, with its articles often drawing a straight line between operations against the West and the caliphate's return. The unnamed author of one early article described "establishing the Global Islamic Caliphate through jihad" as one of the "principles of Islam."[83] In a confessional titled, "I Am Proud to Be A Traitor," Samir Khan described the quest for a caliphate as his central motivation for waging war against his native country, the United States.[84] Khan even contrasted his belief in what can fairly be described as Islamic imperialism with his objections to American foreign policy, writing that the former was at the core of his "religious convictions in the absence of politics."[85] The Prophet Muhammad, Khan reasoned, had sought to bring "Islam to the world," and Islam contained a "working system of government that would shape entire societies based on the guidelines of Qur'an and Sunnah." In Khan's view, jihad would "remain individually obligatory (fard 'ayn) upon all the Muslims of the world until all of our lands are recaptured from the occupiers."[86]

Anticipating the argument that he needed religious sanction from an "esteemed scholar" to justify his views, Khan explained he had "irrefutable" evidence of the rightness of his path in the form of Abdullah Azzam's fatwa. The U.S. military has "military and intelligence bases spread throughout our lands in order to help protect their client governments from Muslims who work for Islam's establishment," Khan explained. Thus, Khan wrote that he had he sworn allegiance to bin Laden and declared that he and his companions would "wage jihad for the rest of our lives until either we implant Islam all over the world or meet our Lord as bearers of Islam."[87]

Khan's dream of resurrecting the caliphate became one of Inspire's recurring themes. AQAP emir Nasir al-Wuhayshi elaborated on this point in the magazine's first issue, explaining: "Our objectives are driving out the occupiers from the Arabian Peninsula and purifying its land from them, establishing the law of shariah, the establishment of khilāfah, spreading the call to the oneness of Allah."[88] One issue later, Wuhayshi's deputy, Said al-Shihri, said that AQAP did not seek "to remove these petty states" throughout the Middle East and North Africa "only to replace them with other petty states." Instead, he stated that AQAP intended "to unify the Muslim lands under shari'ah."[89]

Like bin Laden and Zawahiri, AQAP's leaders believed this couldn't be accomplished as long as America stood in the way. Inspire thus identified the United States as al-Qaeda's main target. Note that although the reason given for reestablishing the caliphate by force is ideological, the case articulated for prioritizing the fight against the United States is more pragmatic. It is thus the kind of organizational decision that could be subjected to learning processes and, hence, altered if the group's strategic calculus changed. At the time, AQAP prioritized the fight against the far enemy even though it had been years since 9/11. Striking America had become logistically daunting, but individual terrorists were more difficult to stop. Wuhayshi and Shihri called for lone attacks in *Inspire*'s earliest issues. Wuhayshi suggested a number of possible methods of attack, including by "a man with his knife, a man with his gun, a man with his rifle, a man with his bomb, by learning how to design explosive devices, by burning down forests and buildings, or by running over them with your cars and trucks."[90] His list prefigured the many ways that lone terrorists would strike in Europe and the United States in the years to come.

Awlaki and Khan had to explain why it was necessary for individual extremists to take up the banner of jihad in their home countries. For practical justifications they turned to the writings of Abu Musab al-Suri (see chapter 3). *Inspire*'s first issue mentioned Suri's writings, which were also featured in later issues. Suri was captured in Pakistan in 2005 and rendered to his native Syria, where he remained imprisoned at the time of *Inspire*'s launch.

Suri's magnum opus was a 1,600-page treatise titled *The Global Call to Islamic Resistance*, which first appeared online in late 2004.[91] In this work, Suri provided his history of the jihadist cause, surveying past successes and failures to determine the best course of action. Events he explored included the toppling of the Taliban's Islamic Emirate in Afghanistan and Saddam Hussein's regime in Iraq. Suri argued that both wars proved the superiority of the American military, and it was pointless for a jihadist organization to openly contend with such a superior adversary. There were thus only "three schools of jihad" available, Suri contended: the "school of secret military organizations (regional-secret-hierarchical)," the "school of open fronts and overt confrontations," and the "school of individual jihad and small cell terrorism."[92] He evaluated each of these schools by several criteria. On the military front, he examined whether the various methods allowed meaningful operations. On security, he assessed whether the schools allowed jihadists to evade capture or infiltration by intelligence forces. Other criteria included success in conducting *dawa* and education.

From Suri's perspective, the school of clandestine militant groups was a "complete failure on all levels." The second school, that of "semi-regular guerrilla warfare," had some achievements, especially in Afghanistan. But the third school, individual and small group-based jihad, had been a resounding success, Suri wrote, because it had awakened the umma, turning Muslims around the world into potential foot soldiers. In practice, the dividing line between these three schools was not always clear: Al-Qaeda itself has used all three methods. But Suri insisted that the first school was no longer an option, that the era of massive covert jihadist mobilization was over. "It is no longer possible to operate by the methods of the old model, through the 'secret-regional-hierarchical' organizations, especially after the September 11th events and the onset of the American campaigns, where the great majority of the existing secret organizations were destroyed," Suri wrote in a passage excerpted for *Inspire*'s readers.[93]

There was an incongruity in *Inspire*'s presentation of Suri's arguments that was likely lost on most readers. While Suri thought top-down organizations were outmoded, neither bin Laden nor Zawahiri agreed, nor did the leadership of AQAP, whose online magazine excerpted his argument. Al-Qaeda never ceased to operate as a "secret-regional-hierarchical" organization. The files recovered in bin Laden's compound show that his group remained highly secretive until his dying day, often hiding basic aspects of its operations from even its followers. The network maintained its top-down character. For instance, documents from Abbottabad show that bin Laden continued to personally oversee the efforts of Younis al-Mauritani, a top operative in al-Qaeda's external operations arm.[94] Awlaki himself helped to shape plots in secret, a reflection of how al-Qaeda's affiliates were also organized as a hierarchical secret army. In short, in no way had al-Qaeda adopted Suri's philosophy for waging jihad.

Suri's writings were still useful to the group, though. They dealt with a vital component of al-Qaeda's operations, its campaign to encourage individual terrorism. Remotely inspired attacks have often been described as "lone wolf" terrorism, but Suri himself rejected the idea that individual jihadists could ever truly be loners. One excerpt from Suri's writings in *Inspire* is titled "The Idea of Belonging to the Whole Islamic Nation and Its Necessity for Jihad."[95] In it, Suri argued that a jihadist's "personal sense of belonging" needed to occur at "the level of religious belief" and could not be based on artificial geographical boundaries. Suri complained that if most Muslims were asked where they were from, they would answer by mentioning their country, revealing a commitment "to the borders of Sykes-Picot, drawn in his mind by colonialism." Suri wanted his audience to instead see themselves as part of a global "brotherhood."

Suri placed great emphasis on a series of small-scale attacks and failed plots in the early 1990s, seeing them as proof that the West would cave to jihadists' demands if a wave of individual terrorists struck. He pointed to El Sayyid Nosair's 1990 assassination of Meir Kahane, a right-wing Jewish rabbi, and Ramzi Yousef's attempt to bring down the World Trade Center's twin towers in 1993 as evidence that even individual assassinations and failed attacks could take a toll on the United States. Suri pointed out that a series of Palestinian terrorist attacks on Israeli targets had forced President Bill Clinton and other world leaders to attend a conference in Sharm El Sheikh, Egypt, in the mid-1990s. Suri claimed that there were no operational connections between the individuals responsible for these attacks and that this provided an advantage: Even if authorities stopped one cell or person, the setback wouldn't lead to subsequent arrests. "These spontaneous operations performed by individuals and cells here and there over the whole world, without connection between then, have put the . . . intelligence apparatus in a state of confusion, as arresting the [members] of aborted cells does not influence the operational activities of others who are not connected to them," Suri wrote.[96] Attacks by individuals or small cells would make it possible for the jihadists to open additional fronts, wearing down an enemy unaccustomed to fighting such an omnipresent yet seemingly disconnected opponent. After waves of individual attacks had weakened America, Washington would no longer be able to sustain allied governments in the Muslim-majority world, leading to more open battles against the near enemy that would be fought on better terms for the jihadists. In *Inspire*, Awlaki elaborated on Suri's narrative, updating his arguments as circumstances warranted.

OPEN SOURCE JIHAD

One innovative recurring section in *Inspire* was titled "Open Source Jihad," which the publication described as a "resource manual for those who loathe the tyrants."[97] The section offered how-to instructions for "bomb making techniques, security measures, guerrilla tactics, weapons training and all other jihad activities."

With "Open Source Jihad," *Inspire*'s authors repurposed a popular technique for accelerating organizational learning in the field of software development: open-source coding. In open-source coding, developers publish existing code for products on free and accessible platforms like Linux and GitHub, which allow users to download and edit the original developers' code.[98] Publishing the existing code not only allows the producer to decentralize the original developers' knowledge but also facilitates a relatively low-cost process of experimentation. When independent coders upload their edited versions to the same platform, the developer and community of coders will better understand what works and what does not. The result is often a superior software program.

That process for accelerating organizational learning has shown similar promise for jihadists. By publishing tips and techniques for bomb-making and attacks, AQAP helped its supporters conduct attacks using AQAP's existing organizational knowledge. Based on the success or failure of attacks by AQAP supporters using "Open Source Jihad," AQAP could refine its own techniques and its public tips.

Inspire is not the first publication to disseminate material that could be used for violent ends. *The Anarchist Cookbook*, published in 1971, provides readers with advice on "handling firearms, making bombs, and hacking phones."[99] Investigators have linked the book to numerous attacks, including the 1995 Oklahoma City bombing and the 1999 Columbine High School shooting.[100] William Powell, the author of *The Anarchist Cookbook*, renounced his work soon after its publication and never updated it. Thus, the iterative nature of "Open Source Jihad" made this part of *Inspire* a novel way for a terrorist group to accelerate its organizational learning.

The inaugural issue's "Open Source Jihad" section contained two parts, including a now-infamous guide on how to "Make a Bomb in the Kitchen of Your Mom."[101] The colorful pages presented a step-by-step process for constructing either a pipe bomb or a pressure-cooker explosive. Both kinds of bombs relied on commonly available parts and could be detonated with an electronic circuit built from a household clock.

The manual caught the attention of aspiring terrorists in the United States. Three people died and 264 were wounded when a pair of pressure-cooker bombs were detonated at the finish line of the Boston Marathon on April 15, 2013. The devices were built by two brothers who had been drawn to *Inspire* and Awlaki's teachings. The eldest, Tamerlan Tsarnaev, was killed in a shootout with police hours after the attack, while his brother, Dzhokhar, was arrested after a citywide manhunt. During Dzhokhar Tsarnaev's trial, an FBI computer expert explained that issues of *Inspire*, including the issue that contained bomb-making instructions, were found on Dzhokhar's computer, as were audio files containing Awlaki's lectures.[102] Just a few weeks before the bombings he tweeted that people could "gain an unbelievable amount of knowledge" by listening to Awlaki's Hereafter lecture series.[103] Dzhokhar reportedly admitted to authorities that the pair had used the *Inspire* guide to build their own pressure-cooker bombs.[104]

"Make a Bomb in the Kitchen of Your Mom" has been found in the possession of other would-be terrorists. Pfc. Naser Jason Abdo, who planned to detonate similar explosives at a restaurant frequented by soldiers stationed at Fort Hood, was sentenced to life in prison for his plan.[105] Abdo yelled out Nidal Hasan's name during the opening day of his trial, an indication that he wanted to follow in the Fort Hood shooter's footsteps.[106]

The bomb-making guide that the Tsarnaev brothers had used to such deadly effect was credited to an author writing under the pseudonym "AQ Chef." In subsequent issues of *Inspire*, AQ Chef shared other ideas, including instructions for setting forest fires, thus inflicting "economic losses" on firms that sell "wooden products" as well as on insurance companies.[107] The writer sometimes took his cues from actual plots, including Faisal Shahzad's 2010 attempt to detonate a car bomb in New York City's Times Square. In the twelfth issue of *Inspire*, released in 2014, AQ Chef provided readers with a "simple" guide for building a car bomb, with the instructions placed beside images of Times Square. Shahzad had received first-hand instruction from the Pakistani Taliban in Waziristan several months before he loaded a Nissan Pathfinder with explosives.[108] Shahzad was a fan of Awlaki's lectures, telling authorities that the cleric's sermons had helped transform his thinking.[109] *Inspire*'s first issue included a quote from Shahzad advocating violence in the face of America's "Crusade."[110]

Inspire sometimes explained the bomb-making processes in unnervingly specific detail. An explosives expert identified as "Dr. Khateer" walked readers through the production of acetone peroxide, a "fatal formula with ingredients that are widely available." In two separate editions of the magazine, he gave instructions on building remote-controlled bombs.[111] For less ambitious terrorists, *Inspire* provided cursory lessons on using assault rifles and handguns.[112]

Although AQAP wanted supporters to be able to use its tactical advice to launch attacks without assistance, the group also encouraged readers to contact them. Awlaki himself answered questions from readers. *Inspire* also gave readers a short manual for using the encryption software Asrar al-Mujahideen (Mujahedin Secrets). Indeed, the first "Open Source Jihad" section contained screenshots of the software along with advice on how to use it.[113] Readers were advised that the application wasn't foolproof and that it was better to communicate outside the digital realm if possible. Nonetheless, AQAP advertised its public key for encrypted communication and encouraged readers to get in touch. *Inspire* specifically sought production assistance in the form of graphics, news clippings, and other materials that could be included in future editions.

INSPIRE'S IMPACT

Awlaki and Khan spurred a new generation of terrorists to action through *Inspire*. Even if most plots that the publication seeded were thwarted or failed of their own accord, these efforts tied up precious security resources. AQAP's decision to promote individual terrorism through *Inspire* was rooted in a new operational reality. The Western counterterrorism apparatus had thwarted a series of centrally directed plots, and AQAP viewed "lone" terrorists or small cells as an efficient way to get around the security and surveillance barriers erected after 9/11. Awlaki and Khan packaged their practical and ideological guide to jihad in a format that made it easy for would-be recruits to follow.

After their deaths, AQAP claimed that Awlaki was merely "the guest writer" in *Inspire*, while the "most active one was brother Samir Khan," who "exploited all of his energy and effort for this sake."[114] Even if Khan might have put more work into *Inspire* than Awlaki, he lacked the cleric's eloquence. Undergirding all the tactical advice in *Inspire* was Awlaki's argument for terrorism against civilians.

Awlaki's Operational Planning

Verbal incitement was not the only avenue Awlaki took to influence future attacks. It became clear over time that Awlaki was also involved in specific AQAP plots.

In 2009 Awlaki personally counseled Umar Farouk Abdulmutallab as he prepared to launch the underwear bomb plot (see chapter 4).[115] While other

AQAP operatives were also involved, Abdulmutallab told authorities that Awlaki served as his spiritual mentor. Awlaki told Abdulmutallab to "pray for religious guidance concerning the right time to make the flight and then to travel when he was ready."[116] The would-be mass murderer explained to authorities that he had followed Awlaki's guidance. Years after the underwear bomb plot, AQAP released images of Awlaki and Abdulmutallab standing side by side, underscoring the close relationship between the two.[117]

Today end-to-end encryption software is freely available on most smartphones. But that wasn't the case when Awlaki was alive. Al-Qaeda had to distribute its own encryption software, which, as previously noted, was dubbed Asrar al-Mujahideen. Awlaki made creative use of this program, combining encrypted messages, couriers, and multiple email accounts to mask his work.[118]

In 2009 and 2010 Awlaki corresponded with a Bangladeshi-born British Airways computer expert named Rajib Karim. Awlaki wanted Karim to attack U.S.-bound aviation. The pair went to extraordinary lengths to conceal their communications, with Awlaki passing encrypted messages through Karim's Yemen-based brother.[119] After Karim was arrested in 2010, authorities likened his secret messaging system to a series of "Russian dolls," with one message hidden inside another.[120] It took the British government's experts nine months to crack into Karim's computer, with police describing the encryption mechanism as "the most sophisticated they had seen in a British terrorist case."[121] Karim and Awlaki's communications involved pasting text into an Excel worksheet, which was then encrypted and copied into a Microsoft Word document.[122] After that, the Word document was protected with a unique password, loaded into a RAR program for further compressing and encryption, and further manipulated via various hosting sites.

Karim's arrest in February 2010 didn't end Awlaki's attempts to attack aviation. No less a figure than President Obama has stated that Awlaki personally directed AQAP's attempt to blow up two U.S.-bound cargo planes in October 2010 (see chapter 4).[123]

The cleric's fingerprints would soon appear on another planned massacre. In December 2010 a British man named Minh Quang Pham traveled from London to Yemen, swore allegiance to AQAP, and pledged that he would be willing to martyr himself for its cause.[124] Awlaki quickly recognized Pham's potential. Pham put his college education in graphic design and animation to use for *Inspire*, working directly for Awlaki and Samir Khan.

But Pham didn't intend to stay in Yemen. At first Awlaki wanted him to act as an AQAP recruiter upon his return to Britain. But Pham decided he would rather "sacrifice" himself than surreptitiously recruit others. Awlaki agreed to guide Pham, showing him how to build a bomb using commonly available chemicals and advising him on a potential target. Awlaki said it would be best for Pham to kill himself near or inside the arrivals section of Heathrow International Airport in London. The cleric "instructed Pham to carry an explosive in a concealed backpack and target the area where flights arrived from the United States or Israel," according to the U.S. Department of Justice. Pham never got the opportunity. He was arrested upon returning to Heathrow from Yemen in July 2011 and eventually extradited to the United States, where he plead guilty to terrorism-related charges and was sentenced to forty years in prison.

The Cartoon Jihad
THE CHARLIE HEBDO ATTACK

On the morning of January 7, 2015, the staff of *Charlie Hebdo*, a weekly satirical newspaper based in Paris, gathered for an editorial meeting at their offices in the 11th Arrondissement. The publication had stoked controversy throughout its existence, incessantly lampooning political, cultural, and religious figures. On that morning two terrorists—brothers Saïd Kouachi and Chérif Kouachi—knocked on the door of a nearby office looking for the newspaper's headquarters, which they found after a second attempt. The pair shot a guard in the lobby and headed for the second floor, where the staff meeting was held.

"Allahu Akbar . . . where is Charb?," one brother called out, using the nickname of Stéphane Charbonnier, the paper's editor. Within minutes, the brothers had murdered Charbonnier and ten others. The Kouachis didn't kill everyone they came across. "I won't kill you. You're a woman, we don't kill women. But think about what you do, what you do is bad. I'm sparing you and because I've spared you, you will read the Qur'an," writer

Sigolène Vinson recalled one of them saying.[125] In contrast, moments earlier the terrorists had killed columnist Elsa Cayat, showing they were in fact willing to kill women. (Cayat's Jewish ethnicity may have influenced their decision to kill her.) After fleeing, the terrorists clashed with police at least three times. The pair were hunted down two days later, when French police killed them in a shootout after a short hostage standoff north of Paris.

Confusion surrounding the culprits and their affiliation lingered long after the massacre. Some claimed that the Kouachis were sent by ISIS. Indeed, the narrator in *Three Days of Terror: The Charlie Hebdo Attacks*, a popular documentary that aired on HBO, incorrectly described the assault on the newspaper as ISIS's "first" attack in France.[126] This confusion stemmed in part from one of the brothers' friends, Amedy Coulibaly, carrying out his own terrorist attack at a kosher market in Paris after recording a video pledging allegiance to Abu Bakr al-Baghdadi. In previous years, the Kouachis and Coulibaly were part of the so-called Buttes-Chaumont network, which recruited youth to fight for al-Qaeda in Iraq, ISIS's predecessor organization.[127] But the Kouachis were al-Qaeda men. More specifically, they were disciples of Anwar al-Awlaki.

The brothers identified themselves as al-Qaeda members and even mentioned Awlaki by name during the massacre. "I was sent, me, Chérif Kouachi, by al-Qaeda of Yemen," the junior brother later told French television during the siege in Dammartin-en-Goële.[128] "I went over there and it was Anwar al-Awlaki who financed me," Chérif added. Both Kouachi brothers spent time in Yemen. Saïd, the older of the two, lived there for nearly two years, reportedly meeting Umar Farouk Abdulmutallab at the Sana'a Institute for the Arabic Language, where they both studied.[129] According to intelligence officials, Saïd also received firearms training from AQAP and met directly with Awlaki.[130] Peter Cherif, a U.S.- and UN-designated terrorist who fought for al-Qaeda in Iraq before being captured and extradited to France, also connects the brothers to AQAP. French officials have identified Cherif, who worked for AQAP after his release from an eighteen-month prison stint in France, as a key enabler of the Charlie Hebdo massacre, although the details of his role remain murky.[131] According to one report sourced to U.S. and French officials, Cherif provided the junior Kouachi with funds and provided a short course of training.[132]

The attack on Charlie Hebdo was the deadliest chapter in the "cartoon jihad," a long-standing campaign orchestrated by al-Qaeda's senior leadership, with major assists from AQAP and Awlaki. This effort was meant to add moral weight to al-Qaeda's terrorism. In avenging perceived insults against the Prophet Muhammad, the jihadists could portray themselves as true defenders of the faith.

The Kouachis, AQAP, and al-Qaeda's senior leadership all claimed that the attack on Charlie Hebdo was justified because the newspaper had smeared the Prophet by republishing controversial satirical cartoons of him. "We avenged the Prophet Muhammad! We killed Charlie Hebdo," one of the Kouachis shouted in French after the slayings.[133] AQAP took credit for the operation a week later. "We, al-Qaeda in the Arabian Peninsula, claim responsibility for this operation as vengeance for the messenger of Allah," Nasser bin Ali al-Ansi, a senior member of the group, said in a video. Ansi claimed that AQAP's leadership "chose the target and plotted and financed the plan" in accordance with orders "by our general chief Ayman al-Zawahiri."[134]

THE *JYLLANDS-POSTEN* CONTROVERSY

The origins of the grievance that sparked the Charlie Hebdo attack could be traced to a controversy that erupted nearly a decade earlier. In September 2005 the Danish newspaper *Jyllands-Posten* published twelve satirical cartoons of the Prophet Muhammad. Flemming Rose, the paper's cultural editor, had commissioned the images as a direct challenge to what he saw as an area of self-censorship. Rose believed that Islamic attitudes, which he saw as resistant to satire or criticism, were making Danish society less open. "At the end of September [2005], a Danish standup comedian said in an interview with *Jyllands-Posten* that he had no problem urinating on the Bible in front of a camera, but he dared not do the same thing with the Koran," Rose explained in his defense of the cartoons. "This was the culmination of a series of disturbing instances of self-censorship," Rose explained, citing a string of similar episodes.[135]

The most inflammatory cartoon featured the Prophet Muhammad wearing a bomb-filled turban. The newspaper's editor knew the images would be controversial. Indeed, he published them to provoke a reaction. But the reaction ended up being both global and geopolitical. Protesters stormed Danish embassies, boycotted businesses around the globe, and lives were lost in the unrest.

Al-Qaeda was watching these events and sought to exploit them for years to come. The group's strategy was to launch a "cartoon jihad," a campaign to exact revenge on those who they believed had slandered Islam's central figure. Mullah Dadullah, an al-Qaeda-linked Taliban commander, offered 250 pounds of gold to anyone who assassinated Kurt Westergaard, *Jyllands-Posten*'s main cartoonist.[136] In February 2008 two Tunisians and a Dane of Moroccan descent were arrested for plotting to kill Westergaard in his home city of Aarhus.[137] Nearly two years later a Somali man made another attempt on Westergaard's life, breaking into the cartoonist's home with an ax and knife.[138] Westergaard was forced to hide in a panic room until authorities arrived.

Lars Vilks, a Swedish man, was among the few European cartoonists whom such threats failed to deter. Following in Westergaard's footsteps, Vilks produced another controversial image of the Prophet Muhammad, depicting him with the body of a dog. The jihadists took notice. In September 2007, Abu Omar al-Baghdadi, the head of the Islamic State of Iraq, offered a bounty to anyone who assassinated Vilks. The reward ranged from $100,000 to $150,000, with the greater sum being paid if the killer managed to slaughter Vilks "like a lamb." Baghdadi also offered $50,000 to anyone who killed Ulf Johansson, the editor of *Nerikes Allehanda*, which printed one of Vilks's cartoons. If the "crusader state of Sweden" didn't apologize for this offense, Baghdadi vowed, then his men would begin targeting Swiss companies.[139]

Baghdadi was following the course that al-Qaeda's senior leadership had set. In an April 2006 message first aired by Al Jazeera, bin Laden portrayed the cartoons as part of the West's war against Islam. He appealed to the entire umma "to support our prophet Muhammad, and to punish the perpetrators of the horrible crime committed by some Crusader-journalists and apostates."[140] Bin Laden claimed that the "umma has reached a consensus that he who offends or degrades the messenger would be killed." It was a theme he and other al-Qaeda leaders returned to repeatedly.

Al-Qaeda's pivot to targeting cartoonists depicting the Prophet Muhammad exemplified the group's capacity for organizational learning at the strategic level. Muslim scholars, including many Salafist clerics, heavily criticized the 9/11 attacks because they indiscriminately killed civilians. Al-Qaeda faced additional criticism for the high proportion of Muslims killed by its attacks.[141] The cartoon jihad was not only more discriminate but also represented an attempt to focus on targets who would be deemed universally acceptable by the audience to which al-Qaeda tried to appeal.

Bin Laden's top lieutenant kept returning to the cartoon jihad in his statements. In early 2008 Zawahiri released a lengthy tract titled *The Exoneration.*[142] In it, Zawahiri argued that "Western peoples and governments believe that any writer or artist has the right to ridicule the Prophet (may God bless him and grant him peace), as happened with the cartoons insulting the prophet's honor that were published in a number of Western countries." Bin Laden's second-in-command inveighed against Western laws that protected those who lampooned the Prophet. Because these laws were illegitimate, Zawahiri argued, Muslims traveling through the West had the right to "kill Salman Rushdie and the cartoonists who ridiculed the Prophet (may God bless him and grant him peace), regardless of any visa, safe-conduct, or treaty." Zawahiri argued that a Muslim "may punish" an "entire country or people" if they reviled the Prophet, "participated in it, or colluded in it."

Bin Laden never lost focus on the offense he believed the cartoonists, their enablers, and their countrymen had committed. "Your publication of these drawings—part of a new crusade in which the Pope of the Vatican had a significant role—is a confirmation from you that the war continues," bin Laden said in March 2008.[143] The al-Qaeda founder claimed that the Europeans were "testing Muslims" and he promised more attacks in return. Indeed, bin Laden described publication of the cartoons as a "bigger catastrophe" than the "bombing of modest villages" in Afghanistan and Iraq. Zawahiri reiterated bin Laden's threat the following month, saying: "I admonish and incite every Muslim who is able to do so to cause damage to Denmark in order to show your support for our Prophet, may Allah bless him and grant him salvation, and to defend his esteemed honor."[144]

Danish police arrested eight men in September 2007, saying they had ties to "high-ranking members of al-Qaeda."[145] The cell had been trying to procure chemicals for a mass-casualty bombing. The arrests didn't end al-Qaeda's appetite for revenge against Denmark or Danish targets.

In June 2008 an al-Qaeda suicide bomber detonated an explosives-laden car outside the Danish Embassy in Islamabad, killing six people. Al-Qaeda issued a statement saying the bombing was revenge against Denmark for allowing a newspaper to publish "degrading drawings of the Prophet."[146] The announcement repeated a warning from bin Laden: "If there is no check on your freedom of words, then let your hearts be open to the freedom of our actions."

JIHAD JANE

The cartoon jihad soon had an American element. In early 2009 U.S. officials learned that an American woman, Colleen LaRose (a.k.a. "Jihad Jane"), was communicating online with an al-Qaeda handler who wanted her to travel to Sweden and murder Lars Vilks.[147] LaRose traveled to Europe in 2009 but gave up and returned to Philadelphia, where law enforcement arrested her.[148] Before her capture LaRose had helped spread Awlaki's posts by sharing them on message boards.[149]

LaRose was an amateur even among aspiring terrorists, but al-Qaeda had more effective killers at its disposal. The group dispatched a reconnaissance man, an American named David Coleman Headley, to Denmark in the summer of 2009.[150] Headley was an established operative, and had surveilled hotels and other targets in Mumbai in advance of Lashkar-e-Taiba's November 2008 urban-warfare assault on the Indian city. A few months later, he rode around Copenhagen on a bicycle, pointing his video camera at government buildings, embassies, restaurants, and tourist spots, along with the city's main train station and the offices of *Jyllands-Posten*. Headley also contacted the newspaper, posing as a businessman who wanted to buy advertising space. Headley's reconnaissance reports were then passed to an al-Qaeda commander known as Ilyas Kashmiri, who reported directly to bin Laden.

Kashmiri and Headley devised a plan of attack. A small team of terrorists would infiltrate the newspaper's offices, take hostages, then behead them, making a public spectacle of the blasphemers' deaths.[151] If the assault on *Jyllands-Posten* failed, the al-Qaeda team would regroup and strike another target that Headley had monitored. It was an audacious plan, but like so many of al-Qaeda's professional plots it was eventually thwarted. Headley was arrested in October 2009.

AWLAKI ENTERS THE FRAY

Awlaki weighed in on the cartoon controversies shortly after his December 2007 release from Yemeni prison. In May 2008 Awlaki resumed posting on his eponymous blog, with one of his first entries titled "The Dust Will Never Settle Down." The post announced a talk he would deliver with the same title. In that lecture, Awlaki discussed what should be done about the cartoons and other purportedly offensive material.

"There has been recently an increase of unacceptable behavior from the kuffar towards our beloved Prophet," he wrote on his blog. He then asked rhetorically: "So what is the ruling of sharia on such incidents and how did the Sahaba [companions of the Prophet] deal with such people and what do our scholars say about them?" Awlaki answered the question in his lecture: "This was the impression that the disbelievers would get when they would see the Muslims, that *they would never give him up! That they would never betray him! That they would never leave him! That they would fight until the last man for his protection!*" Awlaki complained that "when the Danish cartoon controversy happened" in 2005, the "Muslim world was on fire," but when the offense was repeated in Sweden, with Vilks's cartoon, "the reaction was less." Awlaki never let go of this theme in *Inspire*.

The inaugural issue included an entire section modeled after Awlaki's then-two-year-old lecture that bore the same threatening title, introducing "The Dust Will Never Settle Down Campaign."[152] The section included a "hit list for the ummah to take out pertaining to the figures related to the blasphemous caricatures." A two-page timeline summarized events from the original September 2005 publication of the cartoons in *Jyllands-Posten* to a May 2010 attack on Lars Vilks at Sweden's Uppsala University. The feature noted several well-known personalities—Salman Rushdie, Ayaan Hirsi Ali, Taslima Nasrin, Bernard-Henri Lévy, Irshad Manji, and Ibn Warraq—who had signed a statement decrying Islamic "totalitarianism" that appeared in the pages of *Charlie Hebdo*. It was implied that these people were on al-Qaeda's hit list.

The issue's main feature was an essay by Awlaki, "May Our Souls Be Sacrificed for You!"[153] Defending the Prophet, he wrote, is an "issue that should unite the efforts of Muslims worldwide." He congratulated himself on the prescience of his lecture two years earlier, as he said he knew the "cartoon controversies" were not "some isolated incidents that would just fade away." Awlaki attacked laws protecting free speech in the West, claiming that the "defamation of Islam is not only protected but promoted." Awlaki blasted the entire Western legal and political system for "protecting and promoting the defamation of Muhammad." This made attacks on "any Western target legal from an Islamic viewpoint," Awlaki reasoned, since the whole Western world was complicit in attacks on the Prophet by virtue of its legal protection of insults against Islam. This was the same argument that Zawahiri had made in *The Exoneration* in 2008.

Part of Awlaki's rhetorical skill lay in his ability to weave interpretations of Islamic history into current events like the cartoon controversies. In the first issue of *Inspire*, he connected his call for violence to avenge the Prophet to Islam's earliest days, claiming there was a "blacklist of names of people in" Mecca who were to be killed for committing various offenses during the Prophet's time, among them "women who sang poetry defaming" Allah's messenger. Awlaki had a more contemporary woman in mind when he wrote those words.

"COMEDY CENTRAL TOTALLY FUCKING PUSSED OUT": SOUTH PARK ENTERS THE FRAY

In the spring of 2010 a previously little-known American cartoonist named Molly Norris used her Facebook account to announce an "Everybody Draw Mohammed Day," which was intended to protest Comedy Central's self-censorship of a *South Park* episode dealing with the cartoon controversies. The irreverent creators of *South Park*, Trey Parker and Matt Stone, had wanted to express solidarity with *Jyllands-Posten* by including an image of Muhammad in a 2006 episode of the show. But their network, Comedy Central, forced them to hide the cartoon figure behind a box that read "censored." Stone later commented that "Comedy Central totally fucking pussed out."[154]

Parker and Stone later decided to include the Prophet Muhammad as a character in the 200th episode of their show. Islam's central figure was initially depicted in a bear costume, thus avoiding direct representations of him. In the following episode, Parker and Stone intended for Muhammad to leave the bear costume and appear on-screen. Comedy Central not only censored Muhammad's appearance but literally bleeped the word *Muhammad* out of the entire episode. Parker and Stone explained in a statement afterward: "In the 14 years we've been doing South Park we have never done a show that we couldn't stand behind. We delivered our version of the show to Comedy Central and they made a determination to alter the episode. It wasn't some meta-joke on our part. Comedy Central added the bleeps. In fact, Kyle's customary final speech was about intimidation and fear. It didn't mention Muhammad at all but it got bleeped too."[155]

It was in the context of this tilt toward almost parodic levels of self-censorship that Norris, like *Jyllands-Posten* before her, took a brief stand for free speech. She figured that the kind of fear on display, as well as the threats of violence, could be rendered moot if millions of people simply drew Muhammad. But Norris quickly backed away from her "Everybody Draw Mohammed Day" concept when it became clear that the threats of physical harm were real.

Awlaki wasn't in a forgiving mood. In the first issue of *Inspire*, he wrote that Norris "should be taken as a prime target of assassination along with others who participated in her campaign."[156] Norris remains in hiding to this day.

Awlaki's American fans in fact played a critical role in provoking Comedy Central's impressive display of cowardice. Comedy Central had decided to strike the image of Muhammad and ultimately bleep out the word Muhammad from *South Park* after a small group known as Revolution Muslim threatened Parker and Stone.[157] Jesse Morton, an American convert to Islam, had founded Revolution Muslim in December 2007 and promoted propaganda from al-Qaeda's senior leadership, Awlaki, and various other extremists. In April 2010 Morton and co-conspirator Zachary Chesser encouraged anyone who wanted to punish Parker and Stone to "pay them a visit," and shared the *South Park* creators' home addresses. Chesser had been following Awlaki's work for years and had been a commenter on the cleric's blog. The pair's pronouncements cited Awlaki's lectures, "which explained the Islamic justification for killing those who insult or defame" Muhammad.[158] When Awlaki used *Inspire* to threaten Norris in July 2010, Morton and Chesser quickly amplified his threats. They promoted *Inspire* online, including its hit list naming Norris and others. Morton justified this incitement campaign, claiming that "Islam's position is that those that insult the Prophet may be killed."[159]

Both Morton and Chesser landed in prison, with Morton later renouncing his worldview and emerging as a counterextremist. But the threats in *Inspire* continued.

An early 2011 article praised Taimour Abdulwahab al-Abdaly, who blew himself up in Stockholm in December 2010, as a "hero" and "shahid" (martyr). The magazine gushed that Abdaly had "fulfilled his individual duty towards Allah in an operation that was long overdue to remind Sweden that its blasphemy against the Messenger of Allah and its participation in the occupation of Afghanistan will not go unpunished."[160] The same edition trumpeted Western news coverage of Awlaki's threats against Norris and others.

VENGEANCE FROM THE GRAVE: *INSPIRE*'S POST-AWLAKI CARTOON JIHAD

In March 2013, a year and a half after Awlaki and Khan were killed, *Inspire*'s new editors published yet another "wanted" list of individuals who had committed "crimes against Islam." AQAP added a new name to the roll of people it wanted dead: Stéphane Charbonnier, the editor of *Charlie Hebdo*. Figure 5.1 shows the graphic, which marked "Charb" and ten others for death.

FIG. 5.1 The graphic in AQAP's *Inspire* magazine marking several public figures, including "Charb," for death

This graphic would come to be emblematic of what made Awlaki's magazine so dangerous. *Inspire* garnered media attention in the West because of its ability to further violence without direct operational connections to the attackers. Still, as we have shown, the January 2015 *Charlie Hebdo* massacre was not exactly an inspired attack. The Kouachi brothers had concrete ties to professional AQAP terrorists. In this way, the plot provides an important wrinkle in our understanding of al-Qaeda's terrorism and Awlaki's role in it. AQAP's men went from encouraging unknown supporters to carry out murder to directly facilitating the operation themselves. While AQAP wanted to offer wannabes a model for do-it-yourself terrorism, they also wanted to follow through on al-Qaeda's many threats related to the Muhammad cartoons without having to wait for an aspiring terrorist to do it for them.

This two-track strategy can be seen in the fourteenth issue of *Inspire*, released in September 2015. The cover story encouraged readers to carry out assassinations of well-known personalities and influential people in the United States and elsewhere. But the issue also celebrated the "Paris Operation," with one article containing a "military analysis" of the *Charlie Hebdo* attack.[161] The assessment appeared under the byline of Ibrahim Ibn Hassan al-Asiri, AQAP's chief bomb maker and a key figure in the 2010 cargo plane plot. Al-Qaeda's "central leadership began by selecting a particular target—in this case, caricature artists defaming the religion and the Prophet Mohammed," Asiri wrote. The group's leaders then selected "two methods" for killing the guilty parties. The first was the "lone jihad" method, in which al-Qaeda would have "no direct connection" to the terrorists except for "inspiring and guiding" them. Because that route failed, the group turned to the second method, an "operation organized by a jihadi group" that worked by "assigning specific persons to target the cartoonists." Al-Qaeda readied Saïd Kouachi for the attack by "giving him necessary training that will prepare him militarily and psychologically to successfully execute the operation." Asiri explained that while Kouachi was given latitude to determine how to best conduct the shootings, al-Qaeda had laid the groundwork and set the plan in motion.

Awlaki's cartoon jihad legacy wasn't confined to AQAP. The al-Qaeda organization continued using his ideas about the cartoon jihad to justify terrorism and assassinations even after he had been dead for several years. In May 2015 the emir of al-Qaeda in the Indian Subcontinent, Asim Umar, released a speech evocatively titled "The Dust Will Never Settle Down."[162] The video accompanying Umar's talk opened with audio from Awlaki praying for God to "raise among us men and women [who] do not fear [for] the sake of Allah the blame of the blamers, who would make the *kuffar* realize that they, by committing blasphemy against our beloved Muhammad, have actually walked straight into a hornets' nest and the dust of this will never settle down." The video repeated the words "the dust of this will never settle down" with an echoing effect.

In the video Umar claimed responsibility for a string of murders targeting "blasphemers," men and women in Bangladesh and Pakistan who he said had defamed Islam and the Prophet. These victims included Avijit Roy, a prominent atheist blogger murdered in February 2015; Rajib Haider, a blogger murdered in February 2013; Muhammad Shakil Auj, dean of Islamic Studies at the University of Karachi who was shot to death in September 2014; Shafiul Islam, a professor at Rajshahi University killed in September 2014; Aniqa Naz, a Pakistani blogger; and Washiqur Rahman, a blogger murdered in March 2015. Several of the victims were brutally hacked to death with machetes, knives, or meat cleavers. All these murders, Umar said, had been conducted in accordance with the orders of Zawahiri and bin Laden, specifically the al-Qaeda founder's threat against the cartoonists and other blasphemers. Umar crowed that the jihadists "have taught a lesson to blasphemers in France, Denmark, Pakistan and now in Bangladesh." He portrayed all these murders as retaliation in the "same war," whether the jihadists' enemies "fought with drones [in northern Pakistan] or with the cursed pens of *Charlie Hebdo*."[163] The video underscored this claimed connection between the *Charlie Hebdo* attack and the murders of "blasphemers" in Bangladesh and Pakistan by including footage of AQAP's Nasser bin Ali al-Ansi claiming responsibility for the "Paris Operation."

It would not be surprising if al-Qaeda returns to the themes of the cartoon jihad in future operations, specifically by targeting men and women alleged to have offended Muslims through legal acts of self-expression. Such a campaign would advance the group's strategy of dividing the world into warring Muslim and non-Muslim camps, and would continue along its path of organizational learning by focusing on certain discrete and "acceptable" targets. From the very beginning, *Inspire* crystallized the issue of avenging insults against Islam.

But as this brief history of the cartoon jihad also shows, *Inspire* was merely amplifying (albeit in an innovative way) the arguments that bin Laden, Zawahiri, AQAP's leaders, and other high-level jihadists were already making. Al-Qaeda eventually decided that its attempts at remotely inspiring deadly attacks as part of the cartoon jihad weren't working as the group had hoped, leading to the Kouachi brothers' more professionalized massacre in Paris. Later jihadists would eventually employ Awlaki's work for their own purposes. The men of the Islamic State made significant use of the cartoon campaign to inspire individual jihadists to lash out in the West. Years after the American cleric's death, ISIS gave Awlaki's messages a new, lethal urgency.

ISIS's Calls to Attack

When ISIS's leaders announced their caliphate in the summer of 2014, they called on all the world's Muslims to join what they believed to be a world historical project. "So rush O Muslims and gather around your *khalīfah*, so that you may return as you once were for ages, kings of the earth and knights of war," the group's spokesman, Abu Muhammad al-Adnani, pronounced.[164] Like Awlaki, the upstart jihadist group aimed much of its messaging at disaffected Muslims living far beyond the Middle East.

Abu Bakr al-Baghdadi echoed Adnani's words several days later in the speech he gave after publicly accepting the title of caliph. "So rush, O Muslims, with your religion to Allah as *muhājirīn* (emigrants)," he urged listeners outside the caliphate.[165] Baghdadi made a special call for assistance from skilled supporters, including scholars, preachers, experts in Islamic jurisprudence, "judges, as well as people with military, administrative, and service expertise." Muslims from all of these professions should fulfill the "*wājib 'aynī*" (individual obligation) and emigrate to the new caliphate, Baghdadi said.

But ISIS was also intent on wreaking destruction outside the caliphate's borders. A few months after the caliphate declaration, ISIS's leaders instructed followers in the West to strike in their home countries, killing anyone they could. "If you can kill a disbelieving American or European— especially the spiteful and filthy French—or an Australian, or a Canadian, or any other disbeliever from the disbelievers waging war, including the citizens of the countries that entered into a coalition against the Islamic State, then rely upon Allah, and kill him in any manner or way however it may be," Adnani said in September 2014. "Do not ask for anyone's advice and do not seek anyone's verdict. Kill the disbeliever whether he is civilian or military." He said the blood of Western citizens was "like the blood of a dog," and "there is no sin . . . in spilling it."[166]

Awlaki's words echoed in Adnani's fiery rhetoric. The late American cleric had framed his own calls for individual terrorism in much the same terms. In the years that followed, authorities would discover time and again that ISIS supporters had embraced Awlaki's teachings at some decisive point on their path.

Just two days after Adnani's speech, an eighteen-year-old named Abdul Numan Haider stabbed two counterterrorism officers in Melbourne.[167] Haider had offered to help with ongoing investigations, although this turned out to be a ruse. Haider was quickly shot to death upon launching his attack, and both officers survived. The timing of Haider's assault was conspicuous. The stabbings marked the first terrorist attack by an ISIS supporter in the West in the wake of Adnani's call.

The following years brought a wave of attacks by individuals or small cells acting in ISIS's name. It was often difficult to determine whether the caliphate's calls for freelance terrorism had spurred the attackers or if there were deeper operational links. In some cases the perpetrators had truly acted on their own. In other instances (see chapter 10), ISIS handlers offered online guidance from overseas, communicating with would-be terrorists via secure means.

CONTEXTUALIZING ISIS'S SUCCESS: BEYOND EARLY ADOPTION

To understand how ISIS was able to achieve its breakthrough in inspiring attackers throughout the world, it is helpful to recall our violent non-state-actor technology adoption curve, and how technological improvements emerge after the early-adoption phase. Social media platforms did not drastically evolve between the period of Awlaki's prominence and the rise of ISIS's online campaign. But three distinct changes occurred. First, the unique capabilities of social media became better understood and best practices for engaging followers on social media became increasingly distinct from those employed in the Web 2.0 world. Second, far more people worldwide were drawn to social media. Third, advances in encryption allowed secure conversations between jihadist influencers and operatives that would likely have resulted in arrests during Awlaki's prime.

At the beginning of this chapter, we described the internet's evolution from Web 1.0 to Web 2.0 to the social web. Awlaki rose to prominence as Web 2.0 was giving way to the social web. But he used the social web largely the way content producers used Web 2.0. His content was the primary message, and interactivity with his audience was of secondary concern. Techniques for gaining a loyal and devoted audience and for cultivating personal relationships via the social web that seemed deep and meaningful became further refined after Awlaki's death. ISIS emerged in the context of this deeper realization of the social web's potential not only for entertainers like Taylor Swift or Justin Bieber but also for social entrepreneurs like ISIS.[168] ISIS's use of the social web was genuinely innovative, but the group benefited heavily by traveling paths that others had already blazed outside of the terrorism context, in part because many of its young devotees were highly familiar with the milieu of social media.

The second major change from early adoption to the iteration and breakthrough phase in the violent non-state-actor technology adoption curve is that between 2010 and 2014 the number of social media users grew. Facebook had 608 million monthly users at the end of 2010. By the end of 2014, that number had soared to nearly 1.4 billion.[169] Over the same time period, Twitter's user base increased from 54 million to 288 million. Thus, the potential reach of ISIS's propaganda vastly surpassed that of Awlaki's YouTube videos.

The third change was significant improvement in secure user-to-user communication, which we discuss in chapter 10. Suffice it to say, for now, that the widespread diffusion of end-to-end encryption technologies helped facilitate the virtual plotter model.

DABIQ

ISIS emulated al-Qaeda in other ways that revealed Awlaki's lingering influence. In July 2014 ISIS released its own English-language magazine, Dabiq. The title was the name of a small town in northern Syria central to Islamic eschatology. Dabiq is said to be the future location of an end-times battle between good and evil. ISIS was promoting an end-of-the-world fantasy to its readers in choosing this name for its flagship English-language publication, positioning itself as a central end-times actor. But after ISIS controlled the town of Dabiq for a brief period, it fell to U.S.-backed forces. To ISIS's embarrassment, the anticipated final battle for the fate of the world never materialized. Never one to admit error, ISIS quickly changed the name of its English-language publication to *Rumiyah*, or Rome. It did so with no notice or explanation. Fifteen issues of *Dabiq* were posted online between July 2014 and July 2016.

Like *Inspire*, *Dabiq* had an American editor, Abu Maysarah al-Shami. The Boston native came to loathe al-Qaeda and used *Dabiq* to undermine Abu Bakr al-Baghdadi's rivals (see chapter 8). *Inspire* told readers that the caliphate would one day be a reality, but *Dabiq* declared that Muslims were required to pledge their fealty to a caliphate that already existed.

The first two issues of *Dabiq* focused on the call for *hijrah* (migration) by Western recruits, with incitement to lone attacks gaining prominence as ISIS began to lose territory. The third issue was posted in October 2014, a few weeks after the beginning of the American-led anti-ISIS air campaign in Iraq and Syria. The issue ramped up ISIS's anti-American rhetoric while retaining the call for *hijrah*. The fourth issue, published the same month, focused largely on Adnani's call for individual attacks in the West. It was no accident that the same issue included *Dabiq*'s first mention of Awlaki.[170] Adnani's incitement of attacks became an increasingly prominent feature in the magazine from the fifth issue onward. *Dabiq* celebrated people who attacked in ISIS's name across the globe.

Dabiq's editorial team buttressed the argument for compulsory loyalty to Baghdadi by republishing an article that had first appeared in AQAP's *Sawt al-Jihad*, the publication that predated Awlaki's tenure with the group.[171] *Dabiq* informed readers that the piece, titled "Advice to the Mujahidin: Listen and Obey," was written before AQAP became "the partisan Yemeni branch," a bitter concession that AQAP had rejected Baghdadi's role as caliph. Still, *Dabiq*'s editors pressed the old article into service out of appreciation for its theme of fealty to an earthly caliph. "The first piece of advice—following my advice to fear Allah and be mindful of Him—is to listen to and obey those whom Allah has given authority over the affairs of the mujahidin," the AQAP author advised. He cautioned that disobeying one's emir was akin to disobeying the Prophet. The article had nothing to do with Baghdadi, but its arguments could be repurposed to show that even al-Qaeda recognized the need for unwavering loyalty to a Baghdadi-like figure.

Thus, potential recruits in the West were increasingly exposed to a combination of calls by both ISIS and al-Qaeda for individual or small-cell attacks. The dangers of these two competing yet mutually reinforcing channels of incitement quickly became evident.

ISIS ATTACKS, WITH A TABLESPOON OF AWLAKI

Around the same time as Abdul Numan Haider's attack, another Australian ISIS recruit, Mohammad Ali Baryalei, sparked a massive counterterrorism investigation with a message he sent from the caliphate urging his comrades to kidnap and behead a random civilian. Baryalei had a history of drug abuse and excessive gambling but had found personal redemption through an extremist interpretation of Islam, which he came to in part through the lectures of Anwar al-Awlaki. In one of Baryalei's favorite videos, Awlaki explained that Australia was the enemy of Muslims in a "long protracted war that will . . . end up with the Muslims ruling the world."[172] Baghdadi and Adnani's caliphate claimed to be on the path to precisely this objective. Baryalei relocated to the caliphate to assist their project.

Working along the border of Syria and Turkey in 2014, Baryalei tried to instigate murders back in Australia. He wanted ISIS supporters to reproduce the grisly beheadings that a British transplant named Mohammed Emwazi (a.k.a. "Jihadi John") had carried out in Syria, except without their ever traveling to the Middle East. At that point, Emwazi had already beheaded Americans James Foley and Steven Sotloff as well as two British men, David Haines and Alan Henning. Baryalei failed to instigate copycat killings in Australia. Authorities intercepted his phone call to Omarjan Azari, a twenty-two-year-old tasked with carrying out these attacks, leading to a wave of raids in Sydney and Brisbane three days before Haider's knife assault in Melbourne.[173]

Haider had been known to law enforcement prior to his stabbing attack. He allegedly threatened Australian officials while brandishing ISIS's black banner at a local mall.[174] The government then revoked his passport, preventing him from traveling abroad for jihad. This made Haider one of the earliest examples of the so-called frustrated traveler phenomenon, where men and women prevented from joining ISIS's caliphate decided to strike in their home countries instead. ISIS actively encouraged this practice. Adnani told followers that if foreign governments "have shut the door of hijrah in your faces," ISIS's supporters should "open the door of jihad in theirs."[175]

On the morning of October 20, 2014, another frustrated traveler, Martine Couture-Rouleau, rammed his car into two Canadian servicemembers in a parking lot in Saint-Jean-sur-Richelieu, Quebec. One victim later succumbed to his injuries. Like Haider, Couture-Rouleau was known to authorities. The Royal Canadian Mounted Police had seized his passport in July 2014 and placed him on a list of high risk travelers, thwarting his planned journey to Turkey and then on to the caliphate.[176] In the days and weeks that followed, ISIS supporters shot and killed a Canadian servicemember at the National War Memorial's tomb of the unknown soldier in Ottawa and opened fire in the nearby national Parliament building;[177] charged police officers in Queens, New York wielding a hatchet;[178] seized hostages at a Lindt chocolate café in Sydney, Australia, killing two during the standoff;[179] drove a vehicle into a crowd of pedestrians in Dijon, France;[180] assaulted police officers in Joué-lès-Tours, France, with a knife; and rammed another vehicle into a Christmas market in the French city of Nantes.[181] The death toll from these attacks was relatively low, and authorities cited a history of psychological problems or other factors in several cases. But Adnani and his comrades had successfully amplified the message that al-Qaeda and Awlaki had first promulgated. Years earlier, Awlaki had called for individual attacks in the West. Adnani and ISIS had renewed that call and blood was being spilled.

On May 3, 2015, two men, Elton Simpson and Nadir Soofi, drove from Arizona to Garland, Texas, where they opened fire outside an event called the "Muhammad Art Exhibit and Contest." Only Simpson and Soofi were killed in the shootout, although a security guard was wounded.

Both Simpson and Soofi advertised their admiration for Awlaki, emphasizing their devotion to him in their final moments. Soofi penned a handwritten letter before the attack saying that he was inspired by Awlaki's teachings.[182] Simpson maintained a Twitter account named "Shariah is Light" that had a picture of the late cleric as its profile image. On Twitter, Simpson followed Junaid Hussain, an online ISIS recruiter. One of Simpson's last tweets, posted mere hours before he launched his attack, implored his followers to follow @_AbuHu55ain, the Twitter handle Hussain employed at the time. Simpson's final tweet read: "The bro with me and myself have given bay'ah to Amirul Mu'mineen [Baghdadi]. May Allah accept us as mujahideen. . . . #texasattack."

Junaid Hussain, who may have been in direct contact with Simpson, had agitated for attacks against the Garland event, and he celebrated Simpson and Soofi's attack immediately after it was launched. ISIS quickly declared responsibility for the attack.[183] The group's first claimed operation in the United States had come from two of Awlaki's devoted fans.

The Garland shooters were part of a pattern of Awlaki enthusiasts throwing in with the caliphate. A far deadlier jihadist attack on U.S. soil soon underscored the continuity between Awlaki's ideas and those of ISIS. On the morning of December 2, 2015, the San Bernardino County Department of Public Health in Southern California held a training event that was supposed to double as a light-hearted holiday party. Syed Rizwan Farook and Tashfeen Malik, a married couple, turned the event into a massacre. By the end of their rampage, fourteen people lay dead and twenty-two were wounded. The couple made it clear that they had carried out the massacre in Baghdadi's name.[184]

Farook had worked as a food inspector for the county public health department; the victims at the party he terrorized were his coworkers. Farook had become radicalized years earlier by watching Awlaki's videos and reading *Inspire*, and he in turn helped to indoctrinate a friend named Enrique Marquez Jr. In 2011–2012 Marquez illegally purchased the assault rifles that Farook and Malik used in their assault. Farook and Marquez had originally planned to attack the library or cafeteria at Riverside Community College, where both men had attended classes. Alternatively, the friends considered targeting commuter vehicles traveling on State Route 91. Farook would throw pipe bombs onto the highway, and the pair would shoot motorists after traffic came to a standstill.

As he fantasized about killing his classmates or random commuters, Farook developed an obsession with al-Qaeda's regional branches. He considered joining AQAP, watched al-Shabaab-produced videos, and reportedly had ties to members of al-Nusra Front in Syria. When Farook introduced Marquez to his radical beliefs, he expressed a "disdain towards Muslims in the U.S. military who killed other Muslims," a recurring theme in Awlaki's work that had particular influence on Nidal Hasan. After ISIS's territorial gains in 2014, Farook and his wife, Tashfeen Malik, gravitated to the caliphate as an inspiring beacon of jihadist success. On the day of their massacre in San Bernardino, a post on Malik's Facebook page read: "We pledge allegiance to Khalifa bu bkr al bhaghdadi al quraishi," a typo-littered rendering of Khalifa Abu Bakr al-Baghdadi al-Quraishi.[185]

The married couple became obsessed with using pipe bombs in a multipronged attack. They relied on *Inspire*'s instructions to make crude devices intended to kill emergency workers and policemen. Luckily, they failed to detonate.[186] But AQAP and Awlaki's earlier work helped these terrorists to experiment with bomb-making in the first place. In interviews with authorities, Marquez "described his familiarity with the use of remote-control devices to detonate IEDs, and said he and Farook reviewed instructions on how to make IEDs that were in Inspire Magazine."[187] Their homemade IEDs employed readily available objects like Christmas lights and remote-control car parts, just like those promoted in *Inspire*.

Within hours of committing mass murder, Farook and Malik were hunted down in their rented SUV and killed in a shootout. They left behind a baby girl. Marquez was arrested and eventually pleaded guilty to various charges related to his plotting with Farook, along with immigration fraud.

A massacre on the other side of the country would soon serve as an even more lethal example of how jihadist groups could seed attacks from half a world away. Omar Mateen entered the Pulse nightclub in Orlando, Florida shortly after 2 a.m. on June 13, 2016, carrying a semiautomatic rifle and a handgun. He opened fire, then took hostages. Forty-nine people died and dozens were wounded before Mateen fell in a hail of bullets about three hours into his rampage. After the attack, press reports speculated that Mateen may have been gay and struck Pulse, a LGBT-friendly establishment, because of his repressed sexuality.[188] Investigators found no evidence to support this now-widespread interpretation of the massacre. While human psychology is complex and it is difficult to reduce motivations to a single factor, there is a more compelling explanation for Mateen's act of mass murder: He had been influenced by both al-Qaeda and ISIS.

Indeed, Mateen repeatedly communicated his motives while the attack was in progress. During the hostage crisis at Pulse, Mateen called 911 three times and also rang Orlando's *News 13*. He wanted to ensure people heard him swear his loyalty to Abu Bakr al-Baghdadi. "I pledge allegiance to Abu Bakr al-Baghdadi may God protect him . . . on behalf of the Islamic State," Mateen said in response to one of the emergency operator's questions.[189]

"I did it for ISIS. I did it for the Islamic State," Mateen told a *News 13* producer.[190] On the day of the atrocity, Mateen also wrote on Facebook: "America and Russia stop bombing the Islamic state . . . I pledge my alliance [*sic*] to abu bakr al Baghdadi . . . may Allah accept me."

Mateen might have drawn inspiration from the earlier attack in California. He reportedly used his Facebook account to search for information on the San Bernardino terrorists a month before his rampage. Like the San Bernardino killers, Mateen didn't suddenly adopt jihadist views with ISIS's rise. Instead, jihadism was swirling in his head years before Baghdadi became a household name. The FBI had investigated the future terrorist at least twice before the mass slayings at Pulse.[191] He first came across the Bureau's radar in May 2013 when he made threatening comments to coworkers. Mateen claimed then to have family ties to al-Qaeda and boasted, somewhat incongruently, of being a member of Hizballah, their sometimes-rival. He warned that he would "martyr himself" if law enforcement officials ever raided his apartment. The FBI looked into him at the time, interviewing various sources and Mateen himself. Mateen told agents he was mistaken in issuing his threats, and the Bureau closed its investigation in the first half of 2014.

By July 2014 Mateen was back on the FBI's radar. This time his name surfaced during an investigation into Moner Mohammad Abu Salha, an American who blew himself up in May 2014 on behalf of al-Nusra Front in Syria. The FBI found that Mateen and Abu Salha were casual acquaintances. Both had attended the same mosque. Investigators didn't find much more to the relationship. Yet there were signs that Mateen may have been walking a path similar to that of Abu Salha. A witness contacted by the FBI in 2014 reported that Mateen had been watching Awlaki's videos. Yet the witness still saw little cause for concern: Mateen had a wife and child and appeared to live a settled life, so figured that there was likely nothing to worry about.[192] That assumption proved tragically wrong.

In addition to declaring his allegiance to Baghdadi in the course of his massacre, Mateen announced his solidarity with the Boston Marathon bombers and Abu Salha. FBI director James Comey expressed befuddlement at Mateen's references to these latter three individuals because they "were not inspired by" ISIS. For Comey, Mateen's hailing of non-ISIS jihadists added "a little bit to the confusion about his motives."[193] This confusion represents an extraordinarily narrow view of how jihadists find motivation.

The cases where attackers have drawn from both ISIS and al-Qaeda are voluminous, and there should have been nothing confusing about Mateen's affinity for these terrorists, least of all from one of the federal government's top law enforcement officials. The Boston bombers' murderous imaginations had been sparked, at least in part, by Awlaki and *Inspire*; al-Nusra Front, which dispatched Abu Salha on his suicide mission, had once been an arm of the Islamic State. The Kouachi brothers and Amedy Coulibaly had no trouble cooperating in launching attacks in France even though they played for different jihadist teams. From a Western jihadist's perspective, Baghdadi, the Tsarnaevs, and Salha could easily fit within the same ideological ecosystem. Mateen's expression of support for their missions likely reflected his own evolution from an al-Qaeda admirer to an ISIS supporter—the same progression as the San Bernardino couple.

The rash of remotely inspired attacks in the United States that could be traced to Awlaki's ideas still wasn't over. On the morning of September 17, 2016, an improvised explosive device detonated along the route of the Seaside Semper Five Marine Corps Charity 5K race in Seaside, New Jersey.[194] A lucky coincidence prevented the attack from claiming lives: The start of the race had been delayed. If the event had started on time, runners would have been passing by when the bomb exploded. This wasn't the only time residents of New York and New Jersey narrowly avoided tragedy that week. The Afghan American man who placed that bomb, Ahmad Khan Rahami, planted several others too. Later that night, Rahami brought two bombs into New York City's Chelsea neighborhood, leaving one on Twenty-Third Street and the second on Twenty-Seventh Street. The bomb on Twenty-Third Street, left between Sixth and Seventh Avenues, was placed in or near a dumpster that was sent tumbling through the air when the explosive detonated.[195] The windows on a nearby building shattered, and the ground shook for several blocks around the explosion. Twenty-nine people were wounded, but given the ferocity of the explosion, casualties could have been far worse. The other incendiary device, a pressure-cooker bomb, was recovered without incident on Twenty-Seventh Street.

The next evening, September 18, authorities discovered six more of Rahami's devices in a backpack outside a mass transit station in Elizabeth, New Jersey. The bombs were recovered without incident, with one exploding when law enforcement used a robot to neutralize it.

Authorities arrested Rahami in Linden, New Jersey, on September 19, about forty-eight hours after his first bomb detonated. Rahami didn't go quietly: He shot and injured several police officers before he was apprehended. He also left behind ample evidence of what he had been up to and why. The pages of a handwritten journal found in his possession were particularly telling. "The sounds of bombs will be heard in the streets," he wrote, fantasizing about "bombs set off in the streets [where] they plan to run a mile." The pages were bloodied during Rahami's firefight with police, but his praise of jihadist icons like Osama bin Laden, Anwar al-Awlaki, Nidal Hasan, and Abu Muhammad al-Adnani could still be made out, turning the notebook into another instance of terrorists in the West drawing inspiration from both al-Qaeda and ISIS figures. Rahami had even paired Awlaki's guidance with Adnani's advice, noting that they both said to "clearly attack the Kuffar in their backyard." Although Rahami employed several designs for his bombs, authorities detected a similarity to the instructions found in *Inspire*. Indeed, authorities found a copy of *Inspire*'s "Make a Bomb in the Kitchen of Your Mom" on Rahami's laptop.[196]

By now this was a familiar story: The United States had seen a series of cases where extremists first influenced by al-Qaeda, *Inspire*, and Awlaki became enthralled with the caliphate. In 2015 the FBI arrested nine Minnesotans of Somali heritage who intended to join ISIS's overseas ranks. Abdirizak Warsame, the ringleader, testified that they had listened to Awlaki's lectures as part of their indoctrination process.[197] On November 28, 2016, ISIS quickly claimed responsibility for an attack that Abdul Razak Ali Artan, a Somali refugee, carried out at Ohio State University. Artan rammed his vehicle into a crowd of pedestrians, then jumped out and began stabbing people, wounding thirteen in the assault. He had drawn inspiration from both ISIS and Awlaki, whom he called a "hero" in a Facebook post.[198]

The trend of American jihadists using the long-dead Awlaki as a gateway into support for ISIS continued even after much of the caliphate had fallen. In February 2018 Sajmir Alimehmeti, a native Albanian, pleaded guilty to attempting to provide material support to ISIS.[199] Awlaki's lectures on martyrdom were found on Alimehmeti's laptop.[200] In December 2018 the FBI arrested a twenty-one-year-old Ohio man, Damon M. Joseph, who was conspiring to attack a synagogue in Toledo.[201] Joseph's online activities had attracted the attention of authorities earlier that year when he posted messages praising both ISIS's caliphate and Awlaki. He had also created video mashups that mixed Awlaki's lectures with ISIS imagery, an illustration of the continuity many jihadists perceived from the late Yemeni American cleric to the caliphate. In one such homemade production, Joseph implored viewers to heed Awlaki's call to arms, including recognizable statements such as "44 ways of jihad, have you contributed? Do your part to help your brothers" and "Whatever country you are in, gather with eachother [sic] and do what you can, Allah will reward you for any 44 ways of jihad you can do." In conversations with a person he thought was a fellow extremist, Joseph described his crude videomaking as a form of "virtual jihad" and said he was considering moving on to violence. Unbeknownst to Joseph, this ostensible comrade was an undercover FBI operative. The "virtual jihad" would be Joseph's last.

All these examples show that Awlaki's death and the caliphate's decline did not stop the cross-pollination of their ideas from spurring acts of violence. Whatever setbacks befell AQAP or the caliphate, their call to jihad remained compelling.

The Evolution of Individual Terrorism

Terrorist threats surged across the world in the wake of ISIS's June 2014 caliphate declaration. Although data on this increase can be difficult to interpret, a report prepared by Europol found that 395 suspected jihadists were arrested across mainland Europe in 2014, with the figure spiking to 687 arrests in 2015.[202] The number then rose to 718 in 2016, before leveling off at 705 in 2017 and declining to 511 arrests in 2018. The timing of this surge tracks with ISIS's rise and its emphasis on individual jihad in the West. There was a 74 percent continent-wide increase in arrests of suspected jihadists the year after Adnani declared his boss to be "Caliph Ibrahim" and called on believers to strike across Europe.

This data comes with a number of caveats. Arrest statistics for Britain, which also experienced a surge in jihadism, were not included in Europol's tabulation. Personal motivations for violent extremism can be complex, and it shouldn't be assumed that all these suspects were ideological automatons nor that they all had links to "other radicalised individuals or terrorist groups," Europol noted.[203] Not all of these suspected jihadists were

ISIS enthusiasts, and not all arrests lead to convictions. Other types of terrorist threats—including ethnonationalists and separatists, as well as right-wing and left-wing extremists—figure prominently in these figures as well.

Europol's reporting nevertheless points to a spike in jihadism following the caliphate declaration. Europol counted twenty-three completed or thwarted jihadist terrorist plots in 2018, in which the "majority of the perpetrators . . . were acting or were planning to act alone."[204] This doesn't mean the plotters had no outside support, as extremist networks, family members, and friends may have provided encouragement or other forms of assistance. But, with few exceptions, these plots were not planned by groups. ISIS claimed that one of its "soldiers" carried out four of the seven successful attacks in 2018.[205] Three of these occurred in France, the fourth in Belgium. By comparison, al-Qaeda did not claim any terrorist attacks in Europe in 2018.

There's little question that ISIS surpassed al-Qaeda as a motivator of individual terrorism in the United States and Europe from 2014 onward. Even a cursory glance at operations during this time reveals dozens of small-scale attacks attributable to ISIS's influence. Even AQAP has been forced to recognize its rival's success in inspiring individual terrorism. In both *Inspire* and a series of special *Inspire* "guides," AQAP lauded numerous attacks by caliphate supporters, including the June 2016 Orlando massacre; the 2016 Bastille Day attack in Nice, France, that left more than eighty people dead; stabbings at a mall in Minnesota and bombings in New York and New Jersey in September 2016; and a vehicular assault near the British Parliament in March 2017. AQAP did not have a similar track record to boast about. AQAP quibbled with some of these operations even though *Inspire* saw fit to laud them. The group complained, for instance, that Omar Mateen erred in targeting a nightclub where "most of the individuals present . . . were Latino" and gay because it "is better to avoid targeting places and crowds where minorities are generally found in America." Instead, the jihadists should instead target "areas where the Anglo-Saxon community is generally concentrated" because this "class of the American community is the majority and it is the one that is in the American leadership."[206] ISIS expressed no such reservations.

This lack of discrimination in endorsing targets and types of attacks may point to one reason ISIS has had more success than AQAP with respect to individual terrorism. As the caliphate grew in influence, AQAP began to advocate increasingly complex operations for would-be terrorists, like derailing commuter trains, carrying out professional-level assassinations, or waging military-style assaults like the one at *Charlie Hebdo*'s offices. ISIS instead focused on inspiring attacks on anyone using any means while also directly orchestrating other operations (see chapter 10). AQAP itself began to realize the deficiencies in its approach. Followers shouldn't "complicate matters" but instead should "take it easy and simple," AQAP emir Qasim al-Raymi said in 2017, perhaps envying the effectiveness of ISIS's simpler course.[207]

Awlaki's long afterlife suggests that individual terrorism isn't likely to disappear regardless of whatever setbacks AQAP and ISIS encounter in the coming years. Awlaki and AQAP exported the concept of remotely inspired attacks after learning how difficult it was for professional terrorists to strike in the post-9/11 environment. ISIS built on this work. Compared to a more organized plot, individual terrorism is difficult for authorities to detect and to stop. The legacy of Awlaki is likely to continue looming behind future atrocities. Awlaki was a pioneer, using new tools and new media to spread ideas and tactics.

In 2011 a new source of opportunity came onto the scene, one that would have an even more lasting impact on jihadist organizations than Awlaki's work. As Awlaki was preparing the last issues of *Inspire* to be published during his short life, al-Qaeda was adapting to the new opportunities and challenges posed by the Arab Spring, revolutions that would change the region's governments and destabilize geographic spaces.

6

Strategic Learning
Al-Qaeda and Jihadism in the Arab Spring

On December 17, 2010, a twenty-six-year-old street merchant named Mohamed Bouazizi set himself on fire in the hardscrabble Tunisian town of Sidi Bouzid. A policewoman and her colleagues had recently confiscated Bouazizi's fruit and vegetable cart, the source of his income, because he lacked a license.[1] This wasn't the first time power-tripping local authorities had seized Bouazizi's cart. As on other occasions, Bouazizi reportedly offered to pay a fine, but this time a compromise was rejected. Fayda Hamdy, the policewoman, claims she had warned Bouazizi the day before that he had to move his cart and that he became belligerent.[2] According to popular lore, Hamdy slapped Bouazizi in the face and insulted him, something Hamdy has repeatedly denied. Whatever happened, an obviously distraught Bouazizi traveled to the Tunisian government's provincial headquarters to dispute his equipment's confiscation, only to be turned away. Unsettled by this series of petty humiliations, the young Tunisian doused himself in gasoline and set himself aflame outside the provincial governor's office. He died a few weeks later, on January 4, 2011.

Although no one anticipated it at the time, Bouazizi's suicide became the catalyst for a political revolution that swept through much of the Middle East and North Africa. Tunisian president Zine El Abidine Ben Ali, who had ruled comfortably for more than two decades, was forced to flee his

longtime fiefdom less than a month after Bouazizi's death. Other authoritarian rulers, including Egypt's Hosni Mubarak, Libya's Muammar al-
Qaddafi, and Yemen's Ali Abdullah Saleh, lost their grip on power in the
following months. In Syria, peaceful protests against Bashar al-Assad
evolved into a bloody insurgency.[3] A decade later, the country is still
at war.

In Washington, these events, which became known as the Arab Spring,
were initially viewed as the beginning of a new democratic era for the
Muslim-majority world. Earlier in this book we described the widespread
misreading of the regional upheaval as one of the key consensus errors that
gripped our field in recent years. Experts and policymakers widely believed
that this political opening would free tens of millions of people from
oppressive governments while sounding the death knell for al-Qaeda and its
ideology. Former CIA official Michael Morell's agency had initially embraced
the idea that the revolutions would be debilitating for the jihadist movement. Something close to the opposite in fact occurred. The determination
that the wave of popular protests would weaken or destroy al-Qaeda was
the "most important" of "all the [CIA's] analytic missteps during the run-up
to what became known as the Arab Spring," Morell wrote. Instead of usher-
ing in the end of al-Qaeda, he continued, "the Arab Spring was a boon to
Islamic extremists across both the Middle East and North Africa."[4]

Al-Qaeda neither predicted nor sparked the revolts of 2011. The group's
leadership would later absurdly claim that the protests were a direct result
of the 9/11 hijackings. But unlike officials in Washington and Langley, al-
Qaeda's leaders quickly realized that the turmoil presented new opportunities to win adherents to their cause. Bin Laden wrote in his personal
diary in early 2011 that the "chaos and the absence of authority" provided
an ideal environment for spreading al-Qaeda's ideology.[5] Mere days before
a team of Navy SEALs killed him in May 2011, bin Laden correctly surmised
that Islamist political parties would rise from the ashes of fallen dictatorships. A little over a year later, the Muslim Brotherhood in Egypt and the
Islamist Ennahda party in Tunisia had both taken control of their country's governments. Islamists in post-Qaddafi Libya also began to participate in politics and win supporters. Although al-Qaeda often quarreled
with these same Islamists, bin Laden did not want to highlight their differences at the outset of the Arab Spring. The al-Qaeda leader wanted to concentrate on seizing new opportunities to spread the group's message.

"It would be nice to remind our brothers in the regions to be patient and deliberate, and warn them of entering into confrontations with the parties belonging to Islam," bin Laden wrote in a memo dated April 26, 2011. "It is probable that most of the areas will have governments established on the remnants of the previous governments, and [it is] most probable these governments will belong to the Islamic parties and groups, like the Brotherhood and the like." Al-Qaeda's duty during the tumult, bin Laden reasoned, was to watch events closely and avoid squandering the "unprecedented opportunities" they presented. The al-Qaeda head believed that the "more time that passes and the call [dawa] increases, the more the supporters will be of the people, and the more widespread will be the correct understanding among the coming generations of Islamic groups." One conceivable and even likely result of the Arab Spring, he wrote, was "the coming of Islamic governments that follow the Salafi doctrine."[6]

The dawa (proselytism) that bin Laden mentioned became a central part of al-Qaeda's early response to the Arab uprisings. The emphasis on dawa required a shift in al-Qaeda's strategic thinking. For many U.S. analysts, al-Qaeda was defined exclusively by its attacks on America and on Western interests, as though such operations were the organization's raison d'être. Many analysts simply misread al-Qaeda as a strategically static organization. This perception was likely fed by the fact that al-Qaeda prided itself on being ideologically inflexible and hostile to theological innovation (bida). But the group's theological rigidity did not prevent it from adopting new strategies to achieve its broader goals—and, as we have explained (chapter 3), the far-enemy strategy was rooted in strategic assessment rather than theological principles. Indeed, fighting the far enemy was never the totality of al-Qaeda's activities at any given time.

There were always problems with al-Qaeda's political theory, which is hardly surprising. America always possessed a more variegated and complex approach than al-Qaeda wanted its audience to believe. Still, prior to the Arab uprisings, bin Laden and his closest comrades treated American policy like gravity, as if it were an unchanging centripetal force keeping various dictatorships in place. After Bouazizi's suicide by fire in Tunisia and the earth-shaking events that followed, al-Qaeda modified its program for an environment in which the laws of gravity had suddenly changed.

The General Guidelines for Jihad: Al-Qaeda's Post–Arab Spring Approach

Months after the May 2011 Abbottabad raid that resulted in bin Laden's death, his successor, Ayman al-Zawahiri, explained al-Qaeda's new reality. For Zawahiri, the fall of Tunisia and Egypt's rulers were losses for America comparable to the 9/11 attacks. America "was defeated in Tunisia and lost its agent there," and "it was defeated in Egypt and lost its biggest agent there," Zawahiri claimed.[7] In a separate statement, he assessed that in Egypt and Tunisia, new "opportunities have opened up for preaching [but] only Allah knows how long they will last," and thus" the people of Islam and jihad should benefit from them and take advantage of them to report the clear truth and make the Ummah come together."[8]

In September 2013 Zawahiri codified al-Qaeda's updated approach to the turmoil in his "General Guidelines for Jihad."[9] The drafting of the guidelines reveals some of al-Qaeda's inner workings, as the text was shared with the organization's regional arms before it was finalized and published online.[10] A careful reading tells us even more about al-Qaeda, its goals, and the organizational learning it engaged to facilitate its adaptation to the post-2011 world. Zawahiri and his men devised different plans for different countries, reflecting each environment's distinct opportunities and challenges.

Al-Qaeda divided its post-uprising work into two categories: military and propagational. The first grouping would still involve spectacular terrorist attacks, but military work was not limited to plotting against America and its allies. Zawahiri's guidelines stipulated that the "military work firstly targets the head of (international) disbelief, America and its ally Israel," and then, secondly, "its local allies that rule our countries." The "purpose of targeting America" was the same as it had always been: "to exhaust her and bleed her to death, so that it meets the fate of the former Soviet Union and collapses under its own weight as a result of its military, human, and financial losses." Once Washington's empire was in freefall, America's "grip on our lands will weaken and its allies will begin to fall."[11]

To this point, the guidelines read much like al-Qaeda's pre-2011 outlook. But Zawahiri also offered justifications for a broad-based insurgency stretching from West and North Africa, through the heart of the Middle East, and into South Asia. The specifics of the conflict against the various "proxies of America ... differ[ed] from place to place," but Zawahiri consistently tied these present and future local wars back to al-Qaeda's global, anti-American agenda. Thus, the struggle against the Afghan government was "part of the fight against [the] Americans" and directly tied to the situation in Pakistan, where the "struggle ... complements the fight for the liberation of Afghanistan from American occupation." Likewise, Zawahiri explained that al-Qaeda licensed jihadist activity in the Arabian Peninsula because the governments there were "proxies of America." In Somalia, the fight against the country's internationally recognized government was necessary because it was the "spearhead of the Crusader occupation."[12]

But Zawahiri went further, justifying jihad in three countries where American influence seemed to be on the wane. In Iraq, the jihadists continued to fight because their aim was "to liberate the Sunni territories from the Safavid (Shiite) successors of America." By this Zawahiri meant that he expected Iran to supplant America in the wake of the U.S. withdrawal, a realistic assessment. Al-Qaeda's leader conceded that the American presence was "negligible and obscure" in Algeria but said that jihad was still necessary to weaken the government and spread jihadist "influence in the Islamic Maghreb, the West African coastal region, and the countries of the southern Sahara." Despite America's diminishing role in, or outright absence from, these areas, Zawahiri surmised that the "prospect of a conflict with America and its allies" in these regions was becoming "evident."[13]

Then there was Syria. Zawahiri did not even pretend that the rebellion against Assad was tied to a larger war against America. Instead, he explained that "the rulers of Syria do not allow the mere existence of any Islamic entity, let alone a jihadist one, and their bloody history of trying to uproot Islam is a well-known fact."[14]

The military aspects of the 2013 guidelines were very different from the Western notion of al-Qaeda as a terrorist organization myopically focused on killing civilians in America and Europe. Zawahiri had set forth the rationale for waging attacks and insurgencies in a vast range of countries, some of which lacked any real American presence. Indeed, scholars have long assessed that bin Laden rather than Zawahiri was the primary architect of the far-enemy strategy, particularly given that Zawahiri's early jihadist career involved campaigns against the Egyptian regime.[15] Thus, it is possible that, even at the time, Zawahiri intended this explication of the jihadist battle fronts to subtly move away from a predominant focus on the far enemy.

The propagation work that Zawahiri outlined in the guidelines was just as broadly conceived. Zawahiri wrote that the group's "propagational work . . . aims to create awareness in the Ummah regarding the threat posed by the Crusader onslaught, clarify the true meaning of Tawheed [monotheism] in the sense that the rule and sovereignty belongs to Allah alone, and stress upon the importance of brotherhood based on Islam and the unity of all Muslims lands."[16] Such activities included cultivating a "vanguard" of mujahedin to lead the cause while also "creating awareness within the masses" and inciting the people to revolt against their rulers. This work was intended to "serve as a prelude to the establishment of the Caliphate."[17]

Al-Qaeda took concrete steps to spread its ideology in the wake of the Arab Spring. Within months of the uprisings, groups calling themselves Ansar al-Sharia (supporters of sharia) sprouted in Egypt, Libya, Tunisia, and Yemen.[18] American analysts and policymakers initially treated the groups as local entities, wholly separate from al-Qaeda and its anti-Western jihad because they were ostensibly devoted to providing social services and preaching an austere version of Islam locally. That conclusion relied on both an erroneous understanding of al-Qaeda's objectives and a rather perverse eagerness to discount any connections to al-Qaeda unless regional Islamists explicitly employed that name. This eagerness is difficult to explain as anything but a political preference on the part of analysts, given al-Qaeda's past propensity to employ front groups. Indeed, al-Qaeda's own strategic doctrine, set forth in various messages and in its 2013 guidelines, made dawa a strategic priority. And al-Qaeda was not naive enough to believe that evangelists calling themselves al-Qaeda would be met with open arms anywhere. The ties between the various Ansar al-Sharia chapters and al-Qaeda should have been somewhat obvious, not least because al-Qaeda veterans led each of these organizations.

We now turn to how the jihadist movement evolved in the post-revolution environments of Egypt, Libya, and Tunisia as well as in revolutionary Syria. In each country, jihadists engaged in both military and propagational work.

Post-Mubarak Egypt

The fall of Hosni Mubarak in Egypt presented jihadists an opportunity they had long yearned for. Egypt is the most populous Arab country and the native land of many of the movement's leading figures, including Zawahiri. But the country had always been inhospitable to al-Qaeda. As jihadist groups gained strength, the Egyptian government would typically clamp down on them, often with devastating effect.

THE BITTER HARVEST

From 1980 through the start of the Arab Spring, Egyptian jihadists conducted sporadic attacks, some of them significant. But Egyptian society was always more amenable to the Muslim Brotherhood's more pragmatic approach than to the outright terrorism of Ayman al-Zawahiri and other jihadists. Zawahiri often complained about the Brotherhood's compromising ways.

Following Khalid Islambouli's assassination of Anwar Sadat in 1981, Sadat's successor, Hosni Mubarak, cracked down on the networks with which Islambouli was associated. Zawahiri even spent a short time in an Egyptian prison after Sadat's death.[19] The future al-Qaeda emir and his band of revolutionaries dreamed of an uprising, but Zawahiri's Egyptian Islamic Jihad (EIJ) could not muster anything close to a full-fledged rebellion in the 1980s. Nor could Gama'a al-Islamiyya. Both EIJ and Gama'a, as well as their splinter groups, had difficulty operating in the years following Sadat's assassination. An Egyptian jihadist diaspora formed, with extremists relocating first to Afghanistan and Pakistan, then eventually to other locales, including Albania, Azerbaijan, Bosnia, Iran, Sudan, and Yemen.

Zawahiri first met bin Laden in South Asia in the 1980s (see chapter 3). Their partnership blossomed during al-Qaeda's period in Sudan. At the time, Sudan was an ideal staging ground for international conspiracies, especially those aimed at Egyptian interests. A June 1995 assassination attempt against Mubarak had its roots in Sudan, while the November 1995 bombing of the Egyptian embassy in Islamabad killed more than a dozen people. But this violence failed to translate into broader success. Zawahiri and his comrades were wanted men. Foreign security services were well aware of their ongoing attempts to orchestrate attacks.

Ayman al-Zawahiri and his younger brother Mohammed had been partners in jihad since their adolescent years, when they formed their first militant cell.[20] Omar Azzam, a second cousin of Ayman and Mohammed, later told journalist Lawrence Wright that the brothers had been committed to their radical path from a young age. "Bin Laden had a turning point in his life," Azzam told Wright, "but Ayman and his brother Mohammed were like people in school moving naturally from one grade to another. You cannot say those boys were naughty guys or playboys, then turned one hundred and eighty degrees. To be honest, if Ayman and Mohammed repeated their lives, they would live them the same way."[21]

The pair continued their work as EIJ leaders after they grew into adults, with Ayman at the group's helm. Meanwhile, the junior Zawahiri traveled the world, ostensibly working for the World Islamic Relief Organization, a Saudi-run charity.[22] In reality, he was Ayman's chief operator, establishing connections in Bosnia, Indonesia, Malawi, Sudan, and Yemen. In the summer of 1998 American and Albanian authorities broke up a terrorist cell that had the U.S. Embassy in Tirana, Albania, in its crosshairs. Authorities discovered that the cell answered to Mohammed al-Zawahiri.[23] At some point in the next two years Mohammed al-Zawahiri was detained in the United Arab Emirates and quietly rendered back to Egypt, although there are conflicting accounts of this incident.[24] Another jihadist who worked with the Zawahiri brothers, Ahmed Salama Mabrouk, suffered a similar fate. In July 1998 the CIA and local authorities captured Mabrouk in Azerbaijan.[25] Mabrouk's laptop, which contained contact information for militants around the globe, was an invaluable source of intelligence. Like Mohammed al-Zawahiri, Mabrouk disappeared into Egypt's prisons, along with dozens of other EIJ and Gama'a members.

Egyptian jihadists were hounded abroad and marginalized into irrelevance in their own country. But the Arab Spring suddenly offered the chance to change that dynamic. Crucially, al-Qaeda did not declare jihad against the Islamist politician Mohamed Morsi or his short-lived government after they were elected to power, despite the vitriol Zawahiri had directed at the Muslim Brotherhood.

THE BUMPER CROP: THE MORSI YEARS

Morsi's election was a dramatic break from modern Egyptian politics. Mubarak had ruled Egypt with an iron fist after Sadat's assassination. Mubarak was ultimately toppled by widespread protests in February 2011. Nearly a year and a half later, in June 2012, Morsi won Egypt's first openly contested presidential election. Morsi's rise to power, and the similar electoral triumph of an Islamist party in Tunisia, convinced many observers that al-Qaeda's reason for existence had been invalidated. But the Brotherhood's electoral viability did not turn jihadism into a relic of an earlier era. Al-Qaeda and like-minded jihadists engaged in crucial organizational learning. They would adjust to new political realities.

Instead of fighting the Brotherhood's ascent, al-Qaeda took advantage of Egypt's newly open social and political space. Egypt became a place where jihadists could proselytize without much fear of the government stopping them. Jihadists and their allies set up organizations to spread their ideology, including Ansar al-Sharia Egypt, which advocated for hardline Islamic law. Ahmed Ashush, a former EIJ member who had joined the jihad in Afghanistan and remained openly loyal to al-Qaeda, headed the group.[26] Ansar al-Sharia Egypt held rallies and events where two of the star speakers were none other than Mohammed al-Zawahiri and Ahmed Salama Mabrouk. Like Ashush, both of them were freed after Mubarak's government collapsed. Other newly released EIJ and Gama'a members joined them in their extremist roadshow.

Ansar al-Sharia's leading figures criticized Morsi for failing to establish sharia-based governance but did not call for his ouster or threaten him. Zawahiri adopted a conciliatory tone, biting his tongue throughout several messages he released that focused on Egypt. Al-Qaeda's lenient policy with respect to the Brotherhood and other Islamists proved controversial in jihadist circles. ISIS later issued a blistering attack on Zawahiri and al-Qaeda not only for calling for "greater cooperation between themselves and the Ikhwan [Muslim Brotherhood]" but also for criticizing "those who pronounced takfir [excommunication] upon the Ikhwan."[27]

The al-Qaeda leader defended his leniency with respect to the Brotherhood. In an early 2017 video he explained that Morsi was different from Mubarak because he "gave plenty of room for freedom of expression," which the "majority of the mujahedin decided" to exploit in order to spread their message. Zawahiri explained that this approach produced "blessed outcomes," including the promotion of "*dawa*, monotheism, and jihad all over Egypt and Tunisia." Zawahiri noted that jihadist sheikhs "held conferences and mobilized protests in downtown Cairo and in Tahrir Square." During these appearances, the sheikhs called "for sharia rule" and jihad—to be waged *elsewhere*, naturally—while "supporting al-Qaeda" and confronting the "falsifications" of America. Zawahiri argued that this "brief opportunity" could not be squandered.[28] The al-Qaeda video accompanying Zawahiri's argument included multiple scenes of Ashush and Mohammed al-Zawahiri preaching on the streets and advocating on al-Qaeda's behalf in their television appearances.

Other examples of this new space for jihadist *dawa* were apparent. At one event outside the French Embassy in Cairo, Mohammed al-Zawahiri's men hung banners of his older brother and bin Laden as they decried France's intervention in Mali, something that no previous or subsequent Egyptian government would have allowed.[29] That rally was a minor event compared to the events of September 11, 2012.

9/11/12: THE EMBASSY RIOT

Initial reports said the crowd at the U.S. Embassy in Cairo was incensed over the trailer for an obscure, low-budget anti-Islam video titled *Innocence of Muslims*.[30] While some were undoubtedly riled up over the video, which had made its way into Egypt's news cycle, it hardly accounts for what transpired. The protest, conspicuously held on the anniversary of the 9/11 hijackings, might better be described as a pro-al-Qaeda riot. Chants of "Obama, Obama, we are all Osama!" rang out as pro-al-Qaeda graffiti was spray-painted on the embassy's walls and on nearby buildings. Protesters stormed the embassy's courtyard, tearing the stars and stripes down. In its place, they hoisted a black banner commonly used by al-Qaeda and similar groups.[31]

Mohammad al-Zawahiri and his newly freed comrades orchestrated the embassy riot.[32] Formerly imprisoned EIJ and Gama'a jihadists called for the protest in the name of Sheikh Omar Abdel Rahman, the imprisoned "Blind Sheikh." The day before the rally Mohammed al-Zawahiri tweeted about the *Innocence of Muslims* video in order to inspire anger, calling on the "sons" of jihad to rally in "support for the Prophet." Also on September 10, 2012, Ayman al-Zawahiri released a video calling on Muslims to exact revenge for the death of Abu Yahya al-Libi, a senior al-Qaeda figure killed in an American drone strike. The al-Qaeda head argued that his group had not been defeated despite the loss of numerous leaders and that its "message has spread amongst our Muslim Ummah, which received it with acceptance and responded to it."[33] The embassy protest that Ayman's younger brother helped plan in Cairo the following day seemed to prove the al-Qaeda emir's argument that in Morsi's Egypt the group was able to propagate its ideology and spur new followers to action.

The U.S. government thought that Morsi's initial response to the protest was unacceptably tepid. President Obama, who was reportedly "fed up" with his Egyptian counterpart, called the following day to demand a "show of support."[34] The White House released a terse statement summarizing the September 12, 2012, call, twice using the word *underscored* to recount Obama's message that Egypt had made commitments to "secur[e] U.S. diplomatic facilities and personnel" in its territory. The president added that "he rejects efforts to denigrate Islam, but underscored that there is never any justification for violence against innocents and acts that endanger American personnel and facilities."[35] In reply, Morsi said Egypt "would honor its obligation to ensure the safety of American personnel."[36]

In the months that followed, Egypt's interior ministry re-arrested some of the jihadists who had once again become active in the country. But Morsi's Egypt remained a permissive environment. Weeks after the embassy protest, a small jihadist media shop released a video celebrating al-Qaeda's role in the riot.[37] The video included footage of Mohammed al-Zawahiri and several other well-known al-Qaeda-linked men inciting the crowd outside the embassy. One of them was Rifa'i Ahmad Taha, a Gama'a leader and signatory of al-Qaeda's February 1998 fatwa establishing an Islamic Front for Jihad against Jews and Crusaders. Although Taha had reportedly disavowed his participation in al-Qaeda's Islamic Front after the fatwa was published, there is no uncertainty concerning his ties to the parent organization. In September 2000 Al Jazeera aired footage of Taha speaking at an al-Qaeda-hosted event in which he and others called for Sheikh Omar's release. Bin Laden and Ayman al-Zawahiri flanked Taha as he spoke about the Egyptian cleric, and Zawahiri then threatened the United States. In October 2000 Taha released a statement lauding the USS *Cole* bombing and threatening

additional attacks on American ships. Morsi's government let Taha operate freely even after al-Qaeda boasted of his role in the embassy riot.

Although some Gama'a figures imprisoned under Mubarak renounced
al-Qaeda, Taha was not among them. Taha fled Egypt after Morsi's 2013
ouster. He made his way to Turkey, then to Syria. Prior to his death in an
American drone strike in Idlib, Taha had been involved in mediation efforts
intended to reconcile cantankerous insurgents within Ahrar al-Sham and
the al-Nusra Front, which was al-Qaeda's official branch in Syria at the
time.[38] In its announcement of Taha's death, U.S. Central Command
described him as a "core" al-Qaeda member.[39] Meanwhile, Ayman al-
Zawahiri remembered Taha as a "lifetime friend" and "brother," saying
that to eulogize him was like "eulogizing a part of my soul."[40]

THE MILITARY DIMENSION

Al-Qaeda's public preaching and protest campaign was just one element
of its evolving strategy for post-Mubarak Egypt. Another EIJ veteran who
had been imprisoned under Mubarak, Muhammad Jamal Abd al-Rahim
Ahmad al-Kashif, began building his own al-Qaeda-linked group, which
American officials came to refer to as the "Muhammad Jamal Network"
as they monitored the operative's training camps in Libya.[41] Jamal had
first received explosives training in al-Qaeda's Afghanistan-based camps
in the late 1980s and served as one of EIJ's most senior military commanders. The United Nations noted that Mubarak's government had
arrested and released Jamal "multiple times" over the years. In 2011 he
was released again.[42]

Jamal was another of the imprisoned EIJ and Gama'a members who
refused to renounce al-Qaeda. After Jamal was freed, Mohammed al-
Zawahiri put him in contact with his older brother, Ayman. American
officials told the Wall Street Journal that Jamal petitioned Ayman al-Zawahiri,
"to whom he has long ties, for permission to launch an al-Qaeda affiliate
and has secured financing from al-Qaeda's Yemeni wing."[43] AQAP provided
key support to Jamal and his men.[44] In his letters to Ayman al-Zawahiri,
Jamal discussed his ambitious designs, saying he had formed "groups for
us inside Sinai" and that he needed more funds for "heavy weapons like
mortars and Grad Missiles."[45] The fighters and weapons were part of
an international plan spanning from Egypt west into Libya.[46] Jamal's

operatives are suspected of taking part in the September 11, 2012, Benghazi attack. Some of them also set up the "Nasr City cell" that Jamal headed, which was accused of planning attacks in Egypt. Although members of the cell were initially accused of plotting to kill Morsi, that charge was later dropped. Instead it appears they had planned to kill Egyptian security officials who had held onto their jobs after Mubarak's ouster. In November 2012 the Egyptian government arrested Jamal. He and his comrades were convicted of various terrorism-related charges. They did not hide their al-Qaeda loyalty during the trial, even holding up pictures of bin Laden inside the courtroom.[47]

At the same time, various al-Qaeda-linked organizations sprouted in the Sinai Peninsula. Muhammad Jamal's network established camps in the Sinai, as did Ansar Bayt al-Maqdis (ABM), which later joined ISIS and became known as Wilayat Sinai. Other militant groups that took root in the Sinai include al-Qaeda in the Sinai Peninsula, Ansar al-Jihad, and the Mujahedin Shura Council in the Environs of Jerusalem. Some of these organizations garnered attention when they were founded because of their ties to larger networks. For example, al-Qaeda in the Sinai Peninsula was headed by Osama bin Laden's former physician, Ramzi Mowafi.[48]

Most of these organizations melted away over time. A noteworthy exception was ABM, which claimed numerous attacks beginning in mid-2011. The group was originally established to fight against Israel rather than against Morsi's government. While there were sporadic clashes between ABM and Egyptian security services in the first two years of the group's existence, its operations mainly focused on targets associated with Israel. One particularly high-profile attack occurred in August 2011, when ABM fighters carried out a cross-border raid on a bus traveling on the Israeli side of the border with Egypt in Eilat. Eight Israelis, including a soldier and a police officer, were killed, along with five Egyptian soldiers. Ayman al-Zawahiri praised the operation, claiming that it exposed the Egyptian military's reliance on the Israelis.[49]

ABM repeatedly bombed gas pipelines running into Israel and launched rockets across the border. Al-Qaeda used its media arms to disseminate the group's propaganda and attack claims. In return, ABM packed its videos with footage of bin Laden, Zawahiri, and other al-Qaeda leaders. ABM's initial leadership was directly tied to Zawahiri through various jihadists who had worked for the al-Qaeda emir since the days he led EIJ. But a series of counterterrorism raids removed many al-Qaeda loyalists from ABM's top tiers, paving the way for the group's eventual defection to ISIS.

ISIS dedicated considerable time and effort to procuring ABM's loyalty. In late 2013 Abu Bakr al-Baghdadi obtained an oath of *bayah* from a small Sinai-based jihadist group known as al-Muhajirun wal-Ansar. The Egyptian daily newspaper *Al-Misri Al-Yawm* reported that upon being captured, al-Muhajirun wal-Ansar founder Adil Ibrahim told authorities that ISIS had promised him $10,000 for his *bayah* pledge. *Al-Misri Al-Yawm* speculated that larger Sinai-based jihadist organizations may have rejected similar offers.[50]

ISIS remained persistent in trying to secure *bayah* from ABM and other Sinai jihadists. The Kuwaiti newspaper *Al-Shahid* reported in September 2014 that ISIS had dispatched Musa'id Abu Qatmah to the peninsula, where he set about trying to win oaths of loyalty.[51] ABM's November 10, 2014, oath of allegiance wasn't the first time jihadists publicly claimed that ABM had pledged fealty to ISIS. Indeed, ABM itself made conflicting statements on this point, which reflected internal jostling between pro-ISIS factions and others that were either loyal to al-Qaeda or else simply unwilling to throw in with the upstart jihadist network. The pro-ISIS factions likely tried to use the group's propaganda apparatus to set a new course for their organization. For example, in June 2014 a Twitter account believed to be associated with ABM posted a message saying that the group had joined ISIS. But ABM swiftly released another statement saying it had no official Twitter feed, thus nullifying the alleged oath.

A similar sequence of events occurred on November 3, a week before ABM's actual oath. A statement pledging loyalty to Baghdadi went out in ABM's name, but within hours ABM denied the statement's validity and scolded the media, telling them to "check the accuracy of their sources and to stick to ABM's official statements."[52] But ABM again declared its allegiance to ISIS on November 10, 2014, this time in an audio message.[53] Unlike the previous public oaths, no subsequent statement was released to walk back the announcement. The oath to ISIS was nonetheless deeply divisive within ABM. The faction that defected to ISIS took on the new name Wilayat Sinai.

In July 2013 the Egyptian military overthrew Morsi and his Ikhwan government in a coup, installing Abdel Fattah el-Sisi as the new president. The jihadists' window of opportunity to spread their message in the open proved to be short-lived, just as Zawahiri had warned. Wilayat Sinai turned its guns on Sisi's forces, sparking a low-grade insurgency in the peninsula. ISIS cells have frequently attacked Coptic and other churches in Egypt's mainland. On November 24, 2017, a large bomb rocked the Al-Rawda mosque, which was associated with Sufis, during Friday prayers.[54] Gunmen then shot congregants as they fled. At least 305 people were killed and more than 100 wounded. The slaughter was typical of the carnage associated with ISIS's provinces, all of which have declared it permissible to kill Sufis for their alleged heresies. Jund al-Islam, an al-Qaeda-linked group in the Sinai, quickly distanced itself from the massacre, declaring it to be a "great sin and transgression to violate the sanctities of Muslims."[55]

Al-Qaeda wanted to use Egypt's post-uprising vacuum to quietly build support for its cause. In contrast, ISIS wanted to shock people into joining its ranks or terrorize them into submission. Ironically, al-Qaeda's strategy in Egypt might have created a local jihadist base that its bloodthirsty rival could eventually exploit. Either way, Sisi's regime does not permit violent ideologues to storm embassies or preach jihad on television. Those days came to an end when Morsi vanished into an Egyptian prison.

Post–Arab Spring Libya

The Libyan state marshaled greater violence than did Mubarak in attempting to crush the local manifestation of the Arab Spring. As the Libyan people rose up, Muammar al-Qaddafi blamed al-Qaeda for the rapidly expanding protests against him. Qaddafi claimed that his dictatorship was the only thing "stopping al-Qaeda from flourishing" in the country.[56] The dictator was deliberately mischaracterizing his opposition. Al-Qaeda did not start the Libyan uprising nor were jihadists the only ones who took up arms against him. Still, many observers were too quick to dismiss al-Qaeda's role out of hand, downplaying the extent of jihadists' footprint in North Africa.

THE UNITED STATES' DECISION TO INTERVENE MILITARILY

The Obama administration was initially skeptical of military intervention in Libya when Qaddafi began to crack down on the uprising. Some of Qaddafi's more outlandish statements include exhorting his loyalists to cleanse the streets of "the greasy rats" who opposed him and praising China's Tiananmen Square massacre.

At the start of the weekend of March 12–13, Defense Secretary Robert Gates—who was outspoken about his opposition to military action in Libya—"spoke for the dominant view within the administration" when he publicly voiced doubts about intervening against Qaddafi.[57] Christopher Chivvis, an author and analyst specializing in national security and foreign policy issues, explains that at the time two major arguments existed within the administration for military intervention. The first was humanitarian: the concern that, if he wasn't stopped, Qaddafi would slaughter Libyan citizens. The second argument related to the Arab Spring uprisings and the fact that "decisive support for the revolution would vividly demonstrate that the United States supported the uprisings across the region and could thereby deter other regional leaders from crushing legitimate civilian protests by force."[58] Although Chivvis does not mention it, another factor that seemingly drove the view that the uprisings were in the U.S. interest was the fight against al-Qaeda and affiliated movements. As we have shown, early in the Arab Spring U.S. analysts overwhelmingly believed that the revolutionary events were devastating for al-Qaeda and other jihadist groups.

Although the arguments for intervention were not persuasive to most of the administration's decisionmakers as the weekend of March 12–13 began, the administration's thinking rapidly reversed in favor of military action. A couple of changes drove this reversal. One was rapid advances made by Qaddafi's forces as they succeeded in "pushing rebels out of the oil port of Ras Lanuf on March 11 and crushing the uprising in Zawiyah."[59] Having secured their hold over both Ras Lanuf and Zawiyah, Qaddafi's forces marched on Benghazi, which was the opposition National Transitional Council's base of operations. These Qaddafi victories resulted in a second change: Alarmed by developments, the Arab League issued a statement asking the UN Security Council to immediately impose a no-fly zone over Libya to protect civilians. Chivvis writes that the Arab League vote "was a critical step on the road toward intervention."[60] The combination of Qaddafi's advances and the Arab League vote swung the administration's preferences toward military action.

America then pushed for a stronger Security Council resolution, and its passage paved the way for NATO's intervention. It didn't take long for

Qaddafi to fall and ultimately meet his gruesome end. The capital of Tripoli fell into rebel hands in August 2011, and Qaddafi was found by rebels, beaten, and shot to death on October 20.

The intervention remained widely regarded as a success for years. In *Foreign Affairs*, Ivo Daalder and James Stavridis described the operation as a "model intervention." They elaborated that "the alliance responded rapidly to a deteriorating situation that threatened hundreds of thousands of civilians rebelling against an oppressive regime. It succeeded in protecting those civilians and, ultimately, in providing the time and space necessary for local forces to overthrow Muammar al-Qaddafi."[61] Oliver Miles, the former British ambassador to Libya, described the intervention as "a great success," stating that although there were many concerns in Britain about the Libya war at the outset, "I think most people are convinced, now, that it was good and the result is good."[62]

In viewing the intervention as a success, these voices were generally dismissive of the role played by jihadists or of militants' ability to exploit the aftermath. American officials told the *Los Angeles Times* in March 2011 that "the U.S. intelligence community has found no organized presence of al-Qaeda or its allies among the Libyan opposition."[63] Stavridis, then NATO's supreme allied commander for Europe and head of U.S. European Command, said the same month that there were only "flickers" of al-Qaeda involvement, amounting to just a "relative smattering of bad guys in Libya."[64] Noman Benotman, a former member of the al-Qaeda-linked Libyan Islamic Fighting Group, told the press that the rebels were moderates. "Who is behind the revolution? It's not the Islamists or the jihadists," Benotman said. "It's ordinary people, moderates, liberals, lawyers and writers."[65] But, as we will show, this wasn't entirely the case.

AL-QAEDA'S DESIGNS ON LIBYA

Meanwhile, in Pakistan, bin Laden and his lieutenants were already plotting to capitalize on Qaddafi's misfortunes. The revolutionaries came from all strata of Libya's fractured society, but this jihadist inner circle assessed that al-Qaeda's men were present from the very beginning.

"The changes that have taken place in the Arab region are enormous," Atiyah Abd al-Rahman, bin Laden's right-hand man, wrote to his boss in April 2011 as Libya plunged into civil war. "Take Libya as an example. The last thing we have heard from the brothers in Libya is that they have started to arrange their affairs. They are engaging in activities and they have a role there, praise God." Atiyah noted that he was already corresponding with 'Urwah al-Libi, a Libyan al-Qaeda veteran who had recently returned to his home country after being freed from some form of arrest in Iran. "We are in contact with him on the net," Atiyah wrote, describing 'Urwah as "an important brother for our field work" and "an outstanding combatant," whom he anticipated would play "a role in Libya."[66]

Not long after Atiyah's letter was written, 'Urwah died in a shootout with Qaddafi's forces, an event that itself undercut claims about al-Qaeda's absence from the conflict.[67] Although 'Urwah was gone, he had already paved the way for other al-Qaeda operatives to relocate to Libya. One was Abu Anas al-Libi, a veteran bin Laden loyalist. Wanted for his role in the 1998 U.S. Embassy bombings in Kenya and Tanzania, Abu Anas was captured during an American raid in Tripoli more than two years after his comrade 'Urwah's demise.

Atiyah was bullish about al-Qaeda's prospects in Libya for other reasons. In his view, the environment had been favorable even before the country's crisis. "There has been an active jihadist Islamic renaissance underway in Eastern Libya (Benghazi, Derna, Bayda and that area) for some time, just waiting for this kind of opportunity," Atiyah wrote. "We think the brothers' activities, their names, and their 'recordings' will start to show up soon."[68] The regime's recent release of some Libyan Islamic Fighting Group (LIFG) "brothers" and others from Qaddafi's jails, including the notorious Abu Salim prison in Tripoli, was deemed especially encouraging.

Less than two years earlier, in September 2009, some LIFG figures had prominently revised their ideology in a lengthy treatise.[69] The imprisoned jihadists had seemingly rejected al-Qaeda's ideology and renounced efforts to overthrow Qaddafi. While this development was widely interpreted as a blow to al-Qaeda, in reality it had only a limited effect. Some senior LIFG personnel, such as Atiyah and his colleague Abu Yahya al-Libi, had already been integrated into al-Qaeda's management team. The treatise was also nonbinding, and many of LIFG's men quickly took up armed struggle against Qaddafi as soon as they had the opportunity to do so in 2011. Indeed, LIFG veterans who had previously joined al-Qaeda were among the first jihadists to join the fight.

One of these LIFG veterans was Sufian Ben Qumu, an ex-Guantánamo detainee who was transferred to Libyan custody before being released in 2010. By early 2011 Ben Qumu had been identified as a key trainer for anti-Qaddafi rebels in Derna. Ben Qumu's leadership in the uprising came at the same time Western officials and analysts were claiming al-Qaeda had little to no presence in the Libyan opposition.[70] While Qaddafi certainly exaggerated al-Qaeda's role in the Libyan revolt, his regime had correctly pointed to Ben Qumu's role in the rebellion, an assertion some commentators dismissed as "not credible."[71] Ben Qumu wasn't the only LIFG veteran who joined the campaign against Qaddafi. Two other former LIFG leaders, Abdel-Hakim al-Hasidi and Salim Derby, established the Abu Salim Martyrs Brigade (ASMB), which fought against the Libyan dictator's forces.[72]

Atiyah Abd al-Rahman and bin Laden weren't the only jihadists convinced of Libya's potential. In February 2011 al-Qaeda in the Islamic Maghreb (AQIM) issued a statement strongly supporting the insurgents. "We were pained by the carnage and the cowardly massacres carried out by the killer of innocents Qaddafi against our people and our unarmed Muslim brothers who only came to lift his oppression, his disbelief, his tyranny and his might," AQIM announced. The al-Qaeda branch added that its men "only came out to defend you [the Libyan people] against these despots who usurped your rights, plundered your wealth, and prevented you from having the minimum requirements of a dignified life and the simplest meanings of freedom and human dignity."[73]

AQIM publicly endorsed the rebels without claiming a single attack against Qaddafi's men. This stance misled many analysts into concluding that AQIM was a nonfactor in the fighting. In reality, AQIM clandestinely backed various groups in Libya and was careful not to reveal its hand. The United States also occasionally launched airstrikes against AQIM leaders, thus exposing the group's unannounced presence on the Libyan battlefield.

Years later AQIM publicly explained its strategy in Libya. The seventh issue of AQAP's *al-Masra* newsletter, published in March 2016, included an interview with senior AQIM leader Abu Abd-al-Iylah Ahmad. Ahmad obfuscated when asked whether AQIM had an official presence in Libya, portraying AQIM as an extension of the Libyan people. At the time of the interview, French special forces were embedded alongside the nationalist general Khalifa Haftar's men. Ahmad stated that AQIM would back the

Libyans against the French, whom he accused of "violating the sanctity of Libya."[74]

According to Ahmad, AQIM was not focused on collecting oaths of *bayah* and thus was not trying to establish a formal Libyan presence. Instead AQIM concentrated its efforts on rallying the people against foreign aggression. Ahmad framed AQIM's war as part of a long tradition dating back to Omar al-Mukhtar, who resisted Italian forces in Libya in the early twentieth century. This icon of an earlier era became a consistent theme in AQIM's propaganda as the group portrayed its men as the progeny of Omar al-Mukhtar.

In a key passage of his *al-Masra* interview, Ahmad revealed who AQIM's specific battlefield partners in Libya were: the Ansar al-Sharia groups and ASMB. One-time LIFG members played leading roles in both organizations. From AQIM's perspective, Ahmad explained, these groups were all fighting for the "establishment of sharia," so there was no disconnect between AQIM's goals and theirs.

An unclassified report published in August 2012 highlighted al-Qaeda's strategy for building up its cadres in Libya. The report, *Al-Qaeda in Libya: A Profile*, was prepared by the Library of Congress's federal research division under an agreement with the Defense Department's Combating Terrorism Technical Support Office. According to the document, al-Qaeda's senior leadership (AQSL) in Pakistan directly oversaw the new effort in North Africa. AQSL "issued strategic guidance to followers in Libya and elsewhere to take advantage of the Libyan rebellion," the report stated, noting that these leaders ordered followers to "gather weapons," "establish training camps," "build a network in secret," "establish an Islamic state," and "institute sharia" in Libya.[75] Other information to which the authors did not have access confirmed this analysis: As files recovered from bin Laden's compound revealed, the organization had discussed how to exploit the Libyan turmoil in early 2011.

"AQSL in Pakistan dispatched trusted senior operatives as emissaries and leaders who could supervise building a network," the report noted.[76] These veteran jihadists were successful in establishing "a core network in Libya" but still acted clandestinely and refrained from using the al-Qaeda name. One such figure was the aforementioned Abu Anas al-Libi, whom the report identified as the "builder of al-Qaeda's network in Libya."[77] Another emissary from al-Qaeda central was Abd al-Baset Azzouz, a lieutenant to

Ayman al-Zawahiri who had worked on al-Qaeda's behalf in Afghanistan, the United Kingdom, and Libya.[78] The State Department would later report that Zawahiri sent Azzouz "to Libya in 2011" in order "to build a fighting force there." Azzouz, who was considered a "key operative capable of training al-Qa'ida recruits in a variety of skills," had "mobilized approximately 200 fighters."[79]

The Library of Congress analysts assessed that al-Qaeda "will likely continue to mask its presence under the umbrella of the Libyan Salafist movement, with which it shares a radical ideology and a general intent to implement sharia in Libya and elsewhere."[80] Many observers of the Libyan scene never internalized this point, even after Abu Abd al-Iylah Ahmad admitted AQIM's game plan.

THE BENGHAZI ATTACK

By now the Benghazi attacks of September 11, 2012, have become infamous. Militants whom the former high-ranking CIA official Michael Morell has described as "Islamic extremists" attacked a diplomatic compound in Benghazi. These extremists then conducted two subsequent attacks on a nearby CIA annex. Morell now acknowledges that these attackers had "connections to al-Qaeda."[81] When the dust settled on September 12, four Americans lay dead, including U.S. Ambassador Christopher Stevens. The attacks and the U.S. government's response became the subject of enormous political controversy. Many members of Congress questioned the U.S. government's response to the attacks. Such questions were amplified by the fact that the Obama administration's initial explanation of the attacks, in particular Ambassador Susan Rice's assertions that the attacks were "violent protests," turned out to be false.[82]

The attacks, in the end, dispelled illusions that al-Qaeda was absent in Libya. In Benghazi, Muhammad al-Zahawi led Ansar al-Sharia, which was at the forefront of the September 11, 2012, attacks. At first Zahawi portrayed himself and his men as local ideologues, not al-Qaeda agents.[83] This ruse was eventually dropped. After Zahawi was killed in late 2014, one of AQAP's top theologians, Harith al-Nadhari, released a glowing eulogy for the fallen Ansar al-Sharia leader. Nadhari explained that Zahawi had personally met with bin Laden in the 1990s and learned from the al-Qaeda founder's methodology.[84] Various al-Qaeda videos, including a eulogy from

Zawahiri, portrayed Zahawi as a martyr for the cause. Moreover, the group's Benghazi and Derna wings eventually dropped any pretense of being separate entities and began releasing their messaging under a single brand.[85] By 2015–2016, Ansar al-Sharia openly relied on al-Qaeda ideologues in its online propaganda and on its radio station.[86]

As the investigation into the September 2012 attacks in Benghazi advanced, it became clear that multiple al-Qaeda-linked groups had been involved. In January 2014 the U.S. Senate Select Committee on Intelligence released its review of the assault, which concluded that "individuals affiliated with terrorist groups, including AQIM, AQAP, Ansar al-Sharia, and the Mohammad Jamal Network, participated in the September 11, 2012, attacks."[87] AQIM and AQAP are both official branches of al-Qaeda's international organization, and their leaders had pledged their loyalty directly to Zawahiri. AQIM and AQAP each enjoyed a safe haven in Libya as early as 2012, but neither advertised their presence in videos or other propaganda.[88] The Muhammad Jamal Network was a nascent al-Qaeda branch in 2011 and, as this chapter has discussed, its leader was loyal to Zawahiri.

Much of the press coverage after the Benghazi attack focused on Ansar al-Sharia, ignoring that three other al-Qaeda groups participated. In November 2014 the UN Security Council finally designated the Ansar al-Sharia groups in Libya and Tunisia as terrorist organizations, explicitly recognizing their al-Qaeda ties. According to the United Nations, the Ansar al-Sharia chapters in Benghazi and Derna were both "associated" with AQIM.[89] They also had operational ties to Ansar al-Sharia in Tunisia, which is discussed in the next section of this chapter. The United Nations revealed that Ansar al-Sharia in Benghazi had been working with Al-Murabitoun, an al-Qaeda group led by Zawahiri loyalist Mokhtar Belmokhtar. Belmokhtar led the January 2013 siege of the In Amenas gas facility in Algeria, in which at least sixty-seven people of various nationalities died. Intelligence provided to the United Nations showed that at least twelve jihadists who participated in the In Amenas operation were trained in Ansar al-Sharia camps in Benghazi.[90]

In the chaos of post-Qaddafi Libya, former Qaddafi-era military official Khalifa Haftar rose to prominence as a militia leader. Haftar had defected from Qaddafi's forces during Libya's ill-fated war in Chad in the 1980s, then during the height of Qaddafi's power he joined the Libyan National Army, a dissident group.[91] At that time anti-Qaddafi agitation appeared hopeless, and Haftar lived in exile in the United States. When the uprising against Qaddafi broke out in 2011, Haftar returned to Libya, hopeful that he could lead the rebel army. Leaders of the National Transitional Council, which was established by anti-Qaddafi forces in Benghazi in February 2011, were suspicious of Haftar for various reasons, including his Qaddafi-era ties, his arrogance, and his apparent authoritarian leanings. They feared he would try to personally dominate a post-Qaddafi government. Thus, after Qaddafi's overthrow, Haftar was overlooked for the position he coveted as the military's chief of staff. Denied power in the new government, Haftar agitated from the outside. His voice found a growing audience due to the country's slide into chaos and the role played by extremist groups like Ansar al-Sharia.

Haftar launched a military campaign in May 2014 that he called Operation Karama (Dignity), which in his words was designed to "eliminate the terrorist movement," first in Benghazi, then in all of Libya.[92] Deteriorating security conditions in Benghazi helped his offensive to gain momentum. Eventually Haftar's forces engaged in a protracted siege of Benghazi, with Haftar gaining the upper hand over time. Ansar al-Sharia eventually folded, as Haftar's siege made it impossible for the organization to continue many of its activities. Its surviving members fought for the Shura Council of Benghazi Revolutionaries and then the Benghazi Defense Brigades.[93] According to the U.S. State Department, AQIM backed both groups in their fight against Haftar.[94] There is strong evidence that AQIM also worked with other groups in Libya, including the Derna Mujahedin Shura Council, a coalition that ASMB and Ansar al-Sharia formed in Derna in late 2014.[95] AQIM has admitted that it previously supported both of these Derna Mujahedin Shura Council constituent groups.[96]

Al-Qaeda's use of front groups in Libya represents an example of continuous learning at an organizational level. The group had adopted this tactic in other theaters to mask its influence and avoid the attention of Western intelligence agencies—going all the way back to the 1990s, when it made sophisticated use of international charity organizations. Al-Qaeda was able to draw on past experiences to refine its approach and adapt its collaboration with front groups to the local context. It should come as no surprise, then, that al-Qaeda adopted a similar approach in Tunisia.

Dawa, *Hisba*, and Jihad: Al-Qaeda's Approach to Tunisia

In addition to the Benghazi attacks, a September 14, 2011, assault on the U.S. Embassy in Tunis badly damaged the building, nearly resulting in its destruction, and American lives could easily have been lost there as well. As in Cairo, demonstrators raised an al-Qaeda-style black banner over the Tunis embassy after pulling down its American flag.[97] Ansar al-Sharia groups were heavily involved in the assault on U.S. embassies in both Benghazi and Tunis. Indeed, Ansar al-Sharia in Tunisia (AST) was the chief organizer of the September 14, 2012, riot.[98]

ORIGINS: THE AL-QAEDA ROOTS RUN DEEP

An al-Qaeda veteran led AST. Abu Iyadh al-Tunisi (born Seifallah ben Hassine) headed that organization after working for various al-Qaeda-related causes. During his exile from Tunisia, Abu Iyadh spent time in Britain, where he associated with the leading al-Qaeda ideologue Abu Qatada al-Filistini. Some jihadist forums described Abu Iyadh as Abu Qatada's "disciple," and one AST member said that Abu Qatada is "probably the most influential" of the theorists who had the group's ear.[99] Abu Iyadh also spent time in Afghanistan and in 2000 was one of the founders of the Tunisian Combatant Group (TCG). According to the United Nations, TCG was created "in coordination with" al-Qaeda: During a meeting in Afghanistan, the group "declared its determination to support" bin Laden.[100]

TCG facilitated the assassination of Northern Alliance leader Ahmad Shah Massoud in Afghanistan just before al-Qaeda executed the 9/11 attacks.[101] Massoud's assassins, two Tunisians pretending to be journalists, had traveled on stolen passports that al-Qaeda's European network had procured.[102] Massoud's assassination was an integral part of al-Qaeda's 9/11 plot. Massoud was a key Northern Alliance leader opposed to the Taliban, and al-Qaeda knew that the United States would likely turn to him in the aftermath of a spectacular terrorist plot hatched on Afghan soil. Massoud's death eliminated an American ally from the battlefield before the fight even began.

Abu Iyadh's TCG also sought to conduct terrorist attacks in Europe. In early 2001 authorities discovered that TCG was plotting to strike the U.S.

Embassy in Rome. Italian investigators identified the chief planner as Sami Ben Khemais Essid, who had "spent two years in Afghanistan and trained as a recruiter for al-Qaeda," according to the U.S. State Department. Italian authorities, according to the State Department report, concluded that Essid "headed al-Qaeda operations in Italy" and "owned a firm that was a front for his recruitment activity and terrorist-attack planning."[103] Essid and another TCG/al-Qaeda operative, Mehdi Kammoun, were arrested in Italy and sentenced to several years in prison.[104]

Abu Iyadh was arrested in Turkey in 2003, and Turkish authorities extradited him to Tunisia. Ben Ali's regime sentenced him to forty-three years of imprisonment. The Italian government deported Essid and Kammoun to Tunisia, where they were imprisoned along with Abu Iyadh. The Tunisian revolution would drastically change their lives.

THE OPENING: AST'S *DAWA*, *HISBA*, AND JIHAD STRATEGY

After Ben Ali's reign ended, all three men were released from prison, along with dozens of other extremists. Rather than dimming their enthusiasm for violence, prison served as an opportunity for bonds and commitments to deepen and for a new organization to take shape. Prison was where AST was truly born.

Hassan Ben Brik, who would head AST's *dawa* committee, spoke publicly about how critical imprisonment was for the group's later growth, explaining that "we got to know each other in prison, and we began our work from there."[105] As the militants were released and set about establishing and growing AST in post–Ben Ali Tunisia, they adopted an organizational design and strategy that maintained a great deal of ambiguity. There was ambiguity about how centralized AST was: the group was frequently described by commentators as "decentralized," and it was often unclear which actions taken by AST members were dictated or sanctioned by senior leaders.[106] There was ambiguity about AST's connections to al-Qaeda. Although the group proclaimed its admiration for bin Laden, Zawahiri, and other Salafi jihadist figures, it claimed to be organizationally independent. This was good enough, it should be said, to fool most American analysts. There was some ambiguity about AST's relationship to violence. Early on Ben Brik described jihad as "certainly part of our political project" but said that AST has "no interest currently in embarking on violent initiatives, or acts of terrorism."[107]

This ambiguity advanced AST's strategy for Tunisia, which was based around *dawa, hisba* (a concept denoting "forbidding wrong," which for AST entailed the enforcement of religious norms, sometimes through the use of violence within the Tunisian Muslim community), and jihad.[108] Of these, AST's *dawa* was overt, and AST benefited from being able to undertake it legally and openly. In contrast, AST's violence was generally not meant to be attributable to the organization because it could jeopardize the group's ability to engage in *dawa* openly. A structure that disguised the leadership's role allowed the group to engage in violence while denying that it was doing so. The vast majority of violence that AST undertook in Tunisia in its earliest days could be categorized as *hisba*, directed at other Tunisians who were seen as opposing the movement's mores. Targets included liberals, secularists, and civic activists; educators; and security officers. Eventually, though, jihad violence became so pronounced in Tunisia that AST lost its ability to operate openly.

In its *dawa* strategy, AST emphasized visibility. AST made its presence felt in some traditional ways, holding *dawa* events, holding public protests, and dominating physical spaces such as cafés near places of worship. But AST also had some innovative approaches to *dawa*, including provision of social services and becoming an early adopter in the jihadist community in its use of social media.

AST's social services included distribution of food, clothing, and basic supplies and sponsoring convoys that provided medicine. These efforts concentrated on areas that were neglected by the government, such as rural and impoverished areas, and AST also provided emergency humanitarian assistance in the wake of such natural disasters as flooding. Typically AST's provision of social services was accompanied by distribution of religious literature. While AST was apparently constantly engaged in distributing social services, these efforts did not reach the same areas consistently. Even though AST regularly undertook humanitarian work, it is not clear that any communities saw AST as a services provider week after week. This was where AST's savvy use of social media was relevant. Almost immediately after it undertook humanitarian efforts, AST posted information about its latest venture, including photographs, to its Facebook page and other websites. Social media thus served as a force multiplier. Although

AST did not provide consistent services to a single area, its social media activity illustrated a rapid pace of humanitarian assistance and helped the group achieve its goal of visibility.

Three things are worth noting about AST's *dawa* strategy. First is the context in which this work was undertaken. The Tunisian economy was faltering and had in fact worsened since the revolution. The country's youth were particularly hard hit. As Monica Marks, a scholar who has undertaken extensive field research in Tunisia, wrote, "across the ideological spectrum, from leftist communists to jihadi Salafis, young people speak of being neglected and deceived by their political leaders. Significant numbers of Tunisian youth hold college degrees but cannot find employment."[109] It was not just dire economic conditions that produced widespread frustration but also the feeling that the system was unfair and failing. Tunisia had suffered from maldistribution of resources for some time. Under Ben Ali, the coastal cities experienced relatively strong economic growth while cities in the interior and south benefited little.[110] Thus, even before the revolution, "marginalised areas" were the most "significant sources of recruits to the Islamist movement."[111] Wealth maldistribution helped AST win sympathy and recruits to its cause in marginalized areas. Essentially, AST positioned itself as a critic of the status quo writ large and as a champion of those whom the system neglected.

A second aspect was that AST's provision of social services helped it to carve out something of a parallel state within Tunisia, in a small way. For a related example, in the wake of politician Chokri Belaïd's February 2013 assassination, AST mobilized what it called public protection committees in various parts of Tunisia, allegedly to provide security on the ground by patrolling neighborhoods, preventing looting, and making arrests.[112]

A third noteworthy aspect of AST's *dawa* was the likelihood that the group received foreign sponsorship for at least some of its activities.[113] This foreign sponsorship came disproportionately from organizations that were known to support al-Qaeda and its affiliates. For example, pictures, videos, and other information AST posted on Facebook showed that, in at least one case, it received medical supplies from the Kuwaiti charity Revival of Islamic Heritage Society, which in Tunisia is known as the Society for Preservation of Islamic Heritage. The U.S. Treasury Department had designated the Revival of Islamic Heritage Society a terrorist organization in 2008 "for providing financial and material support to al Qaeda and al Qaeda affiliates, including Lashkar e-Tayyiba, Jemaah Islamiyah, and Al-Itihaad al-Islamiya."[114] The literature AST passed out at *dawa* events could be traced to at least three publishing houses in Saudi Arabia: Dar al-Qassem in Riyadh, Dar al-Tarafen in Ta'if, and the Cooperative Office for the Call and Guidance and Education Communities in Dammam. It is likely that AST, which had a significant amount of these publishers' literature, had a direct relationship either with the publishers or with a designated intermediary.

Because AST benefited from being able to undertake *dawa* openly, the group did not want to escalate its violence against the state too quickly. But the organization felt it could engage in *hisba* violence, operating openly even while threatening the Islamists' opponents.

The phenomenon of *hisba* violence in Tunisia can best be described as Salafist vigilantism.[115] It is worth recalling the layers of ambiguity surrounding AST, which produce lack of clarity about the group's connection to all the instances of *hisba* violence. Some of the incidents that follow were almost certainly connected to AST and may have been planned by the group's leaders, while other acts of *hisba* violence were doubtless spontaneous, carried out by Salafists unconnected to AST. Despite this ambiguity, our exploration of Salafist vigilantism as a complete phenomenon provides a picture of the kind of violence that AST and al-Qaeda hoped would become more commonplace alongside the group's *dawa* efforts.

One group that felt particularly targeted was Tunisian women, who saw mounting pressures directed at them. Since its independence, Tunisia had one of the most progressive legal systems in the Arab world with respect to women's rights.[116] Until the 2011 revolution, the Tunisian state viewed "the presence or absence of hijab" as "a key component" distinguishing modernity from tradition.[117] In addition to imposing some legal restrictions on women's ability to wear hijab, the state took pains to associate the hijab with traditions that, while deserving of respect, society would leave behind as it embraced modernity: young women who did not wear hijab were portrayed as central to the country's more enlightened and liberated future.[118] After the revolution many Tunisian women perceived increasing pressures and harassment directed at their manner of dress. Some women consequently changed the way they dressed unwillingly, including donning the hijab as a protective measure.[119]

Tunisia's earliest known post-revolution act of vigilante violence targeted female prostitutes. Although *maisons close* (brothels) have been legal in Tunisia since 1942, in February 2011 a crowd of "several hundred out-raged citizens" gathered near a *maison close* in Tunis on a Friday, the Mus-lim day of prayer, to protest the presence of prostitutes.[120] The protesters came armed with "sticks and torches" but were stopped by the Tunisian military and "a militia of pimps, porters and day laborers."[121] Similar attacks quickly spread, with *maisons close* being set aflame in Kairouan, Medenine, Sfax, and Sousse. Prostitutes were beaten in some attacks.

Other women were physically attacked for lesser affronts to public mor-als. In the working-class Tunis neighborhood of Intilaka, a street vendor scolded journalist Zeineb Rezgui for wearing a sleeveless summer dress, referring to her as a prostitute.[122] As Rezgui recounted, "I tried to talk to him, but all of a sudden he jumped and slapped me hard on my neck. I fell on the ground, he started kicking me. About five other men, also with long beards, some wearing long tunics, joined him. They were kicking and punching me all over my body. The rest of the people were just watching and nobody dared to approach." Similar attacks occurred in Jendouba.[123]

Hisba violence rapidly spread to other sectors of society. One critical battlefield related to free expression. AST and other Salafist groups launched attacks and intimidation campaigns against artists and public intellectuals whose work they thought transgressed the standards appro-priate for an Islamic society. One of the earliest attacks occurred on April 9, 2011. Nouri Bouzid, a film director with outspoken anti-Islamist views, was stabbed in the head by a bearded student who shouted "*Allahu Akbar!*" before delivering the blow. Bouzid survived the attack, which he attributed to his "pro-secular stands and rejection of [Islamist] culture."[124] There were numerous subsequent attacks on art-ists. In June 2011 an art-house cinema in Tunis planned to show a movie about secularism that many Salafists viewed as heretical. In response, "a gang of Salafists forcibly entered," then "sprayed tear gas and roughed up the management."[125]

An even more striking series of incidents occurred in October 2011. The television station Nessma showed *Persepolis*, an animated film that many conservative Muslims find blasphemous because it contains a dream sequence in which God is visually depicted, something anathema to stricter interpretations of Islam. Following the controversy, the head of the station, Nabil Karoui, issued an apology for broadcasting it. Nonetheless, numerous preachers devoted their Friday sermons to denouncing Nessma, after which a mob of about three hundred people attacked its studios and tried to set fire to them.[126] This violence was followed a week later by an assault on Karoui's home by an armed mob of "about a hundred men, some of whom threw Molotov cocktails." About twenty were able to get inside. Karoui's family was home, although he was not, and his family barely managed to escape. In a disturbing footnote, the government's response was to call for "respect for sacred things," and in May 2012 it was Karoui rather than his attackers who ended up being fined by a Tunisian court. He was found responsible for "disturbing public order and attacking moral values" by showing the film.[127]

Salafists also sought to dominate discourse in the civil and religious spheres. There were numerous instances of Salafists showing up in mosques and demonizing the previous imams, accusing them of being collaborators with the old regime. This facilitated the Salafi takeover of around four hundred mosques. Islamic practices regarded as deviant were targeted too. For example, Sufi shrines were burned.[128]

Salafi vigilante violence also extended to non-Islamic faiths. In September 2011 a group of Salafists occupied the Christian basilica in El Kef with the intention of turning it into a mosque.[129] In March 2013 Salafists physically attacked two Italians and two Tunisians in the southeastern coastal town of Zarzis under the erroneous impression that they were evangelizing for the Christian faith.[130]

Education was another contested area. At Manouba University, outrage boiled over into violence after university administrators decided to reaffirm the presidential decree issued in 1981 that prohibited female students from wearing the niqab (face covering) in class. Salafists denounced the ban and demanded an end to mixed-sex education.[131] Salafists briefly took Habib Kazdaghli, the dean of the college of letters, as a hostage. "Salafists are not letting us do our job. Whenever us professors try to apply the university's law, we get physically attacked," said English professor Radhia Jaidi. "The Faculté des Lettres is no longer a safe environment for us to teach in."[132] During the ongoing dispute, a Salafist ripped down the Tunisian flag and replaced it with a black banner reminiscent of al-Qaeda's flag.

Similar to the Nessma case, Dean Kazdaghli found himself prosecuted after this ordeal due to a confrontation he had with two veiled female students in March 2012. He told *Der Spiegel* that they "loudly demanded that they be allowed to attend lectures," and one of them angrily swept the papers on Kazdaghli's desk onto the floor.[133] He and his staff "forcibly removed the two furious women," after which they sued him for assault. The trial, which served as a lightning rod in Tunisia's culture wars, eventually resulted in Kazdaghli being acquitted.

Other Tunisian universities, and even secondary schools, saw similar open confrontation between secularists and Salafists.[134] A group of Salafists broke into a secondary school in Menzel Bouzelfa in April 2013 and physically and verbally assaulted the principal, who had barred entry to a female student wearing niqab. The principal was hospitalized.[135]

Another sphere that Salafi vigilantes attempted to control was that of private vice, with attacks on hotel bars and alcohol vendors. In one representative September 2012 incident, about fifty activists burst into a bar in Sidi Bouzid's Hotel Horchani, where they smashed bottles and chased customers while yelling that drinking is a sin. "A young man who tried to film the raid was beaten by members of the group and taken to an unknown location," Agence France-Presse reported.[136]

A final category of *hisba* violence that is worth mentioning was directed at civil society activists. A harrowing letter that Human Rights Watch sent to Tunisian officials documented these assaults. Rajab Magri, who was part of a group that disrupted the aforementioned Salafi occupation of the basilica in El Kef, told Human Rights Watch that he was targeted by Salafists thereafter, first on Facebook and then in person. In May 2012 a number of Salafi activists ambushed him on an El Kef street. "They started kicking and punching me all over my body, they grabbed me by the hair and started hitting my head on the pavement," he reported. "I was almost unconscious. They were insulting me, calling me a kafir and shouting that they will kill me."[137] Other activists had similar stories.

Unfortunately, the police response was often tepid. Human Rights Watch reported on police inaction following multiple attacks. In Magri's case, police took no action after two assaults against him, and one officer told him they could not arrest one of the attackers because "his emir threatened to set the city on fire if they do." Zeineb Rezgui, the female journalist who was attacked in Tunis, reported a similar explanation for police inaction. An officer said her attackers "threatened him and vowed to burn his house and kill his family if they did anything against him."[138] A Human Rights Watch researcher in Tunis told one of this book's coauthors in 2013 that Tunisian authorities had not taken action to prosecute the perpetrators of numerous assaults that her organization had documented.[139]

In one sign of the security forces' belief that they lacked the upper hand against Salafi vigilantes during this period, Tunisian security forces held a rally in November 2012 denouncing attacks against them. They demanded more equipment as well as the right to use "all means necessary" when confronting physical attacks.

THE TURN TO JIHAD IN TUNISIA

Thus, although Salafi jihadists were able to operate openly during the early years after the revolution, they frequently engaged in acts of violence as well, especially *hisba* violence. But jihadist attacks against the state grew too, ultimately resulting in the government banning AST and other jihadist groups.

The clearest inflection point for the growth in jihadist violence against the state was December 2012, when militants shot and killed Anis Jelassi, an adjutant in the Tunisian National Guard, in the Kasserine governorate.[140] This incident prompted Tunisian authorities to identify, for the first time, a militant group known as Katibat Uqba ibn Nafi, which both Tunisian authorities and the group itself have described as a battalion of AQIM.[141] Jelassi's killing prompted intensified police operations in western Tunisia, particularly around Jebel el-Chaambi. These intensified operations resulted in Tunisian authorities getting into occasional firefights with militants running arms and other items across the border. There were several escalations in violence perpetrated by militants in western Tunisia, including an intensifying use of improvised explosive devices against security forces.[142]

Another escalation was the assassination of Tunisian politicians. On February 6, 2013, gunmen shot and killed secularist politician Chokri Belaïd outside his Tunis home. For more than a year prior to his death, Belaïd had been subjected to a campaign of surveillance and intimidation. Six months after Belaïd's murder, on July 25, secularist politician Mohammed Brahmi was gunned down in Tunis. This second assassination occurred the same week that a jihadist ambush in Jebel el-Chaambi left "eight soldiers dead—five with slit throats."[143] These two bloody incidents, occurring so close together, represented a point of no return. Tunisia banned AST and launched a crackdown on domestic jihadist networks.

After the state's crackdown, jihadist attacks were confined mainly to the western part of Tunisia, near its border with Algeria. But jihadists' desire to kill tourists in urban centers became clear, and by 2015 two major attacks on tourist targets shocked the country. In March 2015 an attack at the Bardo National Museum in Tunis left twenty-one tourists and a Tunisian dead. The Bardo attack was followed three months later by a horrific beach attack in Sousse that killed thirty-eight.

Al-Qaeda's operations in Tunisia are an example of its capacity for discontinuous organizational learning at the strategic level. In neighboring Libya, the state was never put back together after the war against Qaddafi. Thus, in that theater al-Qaeda could draw on its experiences operating in similar conflict zones, like Afghanistan and Iraq. But Tunisia, as bin Laden noted, represented an unprecedented opportunity—with an emphasis on *unprecedented*. Al-Qaeda did not have a clear template, in either the group's past experiences or operational doctrine, for taking advantage of it. Although al-Qaeda operated with few restraints in Sudan for part of the 1990s, al-Qaeda had little experience operating in a Muslim-majority country with a strong civil society that nonetheless provided jihadists the opportunity to openly proselytize. To capitalize on the novel situation, al-Qaeda openly engaged in *dawa* to build a base of support while covertly engaging in a campaign of violence against civil society figures and activists. In doing so, for a time AST and other jihadists obscured their involvement in attacks. This strategy was imperfectly executed: Tunisian jihadists almost certainly triggered a state clampdown before senior-level strategists would have liked.

But in other ways the strategy worked. The success of this approach can be seen in the fact that most Western analysts failed to understand al-Qaeda's approach in Tunisia and indeed believed that al-Qaeda had no presence there. Why? Part of the analytic failure was likely due to an underestimation of al-Qaeda's capacity for discontinuous learning at the strategic level.

Syria

The protest movement that erupted in North Africa quickly spread to Syria, which the Assad family had dominated since the early 1970s. Since he became Syria's president in 2000, many in Washington considered Bashar al-Assad, the heir to the family's autocracy, to be a potential reformer. This assessment was quickly put to the test in the spring of 2011, when the

Syrian people rose up to demand a less repressive government. Assad opted to crush these early protests with overwhelming force.

Faced with the regime's brutality, the protest movement began to morph into an insurgency, with militias and other armed units organizing. Some senior regime officials and military officers defected, with some joining the loosely configured Free Syrian Army (FSA), an antiregime coalition founded in July 2011. The FSA failed to form a cohesive fighting force or establish a unified chain of command. Instead the FSA became a brand that various armed opposition groups adopted, some of which wanted to replace Assad's tyrannical regime with their own Islamist autocracy. As with every other Arab Spring upheaval, al-Qaeda did not foresee or instigate the Syrian uprising. Still, by the end of 2011 the jihadists were already conducting some of the fiercest attacks against Assad's regime.

BLOWBACK

On December 23, 2011, two suicide bombers detonated explosives-laden cars near Assad's state security offices in Damascus.[144] The bombings were the first known suicide attacks in Syria since the protests-turned-rebellion began nine months earlier. The attack killed at least 44 people and wounded more than 160. For years after the explosions, Syrian opposition sources would claim that the bombings were actually a regime false-flag operation, with Assad striking his own facilities.[145] Zero evidence supports this theory. According to the U.S. government's National Counterterrorism Center, it is likely that two female suicide bombers deployed from Iraq were responsible for the strike.[146]

Proponents of the false-flag hypothesis seized on the fact that no group immediately claimed responsibility for the bombings. But just two weeks later, on January 6, 2012, Jabhat al-Nusra (or al-Nusra Front) carried out a third suicide attack in the Syrian capital, killing more than two dozen people.[147] Al-Nusra Front, an arm of al-Qaeda in Iraq (AQI) at the time, would later claim that bombing as well as a series of other suicide operations targeting the Assad regime in Aleppo, Damascus, Hama, and elsewhere throughout 2012.

In a sense, the jihadists were turning against a former ally. At the height of the Iraq War, Bashar al-Assad's regime had hosted a key gateway for foreign fighters seeking to combat American forces. U.S. officials, including Gen. David Petraeus, warned Assad through intermediaries that he risked blowback by helping the extremists: One day the same jihadists transiting through Syrian soil could turn their guns on Assad.[148] The Syrian dictator didn't care. He supported them not out of any love for the jihadists but due to a desire to see the United States defeated in Iraq. This was articulated explicitly by Syrian officials from the earliest days of the U.S. invasion. Addressing the country's parliament in March 2003, the month of the U.S. invasion, Syria's foreign minister, Farouq al-Sharaa, said that "Syria has a national interest in the expulsion of the invaders from Iraq."[149]

Some of Assad's closest comrades oversaw the jihadists' pipeline into Iraq, sometimes interrupting the flow of fighters but never fully stopping it. Syria's role as the primary transit point for militants during the Iraq War, as well as a permissive operating environment for militants stationed there, has been outlined and verified by insider accounts, official U.S. government statements, captured documents and data, and contemporaneous open-source reporting. For example, a June 2005 *Washington Post* article provides the account of thirty-two-year-old trafficker Abu Ibrahim, who had smuggled foreign fighters from Syria into Iraq since as early as 2003. Abu Ibrahim detailed his work for Abu Qaqaa, a Syrian cleric who is best known for his role in recruiting AQI fighters.[150] Describing himself as Abu Qaqaa's "right-hand man," Abu Ibrahim explained the latitude that Abu Qaqaa's operation enjoyed in Syria. According to Abu Ibrahim, mere weeks after the 9/11 attacks, "the group felt bold enough to celebrate in public in Aleppo with a 'festival,' as it was called, featuring video of hand-to-hand combat and training montages of guerrillas leaping from high walls."[151]

Abu Qaqaa was arrested for sponsoring this festival, as it came at a sensitive time, less than a month after the 9/11 attacks, when the United States enjoyed its maximum ability to exert pressure internationally. But even at that charged time, Abu Qaqaa was released in mere hours. Abu Ibrahim recalled that by 2002 these festivals were held biweekly and were even attended by "Syrian security officials and presidential advisors." Abu Qaqaa and his supporters came to possess a level of authority that "rivaled that of the Amn Dawla, or state security."[152] This included leeway to engage in *hisba*-oriented violence and intimidation.

Syria's support for insurgents quickly became apparent to U.S. officials. America invaded Iraq in March 2003, and before the end of that month U.S. Secretary of Defense Donald Rumsfeld had already "accused Syria of allowing military supplies to be transported across its border to Iraq."[153]

A month later, on *Face the Nation,* Rumsfeld described "busloads of people coming out of Syria into [Iraq]."[154] The undersecretary of state for arms control and international security, John Bolton, was even more blunt in his assessment. Testifying before the House International Relations Committee (now known as the House Foreign Affairs Committee) in September 2003, Bolton declared that "we have seen Syria take a series of hostile actions toward coalition forces in Iraq. Syria allowed military equipment to flow into Iraq on the eve of and during the war. Syria permitted volunteers to pass into Iraq to attack and kill our service members during the war, and is still doing so."[155] The same month, the administrator of the Coalition Provisional Authority in Iraq, Amb. L. Paul Bremer, testified to the same committee that "out of the 278 third-country nationals who were captured by coalition forces in Iraq, the 'single largest group are Syrians.'"[156]

Assad's support for anti-U.S. fighters remained extensive enough that the United States felt compelled to take unilateral action. On October 26, 2008, an American special forces team swooped into the town of Sukkariya in eastern Syria. During a brief gun battle, the Americans killed a senior AQI facilitator called Abu Ghadiya.[157] A native of Mosul, Abu Ghadiya had managed the Syrian pipeline since 2004 with the help of his brother and two cousins.[158]

Flashing forward to 2011, just as U.S. officials had warned, the men who relied on AQI's Syrian safe haven eventually sought to unseat their former patron, Assad.

ISIS AND AL-NUSRA FRONT IN THE SYRIA JIHAD

ISIS is the direct descendant of AQI. In addition to seeding Abu Bakr al-Baghdadi's caliphate, AQI was crucial to the rise of the al-Nusra Front. Al-Qaeda's Syrian franchise grew into the strongest Syrian rebel faction outside of ISIS itself.

The founder and former emir of al-Nusra Front—a name that is no longer employed on the Syrian battlefield as of this writing, consistent with militant groups' tendency to morph and take on new names—is a Syrian former Baghdadi lieutenant known as Abu Muhammad al-Julani. In 2011 Baghdadi dispatched Julani and a small cadre to Syria, providing them money, arms, and assistance with facilitation.[159] Julani's nom de guerre means he is originally from the Golan Heights or the area immediately surrounding it. Julani was able to activate what was left of AQI's original facilitation network inside Syria, the same enterprise that Assad once abetted.

At first al-Qaeda's senior leaders sought to hide their hand in the Syrian insurgency, calculating that any group openly operating as an al-Qaeda affiliate or arm of the Islamic State of Iraq would garner unwanted scrutiny. Baghdadi's men complied with this directive, at least through the end of 2012. Julani's al-Nusra Front did not openly flaunt its ties to the Islamic State of Iraq, initially marketing itself as an entirely new militant endeavor. Al-Nusra continued with this independent, Syria-focused branding even as the role of foreign fighters in its ranks and its suicide operations became more prominent.

Al-Qaeda took other steps to conceal its place in the insurgency. Al-Qaeda veterans were embedded in multiple groups, including those with a more Syria-focused, ostensibly nationalist orientation. Chief among these was Ahrar al-Sham ("Free Men of Syria"), which became a prominent player and often fought alongside al-Nusra Front. Some within the U.S. State Department even reportedly met Ahrar al-Sham's leadership and may have considered the organization a possible partner inside Syria, where the United States backed various rebel factions against Assad's regime.[160] At one point a political liaison for Ahrar al-Sham penned op-eds in Western newspapers claiming that his organization was not connected to al-Qaeda in any way. This argument, published in the *Washington Post* and the *Telegraph*, was a lie.[161]

One of Ahrar al-Sham's most senior figures was a jihadist known as Abu Khalid al-Suri. Beyond working with AQSL in Afghanistan prior to 2001, Abu Khalid may have physically delivered surveillance tapes of the World Trade Center and other American landmarks to bin Laden.[162] Abu Khalid's role as bin Laden's courier was first revealed by a Spanish court, which tried him in absentia after the 2004 bombings in Madrid.[163] Despite some disagreements with bin Laden's approach to waging jihad prior to 9/11, Abu Khalid was obviously an al-Qaeda operative. The Spanish court found that he had served al-Qaeda's founder as a trusted courier and that bin Laden's successor relied on him as well. After Abu Khalid was released from one of Assad's prisons in the wake of the uprising, he communicated regularly with Zawahiri, who welcomed Abu Khalid back into the al-Qaeda fold. Abu Khalid was so trusted by Zawahiri that the al-Qaeda head named him the group's chief representative in the Levant, later relying on

Abu Khalid to arbitrate a nasty dispute that was brewing between Abu Muhammad al-Julani and his one-time boss, Abu Bakr al-Baghdadi.[164] Abu Khalid failed in that mission and was ultimately assassinated by an ISIS suicide bomber in February 2014. Zawahiri and al-Qaeda effusively praised Abu Khalid in the years that followed, repeatedly confirming that he was one of Zawahiri's most trusted advisers in Syria.[165] Nor was Abu Khalid the only al-Qaeda veteran embedded in Ahrar al-Sham. The group's secular-nationalist facade concealed al-Qaeda's strategy for gaining prominence within the anti-Assad movement.

In April 2013, after his men had established a beachhead in Syria, Abu Bakr al-Baghdadi announced that his Islamic State of Iraq would add al-Sham (Syria) to its name to tout its presence in the Levant region. This is when the group began to be known by the acronym ISIS.[166] Baghdadi ordered Julani's al-Nusra Front to merge with his group. Julani refused, stating that he owed fealty to Zawahiri directly.[167] In May 2013 Zawahiri issued a public ruling stating that Baghdadi's operation should return to Iraq while Julani would remain in charge of al-Qaeda's arm in Syria. However, Zawahiri also upbraided Julani for revealing the nature of his al-Qaeda associations without permission. This indicates that AQSL wanted the group's presence in Syria to remain a secret.

Initially ISIS didn't even reply to Zawahiri's decision. Months of ensuing jihadist diplomacy couldn't stop Baghdadi and his men from going rogue. Zawahiri lost any measure of control over Baghdadi's operation, and ISIS's animosity for bin Laden's successor only grew. The split between al-Qaeda and ISIS produced the most significant internecine conflict in jihadist history.

In June 2014 ISIS rebranded itself once again. Baghdadi's men swept through much of northern Iraq, capturing Mosul and other significant territory. In declaring that it had reestablished the caliphate (the jihadists' longtime goal), the group said it would henceforth be known simply as the Islamic State. No longer a mere militant group, ISIS now commanded the allegiance of various "provinces" around the world. In the months that followed, ISIS repeatedly stated that all al-Qaeda-affiliated groups had been rendered illegitimate and that their fighters owed their loyalty to Caliph Ibrahim, as Baghdadi now dubbed himself (see chapter 7). The ISIS-al-Qaeda feud would spread from West Africa through Southeast Asia, with ISIS challenging al-Qaeda's traditional dominance over the global jihadist movement. But the tension began in Syria, with Julani's refusal to bend his knee once more to Baghdadi.

ISIS's surge threatened al-Qaeda's project in the Levant but did not end it. Al-Qaeda regrouped, attempting to hold off the caliphate's men while also taking the fight to Assad. The uprising in Syria, as in Libya and Tunisia, gave al-Qaeda a chance to spread its doctrine and expand its operation, even if these opportunities came with their own risks.

For one thing, the Syria conflict gave al-Qaeda the chance to acquire strategic territory. In the West, it was often assumed—due to its adoption of the far-enemy doctrine—that al-Qaeda did not really care about conquering land. This wasn't true. In fact, al-Qaeda's leaders repeatedly said their primary goal was building a new caliphate. Unlike Baghdadi, bin Laden and Zawahiri considered this a long-term project and understood the dangers that would arise as soon as a caliphate was declared. Bin Laden and Zawahiri believed that once jihadists declared themselves rulers over an Islamic state in any part of the world, a U.S.-led international alliance would quickly move to unseat them. ISIS's decision to declare itself a caliphate arguably proved al-Qaeda's strategic calculus correct. By the end of 2018 the United States and its allies had ejected Baghdadi's men from their strongholds in Mosul, Raqqa, and elsewhere, ending ISIS's claim to rule a territorial caliphate.

Meanwhile, al-Qaeda was securing its own territory in Syria's northwestern Idlib province, away from the counter-ISIS fight. Long before the 9/11 attacks, Zawahiri had eyed the Levant as key terrain. In his book *Knights Under the Prophet's Banner*, he opined that the West had established Israel between Egypt and Syria to prevent the rise of a new caliphate encompassing the region. Zawahiri returned to this conspiratorial reading of Israel's history in a 2005 letter to Zarqawi. Zawahiri added that it had "always been my belief that the victory of Islam will never take place until a Muslim state is established in the manner of the Prophet in the heart of the Islamic world, specifically in the Levant, Egypt, and the neighboring states of the Peninsula and Iraq; however, the center would be in the Levant and Egypt."[168] As we have shown, Egypt was nowhere close to an ideal place to raise al-Qaeda's black banner permanently, even after Mubarak fell. The best location for al-Qaeda's envisioned caliphate was inside a chronically weak state or a conflict zone as close to the center of the Middle East as possible. Syria thus became, in many ways, the ideal incubator for al-Qaeda's long-term program. Assad's ceaseless brutality and mass murder horrified or demoralized many Syrians. The jihadists could offer an alternative: join us and we will take the fight to your oppressor, together. But over time al-Qaeda faced new management challenges in Syria even beyond the menace of Baghdadi's caliphate.

AL-QAEDA'S SYRIA STRATEGY

From the beginning of the conflict, al-Qaeda focused its attention on Assad. Julani only revealed his allegiance to al-Qaeda in April 2013, when he appealed to Zawahiri to intercede on his behalf against Baghdadi. In the months that followed, it became clear that al-Qaeda had seeded al-Nusra's senior ranks with veterans who were tasked with leading men into battle while crafting the group's strategic vision. These al-Qaeda veterans had impressive jihadist pedigrees. For example, Abu Hammam al-Shami, an expert in guerrilla warfare, set up training camps in Syria similar to those he ran in Afghanistan prior to 9/11. Abu Firas al-Suri helped build al-Qaeda's network in Pakistan before serving in Yemen. Once in Syria, Abu Firas became al-Nusra's spokesman, positioning the group as a jihadist foil to ISIS. Ahmed Salama Mabrouk, who was recently freed from an Egyptian prison, also joined al-Nusra in a senior capacity. A younger yet experienced member of al-Qaeda known as Sanafi al-Nasr relocated from South Asia to serve as one of al-Nusra's chief strategists.[169] While these men found Syria receptive to al-Qaeda's mission, their roles as known agents of the organization meant they were constantly hunted. By 2016 American drone strikes had killed three of the four men. Only Abu Hammam al-Shami lived on to keep fighting, and he eventually became embroiled in a leadership dispute with Julani.

Al-Qaeda drew thousands of people to its cause with a strategy very different from ISIS's program. Abu Firas al-Suri explained this strategy in a 2015 al-Nusra video trumpeting the organization's role in al-Qaeda. Al-Qaeda's goal was to develop an "erupting jihadi center" in the Levant and elsewhere, Abu Firas explained. He said the "concept of jihad in the Levant was absent from people's minds" after the fall of the Ottoman caliphate. Abu Firas then echoed points Zawahiri raised in *Knights Under the Prophet's Banner* and in his letter to Zarqawi. "The Levant is regarded [as] one of the most important centers in the Islamic world due to its close proximity to

Palestine, to the Hijaz [Saudi Arabia] and being in the center of the Islamic world," Abu Firas stated. The al-Qaeda veteran drew on Marxist revolutionary theory to elaborate on Syria's importance, explaining that even "Western theorists, such as Frenchman Régis Debray," had concluded that it was necessary to develop a "continually erupting center for revolutions." Abu Firas clarified that al-Qaeda could not consider Debray a "role model" or idolize leftist militants like Fidel Castro or Che Guevara. But al-Qaeda could still analyze and learn from other ideological movements' innovations in asymmetric warfare, a topic Debray had expounded upon in detailed treatises about mid-twentieth-century communist revolutionary struggles in Latin America.[170] This underscores a point we made in chapter 2 about jihadist organizational learning: It will be impeded in areas that are theological or that can otherwise be classified as doctrinal, but jihadist groups are more inclined to engage in broad-based learning about matters that can be classified as purely strategic. In Debray's case, there was much al-Qaeda could glean from his examination of the insurgencies that toppled regimes throughout Latin America and replaced them with communist governments. This paralleled al-Qaeda's own quest in Syria.

By 2015 al-Nusra Front had grown into a formidable guerrilla army. Early that year, al-Nusra, Ahrar al-Sham, and their allies created a new force that would go on the offensive against Assad. The Jaysh al-Fatah ("Army of Conquest") coalition pooled the resources of various rebel factions, including some FSA-branded groups that had received American arms and support. Al-Nusra and Ahrar al-Sham were not the only al-Qaeda-connected jihadist groups to participate in Jaysh al-Fatah. Jund al-Aqsa, a hardline group established by al-Qaeda veterans, stormed Assad's positions as a Jaysh al-Fatah member.[171] Formed in 2014, Ansar al-Din Front brought together foreign fighters from several smaller jihadist groups that had entered the war earlier. The organization's men fought alongside al-Nusra as part of Jaysh al-Fatah. The Turkistan Islamic Party (TIP), composed predominantly of Uighur jihadists, also established a branch in Syria. TIP's men in Afghanistan had been loyal to the Taliban and al-Qaeda long before the 9/11 hijackings and continued to maintain a foothold in South Asia despite the U.S.-led military campaign in the region. TIP, which did not hide its admiration for al-Qaeda's leaders, sent a contingent to Syria that became increasingly significant on the battlefield. Additional ethnic fighting formations—made up of Chechens, Turks, Uzbeks, and others—also joined the conflict alongside Jaysh al-Fatah. In some cases only a little detective work was needed to see these groups' al-Qaeda links.

At first Jaysh al-Fatah enjoyed stunning success, sweeping through Idlib province in weeks. Al-Qaeda's branches around the globe cheered these gains and Zawahiri dispatched additional lieutenants to Syria to bolster the group's leadership ranks. At first it looked as if al-Qaeda was going to mirror ISIS's territorial gains, albeit on a lesser scale and using a different strategy. But Jaysh al-Fatah's conquests never reached beyond northwestern Syria. In time Jaysh al-Fatah and other rebel configurations lost battle after battle. By late 2017 Idlib was the last redoubt for the insurgency, as Assad's forces and their Russian and Iranian backers brutally eliminated the armed opposition.

FRAGMENTATION

In July 2016, with the fight against Assad flailing in the wake of Russia's military intervention nine months earlier, Abu Muhammad al-Julani implemented a plan intended to unify the Syrian opposition under his command. Julani held a press conference to announce that al-Nusra Front was abandoning its name and would now be known as Jabhat Fatah al-Sham ("Conquest of the Levant Front").[172] Julani said that Jabhat Fatah al-Sham would not be affiliated with any "external" entity. This ambiguous phrasing was widely reported throughout the media as al-Nusra breaking from al-Qaeda. While the move would ultimately set off a leadership dispute between Julani and various al-Qaeda loyalists in Syria, there are good reasons to suspect that this alleged break was not what it appeared to be.[173]

The history of this purported split establishes the reason for skepticism. Shortly before Julani's announcement, Zawahiri deputy Abu al-Khayr al-Masri publicly approved al-Nusra Front's rebranding in an audio message, saying it was consistent with Zawahiri's directives regarding Syria.[174] Masri was subsequently killed in a U.S. drone strike in early 2017, and his death may have contributed to the leadership disputes that followed. Julani heaped praise on al-Qaeda's senior leaders in his statement announcing Jabhat Fatah al-Sham. Various pro-al-Qaeda observers noted on social media that at the press conference, Julani dressed in stylized garb that was clearly intended to evoke the person of Osama bin

Laden. As he read his announcement, Julani was flanked by two men: Ahmed Salama Mabrouk and Abu Abdullah al-Shami. Mabrouk, who died in a U.S. drone strike in Idlib mere months later, had been a Zawahiri confidant since the 1980s.[175] It is difficult to imagine such a figure personally blessing a true break in al-Nusra's loyalty. Abu Abdullah would eventually say that Julani's move was the beginning of a real separation. But that was seemingly not his perspective at the time. In late 2017, over a year after Jabhat Fatah al-Sham's birth, Abu Abdullah described the break as deceptive. He explained that the idea of al-Nusra's relaunch as Jabhat Fatah al-Sham "was to change the name of the group . . . and announce what would be understood in the media as breaking the ties with" al-Qaeda.[176] According to Abu Abdullah, in July 2016 and the months that followed "there would remain a secret undisclosed allegiance to them [al-Qaeda], in a state which would resemble the situation before our dispute with ISIS."[177] Recall that Zawahiri had not wanted al-Nusra to reveal its relationship with al-Qaeda in the first place, and when he weighed in on the ISIS-Nusra dispute, the al-Qaeda boss rebuked Julani for making this relationship public. Although Abu Abdullah said the break was deceptive, he blamed poor communication for the fake split growing into a real conflict. Zawahiri thought Jabhat Fatah al-Sham had "actually broke[n] its ties," Abu Abdullah said, insisting that "this was not the case from our side."[178]

In January 2017 Jabhat Fatah al-Sham announced that it had merged with four other groups to form still another entity, Hay'at Tahrir al-Sham (the Assembly for the Liberation of the Levant, or HTS). This group also marketed itself as an independent enterprise. Dissent in the jihadists' ranks grew. Some al-Qaeda veterans had objected to Julani's July 2016 announcement at the time, and still other dissenters emerged throughout 2017. Eventually Julani's men detained two high-profile critics who had argued that the al-Nusra chief had broken his *bayah* to Zawahiri.[179] The two Zawahiri loyalists were eventually released after an arbitration committee, headed by another al-Qaeda veteran, secured their freedom.[180]

In establishing HTS, Julani had hoped to unify the beleaguered insurgency against Assad under common leadership. Instead, HTS fractured within months. Some groups that had fought side by side with Julani's men since the beginning, like Ahrar al-Sham, refused to even join HTS.[181] Still others joined and then broke away, including the Nur al-Din al-Zanki

Movement, which was one of HTS's five original constituent groups. Another founding member of HTS, the aforementioned Ansar al-Din Front, broke from HTS in February 2018. Other dissatisfied factions within HTS split to form the Guardians of the Religion organization, which Abu Hammam al-Sham reportedly leads. Months earlier, Abu Hammam had clashed with Julani on several issues.

Al-Nusra's rebrandings and their consequences amounted to a serious disruption in al-Qaeda's chain of command and left many unanswered questions for the transnational jihadist organization. Zawahiri has criticized HTS, indirectly accusing it of pursuing a "nationalist" agenda—in lieu of al-Qaeda's global jihad.[182] In late 2017 Zawahiri rebuked anyone in Syria who thought he had granted any group permission to break its oath of fealty to him.[183] Although Zawahiri didn't name Julani in his message, he clearly had HTS in mind. Yet the U.S. government still considered HTS an "affiliate" of al-Qaeda, insisting that its various moves did not amount to a real break from AQSL.[184] This remained the official American position as of late 2021, more than three years after HTS first formed.

HTS still portrays itself as outside the al-Qaeda fold. Whatever the future holds for the HTS–al-Qaeda relationship, it is clear that plenty of jihadists in Syria remain beholden to Zawahiri and his lieutenants.

This section thus shows how al-Qaeda engaged in organizational learning processes in Syria. As we discussed (chapter 2), organizational learning need not always result in positive outcomes. In Syria, al-Qaeda had a clever strategy rooted in obfuscation, similar to the strategy it employed in Tunisia and Libya. That strategy helped the militant group in some ways. The initial obfuscation of al-Nusra's connections with al-Qaeda initially allowed al-Nusra to gain a foothold in the Syrian insurgency that likely would not have been possible had it been open about its al-Qaeda affiliation. Abu Abdullah al-Shami, who had inside knowledge about the ostensible split between al-Qaeda and Jabhat Fatah al-Sham, has said that this "break" was deceptive. If so, it fooled many outside observers—but also fooled key leaders in al-Qaeda itself.

While there is certainly much more to learn about the organizational events that al-Qaeda set in motion in the Syria theater, from the current vantage point it seems that key al-Qaeda decisionmakers assumed more perfect information throughout the organization than existed. But, as we have explained, imperfect information-sharing and communication throughout an organization are inherent challenges for organizations with al-Qaeda's design. Yet the group did not sufficiently account for imperfect communication between the leadership of the group's Syria-based affiliate and members of AQSL, including Zawahiri. They did not account for the possibility that health issues, for example, could cause lapses in communication. There also may have been an assumption that participants close to al-Qaeda in the Syria theater and beyond would either understand the nature of the deception or would remain impassive and unemotional in the face of apparent organizational fragmentation. It appears that none of these assumptions proved accurate.

Striking the Far Enemy from Syria

For jihadists, the Syria conflict is more than just a laboratory for state-building schemes or an opportunity to overthrow a heretical regime. Syria also became the perfect staging ground for external attacks.

From 2014 onward, ISIS frequently plotted to strike the West, and often succeeded. In some of these plots, such as the November 2015 Paris attacks, the group dispatched terrorists to Europe directly from Iraq and Syria. Meanwhile, al-Qaeda's actions and intentions toward far-enemy targets from Syria have been more ambiguous. There is no question that in Syria, Zawahiri and his advisers prioritized the guerrilla war against the near enemy (Assad's regime) over attempts to terrorize the far enemy.

During an interview that aired on Al Jazeera in May 2015, Julani made clear that Zawahiri had made a calculation regarding the use of Syrian territory as a base for attacks outside the country.[185] The "directives that come to us from Dr. Ayman, may Allah protect him, are that the al-Nusra Front's mission in Syria is to topple" Assad's regime and defeat its allies, especially Hizballah, Julani said. Should Assad fall, al-Nusra was to reach "a mutual understanding with other factions to establish a righteous Islamic rule."[186] Julani elaborated: "We have received guidance to not use Syria as a base for attacks against the West or Europe so that the real battle is not confused." The al-Nusra leader conceded that "maybe" the larger al-Qaeda organization is plotting against the West—just "not from Syria."

Still, Julani explained that these directions could change if American air-strikes made retaliation necessary.

But this doesn't mean that al-Qaeda had in fact abandoned the idea of using Syria as a launching pad for attacks in the West. It was clear that al-Nusra shared al-Qaeda's anti-Americanism. In June 2015, weeks after Julani's interview aired, the group released a video titled "The Heirs of Glory" that celebrated the 9/11 hijackings and portrayed al-Nusra as part of the jihad that Osama bin Laden had launched against the United States.[187] And there was concrete plotting behind closed doors.

When the Obama administration announced the beginning of the Amer-ican air campaign against ISIS in September 2014, it said the United States was also targeting another organization in Syria: the "Khorasan group." Few had heard of this entity outside of U.S. intelligence and counterter-rorism circles. In the ensuing confusion, some observers claimed that Khorasan was an al-Qaeda offshoot or an entirely new terrorist group. In reality, the so-called Khorasan group was a specific command structure within al-Qaeda. According to U.S. intelligence officials, the name was derived from the "Khorasan Shura," an elite advisory body within al-Qaeda that oversaw some of its most sensitive tasks, and whose members were partially based in Syria.[188] One of its missions was to lay the groundwork for plots against the West that al-Qaeda could eventually execute. It appears that Khorasan was never given the green light to carry out a mass casu-alty attack, but the group's work was designed to allow al-Qaeda to push the "go" button at any time.

Zawahiri ordered trusted operatives who had been based Afghanistan, Chechnya, Europe, Iran, Pakistan, Yemen, and North Africa to relocate to Syria.[189] These were the al-Qaeda men who later comprised the Khorasan group. Some of the group's members were trained by Ibrahim al-Asiri, AQAP's expert bomb maker.

One of the Khorasan group's most senior figures was Muhsin al-Fadhli, a Kuwaiti who fought in Afghanistan and Chechnya, had been implicated in a string of al-Qaeda plots since the early 2000s, and may have had fore-knowledge of the 9/11 hijackings.[190] Fadhli had been tied to the October 6, 2002, attack on the French ship MV *Limburg* as well as the October 8, 2002, attack against U.S. Marines stationed on Kuwait's Faylaka Island. By early 2013 Fadhli had relocated to Syria after temporarily heading al-Qaeda's Iran-based facilitation network.[191] The press in Fadhli's native Kuwait quickly reported his move to Syria. Counterterrorism officials were watching him closely too. In May 2013 Egypt broke up an al-Qaeda plot targeting Western embassies in Cairo.[192] Egyptian authorities claimed that the cell responsible for the plan was part of the Muhammad Jamal Network and had been in contact with a Syria-based jihadist known as Dawood al-Assadi (one of Fadhli's known aliases), who was "responsible for receiving terrorist elements on" Turkey's borders.[193]

The CIA continued to hunt Fadhli after it discovered his involvement in the Egyptian plot. U.S. forces finally caught up with him in July 2015, when a drone struck Fadhli's car in Sarmada, a town in Idlib province.[194] It appears that Fadhli was not the overall head of the Khorasan group but rather in charge of its "external work," meaning terrorist plots against major targets abroad. U.S. officials have identified another al-Qaeda veteran, Mohammed Islambouli, as the Khorasan group's top leader. As the brother of Anwar Sadat's assassin, Islambouli was like royalty in jihadist circles. He remained safely ensconced in Turkey, whose government allowed him to live and operate despite being well-known to security services the world over since the 1980s.

Other al-Qaeda operatives joined Fadhli as members of the Khorasan group in Syria. They included Sanafi al-Nasr, a Saudi who was a distant cousin of Osama bin Laden; and French explosives expert David Drugeon. Like Fadhli, Nasr was a former head of al-Qaeda's Iran-based network. As chief of al-Qaeda's Victory Committee, Nasr was also tasked with developing the global network's policies. Nasr's career demonstrates that there are often no firm lines dividing al-Qaeda's insurgent operations from its terrorist plotting against the West. On his popular Twitter feed, Nasr announced that he would love nothing more than to strike the United States. Once he arrived in Syria, Nasr's work took on a dual focus: He was involved in both the Khorasan group's international plotting and in the development of al-Nusra's overall strategy for the war in Syria.[195] Drugeon, meanwhile, was an advanced bombmaker who communicated with some of al-Qaeda's new European recruits. Neither Nasr nor Drugeon ever succeeded in attacking the West. They were killed in separate drone strikes in 2015.

Al-Qaeda operatives were still plotting against the West from Idlib, Syria, more than two years after the United States began bombing Khorasan group targets. On October 17, 2016, the United States killed Haydar Kirkan in an airstrike. It is not clear what Kirkan was planning at the time of his death, but the Defense Department connected him to al-Qaeda's global campaign against the West. In its statement announcing Kirkan's death, the Pentagon described him as al-Qaeda's "senior external attack planner in Syria, Turkey and Europe," adding that he had also served as an "experienced facilitator and courier for al-Qaeda in Syria."[196] Kirkan had attended al-Qaeda training camps in Afghanistan in 1999 and had maintained a network inside Turkey as early as 2007.[197] After the al-Nusra-led Jaysh al-Fatah coalition took over Idlib in 2015, Kirkan relocated his operations into the Syrian province.

Although details remain murky, there are two possible known instances of Syria-based al-Qaeda operatives plotting external attacks as retaliation for Russia's involvement in the Syrian war. On the evening of December 19, 2016, Andrei Karlov, Russia's ambassador to Turkey, was assassinated at point-blank range at a modern art center in Ankara. Karlov had been invited to speak at an event celebrating a collection of photos taken inside Russia. No group ever claimed responsibility for the murder, which had all the signs of a professional hit job. The assassin, Mevlüt Mert Altıntaş, was an off-duty Turkish police officer who managed to plant himself next to Karlov.[198] Before he was killed, Altıntaş smashed some of the photographs and protested Russia's bombing of Aleppo. At the time, jihadists and other insurgents were attempting to stop Assad and his allies from retaking the city, an effort that eventually failed. Al-Qaeda's propagandists celebrated the ambassador's assassination, portraying it as part of a series of attacks the group had either inspired or directly conducted. These videos do not prove that al-Qaeda was responsible. There are other explanations for the ambassador's murder, and Altıntaş may have simply taken up the cause of Aleppo for his own personal reasons.[199] But al-Qaeda has repeatedly featured footage of the assassination in its productions, including accompanying messages from Osama bin Laden's son, Hamza.[200]

Less than four months after Karlov's death, on April 3, 2017, a bomb detonated on a metro train in Saint Petersburg, Russia, killing fifteen people. Russian authorities identified the perpetrator as Akbarjon Jalilov, an ethnic Uzbek born in Kyrgyzstan. It would be several weeks before a group claimed responsibility for the attack, when a previously unknown organization called Katibat Imam Shamil said it had dispatched Jalilov.[201] In a statement posted on al-Qaeda-affiliated social media channels and republished in AQAP's *al-Masra* newsletter, the group claimed that Jalilov had been dispatched "under the directives of Sheikh Ayman al-Zawahiri."[202] The authors of the message stated that the bombing was revenge for Russia's support for the "criminal" Assad regime in Syria, along with Moscow's other atrocities in Chechnya and Libya. Many details surrounding the Saint Petersburg metro bombing, including whether Katibat Imam Shamil was a real outfit or a front group, remain unclear. It is also possible that ISIS, which has conducted its own attacks in Saint Petersburg and elsewhere in Russia, was the real culprit. But the statement from Katibat Imam Shamil may well have been legitimate, since al-Qaeda-linked Uzbek fighting factions are active in both Afghanistan and Syria. It is quite likely that the bombing could have been a deadly payoff for al-Qaeda's long-standing strategy of using the Syrian vacuum to advance its war against far enemies.

The Challenges Ahead for al-Qaeda

Al-Qaeda defied expert predictions that the Arab Spring would weaken or destroy the organization. Yet Zawahiri did not view the uprisings as an unmitigated positive development. In his various public releases about the revolutions, Zawahiri was cautiously hopeful early on—one series of his messages was titled "The Islamic Spring"—but his commentary became more pessimistic as events developed. In January 2018, seven years after the protests first shook much of the Middle East and North Africa, As Sahab released a message from Zawahiri that was especially grim. In his speech, titled "Seven Years Later, Where Is the Salvation?," Zawahiri complained that "all of the revolutions were suppressed except Syria, which entered the spiral of international solutions," meaning that powerful countries were now dictating the course of events there. The "reigning regimes in Tunisia, Egypt, Yemen and Libya" have all "returned," only "more ferocious and corrupt" than before. Zawahiri said that the jihadists should learn from this "bitter experience."[203] In his view, the Arab Spring proved that jihadists cannot compromise on their ideology the same way that various Islamist parties had, especially the Muslim Brotherhood.

Zawahiri offered a highly selective account of recent history. He claimed that the Muslim "masses" had demanded the implementation of sharia but that Islamist parties betrayed them and cut deals with international actors instead. In reality, the region's secularists often appeared "outmanned, out-organized, and outmaneuvered" politically and otherwise, but "in numerical terms they probably represent the largest proportion of the population in most countries."[204] Much of the secularists' early disorganization relates to their relative ability to organize prior to the revolutions. The regimes' suppression of secularists was often more ruthlessly effective than it was of Islamist groups. Further, secularist groups were not united under a single banner but rather were "divided ideologically among liberals, socialists, communists, nationalists, and the like."[205]

Al-Qaeda's footprint greatly expanded as a result of the Arab uprisings. Yet the Arab Spring has nevertheless posed a number of long-term challenges for the group. Zawahiri's relative pessimism wasn't unwarranted. Strongmen stand in al-Qaeda's way in Libya and Syria. In Syria, Assad has pounded the jihadists with Russian and Iranian backing. Al-Qaeda's affiliates once conducted guerrilla-style operations throughout the country but have seen leadership disputes and battlefield losses reduce their fighting capability. Al-Qaeda would have to jump-start the rebellion for Syria to continue being the "erupting jihadi center" that Abu Firas al-Suri had envisioned. Zawahiri believed that the Levant could be the incubator that jihadists needed to gain political and administrative experience, but going by their own criteria the extremists' record in the country has been decidedly mixed. The "Salvation Government" in northwestern Syria, which is associated with HTS, has been incapable of firmly ruling the territory it supposedly governs. The Syrian insurgency remains disjointed despite al-Qaeda's attempts to unify opposition to Assad under its command. Russian and Syrian jets regularly bomb the country's last surviving opposition enclave in southern Idlib province. The threat of a large-scale operation looms.

In Libya, Khalifa Haftar has waged his own scorched-earth campaign against Islamist extremists. Like Assad, he brings to bear superior firepower, including warplanes. Ansar al-Sharia and the Derna Mujahedin

Shura Council, both of which were al-Qaeda projects, once ruled over the eastern Libyan cities of Benghazi and Derna. In 2016 the Derna Mujahedin Shura Council was strong enough to eject their ISIS-affiliated rivals from the city and its outskirts. The Shura Council was so firmly rooted within the fabric of the city, which was long a hotbed for extremism, that locals viewed Baghdadi's representatives as unwelcome usurpers. But Haftar's Libyan National Army pounded Benghazi and Derna throughout 2016 and 2017, forcing the al-Qaeda-aligned groups to temporarily give up their local governance project. As in Syria, al-Qaeda will have to regroup to reignite the Libyan insurgency. ISIS, which initially surged in parts of Libya, notably Sirte, has receded after a fighting coalition dislodged Baghdadi's men from their strongholds. Both ISIS and al-Qaeda-aligned groups retain a presence in Libya, but it isn't clear how strong they now are.

Aside from this anti-jihadist military pressure, al-Qaeda faced opposition from ISIS, which disrupted al-Qaeda's response to the Arab uprisings. Al-Qaeda did not suffer the defections of major branches that most analysts predicted, but Baghdadi's enterprise still drew resources, manpower, and critical energy away from Zawahiri's network. As ISIS rose to prominence, AST's Abu Iyadh even suggested to Zawahiri that the al-Qaeda leader join Baghdadi's project.[206] Abu Iyadh portrayed such a move as an effort to reform ISIS from within. But there was desperation in his proposal, as he clearly feared that the caliphate's sway was too strong for many jihadists, especially the youth, to resist. This was likely related to some specific elements of Tunisian jihadism, as Tunisian foreign fighters had disproportionately aligned themselves with ISIS in Syria. Abu Iyadh quickly reversed his suggestion, recognizing that it was foolish to think the two sides could reach accommodation.[207] While Abu Iyadh and others remained loyal to al-Qaeda, they couldn't stop some of the group's cadres from joining ISIS.

Al-Qaeda suffered even worse defections in Egypt. As this chapter details, in late 2014 Ansar Bayt al-Maqdis announced that it had pledged allegiance to Baghdadi. The organization quickly rebranded as Wilayat Sinai. ABM had clearly been part of Zawahiri's global network even if it had not affirmed its fealty to al-Qaeda in public. The loss of ABM was a blow to al-Qaeda's post–Arab Spring project and must have been especially disappointing for the Egypt-born Zawahiri. Wilayat Sinai remains threatening to this day, challenging the Egyptian state in the northern Sinai and operating elsewhere in the country. While the loss of ABM was a significant development, al-Qaeda still has loyalists with an eye on Egypt. One such operative who worked to build the group's Egypt-based network was Hisham Ashmawi, a former Egyptian special forces officer implicated in a series of assassinations in Egypt who was eventually captured in Derna in late 2018.[208]

The Arab uprisings led al-Qaeda to deprioritize attacks in the West. This doesn't mean that the group stopped plotting against the United States and Europe entirely, and al-Qaeda's presence in each Arab Spring country arguably magnified the group's ability to strike Western targets. For example, in the summer of 2013 the U.S. government was forced to close embassies and other diplomatic facilities in twenty-two countries based on intelligence suggesting that al-Qaeda was coordinating attack plans across several of its entities.[209] Some of the al-Qaeda operatives involved in this disrupted plan were stationed in areas where the organization initially benefited from the Arab revolutions, including in the Sinai. As al-Qaeda moves forward, its leadership may decide to renew the group's previous emphasis on attacks against the West. Since 2014 ISIS has flooded the West's defenses. It seems that, in contrast, al-Qaeda has chosen to lie in wait. It may eventually release similarly destructive energies in new ways.

The Arab Spring created new chances for extremist political and military takeovers. As Zawahiri himself has remarked, none of them ended in a jihadist victory. This doesn't mean al-Qaeda completely lost, though. The group is active throughout the MENA region nine years after the first protests erupted. Al-Qaeda's post-2011 history demonstrates jihadists' ability to engage in organizational learning and should encourage the counterterrorism field to learn from the mistaken assumptions of the recent past.

7

The Islamic State's Rise and Rule

On July 4, 2014, Abu Bakr al-Baghdadi slowly climbed the pulpit of the Great Mosque of Al-Nuri in Mosul, Iraq. Baghdadi's men had just proclaimed him the caliph of all the world's Muslims. His organization had scored a series of stunning military victories in the run-up to this pronouncement. Baghdadi's self-proclaimed caliphate now controlled territory stretching across large swaths of Iraq and Syria, comparable to Great Britain in geographic size even if most of it was uninhabited desert.

Baghdadi specifically chose Al-Nuri, a famous religious and cultural site in one of Iraq's largest cities, to announce his triumph. "O Muslims everywhere, glad tidings to you and expect good," Baghdadi said. "Raise your head high, for today—by Allah's grace—you have a state and Khilafah, which will return your dignity, might, rights, and leadership."[1]

Baghdadi's speech stressed the importance of the word *return*. The need to reestablish a caliphate, an institution that ceased to exist after the Ottoman state's dissolution in 1924, had long been central to Islamist thought. From the Muslim Brotherhood to al-Qaeda and ISIS, a range of Islamist movements saw the caliphate's reestablishment as their overarching goal. By the summer of 2014 Baghdadi, now known to his followers as Caliph Ibrahim, claimed to have succeeded where others had fallen short.

Addressing the assembly at Al-Nuri, Baghdadi painted a bleak picture of the world, a vision consistent with the dark, conspiratorial outlook of Sayyid Qutb, Sayyid Abul A'la Maududi, Osama bin Laden, and other major Islamist figures that had preceded him. Much of the world was conspiring against Muslims, Baghdadi said, with Muslims' rights being "forcibly seized" everywhere, from China to the West. Muslim honor was being violated and Muslim blood spilled, with believers suffering the "worst kinds of torture." Against this backdrop, the entire Ummah was "watching your jihad with eyes of hope," Baghdadi told his audience. He naturally cast his Islamic State in utopian terms, as the only place where Muslims could find justice and respite from the humiliations the world inflicted upon the Ummah. He also portrayed the caliphate as a vehicle for *revenge*—a word he used repeatedly—against all who oppressed Muslims or abused their faith. Baghdadi claimed his caliphate would do nothing less than overturn the existing world order. He described the world as "divided into two camps and two trenches, with no third camp present: The camp of Islam and faith, and the camp of *kufr* (disbelief) and hypocrisy—the camp of the Muslims and the mujahedin everywhere, and the camp of the Jews, the Crusaders, their allies, and with them the rest of the nations and religions of *kufr*, all being led by America and Russia, and being mobilized by the Jews." Baghdadi vowed that ISIS would destroy the camp of disbelief, "trample the idol of nationalism, destroy the idol of democracy and uncover its deviant nature." The day was coming "when the Muslim will walk everywhere as a master, having honor, being revered, with his head raised high and his dignity preserved." Anyone who dared even offend a Muslim "will be disciplined, and any hand that reaches out to harm him will be cut off."

Baghdadi's caliphate reached the pinnacle of its power in the months following this speech. ISIS's message—which combined a millenarian theological narrative with puritanical zealotry, anti-Americanism, anti-Semitism, apocalyptic eschatology, and a bitter sense of grievance—appealed to a disturbing number of people across the world. The caliphate mushroomed in Iraq and Syria and drew tens of thousands of foreign fighters from Europe, the Middle East, North Africa, and elsewhere.[2] Baghdadi's project also sprouted new outposts from West Africa to Southeast Asia.

The territorial caliphate turned out to be short-lived. By early 2019 ISIS had lost essentially all the land it once controlled. Baghdadi's fighters had clung to a small enclave in eastern Syria before losing it to numerically superior and better-equipped enemy forces. Thousands of ISIS fighters surrendered in advance of this defeat.[3] But ISIS only lost the remainder of its land as the result of intense combat that reduced entire cities and towns to rubble. ISIS refused to leave populated areas, forcing the U.S.-led coalition to bomb mosques and hospitals that Baghdadi's die-hards had turned into their makeshift headquarters. Not even the Great Mosque of Al-Nuri, site of Baghdadi's rousing "us versus the world" speech, survived the fighting. ISIS blew up the mosque, built eight centuries earlier, as coalition forces descended in June 2017.[4]

ISIS retains an international network even after the string of defeats that it suffered in Iraq and Syria. Thousands of jihadists fight on as insurgents in both countries while ISIS militants terrorize civilians and battle security forces in other places across the world. Although ISIS's scorched-earth approach may have caused some caliphate-seekers to quit the organization, the urge to resurrect an empire worthy of Islam's glorious past has not died. The utopian dream of a jihadist caliphate is very much alive, however nightmarish the reality may have been.

For many in the West, the idea of a modern-day caliphate ruling the Muslim-majority world may seem fanciful. It certainly appeared that way in the years leading up to ISIS's emergence. During a speech on June 29, 2011, John Brennan, President Obama's senior counterterrorism adviser, dismissed al-Qaeda's "grandiose vision of global domination through a violent Islamic caliphate" as "absurd." Brennan added that the United States was "not going to organize our counterterrorism policies against a feckless delusion that is never going to happen."[5] Three years later to the day, on June 29, 2014, the Islamic State's men declared that they now ruled over a caliphate stretching across vast sections of two countries.

Today Baghdadi is dead, and his men have resorted to guerrilla warfare. But the utopian dream of a caliphate still motivates both the ISIS and al-Qaeda networks. The jihadist worldview and the movement's sense of purpose stem from the goal of capturing territory and governing it according to an austere version of Islamic law. In Iraq the caliphate was a guiding motivation for jihadists from the early days of the U.S. military occupation of the country, over a decade before Baghdadi's declaration. Jihadists adapt, adjust their practices, and engage in learning with the idea of an eventual caliphate in mind. It is impossible to understand jihadism's continuing appeal without a clear sense of the dream that the movement hopes to ultimately realize.

The Iraq War: The Early Origins of ISIS

The beginnings of ISIS's organization and ideology emerged within al-Qaeda's brutal Iraqi affiliates in the years following the U.S. invasion that toppled Saddam Hussein's regime in March 2003. While Saddam's government quickly fell, it proved exceedingly difficult for the United States and its partners to replace Saddam's neo-Stalinist state, which was largely held together by widespread fear of a brutal tyrant. President George W. Bush had argued that removing Saddam from power was necessary to fighting the "global war on terror," but his administration did not appreciate how militants would exploit the political vacuum that Saddam's removal produced.

In many ways al-Qaeda's far enemy had come to the jihadists' backyard in Iraq, making it easier for them to kill and maim American soldiers. It should not be inferred, though, that jihadists or other militants fighting American forces in Iraq were pursuing a far-enemy strategy. As Sohail Hashmi notes, "the invasion and occupation of parts of Afghanistan and later Iraq by American forces ... blurred the distinction between near and far enemies."[6] The war also ultimately made it possible for Iraq-based jihadists to begin building their Islamic state in the heart of the Middle East—which might have been an unlikely development from al-Qaeda's vantage point. Prior to 9/11 al-Qaeda had analyzed the viability of launching a jihadist revolution in a number of countries, and the prospects in Iraq seemed so unlikely that they did not even consider it. An al-Qaeda strategist known as Abu Bakr Naji discussed these assessments at length in a tract titled *Management of Savagery*. Michael W. S. Ryan summarizes Naji's work in his book *Decoding Al-Qaeda's Strategy*, explaining that Naji and al-Qaeda divided nations into "high-priority" and "nonpriority" countries. Al-Qaeda eventually wanted to take over a broad swath of territory with Muslim-majority populations, but only the "more feasible candidates" for jihadist revolution were included in the high-priority category.[7] This division was based on characteristics that included the geography's favorability for guerrilla warfare, the strength of the central government, the population's attitude toward global jihadism relative to competing ideologies, and the availability of weaponry.[8] In the high-priority countries—including Jordan, Libya, Nigeria, Pakistan, Saudi Arabia, Tunisia, and Yemen—al-Qaeda envisioned "three stages of jihad." At first the group would inflict damage with the aim of exhausting the apostate regime. Next the group would focus its efforts on establishing an "administration of savagery in the areas from which the central government has withdrawn its forces," to be followed by the formation of an Islamic state governed according to "al-Qaeda's version of shari'ah."[9]

Nonpriority countries like Egypt and Israel were considered inhospitable to al-Qaeda's revolution. In these lands, the jihadists would carry out terrorist attacks without launching a full-fledged campaign of guerrilla warfare. Naji claimed that these country studies were initially developed three years before the 9/11 hijackings. As we noted, al-Qaeda's assessments did not include Iraq. In the late 1990s al-Qaeda did not foresee an event as disruptive as the United States' war against Saddam. When Naji's treatise was eventually published online in 2004, the year after the U.S.-led invasion, Iraq still didn't show up in the list of high- or low-priority countries.[10]

The Iraq War changed al-Qaeda's priorities. Bin Laden quickly recognized that the Americans had stumbled into a conflict for which they were ill prepared. On the eve of the war, bin Laden even sanctioned cooperation with Saddam Hussein's Baathists, a long-standing ideological opponent of jihadists. "Under these circumstances, there will be no harm if the interests of Muslims converge with the interests of the socialists in the fight against the crusaders, despite our belief in the infidelity of socialists," bin Laden said in a February 2003 audio message. Bin Laden drew justification for this "convergence of interests" from Islamic history.[11] Bin Laden was the most wanted man in the world at the time of this message. The Taliban had lost its emirate in Afghanistan in the aftermath of the 9/11 hijackings. But as U.S. forces rolled into Iraq, and as Saddam Hussein's state melted away, new opportunities presented themselves.

THE FOUNDER: ABU MUSAB AL-ZARQAWI

Al-Qaeda in Iraq's story—and, ultimately, that of ISIS—begins in Afghanistan with a young man, a street thug turned religious militant, traveling there in the late 1980s in the hope of fighting its Soviet occupiers. He arrived a bit too late.

Abu Musab al-Zarqawi, born Ahmed Fadil al-Nazal al-Khalayleh, attained international notoriety for both his brutality and his success as a militant leader. He was born in 1966 in Zarqa, Jordan, to a poor, conservative family belonging to the Bani Hassan tribe.[12] Known as a thug in his early life, he generally did not attend religious services as a youth. In a well-regarded biographical account of Zarqawi, Mary Anne Weaver notes that, of all the interviews about Zarqawi she conducted during her research in Jordan, it was universally acknowledged "that as a teenager al-Zarqawi had been a bully and a thug, a bootlegger and a heavy drinker, and even, allegedly, a pimp in Zarqa's underworld."[13] However, he underwent a religious awakening at Zarqa's al-Falah mosque. Zarqawi's mother first enrolled him in religious classes, "no doubt hoping to keep him out of a life of crime."[14] Following his turn to piety, Zarqawi traveled to Afghanistan in 1989, arriving too late to fight the Soviets, who had already withdrawn.

Despite that, he was able to join the transnational jihadist movement. Bin Laden was also in Afghanistan during Zarqawi's first visit, and Zarqawi trained for combat in the Sada camp, which bin Laden ran.[15] Zarqawi also met fellow Jordanian Abu Muhammad al-Maqdisi (born Isam Muhammad Tahir al-Barqawi). Maqdisi was, and remains, a renowned Salafist cleric who became Zarqawi's ideological mentor.[16] Zarqawi also built relationships with other jihadists in Afghanistan that allowed him to form the "Zarqawi organization," the militant outfit that would undergo several name changes and that would ultimately become known as ISIS almost a decade after Zarqawi's death.

In Afghanistan, Zarqawi and Maqdisi established their own militant group. Composed of around a dozen men, it was known by police and reporters as Bayat al-Imam (Allegiance to the Imam). But members of the group reportedly referred to their organization instead as Tawhid wa-l-Jihad (Monotheism and Jihad).[17] The group's primary goal was to overthrow Jordan's monarchy and replace it with an Islamic government. The group attracted Jordanian authorities' attention upon Zarqawi and

Maqdisi's return to Jordan in 1993. They were arrested the following year. Prior to their arrest, their group "tried several ill-fated attacks," and they were finally apprehended "after members attacked a Jordanian border crossing with Israel, likely in an effort to torpedo the ongoing peace negotiations."[18] Both men were convicted on terrorism charged and sentenced to fifteen years in prison.[19]

Zarqawi's years in Jordanian prison were pivotal to his jihadist career. Journalist Abdallah Abu Rumman, who met Zarqawi during his stint in the same prison in September 1996, recalled that Zarqawi's organization was "amongst the strongest and most influential" associations in the institution.[20] Zarqawi had a strong leadership style, "able to control everyone and organize all the details of relations within the group."[21] Eventually Zarqawi eclipsed even Maqdisi and became the emir of the prison group.[22] Prisoners' family members routinely smuggled out religious tracts written by Maqdisi. Prominent London-based cleric Abu Qatada al-Filistini in turn published writings by Bayat al-Imam members in his magazine *Al-Minhaj*, allowing other jihadists to stay abreast of the activities of their brothers in Jordan's prisons.[23]

In 1999 King Abdullah II declared a general amnesty for Jordanian prisoners, and both Zarqawi and Maqdisi were released. Zarqawi promptly returned to South Asia. He was briefly arrested in Hayatabad, Pakistan, for overstaying a residence permit, after which he left Pakistan for Afghanistan.[24] Two weeks after his arrival in Kandahar, Zarqawi met with Sayf al-Adl, who was then al-Qaeda's security chief.[25] Sayf al-Adl played an important role in facilitating al-Qaeda's partnership with Zarqawi, although there is some dispute among jihadist leaders about how central he was.[26] Regardless of how the negotiations proceeded, it was agreed that Zarqawi would run a militant training camp in Herat, in western Afghanistan. Bin Laden indirectly provided the camp's funding and equipment.[27]

During his time in Herat, Zarqawi developed outreach and recruitment operations in Jordan and Syria and grew the number of militants in his camp. He focused on recruiting fighters from Bilad al-Sham, a region that includes Jordan, Syria, Lebanon, and historic Palestine.[28] Consistent with what would become a pattern of adopting new monikers, the Zarqawi organization's network in Herat became known as Jund al-Sham (Soldiers of the Levant), although the banner above the entrance to the Herat camp continued to read Tawhid wa-l-Jihad.[29] Graduates of the Herat camp later took part in notable terrorist plots, including the 2002 assassination of U.S. diplomat Laurence Foley in Amman.[30]

After the U.S.-led invasion of Afghanistan in October 2001, Zarqawi reportedly spent time on the front lines.[31] He eventually fled Afghanistan through Iran, then made his way to Iraq in 2002, before the U.S. campaign in that country began. An audio file recovered from bin Laden's Abbottabad compound contains a lengthy biography of Zarqawi, recorded by a jihadist who served alongside him known only as Abu Muhammad.[32] Much of Abu Muhammad's testimony tracks with what other secondary sources indicate about Zarqawi's career. Abu Muhammad confirms that Zarqawi set up operations in Iraq before the Americans invaded. Abu Abdullah al-Shafi'i, a leader in the militant group Ansar al-Islam, welcomed Zarqawi when he arrived in Iraqi Kurdistan. Abu Muhammad describes Zarqawi's designs on other countries throughout the region. Initially, he says, Zarqawi tried to establish fronts in Jordan and Syria, shipping weapons to both countries. Although Zarqawi's men conducted operations in both locales, including the murder of Laurence Foley in October 2002, Abu Muhammad says Zarqawi considered these initial efforts to be failures. Zarqawi was busy establishing a network in Mosul as early as 2003. Indeed, eleven years later, Mosul became one of the twin capitals of ISIS's caliphate. The jihadists' networks in Mosul evolved over that span, but Abu Muhammad's account indicates that Zarqawi made establishing a foothold in the city one of his first priorities.

Zarqawi "had an idea to work on something to recruit more young men for jihad in Iraq . . . if Americans attack Iraq," Abu Muhammad explained. About two months before the war, Abu Muhammad and others introduced Zarqawi to a number of clerics in Iraq, as well as "young men" who were presumably their students. At first the Iraq War disrupted Zarqawi's plans. Days before the March 2003 invasion, Zarqawi decided to flee to Iran, where he was briefly detained. Abu Muhammad explained that Iranian authorities told Zarqawi he could travel "to Pakistan or Malaysia or Indonesia or Turkey," but Zarqawi insisted on returning to Iraq. He met with Abu Muhammad and others in Baghdad before absconding to Syria, where he waited for Saddam's regime to fall. Zarqawi then traveled to Mosul and stayed there for three months. He asked other extremists in the city "to prepare for him militants and cars," which he would rely on in the fighting to come.[33]

Name employed	Years used
Bayat al-Imam (aka Tawhid wa-l-Jihad)	c. 1993–1999
Jund al-Sham	c. 1999–2004
Jama'at al-Tawhid wal-Jihad (JTJ)	2004
Tanzim Qa'idat al-Jihad fi Bilad al-Rafidayn (al-Qaeda in Iraq)	October 2004–January 2006
Majlis Shura al-Mujahedin fi-l-Iraq (Mujahedin Shura Council)	January–October 2006
Islamic State of Iraq (ISI)	October 2006–April 2013
Islamic State of Iraq and al-Sham (ISIS)	April 2013–June 2014
Islamic State	June 2014—present

FIG. 7.1 Name changes for Zarqawi's Iraq-based network

Zarqawi's Iraq-based network initially operated under the name Jama'at al-Tawhid wal-Jihad (JTJ). JTJ consisted of both former Iraqi regime officials and dedicated jihadists. The group would undergo a number of name changes, as shown in figure 7.1.[34]

Zarqawi put military and intelligence personnel from Saddam's fallen government in key positions. As native Iraqis who had formerly served a totalitarian regime, these men possessed skills and knowledge that proved helpful. Several ex-regime officials were among Zarqawi's top recruits, including a "member of Saddam Hussein's special guard," a former major in the Fedayeen Saddam, and former chiefs of staff for the Iraqi Intelligence Service and Republican Guard, according to a U.S. Marine Corps study.[35]

ZARQAWI'S RISE

In the summer of 2003, three months into the U.S. occupation, Zarqawi's group announced its role in the Iraq War with a series of spectacular suicide bombings, including an attack on the UN office in Baghdad that killed the United Nations' special representative in the country. The jihadists conducted at least twenty-five "martyrdom" operations in the last nine months of 2003.[36] Suicide terrorism had been relatively rare in the Middle

East at the time of Saddam's ouster, and Zarqawi's prolific use of men willing to sacrifice themselves for his cause was attention-grabbing. This kind of attack quickly became a routine tactic for jihadists in the heart of the region.

Regular suicide bombings weren't Zarqawi's only adaptation to the realities of post-Saddam Iraq. He was just as innovative on the propaganda front. Early in the conflict, the Zarqawi-led JTJ became adept at creating and disseminating high-quality media productions. A jihadist known as Abu Maysara al-Iraqi was central to these efforts.[37] A posthumous biography written by other jihadists stressed Abu Maysara's religious credentials, saying that he had studied theology in Iraq and proselytized for the jihadist cause in Baghdad since well before the war.[38] Saddam's intelligence services arrested Abu Maysara for these activities but released him shortly before the U.S. invasion. After his release, Abu Maysara joined JTJ and was named the group's deputy official for the media department as well as its "official spokesman . . . on the internet and in jihadist forums."[39] This made Abu Maysara a key early adopter as he took advantage of online networks, which would later—in both the *iteration* and *breakthrough* phases of the violent non-state actor technology adoption curve—make it easier for extremists to spread recruitment videos and other media. Some of this content was so gory that al-Qaeda's senior leadership objected: Even veteran militants who had spent their lives plotting attacks in Muslim-majority countries were concerned that Zarqawi's propaganda would offend and alienate too much of the Islamic world.[40]

A troublesome independent streak buffered Zarqawi's emerging sadism. In early 2004 Zarqawi penned a letter that must have flummoxed bin Laden and his comrades.[41] Al-Qaeda had often taken a pragmatic approach toward the Shiites, a community whose treatment remains a controversial subject within Sunni jihadist circles. Al-Qaeda adopted a somewhat forgiving approach to Shiites for ideological and pragmatic reasons, such as protecting the group's tense but sometimes cooperative relationship with the Iranian government. The fact that Zarqawi himself had relied on Iran to transit in and out of Iraq as the war began shows that he understood some of the militant group's pragmatic concerns. Despite this, Zarqawi saw Shiites as his principal enemy in Iraq and pursued an ultraviolent strategy.

In his letter, Zarqawi wrote that if his group was successful in pulling the Shia "into the arena of sectarian war," then "inattentive Sunnis" would "feel imminent danger" and awaken.[42] Zarqawi wanted to ignite a sectarian firestorm in order to radicalize Iraq's Sunnis and recruit more of them to his cause. He saw the Shiites, and not the United States, as his main adversary in Iraq, a complete reversal of al-Qaeda's strategy. In a section of the letter titled "The Work Plan," Zarqawi briefly mentioned the Americans, only to dismiss them as the "most cowardly of God's creatures." He considered U.S. personnel to be an "easy quarry" and ruminated about capturing some Americans "to trade them for our detained sheikhs and brothers." After dedicating just three sentences to the Americans, Zarqawi spent several paragraphs expounding on his animus toward the Shia, who "have declared a secret war against the people of Islam." In Zarqawi's view, the "danger from the Shiites . . . is greater and their damage is worse and more destructive to the [Islamic] nation than the Americans, on whom you find a quasi-consensus about killing them as an assailing enemy." Sectarian warfare was an untapped source of potential for jihadists: The fight against the Shia was a "way to drag the [Islamic] nation into the battle." After all, when "the Americans disappear from these areas," the Shia would still be there.

Zarqawi publicly swore allegiance to bin Laden in October 2004, months after penning his argument for sectarian war in Iraq.[43] JTJ rebranded as al-Qaeda in the Land of Two Rivers and became more widely known as al-Qaeda in Iraq (AQI). According to a U.S. Marine Corps study, Zarqawi's public oath to bin Laden brought tangible benefits, including "increased funding, recruits, logistical support, as well as political and religious backing from al-Qaeda's leadership."[44]

Al-Qaeda's senior leaders still harbored reservations about the bloodthirsty Jordanian despite their newly announced partnership. While Zarqawi was a brutally effective killer, many in al-Qaeda central feared that he lacked the savvy and restraint necessary to translate battlefield success into political victory.

By the end of 2004 Zarqawi led perhaps the deadliest jihadist outfit on the planet. Jihadists were flailing nearly everywhere outside Iraq. The Taliban-led insurgency in Afghanistan was only beginning to regroup; al-Qaeda's attempt to launch a rebellion inside Saudi Arabia in 2003 fizzled. Al-Qaeda began placing special importance on the war in Iraq, which was attracting volunteers from throughout the MENA region. In December 2004, two months after Zarqawi's oath of *bayah*, bin Laden released a message describing Iraq as "a golden and unique opportunity." For bin Laden, Iraq was the central front in a "Third World War, which the Crusader-Zionist coalition began against the Islamic nation." Bin Laden described Baghdad as "the capital of the caliphate." It was in Iraq, the al-Qaeda founder predicted, that jihadists would either achieve "victory and glory" or "misery and humiliation."[45]

Yet even as bin Laden publicly hailed Zarqawi as the chief commander in an apocalyptic battle, al-Qaeda's men privately discussed their misgivings about the Jordanian.

Al-Qaeda's Concerns About AQI

Al-Qaeda's senior leadership outlined their concerns about Zarqawi in letters that the U.S.-led coalition later recovered. In one July 2005 missive Zawahiri outlined a series of "incremental goals," modest in comparison to Zarqawi's fervor for sectarian bloodshed, that he wanted the Jordanian and his followers to achieve.[46] Zawahiri's letter has been the subject of much commentary, mainly because he openly chastised Zarqawi for reveling in the slaughter of Shia civilians and others, actions that Zawahiri thought would alienate al-Qaeda's base of support in Iraq and beyond. Zawahiri's objections seemingly had little to do with the morality of Zarqawi's tactics and were rooted in a broader strategic framework.

Zawahiri wrote that al-Qaeda intended to build a caliphate in Iraq but thought it would be necessary to expel the Americans first. With this enemy vanquished, AQI could "establish an Islamic authority or emirate, then develop it and support it until it achieves the level of a caliphate." Zawahiri cautioned that such a state would face external and internal opposition. But if the jihadists could hold their new state, they could extend their war "to the secular countries neighboring Iraq," then eventually to Israel. Zawahiri raised objections to Zarqawi's approach to the war because he believed the Jordanian was jeopardizing al-Qaeda's long-term vision. Zawahiri pointed to the loss of the Islamic Emirate of Afghanistan, explaining that the Afghan people didn't rally to the Taliban's cause when the Americans invaded. Al-Qaeda's senior leadership had learned from this bitter experience and wanted to avoid a similar fate in Iraq: The key lesson they took from Afghanistan was that only an Islamic emirate buttressed by popular support could survive external challenges. Zawahiri wrote that massacring Shiites and attacking their mosques was not "acceptable to the Muslim populace" no matter how much Zarqawi "tried to explain it," and that the public's aversion to his tactics would only grow. Zawahiri wanted Zarqawi to build good relations with Islamic scholars and establish proto-governance based on *shura*, or consultation. The *shura* might never happen if Zarqawi's bloodbath didn't abate.

In late 2005 another al-Qaeda manager and one of bin Laden's most trusted lieutenants, Atiyah Abd al-Rahman, penned his own critique of Zarqawi.[47] Atiyah, who later died in an August 2011 drone strike, was closely involved in al-Qaeda's attempts to manage its unruly branch in Iraq. Although Atiyah made a point of heaping praise on Zarqawi in his letter, he couldn't hide his displeasure and even suggested that the Jordanian consider stepping aside to allow "someone who is better and more suitable" to take the reins of leadership. This was not an order, Atiyah explained, but a restatement of something he had "previously advised."[48] Atiyah did however command Zarqawi to communicate more frequently, both via courier and the internet. His explanation of why this was necessary dripped with condescension: He explained that Zarqawi could benefit from the superior leadership of al-Qaeda's sheikhs and shouldn't make any "comprehensive" decisions before consulting bin Laden and Zawahiri.

Atiyah, who worried that Zarqawi would alienate Iraqis, offered advice that any student of warfare would recognize: Military action alone is fruitless, and violence cannot be allowed to undermine the political purpose for which it was being wielded. "Policy must be dominant over militarism," Atiyah wrote. "This is one of the pillars of war that is agreed upon by all nations, whether they are Muslims or unbelievers. That is to say, that military action is a servant to policy." The al-Qaeda lieutenant advised that the "important thing is to keep your reputation and that of the mujahedin pure, especially your organization, and to gain peoples' affection and love, and to strive for it."[49]

Both Atiyah and Zawahiri had counseled Zarqawi on the need to mind the political front. On January 15, 2006, Abu Maysara al-Iraqi announced the establishment of the Majlis Shura al-Mujahedin fi-l-Iraq (better known as the Mujahedin Shura Council, or MSC), an umbrella group composed of six Iraqi Sunni militant factions.[50] The group Jaysh Ahl al-Sunnah wa-l-Jama'a, for which ISIS's eventual caliphate Abu Bakr al-Baghdadi served as the emir of the Sharia Committee, joined MSC on January 29.[51]

Although MSC purported to function as a coalition, the group was AQI's brainchild. At the time AQI faced growing criticism from Iraqis for representing a foreign agenda and conducting indiscriminate attacks against civilians, just as Zawahiri anticipated it would. Al-Qaeda viewed MSC as a way to rebrand, highlighting the group's local origins and connections in an effort to regain the support of other Iraqi factions and the population. The person chosen to lead this group was a previously unknown figure called Abdullah bin Rashid al-Baghdadi, who provided an Iraqi face to MSC's leadership.[52] Attacks in Iraq claimed by MSC during its relatively brief existence did not invoke AQI's name, yet AQI quietly remained the dominant player in the Iraqi Salafi jihadist landscape.

Indeed, a document recovered from bin Laden's compound and released by the CIA in 2017 appears to foreshadow the creation of the MSC. It is not clear who authored or received the memo, but it seems to have been written in late 2005. The document lays out the political challenges standing in the way of jihadists' state-building endeavor. According to the memo's author, Zarqawi and his men faced numerous obstacles, chief among them the Americans and their allies. The al-Qaeda author likened Iraq's insurgent groups to children with "one father" but "many mothers." The "common connection between all of these fighters is that they have refused the infidel occupation," he stated, but they have "different opinions, approaches, and visions" for the fight. There were those who wanted to resurrect Iraq's Baathist regime, and others who were fighting "to make God's Supreme Word, and make Islam the only religion, and make the Mesopotamia the base that will lead to liberate the rest of the occupied Muslim countries."[53] This latter grouping included Zarqawi's al-Qaeda branch, as well as another al-Qaeda-linked group, Ansar al-Sunnah.

When the memo was written in late 2005, the jihadists' enemies were looking to capitalize on their opponents' disunity. The author had a solution. He endorsed a plan to create a council of "leaders and scholars, so they can meet and agree on the fundamental concepts, and find ways to execute them." The memo argued that this political front would insulate the jihadists from America's machinations—which was precisely the intent behind MSC's creation. The same memo contains instructions for reforming the "management of the brothers" in Iraq. The author lamented that Zarqawi himself "is not able to make much improvement" in this regard. "If he was able to find experienced brothers in administration, communication, and politics, he would have fixed a lot of these issues," the author wrote of Zarqawi.[54]

MSC did not live up to the hopes that the memo's author had. But the council's creation did formalize some of the long-standing alliances between AQI and lesser-known insurgent groups. However, Zarqawi didn't have the opportunity to correct his course in Iraq. He was killed in a joint U.S.–Iraqi raid in June 2006. The dream of building a state was left to his successors.

The Islamic State of Iraq

The MSC marked a short-lived transitional phase of the insurgency. In mid-October 2006 the MSC and several other insurgent groups announced that they had merged to form the Islamic State of Iraq (ISI). As Brian Fishman notes, while ISI was largely viewed in the West as "just another rebranded AQI," the group in fact "immediately set out to build a scalable bureaucratic framework that would eventually define the Islamic State during the Syrian civil war."[55] Fishman outlines a number of steps that ISI took during this period that later defined ISIS's bureaucracy. Among other things, Fishman explains that the group:

- Named a cabinet, including Ministries of Agriculture and Marine Wealth, Oil, and Health;
- Executed small-scale public works projects, like irrigation canals;
- Managed health and safety regulations, including setting speed limits on roads;
- Created an internal bureaucracy for political and military administration;
- Called on "Muslim brothers around the world, especially those neighboring our dear state" to emigrate, and promised to "provide them with benefits and expertise";
- Enforced strict financial accounting procedures;
- Completely rebranded all of its propaganda;
- Enforced rigorous pay scales and cared for the family of deceased fighters;
- And recruited members with a range of administrative and scientific backgrounds, not just military experience.[56]

Why do this under the auspices of ISI? A spokesman for the new organization explained that Iraq's Sunnis needed a political entity of their own to counterbalance the Kurds and Shiites, who already had their own governments.[57] The spokesman said that ISI would gather Iraq's Sunni Muslims under the leadership of Abu Umar al-Baghdadi, an obscure figure whom he strikingly referred to as the Amir al-Mu'minin, or the emir of the faithful.[58] In invoking this title, the spokesman was employing a weighty concept. The title Amir al-Mu'minin is usually reserved for a caliph.

THE QUESTION OF *BAYAH*

The new head of AQI, Abu Hamza al-Muhajir, declared his own allegiance to Baghdadi. Muhajir was a longtime participant in the jihadist movement who had served Zawahiri as a member of Egyptian Islamic Jihad in the 1980s. In the 1990s Muhajir joined the jihadist scene in Afghanistan, where he reportedly met Zarqawi.[59] Zawahiri would later praise Muhajir for remaining true to al-Qaeda's cause even as the United States bombed Afghanistan in late 2001. According to both the CIA and Muhajir's wife, the veteran Egyptian jihadist made his way to Iraq in 2002.[60] Once there, he helped Zarqawi build the network that evolved into AQI. Muhajir "obtained a farm in Diyala Province through his Iraqi contacts, which he converted into a terrorist training camp for foreign fighters," according to the U.S. Marine Corps. After the war began, Muhajir became one of Zarqawi's "top lieutenants" in Fallujah, an AQI stronghold and site of some of the war's heaviest fighting.[61]

"I tell the venerable sheikh, the brave hero, the Qurayshi Hashemite, who is of a Husayni origin, the leader of the faithful, Abu Umar al-Baghdadi, I pledge allegiance to you to hear and obey during good and bad times, and in pleasant and unpleasant situations, and this is a promise to say the truth wherever we may be, not to fear the criticism of anyone in the cause of Allah," Muhajir proclaimed.[62] Muhajir's description of Baghdadi was carefully worded. The phrasing "Qurayshi Hashemite . . . of a Husayni origin" was intended to emphasize Baghdadi's purported lineage from the Prophet Muhammad's own tribe. One Islamic tradition holds that it is necessary for a legitimate caliph to be of Qurayshi lineage—and a later Baghdadi, Abu Bakr, would emphasize his own claimed Qurayshi lineage when he purported to reestablish the caliphate.[63] Muhajir declared that "all the formations" he commanded were now under ISI's authority. Addressing "mujahedin across the world," Muhajir announced that the "first cornerstone of the Islamic Caliphate project" had been laid.

Years later, after ISIS's men openly defied al-Qaeda's leadership in the lead-up to their split from the organization, both the ISIS faithful and also some counterterrorism analysts claimed that ISI's creation marked the end of al-Qaeda's presence in Iraq.[64] According to this argument, because Muhajir pledged fealty to the previously unknown Abu Umar al-Baghdadi, bin Laden and Zawahiri lost all authority over the jihadist project in the country. Contemporaneous evidence does not support this view.

While the timing of ISI's announcement might have caught al-Qaeda's senior leadership off guard, the organization's long-stated goal was to raise an Islamic emirate inside Iraq. Zawahiri made this clear in an interview released on the fifth anniversary of the 9/11 hijackings in September 2006. Zawahiri explained that their "general concept" was to establish Islamic emirates in Iraq and Afghanistan. These entities would serve as the "launching pad for the defense of Islam and Muslims and a step toward the revival of the caliphate."[65]

If Muhajir had broken his *bayah* to al-Qaeda, it would have precipitated an intra-jihadist crisis that would have been impossible to hide from outside observers. Yet al-Qaeda never accused him of what would have been a treasonous act. The reality was quite the opposite. Bin Laden and Zawahiri continued to publicly praise Muhajir for years to come. Al-Qaeda's senior leadership actively defended ISI against its jihadist critics and encouraged Muslims to swear allegiance to Abu Umar al-Baghdadi. In return, ISI continued to signal its loyalty to al-Qaeda in its videos and statements.

More than anyone else, Abu Hamza al-Muhajir could be considered ISI's true founder. Because Muhajir headed the largest Sunni militant outfit in Iraq at the time, ISI would never have existed without his explicit permission. After Zarqawi's demise in June 2006, AQI moved quickly to name Muhajir its new emir. AQSL openly praised the appointment, with Zawahiri saying that al-Qaeda was "very happy about the transfer of the banner of jihad and resistance" to Muhajir. For his own part, Muhajir made his loyalty to bin Laden a theme of his first speech as AQI's head. "We are waiting for your directives and we are at your disposal," Muhajir said to bin Laden, whom he referred to as "our sheikh and emir."[66] In a September 2006 speech, a few weeks before ISI's founding, Muhajir again emphasized his fealty not only to bin Laden, whom he described as "our emir," but also to Zawahiri ("our sheikh") and to Taliban founder Mullah Omar ("our guardian"). Addressing all three leaders, Muhajir said he and his men were "an arrow in your quiver" and "your obedient soldiers."[67] These are not the words of a man on the verge of breaking his oath of fealty. Muhajir was an al-Qaeda man when ISI was created and would remain one for years to come.

In a July 2007 speech, Zawahiri offered a full-throated defense of Muhajir and ISI. Al-Qaeda's second-in-command described the now-defunct MSC as "a big leap on the road of jihadi action in Iraq." Abu Hamza al-Muhajir, Zawahiri said, "strove with his honorable, sincere brothers . . . to establish the Islamic State of Iraq." ISI's founding was "good news for the Muslims," as "they moved one step closer to the outskirts of Jerusalem and the establishment of the Caliphate," Zawahiri said.[68] The Egyptian doctor went on to criticize those who did not recognize ISI as a legitimate government.

Despite Zawahiri's endorsement, doubts continued to linger among jihadists about ISI's theological legitimacy. This became a serious enough issue that an al-Qaeda representative secretly met with Saudi clerics to gauge their support for the entity.[69] One prominent jihadist critic of ISI was Dr. Hamid al-Ali, a Kuwaiti who had recruited and fundraised for AQI. In December 2006 the U.S. Treasury Department designated Ali a terrorist, noting his role as an AQI facilitator.[70] Despite this, Ali did not back the new ISI project: He loudly called for its dissolution, rankling al-Qaeda's senior leadership.

Correspondence recovered from bin Laden's Abbottabad compound shows how al-Qaeda's senior leaders moved to strengthen ISI's standing and answer its jihadist critics, including Dr. Ali. Needless to say, this is not a favor they would extend to a breakaway branch whose leader had violated an oath of fealty. One letter, seemingly written by bin Laden in August 2007, stressed the importance of bolstering ISI. The missive—which is addressed to Abu Muhammad, one of Zawahiri's known aliases—says that the "effort to remove ambiguity around the subject of the Islamic State of Iraq" is a "very important subject." The author says that the recipient—again, likely Zawahiri—had an "easier" time maintaining contacts with the "media, and the information network," and therefore needed "to plug that gap." Bin Laden advised that the "main axis of your work plan in the coming stage would be the continued support for the truthful mujahedin in Iraq headed by our brothers in ISI, and defending them should be the core issue and should take the lion's share and the top priority in your speeches and statements." Zawahiri needed to make his "support for ISI" both "overt and obvious." Bin Laden set forth a number of reasons that ISI deserved such a loud defense. One point in particular "must be stressed and hammered" repeatedly: The conflict in Iraq was "between two ideologies," one that wanted Iraq to be ruled under sharia, and another that was secular and sought to return the country to the rule of "kings and presidents."[71]

Tellingly, bin Laden referred to ISI as an al-Qaeda project. "Al-Qaeda has become international, praise Allah, and its circle has widened and people entered it in droves, tribes and groups, so in Iraq it had to establish a government, have an emir to rule them, ease their needs and protect the religious goals," bin Laden wrote. ISI's critics had committed a religious error in spurning the group, and Dr. Ali "should have mentioned in his statement the unanimity of the scholars on the necessity of appointing the imam and establishing the government to rule people with Allah's laws, so it was strange that he asked to dissolve and annul ISI." Here bin Laden was replying to Dr. Ali's objection that ISI's emir, Abu Umar al-Baghdadi, was in "hiding" and remained an unknown figure to the Muslims he was supposed to lead. Bin Laden defended Baghdadi and the decision to name him emir. "The trusted mujahedin in Iraq nominated people, established the state, and agreed on an emir for them," the al-Qaeda leader wrote. In other words, while al-Qaeda's senior leadership was unfamiliar with Baghdadi, they did know Abu Hamza al-Muhajir, the "emir of war in Iraq." Muhajir "knew Abu Umar al-Baghdadi and swore allegiance to him."[72] Bin Laden thought this chain of loyalty should satisfy Dr. Ali and other critics.

Al-Qaeda's leadership didn't want to admit that Dr. Ali had a point. Months after ISI's founding, the true identity of Abu Umar al-Baghdadi was unknown to Iraqis, and even to most jihadists. The U.S. military alleged that Baghdadi was a fictional persona essentially being played by character actors. The U.S. military further claimed that after the public became aware of this deceit, Muhajir and ISI appointed a real Iraqi to serve as "Abu Umar al-Baghdadi."[73]

Jihadist sources eventually told a different story. Baghdadi was indeed a real person, and an Iraqi to boot. According to one oft-cited biography posted after Baghdadi's death, his real name was Hamid Dawud Muhammad Khalil al-Zawi, and he had served as a policeman in Haditha under Saddam's regime.[74] Iraqi officials had allegedly removed Zawi from his post in the early 1990s because he had become a Salafist. After the U.S.-led war began, Zawi joined Zarqawi's JTJ, the predecessor of AQI. The future ISI leader served as JTJ's head of security in Baghdad, the jihadists' governor of Diyala province, then as the leader "in charge of all the provinces." Zawi eventually had the role of ISI emir thrust upon him, accepting the title of emir of the believers. None of these details were widely known in October 2006, when Abu Umar al-Baghdadi was named head of the ISI. Some jihadists would continue to wonder why they should pledge fealty to someone who didn't show his face and had little public presence beyond occasional audio messages.

Al-Qaeda's two top leaders repeatedly contended that this ambiguity was a nonissue, defending the claims to legitimacy of Abu Umar al-Baghdadi. In a December 2007 speech bin Laden encouraged all Iraqis to join the Baghdadi-led ISI. At the time, al-Qaeda was alarmed at the Sahwa, the Sunni "awakening" in which local tribal leaders in western Iraq turned decisively against the jihadists. Bin Laden's audio message, which was nearly an hour long, was intended to buttress ISI against this new challenge. Intransigent tribesman aside, al-Qaeda's leader said that many Muslims "were pleased when a number of the emirs of groups" and a "number of chiefs" from the "steadfast and mujahid tribes unified their stand under the banner of monotheism and pledged allegiance to [the] honorable Sheikh Abu Umar al-Baghdadi as emir of the Islamic State of Iraq." The al-Qaeda founder praised Baghdadi and his men for refusing to "bargain over their faith and accept half-solutions."[75]

Bin Laden was speaking with an awareness that some, like Dr. Ali, had raised objections to the shadowy Baghdadi. Bin Laden dismissed this criticism, saying that "ignorance about the affairs of the emirs of the mujahedin in Iraq is harmless . . . if they have been recommended by trusted, fair persons, such as Emir Abu Umar, who has been recommended by trusted, fair mujahedin." Bin Laden argued that Zarqawi and Muhajir had both vouched for Baghdadi. The al-Qaeda chief then took aim at those who refused to swear their loyalty to Baghdadi. "Refraining from pledging allegiance to one of the emirs of mujahedin in Iraq after their recommendation by trusted, fair persons under the pretext of not knowing their conduct leads to great evils, one of the gravest of which is obstructing the establishment of the great Muslim nation under one imam, which is a nullifier," bin Laden said.[76] He couldn't have been any clearer: For al-Qaeda, failing to declare one's allegiance to Abu Umar al-Baghdadi could serve as a nullifier of other Muslims' faith, causing them to apostatize.

In an "open interview" posted online by As Sahab in April 2008, Zawahiri answered a series of questions posed by al-Qaeda's global supporters.[77] Some wanted to know what Zawahiri and bin Laden thought of ISI, with one questioner asking why jihadists should vow "allegiance to the commander of the faithful in Iraq, Abu Umar al-Baghdadi . . . given that he was an unknown person." Zawahiri responded by quoting bin Laden's December 2007 speech at length. Another questioner asked Zawahiri why ISI was announced in the first place, since the jihadists were engaged in a "hit-and-run process and the time for declaring an Islamic state has not yet come." Zawahiri brushed aside this concern, arguing that the first Muslim-ruled states were "not fully consolidated" and faced deep challenges to their rule and cohesion. Zawahiri essentially sneered at reports that Baghdadi was a fictional character. "Perish in your rage," he said to those who spread this claim. Zawahiri would continue to advocate on ISI's behalf in the months to come.[78]

Baghdadi's obscure and secretive persona wasn't the only source of controversy surrounding ISI in jihadist circles. Muhajir's wartime military leadership came under criticism, with even some of his comrades finding him too extreme. Al-Qaeda's senior leadership fielded multiple complaints from Muhajir's fellow jihadists in Iraq and critiqued some of his key decisions. But al-Qaeda addressed these problems from the perspective of superiors dealing with a trusted subordinate who had been given a difficult task. Bin Laden wrote a scorching letter to Muhajir dated October 18, 2007. The ISI military commander had threatened Iran, which bin Laden thought foolish. Muhajir hadn't consulted AQSL first, while bin Laden and his subordinates had their own delicate dealings with the Iranians. "You did not consult with us on that serious issue that affects the general welfare of all of us," bin Laden wrote. "We expected you would consult with us for these important matters, for as you are aware, Iran is our main artery for funds, personnel, and communication, as well as the matter of hostages." Despite constant tensions between the two sides, the Iranian government allowed al-Qaeda to maintain a facilitation pipeline inside Iran. "There is no need to fight with Iran, unless you are forced to because of the great harm caused by them, and unless you are able to inflect them with harm," bin Laden wrote. "Hence, if you are not in the position to deliver either, then my advice is to refrain from attacking them; and devote your total resource to the fortification of the nation, and the fight against the crusaders and the apostates."[79] In keeping with bin Laden's wishes, ISI never attacked Iran directly, although the Sunni jihadists continued to clash with their Shia counterparts in Iraq, some of whom were Iran-backed.

Al-Qaeda's senior leadership ended up weighing accusations by ISI's top judge, Saudi ideologue Abu Sulayman al-'Utaybi, that Muhajir was a weak leader who displayed an eschatological streak that affected his judgment. 'Utaybi warned that ISI's leadership now contained men who "adhere neither to our thought nor to our method, but are totally against us and are not righteous but corrupt corruptors." The Saudi ideologue alleged that these same figures, appointed under Muhajir's authority, "are the biggest danger of all."[80] It isn't clear what al-Qaeda's senior leaders thought of 'Utaybi's accusations, but they asked Muhajir to respond to the charges. This controversy cooled when 'Utaybi was killed in a May 2008 U.S. airstrike in Afghanistan, removing one of Muhajir's chief internal critics.[81] Still, al-Qaeda's correspondence concerning the 'Utaybi–Muhajir dispute revealed that Muhajir was still in the organizational fold. It is the kind of exchange, on both 'Utaybi's part and al-Qaeda's, that only makes sense if ISI is an affiliated and subordinate organization. Further, Zawahiri discussed a number of administrative matters with his longtime subordinate in the exchange and told him to send more frequent updates.

Other jihadists also complained to al-Qaeda's senior leadership. Ansar al-Sunnah regularly communicated with al-Qaeda central.[82] Ansar al-Sunnah remained independent of its larger jihadist cousin in Iraq: Its leadership never trusted ISI, despite repeated attempts at a merger.[83] Muhajir had called upon Ansar al-Sunnah to join ISI upon the latter's founding, but Ansar al-Sunnah refused. This rejection was noteworthy, as Ansar al-Sunnah's emir, Abu Abdullah al-Shafi'i, had helped Zarqawi during the latter's first days in Iraq. At one point Muhajir pleaded with al-Shafi'i, saying that he would kiss al-Shafi'i's "coat a thousand time[s]" while he waited for al-Shafi'i to "join hands" with his brother in the "Islamic State against the infidels and the unbelievers on earth."[84] Al-Shafi'i was unmoved. Ansar al-Sunna's leadership repeatedly warned AQSL that ISI was too extreme and would sully the jihadists' image in Iraq. As in similar cases, al-Qaeda's managers refused to side with the ISI's critics. Instead they encouraged Ansar al-Sunnah to fold its operations into ISI's.

Meanwhile, ISI's media arm continued to portray the organization as a key player in advancing al-Qaeda's global agenda. In March 2007, five months after ISI's establishment, a new militant group announced its presence in Iraqi Kurdistan. In a video released by ISI's Al Furqan Media Establishment, a spokesman for the new outfit, known as al-Qaeda's Brigades of

Kurdistan, made it clear that he and his men were loyal to both Osama bin Laden and Abu Umar al-Baghdadi. The spokesman, identified as Sheikh Abdallah Hassan al-Surani, described his organization as a "division" of al-Qaeda that had "pledged to our emir, Sheikh Osama bin Laden." The Kurdish jihadists were "at the service of the dear brothers" in ISI, Surani said, since they had also pledged fealty to Baghdadi.[85] The fact that Surani and members of al-Qaeda's Brigades of Kurdistan saw *bayah* to both al-Qaeda and ISI as consistent indicates that al-Qaeda and ISI were part of the same organization. The U.S. State Department designated al-Qaeda's Brigades of Kurdistan as a terrorist organization years later, noting its loyalty to both al-Qaeda and al-Qaeda in Iraq (the name the U.S. government still employed to refer to the ever-rebranding Iraqi jihadist enterprise).[86]

Some Al Furqan Media productions featured al-Qaeda leaders, while others celebrated "martyrs" who had sacrificed themselves for ISI's cause. These videos were filled with al-Qaeda imagery and the suicide bombers often expressed their fealty to bin Laden. In a 2009 release, one suicide bomber identified as Abu Hadhayfah al-Ansari spoke directly to bin Laden: "Be happy, you have soldiers that do not accept injustice. You have soldiers that are—by God—as courageous as lions." Other ISI martyrdom videos took a similarly unmistakable al-Qaeda perspective.[87]

In September 2009 ISI reshuffled its cabinet. Abu Hamza al-Muhajir continued as war minister, but ISI announced that it now had ministries responsible for the judiciary and treasury, along with public relations, captive and detainee affairs, health, information, and oil.[88] In the video announcing these changes, several clips appeared before the spokesman for ISI's information ministry read Abu Umar al-Baghdadi's organizational changes. These clips included statements from al-Qaeda's three most senior officials at the time alongside footage of ISI's own two top leaders. This pairing of al-Qaeda bosses with ISI's leadership was typical of ISI propaganda. In his statement appearing in the video, bin Laden lauded that the "emirs of various groups," as well as a number of tribal chieftains, had "pledged their allegiance to the honorable Sheikh Abu Umar al-Baghdadi, emir of the Islamic State of Iraq." In a separate clip, Zawahiri congratulated the mujahedin "on the establishment of the Islamic State of Iraq" and encouraged the Ummah to support "this young, fledgling state" that was the "gateway to the liberation of Palestine and the restoration of the Islamic caliphate."[89]

THE SAHWA, THE SURGE, AND ISI'S SETBACKS

At the height of the Iraq-based jihadist enterprise's power in late 2006, the jihadists consolidated control over territory stretching from Anbar province in western Iraq all the way into parts of Baghdad. Inside the Iraqi capital, ISI clashed with Iranian-backed Shia militias, feeding the country's sectarian violence. Zarqawi had concluded that the jihadists could funnel suicide bombers and other personnel into key operating areas by controlling a number of vital roads, railroads, and residential areas a short distance from central Baghdad.

By December 2006 the group controlled three main paths into Iraq. One stretched from northeastern Syria through the Iraqi border town of Sinjar all the way into Mosul, north of Baghdad. A second path ran through another town on the Syrian border called al-Qa'im, which sits on the Euphrates River in Anbar province. The third funneled through al-Rutbah, another Anbari town located near the Jordanian and Syrian borders. But the primary gateways into Iraq for ISI's martyrs were in eastern Syria. Hundreds of volunteers from throughout the MENA region heeded Zarqawi's call for jihad in Iraq, with a disproportionate number of recruits coming from Tunisia and Libya.

By late 2006 Sunni opposition to al-Qaeda had crystalized into the Sahwa (Awakening), as Iraqi tribal leaders turned against ISI's authoritarianism and violence. In September 2006 around thirty of these leaders held a meeting to voice their opposition to the Zarqawi organization and formed a coalition called Majlis Inqadh al-Anbar, or the Anbar Salvation Council, to combat ISI elements.[90] This was the genesis of what would popularly become known as the Awakening movement.

The tribesmen had good reason to revolt. ISI's laws could be bizarre and oddly specific. According to one account, segregation of the sexes was extended even to produce: Cucumbers had to be kept a safe distance from tomatoes, as the former were considered male and the latter female.[91] Penalties meted out for defying the group were harsh. Amputations, executions, and torture became commonplace.

The United States made two major changes to its approach that contributed to ISI's setbacks: increasing the number of soldiers on the ground (adding thirty thousand troops) and dramatically shifting the way the troops were used. The additional number of troops would not have made a great difference to the conflict if there had not also been a change in the strategic use of this force. Previously the U.S. military had been generally disengaged from the Iraqi population, operating under the assumption that its presence was a cause of insurgent violence and thus American soldiers should be seen infrequently. This led to the creation of massive forward-operating bases that were literally walled off from the rest of the country. Rather than keeping U.S. forces away from Iraqi civilians, the new U.S. strategy called for engaging in more frequent foot patrols, interacting with Iraqis, and putting a more recognizable "face" on the American presence. This approach saw the Iraqi population as the center of gravity in the conflict. America shifted toward protecting Iraqi civilians from insurgents and other dangers, and American forces were better integrated with the Iraqi population through the use of outposts in the districts they patrolled. These outposts had U.S. soldiers living and sleeping in the same districts they were working to secure rather than being confined to their forward-operating bases.[92]

These changes, coupled with the turning of tribes and former insurgents to cooperation with coalition forces, made a difference on the ground in Anbar. A program known as the Sons of Iraq was extended beyond Anbar province. At its height, more than one hundred thousand predominantly Sunni Iraqis participated in the program.

Gen. David Petraeus and Amb. Ryan Crocker explained the changes on the ground to Congress in September 2007 and April 2008 congressional testimony. By the initial testimony in September 2007, the Awakening had already helped to significantly improve Anbar, transforming it from the days when ISI was the dominant actor. General Petraeus said that Anbar had become "a model of what happens when local leaders and citizens decide to oppose al-Qaeda and reject its Taliban-like ideology."[93] In his April 2008 testimony, General Petraeus explained that the Awakening continued to root out ISI and establish local security.[94] Figure 7.2, a Multi-National Force—Iraq graphic, traces the diminishing fortunes of al-Qaeda/ISI over time.

Al-Qaeda had loudly backed ISI's project in Iraq, believing it to be the jihadists' best chance to establish a permanent beachhead in the heart of the Middle East. Four years after the American invasion, al-Qaeda's grim utopian vision for the country seemed to be a failure.

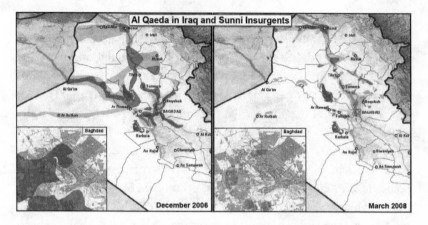

FIG. 7.2 Multinational Force–Iraq map showing al-Qaeda in Iraq's diminishing fortunes

ISIS Rises

In the early hours of April 18, 2010, Iraqi and American forces advanced on a residence outside Tikrit, Saddam Hussein's hometown, where Abu Hamza al-Muhajir and Abu Umar al-Baghdadi were thought to be hiding. Within hours, the U.S. military declared them both dead. "The death of these terrorists is potentially the most significant blow to AQI since the beginning of the insurgency," declared Gen. Ray Odierno, who headed America's military presence in Iraq.[95] A few months later the U.S. military boasted that more than three-fourths of ISI's top leadership had been killed or captured.[96]

In the preceding chapter, we examined al-Qaeda's Syria strategy, one dimension of which was designed to deal with ISIS, the unruly challenger. How did ISIS emerge as a foil to the most powerful jihadist outfit on earth? How was it able to make a credible claim to having established a caliphate just four years after being in such dire straits?

ABU BAKR AL-BAGHDADI TAKES THE REINS

The weak position that the Islamic State of Iraq found itself in following the deaths of Muhajir and Abu Umar al-Baghdadi was anything but illusory, and the road back would be anything but easy. Weeks after the raid near Tikrit, ISI announced its new leader, Abu Bakr al-Baghdadi. Born into a religiously devout family in 1971 (birth name: Ibrahim bin Awad bin Ibrahim al-Badri al-Radawi al-Husseini al-Samarra), Baghdadi had mastered Qur'anic recitation, which he studied at the University of Baghdad, then at the Saddam University for Islamic Studies.[97] The latter was founded during Saddam Hussein's "Return to Faith" campaign in the early 1990s, when the dictator, then under intense international isolation following his failed conquest of Kuwait, suddenly discovered a new appreciation for his religion.[98] Among other things, Saddam funded religious schools throughout the country. During the 1990s the Iraqi state became heavily reliant on paramilitary forces such as the Fedayeen Saddam, whose members were ostensibly zealous believers in the dictator's personality cult.[99] Saddam relied on his Fedayeen to quash dissent, and he deployed them early in the 2003 war. The first Iraqi fighters to confront the U.S. Marines in southern Iraq during their push toward Baghdad were not uniformed members of the Iraqi military but Fedayeen personnel riding in trucks with heavy guns mounted on the back.[100] These fighters were no match for American conventional forces, but many of the surviving Fedayeen melted back into Iraqi society, taking with them a grudge against the Americans and their allies. Many of the Fedayeen, who were trained in paramilitary warfare, became insurgents once the regime fell. Some joined Zarqawi's group. Saddam also invited foreign fighters into Iraq to join his resistance against the U.S.-led coalition. This move, too, helped swell Zarqawi's ranks.[101] Years later, in 2010, Abu Bakr al-Baghdadi inherited an organization that included fighters from many different strains of prewar Iraq, including former Iraqi regime and military personnel.

After the U.S.-led invasion, future ISIS emir Abu Bakr al-Baghdadi cofounded a militant group he called Jaysh Ahl al-Sunnah wa-l-Jama'a.[102] In February 2004 Baghdadi was arrested and detained at Camp Bucca, a facility that housed some of the insurgency's most notorious personalities. The camp became an incubator for jihadism, in part because it gave extremists like Baghdadi the chance to indoctrinate former Baathists.[103]

Baghdadi was released in December 2004 after spending ten months at Camp Bucca. He returned to his career in jihadism almost immediately. In early 2006 Baghdadi's organization joined the MSC. Baghdadi received a promotion when MSC relaunched as ISI in October 2006. He became a member of ISI's *shura* council and oversaw the sharia committees for each of the group's "provinces" throughout Iraq. This meant Baghdadi held one of ISI's most important religious offices.[104]

Although al-Qaeda's senior leadership had endorsed ISI, it is doubtful bin Laden or Zawahiri knew Baghdadi when he ascended to the organization's top spot in April 2010. A memo found in bin Laden's Abbottabad compound mentions a request for the biographies of Baghdadi and ISI's new war minister.[105]

Baghdadi was still openly loyal to al-Qaeda, even if the group's central leadership didn't know much about him. ISI's new leader recorded a glowing eulogy and promised revenge after bin Laden's death in May 2011. Baghdadi addressed "our brothers in the al-Qaeda organization" and the "mujahid Sheikh Ayman al-Zawahiri," as well as Zawahiri's "brothers in the leadership" of al-Qaeda: "You have in the Islamic State of Iraq a group of loyal men pursuing the endeavor of truth" and "they shall never forgive nor resign."[106]

When Baghdadi assumed control of ISI in April 2010, the jihadists controlled little territory, but this lack of territory masked a deeper reality. Iraq was still a powder keg, and the jihadists retained significant capabilities even in their comparatively weak state. Events in the months ahead would prove fortuitous for Baghdadi and his group.

ISI'S OPENING

In December 2011 the United States withdrew the last of its troops from Iraq. With the Americans gone, ISI was able to increase its operational tempo. By early 2012 the group was back to conducting about 75 attacks a week, a figure which rose to an average of 140 by the end of the year.[107] The Iraqi government's growing pro-Shia sectarianism and incompetence, along with the civil war in neighboring Syria, made Iraq's situation precarious after the American departure. Prime Minister Nouri al-Maliki's assurances that his government would be inclusive of Iraq's minority groups gave way to the reality that he was pursuing a pro-Shia sectarian agenda that exhausted the patience of many Iraqi Sunnis by the early 2010s. The government was also unable to adequately defend its prison facilities. A series of ISI-led jailbreaks returned hundreds and possibly thousands of hardened jihadists to the battlefield. As but one example, an estimated five hundred to six hundred jihadists were freed from Abu Ghraib prison and a jail in Taji during just two mass breakouts in July 2013.

With Iraq already boiling, a parallel conflict created new opportunities for ISI in Syria. As we have detailed, in 2011 the Syrian people rose up against Bashar al-Assad's dictatorship. Baghdadi initially sent a small cadre of men into Syria to establish a foothold in the disintegrating country.[108] These jihadists included an ISI lieutenant known as Abu Muhammad al-Julani as well as Zarqawi's brother-in-law, a Jordanian who went by the nom de guerre Abu Julaybib al-Urduni.[109] The ISI arrivals established a group called Jabhat al-Nusra, which neither advertised itself as an extension of Baghdadi's ISI nor revealed that senior al-Qaeda personnel were among their ranks.

Al-Nusra's deceptively al-Qaeda-free branding didn't fool the U.S. government, but its strategy for gaining followers and keeping the Americans off their backs worked, at least initially. Non-jihadist Syrian rebel groups howled in protest when the United States designated al-Nusra Front as an al-Qaeda-affiliated terrorist organization in December 2012.[110] By that point Julani's men had become an integral part of the rebellion. In early 2013 the jihadists led an assault on Raqqa. The provincial capital and future seat of Abu Bakr al-Baghdadi's caliphate fell to the opposition by March.

ISI's Syrian arm was on the rise, but Baghdadi was growing impatient. Al-Nusra leader Abu Muhammad al-Julani was winning battlefield victories but becoming harder for Baghdadi to control. A few weeks after Raqqa's fall Baghdadi decided to act. On April 8, 2013, he addressed the jihad in Syria in a lengthy audio message. He explained that Julani "is one of our soldiers" and had been assigned, along with others, to establish a beachhead for ISI in Syria. After detailing the material support that ISI had given al-Nusra since its inception, Baghdadi said it was now time to prevent any confusion as to al-Nusra's loyalties, so the time had "come to declare before the people of al-Sham and the whole world that Jabhat Al-Nusrah is only an expansion for the Islamic State of Iraq and part of it." Thus, Baghdadi declared that al-Nusra and ISI were now one, united under the name the Islamic State in Iraq and al-Sham, or ISIS.[111]

As we have detailed (chapter 6), Julani had no intention of abiding by this decree. He publicly appealed to Zawahiri to resolve his dispute with Baghdadi. Zawahiri, in turn, issued an official ruling in a May 23, 2013, letter addressed to Julani, Baghdadi, and Abu Khalid al-Suri.[112] Zawahiri largely sided with Julani and ordered Baghdadi to withdraw his forces from Syria. But, as we noted, Zawahiri also reserved some ire for Julani for telling the world about "his links to al-Qaeda without having our permission or advice, even without notifying us." Zawahiri said that Baghdadi and Julani should continue in their role as emirs of their respective groups for a year and should then "submit a report to the general command of [al-Qaeda] about the progress of work." At that time, the general command would decide "whether to extend" their mandates. Zawahiri had named Abu Khalid al-Suri, then a senior official in Ahrar al-Sham, as his chief arbitrator. Abu Khalid was supposed to resolve any dispute between the two emirs "arising from the interpretation" of Zawahiri's ruling.

AL-QAEDA AND ISIS: A MESSY DIVORCE

How powerful had ISIS become? Baghdadi simply ignored Zawahiri's order. He refused to submit to Abu Khalid's authority. At al-Qaeda's behest, veteran extremists from around the globe traveled to Syria to help mediate the ISIS–al-Nusra dispute. Some of these men belonged to the Khorasan Group. Al-Qaeda's leaders also reached out to a Baghdadi-aligned Iraqi jihadist they thought they could trust, Abu Ali al-Anbari. Anbari had once acted as a liaison between Zarqawi and al-Qaeda's leadership in Pakistan. Baghdadi now refused to answer Zawahiri directly, but Anbari could still facilitate an indirect dialogue between the two. In September 2013 Zawahiri wrote to Anbari. Although the al-Qaeda chief complained that it was Baghdadi's duty to respond to him, Zawahiri still addressed a number of arguments Anbari had made on Baghdadi's behalf. The al-Qaeda leader argued that Baghdadi's machinations had disrupted the jihad in Syria. He had revealed al-Qaeda's role, bringing needless international scrutiny. While the Syrian people had once been unambiguously on al-Nusra's side, Zawahiri claimed they were now wondering why al-Qaeda was sowing divisions in the rebellion and courting America's wrath. Other al-Qaeda leaders met Anbari, trying to convince Baghdadi to change course.

Al-Qaeda's last-ditch reconciliation attempt ended in early 2014. On January 23 Zawahiri publicly called for all jihadist factions fighting Assad's regime to let go of their "partisan fanaticism," which undercut the "unity of your ranks."[113] Zawahiri said he believed the jihadists' "brotherhood in Islam" was stronger than any temporary "organizational bonds," and their infighting distracted from the war against their true enemies. The same day, Abdullah Muhammad al-Muhaysini, an al-Qaeda-linked Saudi cleric who had relocated to Syria, announced his own reconciliation plan.[114] Muhaysini's effort, titled the "Initiative of the Ummah," won widespread backing from jihadist and Islamist groups in Syria. Only one major group refused to endorse it: ISIS. But they were the only local jihadist group whose opinion really mattered.

On February 3, 2014, al-Qaeda's general command disowned ISIS. In a terse statement posted online, Zawahiri and his management team announced they now had "no connection" with ISIS, which is "not an affiliate with the al-Qaeda group and has no organizational relation with it." Further, al-Qaeda was "not responsible" for ISIS's actions.[115] ISIS retaliated weeks later, dispatching a suicide bomber who killed Zawahiri's main representative in Syria, Abu Khalid al-Suri. The war between ISIS and al-Qaeda had begun.

Al-Qaeda didn't immediately give up on the possibility of intra-jihadist peace. Even after Abu Khalid's death, the group publicly reached out to ISIS and its supporters while simultaneously working to undermine Baghdadi's authority. In May 2014 Zawahiri released a lengthy message titled "Testimonial to Preserve the Blood of Mujahedin in al-Sham."[116] Al-Qaeda's emir offered an olive branch to Baghdadi, asking him to "listen to and obey your emir once again." Zawahiri said loyalists around the globe had asked him to address the history of Baghdadi's organization and its ties to al-Qaeda. Zawahiri obliged, explaining that while the original Islamic State of Iraq had been established without al-Qaeda's explicit permission, it still remained part of al-Qaeda. According to Zawahiri, Muhajir had sent a message to al-Qaeda's senior leadership, explaining that while the ISI's founding had been forced upon him for "political" reasons, he was nonetheless loyal to al-Qaeda, as was Abu Umar al-Baghdadi. Some of Abu Bakr al-Baghdadi's supporters had countered by claiming that ISIS's emir had never sworn *bayah* to al-Qaeda's leadership. Zawahiri rebutted these arguments, saying that after bin Laden's death in May 2011, ISI had sent a liaison to al-Qaeda central who asked if ISI should "renew its allegiance publicly or secretly as before."[117] Zawahiri reminded his audience that Baghdadi himself had proclaimed that al-Qaeda had "faithful men" in Iraq in his eulogy for bin Laden.

Abu Muhammad al-Adnani, Baghdadi's fire-breathing spokesman, responded to Zawahiri not long after. Adnani tried to persuade listeners that Baghdadi and his forebearers in ISI had never been full-fledged al-Qaeda subordinates.[118] But his case was mired in logical inconsistencies. At times Adnani sounded effusively pro-al-Qaeda. His message even began with a montage of al-Qaeda leaders. He said that bin Laden's vision "runs in our blood" and "has become rooted in our hearts," adding that he and his comrades "revered" and "glorified" al-Qaeda "to the extent that we have not obeyed leaderships other than this leadership." Adnani even wielded one of the same missives Zawahiri introduced as evidence of ISI's former loyalty and ISIS's present disloyalty: a message to al-Qaeda's general command from Abu Hamza al-Muhajir. Adnani conceded that Muhajir had emphasized ISI's "loyalty to the figures of the ummah as manifested in al-Qaeda." Adnani also conceded that ISIS's "emirs used to address al-Qaeda as soldiers address their emirs, students address their mentor sheikhs, and juniors address their seniors." He even admitted that ISIS had refrained from targeting Iran because the group was "acting upon the orders of al-Qaeda to safeguard its interests and supply lines in Iran."[119] ISIS refrained from operating in several countries throughout the Middle East so as not to "disobey the figures and leaders of jihad" in al-Qaeda. After essentially proving that ISIS was once an enthusiastic participant in al-Qaeda's global network, Adnani pivoted in his argument. However wonderful al-Qaeda's senior leadership might be, Adnani said, they didn't really oversee or fund ISIS's operations in Iraq, which meant that neither ISI nor ISIS was ever truly under al-Qaeda's command. Most of ISIS's rank and file didn't care about this argument's obvious weaknesses. After all, ISIS was an organization on the rise.

ALL THE CALIPH'S MEN

ISIS had made a conscious decision not to become overly dependent on al-Qaeda as it expanded into Syria. Abu Bakr al-Baghdadi had other men beside Julani who would ensure that the group's expansion into the Levant was successful, even in the event of a total break from al-Qaeda's network. One such operative was a man known as Haji Bakr, a former military officer in Saddam's regime whose real name was Samir Abd Muhammad al-Khlifawi. Bakr had joined the insurgency in Iraq early on and spent time in American custody at Camp Bucca and Abu Ghraib. After his release, Bakr reportedly relocated to the town of Tal Rifaat in Syria's northern Aleppo province by 2012. A significant cache of papers found in Bakr's home after he was killed in early 2014 included detailed plans for ISIS's future takeover of Syria.[120] In Bakr's dystopian blueprint, religion would be used as a weapon to subjugate populations. Authority would be divided among various regional and district emirs, all of whom would spy on the population and on each other, making internal dissent impossible, at least in theory.

Two other early Baghdadi loyalists in Syria were the brothers Firas and Amru al-Absi. Together they founded an organization known as Majlis Shura Dawlat al-Islam, later renamed Majlis Shura Mujahedin. In July 2012 the Absi brothers and their men seized the strategic Bab al-Hawa crossing between Turkey and northern Syria. This triumph was unmistakable proof that al-Qaeda-linked fighters were a growing presence in the rebellion. Firas al-Absi and his men reportedly belonged to al-Nusra but had remained loyal to Baghdadi throughout the intra-jihadist dispute.[121] Firas was killed by rival rebels in August 2012. His younger brother went on to become a key figure in ISIS. Amru helped woo other jihadists to Baghdadi's cause and established a foothold for the organization in Syria's Aleppo and Homs provinces. Baghdadi appointed Amru, who was killed in a March 2016 airstrike, to head ISIS's media department and serve on its shura council.[122]

Baghdadi's project received a boost when Abu Umar al-Shishani, a commander known for his bravery on the battlefield, announced his allegiance to ISIS.[123] Although his nom de guerre suggested that he was Chechen, Shishani was in fact a Georgian national and former member of his home country's U.S.-backed special forces. Shishani helped found Jaysh al-Muhajireen wa-l-Ansar (JMWA), which drew fighters from the Caucasus region to Syria.[124] JMWA initially tried to remain neutral in the conflict between ISIS and al-Qaeda, but Shishani eventually chose sides. The Georgian and a group of his men broke off from JMWA in mid-2013 and swore allegiance to Baghdadi. We noted that organizational learning can occur through the acquisition of additional talent by a group, and the addition of Shishani provided expertise that enabled a number of prominent ISIS battlefield victories. Further, Shishani's addition to ISIS probably helped convince additional foreign fighters to defect, bolstering Baghdadi. ISIS shuttled Shishani back and forth between Iraq and Syria, making sure he was deployed where he was needed most.

Another foreign fighter named Turki al-Binali provided crucial ideological support to accompany Shishani's muscle. Few major jihadist ideologues approved of Baghdadi's project, and the best-known figures actively criticized it. But Binali, a native of Bahrain, provided Baghdadi with the theological backing that he desperately needed. As early as April 2013 Binali argued in dense religious tracts that ISIS satisfied the criteria to be considered a caliphate and called on Muslims to swear allegiance to Baghdadi.[125] Binali played a significant role in recruiting foreign fighters and tried to convince some of al-Qaeda's branches to defect to Baghdadi's cause. Binali had less success in the latter endeavor, but there is no question that his arguments and pedigree were taken seriously. As a student of Abu Muhammad al-Maqdisi, one of al-Qaeda's intellectual heavyweights, Binali provided Baghdadi with crucial intellectual firepower. Maqdisi fired broadsides against ISIS's caliphate in his writings, but Binali provided the necessary rebuttals. According to the United Nations, Binali was so important that Baghdadi named him his chief religious adviser just months after ISIS's emir relocated to Raqqa in 2014.[126]

The insurgency's gains against Assad undoubtedly influenced Baghdadi's decision to formally expand ISI into Syria. In early 2013 a Jabhat al-Nusra- and Ahrar al-Sham-led consortium of rebel groups began gaining ground in and around Raqqa. By March 2013 these insurgents controlled the city, which was the first of Assad's provincial capitals to fall into the rebels' hands. It was no coincidence that Baghdadi announced his organization's official presence in Syria weeks later. Baghdadi's organization continued to make territorial gains in Syria throughout 2013, sometimes fighting alongside other groups. The group continued to win defectors and kill detractors in Syria well into 2014. At the same time ISIS was on the march across Syria, the group launched a campaign in northern and western Iraq. During this period of expansion, ISIS relied on human intelligence to map the social landscape of territory it sought to conquer in Syria and Iraq, at least in part enabled by ex-Baathist intelligence operatives who mapped cities' key players and power brokers, monitored their pattern of life, and helped ISIS co-opt, kill, or imprison them. The incorporation of ex-Baathists into ISIS further exemplifies a common strategy to enhance organizational learning that applies also to Shishani's role in ISIS: integrate outsiders with specialized knowledge. With this newfound organizational capability, ISIS managed to shock much of the international community and build a nascent state from the ashes of Abu Umar al-Baghdadi's organization.

In this period ISIS also demonstrated its capacity to experiment with emerging technologies like unmanned aerial systems (UAS). In the spring and summer of 2014 the group released propaganda videos featuring aerial shots of suicide vehicle-borne improvised explosive devices.[127] Over time, ISIS refined its UAS capabilities, particularly as commercially available UAS platforms continued to improve, just as the violent non-state-actor adoption curve anticipates. In October 2016 evidence emerged that ISIS was trying to weaponize UASs. As two Kurdish Peshmerga fighters examined a downed ISIS drone, the drone's explosive device, which was disguised as a battery, detonated, killing both fighters.[128] In subsequent months ISIS's weaponized drones proliferated.[129] ISIS settled on a more or less standardized approach to weaponization, which involved retrofitting commercially available drones. While ISIS experimented with fixed-wing versions, their most successful platforms appear to have been quadcopter drones with an underbody modification allowing them to carry grenades.[130] The grenades were dropped from carriers under the drone. ISIS's modifications to commercially available UAS technology may not have transformed the battlefield, but they did demonstrate the group's capacity for tactical creativity.

After announcing its caliphate, ISIS established an elaborate governance structure capable of indoctrinating, taxing, and enslaving a captive civilian population. A *shura* council and a second delegated committee were created as a layer of authority directly beneath Baghdadi. The former consisted of Baghdadi's most trusted advisers, who would consult him on a range of key matters. The latter was charged with carrying out some of the caliph's specific duties and held broad administrative powers. This body oversaw several other committees, along with ISIS's *dawa*-related councils and its various provinces. After conquering much of Iraq and Syria, ISIS appointed additional governors as the rulers of its various provinces in both countries. As the group announced its expansion throughout the Middle East, North Africa, and South Asia, it appointed local governors to preside over the group's conquests, although few of them controlled significant populations.

That governance structure did not emerge overnight. As this book details earlier, the Islamic State of Iraq had put in place a bureaucratic system that it intended to eventually supplant the government. Although ISI's struggles prevented it from truly engaging in the core functions of government, that dynamic rapidly changed as ISIS gained territory. ISIS established a judicial system, a very active police force, and other entities like a consumer protection authority and a department of motor vehicles.[131] It managed electrical systems, water supplies, and other public services in some of the cities it controlled.[132] Throughout its territory, ISIS enforced its rule with trademark brutality. But to create a state that provided effective public services, ISIS needed more than a local monopoly on the use of force. It needed knowledge.

ISIS integrated outside expertise into its ranks to facilitate organizational learning. In areas it conquered, ISIS forced civil servants to return to work—this time under ISIS's banner—or face punishment. Rukmini Callimachi suggests that ISIS's approach toward civil servants in these areas showed that the "militants learned from mistakes the United States made in 2003 after it invaded Iraq, including the decision to purge members of Saddam Hussein's ruling party from their positions and bar them from future employment." She explains that although that "decree succeeded in erasing the Baathist state," it also ended up gutting "the country's civil institutions, creating the power vacuum that groups like ISIS rushed to fill."[133]

ISIS's authoritarian government was to be a temporary feature of the region. Within months of Baghdadi's speech at Al-Nuri, the United States organized an international coalition to liberate the territory ISIS held. In Iraq the United States partnered with the government's forces and Iranian-backed paramilitary groups to drive Baghdadi's men from the northern and western parts of the country. In Syria a predominately Kurdish group, the Syrian Democratic Forces, served as the anti-ISIS coalition's principal ground force. By early 2019, less than five years after ISIS declared its caliphate, Baghdadi's men had lost all their territory in both countries.

ISIS has not been completely defeated. Thousands of its fighters carry on as guerrilla warriors and terrorists, vowing to revive the lost caliphate's glory. Still, the peak of ISIS's power has likely come and gone. The jihadists' caliphate has fallen—at least for now.

Learning from Past Caliphate Failures

Months before his death in May 2011 Osama bin Laden penned a memorandum to al-Qaeda's regional commanders, reminding them of their ultimate purpose. "Our main goal, and yours, is to resurrect the religion of Islam, and to build a caliphate-based state in every Muslim country," bin Laden wrote in the fall of 2010.[134] "We need to concentrate our jihad efforts in areas where the conditions are ideal for us to fight." Bin Laden named Iraq and Afghanistan as "two good examples" of where his men should focus their efforts. But he warned that al-Qaeda shouldn't render its efforts fruitless by focusing on the wrong parts of the world. "We need to fight in areas where we can gain points toward the creation of the caliphate-based state," bin Laden continued. But he warned that their enemies could "easily destroy" any state lacking the "essential foundations to function and defend itself." Although al-Qaeda viewed the United States as a weakened foe, bin Laden reminded his men that the world's only superpower was still strong enough to swiftly crush Saddam's regime and the Taliban's emirate. He warned that a newly declared caliphate would meet the same fate. "Building a state without proper foundations is like building a house in the middle of a torrential stream," he explained. "Every time the water destroys the house, we rebuild, then we rebuild until those who help us with the rebuilding give up on us."

This cycle could be demoralizing, cautioned the al-Qaeda emir. The "public does not like losers," he said, advising al-Qaeda's regional managers to avoid skipping "any of the stages" necessary for building "public support." Bin Laden wrote that "a quick work might be fruitful in the short run, but it is not what we need to do."

Al-Qaeda's failures in Iraq likely informed bin Laden's later thinking about state-building. As we have explained, bin Laden and Zawahiri fully endorsed the Islamic State of Iraq's state-building project. The timing of ISI's announcement might have taken al-Qaeda by surprise, but al-Qaeda's goal in Iraq was still to establish an emirate or caliphate, and AQSL went on to advocate forcefully on ISI's behalf. Four years later, bin Laden concluded that it wasn't wise for his men to declare Islamic states in any region. By that time ISI appeared to be a loser.

Baghdadi's Islamic State grew out of this Iraq crucible. He and his men charted a course that was almost exactly the opposite of what bin Laden and Zawahiri recommended. Since Zarqawi's days, al-Qaeda's leadership had warned militants in Iraq that brutality would alienate the population, making it impossible to maintain the support a caliphate required. ISIS's members ignored this admonition and celebrated violence to a degree that not even the sadistic Zarqawi had dared. Baghdadi's followers drowned, burned, and beheaded their victims on camera. These nightmarish images revolted the vast majority of humanity, but the gory scenes also emboldened new followers. Baghdadi's men also reveled in indiscrim-inate slaughter of Shia civilians, another tactic al-Qaeda warned against. ISIS and al-Qaeda, in other words, took very different lessons from ISI's experience.

The ISIS saga soured al-Qaeda on the idea of assigning caliph-like titles or responsibilities to any would-be militant ruler. Bin Laden and Zawahiri once endorsed Abu Umar al-Baghdadi as the emir of the faithful in Iraq, even though al-Qaeda had considered Taliban leader Mullah Omar to be the emir of the faithful. A second ruler with the same title meant there was a competing claimant. Abu Bakr al-Baghdadi eventually took this title to its logical extreme, as his followers proclaimed him the actual caliph, here and now. For al-Qaeda, the emir of the faithful was always an aspirational position. But by backing this concept in Iraq, al-Qaeda's senior leadership opened the door for a competitor to emerge. After ISIS's initial rise in 2014, al-Qaeda redoubled its claims that the Taliban's leader was the true emir of the faithful. It is not likely that al-Qaeda will endorse another aspiring caliph anytime soon.

But the story of ISIS's rise is more than a story of al-Qaeda's shortcom-ings in Iraq and Syria. It is also a story of ISIS's capacity for organizational learning. The group incorporated ex-Baathists into its ranks, who could leverage their experience in human intelligence. It experimented with emerging technologies like UAS. It relied on the experience of the prior regime's civil servants to provide public services to the populations it ruled and present itself as a normal state. That capacity for organizational learn-ing did not spare ISIS from its ultimate territorial defeats: One might say that ISIS's capacity to learn failed to save it from bd strategic choices. But if ISIS continues to invest in organizational learning, it is not inconceiv-able that the group could emerge in the future every bit as lethal and effec-tive as it was during the caliphate's height—or, chillingly, perhaps even more so.

8

The *Fitna*

ISIS Versus al-Qaeda

On April 29, 2019, Abu Bakr al-Baghdadi appeared on camera for only the second time in his long career as a jihadist standard-bearer.[1] His first on-screen appearance had come nearly five years earlier, when Baghdadi triumphantly embraced his role as the leader of a revived caliphate from the pulpit of the Great Mosque of Al-Nuri, with Baghdadi dressed in a manner evocative of a ruler from the medieval Abbasid dynasties.[2] Baghdadi's garb and surroundings at that time reinforced his stature. But Baghdadi's April 2019 appearance displayed how far his organization had plummeted. Baghdadi sat on the floor, dressed like a common fighter, with a rifle leaning against a wall behind him.

ISIS had lost its last scrap of turf in Baghouz, a ramshackle town in eastern Syria, weeks earlier. The group could no longer claim to be remaining and expanding, ISIS's motto at the height of its power. Instead Baghdadi preached patience and resiliency. He praised his men for standing their ground in Iraq, Libya, and Syria, the caliphate's three former strongholds. Even in defeat, ISIS's fighters "did not abandon their faith, nor did they give away their land to the infidels, except over their corpses and torn body parts." Baghdadi also discussed ISIS's *wilayat* (provinces) further afield, lauding them for carrying out "92 operations in eight countries . . . to avenge their brothers in Syria."[3] One of his henchmen then handed Baghdadi portfolios for each of the organization's wilayat. The files trumpeted

ISIS's continuing operations from West Africa through the heart of the Middle East and into South and Central Asia.

To some, it may have seemed that Baghdadi was merely trying to rally his demoralized foot soldiers after their dream of an ever-expanding caliphate had died. But al-Qaeda's men discerned a menacing undertone in Baghdadi's seemingly pathetic boasting. The speech was another example of ISIS aiming its statements at enemies within the jihadist movement without specifically naming al-Qaeda. When ISIS spokesman Abu Muhammad al-Adnani declared the caliphate's formation five years earlier, he claimed that the "legality of all emirates, groups, states, and organizations, becomes null by the expansion of the khilāfah's authority and arrival of its troops to their areas."[4] This was an attack on al-Qaeda and its allies around the globe, all of which were supposedly outlawed once Caliph Ibrahim's soldiers set foot on their soil.

Although he had lost his territorial caliphate since that first declaration, Baghdadi wasn't backing down in his 2019 video. A prolific al-Qaeda commentator known as Abu Yaman al-Wazzani immediately recognized the implicit threat in Baghdadi's message. In flaunting his provinces around the world, Wazzani asked, wasn't Baghdadi encouraging his followers to continue warring against al-Qaeda in Somalia and Yemen and to keep up the fight against the Taliban in Afghanistan?[5] Wazzani alleged that, in his message, Baghdadi stressed ISIS's anti-al-Qaeda satellite groups, while failing to prioritize war against the "crusaders." Even with his group in freefall, Baghdadi was inflaming the *fitna* that had engulfed the jihadists' ranks.

There is perhaps no dirtier word in the jihadist vocabulary than *fitna*. Although the term's meaning varies depending on context, *fitna* generally refers to strife or discord within the Muslim community. The concept harkens back to the first Islamic empires, an era of frequent challenges to the earliest caliphs' authority. In the jihadist context, the early Afghan militant scene witnessed bitter infighting. But the *fitna* that Baghdadi's project unleashed disrupted the jihadists' ranks like nothing before. The immediate result of Baghdadi's 2013 expansion into Syria was to divide the rebels fighting Assad. Some factions belonging to al-Nusra Front joined Baghdadi's cause, giving him a foothold in northern and eastern Syria—including in Raqqa, the city that would become the caliphate's capital. High-profile militants, such as Abu Umar al-Shishani, declared themselves caliphate loyalists. Shishani's battlefield exploits in Iraq and Syria were legendary, and he had a reputation for leading his men into some of the region's most intense combat. His defection to ISIS's ranks in mid-2013 was significant. Many foreign fighters who admired Shishani followed him to ISIS. Shishani was so important to ISIS that he stood next to Abu Muhammad al-Adnani as bulldozers symbolically erased the border between Iraq and Syria in June 2014. Footage of that scene became central to the ISIS's mythos, marking the moment the group could plausibly claim to be a real, physical political unit cutting across borders that European powers had once imposed. The group celebrated the event with a video titled "The End of Sykes-Picot."

Shishani rose through ISIS's ranks to become one of its top military commanders, battling not only the Assad regime, Iraqi security forces, and U.S.-backed fighters but also his former comrades in al-Qaeda. Shishani's death in a July 2016 airstrike in Iraq was a joyous occasion within al-Qaeda, with an affiliated cleric claiming that Shishani "was responsible for the deaths of hundreds of mujahedin" in Syria and praising Allah for the jihadist icon's demise at the hands of a Western state.[6]

Outside Syria, the expansion of Baghdadi's group into or near the territory of rival jihadists had a lasting effect. When ISIS's chief assumed the title *amir al-muminin* (the emir of the believers), it was a direct challenge to the Taliban, who believed their leader possessed an identical stature. Indeed, a few months after his stirring appearance at Al-Nuri's pulpit, Baghdadi's caliphate had expanded far beyond Iraq and Syria. In November 2014 jihadists in Algeria, Egypt, Libya, Saudi Arabia, and Yemen publicly swore allegiance to the caliph. Baghdadi publicly accepted their oaths of fealty, announcing "the expansion of the Islamic State to new lands." He declared "the nullification of the groups" in the lands into which his caliphate had expanded—in other words, that al-Qaeda and other jihadist competitors had become illegal entities from his caliphate's perspective.[7] Baghdadi's acceptance of these new affiliates thus recapitulated ISIS's original challenge to the legitimacy of other jihadist groups, as the caliphate's authority extended into any land where Baghdadi's loyalists established themselves.

This approach, which continued even after ISIS lost its territorial caliphate, was a power play that produced *fitna* thousands of miles from Syria's borders. ISIS's project was a particular threat to al-Qaeda. The group's constant attacks on al-Qaeda stemmed in part from the fact that both groups were competing for the hearts and minds of militant groups and sympathizers across the globe. To supplant al-Qaeda as the preeminent jihadist group and maintain that status, ISIS needed to outcompete al-Qaeda online and on the battlefield. ISIS's expansion into Central Asia, South Asia, and Africa led to clashes between al-Qaeda affiliates and ISIS's *wilayat*. Despite ISIS's best efforts, al-Qaeda's affiliates retained the upper hand in many of these confrontations. This chapter explores the theory behind each group's approach, examines how it related to their own methods of organizational learning, and provides a detailed account of how the intra-jihadist competition played out worldwide.

Two Competing Jihadist Models

In evaluating the competing models of ISIS and al-Qaeda, it is important to appreciate just how disruptive ISIS's challenge was for al-Qaeda. For almost two decades, al-Qaeda was recognized as the world's dominant Salafi jihadist militant group. Al-Qaeda's competition against its enemies until 2013–2014 can be understood conceptually as a two-player game: Al-Qaeda represented Salafi jihadism, and its opponent was countries and other actors who opposed or failed to live up to its puritanical vision of Islam. This two-player dynamic changed with ISIS's dramatic growth. Differences between the two groups were discernible early on. For one, ISIS was more technology-savvy: It understood social media's ability to mobilize people to its cause in a way that al-Qaeda did not despite Awlaki's influence. ISIS also expected to experience success in a shorter timeframe than al-Qaeda.

Despite similar ideologies and a common objective of creating a caliphate, al-Qaeda and ISIS soon found themselves locked in a fierce competition. What had once been a two-player game had been transformed into a three-player game.[8] ISIS exploited the vulnerabilities inherent to the deliberate approach that al-Qaeda had adopted and portrayed al-Qaeda's patience as indecisiveness. In the classic volume *Makers of Modern Strategy*, John Shy and Thomas Collier define revolutionary war as "the seizure of political power by the use of armed force," with the additional characteristics "that the seizure of power is by a popular or broad-based political movement, that the seizure entails a fairly long period of armed conflict, and that power is seized in order to carry out a well-advertised political or social program."[9] A number of authors, including David Kilcullen and Michael Vlahos, have explicitly adopted the framework of understanding jihadist actors as revolutionaries in their analysis of al-Qaeda.[10] Stathis Kalyvas similarly proposed that ISIS should be considered a revolutionary movement.[11]

The two groups differed in their approach to revolution. Al-Qaeda favored covert actions, unacknowledged affiliates, and a relatively quiet organizational strategy for building a larger base of support. ISIS, in contrast, believed the time for a broader military confrontation had already arrived and combined shocking violence with effective propaganda. A useful framework for understanding these groups' strategies can be found by contrasting the Maoist and Focoist schools of revolutionary thought. Al-Qaeda exhibited a revolutionary strategy that is both implicitly and explicitly based on the works of Mao Tse-tung, whereas ISIS possessed a strategy more consonant with the Focoist approach of Ernesto "Che" Guevara and Régis Debray.[12]

Mao's theory of revolution is rooted in the primacy of politics over warfare. His first two principles are "arousing and organizing the people," and "achieving internal unification politically."[13] In Mao's paradigm, these steps, which constitute his first stage of revolutionary warfare, must occur before the initiation of military action, covert or otherwise. Mao's first stage—of organization, consolidation, and preservation—is followed by a stage of progressive expansion, followed by a third and final stage of decision, or the destruction of the enemy. Only upon a steadfast political foundation, in Mao's view, can guerrilla forces create bases for logistics and operations and build the strength for the final conventional stage of warfare. Mao rarely undertook strategic military offensives outside of areas that were prepared politically.[14]

Under Mao's theory of revolutionary warfare, the early stages do not terminate with the initiation of a new stage. Thus, Maoist revolutionaries continue to emphasize the political stage of organization and consolidation even as they pursue progressive expansion. Consistent with Maoist theory, al-Qaeda and its affiliates focused on building the group's political support. Even in areas where al-Qaeda openly undertook warfare, it was somewhat restrained in its approach to civilian populations and adopted a relatively slow and phased implementation of its hardline version of sharia where it enjoyed territorial control.

Contrary to the Maoist approach is the Focoist approach to revolutionary war. First used successfully in Cuba in the 1950s and attempted unsuccessfully many times since, Focoism holds that the political foundation for revolution can be crafted through violence. Che Guevara essentially flipped Mao's theory by arguing that the use of violence against the state could inspire the peasants to rise up.[15] Focoism accepts great risks in order to inspire support. ISIS in many ways followed the Focoist model. It believed in the power of violence to forge the political opinions of the Muslim masses. ISIS viewed al-Qaeda's more deliberate Maoist-style approach as too slow. ISIS was willing to take significant risks for propaganda purposes and was happy to win today and lose tomorrow if today's win created a large enough subject for propaganda.

This framework of Maoist versus Focoist models of revolutionary warfare should not be seen as a complete explanation of either al-Qaeda or ISIS. Neither group was perfectly Maoist or Focoist, but they can be understood as having largely adhered to one or the other revolutionary paradigm.[16] One virtue of this framework is that it places al-Qaeda and ISIS within the broader revolutionary history in which they reside and thus illuminates certain aspects of their respective strategies.

Examining the implications of the two groups' approaches, al-Qaeda's use of Maoist strategy was designed to be low risk and to yield long-term results. This is consistent with al-Qaeda's conception of its conflict with the West as existential and generational in nature. The group took steps to ingratiate itself with local populations and reduce its exposure to counterrevolutionary forces. Jabhat al-Nusra even convinced some U.S. allies—namely Qatar, Saudi Arabia, and Turkey—that it should be viewed as a partner in the fight against ISIS and also Assad's brutal regime. ISIS's use of a more Focoist strategy carried greater risks. The group's extreme violence and imposition of repressive governance alienated populations under its control, as ISIS knew it would. ISIS employed repression to deal with this problem, making an example of would-be opponents. The riskiness of this approach is the primary reason that Focoist revolutions have experienced very limited success outside of Cuba: Focoism inherently exposes revolutionary forces to counterrevolutionaries, who are often better equipped.[17]

Although ISIS correctly discerned a vulnerability in al-Qaeda's approach that allowed the challenger to rapidly gain market share in the world of jihadism, bin Laden and Zawahiri were nevertheless correct in warning that the United States and its allies could easily destroy any jihadist state. The United States dislodged Baghdadi's men from their strongholds by working with and through allies, proxies, and an airpower campaign without having to mobilize the large-scale forces deployed at the height of the Iraq War. For more sophisticated jihadists, the lesson of the caliphate's impatience will be obvious. ISIS failed to become the empire its members and supporters had dreamed of. Instead, the organization now survives as an insurgency and terrorist operation.

Another difference between the two was ISIS's obsession with *bayah*, which relates to its Focoist approach that emphasizes the visibility of the group's efforts. ISIS constantly marketed scenes in which followers in various hotspots swore fealty to Baghdadi. In mid-2019, for instance, ISIS's propagandists produced a series of videos titled "And the Best Outcome is for the Pious" featuring men in Afghanistan, Azerbaijan, Bangladesh, the Caucasus, the Democratic Republic of the Congo, Iraq, Libya, Mozambique, the Philippines, Somalia, Syria, Tunisia, Turkey, West Africa, and Yemen renewing their oaths of allegiance to Baghdadi. At the time ISIS controlled little to no territory in these places. But the presence of the group's "soldiers" was enough for ISIS to make claims on power and declare that fealty remained a religious necessity for all Muslims. In contrast, al-Qaeda has often been reluctant to publicly acknowledge its foreign branches.

The two groups' differing approach influenced not only the output of their propaganda but even their propaganda apparatuses—although al-Qaeda's propaganda efforts came to more resemble those of ISIS over time. ISIS portrayed its branches as parts of a singular entity, with common color schemes, labeling, and online media distribution points. Amaq News Agency efficiently packaged short video clips from around the globe into uniform-looking productions. A supporter of the caliphate could download similar-looking videos originating from places as far from one another as West Africa or Southeast Asia. In comparison, al-Qaeda's media were more diffuse. Each of al-Qaeda's regional branches had its own media shop, so the global network's messages and videos were not always disseminated through a common channel. Most recently, al-Qaeda's As-Sahab Media tried to get these regional outlets to operate on a common platform. Videos from both al-Qaeda's senior leadership and its foreign branches now feature graphics with the logos for As-Sahab alongside all the emblems of the local affiliates' various media arms: Az-Zallaqa (Jama'at Nusrat al-Islam wa-l-Muslimin), Al-Andalus Media (AQIM), Al-Malahem Media (AQAP), and Al-Kataib Media (al-Shabaab).[18] This is illustrative of increasing media coordination, but al-Qaeda still hasn't approached the frequency or consistency of ISIS's messaging.

Perhaps most importantly, the two rivals evolved distinctly different approaches to violence. ISIS's broad application of *takfir* justified violence on a massive scale. Unlike al-Qaeda, the caliphate's men gleefully shared the goriest of images, while ISIS's *takfiri* policies led the group to declare a broad segment of the Muslim population to be apostates. Al-Qaeda cautioned against this course of action, warning that it could alienate locals and lead to an endless hunt for internal enemies. This, indeed, proved to be the case, with the rise of an ultraradical school within the Islamic State, the Hazimis, which this book discusses later.

The *fitna* that began in 2014 caused turmoil throughout al-Qaeda's ranks, but it didn't break the group. Today al-Qaeda's regional branches are actually stronger than ISIS's provinces in several parts of the world. Fleshing out the differing approaches of ISIS and al-Qaeda, we now turn to the competition between the two groups' regional branches.

ISIS's Provinces Versus al-Qaeda's Regional Branches

In a 1997 interview bin Laden explained why Muslims should trust al-Qaeda instead of the dictators ruling the MENA region. "Muslims need a leader who can unite them and establish the 'pious caliphate,'" which would "start from Afghanistan," bin Laden argued. In his first post-9/11 interview, bin Laden said that al-Qaeda wanted "the revival of this nation under the Islamic caliphate, as predicted by the Prophet in his traditions." Other al-Qaeda leaders similarly emphasized the caliphate's eventual revival.[19]

The quest to resurrect the caliphate was central to al-Qaeda's organization, propaganda, and self-image long before ISIS earned worldwide infamy. This is one reason that the group was so alarmed at Baghdadi's claim in 2014 that, with ISIS's military advance from Syria into Iraq, the Muslims now "have a state and *khilāfah*, which will return your dignity, might, rights, and leadership."[20] By declaring his caliphate, Baghdadi claimed to have delivered the victory that al-Qaeda's leaders repeatedly said was necessary to restoring Islam's stature and power. Al-Qaeda often discussed the oppression of Sunni Muslims at the hands of various nefarious forces, but Baghdadi now claimed to have liberated them, delivering a state that would protect their interests and govern according to the jihadists' puritanical version of Islam. Baghdadi and his men not only sought to undermine Zawahiri's authority as the "wise man of the umma," as his followers called him, but also encouraged al-Qaeda loyalists around the globe to defect to their side.

ISIS's provincial model was one method ISIS employed to undermine al-Qaeda, which already had its own province-like entities. Although al-Qaeda's senior leadership advocated a patient approach to caliphate-building, these leaders were still laying the groundwork for an international jihadist state, however far off it might be. In the years following the 9/11 hijackings, al-Qaeda expanded to include regional franchises across Africa, the Middle East, and South Asia. In the West, these groups are often called al-Qaeda's "affiliates," but they can also be referred to as "branches" that possess a clear operational connection to the group's central leadership.[21] These groups include al-Qaeda in the Arabian Peninsula (AQAP), al-Qaeda in the Islamic Maghreb (AQIM), the AQIM-established affiliate Jama'at Nusrat al-Islam wa-l-Muslimin (JNIM) in West Africa, al-Qaeda in the Indian Subcontinent (AQIS), and al-Shabaab in Somalia. Until July 2016 al-Nusra Front was al-Qaeda's official branch in the Levant. Each al-Qaeda branch is headed by an emir who has sworn *bayah* to al-Qaeda's overall leader. In Syria the leadership of Tanzim Hurras al-Din is also faithful to Zawahiri. Al-Qaeda and its regional branches sometimes work with or through other front groups that are not themselves openly part of the al-Qaeda organization. The Ansar al-Sharia organizations that sprouted in North Africa and beyond following the 2011 Arab uprisings are a revealing example of this practice. Al-Qaeda has also maintained close ties to various other jihadist groups, such as the Pakistani Taliban. ISIS would try to lure all of these organizations away from al-Qaeda's orbit.

In al-Qaeda's model, each of its regional branches is responsible for laying the groundwork for a future emirate. The branches are principally insurgent groups intent on transforming local political structures so a government adhering to al-Qaeda's version of sharia can rise in their place. In the future, al-Qaeda believed, these emirates would join together to form a contiguous caliphate. Al-Qaeda's ambition stretches all the way to Spain, which the jihadists still call by its Arabic name of Al-Andalus. Abdullah Azzam ruled in a famous fatwa that jihad was an individual duty for all Muslims until the reconquest of Al-Andalus and all other territory that had once been under the dominion of past caliphates.[22] That remains al-Qaeda's mission, even if it sounds far-fetched to Western ears.

HOW AL-QAEDA'S REGIONAL BRANCHES WERE FORMED

To illuminate how ISIS's model was so threatening to al-Qaeda, we now concisely review how al-Qaeda's regional branches were born and developed. Al-Qaeda's regional branches share the senior leadership's goal of establishing a pan-Islamic caliphate. In October 2004 Abu Musab al-Zarqawi swore allegiance to bin Laden on behalf of himself and his organization, Tawhid wa-l-Jihad. Zarqawi's operation was quickly renamed al-Qaeda in the Land of Two Rivers, even though it was more popularly known as al-Qaeda in Iraq. "Land of Two Rivers" was a reference to the Euphrates and Tigris, which cut across Iraq's interior. Zarqawi's oath to bin Laden specifically referred to Iraq's historic role as the seat of power for past caliphates, describing the country as "the land . . . of the Caliphs" and declaring that a caliphate following the "guidance of Prophethood" would be resurrected.

The second al-Qaeda regional branch was established in September 2006, when the Algeria-based Salafist Group for Preaching and Combat (GSPC) negotiated its admission into the jihadist network. In 2007 GSPC rebranded as al-Qaeda in the Islamic Maghreb and the group's emir, Abdelmalek Droukdel, announced his fealty to bin Laden.[23]

GSPC's founding charter, which the group published online after joining al-Qaeda, listed several objectives. GSPC said it was established to carry out "phased means" toward "establishing a group of Muslims—the caliphate," which it described as a "sacred goal that all Muslims must strive to attain."[24] After the group rebranded as AQIM, a GSPC veteran known as Younis al-Mauritani explained that a future caliphate remained one of the organization's chief goals. In an August 2007 letter recovered from bin Laden's Abbottabad compound, Mauritani summarized the state of the jihadists' project in Algeria, where the government had ruthlessly suppressed AQIM. Mauritani viewed the merger of GSPC with al-Qaeda as a potential boon because it "had changed the balances, and confused the accounts of the local, regional and international foes." This "unity and consolidation of the ranks under the term *Al-Tawhid* created a support that the Caliphate state was based upon," al-Mauritani elaborated.[25]

Mauritani was a true al-Qaeda insider when he penned this letter. He had served as GSPC's liaison to al-Qaeda's core leadership in Pakistan and negotiated the merger between the two groups.[26] His letter illustrates the relationship between al-Qaeda's regional branches in Iraq and Africa at the time. Zarqawi's "students" had arrived to buttress AQIM's ranks, Mauritani noted, adding that they "would not be satisfied with anything other than the VBIEDs [vehicle-borne improvised explosive devices] and the suicide attacks."[27] Zarqawi played a "pivotal role" in the "first phases" of GSPC's merger with al-Qaeda, according to Droukdel.[28]

Al-Qaeda announced the merger of its operations in Saudi Arabia and Yemen into the new al-Qaeda in the Arabian Peninsula in January 2009.[29] AQAP quickly gained notoriety for its efforts to attack the United States, and its leadership was stocked with jihadist veterans determined to strike the far enemy. All four of AQAP's founders had been imprisoned in the years following the 9/11 hijackings but either had been freed or had escaped. Nasir al-Wuhayshi had been bin Laden's aide-de-camp. Wuhayshi and fellow AQAP cofounder Qasim al-Raymi had been imprisoned in Yemen but escaped in a 2006 jailbreak. They quickly got to work rebuilding al-Qaeda's footprint in the country. Wuhayshi was named AQAP's emir, a position he held until his death in an American airstrike in June 2015. Wuhayshi simultaneously served as one of al-Qaeda's top global deputies, a dual role that shows how the organization's branches are part of an integrated network. Raymi was initially named AQAP's military commander but became AQAP's overall emir in mid-2015 after a series of leadership losses, including Wuhayshi's death. AQAP's other two cofounders, Said al-Shihri and Abu al-Harith Muhammad al-Awfi, had been Guantánamo detainees. The two were transferred from Guantánamo to their native Saudi Arabia, where they were enrolled in a rehabilitation program. The program didn't work: The pair absconded to Yemen, where they helped relaunch AQAP.

Shihri served as AQAP's first deputy emir. He explained al-Qaeda's objectives in the Arabian Peninsula in the January 2009 video that announced the group's creation.[30] The organization's men were following the path of the martyrs, he said, until they could "establish the state of Islam and a righteous caliphate according to the guidance of our prophet." Either this utopia would be realized or Shihri and his comrades would be martyred trying to build it, the deputy emir promised. The latter desire was granted, as Shihri died in an American drone strike in 2013.[31]

Al-Qaeda also expanded its reach into other parts of Africa. In February 2012 the Somali militant group al-Shabaab and al-Qaeda publicly announced their merger, with al-Shabaab serving as the organization's proto-emirate in East Africa. There has been some confusion in analytic circles over the Somali group's role in al-Qaeda. Most prominently, the analysts who were given the first opportunity to view documents seized from bin Laden's Abbottabad compound and write about them in the public sphere, who were based at West Point's Combating Terrorism Center (CTC), concluded that the al-Qaeda leader had "denied" al-Shabaab's "request for formal unity."[32] Based on a single August 2010 letter written by bin Laden, CTC's analysts concluded that the emir "discouraged" official unification, and "politely declined" such an offer from al-Shabaab leader Ahmed Abdi Godane (a.k.a. Mukhtar Abu al-Zubayr).[33] The authors of the CTC analysis wondered why bin Laden would deny al-Shabaab "official membership in" al-Qaeda "yet still honor Abu al-Zubayr with a personal and cordial letter that he could have asked" his right-hand man "to write on his behalf."[34] The analysts then launched into a lengthy speculative analysis seeking answers to this question, which was itself based on an inaccurate reading of the 2010 letter. Bin Laden had not denied al-Shabaab's request for unity: He had simply told al-Shabaab's leader to keep their union secret for pragmatic reasons.

In fact, parts of the missive strongly implied that al-Shabaab was part of al-Qaeda's larger organizational structure. In the same letter to Zubayr, bin Laden specifically addressed "the issue of unity," writing that "this obligation should be carried out legitimately and through unannounced secret messaging."[35] News of the groups' relationship was to be spread "among the people of Somalia, without any official declaration by any officers on our side or your side, that the unity has taken place." Bin Laden further advised that his allies in Somalia should "say that there is a relationship with al-Qaeda, which is simply a brotherly Islamic connection and nothing more," a vague formulation that could be neither denied nor proven—and one that the post–Arab Spring Ansar al-Sharia groups would employ in a slightly modified form. Bin Laden carefully explained his reasoning, telling Zubayr that if "the matter [of unity] becomes declared and out in the open," then "it would have the enemies escalate their anger and mobilize against you," a fate similar to "what happened to the brothers in Iraq or Algeria" previously. Regardless, it was "true that the enemies will find out inevitably" about their ties because "this matter cannot be hidden, especially when people go around and spread this news." If bin Laden had denied Zubayr's request for unity, then there was nothing that needed to be hidden in the first place. An "official declaration remains to be the master for all proof," the al-Qaeda founder acknowledged. Still, bin Laden explained that by keeping the merger secret, Muslims throughout the region could continue to do business with al-Shabaab's upstart emirate without the consequences that come from cooperating with al-Qaeda.

Bin Laden's letter to Zubayr was an attachment to a longer message written for bin Laden's right-hand man, Atiyah Abd al-Rahman.[36] This longer letter wasn't released to the public until a 2015 terrorism trial in Brooklyn. In the longer letter, bin Laden explains to Atiyah what al-Shabaab's *bayah* to him should entail. "As for the pledge of allegiance from the brothers in Somalia, let it be based on waging jihad to establish the caliphate," bin Laden wrote. Bin Laden also explained why Abu Yahya al-Libi, a top al-Qaeda ideologue, needed to help al-Shabaab "now that they have joined us." Libi shouldn't be kept busy "with administrative work instead of conducting scholarly research due to its importance and our huge need for his efforts, especially after our brothers in Somalia have had the upper hand." After all, al-Shabaab now controlled "an Islamic emirate on the ground with millions of subjects," heavy responsibilities that demanded "close follow-up" from AQSL. The "gravity of the responsibility upon our shoulders now that they have joined us" meant that Libi should "dedicate a big part of his time for this mission, and not just to prepare the research they ask him for, but also to anticipate what they will need and prepare it for them."

Bin Laden clearly considered al-Shabaab to be one of al-Qaeda's regional branches when he wrote those August 2010 missives. The al-Qaeda founder repeatedly referred to al-Shabaab's territory in Somalia as an emirate and advised Zubayr to refrain from openly declaring an Islamic state: If al-Shabaab prematurely announced its emirate and failed to deliver on its vision, bin Laden argued, the population's expectations would go unmet, fueling discontent. After bin Laden's death, his successor, Zawahiri, decided that AQSL would no longer keep the nature of their relationship with al-Shabaab a secret. In February 2012, al-Qaeda and al-Shabaab announced their union, and Zawahiri publicly accepted Zubayr's bayah.

Al-Qaeda's strategy of viewing affiliates as vehicles for long-term caliphate-building extended into South Asia. In September 2014 Zawahiri announced the formation of AQIS, which incorporated elements of various preexisting al-Qaeda-affiliated groups throughout Afghanistan and Pakistan. Nearly three years later, in June 2017, AQIS released its "code of conduct." AQIS explained that its key objectives included "striving to implement the *Shari'ah* of Muhammad and to establish *Khilafah* in compliance with the Prophetic method," and that "strengthening and defending of [the] Islamic Emirate of Afghanistan is part of this objective."[37] The Taliban's Islamic Emirate had been a key part of al-Qaeda's imagined caliphate. Although the Taliban's emirate was lost as the result of the post-9/11 U.S. invasion, al-Qaeda and its closest allies in the region have been fighting to reclaim it ever since. Figure 8.1 provides a timeline of al-Qaeda's global expansion.

Ayman al-Zawahiri had sworn his own *bayah* to the Taliban's leader, keeping with a tradition that bin Laden began. The first Taliban emir to secure al-Qaeda's loyalty was Mullah Omar, a reclusive figure who died in

Prior Group Name	Al-Qaeda Affiliate Name	Date Affiliate Announced as Part of al-Qaeda
Jama'at al-Tawhid wa-l-Jihad	Al-Qaeda in Iraq (AQI)	October 2004
Salafist Group for Preaching and Combat (GSPC)	Al-Qaeda in the Islamic Maghreb (AQIM)	September 2006
Preexisting al-Qaeda-linked groups	Al-Qaeda in the Arabian Peninsula (AQAP)	January 2009
Al-Shabaab	Al-Shabaab	February 2012
Preexisting al-Qaeda-linked groups	Al-Qaeda in the Indian Subcontinent (AQIS)	September 2014

FIG. 8.1 Major announced al-Qaeda affiliates

2013, although the Taliban neglected to announce his death until 2015. Mullah Mansour succeeded Omar. Zawahiri quickly renewed his *bayah* to Mansour, whom the United States then killed in a May 2016 airstrike. Hibatullah Akhundzada, who sacrificed his own son in a suicide bombing in southern Afghanistan in 2017, then took over as Taliban chief. Naturally, Zawahiri swore *bayah* to Akhundzada too. Al-Qaeda's regional branches have formally recognized that Zawahiri's *bayah* to the Taliban's leader also applies to them. Senior figures in AQAP, AQIM/JNIM, AQIS, and al-Shabaab have all described the Taliban's top man as the emir of the faithful.

Abu Bakr al-Baghdadi claimed that same title for himself in mid-2014, then decreed every jihadist group other than ISIS to be illegitimate. ISIS's caliphate declaration was a frontal assault on al-Qaeda's system of proto-emirates. In addition to providing material incentives to leave al-Qaeda's orbit, ISIS effectively asked al-Qaeda's affiliates: *Why wait for the caliphate to be reestablished in the future when we have resurrected it now?*

THE MEDIA WAR

ISIS produced a torrent of anti-al-Qaeda messaging. Abu Muhammad al-Adnani led the charge, repeatedly blasting al-Qaeda. For example, in a May 2014 message titled "Apologies, Emir of al-Qaeda," Adnani claimed that Baghdadi had never been an al-Qaeda man and that the Islamic State of Iraq was never really an al-Qaeda branch.[38] In chapter 7 we dissected this document's weaknesses and inconsistencies. It isn't clear why Adnani or his supporters thought "Apologies, Emir of al-Qaeda" helped their cause. But for Baghdadi's diehards, a litigation of the past held little interest, as the caliphate's siren call was enough.

Zawahiri set forth his own version of events in his eventual rebuttal to Adnani's revisionist history, citing evidence that Baghdadi and ISI were part of al-Qaeda's global network before they disobeyed their emir.[39] Al-Qaeda also relied on high-profile clerics, including Abu Qatada al-Filistini, Abu Muhammad al-Maqdisi, Hani al-Sibai, and Tariq Abdul Halim, to undermine ISIS's caliphate claim. Other lesser-known figures jumped into the rivalry as well. Ahmad Abousamra, an American graduate of the University of Massachusetts in Boston, was one who entered the fray.[40] In December 2013 Abousamra, who adopted the name Abu Maysara al-Shami, was added to the FBI's Most Wanted Terrorists List, along with a

$50,000 reward for information leading to his arrest.[41] Abu Maysara was living in Aleppo when the uprisings against Assad began in 2011. He joined al-Nusra Front but didn't remain in al-Nusra's ranks when its leader, Abu Muhammad al-Julani, openly defied Baghdadi in April 2013. Instead Abu Maysara stayed loyal to the future caliph.

Indeed, Abu Maysara became one of al-Qaeda's most persistent and vicious critics. According to an ISIS hagiography published after Abu Maysara's death in a 2017 airstrike, a member of Baghdadi's inner coterie first recognized the former Bostonian's potential as an ideological brawler. That man was an Iraqi known as Abu Mohammed al-Furqan, who may have earned his nickname because he headed Al Furqan Media, which had served as the central media arm for the group's senior leadership since the days of al-Qaeda in Iraq. He also "played a leading role" in setting up the Amaq News Agency and launching ISIS's magazine *Dabiq*.[42] In addition to serving on ISIS's senior *shura* council, which directly advised Baghdadi, Furqan was the group's minister of information.[43] Furqan oversaw the "production of terrorist propaganda videos showing torture and executions," the Pentagon stated when announcing Furqan's death in September 2016.[44] He also recruited new media talent for his operation, including Abu Maysara.

In ISIS's telling, Furqan realized that Abu Maysara's talents would be wasted if he died as a suicide bomber. Furqan stopped the American from conducting a suicide operation against Assad's forces in Aleppo early in the war, sending another bomber in Abu Maysara's stead. Furqan then recruited Abu Maysara into ISIS's media division. Abu Maysara translated the organization's productions into English and served as the chief editor of *Dabiq*, ISIS's first English-language magazine. The inaugural issue of *Dabiq*, titled "The Return of Khilafah," appeared online on July 5, 2014, just days after ISIS declared its caliphate.

Throughout fifteen issues published online across two years, Abu Maysara's *Dabiq* glorified life in the new caliphate, reinforced the message of war against the rest of the world, and encouraged supporters to conduct attacks in the West. *Dabiq* also became an integral part of ISIS's anti-al-Qaeda propaganda campaign. The online magazine published screeds aimed at their jihadist rivals' leaders and policies. For instance, the cover story of *Dabiq*'s sixth issue, "Al Qa'idah of Waziristan: A Testimony from Within," featured the testimony of an alleged al-Qaeda security official who had decamped for the caliphate.[45] The defector, known as Abu Jarir ash-Shamali, criticized bin Laden for supposedly failing to declare the apostasy of "rulers and their armies" throughout the Muslim-majority world prior to the 9/11 hijackings. Even in the leadup to 9/11, bin Laden hadn't been doctrinaire enough for ISIS.

Abu Maysara personally wrote a number of articles in *Dabiq*, such as "The Jews of Jihad," in which he alleged that al-Qaeda's branches devised a plan to infiltrate Baghdadi's caliphate and reform it from within. "Jews of Jihad," which associated al-Qaeda with anti-Semitic tropes, became a popular insult employed by ISIS's followers in early 2016, and the essay was shared widely across the group's social media channels.

ISIS's *al-Naba* newsletter became a regular source for Arabic-language anti-al-Qaeda commentary. *Al-Naba*'s editors chafed at the allegation that ISIS was unlawfully killing Muslims in comparison to al-Qaeda's jihad. According to *al-Naba*, al-Qaeda and its branches had committed a number of "violations in sharia policy," ranging from excessive leniency toward "polytheists" (meaning Shias and also non-Muslims) to their willingness to ally "with bands of apostates" who were "facilitating their victory over the Muslim soldiers of the Islamic State." *Al-Naba* charged that al-Qaeda's men had warred against ISIS's Muslims while "allying with idolators" in Syria, Libya, the Khorasan, Somalia, and Yemen. In contrast, *Al-Naba* claimed, ISIS fought and killed "all unbelievers and polytheists" no matter who they were.[46]

ISIS tried to poach al-Qaeda's regional branches. But not one of al-Qaeda's major branches broke with Zawahiri in its entirety. These branches and their allies fought Baghdadi's men both on the ground and in the realm of ideas. We now turn to the competition between ISIS and al-Qaeda in four key places: the Khorasan (an area encompassing Afghanistan, Pakistan, and parts of the surrounding countries), the Arabian Peninsula, North and West Africa, and East Africa. Baghdadi's men ran into stiff opposition in each region.

Fitna in the Khorasan Region

On January 26, 2015, Abu Muhammad al-Adnani announced ISIS's expansion to Khorasan in a speech bluntly titled "Say, Die in Your Rage."[47] Adnani claimed that Afghanistan's mujahedin now had the chance to enter a "new

fight" as part of ISIS's Khorasan province. The region's jihadists had battled the British, the Russians and the Americans since the mid-nineteenth
century, Adnani said, but they could now fight to "enforce *tawhīd* (monotheism) and vanquish *shirk*," or idolatry and polytheism. Although the ISIS
spokesman didn't address the Taliban directly, he was clearly speaking to
its rank and file, accusing the group of not following a purely monotheis-
tic creed and of being too merciful toward Shias. In his broadside, Adnani
sought to leverage one of the major differences in strategy between ISIS
and al-Qaeda to draw followers away from the Taliban. Prior to 9/11 the
Taliban had massacred thousands of Hazaras, Afghans who adhere to a version of Shia Islam.[48] But in more recent years, the group had adopted a
hesitancy toward sparking sectarian war and generally refrained from
directly targeting Hazara civilians. Restraint on the part of rival militants
presented ISIS with an opportunity. Adnani and his comrades could cor-
ner the market on anti-Hazara violence. ISIS's Khorasan province has
frequently launched suicide bombings against Shia targets in Kabul and
throughout Afghanistan and Pakistan.

Taliban leader Mullah Mansour answered Adnani's challenge several
months later, in a letter addressed to Baghdadi.[49] Mansour opened his missive with a tribute to the "heroes" of the modern era of jihad, all of whom
had "graduated" from the Afghan school of militancy. He named Abdullah Azzam, bin Laden, and Zarqawi. Mansour then explained that the Taliban's men had made many "sacrifices" in their fight against the United
States and its allies. The international *kuffar* couldn't tolerate an Islamic
emirate that governed according to sharia, and American defeat in Afghanistan would be a crushing victory over Crusaders the world over. The fight
was too urgent for there to be a split in jihadist ranks, Mansour claimed.
It is "important to bring to your attention that the Islamic Emirate's jihadist policy against the Crusaders and the international *kuffar*" relies on a
"unity of lines," Mansour wrote. Mansour prayed that Baghdadi's men
would not sow further divisions or incite new "disputes." But if they did
create problems, Mansour continued, Muslims "all over the world would
be unhappy." Underscoring the gravity of his warning, Mansour's message
was disseminated in Arabic, Dari, English, Pashto, and Urdu.

Baghdadi and Adnani paid little attention to Mansour's admonition.
Within months of Wilayah Khorasan's formal establishment, the two sides
were clashing in the country's western Farah province and the eastern

province of Nangarhar, along with Helmand and Zabul in the south.[50] In most of these areas ISIS's fighters were no match for the Taliban's special forces, elite commando units originally equipped to combat NATO soldiers and their Afghan allies. ISIS put up a credible fight, though. Wilayah Khorasan even turned the Tora Bora Mountains, site of Osama bin Laden's hideout in late 2001, into a contested front, losing and then regaining ground on multiple occasions.[51] The Taliban's jihadist opponents also established a foothold in the northern Jowzjan province. That move was also met with stern resistance. In the summer of 2018 Taliban commanders overran ISIS's positions in Jowzjan, killing or capturing hundreds of fighters and forcing others to surrender to the Afghan government.[52] ISIS managed to survive the Taliban's onslaught and carve out a small safe haven in eastern Afghanistan that included parts of Nangarhar and Kunar provinces. ISIS also established cells in neighboring countries.

The Khorasan-based competition between the two sides has been similarly intense on the internet. ISIS's propaganda machine set its sights on the Taliban, repeatedly issuing condemnations of the group and its longstanding alliance with al-Qaeda. In *al-Naba*, Baghdadi's propagandists labeled the Taliban a nationalist and apostate movement, blasting it for being overly willing to accommodate the "polytheist states" surrounding Afghanistan.[53] ISIS's propagandists argued that the Taliban had become a "servant" and "watchdog" for apostate governments by assuring them that territory under Taliban control would not be used to conduct "new attacks" abroad. Moreover, ISIS alleged, the Taliban received guidance from the "Pakistani intelligence services" and even developed a "close relationship" with Iran and Russia. *Dabiq* similarly railed against the Taliban. In a special issue devoted to demonizing the Shia, *Dabiq*'s editors compared the Taliban's lenient posture toward the Muslim religious minority to al-Qaeda's own policy.[54]

There was some truth to each of these critiques. The Taliban has a longstanding working relationship with sections of Pakistan's military and intelligence services. This has created a messaging problem for al-Qaeda, which naturally positions the Pakistani state as its enemy.[55] Still, al-Qaeda works closely with the Haqqani Network, an integral part of the Taliban that has its own history of cooperating with Pakistani intelligence. Members of the Taliban's senior leadership, including the Haqqanis, have hidden out in Pakistan-based safe havens ever since the U.S.-led war in

Afghanistan began in October 2001.[56] The Taliban has also evolved an approach to diplomacy that permits collaboration with Pakistan's government, viewing Islamabad as a means to the goal of resurrecting its emirate. This philosophy extends to a host of other states. The Taliban has engaged in talks with Iran, Russia, and the United States, something ISIS's propagandists enjoy pointing out. (The treaty that the Taliban ultimately entered into with the United States is discussed further in chapter 9.) The Taliban has treated ISIS as a common enemy in its dealings with Iran and Russia and reportedly assured American diplomats that it will prevent Afghan soil from being used to plan another 9/11-style operation.[57] Even if this is an empty promise, the Taliban is willing to at least feign minimal cooperation on counterterrorism issues in exchange for Western withdrawal from Afghanistan. These moves require a pragmatism that ISIS deems inconsistent with its doctrine.

Wilayat Khorasan quickly got to work exploiting this gap, convincing disaffected commanders of established groups to join its cause. The organization's first leader was Hafiz Saeed Khan, a former Pakistani Taliban commander. His deputy, Abdul Rauf Khadim, was an ex-Afghan Taliban commander whom the United States had detained at Guantánamo.[58] These leaders' selection was no accident as their two former groups—the Afghan and Pakistani Taliban—were Wilayah Khorasan's principal recruiting targets. Over time, the caliphate's province in Afghanistan would become one of the group's strongest outposts outside Iraq and Syria. But the province has suffered through a bumpy ride and has not come close to dethroning the Taliban. Meanwhile, al-Qaeda's decades-old strategic relationships with the Taliban and like-minded groups throughout the region are still paying dividends.

ORIGINS OF THE KHORASAN *FITNA*

Wilayah Khorasan's evolution helps explain why ISIS has proven so resilient. The first noteworthy defections from al-Qaeda to ISIS came months before Baghdadi was proclaimed caliph. In April 2014 a group of nine al-Qaeda veterans, including the brother of Abu Muhammad al-Maqdisi, signed a letter protesting Zawahiri's rejection of ISIS's expansion from Iraq into Syria.[59] The letter was consistent with the rhetorical attacks ISIS would launch against al-Qaeda in the months and years that followed. The defectors objected to various al-Qaeda policies, including the group's leniency with respect to the Shia, hesitancy to brand other Muslims as apostates (*takfir*), endorsement of the Arab Spring uprisings and encouragement of the nonviolent protesters who launched them, relatively positive view of Egyptian president Mohamed Morsi, and "lack of courage" in implementing the jihadists' version of sharia.[60] When an al-Qaeda ideologue publicly responded to these charges, it hardly quelled the controversy.[61]

Another high-profile defection came on July 1, 2014, just two days after ISIS's caliphate announcement. A former Guantánamo detainee and senior Afghan Taliban leader named Abdul Rahim Muslim Dost declared his allegiance to Baghdadi.[62] Dost had served as a Taliban commander in Kunar and Nuristan, eastern provinces that have long been al-Qaeda sanctuaries. Dost distributed a short Pashto- and Dari-language booklet titled *Fateh*, meaning *victory*, in refugee camps, hoping to draw Afghans to ISIS's cause.[63] Dost also wrote a book in Arabic lauding the caliphate and its leadership.[64] As a footnote to this early defection, two years later Dost switched sides once again and reemerged as an ISIS critic.[65]

A number of mid-level Pakistani Taliban commanders, including the group's spokesman, announced their fealty to Baghdadi in October 2014.[66] These same figures, along with a few new defectors, also swore allegiance to Baghdadi in a video released on January 10, 2015.[67] In response, the Pakistani Taliban made the absurd claim that its traitorous spokesman never existed, explaining that Shahidullah Shahid was an "imaginary" name.[68] The Pakistani Taliban also publicly renewed its oath of fealty to Taliban emir Mullah Omar (although he was in fact already dead at that time). In May 2015 the Pakistani Taliban released a lengthy treatise declaring Baghdadi's "self-professed caliphate" illegitimate and praising the Afghan Taliban and AQSL.[69] According to one assessment that the UN Security Council published in mid-2019, the Pakistani Taliban has around 3,500 fighters deployed to Taliban strongholds in eastern Afghanistan.[70] Still, Wilayat Khorasan poached enough of the group's cadres to establish its own beachhead in Afghanistan and Pakistan.

But Baghdadi's caliphate failed to attract followers from Pakistan's largest jihadist organizations, such as Lashkar-e-Taiba and Jaish-e-Mohammed.[71] Instead of relying on defectors from these groups, Wilayah Khorasan developed strategic relationships within other, smaller organizations that enhanced its operational capacity. Two such outfits have jointly claimed attacks with Wilayah Khorasan: Lashkar-e-Jhangvi (LeJ) and Jamaat-ul-Ahrar (JuA). According to a study by Amira Jadoon, "72% of all deaths and 84% of all injuries" that Baghdadi's group in Pakistan caused "between January 2014 and July 2018" were a "result of jointly claimed attacks with LeJ or JuA."[72] While some of these operations were aimed at security forces, others targeted civilians from Pakistan's religious minorities, including Shiites.

Although LeJ has its own historic ties to al-Qaeda, it is a natural ally for ISIS because of their shared anti-Shia fanaticism.[73] The reasons behind JuA's attraction to the local ISIS affiliate is a more complicated story. JuA's top leaders are known to be close to al-Qaeda, but the group is an offshoot of the Pakistani Taliban, which has undertaken numerous potentially frustrating reorganizations over the years. JuA might have also collaborated with ISIS because of their common geography, as both are based in Nangarhar.[74]

Another defection to ISIS occurred in mid-2015, when the Islamic Movement of Uzbekistan (IMU) officially joined Abu Bakr al-Baghdadi's caliphate. On August 6, 2015, IMU released a video in which the group's leader, Uthman Ghazi, swore allegiance to Baghdadi alongside numerous IMU fighters. At first Ghazi's decision to quit the Taliban–al-Qaeda axis looked like one of ISIS's most important gains in South and Central Asia. IMU was one of the region's oldest jihadist organizations and had fought alongside al-Qaeda and the Taliban since the 1990s. IMU commanders had even been integrated into the Taliban's political and military command structure.[75] IMU's defection had likely been in the works for a year before the announcement, and IMU's signaling strongly foreshadowed the move. Ghazi had repeatedly praised ISIS and questioned Mullah Omar's status just weeks before the Taliban's July 2015 admission that its founder had been dead for two years.

But ISIS ended up gaining little from IMU's realignment. In late 2015 the Taliban moved against Ghazi at his base in Zabul province, ruthlessly attacking the defector and his men. After what can only be described as a rout of IMU, the Taliban disseminated photos online that appeared to show Ghazi's corpse.[76] Ghazi's disloyalty to the Taliban led to the effective liquidation of his group. A new IMU faction emerged in mid-2016 and promptly proclaimed its fealty to the Taliban.[77] Another IMU splinter group known as the Islamic Jihad Union remained loyal to the Taliban–al-Qaeda axis all along.

Wilayah Khorasan's attempts to attract Central Asian jihadists didn't end with its IMU misadventure. On July 30, 2018, ISIS claimed responsibility for the murder of four foreign tourists who had been cycling through Tajikistan.[78] The young terrorists responsible for the slayings had pledged allegiance to Baghdadi beforehand and sent footage of their oath-taking to Amaq News Agency. The killings in Tajikistan signaled ISIS's intention of growing its presence in the former Soviet republic. The group was also implicated in deadly prison uprisings in Tajikistan, including incidents in November 2018 and May 2019.[79] A Tajik national named Sayvaly Shafiev leads a group of about two hundred pro-caliphate fighters from Central Asia and is trying to recruit more extremists to his cause. According to an expert monitoring team that reports to the UN Security Council, Shafiev has been based in the eastern Nangarhar province, where he is a member of Wilayah Khorasan's *shura* council.[80]

The U.S. military and NATO have conducted a high-value targeting campaign against the leadership of Wilayah Khorasan with the help of Afghan forces. As a result, the leadership of ISIS's Khorasan province has experienced a great deal of attrition. Abdul Rauf Khadim, the group's first deputy, was killed in a February 2015 drone strike in Helmand province after less than a month on the job. A July 2016 drone strike in Nangarhar's Achin district killed Hafiz Saeed Khan, Wilayah Khorasan's founder and first emir. Khan's replacement, Abdul Hasib, was killed during a raid in Achin in April 2017. Hasib's successor, Abu Sayed, died in a U.S. airstrike in neighboring Kunar province three months later, in July 2017.[81] Abu Saad Orakzai took over the group's leadership before meeting his demise in an August 2018 airstrike in Nangarhar.[82] Mawlawi Zia ul-Haq inherited control of the ISIS affiliate. By comparison, the death of Mullah Mansour in a 2016 drone strike is the only time the United States has killed one of the Taliban's top two leaders in recent years.

THE RELATIONSHIP BETWEEN WILAYAH KHORASAN AND ISIS'S CENTRAL LEADERSHIP

Wilayah Khorasan has maintained ties to ISIS's mothership throughout its battles with U.S.-led forces and the Taliban. Hafiz Saeed Khan "went through the application process" that the caliphate set up for recognizing new branches, according to Gen. John W. Nicholson Jr., the commander of NATO's Resolute Support and U.S. Forces Afghanistan from 2016 to 2018.[83] ISIS's central leadership in Iraq and Syria then gave its Khorasan arm advice, publicity, and "some financial support," Nicholson added. ISIS's central media team has encouraged followers to emigrate to Khorasan if other battlefields were unreachable, while the group's leadership in Syria and Iraq has directed specific personnel to the region.

There is other evidence indicating that ISIS's senior leadership has actively overseen the management of its Khorasan branch. In April 2019, according to the UN Security Council's expert monitoring group, a "core delegation" visited the Khorasan region to review the status of the caliphate's loyalists in the area. Mawlawi Zia ul-Haq led ISIS's Khorasan province at the time. ISIS central must not have liked what they saw: Haq was soon "dismissed and replaced by Mawlawi Abdullah," per the UN report. Haq was demoted "due to poor performance in the context" of the group's "setbacks in Nangarhar in the second half of 2018." The leadership switch underscores the "direct relationship between" Wilayah Khorasan and ISIS's "core in Iraq and the Syrian Arab Republic," according to the UN monitoring team.[84]

Wilayah Khorasan has pursued the caliphate's objectives through unrelenting attacks on Shia civilians, especially in Kabul. ISIS is actively stoking sectarian conflict in Afghanistan, just as Adnani warned would happen in his January 2015 proclamation of ISIS's expansion into Afghanistan. For instance, on July 23, 2016, Wilayah Khorasan dispatched three suicide bombers to strike a peaceful demonstration that thousands of Hazaras attended in Kabul, killing at least eighty people and wounding dozens more.[85] Other targets have included Shia mosques, the Iraqi Embassy in Kabul, a Shia cultural center, and a hotel hosting a Shia wedding. Wilayah Khorasan typically justifies these operations by depicting the victims as "polytheists."

In June 2019 ISIS released a video celebrating the continued allegiance of fighters in Afghanistan and the broader region. The production featured jihadists in eastern and western Afghanistan, Iran, Kashmir, and Pakistan trumpeting their fealty to Abu Bakr al-Baghdadi. While the video is too propagandistic to serve as proof of the group's actual reach, ISIS's men have claimed operations in each area the video mentions.

EVALUATING WILAYAH KHORASAN

ISIS's campaign to supplant the Taliban has not succeeded. Wilayah Khorasan is believed to have between 1,000 and 2,500 fighters as of 2021, a fraction of the Taliban's army of 60,000 or more fighters.[86] Manpower estimates for militant groups are inherently suspect, and ISIS's total membership has been undercounted before. Still, these figures are consistent with observable realities in Afghanistan. The Taliban today claims control over all provinces in Afghanistan.[87] In contrast, Wilayat Khorasan largely operates as a territory-free terrorist network elsewhere in the country. But Wilayah Khorasan has created durable streams of income despite lagging behind in its competition with the Taliban. According to American military officials, Wilayah Khorasan has "approached self-sufficiency by extorting money from locals along with smuggling timber, drugs and raw earth material, such as lapis lazuli."[88] In some regions of Afghanistan, the caliphate's fighters are paid hundreds of dollars more per month than their Taliban rivals. The local ISIS branch still can't match the Taliban's funding apparatus, though.

Directly comparing Wilayah Khorasan's strength to al-Qaeda's is difficult because of a fundamental operational difference between the two. ISIS's men are vocal about their presence in South and Central Asia. Sometimes they exaggerate their activities, declaring provinces in places where they have nothing more than terrorist cells, such as Kashmir and India. Al-Qaeda has adopted the opposite approach, as Zawahiri's men rarely announce their operations in Central and South Asia. In Afghanistan, for instance, al-Qaeda fights under the Taliban's banner, operating behind decades-long partnerships with groups like the Haqqani Network (see chapters 3 and 9) as well as Central Asian, Pakistani, and Uighur organizations.

A series of monitoring team reports submitted to the UN Security Council between 2017 and early 2019 map out the ongoing alliance between al-Qaeda and the Taliban. "Many Al-Qaeda-affiliated fighters from the Afghanistan-border area have integrated into the Taliban, leading to a marked increase in the military capabilities of the movement," one report concluded.[89] In other documents, this group of experts determined that there may be "more than 7,000 foreign terrorist fighters" waging jihad on behalf of the Taliban and al-Qaeda, while al-Qaeda "continues to cooperate with the Taliban in return for sanctuary and operating space."[90] AQIS fighters serve as "advisers and trainers" for the Taliban, with whom al-Qaeda's broader organization remains "closely allied."[91] Al-Qaeda continues to benefit from its ties with the Taliban: The group "considers Afghanistan a continuing safe haven for its leadership, relying on its long-standing and strong relationship with the Taliban leadership." The Taliban gains from its relationship with al-Qaeda too. Al-Qaeda "members continue to function routinely as military and religious instructors for the Taliban," per the UN experts.[92]

Al-Qaeda will gain in status and operational latitude if the Taliban rebuilds its emirate, even if it fails to reclaim the whole of Afghanistan. Such a restoration would come at the expense of Wilayah Khorasan, which has remained unwaveringly anti-Taliban and anti-al-Qaeda. But the local ISIS branch could likely survive the return of the Taliban's emirate, thanks to Wilayah Khorasan's resilient presence amid a vast array of enemies in Central and South Asia.

The Arabian Peninsula

The Arabian Peninsula, Yemen in particular, served as an al-Qaeda base of operations before the 9/11 attacks. Al-Qaeda-linked militants bombed the USS *Cole* in October 2000 and unsuccessfully tried to strike the USS *The Sullivans* in January 2000.[93] Yemen's widespread poverty, faltering government, and internal strife created an environment in which al-Qaeda's clandestine operations could thrive. Prior to the Arab Spring, Yemen was the poorest Arab country.[94] In addition, the country has faced critical shortages of water and food.[95] Yemen's government was also challenged by secessionist movements in the north and south. Until the country's unification in 1990, Yemen had been largely split between the north, largely occupied by the Zaydi Shia sect, and the south, a British colony turned Marxist enclave. Although the north had a larger population, the south had the country's most lucrative natural resource, oil. The southern part of the country thus came to resent its junior political role in the unified Yemeni state, leading to a civil war in 1994. Although this conflict was brief, southern grievances endured. At the same time, the Houthis, a Zaydi political movement from the north, resented Sanaa's control of its land and launched an insurgency in 2004 after Yemen's government tried to arrest one of the movement's leaders.[96] Al-Qaeda was able to operate in this context and exploit local populations' grievances.

The 2011 Arab uprisings created new opportunities and challenges for jihadists in Yemen. The Middle East's revolutionary turmoil unseated Yemen's longtime ruler, Ali Abdullah Saleh, in February 2012. The United States had allied with the duplicitous Saleh in the fight against AQAP and its predecessors. Saleh was forced to abdicate in favor of his vice president, Abd Rabbuh Mansour Hadi, whose brief reign also proved tumultuous. With Yemen's government fragmented and weakened, Houthi rebels from the northern governorate of Sa'ada saw a chance to grab power. The Houthis, who are named after the tribe that leads the movement, are predominately Zaydis. Hussein al-Houthi and his son, Abd Malik al-Houthi, commanded the rebels and had fought Yemen's government on and off since 2004. After the shakeup in Yemen's presidency, the Houthis, who benefited from increasing amounts of aid from Iran, allied with former president Saleh and his son, who wanted to reclaim power.[97] The Houthis seized the capital of Sanaa in January 2015, forcing Hadi and his ministers into exile in the southern city of Aden. Hadi fled to Saudi Arabia and brokered a deal to form a coalition of foreign forces to combat the Houthis. In March 2015 a Saudi-led coalition, backed by the United States and Britain, joined the fray, launching Operation Decisive Storm with the intent to reinstall Hadi.[98]

Against this tumultuous backdrop, ISIS discerned an opening. When Baghdadi announced ISIS's expansion into Yemen in a November 2014 speech, he took a direct swipe at AQAP, which was perhaps al-Qaeda's most important affiliate. In Baghdadi's estimation, AQAP's decision to show restraint vis-à-vis the country's Shias all but guaranteed the Houthi rebels' success. He said that if the Houthis "had found *muwahideen* [Muslims devoted to monotheism] to fight them, their evil would not have festered." The caliph implored his followers in the Arabian Peninsula to strike the Houthis' *shirk* (polytheism) with their own *tawhid* (monotheism), which would lead God to break the enemy's strength.[99] Four months later, on March 20, 2015, not long after the Houthis captured Sanaa, ISIS carried out its first attacks in Yemen when four suicide bombers detonated themselves at a pair of mosques Shias frequented in Sanaa, killing over one hundred people. The near-simultaneous bombings were also intended to undercut

AQAP, which was generally opposed to slaughtering Shia civilians. AQAP distanced itself from the bombings, saying the massacres were inconsistent with the guidelines for jihad Zawahiri had issued in 2013.[100]

In the coming months, Baghdadi and his followers indicted AQAP on the grounds that it was soft as it refused to indiscriminately kill Shias and was lax in implementing sharia. ISIS's attacks came at a perilous time for AQAP as the group was already fending off a range of high-powered international adversaries, including a U.S.-led drone campaign. Like al-Qaeda's other branches, AQAP survived every challenge.

It is worth emphasizing why the battle for jihadist supremacy in Yemen was so important to al-Qaeda. By the time ISIS's local affiliate was established in November 2014, the line between AQAP and AQSL had started to blur. In several important respects, al-Qaeda's operational and ideological center of gravity had shifted to the southern Arabian Peninsula after bin Laden's death. AQAP first grabbed Americans' attention through a series of innovative terrorist plots, beginning with its attempt to down a Detroit-bound airliner on Christmas Day 2009. Such plots were only one facet of AQAP's overall operation. The al-Qaeda branch coalesced under the leadership of veteran jihadists, including Nasir al-Wuhayshi, bin Laden's one-time aide-de-camp. As we noted earlier, Wuhayshi served as both AQAP's top leader and deputy emir of al-Qaeda's global network, a position that made him second only to Zawahiri in al-Qaeda's hierarchy. Wuhayshi surrounded himself with prominent al-Qaeda ideologues who articulated and defended the organization's global ambitions.

THE WAR OF WORDS

ISIS's expansion into Yemen was an attack on AQAP and on al-Qaeda as a whole. A jihadist scholar whose feelings about ISIS oscillated between admiration and alarm was Ma'moun Abdulhamid Hatem. Once one of ISIS's most zealous supporters in Yemen, Hatem used his often-suspended Twitter feed to praise ISIS. He encouraged Baghdadi to proclaim himself caliph after his men swept through much of Iraq and Syria. But Hatem's attitude seems to have changed after Baghdadi announced the formation of a Yemeni province. Hatem refused to endorse the group of unknown mujahedin in Yemen who swore allegiance to Baghdadi, dismissing them as mere "students."[101] In a series of more than twenty tweets, Hatem admitted that he had tried to get AQAP to switch allegiance from Zawa-hiri to Baghdadi. The effort had failed, and the former ISIS enthusiast was now concerned that the caliphate's growth in Yemen would exacerbate the difficulties AQAP faced. He cited the American-led hunt for AQAP's lead-ers and the war against the Houthis as sources of angst for the group. Although Hatem claimed he still wanted ISIS to expand in the Arabian Peninsula, he fretted that Baghdadi's actions would divide the jihadist cause. Hatem never defected to ISIS and continued to serve AQAP until his death in an American drone strike in May 2015.

Hatem was the highest-profile AQAP ideologue to flirt with ISIS. Other more senior figures were firm in their dismissals, and AQAP swiftly rejected ISIS's expansion. The al-Qaeda arm's response to ISIS's expansion into Yemen was delivered by a young, charismatic theologian named Harith bin Ghazi al-Nadhari. In a solemn video address, Nadhari explained that AQAP did "not want to talk about the disagreement and *fitna*" in Syria since the jihadists were in a "sensitive stage during which the enemies of Islam, the crusaders, the Safavids [Iran and its sub-state allies], and the *murta-din* [apostates]" were waging war against the Ummah. AQAP had made its "best effort among our members and in our media not to engage in the disagreement that happened in al-Sham," and wanted Syria's jihadists to settle the dispute in a common "sharia court for arbitration."[102]

It was telling that AQAP even felt the need to respond to Baghdadi's speech. Clearly the al-Qaeda branch understood the threat ISIS posed to it. Nadhari rebuked Baghdadi's demand for loyalty, saying that AQAP's lead-ership had already sworn *bayah* to Zawahiri. Nadhari renewed this pledge during his message, adding that al-Qaeda had also maintained an oath of fealty to Mullah Omar for "almost two decades." The AQAP ideologue explained that he and his comrades hadn't "seen anything from either" al-Qaeda or the Taliban that "would require breaking the vow." Nadhari reminded his audience that "living under a rightly-guided caliphate" had been AQAP's goal and mission ever "since the first day." But ISIS's caliphate announcement was premature and illegitimate, he argued, since Baghdadi and his men had not sought "the advice of the influential and authoritative people among the Ummah or at least some of the truthful *ulema* (scholars) and leaders of the jihadist groups."[103]

Nadhari's rejection of Baghdadi's project drew a harsh reply from Abu Maysara al-Shami, the American citizen who edited *Dabiq*. In the magazine's sixth issue, released in December 2014, Abu Maysara contrasted Baghdadi's short declaration of expansion into Yemen, which "did not exceed one minute in length," with Nadhari's "longwinded" rebuttal, in which the AQAP cleric "rambled on" for half an hour.[104] Abu Maysara alleged that Nadhari's message was filled with contradictions and wrote that the AQAP theologian had displayed al-Qaeda's hesitancy to declare takfir on the Shias.

Nadhari died in a January 2015 U.S. drone strike. His death was part of a campaign against AQAP's leadership that had the unintended effect of undermining al-Qaeda's efforts to combat ISIS's rise. Leading AQAP ideologues, including some of the caliphate's harshest jihadist critics, were hunted down throughout 2015.[105] AQAP figures who died—such as Ibrahim al-Rubaish, Nasser bin Ali al-Ansi, and Wuhayshi—had been central to al-Qaeda's initial efforts to contain the spread of Baghdadi's jihadist empire in Yemen and beyond.

For example, AQAP leaders had worked to stave off ISIS's expansion into the Caucasus. In late 2014 a group of jihadists in the region announced their fealty to Baghdadi.[106] Some of these men had served as mid-level commanders in the Islamic Caucasus Emirate (ICE), an al-Qaeda-affiliated group. AQAP's Nadhari and Rubaish helped coordinate a global response the following month, declaring in a statement that ISIS's caliphate was "invalid."[107] Eight al-Qaeda-linked figures in Syria also signed the document. This group of ISIS opponents encouraged jihadists in the Caucasus to resist Baghdadi's "sedition" and remain loyal to ICE emir Ali Abu Muhammad al-Dagestani. Dagestani himself died within months: Russian forces killed him in an April 2015 raid, then killed a string of other ICE leaders throughout 2014 and 2015, inflicting a series of blows from which the group never fully recovered.[108] ISIS cobbled together its upstart Caucasus affiliate by poaching from ICE's remaining cadres and recruiting young men in the region.

Back in Yemen, AQAP replaced the leaders killed in American strikes with several other al-Qaeda veterans. Khalid Batarfi, who had been freed from a prison in the southern port city of Mukalla in early 2015, was a longtime jihadist who received a promotion as a result of the drone campaign. Part of his new role was serving as AQAP's chief anti-ISIS spokesman. In October 2015 Adnani delivered a lengthy harangue against ISIS's rival jihadists. Adnani mocked al-Qaeda's oath of allegiance to Mullah Omar:

"A person who pledges allegiance to a dead man and calls the Ummah to pledge allegiance to a dead man, does such a person deserve a response?" He continued: "We will fight the movements, assemblies, and fronts. We will tear apart the battalions, the brigades, and armies, until, by Allah's permission, we bring an end to the factions, for nothing weakens the Muslims and delays victory except the factions. Yes, and we will liberate the 'liberated' places, because if they are not ruled by the law of Allah, then they have not been liberated."[109]

Within days of Adnani's diatribe, Batarfi issued a video rebuttal. Reading from a script, Batarfi calmly inveighed against Adnani and ISIS for stirring dissent within the jihadists' ranks. Batarfi lamented that Adnani had "declared war on all groups and factions everywhere" while "threatening to fight and shed their blood." Adnani's threat displayed ISIS's "deviation and misguidance," Batarfi argued. "Instead of directing their fight towards the enemies of the ummah" and aiming "their arrows towards the Jews and Christians, they chose to direct their arrows towards the chest of Muslims."[110] To Batarfi, ISIS had betrayed the legacy of the modern jihad's first leaders, including bin Laden, while claiming to have a purer methodology.

Despite Batarfi and the AQAP senior leadership's continuing loyalty to Zawahiri, nothing they said throughout 2014 and 2015 could put an end to ISIS's uprising in Yemen. ISIS's loyalists fired back at their critics in AQAP, releasing their own videos and articles decrying the al-Qaeda branch's supposedly soft approach toward jihad. At first the two sides mostly waged this war of words in the digital realm, largely avoiding armed conflict. That eventually changed in mid-2018.

One key issue in the rhetorical battle has been AQAP's gradualist approach to governance, including the implementation of sharia punishments (*hudud*) and hesitancy to hold territory. As noted, when Adnani threatened other jihadist groups in his October 2015 speech, he said that territory not ruled by sharia has "not been liberated." In ISIS's view, the territory AQAP controlled in southern Yemen belonged in this category. AQAP has twice seized a band of territory across southern Yemen.[111] In 2011–2012 AQAP rebranded itself as Ansar al-Sharia in areas where it held power, a move intended to distance the group and its nascent local government from al-Qaeda's brand without breaking its allegiance to al-Qaeda's emir.[112] This early effort at governance was a failure. One lesson AQAP's leadership drew from the attempt was that the Yemeni people were not ready for the jihadists' version of sharia. AQAP modified its strategy during its second period of rule in 2015–2016, operating as the "Sons of Hadramawt" and branding itself as a governing council that included local representatives.[113] Much of the group's overt activities in Mukalla, the capital of Hadramawt province and one of Yemen's largest cities, focused on *dawa*. During a two-day rally in early 2016 AQAP's men passed out al-Qaeda literature and hosted religious-themed contests that drew participation from students of the Qur'an. The group gave motorcycles and other prizes to the winners.[114]

In April 2016 AQAP retreated from Mukalla as a United Arab Emirates–led coalition advanced on the city. AQAP's men disappeared into the countryside, declaring that it was better to save the city and live to fight another day. "We only withdrew to make the enemy miss the opportunity to take the battle to your houses and markets, and your roads and mosques, for those people do not care about the believers," AQAP announced.[115] Unlike ISIS's men in Mosul, Raqqa, and Sirte, AQAP wasn't willing to risk the city's destruction in the name of religious governance.

ISIS went on the rhetorical offensive again, claiming AQAP's decision had been made out of weakness. The foreword in the thirtieth issue of *al-Naba*, released in May 2016 (less than two weeks after AQAP's withdrawal from Mukalla), was titled "A Failed Experiment or a Corrupt Method." *Al-Naba*'s editors blasted AQAP for seeking to win the affection of the people and for treating Yemen like a "popular incubator." This approach had failed, the publication argued, because AQAP "found itself alone in the face of its enemies, and discovered that the people . . . had not only left it, but stood in the line of the disbelievers against it." ISIS argued that AQAP's men had betrayed their ideology by delaying the implementation of sharia. "Despite their having control over several towns and areas in the country, they were running away from establishing the religion and empowering the sharia of Allah in it, fearing to vex the hypocrites and provoke the apostate tyrants," *Al-Naba* editorialized.[116]

On May 12, 2016, an ISIS suicide bomber drove his explosives-laden vehicle into a Yemeni military headquarters in Mukalla.[117] Three days later another suicide bomber detonated himself at a security compound in the port city, killing and wounding dozens of people, including policemen and new recruits.[118] In June 2016 ISIS claimed responsibility for a series of suicide bombings targeting military and security forces in Mukalla, killing at least forty-three people.[119] The message behind these attacks was clear: AQAP may have retreated from the city, but ISIS would fight on.

AQAP'S GRADUALISM EXPLAINED

ISIS thus tried to capitalize on dissent toward AQAP's relative patience. AQAP's leaders justified their gradualist approach in a series of speeches and letters, taking a stance consistent with bin Laden's advice on how to build an emirate. The reasoning behind al-Qaeda's more gradual approach to state-building can be found in a letter bin Laden wrote to Atiyah in 2010.[120] In it, bin Laden expressed concern that AQIM had become too concerned with "fighting the local enemy," instead counseling that AQIM put more effort into "attacking the American embassies" and oil companies. After briefly surveying AQIM and AQAP's operations, bin Laden stressed the "importance of timing in establishing the Islamic state." The al-Qaeda founder was concerned that "planning for the establishment of the state" must not get ahead of "exhausting the main influential power that enforced the siege on the Hamas government, and that overthrew the Islamic Emirate[s] in Afghanistan and Iraq." Although America's power has been depleted, it "still has the capacity to lay siege on any Islamic state." Bin Laden worried that if his men declared themselves rulers over emirates in Yemen, North Africa, or elsewhere, the United States would quickly move to destroy these statelets.

Bin Laden's concerns were well placed. Two separate offensives ended AQAP's state-building experiments in 2012 and 2016. A French-led coalition ejected AQIM and its allies from their proto-emirate in Mali in 2013, while a U.S.-led coalition destroyed Baghdadi's caliphate over the course of five long years.

AQAP's caliphate strategy was set forth in two letters that Nasir al-Wuhayshi wrote to AQIM's Abu Musab Abdel Wadoud (a.k.a. Abdelmalek Droukdel) in 2012. In the letters, Wuhayshi recounted AQAP's experiences governing territory in Yemen in 2011–2012. Although the local al-Qaeda branch wanted to begin laying the groundwork for an emirate in Yemen, AQSL didn't want to announce that a state had been founded. "As soon as we took control of the areas, we were advised by General Command here not to declare the establishment of an Islamic principality," Wuhayshi wrote in August 2012. Wuhayshi listed the reasons al-Qaeda's general command didn't want AQAP to declare an emirate. "We wouldn't be able to treat people on the basis of a state since we would not be able to provide for all their needs, mainly because our state is vulnerable," the AQAP head explained. "Second: Fear of failure, in the event that the world conspires against us. If this were to happen, people may start to despair and believe that jihad is fruitless."[121]

Even though AQAP did not declare an emirate in southern Yemen, the group was clearly working to establish one over time. Wuhayshi explained that AQAP was implementing sharia gradually. Wuhayshi reasoned that the Yemeni people needed to carefully be reintroduced to al-Qaeda-style sharia law. "Only after monotheism took hold of people's hearts did we begin enforcing these punishments," the AQAP cofounder wrote. Wuhayshi noted that there is widespread confusion over what Islamic law really entails. "Sharia rule doesn't mean enforcing punishments, as some people believe," he wrote to Wadoud. "We have to correct this misconception." That meant dialing back some of the harsher aspects of the religious legal code. The jihadists should "try to avoid enforcing Islamic punishments as much as possible, unless you are forced to do so," while showing "patience, leniency and wisdom" for the "smaller sins and offenses," which can "be addressed gradually."

In keeping with Wuhayshi's advice, AQAP has rarely advertised its implementation of sharia. Even when Ansar al-Sharia, AQAP's front group, produced photos of "Islamic punishments," the images did not depict stonings for adultery or amputations for theft.[122] The contrast with Baghdadi's caliphate is striking. ISIS reveled in sharing photos of its men carrying out *hudud* punishments, eagerly sharing photos of accused homosexuals being thrown off rooftops, people being stoned, and others having limbs and heads severed. Wuhayshi counseled Droukdel that he should try to win the people over "through the conveniences of life and by taking care of their daily needs like food, electricity and water." Before his death in June 2015, Wuhayshi recorded a video explaining the benefits of AQAP's comparatively restrained and gradualist approach to governance.[123] Although Wuhayshi didn't name ISIS, his lecture was clearly intended as a rebuttal of that group. According to the former bin Laden aide, "many of our brothers" had adopted a very narrow definition of sharia, thinking that it "consists only of removing indecent pictures, stopping music, obliging the women to wear hijab." If these measures aren't enacted, Wuhayshi elaborated, some think the sharia isn't being implemented at all. This was both a "shortsighted view" and "crooked understanding," according to Wuhayshi: For AQAP's emir, sharia had a more far-reaching meaning, including "calling people to *tawheed*" and "repelling the transgressing enemy." The Yemeni people, Wuhayshi said, had "just recently left" a state of ignorance, so it was necessary to start with the basics and to be lenient. Wuhayshi believed the transformation of Muslim societies would have to begin with the fundamentals. For the AQAP leader, punishing wayward believers for minor infractions made little sense in a world so far removed from the utopia he and his allies envisioned.

In a 2017 interview Wuhayshi's successor as AQAP's emir, Qasim al-Raymi, returned to this theme. Raymi was asked if it was possible to focus on "administration and control" during times of "conquest and liberation."[124] Can jihadists govern while they are still fighting? Raymi responded that he and his men did not want to rule over others. "Our main goal is to be governed by the Islamic sharia," Raymi said, whether AQAP is the ultimate authority or others earn that role. "During conquest, it is [incumbent] upon the mujahedin to not seize and occupy matters concerning people without consulting them," Raymi said. First and foremost to consult, the AQAP emir added, were "the people of authority from among the scholars, commanders and [people] with a field of specialization." Raymi's view is the opposite of ISIS's. Instead of immediately enforcing a strict religious legal code, AQAP's men preached the necessity of consulting scholars and other knowledgeable people in the lands they came to control.

This critique of ISIS's harshness extended to its battlefield tactics. In the summer of 2016 jihadists shared an alleged ISIS letter authorizing Baghdadi's commanders to kill any fighters who fled the battlefields or who were otherwise "bewitched and cannot be cured."[125] *Al-Masra*'s editors promoted the letter, hoping it could undermine the morale of Baghdadi's followers. The same issue of *al-Masra* reproduced a statement from Abu Zar al-Burmi explaining why he withdrew his pledge of allegiance to ISIS and criticizing the group's brutal methodology.[126] Burmi had been a senior scholar in the IMU, and his initial support for Baghdadi's project was a win for ISIS in Central and South Asia.

In early 2017 *al-Masra* published a lengthy survey that claimed to document the opinions of eighteen leading Saudi pro-jihadist ulema, or scholars.[127] Many of them had been imprisoned in the kingdom for years, so it was difficult to know what they thought at any given time. The article's author, identified as Suhayb Rami, explained that many of the top Saudi pro-jihadist clerics opposed ISIS. One of these critics was Sheikh Abd-al-Aziz al-Tarifi, a former employee of Saudi Arabia's Ministry of Islamic Affairs who had gained a wide audience before running afoul of the royals and landing in prison in 2016. Rami explained that Tarifi was popular among Syria's fighting factions—except for ISIS, as he had declared it impermissible to join Baghdadi's organization.[128] Rami then described the opinions of another leading Saudi cleric, Sheikh Sulayman al-Alwan. Alwan had lauded ISIS's operations when they were confined to Iraq but had since criticized Baghdadi for attempting to coerce people to pledge fealty to him. In Alwan's view, Baghdadi was merely the leader of a single fighting faction and not the caliph of Muslims since he lacked the widespread support needed to claim that title.

The overall point of Rami's article was that few influential pro-jihadist Saudi clerics advocated on Baghdadi's behalf. Most opposed ISIS's project. Rami's summary identified some real ideological tensions within the self-declared caliphate's program. ISIS hadn't been able to win over even the extremist fringe of religious scholars. The popularity of an ultraradical named Ahmad al-Hazimi within ISIS might have been particularly off-putting. Rami described Hazimi as "one of the most controversial sheikhs," and for good reason.

THE HAZIMI TREND

Ahmad al-Hazimi's teachings initially found a strong base of support among Tunisian militants belonging to Ansar al-Sharia in Tunisia, some of whom would later join ISIS.[129] Following their pledge of *bayah* to ISIS, these militants brought Hazimi tendencies to Iraq and Syria. Hazimi himself has not overtly supported any particular organized jihadist group, as his arrest in April 2015 by Saudi authorities limited his ability to do so.

Hazimi took perhaps the hardest possible line on a major point of ideological divergence between ISIS and al-Qaeda. The two groups have foundational disagreements regarding *takfir*, the excommunication of other Muslims. Al-Qaeda has adopted a comparatively forgiving approach to *takfir*. According to al-Qaeda, only qualified individuals are permitted to declare *takfir*, and when they do so it must be in response to a major act of disbelief. ISIS, in contrast, defines *takfir* so broadly that the caliphate's men often use the concept as grounds for excommunicating their ideological cousins, including jihadists who agree with them on nearly everything. Illustrating this, in mid-2017 *al-Naba* described the Muslim Brotherhood's founder, Hassan al-Banna, as an apostate.[130] Although al-Qaeda often criticizes the modern Muslim Brotherhood for participating in elections, the group still holds al-Banna in high esteem.[131] *Al-Naba*'s editors, in contrast, declared *takfir* on the long-dead Brotherhood founder, further describing the late al-Qaeda leader Atiyah Abd-al-Rahman and the ideologue Abu Musab al-Suri as "sheikhs of misguidance" and "heads of *fitna* and corruption."[132] This caused some embarrassment in ISIS circles, as Baghdadi himself had once eulogized Atiyah in glowing terms, not knowing that Atiyah had been critical of ISIS in his private correspondence.[133]

But ISIS's *takfiri* practices were not expansive enough for Hazimi and his followers, who have come to be referred to as the Hazimi trend.[134] This group found its intellectual cornerstone in Ahmad al-Hazimi's work, specifically his book *Ignorance Is Not an Excuse in Islam*.[135] For Hazimi and his followers, Muslims who are unaware of the jihadists' teachings and laws did not get a pass. Whatever their intentions, they were still apostates deserving of death. Further, the Hazimis hold that if an individual does not declare *takfir* on a perceived transgressor, that individual is an "excuser" and can himself be declared an apostate. The idea that excusers have themselves committed apostasy is known as *takfir al-adhir*. This creates the possibility of "chain *takfir*," an unending chain of declarations of apostasy, as *takfir* is declared not only on Muslims who may have committed unwitting offenses but also on every single person who similarly refuses to declare takfir on them. The Hazimis' practice thus threatened the organizational unity of ISIS by virtue of the fact that one cannot disagree yet remain effectively neutral. Anyone who rejected the Hazimis' interpretation of takfir was subject to charges of apostasy.

In effect, Hazimi created a viral doctrine that could be used to condemn broad swathes of Muslims as apostates. Opponents of Hazimi's doctrine in ISIS argued that the doctrine could excommunicate so many that few Muslims would remain to fight for ISIS. Indeed, several adherents to the Hazimi trend declared *takfir* on major jihadist leaders. Turki al-Binali emerged as a champion of the anti-Hazimi perspective. Further, in 2014 ISIS began an internal purge that was seemingly unrelated to the Hazimi trend but that swept up a number of Hazimi leaders and adherents, including the detention of three major Hazimi players: Abu Jaffar al-Hattab, Abu Umar al-Kuwaiti, and Abu Musab al-Tunisi.[136] All three were arrested in August 2014 and likely executed shortly thereafter. A number of regional ISIS emirs who were adherents to the Hazimi trend—Abu Asid al-Maghrebi, Abu al-Hawra al-Jazaeri, Abu Khaled al-Sharqi, and Abu Abdullah al-Maghrebi—were also arrested in 2014.[137]

By 2016 it appeared on the surface that ISIS had the Hazimi threat under control. But this changed rapidly. On May 29, 2016, ISIS's Central Office for Monitoring the Sharia Bureaus—which was two bureaucratic steps down from Baghdadi—issued a memo clarifying the organization's position on *takfir*. The Middle East Media Research Institute explained that the statement "rejected the application of *takfir* to Muslims who are not themselves guilty of heresy but who refrain from making this accusation against people who are, since this would lead to an endless chain of *takfir*. The statement forbade ISIS members to engage in theological disputes that can lead to accusations of heresy against fellow members of the organization."[138]

In October 2016, in its English-language publication *Rumiyah*, ISIS further clarified its stance on takfir. Like the May 2016 memo, *Rumiyah* tried to place ISIS squarely between the positions on *takfir* held by al-Qaeda and the Hazimi trend. However, in May 2017 ISIS's Delegated Committee, which answered directly to Baghdadi, issued a fatwa titled "That Those Who Perish Would Perish Upon Proof and Those Who Live Would Live Upon Proof."[139] This fatwa effectively espoused the Hazimi ideology of rejecting the "excuse of ignorance" and promoted *takfir al-adhir*.[140] In response, Turki al-Binali released a detailed missive arguing against the Delegated Committee's endorsement of a Hazimi-style view of *takfir*. But Binali was killed by a U.S. airstrike several weeks thereafter. Another purge in ISIS seemingly took place following Binali's death, this time directly related to combating the Hazimi trend. The impact of the purge could be seen in September 2017, when the Delegated Committee's endorsement of Hazimi-style *takfir* was rescinded by ISIS's leadership.[141]

The editors of AQAP's *al-Masra* newsletter were bemused by the rancor in ISIS's ranks caused by the Hazimi trend, and tried to capitalize. *Al-Masra*'s fifty-seventh issue, released in July 2017, included the summarized testimony of a purported former ISIS sharia official who went by Khabib al-Jazrawi.[142] In a letter circulated by ISIS's supporters online, Jazrawi decried the Delegated Committee's "excessive extremism" and said he was fleeing his former brethren. *Al-Masra*'s editors knew that, even if ISIS would ultimately be able to tamp down on the Hazimi trend, their rivals' excessive use of *takfir* had empowered that trend. The results would seem absurd and horrifying to al-Qaeda's followers, and potentially even to ISIS devotees.

The Hazimi trend demonstrates some of the challenges to organizational learning that highly ideological organizations face (see chapter 2). ISIS attacked al-Qaeda as too gradualist—but the very ideology it promoted could also encourage greater extremism in its own ranks that diminished the degree of control exerted by ISIS's leadership. The Hazimis were so extreme that ISIS's leaders feared that their agenda, if enacted, would undermine the organization—and certainly would have nullified its ability to engage in effective organizational learning that was fundamental to its ability to seize and hold territory. For example, if ISIS had embraced the Hazimi trend, the group would likely have executed Sunni civil servants in the lands it conquered rather than exploiting their knowledge to provide public services. This example illustrates how highly ideological violent non-state actors struggle to maintain a theoretically coherent organization while interacting pragmatically with the world.

THE FUTURE OF THE *FITNA* IN THE ARABIAN PENINSULA

Until the summer of 2018 the conflict between ISIS's Yemeni arm and AQAP was mainly rhetorical. There were few signs of on-the-ground fighting, and the two sides reportedly maintained a nonaggression pact. The intra-jihadist stalemate lasted until July 2018, when fighting erupted in the Qayfah area of Yemen's al-Bayda governorate, ISIS's main hub of activity in the region.[143] The battle seemed to come to an end when Ansar al-Sharia, AQAP's front group, posted a statement calling for a cessation of hostilities. The pause in fighting didn't last: By the end of 2018 AQAP was regularly declaring its operations against ISIS's men.

Despite AQAP's best efforts, a small cadre of its fighters eventually swore allegiance to ISIS's caliphate. In June 2019 Saudi Arabia announced that the alleged head of ISIS's Yemeni province, a man identified as Abu Osama al-Masri, had been captured in a raid conducted jointly with Yemeni authorities. According to the Saudis, al-Masri had been an AQAP commander from 2010 until his defection in 2015, after which he quickly ascended in ISIS's ranks. The caliphate's Yemen-based leaders have endured internal challenges to their authority as well. In December 2015 a group of dissenters sent a letter to ISIS's central leadership bemoaning the choice of *wali* (governor) for Yemen.[144] The disgruntled caliphate followers complained that the governor had committed a number of sharia violations, like providing insufficient resources during one of their battles. A senior ISIS figure quashed the attempted coup and ordered the complainants to fall in line.

In more recent years AQAP has posed a bigger threat to ISIS's enterprise in Yemen than have disaffected ISIS fighters. By early 2019 AQAP had raised the heat on its rivals, offering a bounty for one of ISIS's leaders and raiding its bases in al-Bayda. In return ISIS dispatched suicide bombers to strike AQAP positions.[145] AQAP used a propaganda outlet named Al Hidayah Establishment for Media Production to disseminate clips of defectors apologizing for betraying their al-Qaeda brethren in the name of the caliphate.[146] As the rivalry became bloodier, these productions increased in frequency. At one point AQAP was able to release out-takes of ISIS jihadists fumbling over the words of an oath to Baghdadi.[147] This footage revealed how heavily scripted many fealty pledges to Baghdadi were.

AQAP is well positioned to survive ISIS's challenge in Yemen. According to one UN estimate, AQAP may have as many as six thousand to seven thousand fighters in its ranks as of mid-2018, while the caliphate's representatives totaled in the low hundreds.[148] There is always uncertainty in such manpower estimates, but there is little doubt that AQAP has entrenched itself in the fabric of Yemen's complex, fractious environment.

The *Fitna* in Africa

Jihadists have found fertile ground in Africa. The continent's numerous conflicts, faltering governments, and widespread economic misery has helped them to find an audience. For al-Qaeda, Africa had been something of a second home. In the 1990s, bin Laden and al-Qaeda found refuge in Sudan and conducted attacks on U.S. embassies in Kenya and Tanzania. With the incorporation of the Algeria-based Salafist GSPC and the Somalia-based al-Shabaab into its ranks, al-Qaeda developed a substantial presence on the continent. But as ISIS expanded, it similarly identified Africa as a land of opportunity.

As ISIS gained a foothold on the continent, Africa became a major the-ater of intra-jihadist conflict. In North Africa, al-Qaeda's pragmatic, low-profile approach to the Arab Spring clashed with ISIS's highly visible approach. In West Africa, al-Qaeda's pragmatism allowed it to build a potent jihadist coalition while ISIS initially struggled with less reliable proxies. In East Africa, al-Qaeda's relationship with al-Shabaab paid dividends as the latter group aggressively opposed ISIS's attempts to gain a foothold.

AL-QAEDA VERSUS ISIS IN NORTH AFRICA

The small, dusty city of Sirte has, perhaps surprisingly, served as a center of power for centuries. Virgil referred to the city as "unfriendly" in the *Aeneid*.[149] Over a millennium later the city served as the Ottoman Empire's foothold in the region.[150] As part of Italy's Libyan colony, Sirte was hotly contested in World War II, and the Gulf of Sirte saw two separate naval battles.[151]

Sirte has seen numerous cycles of decline and revival since its birth, and its latest revival came during the Qaddafi era. Muammar al-Qaddafi was born there in 1942—and would ultimately die in Sirte too. During his rule Qaddafi sought to transform his home city. He made Sirte home to gov-ernment departments and to the Libya's parliament for a time.[152] It was a key location in his typically grandiose and unworkable "United States of Africa" vision. When African leaders came to Libya, Qaddafi received them in Sirte, entertaining them in the city he helped to revive. Sirte, in short, was Qaddafi's gem.

That was the latest of Sirte's periodic processes of revival. Its decline proved to be more dramatic and gruesome, coming just after the death of the city's great champion, Muammar al-Qaddafi. At the height of its power in North Africa, ISIS considered Sirte to be one of the caliphate's three cap-itals, alongside Mosul and Raqqa. The jihadists conquered Sirte in May 2015 after sweeping through the towns of Libya's agriculturally fer-tile and oil-rich central coast. The extremists' campaign to take the city coincided with victorious assaults on Ramadi, Iraq, and the ancient city of Palmyra in Syria. It appeared that ISIS's caliphate truly was expanding on totally different sides of the greater Middle East. But by the end of 2016 Sirte lay in ruins, and ISIS's hold over the city had been broken. On August 1, 2016, the United States launched Operation Odyssey Lightning, an air campaign targeting ISIS's fortifications and weaponry. Across four and a half months, 495 American airstrikes provided cover for Libyan militiamen tasked with dislodging the jihadists on the ground.[153] Block-to-block combat unfolded across a gradually shrinking urban battle zone. ISIS's men eventually ran out of hospitals and schools in which to hide. Sirte was freed from their grip. The caliphate had lost its third most important city.

The fall of Sirte wasn't the end of ISIS in Libya—many of its fighters managed to retreat to the remote southern deserts—but it was a significant blow. Men dispatched from Iraq and Syria had overseen this initial effort to expand the caliphate into Libya. One of them was an Iraqi known as Abu Nabil al-Anbari (a.k.a. Abul Mughirah al-Qahtani) who had been imprisoned with Baghdadi during the U.S occupation of Iraq. Anbari waged a brutal campaign to terrorize Sirte's populace into submission. He may have been the chief murderer featured in a particularly hideous February 2015 video titled "A Message Signed with Blood to the Nation of the Cross."[154] In it, the caliphate's men beheaded twenty-one Egyptian Coptic Christians whom they had captured.

Libya and Tunisia had been hotbeds of jihadist recruitment during the Iraq War. This proved to be of great service to ISIS, which repurposed existing facilitation networks for its caliphate project. For instance, the notorious Battar Brigade, composed of hundreds of Libyans who had fought in Iraq and Syria, sent a contingent back to their hometown of Derna in the spring of 2014.[155] There they formed the pro-ISIS Islamic Youth Shura Council (IYSC), which gave ISIS a formal presence in Derna, and ISIS managed to use that presence to convince the media that—contrary to facts on the ground—it controlled the city.[156]

At the time of IYSC's arrival, several other jihadist factions, including Ansar al-Sharia and the Abu Salim Martyrs Brigade, had strong roots in the city. IYSC immediately sought to demonstrate that it was superior militarily. In April 2014 IYSC held a military parade in which fighters toting rocket-propelled grenades drove through the city's streets.[157] Pictures of the parade were immediately uploaded to IYSC's Facebook page as IYSC leveraged its messaging apparatus to highlight people who had joined the group, including posting repentance statements from former members of the Libyan security services who had supposedly come voluntarily to atone for their sins.[158]

In early October 2014 IYSC posted videos and images on social media of armed militants parading down the streets of Derna while waving ISIS flags and shouting ISIS slogans.[159] In late October, residents of Derna gathered in public and pledged allegiance to ISIS. ISIS's online supporters circulated pictures and video of the event.[160] IYSC's shows of force and propaganda created the perception that ISIS had full control of Derna. Several mainstream press outlets reported ISIS's ostensible control over the city.[161] This reporting was inaccurate. Derna was actually divided among various militant factions. The fact that the group managed to deceive the international media in Derna attests to the effectiveness of ISIS's propaganda apparatus and its capacity for learning and innovation. ISIS was able to take advantage of its growing proficiency with social media, along with (1) the lack of social media penetration into Derna, which stood on the way of messaging testifying to the lack of ISIS control; (2) competing militant organizations' reticence to assert their presence; and (3) the unsafe conditions in Derna, which posed a barrier to further investigation of the situation on the ground by journalists. This deception was of strategic consequence as it helped ISIS demonstrate its strength to African militant organizations it was trying to woo into its network, like Boko Haram. ISIS's initial phantom victories in Africa helped the group's network to grow on the continent.

Despite this propaganda victory, Baghdadi's men ran into an insurmountable hurdle in Derna, in the form of militant groups claiming affiliation with al-Qaeda. Early on in its Libya endeavor, ISIS claimed to have carved out three provinces in the country: Barqa (east), Tripoli (west), and Fezzan (southern Libya). In truth, the caliphate controlled little territory in the North African country. Ultimately, a combination of opponents foiled ISIS's expansion plans for Libya. The United States systematically targeted leadership figures like Anbari, who died in a November 2015 airstrike, and worked with Libyan allies to liberate key territory like Sirte from ISIS.[162] AQIM and its allies also moved against Baghdadi's men.

AQIM firmly rejected ISIS's caliphate claim in the summer of 2014. We "confirm that we still adhere to our pledge of allegiance to our sheikh and emir, Ayman al Zawahiri, since it is a sharia-accorded pledge of allegiance that remains hanging on our necks," read an AQIM statement circulated online in July 2014. The al-Qaeda branch explained that ISIS had forced AQIM's hand by demanding the allegiance of all Muslims.

AQIM questioned what ISIS's unilateral claim to authority meant for groups like the Taliban, the Islamic Caucasus Emirate, and all of the "al-Qaeda branches in other regions." The Zawahiri loyalists explained that while "every honest mujahid" seeks the "establishment of the rightly-guided caliphate," Baghdadi's caliphate wasn't it. AQIM criticized ISIS for failing to receive the blessing of a critical mass of Islamic scholars and jihadist leaders. The "serious step" of declaring a caliphate should not have been taken until after an "expansion of consultation."[163]

ISIS's attempted power grab interfered with al-Qaeda's strategy for post-Qaddafi Libya. AQSL and AQIM had concluded that a deliberate long-term strategy was needed there. Al-Qaeda's men opted for a covert path, slowly building their cadres and indoctrinating Libyans into their version of Islam. This cautious approach was advocated, for example, by bin Laden's chief lieutenant, Atiyah, a native of Libya.[164] Other al-Qaeda-linked thinkers similarly endorsed a clandestine and gradualist approach. Hamzah bin Muhammad al-Bassam advocated in February 2011 for "constructive dis-arrangement," an approach by which the jihadists would operate in the shadows, distracting rivals "from the real size of the work we are doing."[165] Only when the time was right would the "sound assembling take place," Bassam assessed. AQIM put these ideas into practice. In 2016 an AQIM leader known as Abu Abd-al-Iylah Ahmad explained that the al-Qaeda branch had rejected a proposal to establish an emirate in Libya shortly after the rebellion toppled Qaddafi's regime.[166] Instead AQIM decided to back front groups like Ansar al-Sharia and the Abu Salim Martyrs Brigade. Al-Qaeda did not publicly recognize any of these groups as part of its web. Ahmad emphasized that AQIM was concerned with building a "popular base" of support in North Africa.

Al-Qaeda thus treated this chaotic region as the site of a multiphase, long-term project. In the immediate aftermath of the 2011 uprisings, AQSL viewed North Africa as a land for *dawa* efforts to build the popular base that al-Qaeda and AQIM deemed crucial to long-term success. Early in 2011 Atiyah described the new political reality as a "historical opportunity," saying al-Qaeda's followers should "spring into action and initiate or increase their preaching, education, reformation and revitalization in light of the freedom and opportunities now available in this post-revolution era."[167] Both bin Laden and Zawahiri quickly recognized the logic of a *dawa*-based strategy in this new environment. In an August 2011 message

Zawahiri remarked that "opportunities have opened up for preaching" in Egypt and Tunisia, but "only Allah knows how long they will last." The "people of Islam and jihad should benefit from" the newfound freedom to spread their teachings, Zawahiri added.[168]

Al-Qaeda's *dawa* efforts were advanced through Ansar al-Sharia chapters in Egypt, Libya, and Tunisia (see chapter 6). For instance, al-Qaeda veterans who had a history of plotting attacks in Europe led Ansar al-Sharia in Tunisia. Ansar al-Sharia's men preached in the markets and universities, orchestrated protests, and situated themselves near mosques. They provided social services. A similar story unfolded in Libya, where the Ansar al-Sharia chapter in Benghazi was led by Muhammad al-Zahawi. Ansar al-Sharia Libya coordinated blood drives, sponsored an anti-addiction campaign for drug users, hosted contests for students of the Qur'an, and organized humanitarian convoys to deliver charitable provisions abroad, including to Gaza, Syria, and Sudan.[169] There is substantial evidence that Ansar al-Sharia in Tunisia orchestrated a *hisba* campaign to enforce its moral code alongside these more overt efforts.

The Ansar al-Sharia organizations in Libya and Tunisia became prime targets for Baghdadi's expansionism. But neither organization joined ISIS. In July 2014 Ansar al-Sharia in Tunisia (AST) used its Facebook page to endorse AQIM's explicit rejection of the caliphate.[170] But behind closed doors, AST leader Abu Iyadh al-Tunisi made an awkward proposal to Zawahiri and AQSL.[171] Abu Iyadh suggested that Zawahiri and his men swear allegiance to Baghdadi's caliphate so they could reform it from within. Although Abu Iyadh quickly abandoned this impractical idea, the fact that he raised it spoke to the immediate attraction the caliphate claim held for jihadists, especially the young. AQIM's Abu Abd-al-Iylah Ahmad later lamented the many youths who had been drawn to Baghdadi's promises.[172] While there was no wholesale defection from the Ansar al-Sharia groups to the caliphate, they still suffered some betrayals. One former AST cleric joined ISIS's Hazimi faction, ultimately becoming embroiled in the intra-ISIS ideological battle over takfir.[173] Boubaker al-Hakim, a French-Tunisian national wanted for his suspected involvement in two high-profile political assassinations in Tunisia, also joined the caliphate's cause before meeting his end in a December 2016 airstrike in Raqqa.[174]

ISIS ran into resistance from other parties in Libya too. The Derna Mujahedin Shura Council (DMSC), a consortium of several groups that included various al-Qaeda-linked personalities, proved to be one of the country's most important anticaliphate extremist organizations. Among the DMSC's more prominent factions was the aforementioned Abu Salim Martyrs Brigade. Tensions between the media-savvy IYSC and DMSC escalated early in 2015 and came to a head in May of that year, when an IYSC-affiliated preacher in a Derna mosque said in a sermon that ISIS was the only legitimate force in the city. In response, DMSC issued what it dubbed a "final warning" to IYSC.[175] IYSC answered by killing a key DMSC leader, triggering a bout of intense conflict. But IYSC's bark proved to be more potent than its bite: Two weeks after the clashes erupted, IYSC militants were forced to withdraw from Derna to the suburbs. AQIM openly backed DMSC in this dispute.[176] In April 2016 the remaining IYSC forces in and around Derna withdrew from the city.[177] The would-be caliphate only managed to take possession of Sirte, a city it still ultimately lost.

In a notably bitter interview given to *Dabiq* in September 2015, ISIS's Abul Mughirah al-Qahtani (a.k.a. Abu Nabil al-Anbari) expressed his frustrations with Libya's fickle and ideologically lukewarm jihadists. "Many of the leaders and soldiers of [Ansar al-Sharia] were from the first to pledge [*bayat*] in Libya to the Islamic State," Qahtani claimed. And there were men within Ansar al-Sharia's ranks who continued to pine for ISIS's immediate implementation of sharia. But overall, Ansar al-Sharia preferred "division to unity," Qahtani said. After all, the group refused to swear *bayah* to Baghdadi and aligned itself with movements that worked with the "apostate regime" in Tripoli, he fumed, blaming the closeness of some of Ansar al-Sharia's leaders to AQIM for this predicament. Qahtani blasted former members of the Libyan Islamic Fighting Group for engaging in democratic-style politics, a betrayal of their ideology. "Many of these leaders had once accompanied Sheikh Osama bin Laden in Afghanistan," Qahtani remarked, but they had now apostatized themselves by participating in democratic politics.[178]

Qahtani was correct that al-Qaeda's men in Libya preferred to work with other Islamist parties instead of scolding them and demanding allegiance. Al-Qaeda and AQIM took a gradualist approach to transforming Libyan society, adopting the course that AQSL had recommended at the outset of the uprisings. In March 2015 an al-Qaeda-linked theorist known as Abdallah bin Muhammad described the group's posture as "political guerrilla warfare" and praised the decision of former LIFG members to manipulate democratic institutions to their own ends. At the same time, al-Qaeda-linked jihadists were keeping themselves prepared for more literal forms of war, integrating their fighters into Libya Dawn, a predominately Islamist coalition involved in the country's civil war, which was fighting against Gen. Khalifa Haftar.[179] Such nuances in policy would be unthinkable to Qahtani.

Haftar was precisely the type of secular reactionary that al-Qaeda had worried about from the beginning of its Libyan efforts. His men inflicted numerous setbacks on al-Qaeda and its unannounced affiliates, including in Derna and Benghazi. Ansar al-Sharia Libya was forced to formally dissolve in May 2017.[180] Other fighting configurations, including the Benghazi Revolutionaries Shura Council (BRSC), a coalition that included Ansar al-Sharia, have been no match for Haftar's Libyan National Army (LNA), which enjoys aerial superiority. In an interview published by AQAP's *al-Masra* newsletter in late 2016, a senior BRSC leader known as Muhammad al-Darsi explained that his venture had suffered due to senior leadership losses, the intervention of European powers, and the LNA's cunning.[181] Darsi conceded that the BRSC had cooperated with ISIS's arm but said that any alliance was now over. He also admitted that Baghdadi's caliphate declaration had initially drawn young militants away from other jihadist projects in Libya. These factors still didn't produce an ISIS victory in Benghazi. But that doesn't mean al-Qaeda achieved its aims either. A multigroup jihadist and Islamist front established in mid-2016 called the Benghazi Defense Brigades failed to eject Haftar from Benghazi.[182] Ultimately, Haftar was able to expel jihadists from the city.

The al-Qaeda-affiliated jihadists in Derna haven't fared any better. In June 2018 Haftar's LNA declared victory over the jihadists who controlled the city.[183] Although sporadic fighting continued in the months that followed, Haftar's men remained in control of Derna. In November 2018 the LNA captured a major al-Qaeda figure, Hisham Ashmawi, who had served in the Egyptian military before taking up the jihadists' cause.[184] Ashmawi rose through al-Qaeda's ranks in North Africa to lead his own network, Al-Murabitoun, which was implicated in attacks in Egypt and Libya. Ashmawi also earned the enmity of Baghdadi's supporters for his opposition to ISIS.

AQIM still maintains a presence in Libya and Tunisia, but because of its strategy of secrecy, it is difficult to gauge how deep and wide the group's network is. There is no question that the losses in Benghazi and Derna were blows to AQIM's project. A small extension of AQIM, the Uqbah ibn Nafi Battalion, also continues to carry out sporadic attacks in Tunisia, although the group has never proven capable of seizing or holding territory.

It is also difficult to assess ISIS's surviving network in Libya. After losing control of Sirte, the caliphate's men reverted to what they called a "war of attrition."[185] As of mid-2019 there were signs of a resurgence. A monitoring group report submitted to the UN Security Council in June 2019 warned that Baghdadi's forces in southern Libya had "gained momentum as a consequence of the preoccupation of the Libyan National Army with the battle around Tripoli."[186] This report was referring to the fact that Haftar's LNA had begun an offensive against the internationally recognized Government of National Accord in Tripoli in April 2019. This fighting provided ISIS's Libyan fighters the operating space needed to launch a series of attacks in the cities of Zillah, Fuqaha', and Fezzan, and to free imprisoned comrades from LNA's prisons.[187]

ISIS retains an operational capacity in neighboring Tunisia, where it occasionally attacks security forces. A pro-ISIS group known as Jund al-Khilafah Tunisia sprouted in early 2014 and swore allegiance to Baghdadi later that year.[188] Jund al-Khilafah put barbarism at the center of their appeal, carrying out and publicizing such appalling acts as the beheading of a shepherd in November 2015. ISIS has claimed responsibility for attacks on locations frequented by tourists, including the March 18, 2015, massacre at the Bardo National Museum in Tunis and a mass shooting at a beach resort north of Sousse on June 28, 2015. The two attacks killed dozens of people, although Tunisian authorities blamed AQIM's Uqbah ibn Nafi Battalion for the Bardo attack.[189]

The *fitna* in Libya exemplified the strengths and weaknesses of both groups' approaches. ISIS exaggerated its presence in places like Derna. While those exaggerations were later exposed, ISIS garnered substantial media attention in the West and used its presence in Derna to reinforce its online narrative of strength. Although that media attention helped produce an onslaught of American airstrikes, its propaganda victories likely helped convince some African militant groups like Boko Haram to join ISIS's ranks. At the same time, al-Qaeda's subtler strategy ensured that American attention remained on ISIS, but it failed to convert its superior fighting strength in places like Derna into a propaganda victory. As previously discussed, al-Qaeda sought to ward off the kind of international interventions that disrupted its work in Iraq and Afghanistan while ISIS saw the potential of a propaganda blitz and expanding caliphate to win the hearts and minds of jihadists across the world. In some ways, those approaches carried over to West Africa.

WEST AFRICA: BOKO HARAM'S WANDERINGS

West Africa is home to some of the world's fastest-growing militant groups. The evolution of al-Qaeda and ISIS's West African branches has been circuitous, with each experiencing critical setbacks only to reemerge from the turmoil in a new and still-dangerous form.

In March 2015 Abubakar Shekau, leader of the notoriously brutal Nigerian jihadist group Boko Haram, declared his allegiance to ISIS. "We announce our allegiance to the caliph of the Muslims . . . and will hear and obey in times of difficulty and prosperity, in hardship and ease, and to endure being discriminated against, and not to dispute about rule with those in power, except in case of evident infidelity regarding that which there is a proof from Allah," Shekau said. Boko Haram translated the message into three languages (Arabic, English, and French), ensuring it would gain as wide an audience as possible among West Africa's multilingual population and globally. ISIS spokesman Abu Muhammad al-Adnani wasted little time in publicly accepting Shekau's oath of fealty.[190] Shekau's operation was soon rebranded as the Islamic State's West Africa Province (ISWAP).

At the time Shekau's decision to throw in with Baghdadi's cause was a high-profile coup for the caliphate. Shekau was the most notorious militant outside of Iraq and Syria to proclaim his fealty to Baghdadi. His men controlled ground in northeastern Nigeria and were operating in the surrounding countries. Shekau's oath gave ISIS an instant territorial presence in West Africa—an important win for the organization, which frequently boasted that its caliphate was "remaining and expanding." Despite pledging to solemnly follow ISIS's orders, Shekau's reign as the head of ISWAP didn't last long. Just over a year later, in August 2016, ISIS's media team announced that Africa's most feared jihadist had been replaced as ISWAP's emir. Why was Shekau replaced? It is worth delving into his conflict-prone background to understand why even ISIS found him too difficult.

Shekau's decision to join ISIS represented a defection from al-Qaeda's orbit, even if Boko Haram had never been a formal affiliate. After taking control of Boko Haram in 2009, Shekau reached out to al-Qaeda's senior leadership. In a letter recovered from bin Laden's Abbottabad compound, Shekau wrote that he had listened to "tapes of al-Qaeda and its sheikhs," and found them compelling. Shekau wanted to fight "under one banner" with al-Qaeda.[191] AQIM supported Boko Haram's operations, providing Shekau's men with financing, training, and weapons.[192] Other parts of al-Qaeda's international network, including al-Shabaab in East Africa, similarly assisted Boko Haram.[193]

Although al-Qaeda's network assisted Shekau and Boko Haram, al-Qaeda's leaders never publicly admitted him into their fold. They might have been reticent over Shekau's erratic and pugnacious behavior, which his own comrades often complained about. Indeed, in 2012 a small group of Shekau's men broke away from Boko Haram to form their own faction, Ansaru, whose creation AQIM seems to have helped orchestrate.[194] In letters to AQIM officials, Ansaru's leaders repeatedly complained about Shekau's behavior, seeking a way to wage jihad without having to deal with their unpredictable, and perhaps outright psychotic, boss. Ansaru's men complained that Shekau was quick to declare *takfir* on other Muslims and refused to prioritize attacks on non-Muslims over his co-religionists. Shekau bizarrely insisted that his men describe him as the "greatest imam." They risked execution if they failed to do so.[195] Ansaru emphasized that its men, unlike Shekau's jackboots, would not attack "Muslims and public places such as mosques, markets, and motor parks."[196] In this respect, Ansaru's code of conduct echoed al-Qaeda's guidelines for waging jihad. But during Boko Haram's salad days with al-Qaeda, this initial coup against Shekau soon lost momentum. Ansaru limped on for several years, conducting only occasional operations and sporadically releasing messages. Meanwhile, Shekau grabbed international headlines and earned infamy with his audacious acts, including the kidnapping of 276 female students taking high school exams in Chibok, Nigeria, in April 2014.

This mass kidnapping boosted Shekau's global profile, and his decision to join ISIS less than a year later seemed like a boon for the caliphate. But, although the full story behind Shekau's falling out with ISIS's leadership remains largely unknown, Shekau quickly proved to be a problematic ally for Baghdadi. ISIS announced Shekau's demotion in its weekly *al-Naba* newsletter in August 2016.[197] Notice of this move in an official propaganda organ was unusual for someone of Shekau's stature. Abu Musab al-Barnawi, the son of Boko Haram's founder, was named his successor. Shekau and his men then reverted to their original Boko Haram branding, although they apparently still considered themselves part of Baghdadi's caliphate project. In another leadership twist, Barnawi was himself replaced in early 2019 when another militant, Abu Abdullah Ibn Umar al-Barnawi, was named ISWAP's governor.[198] The two Barnawis do not appear to be related: The name Barnawi simply indicates that both men are from Borno.

Compounding this leadership turnover was ISWAP's battlefield losses. Just before the time of its pledge, the group then known as Boko Haram was the dominant military force in Nigeria's Borno State, and its fighters were bearing down on the regional capital of Maiduguri. But it lost much of the territory it held soon after aligning itself with ISIS. The group came under pressure in 2015 from the militaries of Nigeria, Niger, Cameroon, and Chad. Yet neither the group's leadership turnover nor its battlefield setbacks stopped ISIS's West Africa province from quickly becoming one of the caliphate's strongest outposts beyond Iraq and Syria. Estimates of ISWAP's force strength vary greatly, but it is likely that the organization has several thousand members.[199] After experiencing reversals in 2015–2016, ISWAP was seemingly able to regroup and regain the capability to carry out frequent attacks. In late 2018 and early 2019 ISWAP's fighters launched a major campaign in northeastern Nigeria.[200] The offensive began with ISWAP fighters targeting a military base near the town of Magumeri in Borno state. The following day, ISWAP assaulted Rann, a makeshift town for displaced persons that the Nigerian military controlled. Rann sits close to Nigeria's border with Cameroon. ISWAP's offensive forced thousands of civilians to flee their temporary homes for a safe haven across the border.

In addition to netting Boko Haram, in May 2015 ISIS persuaded another veteran African militant to throw in his lot with the caliphate. Adnan Abu Walid al-Sahrawi proved to be a more reliable partner than Shekau, even if the caliphate didn't recognize the Western Saharan militant leader's *bayah* to Baghdadi until a year and a half after he offered it.[201] Sahrawi previously served as spokesman for the Movement for Oneness and Jihad in West Africa (MUJAO) and al-Murabitoun, an al-Qaeda joint venture that brought the Movement for Oneness together with Mokhtar Belmokhtar's al-Mulathameen Brigade. When Sahrawi swore fealty to Baghdadi, he claimed to do so on behalf of the entire al-Murabitoun organization. This proved false as Belmokhtar's outfit immediately disassociated itself with Sahrawi and remained loyal to al-Qaeda.[202] Belmokhtar's men had conducted some of the highest-profile terrorist attacks in the region, including a January 2013 raid on a gas facility in In Amenas, Algeria.

Even if the caliphate hadn't drawn al-Murabitoun to its cause, Sahrawi proved an adept leader despite early setbacks he faced when his former al-Murabitoun allies turned their arms on his faction. His group eventually became known as the Islamic State in the Greater Sahara (ISGS). On October 4, 2017, ISGS members ambushed a convoy carrying Nigerien and American soldiers near Tongo Tongo, Niger.[203] Four U.S. soldiers and five Nigeriens were killed in the attack, which earned Sahrawi's operation widespread acclaim in jihadist circles. ISIS's online supporters circulated a video that included footage recorded from at least one of the Americans' helmet cameras.

Al-Qaeda has backed its own strong horse in the Sahel. On March 2, 2017, al-Qaeda announced a merger of its affiliate groups in the area. The Group for the Support of Islam and Muslims (Jama'at Nusrat al-Islam wa-l-Muslimin, or JNIM) joined four existing al-Qaeda-linked organizations under one banner: Ansar Dine, al-Murabitoun, AQIM's Sahara branch, and the Macina Liberation Front (an extension of Ansar Dine). Iyad Ag Ghaly, a Malian Tuareg militant, was named the new organization's chief. As the longtime leader of Ansar Dine, Ghaly had been closely involved in AQIM's efforts to lay the groundwork for an emirate in Mali after al-Qaeda's men and their allies captured significant territory in the country in 2012. But in early 2013 France led the Operation Serval offensive to dislodge the militants from Malian territory, ending their nascent emirate. AQIM had plotted its return in the years since, and JNIM was the culmination of this planned comeback.

"On this blessed occasion, we renew our pledge of allegiance [*bayah*] to our honorable emirs and sheikhs: Abu Musab Abdel Wadoud, our beloved and wise sheikh Ayman al-Zawahiri and . . . the emir of the Islamic Emirate in Afghanistan Mullah Haibatullah," Ghaly proclaimed when announcing JNIM's formation.[204] ISIS had tried to delegitimize any al-Qaeda state-building effort, often by attacking the notion that the Taliban's leader was the emir of the faithful. It was thus significant that Ghaly's oath reinforced his men's loyalty not only to AQIM's Wadoud and Zawahiri but also to the Taliban's Hibatullah Akhundzada. Ghaly was declaring that al-Qaeda's network had held in the face of Baghdadi's challenge. He would repeat and defend this *bayah* formulation on another occasion.

JNIM is waging a guerrilla war in Mali, and there are signs the group has put down some deep roots. One UN Security Council report found that JNIM has control of "approximately 650 schools" in one region of Mali, with these facilities advancing a program "to transform society in accordance with the group's teachings."[205] JNIM has also expanded its terrorist portfolio throughout the region, conducting brazen operations in neighboring Burkina Faso. Despite the rivalry between al-Qaeda and ISIS, there are indications that JNIM and ISGS may have cooperated in carrying out some attacks.[206]

AL-QAEDA VERSUS ISIS IN THE HORN OF AFRICA

On September 9, 2015, al-Qaeda released the first episode of Zawahiri's "Islamic Spring" series.[207] In it, al-Qaeda's leader tore into Baghdadi's caliphate. The Islamic State wasn't established based on the "prophetic method," Zawahiri argued, and lacked the approval of the leading jihadist religious authorities. But al-Qaeda's chief wasn't entirely negative in his assessment. Although ISIS had made serious mistakes, and although he didn't recognize the caliphate's legitimacy, Zawahiri claimed that if he were based in Iraq or Syria, he would join Baghdadi's men hand-in-hand to fight their common enemies, including the "Crusaders," the Shia, Iraq's government, and assorted secularists. It was an olive branch from Zawahiri in an otherwise harsh critique.

Zawahiri claimed that until that point he had pulled his rhetorical punches in the standoff with Baghdadi's group because he didn't want to inflame the fitna in the jihadists' ranks. His account was partly self-serving: It made him seem like a loftily detached voice of reason. In his message the elderly Egyptian recounted his correspondence with Ahmed Abdi Godane (also known as Mukhtar Abu al-Zubayr), the first emir of al-Shabaab, al-Qaeda's branch in Somalia. Godane had been killed a year earlier in an American airstrike in the early morning hours of September 1, 2014. According to Zawahiri, Godane had been very concerned about ISIS. Zawahiri recounted that, in the summer of 2013, Godane sent Zawahiri a letter explaining that al-Shabaab was aghast at the "behavior of the brothers in" ISIS, adding that their disagreements with al-Qaeda's men were misplaced. Al-Shabaab strove "day and night" for the "return of the Islamic Caliphate," Godane wrote, but Godane didn't think Baghdadi's project qualified as a real caliphate. Godane asked Allah "to forgive the brothers" in ISIS for their transgressions and to "restore them to the truth." Godane likewise encouraged Zawahiri, whom he referred to as "my sheikh," to be patient with Baghdadi's loyalists and to seek reconciliation with them.[208]

By the time Zawahiri replied to Godane's letter in the spring of 2014, the al-Qaeda leader's patience with his upstart jihadist rivals had run out. "I know how sad you are about what is happening in the Levant, the eruption of blind strife there, the disdain for holy sanctities, the disavowal of settled matters such as the State's pledge of allegiance to al-Qaeda, their duplicity in this respect," Zawahiri wrote. In arguing that reconciliation was likely impossible, Zawahiri pointed out that Baghdadi's men "deem it permissible to practice takfir against their opponents" and noted that he had even found a video on the Internet "debating whether Allah's humble servant, "as Zawahiri referred to himself, "is an infidel." The "one who declares Allah's humble servant to be an infidel and blows up Abu Khalid al-Suri, may Allah have mercy on him, will not abstain from blowing up, or declaring to be an infidel, anyone who criticizes him or opposes his projects," al-Qaeda's top leader continued.[209] (As discussed in chapter 7, al-Qaeda veteran Abu Khalid al-Suri was Zawahiri's representative in Syria and AQSL's top mediator in the dispute between ISIS and al-Nusra.)

Zawahiri believed a negotiated truce with Baghdadi would likely be a dead end. Zawahiri recalled to Godane that he had ordered al-Nusra Front to avoid aggression against ISIS while encouraging Baghdadi's organization to return to Iraq for the sake of unity. Zawahiri urged Godane and al-Shabaab to follow a similar path. After summarizing these messages to and from Godane, Zawahiri eulogized al-Shabaab's fallen emir.

Turning to more recent events, Zawahiri used his first appearance in the Islamic Spring series to address his "brothers, the lions of Islam in East Africa." Zawahiri voiced his approval of Godane's successor as al-Shabaab's leader, Shaykh Abu Ubaydah Ahmad Umar, saying "I request of him to exert all of his efforts to institute sharia as the undisputed ruler and master in East Africa." Ahmad Umar remained openly loyal to Zawahiri in the years that followed and would prove critical to suppressing ISIS's insurrection in East Africa.

ISIS was aggressive in its efforts to win the loyalty of al-Shabaab's fighters. From late 2015 to early 2016, the caliphate released a series of propaganda videos encouraging Somali jihadists to switch their allegiance. The videos showed militants in Iraq, Libya, Nigeria, the Sinai, Syria, and Yemen declaring their fealty to Baghdadi. But this campaign met little success. At first only one small faction of former al-Shabaab fighters managed to establish a foothold for ISIS. It is likely that more jihadists in Somalia would have switched to Baghdadi's side had al-Shabaab's leadership not responded decisively to this new threat. In early September 2015, around the same time Zawahiri released his Islamic Spring video, al-Shabaab's leaders circulated an internal memo charting their reaction to Baghdadi's challenge. There was no question of changing sides. Ahmad Umar and his coterie would with dissenters harshly. Al-Shabaab's leaders warned that all public messages about the organization's business and policies could only be released through the group's official media arm.[210] This policy was designed to stanch the ability of ISIS supporters to create confusion about al-Shabaab's loyalty through social media posts, a practice that ISIS actively encouraged.

Al-Shabaab couldn't prevent every message of support for Baghdadi from getting out. The highest-profile al-Shabaab defector was a mid-level commander named Abdiqadir Mumin, whose base of operations was in the Puntland region. In October 2015 Mumin released an audio message pledging *bayah* to Baghdadi on behalf of "the mujahedin of Somalia."[211] The vast majority of al-Shabaab's thousands of fighters across Somalia declined to join him. Mumin even failed to garner support from his own men. Only about twenty jihadists of the three hundred or so operating in the remote Galgala hills of Puntland, where Mumin was based, followed him into ISIS's ranks.

Mumin's change in allegiance provoked an immediate backlash. On October 24 a group of foreign fighters in East Africa known as al-Muhajiroun (the emigrants) released a biting English-language statement, objecting to the "unhelpful pronouncement of a minority of individuals and their so-called bayah to those that have thus far failed to follow the Sunnah but expect to [unite] the Mujahideen."[212] The message was clearly aimed at Mumin and ISIS. Al-Shabaab's spokesman, Sheikh Ali Mahmud Rage, issued stern warnings against joining Mumin. In November 2015 Rage delivered a fifty-minute speech on the al-Shabaab propaganda outlet Radio Andalus warning against disunity in the ranks. Only an infidel sows division, which gives the enemy the ability to "defeat the Muslims." This was meant as a deterrent to anyone thinking about declaring Baghdadi his master.

Despite Rage's warning, others did try to follow in Mumin's footsteps. Al-Shabaab's *amniyat*, the group's notorious secret police, moved swiftly to quash the nascent insurrection. Within al-Shabaab, and in al-Shabaab-held areas, the *amniyat* serves to protect the group's leader, ferret out threats, and ruthlessly eliminate insubordinate members.[213] AQSL might have had a hand in developing al-Shabaab's *amniyat*.[214] Dozens of ISIS sympathizers were killed or imprisoned during the *amniyat*'s late 2015 purge.[215]

On November 10, 2015, al-Shabaab's *amniyat* came calling on Bashir Abu Numan, a veteran fighter commanding a small group in the Middle Juba region. Al-Shabaab had learned that Abu Numan was preparing to defect and launched its own version of a sting operation. Several *amniyat* agents posed as ISIS members and asked to join him. Abu Numan was eager to do so. Al-Shabaab had him assassinated the next day, along with several of his men.[216] ISIS's Somali arm later named a training camp in Numan's honor.

Later that month the *amniyat* ambushed Hussein Abdi Gedi and four others.[217] Gedi had also been stationed in the Middle Juba region and was reportedly part of a group that wanted al-Shabaab to defect from al-Qaeda.[218] In December 2015 the *amniyat* hunted down and killed Mohammed Makkawi Ibrahim, who had once been part of al-Qaeda's network but had recently decided to swear fealty to Baghdadi. Other local ISIS supporters fled, including an American named Abdul Malik Jones, who had reportedly fought in al-Shabaab's ranks for four years before embracing the caliphate.[219] A native of Baltimore, Jones turned himself in to African Union forces in December 2015 rather than risk al-Shabaab's punishment.[220]

One key al-Shabaab defector who survived the crackdown was Abdiqadir Mumin. Since Mumin had been a relatively prominent figure in al-Shabaab, the group's leadership considered his defection to be an act of war. On March 13, 2016, al-Shabaab dispatched an expedition to kill Mumin and his men.[221] Five dhows transported the fighters, including child conscripts, to Mumin's stronghold. The battle became a fiasco for al-Shabaab. Local security forces intercepted the assault force, killing around three hundred al-Shabaab fighters.[222] Dozens of al-Shabaab militants were captured. The UN Monitoring Group later described the failed assault as the "only major maritime operation" in al-Shabaab's history, underscoring how important killing Mumin was for the group.[223] Luckily for ISIS, Mumin was untouched and proved to be adept at avoiding al-Shabaab's vengeance in the years that followed.

A native of Somalia, Mumin had lived in Sweden and Britain, earning a reputation as a charismatic and radical imam in the latter country. He reportedly arrived in London in the mid-2000s, serving as a guest speaker at a Greenwich mosque that was attended by future terrorists like Michael Adebolajo and, possibly, Mohammed Emwazi.[224] Adebolajo and an accomplice used a car to run down a British soldier, Fusilier Lee Rigby, then hacked him to death on a London street in May 2013. Emwazi went on to earn special infamy as "Jihadi John," one of ISIS's chief executioners in Syria. The extent of Mumin's ties to other London extremists isn't clear, but he reportedly fled the United Kingdom for Somalia in 2010 just as Britain's MI5 was investigating his possible terrorist ties.

After decamping from al-Qaeda in 2015, Mumin and his followers succeeded in expanding their operations in Somalia, in part because of support they received from other arms of Baghdadi's enterprise. This mirrored al-Qaeda affiliates' strategy of helping one another. Members of ISIS's Yemeni arm have aided their brethren on the other side of the Gulf of Aden. Mumin's stronghold in Puntland in northeastern Somalia is well suited for such cross-affiliate coordination as it sits directly across the Gulf from Yemen. Mahad Moalim, who served as Mumin's deputy until Moalim's death in 2018, oversaw the shipment of arms and fighters from ISIS elements in Yemen to their brethren in Somalia.[225]

The caliphate's cadres in Yemen also provided the Somalia branch input on governance and organization. ISIS's Yemen branch coordinated the establishment of its sister group in Somalia and facilitated defections from al-Shabaab, according to an expert report submitted to the UN Security Council in 2017. ISIS in Somalia was "dependent on support from sympathizers within Somalia" while also receiving critical help from "affiliates in Yemen and Libya," according to the report—including weapons from Yemen, and funding and trainers from Libya.[226]

Mumin and his confederates have also profited from the "Magafe" kidnap-for-profit operation. Members of the Magafe criminal enterprise held Somali migrants hostage in Libya, freeing them once their loved ones paid a ransom.[227] In March 2017 Kenyan police arrested a Somali named Ali Hussein Ali, alleging that he was a major figure in Magafe who was also linked to ISIS's Africa network. Among other activities, Ali allegedly facilitated migrant travel from across Africa to Libya.[228] Once in Libya, criminal gangs would hold many of the migrants for ransoms that constituted significant sums for the families of poor migrants traveling to find better economic opportunities. Migrants who couldn't produce a ransom were often sold into slave labor.

Mumin continued to draw support from within Somalia too. His organization reportedly expanded its extortion and taxation racket from Puntland's rural areas into Bosaso, a port city and the region's economic center. Mumin's group enriches itself through commercial enterprises in the area. In February 2018 the U.S. Treasury Department sanctioned Mohamed Mire Ali Yusuf and two of his companies suspected of acting as fronts for Mumin's operation. Yusuf has served as an ISIS financial operative, providing much-needed cash to Mumin since at least 2016. According to the U.S. government, Yusuf also does business in Dubai, a further indication of how far ISIS's financial network stretches.[229]

This financial groundwork allowed ISIS to steadily expand its operations throughout Somalia. By mid-2018 Mumin had established cells in the country's south-central region, including in neighborhoods surrounding Mogadishu. Although it is often difficult to verify claims made by Mumin's men, they have undoubtedly conducted operations far from Puntland, including dozens of assassinations in and around Mogadishu.[230] Footage of these killings has been disseminated by ISIS's Amaq News Agency. The videos' first-person perspective dramatizes the murders. The assassins often creep up behind their targets, gun barrels drawn, creeping closer until they pull the trigger. Mumin's reach into Mogadishu has clearly complicated the Somali government's already daunting counterterrorism mission. Still, there is little danger of ISIS supplanting al-Shabaab as the primary threat to Somalia's stability.

Ever since the outbreak of the intra-jihadist civil war, ISIS and al-Qaeda have engaged in fratricidal clashes that splintered the jihadist front and inflicted numerous casualties on both sides. Although it marks a time of profound discord, the *fitna* between these two leading franchises of global jihad offered important opportunities for organizational learning. In their fight for supremacy, ISIS and al-Qaeda were pressured into reassessing their operational and organizational resilience vis-à-vis their main competitor. This internecine struggle prompted both groups to learn from each other throughout the process.

In the case of ISIS, the group's attempt to supplant al-Qaeda's regional branches with its own provinces exemplifies the newcomer's ability to emulate the early successes of a well-established rival. In Afghanistan, for example, ISIS replicated al-Qaeda's ambidextrous organizational model, allowing its local cadres to act independently while providing financial assistance and organizational direction from its central leadership. For al-Qaeda, ISIS's aggressive approach to both battlefield exploits and propaganda constituted a threat but also an opportunity. Al-Qaeda was quieter than ISIS in many ways to keep itself off the Western counterterrorism radar but was also able to launch loud anti-ISIS propaganda campaigns aimed at a pro-jihadist audience. The offensive that AQAP launched against ISIS in Yemen shows how, by systematically stigmatizing ISIS in its mass media campaigns, AQAP inflicted severe reputational damage on its rival.

Skillful exploitation of a rival's perceived vulnerabilities is another area where organizational learning can occur at times of rivalry. ISIS was able to encourage al-Qaeda leaders who were dissatisfied with the organization to defect and join the ranks of the caliphate. ISIS also found messaging opportunities focused on al-Qaeda's areas of perceived weakness. In Yemen, al-Qaeda's decision to show restraint in the fight against "apostates" allowed ISIS to portray its rival as soft. Yet ISIS's ability to portray al-Qaeda as soft was a double-edged sword. Knowing that ISIS's meteoric rise would trigger an immediate response from local governments and Western states, al-Qaeda kept a low profile, ensuring that these forces focused mainly on fighting ISIS. This was certainly the case in Afghanistan, where ISIS's constant trumpeting of its presence gave the U.S. and NATO forces a far easier target than its quieter counterpart.

The rivalry between al-Qaeda and ISIS continues to rage. Notably, the Taliban, which has enduring connections to AQSL, is engaged in an intense fight with ISIS's Khorasan province. The differing approaches to intra-jihadist competition in Afghanistan and West Africa suggest, at the moment, that both organizations' senior leadership could be either adopting different region-by-region approaches or else decentralizing their approach to the intra-jihadist competition.

9

How al-Qaeda Survived
the War in Afghanistan

On October 23, 2016, an American drone struck a small gathering of al-Qaeda operatives in eastern Afghanistan. The drone had a senior leader in its crosshairs: Faruq al-Qahtani, a veteran jihadist responsible for overseeing some of al-Qaeda's most sensitive missions. When the Defense Department confirmed his death in November 2016, it made a stunning claim that should have received more attention. Qahtani, the Pentagon said, had been planning attacks against the United States from inside Afghanistan.[1] And that threat didn't disappear the day Qahtani died. The U.S. military later confirmed that the group continued plotting against various targets in the months following that drone strike in Kunar province.[2] In other words, more than sixteen years after the 9/11 hijackings, al-Qaeda still threatened the United States from Afghan soil. How had al-Qaeda survived America's response to the 9/11 attacks, the killing of its founder and dozens of other high-level operatives, the rise of a potent challenger in ISIS, and a variety of other challenges? It wasn't easy.

All looked lost when Osama bin Laden and his comrades were holed up in the Tora Bora Mountains in late 2001. But when the Navy SEALs came calling nearly ten years later, in May 2011, the world looked very different. Bin Laden and his lieutenants had built and managed a sprawling global network in the years since the al-Qaeda founder fled Tora Bora. Al-Qaeda had regional branches and covert groups operating everywhere from West Africa through the heart of the Middle East and into South Asia. Files recovered from the Abbottabad compound show that bin Laden was regularly communicating with subordinates around the globe, often micromanaging their operations. Even as the drones rained down in northern Pakistan, al-Qaeda still maintained a foothold in South Asia.

The story of how al-Qaeda managed to survive and rebuilt its network in Afghanistan and Pakistan demonstrates the group's adaptiveness and resilience. Al-Qaeda has exploited gaps in America's understanding of the group and its goals, an interpretive gulf that persists. In doing so, al-Qaeda has demonstrated its capacity for organizational learning at the strategic and tactical levels.

Several factors contributed to al-Qaeda's resilience in South Asia. Most importantly, bin Laden, Zawahiri, and their subordinates invested heavily in their relationship with the Taliban. Al-Qaeda and the Taliban fought in the same trenches against the United States and the government in Kabul for two decades. Their alliance remains unbroken, and the Taliban's stunning victory in August 2021 should be understood also a victory for al-Qaeda, which had fought to resurrect the Taliban's Islamic Emirate ever since it was toppled in late 2001. Al-Qaeda also developed close working relationships with an alphabet soup of Pakistani jihadist groups. These relationships paid dividends in September 2014, when Zawahiri announced the launch of a new branch, al-Qaeda in the Indian Subcontinent (AQIS).

For years al-Qaeda has worked under the Taliban's protection in Afghanistan, conducting joint operations but seldom advertising its presence. This policy intends to cloud America's vision and mislead the group's battlefield enemies. Al-Qaeda's men in Afghanistan rarely produce the kind of photos and videos that analysts have become accustomed to seeing elsewhere. In 2015 the United States uncovered two massive training complexes in southern Afghanistan, one of which was perhaps the largest al-Qaeda camp in the country's history. Yet al-Qaeda did not release a single photo or video to market the camp's existence to would-be recruits. The group hoped to keep the camp in the shadows.

In this chapter we shed light on these dark spaces by tracing al-Qaeda's network in South Asia. Al-Qaeda developed a guerrilla army in the region, sustaining a surprisingly vast insurgent footprint. The United States and its allies have repeatedly neutralized al-Qaeda's "external operatives" only to find them quickly replaced. Faruq al-Qahtani himself was the latest in a long line of similar operatives. While al-Qaeda suffered significant personnel losses as a result of America's drone strikes in northern Pakistan, the United States often underestimated the extent of the militant group's network. Al-Qaeda survived the drones' onslaught by moving personnel back into Afghanistan or other parts of Pakistan outside the drone campaign's apparent strike zone. Some senior al-Qaeda figures have been stationed in Iran, a country whose territory the United States is extremely hesitant to reach into. This Iran-based network ties al-Qaeda's management team in South Asia to points throughout the Middle East and beyond. Meanwhile, al-Qaeda has groomed a new generation of talent.

Al-Qaeda's survival in Afghanistan is largely a story of organizational learning. Realizing that the attention of the U.S. military and intelligence community was inflicting substantial losses on its ranks, al-Qaeda tried to conceal its presence. The effectiveness of the group's learning is borne out by the fact that the United States has consistently underestimated al-Qaeda's fighting strength in the country and the broader region. This created openings for al-Qaeda to exploit. As the United States zeroed in on al-Qaeda fighters in northern Pakistan, al-Qaeda identified places like Iran and eastern Afghanistan to move fighters, where the United States either would not pursue them or would find it difficult to do so. The jihadist group's measures—concealing the presence of fighters and finding safe havens—were the product of organizational learning and were key ingredients in al-Qaeda's survival strategy in Afghanistan. To understand the most critical element of that survival strategy, we must examine the organization's closest and longest-standing ally: the Taliban.

The Islamic Emirate of Afghanistan

The loss of the Taliban's Islamic Emirate after the U.S. invasion of Afghanistan in late 2001 was a blow to the jihadist cause. Bin Laden's decision to target the United States in the 9/11 attacks led directly to the loss of this first "emirate." A handwritten note recovered in Abbottabad mentioned that other extremists accused al-Qaeda's leaders of squandering the group's statelet through their strike against America. The letter's author responded to this criticism by maintaining that attacks on America should be the group's highest priority. The "American idol has penetrated and forced itself upon the Islamic world," the author complained. Thus, "it was necessary to conduct an act to break the prestige of this plague and remove this myth from the hearts of Muslims whom shall wake up from their sleep and weakness." The letter's author dismissed complaints about the initial loss of the Afghanistan-based emirate, asserting that the United States would have overthrown it even had the 9/11 attacks never occurred.[3]

The author's first claim, regarding the United States' domineering influence over the Muslim-majority world, carried great weight with Taliban founder Mullah Omar. In an interview with Voice of America two weeks after the 9/11 hijackings, Omar fiercely defended his decision to harbor bin Laden and al-Qaeda. "This is not an issue of Osama bin Laden," Omar replied when asked why he wouldn't expel the world's most notorious terrorist. "It is an issue of Islam," he continued. "Islam's prestige is at stake. So is Afghanistan's tradition." Omar continued that "America controls the governments of the Islamic countries. The people ask to follow Islam, but the governments do not listen because they are in the grip of the United States." If America "stops supporting those governments and lets the people deal with them, then such things won't happen."[4] By *such things*, Omar was speaking about 9/11 and possible future attacks.

The Abbottabad letter's second claim, that America would topple the Taliban regardless of al-Qaeda's actions, was self-serving. Afghanistan was often dangerously distant from the minds of American strategists, whose eventual plan to confront the Taliban stopped well short of countenancing an invasion. Following repeated al-Qaeda provocations, on September 10, 2001, U.S. officials agreed to a "three-phase strategy" in which the Taliban would be offered a final chance to eject bin Laden.[5] If that failed, the United States would ratchet up diplomatic pressure while covertly supporting allied forces in Afghanistan. These allies would "stalemate" the Taliban in Afghanistan's ongoing civil war while attacking al-Qaeda bases. If this second phase didn't succeed in forcing a break between the Taliban and the transnational jihadists they sheltered, the United States "would try covert action to topple the Taliban's leadership from within." Even this hypothetical last resort fell well short of the full-scale invasion that unfolded a few weeks after the 9/11 hijackings.

Like the Taliban's eventual ouster, the limited plan of action conceived on September 10, 2001, was the result of al-Qaeda's own actions, including the 1998 U.S. Embassy bombings in Africa and the 2000 USS *Cole* bombing. Absent such provocations, there is no reason to think the United States would have found a reason to overthrow the Taliban. The letter's author wanted to disingenuously deflect the criticism that al-Qaeda had awoken a sleeping giant, costing the world's jihadists the only emirate that came close to implementing their austere religious laws.

But the Taliban were also responsible for the 2001 invasion. There is little doubt that Afghanistan's fundamentalist rulers knew what their guests were up to. The Taliban nonetheless repeatedly stood by bin Laden and his men. In an April 1998 meeting with Bill Richardson, the U.S. ambassador to the United Nations, Taliban officials evasively declined American demands that bin Laden be expelled. The Taliban's representatives told Richardson that they didn't know bin Laden's whereabouts and assured him that the al-Qaeda emir "was not a threat to the United States."[6] These were blatant lies: Bin Laden had declared war on America in 1996 and renewed his call to arms in March 1998. Al-Qaeda struck the U.S. embassies in Kenya and Tanzania mere months after the Taliban's representatives played dumb with Ambassador Richardson.

America and its allies continued to pressure the Taliban in the months leading up to the 9/11 hijackings. The group proved immovable in its commitment to bin Laden. While bin Laden's relationship with the Taliban was "sometimes tense," the 9/11 Commission found that its "foundation was deep and personal."[7] In late 1999, not long after the embassy attacks, the Taliban's Council of Ministers "unanimously reaffirmed that their regime would stick by" bin Laden.[8] Mullah Omar even had at least one subordinate executed for objecting to his alliance with al-Qaeda's emir.[9] The Taliban similarly rejected Saudi attempts to negotiate the troublesome dissident's return to his home country.[10] Mullah Omar also stood firm against the pressure of U.S. sanctions.[11] Following the 9/11 attacks, Omar refused the opportunity to turn bin Laden over, a move that might have prevented the United States from invading. This says much about the Taliban's relationship with al-Qaeda. Bin Laden and his followers were more than just guests: Al-Qaeda and the Taliban were battlefield allies.

Prior to 9/11 al-Qaeda invested in the Taliban's war against the Northern Alliance, with bin Laden contributing $10–$25 million per year.[12] The al-Qaeda leader also personally oversaw the "Arab 055 Brigade," which recruited militants to train and fight alongside the Taliban's men. The Arab 055 Brigade evolved following 9/11, but it has always been aimed at bolstering the Taliban.[13] Al-Qaeda also took steps to shore up the Taliban's emirate in the days before the hijackings. On September 9, 2001, a suicide bomber killed longtime Northern Alliance leader Ahmad Shah Massoud. The carefully planned assassination was al-Qaeda's way of delivering the Taliban a tangible gain just forty-eight hours before its hijackers struck America. The following day al-Qaeda and the Taliban led a joint offensive against Massoud's shocked loyalists. The operations were intended to preemptively drive back the anti-Taliban Northern Alliance, which would serve as a key American ally in the coming months. Al-Qaeda's strategy failed to save the Taliban's regime, but these steps helped bin Laden's men earn goodwill from their hosts.[14]

But bin Laden had already taken other steps to ensure that the Taliban would remain allied with al-Qaeda. Well before 9/11, bin Laden swore *bayah* to Mullah Omar. The al-Qaeda leader called on Muslims around the world to do the same. Omar and bin Laden likely had different ideas about what the oath meant in practice. Although the pledge could have been read as binding al-Qaeda to Omar's every command, bin Laden may not have interpreted it that way. According to al-Qaeda sources, bin Laden believed that he retained the right to pursue his own policies outside Afghanistan.[15] In practice, Mullah Omar stood by bin Laden even as the American juggernaut set a course for Afghanistan.

The *bayah* that bin Laden and al-Qaeda's men took to Mullah Omar became a significant issue over a decade later, when the rivalry between al-Qaeda and ISIS began to split the world's jihadists. After Baghdadi's men declared him caliph in June 2014, they argued that Muslims owed Baghdadi their allegiance, thus contradicting al-Qaeda's claims about Omar. Two weeks after ISIS's caliphate declaration, on July 13, 2014, al-Qaeda countered by releasing a video of bin Laden discussing his oath to Omar.[16] The footage had been recorded in the summer of 2001. "My pledge of allegiance to the emir of the believers [Mullah Omar] is the great pledge of allegiance, which is mentioned in the chapters of the Qur'an and the stories of the Sunnah," bin Laden said. "Every Muslim should set his mind and heart and pledge allegiance to the emir of the believers Mullah Muhammad Omar."

Al-Qaeda restated its loyalty to Omar in July 2014, with the organization stating that all of its men were soldiers under the Taliban leader's command. Al-Qaeda stopped short of describing Omar as a caliph, but by labeling Omar the emir of the believers, al-Qaeda was clearly portraying the Taliban founder as an alternative to the newly ascendant Baghdadi. A little more than a year later—on July 30, 2015—the Taliban was forced to concede that Omar was actually dead. It turned out Omar had passed away after a long-term illness in April 2013. This should have been extremely embarrassing for Zawahiri and his followers as the Taliban had maintained a *Weekend at Bernie's*-style charade with their leader for more than two years, meaning that al-Qaeda had professed its loyalty to a dead man. This somehow didn't bother Zawahiri, who did not hesitate to renew his binding oath with the Taliban even amid mockery from other jihadist groups.

The Taliban's *shura* council named Mullah Akhtar Mohammad Mansour as Omar's successor. Mansour's election proved controversial as other figures in the Taliban initially objected to his promotion. But Mansour could count on Zawahiri's loyalty: On August 13, 2015, al-Qaeda's propagandists released an audio message from Zawahiri in which he swore fealty to the new Taliban leader.[17] Mansour thanked Zawahiri the next day in a message posted on the Taliban's Voice of Jihad website.[18] Mansour's public recognition of Zawahiri's *bayah* was noteworthy. While the Taliban has never renounced al-Qaeda, it has sought at times to obscure its relationship with the jihadist group. Mansour was clearly an al-Qaeda man, though: Previously, he had described al-Qaeda's leaders as the "heroes of the current jihadist era" and bin Laden as the "leader of mujahedin."

Sirajuddin Haqqani, Mansour's top deputy, was also a longtime al-Qaeda ally. Haqqani's father, Jalaluddin, was one of bin Laden's first comrades in South Asia, and the Haqqanis never abandoned al-Qaeda, even after bin Laden became the most wanted man on earth. After the loss of the Taliban's Islamic Emirate, the Haqqanis' turf in northern Pakistan served as a crucial safe haven for al-Qaeda, with counterterrorism officials tracing a series of international plots to Haqqani-controlled territory in Loya Paktia and North Waziristan. These thwarted attacks included a plan to assault the American military's Ramstein Air Base in Germany, a plot against targets in Denmark, and a planned attack against the Long Island Railroad.[19]

In May 2016 the United States killed Mullah Mansour in a drone strike in Pakistan's Baluchistan province. Mansour had just returned from a meeting across the border in Iran when a bomb struck his car. The Taliban selected the ideologue Hibatullah Akhundzada as Mansour's successor, with Sirajuddin Haqqani staying on as Akhundzada's deputy. Zawahiri swore loyalty to yet another new Taliban leader. Although Akhundzada did not publicly reciprocate Zawahiri's statement of allegiance as Mansour had, the Taliban emir privately told his men they should "continue to work with" al-Qaeda.[20]

Under Akhundzada's leadership, the Taliban celebrated its history with al-Qaeda in a December 2016 video titled "Bond of Nation with the Muja-hedin." The video displayed an image of Mullah Omar and bin Laden side by side in order to underscore this bond. An al-Qaeda veteran based in Yemen, Khalid Batarfi, also praised the Taliban in the video. "Muslim broth-ers! Our beloved Afghan brothers who greatly supported [the] religion of Allah are indeed an excellent example for you," Batarfi said. "The entire world saw how Amir-ul-Mumineen [emir of the faithful] Mullah Omar, the Taliban and all the Afghan people bravely stood and are still standing alongside their mujahid brothers and Arab and non-Arab migrants." Batarfi heaped praise on the Taliban for standing by bin Laden and al-Qaeda and promised that Afghanistan's jihadists would "destroy the biggest idol and head of *kufr* [disbelief] of our time, America."[21]

Zawahiri's *bayah* to the Taliban's leader remains in effect to this day. For the most part, al-Qaeda's branches outside of South Asia have respected this pledge, at least rhetorically. The leaders of al-Qaeda in the Arabian Pen-insula, al-Qaeda in the Islamic Maghreb, al-Qaeda in the Indian Subconti-nent, the Jama'at Nusrat al-Islam wa-l-Muslimin (an al-Qaeda organization established in West Africa in 2017), and al-Shabaab have all stated and restated their loyalty to Zawahiri—meaning that through him they are loyal to the Taliban's leader as well.

America's initial success in dislodging the Taliban from its base of power in late 2001 obscured a problem: Much of the senior leadership of both al-Qaeda and the Taliban survived the American onslaught. Al-Qaeda regrouped just south of Afghanistan, in Pakistan's lawless tribal frontier. The United States conducted a prolific drone campaign to suppress the threat emanating from northern Pakistan but was slow to recognize al-Qaeda's enduring presence in Afghanistan itself. Numerous jihadists from northern Pakistan eventually made their way back into the country, an effort that Faruq al-Qahtani spearheaded.

From June 2010 until early 2016, the U.S. intelligence community and military insisted there were only fifty to one hundred al-Qaeda operatives in Afghanistan at any given time.[22] This range was curiously static. No matter how many al-Qaeda men were killed or captured in any given operation, the lower and upper bounds remained unchanged. Throughout much of this period, the NATO mission in Afghanistan regularly announced that its counterterrorism raids had targeted al-Qaeda loyalists in the country. Still, the U.S. intelligence community's estimates were never updated to reflect new evidence.

Bin Laden's papers demonstrate how flawed U.S. assessments of the group were. Al-Qaeda was present throughout the county. In a June 2010 memo Atiyah noted that al-Qaeda had what he called "groups" in at least eight Afghan provinces: Paktia, Paktika, Khost, Zabul, Ghazni, Wardak, Nuristan, and Kunar. A "full battalion in Nuristan and Kunar," he explained, had "around 70 individuals." In other words, just one of these groups exceeded the U.S. intelligence community's minimum estimate for al-Qaeda's *total* manpower in Afghanistan. That same battalion in Nuristan and Kunar was led by Faruq al-Qahtani. This countrywide presence was hardly a new development. "Our groups inside Afghanistan are the same for every season for many years now," Atiyah explained.[23]

In his memos to bin Laden, Atiyah highlighted al-Qaeda's ongoing cooperation with the Haqqani Network. "We have very strong activity in Afghanistan, many special operations, and the Americans and NATO are being hit hard," Atiyah wrote. In one such, operation, "we cooperated with Siraj Haqqani and another commander." The operation to which he referred was a suicide assault at Bagram Air Base in Parwan province. Bagram Air Base, as the effective center of the U.S. war effort, was a symbol of American power in Afghanistan. The old Soviet installation was home to thousands of American troops and other soldiers, making it one of the largest concentrations of U.S. military might in the country. This made it a frequent target for Taliban attacks. Early in the morning of May 19, 2010, Taliban militants stormed Bagram's fortified perimeter, attacking with small arms, explosives, and suicide vests. While the number of attackers is unclear, the insurgents killed a U.S. contractor and wounded another nine in the attack, which lasted a number of hours. Atiyah identified the attackers' leader as Abu Talha al-Almani, a young German-Moroccan al-Qaeda leader. Almani, who worked with the al-Qaeda-affiliated Islamic Jihad Union and the Haqqanis, had insisted on becoming a martyr—and got his wish.[24]

While the United States was undercounting al-Qaeda in Afghanistan, it was simultaneously misjudging al-Qaeda's presence in Pakistan. U.S. planners assumed that the remainder of al-Qaeda's men were cowering from drones in Waziristan. Once again, bin Laden's memos showed this was a mistaken assumption. There is no question the U.S. drone campaign eliminated many important al-Qaeda operatives. With rare exceptions, the drones struck mainly in North and South Waziristan, which are part of Pakistan's Federally Administered Tribal Areas (FATA). But al-Qaeda's Pakistani network was never confined to this part of the FATA. At the height of the drone campaign, al-Qaeda had men stationed throughout Pakistan, in cities and rural terrain far from the "kill box" in Waziristan. The drones were simply never as devastating as the American government wanted to believe, in part because al-Qaeda made sure to keep a significant part of its forces out of their crosshairs. In a letter recovered in Abbottabad, bin Laden or one of his lieutenants wrote that the group's "reserves" would be kept away from the "front lines," meaning risky locations like Waziristan, to ensure they would live to fight another day.[25] At the peak of the drone campaign in mid-2010, Atiyah complained that he was losing important personnel to the drones "because we continue to make mistakes." But Atiyah also reported that al-Qaeda was still operating at a "medium tempo" in other areas.[26] This is an indication that, while the drones left al-Qaeda feeling somewhat constrained, the United States' unmanned aircraft were hardly debilitating for the group.

Bin Laden ordered many of his men to relocate from Waziristan back into Afghanistan. In an October 2010 letter, bin Laden told Atiyah that "most of the brothers" could be moved from Waziristan to the eastern Afghan provinces of Nuristan, Kunar, Ghazni, and Zabul.[27] In another memo, dated December 3, 2010, bin Laden insisted that "the brothers quickly" leave "Waziristan for Afghanistan and Pakistan, and they should enter Afghanistan in small groups."[28]

Not all of al-Qaeda's important figures escaped northern Pakistan. The drones killed a series of high-profile leaders, several of them crucial to the group's operations. In May 2010 an American missile killed Mustafa Abu Yazid (a.k.a. Saeed al-Masri), who had been al-Qaeda's chief financial manager and served bin Laden for years. Yazid had been well known in jihadist circles. The Taliban quickly sent condolences, describing him as a "heroic fighter and veteran leader."[29]

Yazid was hardly the only bin Laden senior lieutenants to die in the U.S. drone campaign, but plenty of others fled the kill zone and survived. Faruq al-Qahtani had prepared Afghan safe havens for the once-Pakistan-based militants that the drone campaign endangered. "As I have reported before, we have a good battalion over there led by brother Faruq," Atiyah wrote in July 2010. "He recently sent us a message telling us that he has arranged everything to receive us; he said the locations are good, there are supporters and everything."[30] The locales were so good, in fact, that Qahtani survived for more than six years after al-Qaeda began relocating men from northern Pakistan to eastern Afghanistan.

Qahtani wanted to wage attacks against the United States. But in the meantime, he continued to support the Taliban's insurgency. This kind of dual role should, but often does not, factor heavily in assessments of al-Qaeda's strength. Qahtani's dossier demonstrates how al-Qaeda's guerrilla army allows it to thrive in Afghanistan and continue threatening the West. When the U.S. Treasury Department designated Qahtani as a terrorist in February 2016, it noted that he was "responsible for planning attacks against U.S. and Coalition forces in Afghanistan, contributing to al-Qaeda's external operations planning, and fundraising on al-Qaeda's behalf." Qahtani also "directed the delivery of funds and weapons to Taliban associates in Afghanistan for use in future attacks" while "consulting on al-Qaeda operations worldwide" since 2011.[31] In its eulogy for Qahtani, al-Qaeda praised him for fighting alongside the Islamic Emirate of Afghanistan.[32]

In early 2016 the United States finally conceded that the "fifty to one hundred" estimate of al-Qaeda's strength in Afghanistan was an undercount. In September 2016 Gen. John W. Nicholson explained that the United States and its Afghan allies were still hunting al-Qaeda and AQIS throughout Afghanistan, including in "Zabul, Paktika, Ghazni area in the Southeast and then up in the areas to the Northeast . . . Kunar, Nuristan, Nangarhar." He explained that the mountainous area in these provinces "lends itself to a sanctuary."[33] Those were some of the same areas identified as safe havens in bin Laden's correspondence recovered in Abbottabad over five years earlier. Afghan forces led an operation against an al-Qaeda camp in Zabul province that same month.[34]

Al-Qaeda was eager to keep the extent of its footprint in Afghanistan quiet, perhaps because the United States had been aggressively hunting its operatives. General Nicholson revealed in December 2016 that America had killed or captured 250 al-Qaeda figures during that calendar year, including 50 leaders and 200 other members.[35] In other words, during the previous twelve months, America and its allies had killed or captured two and a half times the long-standing high-end public estimate used for al-Qaeda's total manpower in Afghanistan.

The Iran and Pakistan Facilitation Networks

Al-Qaeda's extensive facilitation networks in Iran and Pakistan helped the organization regenerate its footprint in Afghanistan. These pipelines were essential to the group's survival, and al-Qaeda eventually learned to plan around the reality that its key leaders might not be around long. In a November 2010 memo to bin Laden, Atiyah discussed a new generation of al-Qaeda commanders who were being groomed to replace fallen comrades. One budding jihadist particularly impressed Atiyah: Abu Hamzah al-Khalidi, who led a brigade in Afghanistan.[36]

Khalidi rose through al-Qaeda's ranks in the years after Atiyah's glowing review. In 2016 the U.S. Treasury Department designated Khalidi and two other al-Qaeda leaders as terrorists, noting that all three were based in Iran.[37] By 2015 Khalidi had been named al-Qaeda's military commission chief, according to his Treasury Department terror designation—a position that gave him a large say over the jihadists' warfighting in Afghanistan and elsewhere.

It is hardly surprising that Khalidi and his comrades were based in Iran. Despite its Shia identity, Iran has at times provided significant support to al-Qaeda, a phenomenon that began well in advance of the 9/11 attacks. To understand Iran's post-9/11 support to al-Qaeda, it is helpful to delve into the Islamic Republic's history of support for the Sunni jihadist group.

IRAN'S PRE-9/11 SUPPORT FOR AL-QAEDA

Ties between Iran and key al-Qaeda leaders date back to the early 1990s, when Zawahiri, then emir of Egyptian Islamic Jihad, secured an agreement in which Tehran would provide financial and training support to assist EIJ in its fight against Egypt's Hosni Mubarak regime.[38] At the time, Zawahiri's

EIJ and al-Qaeda were closely linked by virtue of Zawahiri's connections to bin Laden. As we discuss in chapter 3, Zawahiri and bin Laden first met in the 1980s while supporting mujahedin efforts in Afghanistan, and Zawahiri served as one of bin Laden's most trusted confidants from this time onward. This close relationship often made it difficult, even before the al-Qaeda–EIJ merger, to practically distinguish between the two organizations. Illustrating this, around 1992 the talks between EIJ and Iran began to include al-Qaeda as well. These discussions culminated in an informal understanding between Iran, al-Qaeda, and EIJ that they would coordinate politically and militarily to confront the United States and Israel and undermine Arab regimes that they viewed as supporting these two states.[39]

In executing this informal agreement, Iran made considerable use of Hizballah as a conduit for channeling covert support to al-Qaeda. Hizballah—a Shia militant organization based in Lebanon that has a global presence—has long played a unique and central role in Iran's foreign policy. Tehran can disavow terrorist operations linked to Hizballah, rather than specifically to Iran, if they prove costly or politically inconvenient. In 1992 bin Laden held initial talks on tactical cooperation with Imad Mughniyeh, the commander of Hizballah's department of military affairs and the mastermind of the October 1983 U.S. Marines barracks bombing in Beirut that killed 241 American servicemen.[40] That bombing contributed to President Ronald Reagan's decision to withdraw American troops from Lebanese soil in February 1984. During the 1990s Iran's material assistance to al-Qaeda included training in explosives, suicide operations, intelligence gathering, surveillance, and communications, much of which was provided at Hizballah camps in Lebanon's Bekka Valley.[41]

Al-Qaeda leveraged the tactical instruction it received from Hizballah to carry out its 1998 bombings of American embassies in Nairobi and Dar es Salaam. Al-Qaeda dispatched senior operatives, including Sayf al-Adl, to train with Hizballah before executing those bombings.[42] According to the 9/11 Commission Report, "al Qaeda had begun developing the tactical expertise for such attacks months earlier, when some of its operatives—top military committee members and several operatives who were involved with the Kenya cell among them—were sent to Hezbollah training camps in Lebanon."[43] The training they underwent focused on how to carry out mass casualty bombings. As a U.S. district court opinion has noted, following one such training, al-Qaeda operatives who were involved in the

Nairobi attack returned "to Sudan with videotapes and manuals 'specifi-cally about how to blow up large buildings.' "[44] In February 2001 al-Qaeda defector Jamal al-Fadl testified that he spoke with Abu Talha al-Sudani, an al-Qaeda operative tied to the bombings, about Sudani's participation in the Hizballah trainings. Fadl recounted that Sudani described the train-ings as "very good" and said he had received instruction on how to blow up "big buildings."[45]

Iran also played an important role in facilitating al-Qaeda's pre-9/11 activities in the Arabian Peninsula, helping the group expand its network in the Gulf. Al-Qaeda exercised some influence in Yemen as early as 1988, supporting anticommunist jihadists during the country's civil war.[46] Iran helped transform this limited influence into a more potent operation by serving as a transit route for al-Qaeda members traveling to and from the Gulf. The groundwork for this travel facilitation was laid in the mid-1990s, when senior al-Qaeda associate Mustafa Hamid (who later became a dis-sident offering harsh critiques of the organization) "negotiated a secret relationship between Usama Bin Laden and Iran, allowing many al Qaida members safe transit through Iran to Afghanistan."[47] Iran held up its end of the bargain by allowing al-Qaeda to "establish a series of guest houses for its fighters making the long journey through [Iranian] territory."[48] Sayf al-Adl identified Iran in 1999 as a "safe passage for the fraternal brothers after the Pakistani authorities began to tighten the noose around our movement."[49]

During this period, Abu Musab al-Zarqawi's association with al-Qaeda allowed him to take advantage of Iran's permissive attitude toward Sunni jihadists. Brian Fishman writes that al-Qaeda agreed that it would "would arrange start-up money for Zarqawi to build a camp near Herat, along the Iranian border, and provide logistical support through a network of safe houses in the Iranian cities of Tehran and Mashaad."[50] These safe houses may have been the same as those used by al-Qaeda operatives traveling between Afghanistan and the Gulf. Fishman further explains that Iran's permissiveness was an explicit and deliberate policy.[51]

POST-9/11 IRANIAN SUPPORT FOR AL-QAEDA

Iranian support to al-Qaeda continued following 9/11. Acting through a deal that Abu Hafs al-Mauritani (born Mahfouz Ibn El Waleed) brokered with the Islamic Revolutionary Guard Corps' elite Quds Force, Tehran gave safe passage and sanctuary to hundreds of jihadists fleeing Afghanistan in the wake of the U.S.-led invasion.[52] Fighters in the first wave fleeing Afghanistan were detained but deported to countries of their choice after being documented, with some issued special traveling papers by Iran. While detained, these fighters were provided comfortable accommodations rather than being held in military or prison facilities.[53] Indeed, Gen. Qassem Suleimani, the head of the Quds Force, reportedly took "personal responsibility" for tending to the fleeing family of Osama bin Laden, as well as senior al-Qaeda members, when they "sought sanctuary in Iran in 2002."[54]

In addition to foot soldiers and volunteers, Iran permitted entry to some of al-Qaeda's highest-ranking members, including Sayf al-Adl, Abu Muhammad al-Masri (a leading al-Qaeda figure who was involved in the 1998 East Africa embassy attacks), Abu Musab al-Suri, and Sa'ad and Hamza bin Laden (Osama's sons).[55] Other al-Qaeda figures who found refuge in Iran after fleeing Afghanistan included Abu Anas al-Libi (a prominent Libyan member who played an important role in the 1998 East Africa embassy bombings), 'Urwah al-Libi, Atiyah Abd al-Rahman, Thirwat Salah Shihata (a former deputy to Zawahiri), and Mohammed Islambouli (an Egyptian fighter and a prominent al-Qaeda member).[56] Iran monitored and surveilled al-Qaeda members in its territory, with the goal of maximizing the utility al-Qaeda could offer to Iranian foreign policy objectives while staving off the dangers that the militant group might pose to Iran. The movements and residences of these al-Qaeda members were restricted, and they were sporadically detained.[57] Even so, Iran did little to prevent some of these operatives from carrying out their duties to al-Qaeda. As Fishman notes, Sayf al-Adl was "living freely in Shiraz when the United States invaded Iraq," and "he continued to play a key role in al-Qaeda's broader command structure." Adl's "captors clearly gave him leeway to remain a productive member of al-Qaeda's leadership" during this period.[58]

The Iran-based al-Qaeda hub rapidly established a "management council" charged with providing strategic assistance to al-Qaeda's senior leadership, which had regrouped in Pakistan. This cadre helped plan and direct the October 2003 truck bombing of a Western housing complex in Riyadh, suicide strikes against multiple targets in Casablanca that same month, and the bombing of the El-Ghriba synagogue in Djerba, Tunisia, in 2002.[59]

Primarily due to pressure from the United States and other Arab states in the wake of these attacks, Iran detained several leading al-Qaeda figures sheltering in the country—but it never specified who these operatives were. Further, subsequently uncovered evidence revealed that key management council members—including Atiyah and Mohammed Islambouli—were still allowed to operate with relative impunity. It is now known that, for the most part, the detained al-Qaeda figures were held under a loose form of military house arrest that afforded a relatively high degree of movement. Moreover, Tehran continued to allow recruits making the journey to South Asia to access guest houses in Iran.[60] Repeated reference to these sanctuaries being used to facilitate the travel of al-Qaeda to and from Afghanistan is made in reports prepared at the Guantánamo Bay detention facility that have been either declassified or appeared in press reporting.[61] According to one document, dozens of Guantánamo detainees were found to have traveled through the Islamic Republic en route to al-Qaeda's training camps in Afghanistan: "Travel through Iran is a known modus operandi for al Qaeda operatives to get into Afghanistan via a chain of safe-houses and operatives."[62] This route was used by Yasin al-Suri, a key al-Qaeda facilitator, since at least 2007. Tehran maintained ties with Suri, allowing him to operate in the country.[63] Another paper similarly asserts that access to guest houses operated by Tehran directly supported the operations of prominent al-Qaeda leaders and facilitators like Abu Zubaydah and Hussein Salem Mohammed.[64]

Beside safe houses, Iran has allowed key al-Qaeda facilitators to operate from its territory. In 2005 the U.S. Treasury Department designated Muhsin al-Fadhli, an Iran-based confidant of bin Laden, as a terrorist for providing financial and material support to underwrite attacks against American and coalition forces in Iraq.[65] In 2009 the United States sanctioned several top al-Qaeda operatives based in Iran, including bin Laden's son Sa'ad and Mustafa Hamid, one of the main people responsible for channeling strategic and tactical communications to and from Afghanistan during the 1990s.[66] In July 2011 the U.S. Treasury Department for the first time formally accused Tehran of forging an alliance with al-Qaeda to move money and recruits from the Persian Gulf to the group's leadership in Afghanistan, Pakistan, and Iraq, with these personnel and assets moving through Iran. Yasin al-Suri was identified as the chief architect behind this enterprise, which drew on a logistical and financial network that operated in tandem with donors and contributors based in Qatar and Kuwait.[67] The next year the U.S. Treasury named Adel Radi Saqr al-Wahabi al-Harbi as Fadhli's chief deputy inside Iran and the main person responsible for assisting with the transfer of jihadists to the Middle East and raising funds in support of al-Qaeda attacks.[68]

The importance of these Iran-based facilitators is reflected in papers seized during from bin Laden's Abbottabad compound. Among the documents was a letter that al-Qaeda's emir wrote in 2007 to a jihadist referred to as "Karim," likely Abu Ayyub al-Masri, who was then the head of the Islamic State of Iraq. In it, bin Laden highlighted Tehran's criticality to his movement's operations, commenting that "Iran is our main artery for funds, personnel, and communication. . . . There is no need to fight with Iran unless you are forced."[69]

Bin Laden had a good reason to admonish al-Masri: Al-Qaeda had negotiated a nonaggression pact with the Iranian government. According to a statement from the U.S. Treasury, under the terms of this agreement, al-Qaeda was required to desist from conducting operations on Iranian soil, including recruiting operatives, while keeping authorities apprised of its activities. In return, the Islamic Republic would afford al-Qaeda operatives based in the country and their families with freedom of movement and an uninhibited ability to travel.[70] The benefits of the arrangement appear to have been substantial for al-Qaeda, providing it a secure base of operations and insulation from U.S. drone attacks.[71]

Iran's relationship with al-Qaeda continued thereafter. In 2016 the U.S. Treasury imposed sanctions on three senior al-Qaeda members, all of whom were based in Iran: Faisal Jassim Mohammed al-Amri al-Khalidi, Yisra Muhammad Ibrahim Bayumi, and Abu Bakar Muhammad Ghumayn. The trio had carried out a range of activities for al-Qaeda, including gathering intelligence, raising and transferring funds, procuring weapons, and facilitating liaisons with the Tehrik-e Taliban Pakistan (TTP) militant group.[72] In its 2017 *Country Reports on Terrorism*, the U.S. Department of State singled out Iran's ongoing support for al-Qaeda as a serious issue.[73] In July 2018 a report produced by the UN Security Council concluded that "al-Qaida leaders in the Islamic Republic have grown more prominent, working with Aiman al-Zawahiri and projecting his authority more effectively than he could previously."[74] The same report concludes that senior al-Qaeda leaders based in Iran have been able to exert influence on the evolving situation in northwestern Syria.[75] In January 2021 the U.S. State Department revealed that another senior al-Qaeda leader, 'Abd al-Rahman al-Maghrebi, is based inside Iran. Al-Maghrebi, the son-in-law of Ayman al-Zawahiri, is the "longtime director" of As-Sahab, al-Qaeda's central media arm. He has also served as the group's general manager for Afghanistan and Pakistan. The State Department noted that al-Maghrebi "continued to oversee al-Qaeda activities worldwide" after relocating to Iran and, as "head of al-Qaeda's External Communications Office," he "coordinates activities with al-Qaeda affiliates."[76]

Thus, although Iran detained some al-Qaeda figures for years after the 9/11 hijackings, others were allowed to operate. Fundraisers throughout the Gulf were permitted to shuttle money to al-Qaeda through Iran. This coincided with a period in which the Taliban and their allies were able to regroup and reclaim lost territory against the U.S.-led military coalition and a still-nascent Afghan government.

AL-QAEDA'S NETWORK IN PAKISTAN

Al-Qaeda's network in Pakistan proved equally important. The extremists could still use madrassas in the northern part of the country as a focal point for their activities, as they had ever since the anti-Soviet jihad in the 1980s. In 2009 the U.S. government designated the head of Peshawar's Ganj Madrassa, Fazeel-a-Tul Shaykh Abu Mohammed Ameen al-Peshawari (a.k.a. Sheikh Aminullah), as a terrorist, describing him as an al-Qaeda facilitator. Peshawari has provided al-Qaeda and Taliban "martyrs" with suicide vests and organized financial support for the bombers' families. Like other jihadist facilitators in Pakistan, Aminullah and his lieutenants serve multiple organizations at once.

Al-Qaeda also uses other jihadist hubs in Pakistan, some of which operate further from the Afghan border. Pakistani counterterrorism officials in Karachi warned in 2016 that they had "a list of several hundred active al-Qaeda members, which makes them assume there are at least a few thousand on the streets" of Pakistan's coastal mega-city.[77] Al-Qaeda's persistence in Pakistan hints at another analytical lapse contributing to the United States' long-standing low-ball estimate of the group's strength in Afghanistan: With Pakistan serving as a rear base for the jihadist group, al-Qaeda's men could regularly shuttle between the two countries, obscuring their actual strength in both places. The picture of al-Qaeda's numbers in Afghanistan was always incomplete without taking its Pakistan-based fighters into account.

Al-Qaeda's Ethnic Fighting Groups

Al-Qaeda survived in Afghanistan partly because of its success in attract-ing and organizing fighters from the surrounding region. Ethnic brigades composed of Central Asian and Uighur fighters bolstered the Afghan insur-gency. The soil on which these strategically advantageous relationships grew had been tilled years before. In the 1990s bin Laden and Zawahiri cul-tivated relationships with jihadists from Uzbekistan, Tajikistan, and west-ern China. The Islamic Movement of Uzbekistan (IMU) grew out of these efforts. According to the United Nations, al-Qaeda's leaders encouraged Uzbek jihadists to form the IMU in 1998, with bin Laden providing seed money. The IMU repaid this support, maintaining "close ties" to al-Qaeda and the Taliban after the 9/11 attacks and participating in the fight against the U.S.-led coalition.[78]

The al-Qaeda dissident Mustafa Hamid has alleged that the group held little sway over the IMU in pre-9/11 Afghanistan. But much evidence con-tradicts Hamid's claims. Both the U.S. government and the United Nations designated the IMU as a terrorist organization precisely because of its documented ties to al-Qaeda, while IMU recruits were integrated into al-Qaeda's operations.[79] Moreover, in a letter recovered in Abbottabad, al-Qaeda privately rebuked Hamid for his "false accusations that have no basis in truth." That document, dated August 22, 2009, was authored by Abu al-Khayr al-Masri, a senior member of al-Qaeda's management team. "You know that the mujahedin from Tajikistan and Uzbekistan whom you com-mend intellectually and militarily and organizationally were trained in al-Qaeda's camps," Masri wrote to Hamid. "You personally gave them political courses in these camps." Masri added that al-Qaeda's "financial support, within the bounds of its limited capability, continued to the Uzbek brothers and their emir Muhammad Tahir after that." Masri accused Hamid of lying about the extent of the relationship between the two jihadist groups. "It is assumed, by virtue of your ties with both sides, that you are knowledgeable of that," Masri wrote in reference to al-Qaeda's financial support for IMU.[80]

IMU fractured amid a worldwide jihadist split in 2015, with one faction renouncing its historical allies to join Baghdadi's ascendant Islamic State. Despite this setback, the Taliban and al-Qaeda still command the loyalty of various Uzbek factions in Afghanistan. IMU splinter groups like the

Islamic Jihad Union and the Imam al-Bukhari Brigade, which also has a presence in Syria, continue to serve the Taliban-led insurgency.

As Masri noted in his rebuttal to Hamid, al-Qaeda also cultivated ties to Tajik jihadists, many of whom had first been IMU members. On September 3, 2010, a suicide bomber driving an explosives-laden car struck a police building in Khujand, Tajikistan's second-largest city. Authorities identified the bomber as Akmal Karimov, who was "trained in al-Qaeda camps in Afghanistan and Pakistan." More than fifty people were jailed in the security crackdown that followed, with a Tajik court deeming all the defendants to be IMU members.[81] Some Tajik fighters have operated under the name Jamaat Ansarullah, which the government of Tajikistan treats as an arm of the IMU.[82]

Another prominent ethnic-based militant group fighting under al-Qaeda's umbrella is the Turkistan Islamic Party (TIP), previously known as the Eastern Turkistan Islamic Movement (ETIM). TIP's relationship with al-Qaeda dates to the 1990s. Its members are primarily Uighurs from western China. The Uighur opposition in China is composed of multiple factions, but TIP remains the region's only al-Qaeda-affiliated enterprise. Some TIP members attended camps in the Tora Bora Mountains prior to the 9/11 hijackings. Two al-Qaeda-affiliated terrorists conducted the trainings: TIP/ETIM emir Hassan Mahsum and Abdul Haq al-Turkistani. Mahsum, who was killed in northern Pakistan in October 2003, has been lionized in al-Qaeda propaganda. In 2015 TIP released an image of Mahsum sitting next to Zawahiri, emphasizing the two jihadists' close relationship. Abdul Haq succeeded Mahsum as TIP's emir, and he was appointed to al-Qaeda's elite shura council by 2005.[83] Abdul Haq was reportedly killed in an American drone strike in 2010, but it later emerged that he survived the attack.[84]

It was fortunate for al-Qaeda that Abdul Haq lived. He became a key voice in al-Qaeda's campaign against ISIS. While some Uighur jihadists were drawn into Baghdadi's camp, Abdul Haq held the al-Qaeda line. In June 2016 Abdul Haq released a lengthy critique of ISIS, stating that the Baghdadi-aligned IMU fighters had been vanquished. The video accompanying Abdul Haq's message reinforced TIP's place in al-Qaeda's network and lionized various al-Qaeda figures. TIP continues to fight in Afghanistan and boasts a significant branch in Syria. While some TIP members have defected to ISIS, Abdul Haq's loyalists continue to run their own active operation, giving al-Qaeda another avenue for participating in the Syrian jihad.

The role of al-Qaeda's ethnic fighting units in the larger jihadist organization is underappreciated. From al-Qaeda's perspective, these ethnic outfits buttressed the Taliban's efforts to resurrect their lost Islamic Emirate. The Uzbek, Tajik, and Uighur groups also recruit throughout Central Asia. While some recruits are likely drawn into militancy because of grievances against repressive regimes in their home countries, they often find themselves fighting for the larger, world-spanning global jihadist cause as well.

Al-Qaeda in the Indian Subcontinent

In early September 2014 Ayman al-Zawahiri announced a new branch of his organization. For more than two years, Zawahiri explained, al-Qaeda had worked to unify elements of several Pakistani jihadist groups under a common banner, an effort that Zawahiri's son-in-law, Abu Dujana al-Basha, had personally led. The result was AQIS, a branch that would extend the organization's reach across South Asia. Not long after Zawahiri's announcement, AQIS claimed responsibility for one of the most audacious plots in al-Qaeda's history.

Under the leadership of two veterans of the Pakistani navy who had defected to the jihadists' cause, an AQIS team attempted to board the PNS *Zulfiqar*, a missile-armed frigate docked in the port of Karachi. According to Pakistani officials, the men never made it on board the ship. AQIS told a different story, claiming that its members engaged in a shootout once they made it onto the vessel. Whatever the truth of the incident, AQIS had a clear plan in mind.[85] Its men intended to hijack the PNS *Zulfiqar* and fire its 72 mm antiaircraft guns at the USS *Supply*, an American oil tanker tasked with refueling other U.S. naval vessels. If this part of the plan succeeded, the AQIS team would proceed to "target the American frigate protecting USS Supply using four anti-ship guided missiles." The jihadists wanted to "destroy any American or coalition warship present in the vicinity, and fight on until attaining martyrdom."[86] A second AQIS team was set to hijack the PNS *Aslat* with the same kind of operation in mind, only with Indian vessels as the eventual target.

If hijacked Pakistani frigates had actually fired on American and Indian warships, there is no telling what would have followed. It is possible that the jihadists' operation would have been misinterpreted as a

Pakistani naval attack. Steve Coll notes that the Indian press added another sinister note to the story, claiming that India's intelligence service had picked up indications that the PNS *Zulfiqar* was carrying a nuclear warhead.[87] This detail has not been confirmed, and it may just be fearmongering. Regardless, U.S. officials have expressed concern that Pakistani nuclear warheads could someday fall into the hands of al-Qaeda or another terrorist organization. Pakistan's changing approach to its nuclear arsenal might make such a scenario more likely. In a May 2017 threat assessment submitted to the U.S. Congress, the Office of the Director of National Intelligence warned that "Pakistan's pursuit of tactical nuclear weapons potentially lowers the threshold for their use." It continued that "early deployment during a crisis of smaller, more mobile nuclear weapons would increase the amount of time that systems would be outside the relative security of a storage site, increasing the risk that a coordinated attack by non-state actors might succeed in capturing a complete nuclear weapon."[88]

AQIS failed to spark a war, but the group displayed alarming capabilities in the course of this unsuccessful plot. Most notably, the PNS *Zulfiqar* affair showed that al-Qaeda had convinced an as-yet-unknowable number of Pakistani military officers to join its cause. In 2016 a Pakistani court sentenced five naval officers to death for their role in the conspiracy.[89] As part of its propaganda effort trumpeting the attempted hijacking, AQIS released a photo purportedly showing one of its men monitoring Gen. Ashfaq Parvez Kayani, the former Pakistani Army chief, as he visited an American warship.

THE PAKISTANI MILITARY AS RECRUITING GROUNDS

In some respects, the Pakistani armed forces may be fertile ground for jihadist recruitment. At their founding, Pakistan's military and intelligence services were heavily shaped by the country's colonial experience. Pakistan's Inter-Services Intelligence agency (ISI) was formed by a British army officer in 1948. The agency was charged with coordinating the intelligence functions of Pakistan's army, navy, and air force. Shuja Nawaz writes in his definitive study of Pakistan's military that Pakistan's army "was saddled at birth with this paradoxical identity: the symbols of Islam but the substance of a colonial force, quite distant from the body politic of the fledgling state."[90]

At its founding, Pakistan's military was primarily composed of the country's secularized elites. Thus, during its early years the military was not close to the country's Islamic parties. Zulfikar Ali Bhutto, who became prime minister in 1973, broadened the ISI by creating an internal wing. He was concerned with bolstering his own power, and his personal leadership had a paranoid strand. Thus, he wanted ISI "to keep surveillance not only on his opponents, but also on his own party men and cabinet ministers. The agency kept dossiers on politicians, bureaucrats, judges and anyone else considered important."[91] Ironically, the internal wing of ISI that Bhutto helped create would play a role in the coup that toppled him from power in July 1977.[92] The coup brought to power Muhammad Zia ul-Haq. Although it was under Zia's rule that the culture of Pakistan's military and ISI shifted in an explicitly Islamic direction, Stephen P. Cohen points out that the army began Islamizing under Zulfikar Ali Bhutto. "Zulfikar himself ordered alcohol removed from the mess," Cohen says, "and one of the reasons that he picked Zia as the army's chief of staff may have been that Zia was seen as a pious general."[93] Bhutto was not motivated by personal conviction in making these moves. He was secular in orientation, but Islamists were ascendant politically at the time. This gesture was designed to placate them.

After executing his coup against Bhutto, Zia ruled Pakistan for around a decade. He had served in the Royal Indian Army prior to Pakistan's creation, and his religiosity was apparent during his military service. As Zia explained: "Drinking, gambling, dancing and music were the way the officers spent their free time. I said prayers, instead."[94] After coming to power, he frequently expressed a sense of divine mission.[95]

Zia's sense of religious mission translated into the adoption of overtly Islamic positions at a public policy level and the government's imposition of religious norms and customs. These changes began immediately after he executed his coup.[96] Zia's government created sharia courts to determine the legitimacy of all laws and invalidate those that they deemed improper, while it tried to create an "Islamic economy" free of interest. Zia also substantially changed the organizational culture of the military and ISI. His reforms of the military went beyond Bhutto's nascent changes in three major ways. First, the military's training came to include Islamic teachings, including at the Pakistan Military Academy and the Command and Staff College.[97] Second, religious criteria were incorporated into the promotion requirements for officers. Many skilled officers with secular outlooks were passed over for promotion.

Fewer officers with secular outlooks reached senior levels in the military, while many officers with conservative religious outlooks reached top levels of command. Third, Zia reinforced these education and promotional policies by mandating formal obedience to Islamic rules. He required not only that soldiers attend the Friday congregational prayers at regimental mosques but also that units bring mullahs with them to the front lines of combat.[98]

At the same time Zia's policies were being implemented, the composition of the officer corps was shifting. The first generation of the officer corps came from the country's social elites, frequently educated in English-language schools, while the new junior officers came from Pakistan's poorer northern districts. Hussain observes that "the spirit of liberalism, common in the 'old' army, was practically unknown to them. They were products of a social class that, by its very nature, was conservative and easily influenced by Islamic fundamentalism."[99] The net effect of Zia's policies and the demographic shift in the junior officer corps was to move the military in a more religious direction.

Perhaps more importantly, soon after Zia came to power, the Soviet Union invaded Afghanistan. The United States and Pakistan cooperated in supporting mujahedin who battled Soviet forces. The ISI grew exponentially during this period, and important relationships between Pakistani officials and Islamic militants developed. While Zia and the ISI controlled much of the Afghan mujahedin's support network, the CIA did have direct relationships with key commanders such as Jalaluddin Haqqani and Gulbuddin Hekmatyar. Haqqani was also Osama bin Laden's chief benefactor in Afghanistan. Jalaluddin, along with his brothers and sons, operated what is widely known as the Haqqani Network, which is an integral part of the Taliban and continued to work with the ISI decades after the CIA broke off the relationship. The Haqqanis are also al-Qaeda's closest allies in Afghanistan and Pakistan. Although the ISI had an official staff of around two thousand prior to the Afghan–Soviet war, after the Soviet withdrawal the ISI retained about forty thousand employees and had a budget of around $1 billion "for maintaining influence among the now-victorious mujahideen groups."[100]

After the Soviet Union retreated from Afghanistan, the fight against the Soviet-backed regime of Mohammad Najibullah continued. The country fell into civil war in 1992, after the mujahedin captured Kabul. The ISI remained involved during this period, and eventually would become a major sponsor of the Taliban. The ISI further supported Islamist militants in the Kashmir conflict through most of the 1990s. During the same period, the ISI also began to support stateless militancy in countries outside the region, funding and backing multiple jihadist groups, for example, that were active in Bosnia and Herzegovina. Husain Haqqani, a scholar and Pakistan's former ambassador to the United States, notes that "the ISI violated the UN embargo on supplying arms to warring parties in Bosnia-Herzegovina and 'airlifted sophisticated anti-tank guided missiles' for the Bosnian Muslims."[101]

Given Pakistan's policy of sponsoring stateless religious militants, it would have taken a sea change to alter this policy at top levels. A sea change did come in the form of the 9/11 attacks and their aftermath. But by that time the state could not completely turn back. Segments of the Pakistani military and intelligence establishment remained sympathetic to the jihadists' cause.

THE MILITANTS WHO COMPOSE AQIS

When Zawahiri announced the creation of AQIS, he did not name the Pakistani jihadist groups that al-Qaeda had recruited and reorganized into its newest arm. He provided some hints though. Al-Qaeda's chief listed several figures who had been instrumental in the AQIS project, each of whom represented one or more established fighting outfits. Zawahiri mentioned Ilyas Kashmiri, a commander in Harkat-ul Jihad-al-Islami (HUJI), who swore his allegiance to bin Laden; along with Badr Mansoor, an al-Qaeda commander who also worked with Harkat-ul-Mujahideen (HuM). Zawahiri's roll call also included Ustadh Amjad Farooqi, another operative affiliated with HUJI and HuM; Dr. Arshad Wahid, who worked with Jundallah, which targets Shia civilians; and Sheikh Ahsan Aziz, a figure linked with the Kashmir-focused Hizbul Mujahideen.[102] It is likely that AQIS also drew its founding cadres from Lashkar-e-Taiba (LeT) and Jaish-e-Mohammed, both of which were established to fight Indian forces in Kashmir. All these organizations have long operated inside Pakistan, often with the approval and assistance of the Pakistani military and intelligence services.

This Pakistani jihadist milieu allowed al-Qaeda to rebuild its organization in South Asia after years of counterterrorism operations, thus enabling it to regenerate its capacity to threaten the West. This phenomenon can be glimpsed in the career of Rashid Rauf, who traveled from Britain to Pakistan in mid-2002.[103] Rauf, a British citizen of Pakistani heritage, made his way into Afghanistan alongside senior Jaish-e-Mohammed figure Amjad Hussein Farooqi in mid-2002. Farooqi's al-Qaeda ties provided a gateway for Rauf to join the group. Just over two years later, Rauf emerged as a key player in al-Qaeda's external operations network, helping stage-manage plots in his home country. He acted as a facilitator for the July 7, 2005, London bombings, which killed fifty-two people, and the failed 2006 transatlantic air plot (see chapter 4). Rauf also met with Bryant Neal Vinas, an American who plotted an attack on the Long Island Railroad, as well as with members of an al-Qaeda cell that planned suicide bombings on the New York City subway in 2009. A U.S. drone strike reportedly killed Rauf in November 2008.

Further, the aforementioned Ilyas Kashmiri was initially known in jihadist circles for spearheading attacks against Indian forces in Kashmir. One photo shared widely on jihadist websites and social media purportedly shows Kashmiri holding the severed head of an Indian soldier. As HUJI's top operational commander, Kashmiri controlled a network that stretched across South Asia. Al-Qaeda had cultivated ties with HUJI beginning in the early 1990s. HUJI members trained in al-Qaeda's camps, and the Pakistani group "provided fighters for the Taliban in Afghanistan." While HUJI is responsible for a string of attacks in Pakistan and India, it is evident that al-Qaeda's anti-Americanism influenced the group, which dispatched a suicide bomber to strike the U.S. consulate in Karachi on March 2, 2006, killing an American diplomat and three others. Despite sharing the Pakistani establishment's animus for India, HUJI often turned its guns and suicide attackers on the Pakistani state, including targeting the ISI, the police, and senior officials.[104]

Kashmiri corresponded with bin Laden and his lieutenants, often seeking instructions. For example, after the Indian media reported in 2010 that Kashmiri's group was an al-Qaeda front, he asked bin Laden whether he should change his organization's name.[105] Recognizing Kashmiri's talents, al-Qaeda made Kashmiri a senior and highly trusted figure in its external operations arm. He was tasked with a far-fetched plan to assassinate President Barack Obama or Gen. David Petraeus during one of their visits to the region.[106] He also oversaw a more feasible plot to attack the *Jyllands-Posten* newspaper in Denmark.[107] That planned attack, which would have

relied on an American named David Headley to conduct pre-attack surveillance, was supposed to exact revenge against the newspaper for printing
cartoons of the Prophet Muhammad in 2005 (see chapter 5). Closer to home,
Kashmiri orchestrated a series of operations against Pakistani officials
before he was eventually killed in a U.S. drone strike in June 2011. Some of
his former subordinates continue to fight under AQIS's banner.

AQIS closely cooperates with the Pakistani Taliban (a.k.a. Tehrik-e Taliban Pakistan or TTP) and has drawn fighters from that organization, a relationship that mirrors the dynamics between similarly affiliated groups in
Afghanistan.[108] According to the State Department, the TTP and al-Qaeda
have maintained a "symbiotic relationship," with TTP receiving "ideological guidance" from al-Qaeda while gaining access to its "global terrorist
network" and drawing on al-Qaeda's "operational experience." In return,
al-Qaeda "relies on TTP for safe haven in the Pashtun areas along the
Afghan-Pakistani border." The result is that TTP acts as "a force multiplier"
for al-Qaeda.[109]

One document recovered in Abbottabad shows that two of bin Laden's
lieutenants reviewed and edited TTP's founding charter.[110] TTP has always
been a coalition of parties in northern Pakistan. The organization
fractured after the death of TTP's leader, Hakeemullah Mehsud in 2014.
Al-Qaeda helped the group through this rough patch and worked to reorganize the TTP by first uniting three key factions under the leadership of
Mati ur-Rehman and then merging this combined venture into the rebuilt
TTP one year after the split.[111]

AQIS HELPED RESURRECT THE ISLAMIC
EMIRATE OF AFGHANISTAN

AQIS's first emir was Asim Umar, a veteran of HuM, one of the Pakistani
jihadist groups that buttressed al-Qaeda's ranks.[112] It is likely that HuM
members were also part of bin Laden's support network in Abbottabad. The
cellphone of bin Laden's courier who unwittingly led the CIA to his boss's
doorstep in May 2011 reportedly contained contacts with Pakistan-based
HuM operatives.[113] Umar eventually graduated from HuM into al-Qaeda's
senior ranks, becoming one of the group's most important figures in South
Asia. AQIS's principal mission since its founding in 2014 has been to help
the Taliban restore its Islamic Emirate. That mission was accomplished in

August 2021, when the Taliban overran Kabul and reinstalled its regime. Under Umar's leadership, AQIS greatly expanded its operations inside Afghanistan and focused much of its activities on improving al-Qaeda and its allies' position in that country. AQIS's assistance helped the Taliban achieve its victory.

AQIS released a new twenty-page code of conduct in June 2017, outlining the organization's basic strategy and chain of command. AQIS "operates in obedience" to the emir of what it calls "al-Qaeda central," meaning Zawahiri. "Ever since its beginning," the charter continues, AQIS "has been engaged in jihad in line with the general guidelines of al-Qaeda." AQIS seeks "to establish Khilafah [an alternative spelling of *caliphate*] in compliance with the Prophetic method," beginning in Afghanistan. "Strengthening and defending the Islamic Emirate of Afghanistan is part of this objective," the group emphasized.[114]

AQIS's code of conduct outlines the organization's responsibility to aid the Afghan Taliban. The document is careful to note that bin Laden swore allegiance to Mullah Omar and that Zawahiri did the same after bin Laden's death. Zawahiri then pledged fealty to Omar's successor, Mullah Mansour, as well as to Mansour's replacement, Hibatullah Akhundzada. Asim Umar, the first emir of AQIS, thus swore his own allegiance to Akhundzada through his *bayah* to Zawahiri. "One of the major objectives of [AQIS] is strengthening the Islamic Emirate of Afghanistan, defending it, and bringing stability to it," the code of conduct reads. To that end, AQIS "engages the enemies of the Islamic Emirate outside Afghanistan, and also takes part in the battles inside it—fighting shoulder-to-shoulder with the mujahideen of the emirate."[115]

This is not mere rhetoric. American military and intelligence officials have found that AQIS was deeply embedded within the Taliban-led insurgency, which ultimately deposed Afghanistan's U.S.-backed government. The chain of loyalty detailed in the code of conduct has had an impact on the Afghan battlefield.

In the summer of 2015 the United States made the shocking discovery that AQIS had built two massive training camps in the Shorabak district of Afghanistan's southern Kandahar province. One of the camps was around thirty square miles in size. The camps' geographic location was just as shocking as their scope. For years, the United States had claimed that al-Qaeda was holed up in the remote eastern provinces of Kunar and Nuristan.

But the two AQIS camps were proof that an arm of al-Qaeda had expanded its operations into the southern part of the country, a place long thought to be free of a significant al-Qaeda presence. "It's a place where you would probably think you wouldn't have AQ," Gen. John F. Campbell, then the commander of NATO's Resolute Support, told the *Washington Post* after the camps were raided.[116]

Dismantling the camps required sixty-three airstrikes over the course of five days in October 2015, a mission preceded by months of advanced planning. Gen. Wilson Shoffner, a U.S. military spokesman, described the raids as "one of the largest joint ground-assault operations we have ever conducted in Afghanistan."[117] This "major al-Qaeda sanctuary" was, Shoffner pointed out, "in the center of the Taliban's historic heartland."[118] General Campbell characterized one of the targets as "probably the largest training camp-type facility that we have seen in 14 years of war."[119]

The Shorabak district had long been contested terrain. But the success of the 2015 operation didn't stop the Taliban from eventually seizing the entire district in February 2017. That same month, the Combating Terrorism Center at West Point published an interview with Gen. John Nicholson, the commander of NATO's Resolute Support and U.S. Forces–Afghanistan. Nicholson explained that AQIS and the Taliban had been "working together" at the camps. He noted that al-Qaeda was careful not to publicly advertise its presence in Shorabak. If anything, its media efforts drew attention *away* from AQIS's secret mega-camps in southern Afghanistan. The Taliban also never admitted who was at the camps, instead decrying the U.S. and Afghan raids in vague language. "With AQIS, in return for the sanctuary and support they get from groups like the Taliban, they do lend assistance to the Taliban," Nicholson said in his interview. "They're lending expertise to the people that we're concerned about inside of Afghanistan."[120]

The United States continued to hunt al-Qaeda operatives in Afghanistan in the months following the October 2015 raids in Shorabak. In May 2016 the U.S. rescued Ali Haider Gilani, the son of former Pakistani Prime Minister Yusuf Raza Gilani, from jihadist captivity.[121] Gilani had been kidnapped in 2013 and held in Afghanistan's eastern Paktika province, a longtime stronghold for the Haqqanis. The U.S. killed one of bin Laden's top lieutenants, Abu Khalil al-Sudani, in a July 2015 airstrike in Paktika. Sudani was so trustworthy that he provided explosives training to Osama's now-deceased son and heir, Hamza bin Laden.[122]

Battlefield events in Afghanistan show how AQIS's men are often commingled with the Taliban. In late 2017 the Afghan government and NATO launched operations against al-Qaeda positions in Ghazni, Paktia, and Zabul. Among those killed was Omar Khetab, a senior al-Qaeda leader who also served as the "second senior leader" in AQIS. In addition, Khetab "was directly involved in fighting against the Afghan government and foreign troops and had a role in advising in the use of heavy weapons such as rockets, mortars and training for Taliban night attacks," NATO's Resolute Support said at the time.[123] The operations killed multiple other al-Qaeda operatives, Pakistani jihadists, and Taliban fighters.[124] Other AQIS commanders have also provided crucial training to Taliban militants. According to a January 2018 UN report, "AQIS fighters operate as advisers and trainers of the Taliban, with 150 to 180 operatives present in southern and eastern Afghanistan."[125] Even that figure may be too low, as the United States has killed or captured far more than 180 AQIS operatives in Afghanistan in recent years.

Perhaps no aspect of al-Qaeda's operations has been as underestimated and misunderstood as its decades-long relationship with the Taliban. The organizations are bound by formal ties of loyalty and use mutually affiliated leaders and their own rank and file to advance each other's goals. Al-Qaeda has taken steps to ensure that its men remain intertwined with the Taliban's armed forces. Al-Qaeda provided crucial support to the Afghan insurgency and received sanctuary in return.[126] Importantly, al-Qaeda continues to export terrorism throughout the Indian Subcontinent from Afghan soil.

Al-Qaeda Operations in the Indian Subcontinent

U.S. and Afghan forces recovered a significant cache of documents and files during the October 2015 raids on the Shorabak camps. This intelligence confirmed that the Shorabak facilities were part of a larger network stretching throughout the region. "We've seen a lot of AQIS interference in Bangladesh," General Nicholson noted during a 2017 interview with the Combating Terrorism Center at West Point. In the Shorabak camps, Nicholson explained, "there were congratulatory notes going back and forth about some of these activities in Bangladesh."[127] Although the document highlighted the group's role in reviving the Islamic Emirate of

Afghanistan, AQIS's 2017 code of conduct also noted that the organization's mission spans "the entire region of the Subcontinent, including Burma, and especially the three large countries, Pakistan, India, and Bangladesh."[128]

AQIS IN BANGLADESH

AQIS has claimed a series of small-scale operations in Bangladesh since 2013, with its militants sometimes working through a front group known as Ansar al-Islam. These attacks are intended to capitalize on an Islamist backlash against convictions related to war crimes committed during Bangladesh's 1971 war of independence against the Pakistani state. In 2010 Prime Minister Sheikh Hasina, leader of the Awami League, established the International Crimes Tribunal to prosecute crimes committed during the war of independence.[129] Three years later, Abdul Quader Mollah, a member of the Islamist Jamaat-e-Islami party, was brought before the tribunal and found guilty of rape and targeted killings against Bangladesh's intellectuals during the revolution. Mollah was deemed responsible for the deaths of 350 civilians. The trial stirred controversy, violence, and protest. The deeply divided country was plagued by unrest in 2013, with over two hundred people dying in related protests.[130] Initially authorities sentenced Mollah to life in prison on February 5, 2013. There was widespread discontent with the sentence, which many deemed too lenient. A series of protests erupted in Shahbag, Bangladesh, shortly after the sentence was handed down. Months later, authorities upgraded his punishment to death. After appeals were exhausted, Mollah was hanged for his crimes on December 12, 2013.

Just before his death, Mollah said he was "proud to be a martyr for the Islamic movement" in the country. Jamaat-e-Islami members and other Islamists claimed him as exactly that. Jamaat-e-Islami dubbed the execution to be a murder and vowed revenge. Rioters firebombed businesses and train stations, and targeted Hindu homes.[131] It is in this context that al-Qaeda and its front groups have claimed a series of assassinations in Bangladesh and Pakistan. The victims have often been hacked to death with machetes. Secular and moderate bloggers were some of Mollah's fiercest critics, using their platforms to criticize Bangladesh's Islamist parties. Rajib Haider, a prominent atheist blogger, helped spark the Shahbag protests.

Machete-wielding assailants murdered Haider on February 15, 2013. Two students of Jashim Uddin Rahmani, an Islamist cleric in Dhaka, were convicted of Haider's killing more than two years later. Rahmani himself was convicted and sentenced to prison for his role in sanctioning the bloodshed but remained unapologetic. Rahmani and other Islamist clerics repeatedly called for attacks against anyone who spoke out against their version of Islam.[132]

A string of other killings followed Haider's murder. The emir of AQIS, Asim Umar, announced in May 2015 that his men had assassinated Haider. Umar also claimed responsibility for the deaths of Muhammad Shakil Auj, who was the dean of Islamic Studies at the University of Karachi when he was shot in September 2014; Shafiul Islam, a professor at Rajshahi University who was also killed in September 2014; Aniqa Naz, a Pakistani blogger who died in 2012; Avijit Roy, a prominent atheist blogger hacked to death in February 2015; and Washiqur Rahman, a blogger killed in March 2015.[133] Some of the killings occurred before the formal launch of AQIS, but it is plausible that the al-Qaeda arm's predecessor organizations carried out the murders. The logic behind AQIS's claimed assassination campaign against the region's secular-leaning writers and scholars is clear.

AQIS wants to portray itself as the true protector of Islam in Bangladeshi society. Most of the country's Islamists are nonviolent, but al-Qaeda hopes to appeal to them regardless. The group portrays the victims of its assassination campaign as blasphemers who have committed offenses that justify their deaths. Al-Qaeda has emphasized its role in the assassination campaign in its propaganda, with Umar describing the campaign as "part of a series of operations initiated by the different branches of al-Qaeda on the orders of our respected leader Sheikh Ayman al Zawahiri." Umar rhetorically linked the series of murders his group carried out to the massacre at the *Charlie Hebdo* offices in Paris in January 2015. The jihadists "have taught a lesson to blasphemers in France, Denmark, Pakistan and now in Bangladesh," Umar claimed.[134]

In April 2016 AQIS expanded its campaign of murder when a team of machete-wielding jihadists posing as deliverymen killed a LGBT activist, Xulhaz Mannan, and his friend Samir Mahbub Tonoy in Dhaka. Ansar al-Islam, the Bangladeshi branch of AQIS, claimed credit. Mannan was the founder of an LGBT magazine in Bangladesh and worked for the U.S.

Embassy for eight years before joining the United States Agency for International Development. AQIS made it clear that the pair were victims of the group's murderous homophobia. "By the grace of Almighty Allah, the mujahedin of Ansar al-Islam were able to [assassinate] Xulhaz Mannan and his associate Samir Mahbub Tonoy," Ansar al-Islam's statement read. "They were pioneers of practicing and promoting homosexuality in Bangladesh," the statement continued. "Xulhaz Mannan was the director of Roopbaan (A cult comprised of the gays and the lesbians) while Samir Mahbub Tonoy was one of its most important activists. They were working day and night to promote homosexuality among the people of this land since 1998 with the help of their masters, the U.S. crusaders and its Indian allies."[135] AQIS assumes that much of its target audience will consider these attacks and the motives for them legitimate.

AQIS BEYOND BANGLADESH

AQIS has had less success outside Bangladesh. A string of arrests has disrupted the group's presence in India, making it difficult to ascertain how many AQIS operatives remain in the country. Al-Qaeda-aligned groups in India include the Indian Mujahideen, which the State Department designated a terrorist organization in 2011, noting that the Indian Mujahideen "played a facilitative role in the 2008 Mumbai attack carried out by LeT [Lashkar-e-Taiba] that killed 163 people, including six Americans."[136]

Whether or not al-Qaeda assisted in the assault on Mumbai—a question that remains unanswered—there is at least one major point of overlap between the attack's planners and al-Qaeda's network in South Asia.[137] A key figure in that plot went on to work for Ilyas Kashmiri, which underscores how fluid the region's jihadist milieu can be. A Pakistani American named David Headley, who had been working alongside LeT figures in Pakistan, conducted surveillance for the Mumbai attacks. In 2009, months after the terrorist siege in India, Headley worked for Ilyas Kashmiri planning an attack on *Jyllands-Posten*. Kashmiri effectively put Headley in charge of the planned assault on the newspaper, but Headley had difficulty assembling the attack team, and the attack soon fizzled. He returned to the United States and was arrested at Chicago's O'Hare Airport in October 2009. Headley confessed to American authorities that he had dealt with a web of threatening personalities, including Kashmiri.[138] Kashmiri was already one of al-Qaeda's chief external planning operatives during this period.

Headley's career trajectory is indicative of how al-Qaeda operates in India and Pakistan. Al-Qaeda has historically maintained close relationships with various Pakistani militant groups opposed to India, such as LeT. Hafiz Saeed, LeT's longtime leader, honored bin Laden as a "hero" after his death and reportedly corresponded frequently with the al-Qaeda founder.[139] It is possible that AQIS might one day cooperate with LeT or similar groups to carry out operations against their common Indian enemies. But there is another dynamic shaping al-Qaeda's strategy in the region. AQIS doesn't just want to cooperate with existing groups but is trying to steer the jihad in the Indian subcontinent in a new direction. To understand this point, it is necessary to take a closer look at the conflict in Kashmir.

Al-Qaeda has supported various Kashmiri jihadists since the 1990s while also building its own presence in Indian-controlled Kashmir.[140] In his correspondence with bin Laden, Ilyas Kashmiri asked an intriguing question: "How can we pull the rug from under the feet of those who conduct Jihad to the benefit of the Pakistani intelligence?"[141]

In 2017 a new al-Qaeda-linked group called Ansar Ghazwat-ul-Hind (AGH) was formed in Kashmir. Its founder was Zakir Musa, a charismatic and handsome young leader who had served as a commander in Hizbul Mujahideen before falling out with his boss, Syed Salahuddin. Although Hizbul Mujahideen had been fighting Indian forces for years, including deploying suicide bombers, Salahuddin had recently sought to distance his group from the global jihadist cause. "This movement is purely local and indigenous. It has no international agenda," Salahuddin declared in May 2017. "Al-Qaeda, Daesh [ISIS] or Taliban have no involvement or role in Kashmir."[142] Musa disputed Salahuddin in an audio message shortly thereafter. Musa explained that, unlike Salahuddin, he would not settle for a purely nationalist struggle against the Indians in Kashmir: He was devoted to implementation of sharia across the disputed region. Musa publicly thanked al-Qaeda for supporting his efforts. Pro-al-Qaeda jihadists celebrated Musa's high-profile break from Hizbul Mujahideen. Haji Mansoor Mehsood, a Pakistani Taliban commander, praised Musa's decision, noting that Musa's previous messages included images of al-Qaeda figures like Anwar al-Awlaki and Abu Hamza al-Muhajir, the deceased leader of the Islamic State of Iraq.[143]

Musa's split with Hizbul Mujahideen is consistent with al-Qaeda's pointed criticism of Pakistani-backed jihadist groups fighting in Kashmir. In its code of conduct, which was released just weeks after Musa's defection, AQIS lambasted jihadist groups that allegedly allowed the Pakistani government to restrain them. "We call on all jihadi groups working under anti-Sharia intelligence agencies in any place to end their dependence on them," AQIS wrote, because the militaries of corrupt governments would destroy the "fruits of these mujahideen's jihad." AQIS even warned that "the Kashmiri Jihad is a clear example of this."[144]

Musa's formation of AGH in 2017 was a sign that AQIS was poaching militant talent from traditional Pakistani militant groups and reorganizing these defectors so they could advance al-Qaeda's agenda. According to some accounts, AGH is drawing members from LeT, even though in practice the newer group continues to cooperate with some of LeT's commanders.[145] Still, AGH has managed to build only a small operational footprint and faces competition from an upstart pro-ISIS outfit that is also trying to win supporters in Kashmir.

AGH has already suffered significant leadership losses. On May 23, 2019, Indian forces killed Zakir Musa after laying siege to a house where he had been staying. The new head of AQIS, Usama Mahmood, glowingly eulogized Musa in a statement released not long after his death. Mahmood said that Musa's life had set an example for all Muslims, serving as an invitation to join the jihadist revolution. AQIS also released a video, "The Soldiers of Ghazwat ul-Hind," which promoted the Kashmiri cause. A few weeks after Musa's demise, another AGH figure, Hameed Lelhari, was named as his successor. In his first speech as AGH's emir, Lelhari called for an independent *shura* council, with members drawn from each of the jihadist groups focused on Kashmir. Lelhari wanted to prevent the jihad from being "exploited by any country or agency," a swipe at the Pakistani intelligence and military establishment. A few days after Lelhari's message appeared online, Zawahiri issued his own statement, "Don't Forget Kashmir." Zawahiri was more explicit than Lelhari in criticizing rival jihadists' chief patron, stating that "the mujahideen must liberate the Kashmiri jihad from the clutches of Pakistan's intelligence agencies."[146]

Kashmir is not the only South Asian battleground where al-Qaeda has tried to expand its influence. The group has also attempted to capitalize on the crisis in Myanmar, although it is not clear how advanced those efforts are. Zawahiri has repeatedly decried the massacre of the country's Rohingya minority, imploring Muslims to defend them. In a September 2017 message, al-Qaeda veteran Khalid Batarfi addressed the situation in Myanmar, calling on "our Muslim brothers in Burma to prepare their apparatus for jihad, and be ready for it, and we call on our Muslim brothers everywhere and especially in Bangladesh and Malaysia and Indonesia to support their brothers in Burma." Batarfi also called on "the mujahedin everywhere" and "especially our brothers in al-Qaeda in the Indian Sub-continent" to strike back against the government of Myanmar.[147]

It is possible that AQIS will seek to do exactly that. Al-Qaeda's general command, which serves as the organization's global management team, has echoed Batarfi's call for jihad in Myanmar.[148] It is unclear how much of a presence al-Qaeda really has in Myanmar. The main insurgent group fighting on behalf of the Rohingya is the Arakan Rohingya Salvation Army, formerly known as Harakah al-Yaqin. The group denies any ties to outside entities.

A Withdrawal Deal

On February 29, 2020, the Trump administration and the Taliban finalized a withdrawal agreement in Doha.[149] Although it was widely reported as a "peace deal," that label was not accurate. The document's title, "Agreement for Bringing Peace to Afghanistan," indicates that its signatories hoped that peace would *result* from the accord, but the accord itself did not provide for a peaceful outcome. For the Taliban, *peace* always meant the resurrection of its Islamic Emirate. Nothing in the deal stood in way of the Taliban achieving its goal by force. Indeed, it was a lopsided accord in which the United States agreed to withdraw all of NATO's forces, including American servicemembers, from Afghanistan in fourteen months in exchange for little—or, really, nothing. The Taliban simply used negotiations with the U.S. government to help achieve its central political and military goal: the restoration of its Islamic Emirate.

Since the Obama administration first began negotiations the Taliban in 2010, the group consistently demanded that the United States exclude the Afghan government, America's ally, from the talks. The Trump adminis-tration acquiesced to this demand in the summer of 2018, moving forward with bilateral talks that sidelined the internationally recognized govern-ment in Kabul.[150] Throughout the on-and-off negotiations that took place over the next year and a half, the Taliban refused to recognize the Afghan government's legitimacy.

The resulting agreement reflected the Taliban's determination to res-urrect its Islamist state. The text of the accord, including its title, includes multiple references to the "Islamic Emirate of Afghanistan." In each instance, the State Department inserted clumsy language intended to underscore that this emirate "is not recognized by the United States." The State Department's actions suggested otherwise. Secretary of State Mike Pompeo flew to Doha to personally meet with the Taliban's political delegation at the signing ceremony, making him the first Cabinet official in U.S. history to meet directly with the group's representatives.

By agreeing to move forward without the Afghan government, the Trump administration validated the Taliban's long-standing claim that the "Kabul administration" was a puppet regime with no authority of its own.[151] To make matters worse, the State Department did not secure any benefits for the Afghan government while granting significant concessions to the Taliban without Afghan president Ashraf Ghani's blessing. These concessions included an uneven prisoner exchange that would see up to five thousand militants released from Afghan prisons in exchange for the Taliban releasing up to one thousand prisoners of its own.[152] This five-to-one swap was to take place *before* the Taliban's representatives attended the first session of "intra-Afghan talks." The Afghan government would take part in these talks as well, but only as one participant among several, as the Taliban refused to recognize its sovereignty. The Afghan government initially balked at this disproportionate swap, concluding that its foes would use the influx of forces to fuel their war. After Secretary Pompeo flew to Kabul to convince President Ghani, while threatening to withhold U.S. aid, the Afghan government began freeing hundreds of prisoners.[153] The United States also agreed to begin working toward the removal of senior Taliban figures from international terrorist sanctions lists once intra-Afghan talks began.[154] That is, the Taliban was to be rewarded just for attending the intra-Afghan talks, regardless of whether they led to peace or end in fiasco. Although the United States did not immediately delist any Taliban figures, this concession, like the uneven prisoner swap, was made by Washington without Kabul's consent.

Pompeo and Special Representative Zalmay Khalilzad argued that, regardless of the accord's obvious weaknesses, it was still a good deal for Americans because they had secured counterterrorism assurances from the Taliban for the first time in history. "The Bush administration and the Obama administration both tried to get the words that were on the paper yesterday that the Taliban would break from al-Qaeda publicly," Pompeo claimed in an interview the day after the agreement was finalized. Pompeo claimed that the Taliban had sworn not only to break with al-Qaeda but also to "work alongside of us to destroy, deny resources to and have al-Qaeda depart from that place."[155]

If the Taliban had agreed to betray al-Qaeda, as Pompeo claimed, it would have been a diplomatic breakthrough. The problem is that none of what Pompeo claimed was true. Nothing he said the Taliban agreed to do was in the written text of the deal. Nor did the Taliban take a single action against al-Qaeda in the months that followed.

Al-Qaeda is mentioned by name in the text twice. Both mentions include the same language. The Taliban claimed it will "prevent any group or individual, including al-Qaeda, from using the soil of Afghanistan to threaten the security of the United States and its allies."[156] But contrary to Pompeo's argument that this was a new commitment by the Taliban, the group had been saying something similar for years, well before the deal was struck in Doha. In February 2019, a year before the deal was finalized, the Taliban assured the world that it does "not allow anyone to use the soil of Afghanistan against other countries including neighboring countries."[157] That supposed commitment was even broader than the one included in the Taliban's deal with the United States, as it technically ensured that jihadists operating in Afghanistan wouldn't strike *any* other countries, whether they were allied with the United States (such as India) or not (such as Iran or Russia). But when the Taliban issued that assurance in February 2019, terrorist groups like al-Qaeda, AQIS, the Pakistani Taliban, Lashkar-e-Taiba, and others were all operating inside Afghanistan, including in areas contested or controlled by the Taliban.[158] Yet some of these same jihadists threatened not only the United States but also Pakistan, India, and other countries. The State Department's agreement didn't explain why the United States should trust the Taliban on this score, given that the group had been dishonest about this issue since the 1990s. The text of the agreement did not include verification or enforcement mechanisms.

Three other provisions could be construed as dealing with al-Qaeda as well as other regional and international terrorist groups, but curiously none of these militant groups were mentioned by name.[159] Per the terms of the agreement, the Taliban supposedly won't cooperate with groups or individuals who threaten the United States or its allies; who allow anti-American entities to recruit, train, or fundraise inside Afghanistan; or who provide travel paperwork for international terrorists. These provisions may have been what Pompeo had in mind when he claimed that the Taliban had agreed to destroy al-Qaeda, even though that's not what the provisions stipulate. Indeed, the text of the agreement is suspiciously vague with respect to what the Taliban is supposed to do. Consider that the Taliban was working with members of AQIS when the deal was negotiated. American and Afghan forces killed Asim Umar, the first emir of AQIS, in the Taliban stronghold of Musa Qala, Helmand, in September 2019.[160] Umar was living in Musa Qala under the protection of the Taliban's shadow governor, yet the group insisted that only civilians had been killed in the raid. The agreement did not explain how the Taliban would uproot AQIS, which is openly loyal to the Taliban's Islamic Emirate. The Taliban also continued to provide safe haven to al-Qaeda's senior leadership well after the deal with the United States was struck. In October 2020 one of Ayman al-Zawahiri's longest serving lieutenants, Husam Abd-al-Ra'uf, was killed in a Taliban-controlled village in Ghazni province, a well-known hub for al-Qaeda.[161]

Per the agreement, the Taliban is supposed to "send a clear message that those who pose a threat to the security of the United States and its allies have no place in Afghanistan."[162] Well more than a year after the agreement was finalized, however, the Taliban still hadn't issued any such message. Hibatullah Akhundzada, the Taliban's leader, declared victory immediately after the accord was signed.[163] In his victory message, Akhundzada said nothing about al-Qaeda or the other jihadist groups in Afghanistan. Nor did Akhundzada renounce Zawahiri's oath of bayah to him. Al-Qaeda's general command hailed the Taliban's victory over America.[164] Curiously, al-Qaeda's senior leaders told their men to abide by the deal—an odd order if the Taliban was truly going to betray al-Qaeda. To date, the Taliban hasn't renounced al-Qaeda, nor has the Taliban turned its guns on its longtime jihadist comrades.

On August 15, 2021, the Taliban seized control of Kabul, Afghanistan's capital. President Ashraf Ghani and most of his inner coterie had fled the country just hours earlier. Although there was some sporadic fighting on the outskirts of Kabul in the days that followed, the end of the nearly twenty-year war was rather anticlimactic. After the fact, U.S. military leaders claimed that no one could have foreseen the swift collapse of the Afghan government. "There was nothing that I or anyone else saw that indicated a collapse of this army, and this government, in 11 days," Gen. Mark Milley, chairman of the Joint Chiefs of Staff, said a week after Kabul fell.[165]

Contrary to General Milley's claim, the dire security situation was obvious to some of those who were paying close attention.[166] Moreover, the Afghan government didn't collapse in just eleven days. Many within the Afghan security forces and military viewed the February 2020 agreement between the United States and the Taliban as a surrender, a sure indication that the Taliban was going to return to power. Demoralized Afghan commanders and local officials agreed to turn over territory to the Taliban in the months that followed, paving the way for the militant group's rapid advances in 2021.[167] The Taliban's final offensive began in early May 2021.[168] The timing was no accident, as the deal between the United States and the Taliban called for all Western forces to be withdrawn from the country by May 1. Even though the U.S. military stayed past that deadline, President Biden confirmed in mid-April that all forces would be withdrawn by September 2021.[169] By mid-August 2021, the entire country was under the Taliban's control.

How al-Qaeda Survived

At the time that the United States was negotiating with the Taliban, the UN Security Council published a series of reports documenting the Taliban's ongoing partnership with al-Qaeda. The UN monitoring team responsible for tracking al-Qaeda found that the organization's "alliance with the Taliban and other terrorist groups in Afghanistan remains firm" and determined that the two were still "closely allied."[170] Al-Qaeda "continues to see Afghanistan as a safe haven for its leadership, based on its long-standing, strong ties with the Taliban," according to the United Nations, which noted that Zawahiri and the Taliban leadership "have repeatedly, in public statements, emphasized the importance of the alliance" between the two organizations.[171] Al-Qaeda has "has grown stronger operating under the Taliban umbrella across Afghanistan and is more active than in recent years," while the Taliban remains the "primary partner for all foreign terrorist groups operating in Afghanistan, with the exception of" ISIS.[172] These partner organizations include the Central Asian, Pakistani, and Uighur groups discussed in this chapter. They compose an essential part of the al-Qaeda-Taliban axis, an alliance that the longest war in America's history did not break.

The durability of that alliance and al-Qaeda's adaptiveness allowed al-Qaeda to endure the American-led onslaught of the past two decades. While the United States has demonstrated the ability to eliminate high-ranking al-Qaeda leaders, the jihadist group has demonstrated its ability to replace those lost commanders and ensure that future leaders become harder to kill. By building strong relationships with Pakistani and Central Asian militant groups, al-Qaeda effectively developed a farm league for new fighters. Al-Qaeda also began to expand its presence in the region by targeting secular-minded Muslims as part of an effort to win support from local Islamists. Al-Qaeda's adaptiveness also had a geographical dimension. When the United States toppled the Taliban-led government and fought al-Qaeda in Tora Bora, al-Qaeda fighters slipped across the Afghanistan–Pakistan border into the relative safety of Pakistan's FATA and Iran. When the United States began to target al-Qaeda fighters in those territories, al-Qaeda moved its fighters to Taliban-held territory in Afghanistan and other safe havens in Iran. These efforts ensured that the United States played a continuous game of "whack-a-mole," striking al-Qaeda in one region only to find the organization popping up elsewhere.

Al-Qaeda frequently worked to conceal its presence in Afghanistan. It did not publicize its massive training camps in Kandahar province. In recent years, the jihadist group played off its competitor ISIS's lust for the media spotlight. The Taliban, with al-Qaeda's help, gained ground while the United States has frequently undercounted the number of al-Qaeda fighters in Afghanistan. Al-Qaeda's adaptiveness has paid dividends, particularly as the Taliban won the war in Afghanistan. To this day, there is no evidence showing that the Taliban has broken with al-Qaeda. Meanwhile, al-Qaeda views the Taliban's defeat of the U.S.-backed government as a "historic victory" and a boon for the global jihadist movement.[173]

10

ISIS's External Operations

A Study in Innovation

On the evening of July 18, 2016, a teenage Afghan refugee named Riaz Khan stepped onto a train in Würzburg, Germany, and began hacking at passengers with an ax. German police shot and killed Khan after he fled the train and attacked a nearby dog-walker.[1] Five people were wounded in the rampage. ISIS quickly claimed credit through the Amaq News Agency, announcing that the terrorist had been the group's "soldier" and that he had "executed the operation in response to calls to target nations in the coalition fighting the Islamic State." The next day Amaq released a video of Khan brandishing a knife as he professed his loyalty to Abu Bakr al-Baghdadi and called on other Muslims to do the same.[2]

Somehow German interior minister Thomas de Maizière still bizarrely described the ax-wielding terrorist as a "lone wolf."[3] The reality was quite different. Khan was not an isolated operator but a shock troop in a larger wave of coordinated atrocities. Khan's attack was part of a series of small-scale attacks that ISIS's virtual plotters orchestrated. The caliphate had teams of jihadists who used social media and secure messaging applications to scout potential operatives, then remotely guide individuals or small cells around the world. The caliphate's virtual plotters have relied on freely available technologies, including Facebook, Twitter, Telegram, WhatsApp, Signal, Snapchat, RocketChat, and TamTam Messenger. The

encrypted chat technology in some of these applications has proven especially useful for ISIS's men, Khan's online handler included.

Less than two months after Khan's attack, the German press released
transcripts of his communications with an unnamed ISIS operative stationed far outside of German, presumably in Syria or Iraq. "What kind of
weapons do you intend to use to kill people?" the caliphate's man asked
Khan via encrypted messages. "My knife and ax are ready for use," Khan
assured him.

"Brother, would it not be better to do it with a car?" Khan's virtual handler asked. Upon being told that Khan did not know how to drive, the
handler suggested that the teenager learn how. "The damage would be
much greater," he assured Khan. Khan explained that "learning takes
time"—and indeed the time and expense involved is far greater in Germany
than it is in the United States. "I want to enter paradise tonight," Khan
explained.

As Khan inched closer to his attack, the handler assured him that "if
you're going to commit the attack, Allah willing, the Islamic State will claim
responsibility for it."

"Pray that I become a martyr," Khan wrote in response. "I am now waiting for the train."

Not long after, Khan followed up: "I am starting now." Khan's guide
responded: "Now you will attain paradise."[4]

As this exchange shows, ISIS directly guided the terrorist assault in
Würzburg, encouraging him through messaging apps until the attack
began. It was not a sophisticated operation that required extensive training. Many attacks that ISIS claimed from 2014 until today have been simple to execute. Still, a professional operative provided encouragement to
the amateur Khan until the moment he struck.

Khan wasn't the only terrorist to receive this kind of virtual assistance.
Counterterrorism officials across the globe found that ISIS frequently managed lone-attacker operations using messaging apps and other forms
of long-distance communication. Even without these attacks killing significant numbers, ISIS's virtual planners forced authorities to expend
valuable resources. Remote-controlled attacks, as European officials
labeled them, were just one of ISIS's diverse methods for threatening the
West. Some of ISIS's most feared operatives were also on the job: The
amniyat, a brutal security service within the caliphate, oversaw a wave of

plots around the world while also working to crush internal threats to Baghdadi's caliphate.

The Islamic State's *Amniyat* and International Plots

The *amniyat*'s name comes from the Arabic word for *security*. The *amniyat* operates in the shadows. The organization, which never advertised its presence or position in ISIS's hierarchy, was only detected through extensive investigative work and reporting. The group was in many ways modeled after the secret police forces (*mukhabarat*) that terrorized the citizens of Saddam's Iraq as well as many other Arab dictatorships. In Iraq and Syria, the caliphate's *amniyat* created a police state that spied widely and crushed dissent.

ISIS's *amniyat* did more than just keep the population in line. The group was actively involved in implementing the caliphate's expansion strategy, furthering the conquest of much of Syria throughout 2012 and 2013 by infiltrating towns and villages, and ensuring local tribal leaders' commitment to Baghdadi's project.[5] The *amniyat*'s mission even reached beyond the caliphate's borders: Some of ISIS's most ruthless operators worked to attack hostile states using any available means.

ISIS's *amniyat* is not a unique phenomenon in the jihadist world. Several al-Qaeda branches have their own version of the same body. Indeed, Shabaab's *amniyat* in Somalia has ruthlessly suppressed support for ISIS within its ranks. But what makes ISIS's *amniyat* noteworthy is its prolific role in overseeing terrorist attacks around the globe.[6] At the height of ISIS's territorial reach, the *amniyat* ensured internal security by conducting counterintelligence operations and rooting out emerging internal threats—yet, simultaneously, a secretive wing of this organization, commonly known as *amn al-kharji*, busied itself conducting external operations. Many of these strikes occurred far from the lands of the caliphate.

Prominent among the *amn al-kharji* officials was Abu Muhammad al-Adnani, a native Syrian who long served as ISIS's spokesperson. The U.S. government found that, in addition to being the caliphate's chief rhetorical firebrand, Adnani "served as principal architect of" the group's external operations until his death in an August 2016 airstrike.[7] A number of foreign fighters served under Adnani, jihadists who could draw on knowledge of their home countries when plotting operations everywhere from Western Europe to Southeast Asia. For instance, one senior figure was a Frenchman known as Abu Sulayman al-Faransi, reportedly a key planner of the group's November 2015 attacks in Paris.[8]

Amn al-kharji explored multiple avenues for conducting terrorist attacks abroad. The group dispatched operatives while also remotely controlling faraway volunteers. These activities dated from the very beginning of ISIS's break with al-Qaeda: European officials first detected the organization's threat to their countries months before Baghdadi was declared caliph. As we explain in chapter 1, on February 11, 2014, French authorities arrested Ibrahim Boudina, a French-Algerian ISIS operative, as he was plotting a terrorist attack. Boudina wasn't the only terrorist ISIS, and its *amniyat* deployed to the West. An exhaustive *New York Times* investigation of European court records and other evidence found that at least twenty-one ISIS operatives had been dispatched to Europe from early 2014 through 2015.[9] On May 24, 2014, a returnee from Syria named Mehdi Nemmouche opened fire at the Jewish Museum of Belgium in Brussels, killing four people. French counterterrorism officials had already deemed Nemmouche a security risk, reportedly placing him under surveillance after he returned from Syria in 2013. Nemmouche was in close contact with an even more notorious operative: Abdelhamid Abaaoud, a member of the ISIS's *amniyat*.[10]

Abaaoud's career bedeviled European counterterrorism officials. He was a known threat who nonetheless succeeded in developing networks in Belgium and France, webs of extremists who later launched two of ISIS's deadliest attacks on European soil. In January 2015 Belgian police raided a safe house in Verviers, targeting a cell Abaaoud had established. A number of suspects were killed, but Abaaoud was nowhere to be found. ISIS's propagandists taunted Belgian officials the following month in their magazine *Dabiq*, which carried an extensive interview with Abaaoud, whom it described as "a mujahid being pursued by Western Intelligence agencies for his jihad in Belgium." Abaaoud bragged in the interview that he and two accomplices had traveled to Europe "in order to terrorize the crusaders." He said Belgium was a target because it "is a member of the crusader coalition attacking the Muslims of Iraq and Shām." Abaaoud mocked Western intelligence services for allowing him to enter Belgium and set up a terrorist cell only to fail to capture him in the Verviers raid. "Allah blinded their vision and I was able to leave and come to Shām despite being chased after by so many intelligence agencies," he boasted. "All this proves that a Muslim should not fear the bloated image of the crusader intelligence. My name and picture were all over the news yet I was able to stay in their homeland, plan operations against them, and leave safely when doing so became necessary."[11]

Astonishingly, Abaaoud succeeded in traveling back into Europe months after this taunting interview in *Dabiq*. This security lapse had lethal consequences. On November 13, 2015, a team of ISIS terrorists dispatched from Iraq and Syria executed the group's largest-ever attack on European soil, killing 129 people and wounding at least 350 more in a series of assaults on crowded locations throughout Paris. Three suicide bombers detonated their explosives near the Stade de France, which was hosting a soccer match between France and Germany. Another team of militants raided the Bataclan theater, where they held hostages until police finally retook the facility. Still other groups of terrorists shot up bars and restaurants. Days after the atrocity, French authorities identified Abaaoud as a principal ringleader. Police soon found him in the Paris suburb of Saint-Denis, where he was killed.[12]

ISIS had long emphasized foreign terrorism, dating from before the caliphate's founding. As the caliphate gained ground across the Middle East in 2013–2014, some argued that the group posed little threat to the West and only cared about seizing territory. In early 2014 President Obama himself argued that ISIS was the "junior varsity" team of terrorism. Implicit in this statement was that idea that it was varsity-level terrorists like those in al-Qaeda's network who were either capable of or interested in launching major attacks around the globe. Obama dismissed the threat ISIS posed, saying the group was "engaged in various local power struggles and disputes, often sectarian," so it wasn't a "direct threat to us or something that we have to wade into."[13] Events in the Middle East ultimately changed the Obama administration's view. Eight months after these statements, the United States sent troops back to Iraq to stanch ISIS's expansion, even though the president had withdrawn all American military personnel from the country during his first term.

Even with the United States deploying thousands of troops to stop ISIS, senior U.S. officials still did not tend to discuss the caliphate as a significant terrorist threat to the West. Ben Rhodes, the top spokesman for

Obama's National Security Council, summarized the administration's conventional wisdom when discussing the beginning of the U.S.-led air campaign against Baghdadi's self-declared state in August 2014. Rhodes, like his boss, tried drew a sharp contrast between ISIS and al-Qaeda. "While both are terrorist forces, they have different ambitions," Rhodes claimed. Al-Qaeda's "principal ambition is to launch attacks against the west and U.S. homeland," he elaborated, while ISIS's "primary focus is consolidating territory in the Middle East region to establish their own Islamic State. . . . So they're different organizations with different objectives."[14]

Neither Rhodes's analysis of ISIS nor his explanation of al-Qaeda would hold up. The Obama administration's interpretation of the groups' differing ambitions and operations reflected a misunderstanding of ISIS. The attempt to use a militant group's ability to hold territory as proof of its lack of ambition to strike abroad didn't withstand logical scrutiny: It is no easy feat to form a guerrilla army capable of conquering territory, and it is not clear why anyone should consider such an adversary to be a lesser foe than a group focused solely on conducting attacks on Western civilians. Further, the idea that al-Qaeda was only interested in spectacular terrorism was always false. In formulating its far enemy strategy, al-Qaeda reasoned that large-scale attacks would weaken America to the point that an Islamic state could rise without foreign interference. Jihadist groups were capable of attempting to militarily engage near and far enemies simultaneously. ISIS took this dual-pronged approach to ever more violent extremes. The *amn al-kharji* maintained multiple channels for incubating strikes, including a team of virtual plotters whose role represents a genuine example of organizational learning and innovation.

The *Amn al-Kharji*'s Virtual Plotters

In the earliest months of its caliphate, ISIS called on prospective followers to perform *hijrah* and migrate to its lands. But the group's approach changed as the international response mounted. By September 2014, as a U.S.-led air campaign pounded ISIS positions in Iraq and Syria, the group's leaders suddenly warned caliphate enthusiasts to stay in their home countries to kill Western citizens. In a September 21, 2014, speech, Abu Muhammad al-Adnani called on international followers to murder Americans and Europeans, along with any other citizen of any country belonging to the anti-ISIS coalition.[15]

ISIS's *amn al-kharji* set up a system for remotely controlling recruits via social media and online messaging applications. Its virtual planners oversaw distinct geographic regions that corresponded with their linguistic abilities. For instance, English-speaking jihadists would look for anglophone recruits. Their involvement in the plots they helped instigate would vary from simple encouragement to providing step-by-step instructions for selecting targets and even building bombs. The threat posed by these faraway operatives became so significant that the United States and its allies waged a campaign specifically designed to kill ISIS's most prominent virtual planners.

THE SHORT HAPPY LIFE OF JUNAID HUSSAIN

One such remote plotter was the target of the first-ever targeted drone strike in the history of one of the world's most storied air forces. On August 21, 2015, Britain's Royal Air Force struck at Reyaad Khan, a British national who was recruiting would-be attackers in his home country. Khan, also known as Abu Dujana al-Hindi, had been operating from ISIS's de facto capital of Raqqa.[16] The Royal Air Force had previously used armed drones as part of larger military campaigns, but the twenty-one-year-old Khan was the first jihadist whom Britain had specifically hunted in this manner. Three days later, on August 24, 2015, Khan's comrade-in-arms, Junaid Hussain, was struck down in an American drone strike in Raqqa.[17] Khan and Hussain had been members of a secretive group within ISIS that the FBI dubbed "the Legion."[18] Its dozen or so members used online applications to bring new recruits into ISIS's fold and plot attacks across the West.

In a speech delivered before the British Parliament in September 2015, Prime Minister David Cameron explained why he saw the two jihadists as such a threat. Khan and Hussain "were British nationals based in Syria who were involved in actively recruiting [ISIS] sympathizers and seeking to orchestrate specific and barbaric attacks against the West, including directing a number of planned terrorist attacks right here in Britain," Cameron said.[19] Neither had concealed their allegiance to the caliphate: Khan had called on Muslims to join Baghdadi's cause in an ISIS video while Hussain repeatedly announced his allegiance online. Behind closed doors, the two were among the caliphate's most prolific virtual plotters.

Khan's career turn would have seemed unlikely in his early life. The Wales-born Khan was "a straight-A student who at one point [harbored] dreams of becoming Britain's first Asian prime minister," according to an April 2017 British parliamentary report on Khan and Hussain.[20] In a video recorded in 2010, Khan "spoke of his desire to rid the world of evil and the problems of growing up in a deprived inner-city area," adding that the British government "was wasting money on illegal wars."[21] He left for Syria in November 2013 and joined Baghdadi's project. From ISIS-held territory, he posted social media messages that boasted "about the people he had killed and his extremist plans," the committee found.[22] In June 2014 Khan appeared in an ISIS video. Within months, British officials were receiving regular updates about the threat he posed. "Through his persistent and prolific efforts to recruit, advise, and encourage operatives in the West to conduct attacks, Khan poses a significant, ongoing and imminent threat to the UK," read one MI5 analysis penned just weeks before his death.[23] Intelligence officials were especially concerned that he had proven effective at providing others the expertise needed to launch attacks inside Britain.

Junaid Hussain's life trajectory was somewhat more straightforward than that of his partner in terrorism. Hussain had been a well-known hacker in his native Britain. In 2011 he stole and published Tony Blair's personal contact information by accessing the email account of one of the former prime minister's staffers. The future ISIS operative was also a member of TeaMp0isoN (pronounced *team poison*), a hacking collective that had once intercepted calls between elite investigators in Scotland Yard and posted the communications online.[24] Hussain relocated to Syria in 2013 after a short stint in British prison. Hussain joined ISIS and reemerged as Abu Hussain al-Britani, putting his small-time hacking abilities to the caliphate's service. Khan and Hussain collaborated so closely in seeding remote-controlled attacks that British officials believed they both needed to be taken out at the same time: They had built their network to be resilient, so the loss of just one of them would not be enough to significantly disrupt the remote-controlled ISIS threat to Britain.[25]

Khan was a charismatic organizer even from afar. His "personal popularity and status online helped attract and influence potential operatives, and he invested significant effort persuading recruits," according to a February 2016 analysis that the committee cited. The pair grew alarmingly effective at convincing people they had never met to carry out acts of mass murder. The committee found that Khan and Hussain were linked to at least some "of the seven major plots thwarted in the UK in 2015."[26]

While Anwar al-Awlaki and AQAP had first advocated for and promoted individual jihadist attacks, with Khan and Hussain's help ISIS had taken remote-controlled terrorism to a deadly new level: The United Kingdom's intelligence and security agencies reported to Parliament that Khan "was prominent in attack planning on behalf of" the caliphate, "directly inciting individuals to conduct attacks," and using "social media to identify potential operatives and then provide them with encouragement and basic capability to enable an attack." Hussain and Khan "did this on an unprecedented scale" in terms of the range and pace of threats.[27] Hussain and Khan, however, were no more creative than was Awlaki. Rather, Awlaki's early experimentation paved the way for Hussain and Khan's success. In line with the violent non-state actor technology adoption curve, Hussain and Khan were able to build off Awlaki's successes and learn from his shortcomings. Awlaki's work spanned the early adoption and iteration phases of the curve while Hussain and Khan helped ISIS reach the breakthrough phase.

ISIS's recruiters could activate plots with alarmingly little advance planning that law enforcement might detect. "It is clear from the intelligence reports that the timescale between Khan contacting an operative, recruiting them and providing targets could be a short period of time," the committee's report reads.[28] The British government emphasized in a memo appended to the report that one of Khan's attacks "could have become a reality at any moment and without warning." Still, all of Khan's plots were "successfully disrupted."[29] The committee credited security agencies with uncovering and stopping Khan's plans, "avoiding what could have been a very significant loss of life."[30]

While MI5 was tracking ISIS's digital recruits in Britain, the FBI also devoted significant resources to counteracting Junaid Hussain. He was involved in a number of terrorist schemes, including at one point releasing personal contact information, including home addresses, of more than a thousand U.S. military personnel. Coming from an organization like ISIS, this kind of doxing was correctly interpreted as a threat. Hussain's method of acquiring the personal information of these servicemembers provides insight into the entrepreneurial model of twenty-first century terrorism. One FBI official described Hussain's process as a form of "crowdsourcing terrorism—using cyber intrusions to obtain information or resources that, when placed in the hands of terrorists, could prove deadly."[31] Although Hussain claimed the soldiers' data was accessed through hacking the victims' mobile devices, he likely used publicly available information for his first list. Later that year he acquired more data from another hacker named Ardit Ferizi. Operating under the handle @Th3Dir3ctorY on Twitter, Ferizi led a Kosovo-based hacking group known as Kosova Hacker's Security, which claimed to have compromised various businesses in Serbia, Israel, and elsewhere before Ferizi decided to assist ISIS.

In April 2015 Ferizi contacted Hussain on Twitter via one of his online aliases, @Muslim_Sniper_D.[32] The Kosovar hacker had quietly posted screenshots that appeared to show credit card numbers and other personal data for dozens of American, British, and French citizens. Ferizi suggested to Hussain that ISIS could use the confidential information that Ferizi had published. In June 2015 Ferizi hacked the Arizona-based server of a U.S. retailer, stealing the personally identifiable information of around 100,000 people.[33] Ferizi then narrowed this information down to a list of 1,351 U.S. servicemembers and other government employees. Ferizi gave the list to Hussain, who posted it to Twitter on behalf of ISIS's hacking division in August 2015.

In a tweet accompanying the stolen information, Hussain claimed that he and his comrades had infiltrated the Americans' "emails and computer systems," warning ISIS's enemies that the caliphate's cyber soldiers "were watching and recording your every move."[34] Hussain proclaimed that ISIS was in the Americans' "emails and social media accounts" and was now extracting their "confidential data." In reality, Ferizi had not broken into the email accounts or computers of more than a thousand people but instead had identified them using information the hacker had stolen from a single third party. Ferizi was captured in Malaysia two months after Hussain posted the list on Twitter, then extradited to the United States, where he admitted his role in this plot.[35]

Hussain had other collaborators throughout his career as a terrorist, including his wife, Sally Jones. Hussain married Jones shortly after she absconded for Syria in 2013. Jones was a curious figure, her radicalism attracting media attention in her native Britain. She had been a guitarist for a punk rock act in London before her conversion to Islam. After arriving in Syria, Jones threatened American and British service members over Twitter and other social media sites. According to some reports, Jones became a leading figure in the female wing of ISIS's secretive Anwar al-Awlaki battalion, which sought to launch attacks in the West.[36] The U.S. State Department designated Jones as a terrorist in September 2015, weeks after her husband's death in a drone strike. The designation noted that Jones had "used social media to recruit women to join" ISIS. Jones reportedly died in mid-2017.

Jones and Hussain had operated at the peak of ISIS's virtual campaign. The couple had been at their most dangerous in 2015, when the caliphate was frequently claiming responsibility for attacks in Western countries. American law enforcement confronted an "explosion" of threats that year, with counterterrorism investigations opened in each of America's fifty states.[37] According to George Washington University's Program on Extremism, two hundred people were "charged in the U.S. with offenses related to the Islamic State" between March 2014 and November 2019.[38] Some fifty-six individuals were arrested on ISIS-related charges in 2015 alone, the most in any single year.[39] The majority of these cases did not result in casualties, which is among other things a testament to U.S. law enforcement's vigilance. The FBI thwarted several of Hussain's plots.

Two of Hussain's remote contacts were arrested in the United States on May 21, 2015. One of them, Nader Elhuzayel, hoped to travel to the caliphate through Turkey. Elhuzayel intended to disguise his final destination and spend a scheduled layover in Istanbul meeting ISIS facilitators who could transport him to Syria. But the FBI arrested Elhuzayel and his co-conspirator Muhanad Badawi, who recorded a video of Elhuzayel swearing allegiance to Abu Bakr al-Baghdadi.

In May 2015 the FBI arrested another of Hussain's online recruits, Munir Abdulkader.[40] Hussain sent the West Chester, Ohio, man the address of an American soldier, advising Abdulkader to kidnap his target and behead him on camera. Abdulkader had initially communicated with Hussain through Twitter direct message, an unsecure platform. Hussain wasn't as careless on other occasions: He frequently used encrypted messaging applications. The Twitter slip-up allowed the FBI to track Abdulkader and eventually place a confidential human source near to him. Abdulkader discussed his murderous intentions in conversations with this FBI plant. After murdering the military employee, Abdulkader "planned to perpetrate a violent attack on a police station in the Southern District of Ohio using firearms and Molotov cocktails."[41] He was soon arrested and pled guilty to terrorism-related charges more than a year later.

ISIS supporters with links to Hussain continued to surface throughout the summer of 2015. On June 2 Usaamah Rahim was shot and killed as he approached a team of FBI agents who were surveilling him.[42] Authorities had detected Rahim's online communications with Hussain months earlier. After Rahim's death, Hussain tweeted that he had encouraged Rahim to carry a knife in case the "feds" tried to arrest him.[43] At first Hussain had instructed Rahim to kill Pamela Geller, a controversial right-wing activist who had organized the Muhammad art contest in Garland, Texas.[44] Rahim instead settled on a different plan and started plotting to kill law enforcement officials.[45] The Department of Justice later confirmed that Rahim had been communicating with other ISIS members abroad in addition to Hussain.[46] At the same time Rahim was hatching plots with Hussain, he also conspired with his nephew, David Daoud Wright, who had drawn up plans for a "Martyrdom Operations Cell." The document was meant to be a blueprint for secretive jihadist militias operating in the United States. After Rahim was killed, Wright scrambled to delete any electronic trail their plans had generated and erased his computer's contents. Wright was ultimately convicted of conspiring to provide material support to ISIS.[47]

On June 13, 2015, Munther Omar Saleh and a co-conspirator were arrested in Queens after they charged at a FBI agent with knives.[48] The FBI had learned that Saleh was conspiring with Hussain to carry out an attack in New York City. Hussain acted as an "attack facilitator," providing instructions for building a pressure-cooker bomb and discussing targets that Saleh and his accomplice, Fareed Mumuni, could strike.[49] Their operation was modeled after the 2013 Boston Marathon bombings, which AQAP had inspired. Saleh also sought and received permission from an ISIS fighter (presumably Hussain) for Mumuni to use the homemade bomb in a suicide attack on the FBI agents trailing them, who had prevented them from traveling abroad to join the caliphate.[50] As during many similar attempts at remote-controlled operations, a confidential source had penetrated the plot before an attack could be launched. Mumuni was arrested in Staten Island on June 17, 2015. He repeatedly stabbed an FBI agent with a kitchen knife in the course of the arrest. Fortunately, the agent was wearing body armor and survived with only minor injuries. Both Saleh and Mumuni plead guilty to terrorism charges in February 2017.[51]

While Hussain was remotely guiding Saleh and Mumuni and encouraging Rahim to target law enforcement in Boston, he had still another American plot in the works. Authorities arrested a nineteen-year-old North Carolina man, Justin Nojan Sullivan, in June 2015. Sullivan's father alerted authorities to his son's increasing radicalism in April 2015 after he destroyed items representing the Buddhist tradition and other religions that didn't comport with his puritanical beliefs. In the ensuing investigation, the FBI uncovered evidence that Sullivan had murdered his seventy-four-year-old neighbor in December 2014.[52] The FBI also discovered that Sullivan had been in touch with Hussain, who discerned the opportunity to harness Sullivan's rage on the caliphate's behalf. Hussain suggested that Sullivan carry out a mass shooting, perhaps at a bar or nightclub. Sullivan agreed. He intended to film the carnage and may have planned on murdering his parents as well. None of this came to fruition as Sullivan shared his agenda with an FBI informant. Sullivan was arrested at his family's home in June 2015 and soon pled guilty to terrorism-related charges, admitting that he had conspired with Hussain to "plan mass shooting attacks in North Carolina and Virginia" with the intent to kill "hundreds of innocent people."[53]

ABU ISSA AL-AMRIKI

Junaid Hussain kept investigators busy, but he wasn't the only one directing operatives who wanted to strike American targets. Another virtual plotter known as Abu Issa al-Amriki was also guiding young caliphate supporters in the United States. One of these would-be terrorists was Emanuel Lutchman of Rochester, New York. Lutchman had amassed a collection of jihadist propaganda and, like many other lone attackers, often watched videos starring Anwar al-Awlaki.[54] Lutchman originally wanted to travel to Syria or Libya to join ISIS. When he told Amriki this plan, the ISIS operative dissuaded him, instead encouraging Lutchman to carry out an attack in the United States on New Year's Eve in 2015. "New years [sic] is here soon," Amriki told Lutchman in one message. "Do operations and kill some kuffar." On December 27, 2015, Amriki and Lutchman discussed possible targets, including bars and nightclubs. On December 30, the day before the planned attack, Lutchman recorded a video in which he swore allegiance to Abu Bakr al-Baghdadi. Addressing his fellow Americans from behind a mask, Lutchman said "the blood that you spill of the Muslim overseas we gonna spill the blood of the kuffar." Lutchman had unknowingly divulged his contacts with Amriki, as well as his intentions, to individuals cooperating with the FBI. He was arrested the same day he recorded his video and later pled guilty to plotting the New Year's Eve attack.[55]

Like Hussain, Amriki was trying to seed multiple attacks at the same time. The virtual planner had also made contact with Mohamed Bailor Jalloh, a former Army National Guardsman.[56] Amriki encouraged Jalloh to carry out an attack, not knowing the FBI was already onto the pair's scheming. Earlier, Jalloh had decided not to reenlist in the National Guard after listening to Awlaki's lectures. Jalloh eventually connected with ISIS both in person and online, meeting ISIS members in Nigeria during a six-month jaunt to Africa and corresponding with Amriki online. One of Jalloh's family members in Sierra Leone helped funnel $700 to Amriki, who was based in the caliphate.[57] After Jalloh returned to America in early 2016, Amriki introduced him to a potential collaborator and fellow jihadist—who, unfortunately for their plans, ended up being a confidential source for the FBI. Under Amriki's guidance, Jalloh resolved to carry out a mass shooting. He bought a firearm in Virginia, later telling investigators that the Awlaki-inspired massacre at Fort Hood was his model. Authorities made sure the weapon Jalloh purchased was disabled before he left the gun shop.[58] In October 2016 Jalloh pled guilty to charges related to the plot.

Other Amriki disciples continued to lurk across the United States. On November 7, 2016, Southern Ohio Joint Terrorism Task Force agents arrested Aaron Travis Daniels at the Columbus airport. Daniels appeared to be en route to Trinidad, although this was allegedly a decoy destination: Daniels's real plan, it seems, was to travel to Libya. According to the Department of Justice, Daniels had been in contact with Abu Issa al-Amriki, who acted as a "recruiter and external attack planner."[59] At one point Daniels said it was Amriki who suggested he go to Libya "to support jihad." The recruit also allegedly "wired money to an intermediary" that was intended to reach Amriki and demonstrate Daniels's value to the caliphate.[60] While the U.S. Attorney's Office did not allege that Daniels planned to commit an attack in Ohio or elsewhere in the United States, his case nonetheless shows how ISIS's virtual plotters can double as travel facilitators.

Amriki's cadre of operatives was able to plot terror on opposite sides of the globe. In June 2016 Indian authorities arrested eight members of a cell in Hyderabad whose ringleader, Mohammed Ibrahim Yazdani, colluded with Amriki online. Yazdani initially contacted Amriki via the ISIS planner's encrypted Telegram channel.[61] Amriki walked Yazdani through the process of swearing allegiance to Baghdadi.[62] Although Yazdani wanted to move his family to caliphate territory, Amriki redirected his energies to a plot in Hyderabad, one of India's leading technology hubs. Amriki and other virtual plotters helped Yazdani vet recruits for his cell and acquire small arms and ingredients for explosives. ISIS's online team even arranged to have ammunition waiting at a dead drop. As with so many of their counterparts in America, Yazdani and his comrades were arrested before they could act.

An American airstrike killed Amriki and his wife, an Australian national, in April 2016 near al-Bab, Syria, a hub for foreign fighters in the northern province of Aleppo.[63] Abu Muhammad al-Adnani, Amriki's boss and head of *amn al-kharji*, was killed in a nearby drone strike several months later. Amriki's remotely guided plots reached into the United States, Canada, and the United Kingdom, the U.S. military said when announcing his death, without mentioning the planned attacks in Hyderabad.[64] Little else is publicly known about the Sudanese national or why he was known as al-Amriki "the American."

RACHID KASSIM

One of the most successful virtual plotters was a failed rapper and former social worker who hailed from France.[65] In July 2016 Rachid Kassim appeared in a propaganda video released by ISIS's Nineveh province in Iraq in which he praised that year's Bastille Day (July 14) truck attack in Nice, France, that killed more than eighty people. It is unclear whether Kassim had any direct ties to the perpetrator, Mohamed Lahouaiej-Bouhlel. ISIS nonetheless claimed the terrorist was a soldier of the caliphate, and with good reason.

France's investigation would later find that Lahouaiej-Bouhlel consumed ISIS propaganda and supported ISIS. Authorities indicated to reporters that, before the Nice attack, Lahouaiej-Bouhlel searched the internet for information on the notorious Orlando nightclub attack carried out by Omar

Mateen, who pledged allegiance to ISIS at the scene of his crimes, and on an attack ISIS's Kassim had previously directed in Magnanville, France, which claimed the life of a police commander and his partner.[66] Data that authorities recovered from Lahouaiej-Bouhlel's computer included "pictures of militants draped in Islamic State flags."[67] The French prosecutor responsible for terrorism cases, François Molin, told the press that one witness recalled Lahouaiej-Bouhlel saying that "he didn't understand why ISIS couldn't have its own territory."[68] Molin also noted that, seven or eight months before he carried out the Nice attack, Lahouaiej-Bouhlel showed an ISIS video of a hostage execution to an acquaintance, who in turn spoke to authorities after the Nice attack.[69] French officials stated repeatedly that ISIS was responsible for the attack, including both French defense minister Jean-Yves le Drian and French president François Hollande.[70] And although it is not conclusive, some evidence suggests that a virtual plotter—perhaps Kassim—may have assisted Lahouaiej-Bouhlel in carrying out the Nice attack. For example, just after the attack Lahouaiej-Bouhlel's uncle said that, according to his relatives in Nice, "his nephew was indoctrinated about two weeks ago by an Algerian member of the Islamic State group in Nice."[71] (Rachid Kassim is French-Algerian and spent a significant amount of time in Oran, Algeria.[72]) Regardless of whether he was directly involved, in the video message he released after the Nice attack, Kassim threatened more attacks in France, then beheaded a captive on camera.

Kassim was a prolific propagandist who urged and organized numerous attacks against his former home country. On July 26, 2016, two young men, Adel Kermiche and Abdel Malik Nabil Petitjean, launched an assault on morning mass at a church in Saint-Étienne-du-Rouvray. The two took hostages and killed an elderly priest before police gunned them down. Amaq News Agency released a video the following day showing the pair swearing allegiance to Baghdadi and identifying them by their noms du guerre, Abu Jalil al-Hanafi and Abu Omar. Afterward French authorities learned that the two had corresponded with Kassim via Telegram.[73] In their conversations Kassim directly incited the pair to carry out their attack. Moreover, Kassim took over Kermiche's Telegram account after the attack, posting audio messages praising the pair's deed and threatening new atrocities in France. Kassim has also been tied to other attackers, both successful and thwarted, including a group of women charged with planning to attack Paris's Notre Dame Cathedral in September 2016 and a team of three fifteen-year-old boys who were allegedly plotting attacks in France.[74]

The caliphate's virtual planners were careful in making sure foreign attacks were clearly branded as ISIS operations. Riaz Khan, the Würzburg train attacker, pledged allegiance to Baghdadi in a video that Amaq released in July 2016. A series of other stylized and branded loyalty declaration videos soon followed. In the months after Khan's video, terrorists in Ansbach and Berlin, Germany; Normandy (the aforementioned pair, Kermiche and Petitjean) and Paris, France; Surgut and Grozny, Russia; Tajikistan; Chechnya; and Sri Lanka all recorded similar allegiance ceremonies prior to their attacks that ISIS then released and distributed over social media.[75] ISIS's virtual plotters had helped orchestrate some of their plots. For example, Mohammad Daleel, a veteran jihadist who had fought in Syria, blew himself up outside of a music festival in Ansbach, Germany, on July 24, 2016. Shortly afterward Amaq released a video from Daleel in which he swore allegiance to Baghdadi. German authorities subsequently learned Daleel had been communicating with an unidentified virtual plotter right up until the moment of the bombing.[76]

The United States targeted Kassim in an airstrike launched near Mosul in February 2017. The ex-rapper likely died in the explosion, although his death wasn't immediately confirmed. Kassim was suspected of guiding more than half of the seventeen plots foiled in France in 2016, according to Jean-Charles Brisard. Kassim's track record makes him one of the most prolific virtual plotters in ISIS's history.[77]

ISIS's Remote-Controlled Plots in Southeast Asia

ISIS's virtual plotter model could be replicated on opposite ends of the earth. ISIS operatives remotely guided plots in Southeast Asia, again using emigrant jihadists to guide attacks in their former home countries. One such operative was an Indonesian named Bahrun Naim, who left for the caliphate's stronghold in northern Syria in late 2014 or early 2015.[78] Naim was a computer guru who once worked at an internet café but spent time in prison after being convicted on weapons charges in 2010.[79] A former member of Hizb ut-Tahrir, a *dawa*-focused organization that seeks to resurrect the caliphate but abstains from overt acts of violence, Naim developed a number of suspicious relationships with extremists. A spokesperson for Hizb ut-Tahrir claimed Naim was expelled from the group when he was discovered carrying a gun.[80] Still, Naim was mainly a minor irritant for local authorities until he reached Syria.

A little over two years after he left for the caliphate, Indonesian authorities and allied governments in Southeast Asia were busy hunting Naim's recruits, scrambling to stop them from killing in ISIS's name. Naim became one of ISIS's most prolific planners of remote-controlled attacks even though most of his operations were thwarted. Naim provided aspiring terrorists in his home country with bomb-making and target selection advice over Telegram and other apps, and partly financed their plans using PayPal and Bitcoin.[81]

Naim assembled teams of jihadists throughout Indonesia using his deep rolodex of extremists, some of whom he knew from interactions in the offline world before his departure for Syria. He augmented these contacts through his prolific use of messaging platforms. There is no doubt encrypted messaging made Naim's job easier, but his in-person ties to a web of Indonesian jihadists bolstered his capabilities as a virtual plotter. Naim's most successful operation came on January 14, 2016, when a group of terrorists executed simultaneous suicide bombings and shootings in a busy shopping area in Jakarta, killing four people and wounding twenty-three.[82] The death toll would have been higher had the assault team been better trained. While Naim had a digital hand in the operation's planning, other militant figures in Indonesia were instrumental in making the attack a reality.

The terrorists had ties to an extremist cleric named Oman Rochman (also known as Aman Abdurrahman), a longtime associate of Naim.[83] Rochman has been imprisoned in Indonesia since 2010 yet still managed to direct ISIS's operations in the country from behind bars for months after Baghdadi's 2014 caliphate declaration.[84] Rochman had been convicted on terrorism-related charges stemming from his support for a camp run by Jemaah Islamiyah, an al-Qaeda-affiliated group. But as Baghdadi's cause accumulated victories in the summer of 2014, splitting the Indonesian jihadist scene, Rochman switched his allegiance to the caliphate.

In January 2017 the U.S. Treasury Department designated Rochman a terrorist, describing him as the "de facto leader" of Indonesia-based ISIS supporters. Rochman used his religious credentials to win supporters for ISIS, requiring them "to obtain a recommendation from him before departing for Syria" and personally blessing their travels. Rochman translated ISIS's propaganda and, according to Treasury, the cleric "issued a fatwa (decree) from prison in Jan. 2016 encouraging Indonesian militants to join" ISIS, in addition to authorizing the Jakarta attack from behind bars.[85]

While Naim directed the Jakarta plot from abroad and Rochman provided a sheen of ideological justification, the muscle for the operation came from a group known as Jamaah Ansharut Daulah (JAD). JAD was created in 2015 as an umbrella organization for "almost two dozen Indonesian extremist groups that pledged allegiance to" Baghdadi, according to the State Department.[86] Rochman's hand guided the process from prison.

JAD provided Naim with personnel ready to carry out his bidding from afar. Naim funded the JAD men responsible for the assault on Jakarta and transferred further sums of cash to help realize his plans for even larger attacks. According to a Reuters investigation, there were at least fifteen foiled attacks and more than 150 terrorism-related arrests in Indonesia in 2016.[87] The most significant conspiracies could be connected to Naim. In August 2016 Indonesian police raided one of Naim's cells on Batam island. His operatives reportedly planned on firing rockets at Singapore's Marina Bay, roughly ten miles across the water. Marina Bay is an affluent area with high-end shopping, a busy casino, and a massive Ferris wheel. The target was apparently Naim's idea. Members of the Batam cell "were in direct contact with Bahrun Naim in Syria" and he had specifically ordered their targets of attack, National Police Chief Tito Karnavian told reporters at a press conference.[88] Naim's machinations kept counterterrorism officials busy even after the Batam crew's capture. His expertise in crafting sophisticated explosives was of particular concern, and he transferred his know-how to followers inside Indonesia and possibly beyond.

While it is not entirely clear currently, these knowledge transfers may turn out to have been something of a breakthrough for the jihadists. Prior to Naim, bomb-makers successfully transferred their knowledge in person, but online efforts to do so were inconsistent, albeit with some success stories, such as the role of *Inspire* in helping Tamerlan and Dzhokhar Tsarnaev execute the Boston Marathon bombings. The reason for this inconsistency is that the online environment allowed for transfers of explicit knowledge, or knowledge easily communicated in writing, but in-person meetings facilitated the transfer of *tacit knowledge*, information difficult to express in written or verbal form. As a result, many would-be attackers who relied on online bomb-making instructions made small technical errors or backed away from their plots, lacking confidence. Naim's use of newer technologies like secure video chat and widespread encryption may have allowed him to confront the tacit knowledge barrier. While it is not clear if this will represent the beginnings of a widespread jihadist break-through, it is clear that Naim's ability to transfer his knowledge to other terrorists had serious consequences for Indonesia.

In November 2016 Indonesian authorities discovered a cell plotting an ambitious attack scheduled for the holiday season that would have included an assault on the country's parliament. According to the *Straits Times*, the ISIS operatives involved had obtained "military-grade explosive material" in large enough quantities to cause "twice the damage done in the 2002 Bali bombings," which had killed more than two hundred people.[89] The next month Detachment 88, Indonesia's elite counterterrorism force, detected a jihadist team plotting to bomb Jakarta's presidential palace. Naim's fin-gerprints were all over the plot, which had produced a completed explo-sive device. "This is a new (terrorist) cell and they had learned to make bombs from Bahrun Naim using the Telegram messaging (smartphone) application," Colonel Awi, an Indonesian official, explained.[90] Local reports drew attention to the ordnance involved in the thwarted attack, noting that the recovered bomb was "more powerful than military-grade TNT."[91]

The plotters reportedly planned to have a woman named Dian Yulia Novi carry the bomb into the palace. Novi's new husband, Nur Solihin, was in on the plot. Naim had recruited Solihin into ISIS and told him to marry a woman capable of carrying out an attack. Solihin was already married to another woman but took Novi as a second wife in accordance with Naim's directions.[92] Novi subsequently confessed that Naim had ordered her to strike a popular changing of the guard ceremony at the palace.[93] "I had been communicating with him for three days, yes, via Telegram," Novi admitted. "He told me which target to bomb, the Presidential Palace Mili-tary Guards."[94]

Bahrun Naim reportedly died in a U.S. drone strike in Syria in mid-2018. Other Indonesian jihadists active on Telegram have carried on his work. The most notable surviving virtual plotter from Indonesia as of this writing is a former Naim confidant and student of Oman Rochman's named Bachrumsyah Mennor Usman. Naim had been Usman's co-leader in Katibah Nusantara, an ISIS unit based in Syria that recruits fighters from Indonesia, Malaysia, and elsewhere in Southeast Asia. In 2014 Usman starred in an eight-and-a-half-minute video titled "Join the Ranks" in which he called on the "brothers in Indonesia" to pledge allegiance to Baghdadi.[95] ISIS showcased Indonesian and Malaysian children receiving weapons training in another video starring Usman that was released in early 2015.

The U.S. Treasury Department describes Usman's web of extremist contacts as an "underground movement" that was exposed only after "Join the Ranks" became a must-watch jihadist video. In addition to drawing recruits to Syria, Usman followed in Naim's footsteps by orchestrating and financing plots in his former home country, sending as much as $105,000 to a unit known as the "Bekasi cell" that plotted against targets in West Java. He "ordered an associate to plan attacks similar" to the Jakarta operation, and also "transferred funds" to the Philippines.[96] Although Usman's digital activities are not as well documented in open-source literature as are Naim's, he likely followed established jihadist best practices by using encrypted messaging apps and similar tools. Usman was reportedly killed in an American bombing in 2018. Supporters eulogized him on Telegram, but the Pentagon still has not confirmed his death.[97]

A Malaysian jihadist named Muhammad Wanndy bin Mohamed Jedi, better known as "Wanndy," forced authorities in his own home country to confront a similar wave of threats. Like his Indonesian counterparts, the caliphate-based Wanndy use Telegram's encrypted chat technology to direct attacks.[98] On June 28, 2016, two jihadists threw a hand grenade at the Movida nightclub near downtown Kuala Lumpur, injuring eight people who were watching a soccer match. Wanndy claimed responsibility on ISIS's behalf, marking perhaps the first successful operation by Baghdadi's network inside Malaysia.[99] But the attack wasn't Wanndy's first attempt at guiding a plot from afar. Three months earlier, in March 2016, Malaysian authorities arrested fifteen accused would-be terrorists whom Wanndy allegedly ordered to conduct attacks.[100] The virtual plotter had threatened top government officials, including Malaysia's prime minister. Wanndy eventually met the same fate as Naim and numerous other ISIS virtual plotters: He was reportedly killed in an airstrike in Raqqa in April 2017.

A Virtually Planned Attack on an Airliner

Many plots discussed in this chapter were relatively simple, involving knives, automobiles, or other ubiquitous means of attack. But remote-controlled plots can reach worrying levels of complexity, with planners imparting bomb-making expertise and other technical know-how to aspiring terrorists. In 2017 off-line personal ties and ambitious planning converged in what is likely the most significant remote-controlled plot to date.

That year Australian authorities learned that ISIS was conspiring to bring down an Etihad passenger plane flying from Sydney to Abu Dhabi.[101] The source of the tip was a foreign counterterrorism service, with Israel's elite military signals intelligence group Unit 8200 reportedly providing crucial assistance.[102] The attack was organized around four brothers, although one of them was an unwitting participant.

The plan was set in motion in April 2017 when a Syria-based ISIS member named Tarek Khayat messaged his brother Khaled in Australia.[103] Tarek, who had been fighting in the Middle East for several years, suddenly wanted his brother's help on a new project. Tarek put Khaled in touch with a caliphate-based virtual plotter who walked him through the steps for constructing an improvised explosive device that could be concealed in a meat grinder. The individual with whom Khaled spoke was later identified as Basil Hassan, an ISIS explosives expert and a leading figure in the group's drone program.[104] Hassan was "an external operations plotter . . . accused of shooting Lars Hedegaard, a 70-year old Danish author and journalist" in 2013, according to a U.S. State Department report.[105] Hedegaard, who gained notoriety as an especially strident critic of the Islamic faith, survived the shooting at his home in Copenhagen. Hassan fled to Turkey after the attempted murder, where he was apprehended in 2014 before being released, allegedly as part of a prisoner exchange agreement between Ankara and ISIS.[106] Prior to working with Khaled, Hassan had worked with ISIS supporters in "Turkey and the Maldives to ship packages containing hidden explosives to countries across the world, including Qatar, Germany, the United Kingdom, and the United States, as an experiment to test their screening systems."[107]

Khaled did as Hassan instructed with the help of another of his brothers, Mahmoud. The two built a bomb that appears to have contained pentaerythritol tetranitrate, one of the two highly explosive substances used in AQAP's Christmas Day 2009 plot. Khaled and Mahmoud did not have to procure most of the bomb components themselves, as an experienced professional terrorist (reportedly Hassan or one of his associates) mailed them the necessary parts in a package originating in Turkey.[108] Khaled and Mahmoud only had to add batteries, wiring, and a timer to the explosive. To help Khaled and Mahmoud with that task, Basil Hassan sent Khaled an audio message through Telegram with instructions on how to wire a bomb, and Khaled responded with photos of the explosive to receive feedback.[109] Hassan also reviewed Khaled's calculations for setting the bomb's timer.

On July 15, 2017, Khaled set out with the fourth of the Khayat brothers, Amer, for Sydney Airport.[110] Unbeknownst to Amer, who was traveling that day, Khaled was planning to kill him in service of the caliphate. Khaled had placed the explosives-packed meat grinder in Amer's checked luggage, explaining that he wanted Amer to bring "gifts for their relatives."[111] Fortunately, the bag turned out to be too heavy for the airline's weight limits and was disallowed. Fearing that Amer's interaction with airline personnel would lead to increased scrutiny of his luggage, Khaled aborted the operation and left the airport with the bomb. Amer boarded the flight anyway, and Khaled and Mahmoud turned their focus to their second plot, which had been in the works since May.[112] This time Hassan and his comrades had an even more audacious idea in mind: They wanted the Khayat brothers to build a chemical weapon.

Australian authorities disbanded the brothers' operation as they tried to build this second device. Australian Federal Police deputy commissioner Mike Phelan explained that while the first improvised explosive device was fully constructed and operational, the second weapon was far from finished and only part of a "hypothetical" plan at the time of the arrests. This second device was "an improvised chemical dispersion device . . . designed to release the highly toxic hydrogen sulfide," Phelan explained, adding that the brothers were "a long way from having a functioning . . . chemical dispersion device." Phelan emphasized that ISIS's involvement in the plot went beyond mere inspiration: "We have been saying for a long time that it is not only the capability of lone actors that we have to worry about, but we also have to worry about sophisticated plots."[113]

In certain cases ISIS has seized on the actions of individual Australian attackers who had no real operational ties to anyone in the caliphate despite their loyalty to Baghdadi. Terrorists like Man Haron Monis, who set off a hostage crisis at a Sydney café in December 2014 in which two people were killed, and Yacqub Khayre, who murdered one person and held another hostage in an apartment building outside Melbourne in June 2017, may have made online contact with ISIS's men, but their attacks required little technical skill. But their actions demonstrate the wide spectrum of complexity in remote-controlled attacks.

Details uncovered during Australia's investigation into the aviation plot provide important insights into ISIS's organizational learning. ISIS was adjusting to, and in some ways overcoming, three key challenges. First, virtual plotters previously provided would-be attackers with bomb-making instructions online. That approach had several downsides. Assailants had to acquire their own materials, creating additional opportunities for authorities to intervene, and they often made small errors in bomb production due to the aforementioned difficulties of transferring tacit knowledge online. Teaching someone to create a bomb from scratch also extended the period in which the plot remained in the planning/preparation phase, thus increasing authorities' opportunities to intervene. Shipping the bomb parts allowed the plotters to sidestep these problems. Second, assailants sometimes ended up getting caught or backing away from plots for psychological reasons. By using an unwitting third party, the Sydney plotters prevented those issues from derailing the plot. Third, in the past, those guided by virtual plotters had carried out attacks themselves, resulting in the operatives' arrest or death. Here neither of the main conspirators planned on carrying out the airline attack. They wanted to sacrifice one of their relatives. This approach would have allowed ISIS to retain two loyal operatives who could continue to plot.

Terror in the Age of Encryption

Al-Qaeda and Anwar al-Awlaki were the first to popularize the concept of lone jihad in the years after the 9/11 attacks, seeking to spur individuals with no operational ties to militant organizations to lash out. ISIS decided to remotely guide men and women around the globe who wanted to act in its name. There was precedent for this approach: Awlaki himself had used encrypted messaging applications to communicate with some of his recruits, including men in the United Kingdom who wanted to strike aviation-related targets. Still, as British intelligence discovered while investigating Reyaad Khan and Junaid Hussain, ISIS's virtual plotters amplified this threat. They established a system for methodically identifying and encouraging willing helpers via social media, sometimes providing them with the tactical expertise needed to move forward with their designs. The result was a steady onslaught of threats.

From the terrorists' perspective, one downside of the virtual plotter model is that it relies on amateurs to do the killing. Would-be attackers have sometimes been sloppy in their use of social media, gifting authorities with investigative leads. Further, encrypted communications haven't always proven impenetrable, and the FBI has used informants to infiltrate the jihadists' ranks.

The virtual plotter model has continued to evolve as ISIS has engaged in organizational learning. The planned 2017 attack on an Etihad airliner represented a significant leap forward. The virtual plotter responsible for the plot, Basil Hassan, introduced new operational practices, including testing the level of scrutiny of several countries' postal services.[114] Although the plot was foiled, Hassan might have had a hand in another, more successful strike on an aircraft. Khaled Khayat reportedly told Australian officials that Hassan helped plan the October 31, 2015, downing of Metrojet Flight 9268 in the Sinai, in which all 224 passengers and crew members died.[115] ISIS claimed to have downed Flight 9268 with a simple bomb hidden in a soda can that was planted by an operative. This is conceptually similar to the planned attack in Sydney, which also relied on explosives concealed in an everyday item.

In this context, jihadists' organizational learning has been primarily reactive. Based on new security measures and the performance of past plots, they have identified weaknesses in the virtual plotter model and tried new techniques, such as shipping bomb parts or using unwitting third parties. Technological developments, like the widespread diffusion of encrypted messaging, have often facilitated that process. Jihadists' approach to honing the virtual plotter model suggests that they will continue to try to use emerging technologies as they become more accessible. The story of virtual plotters is not over yet, and the next phase likely hinges on how new technologies intersect with the virtual plotters' mission.

11

The Past and Future of Jihadist Organizational Learning

As anti-ISIS forces advanced through Mosul, they found a particularly unusual weapons cache that included "retrofitted hobby drones with explosives" and homemade drones produced with "metal pipes, wooden propellers, and repurposed small engines."[1] The soldiers also found simplistic robotic bombs. ISIS's new drone unit, called the Unmanned Aircraft of the Mujahedin, likely operated this workshop.[2] While the weapons were not particularly sophisticated, they demonstrated ISIS's willingness to experiment with new technologies. It appeared that ISIS's engineers were trying to repurpose whatever engines they could get their hands on. For example, several of the weapons had motorcycle engines.[3]

Discoveries like this should correct a popular misconception about jihadists. Jihadist groups do not cultivate the image of being particularly adaptive organizations. They embrace an austere and inflexible ideology. They are notoriously hostile to perceived theological innovation, or *bida*, and insist on practicing Islam as the first three generations of Muslims did fourteen centuries ago. This ideological and theological intransigence belies a strategic and tactical dynamism. This book has shown that these organizations change their strategies and tactics in response to environmental pressures, new opportunities, intragroup disputes, and other factors. It has also shown that jihadists' calls for a return to the way of the *salaf,* or the first three generations of Muslims, have not stopped them from adopting twenty-first century technologies. In the past, many observers have failed to fully appreciate these groups' dynamism and capacity for organizational learning, thus allowing misconceptions to fester, including regarding the Arab Spring, the intra-jihadist competition between ISIS and al-Qaeda, and lone-wolf terrorism. The human and financial consequences of such interpretative errors demand a change in how we think about jihadist organizations.

This chapter has three purposes. First, based on the material in the previous chapters, which provide a sweeping look at these groups' operations and thinking, this chapter charts the evolution of jihadist groups' strategies and tactics. Second, it assesses how their strategies and tactics, particularly their use of technology, may continue to evolve. Third, it outlines a path for analysts and policymakers to better anticipate and respond to jihadist groups' continuing evolution.

Strategic Evolution

Many analysts still draw an unfortunate distinction between al-Qaeda as an organization with a far-enemy strategy and ISIS as an organization that wants to engage in state-building. This book demonstrates (particularly in chapters 3, 6, 7, and 8) why that distinction fails to reflect the diverse ambitions and strategies of these organizations. Although al-Qaeda and ISIS possess sharply differing outlooks, they share the capacity for strategic evolution.

AL-QAEDA'S STRATEGIC EVOLUTION

Al-Qaeda's strategic orientation from its inception through today largely stems from its analysis of external political and military factors. Al-Qaeda initially adopted a strategy focused on the far enemy, specifically the United States, for three principal reasons. First, it saw how regional jihads like those in Algeria, Egypt, and Syria had failed. Second, founding members of the organization played a role in a Muslim insurgency that expelled Soviet forces from Afghanistan, paving the way for the Taliban's eventual takeover of the country. Third, the group saw the United States withdraw troops from Lebanon after the bombing of the U.S. Embassy in Beirut, and from Somalia soon after the ill-fated mission memorialized in *Black Hawk Down* (and in which al-Qaeda may have had a hand).

Al-Qaeda's leadership concluded that Middle Eastern regimes remained resilient due to their Western support. But they believed that if they attacked the United States directly, America might withdraw from the Middle East, just as it withdrew from Somalia and Lebanon. If al-Qaeda could expel the United States from the region, al-Qaeda surmised that it could defeat local regimes and install governments that would govern according to its hardline interpretation of sharia. Conversely, if America intensified its regional presence, the group could use it as a recruiting tool.

Although al-Qaeda did use the intensified American presence following the 9/11 attacks to garner new recruits, its notion that the United States might withdraw following an attack in the United States had a crucial flaw. It conflated the American response to an attack on its personnel far from the American homeland, such as in Lebanon or Somalia, with its response to a devastating attack on American territory. Contrary to bin Laden's expectations, the United States aggressively intervened in Afghanistan and then Iraq. Although al-Qaeda survived American military operations in both countries, al-Qaeda and its allies suffered substantial losses.

Several developments, especially the opportunities presented by the Arab Spring revolutions, convinced al-Qaeda to adopt a different strategy. While the group did not abandon its aspirations to launch attacks in the West, it also recognized the advantages to keeping a lower profile. The group sought to disguise its relationship with affiliates like the al-Nusra Front in Syria, al-Shabaab in Somalia, and Ansar al-Sharia groups in several Middle Eastern states. In postrevolution states that remained stable, like Tunisia and Egypt, al-Qaeda sought to capitalize on newly permissive environments for spreading its message through nonviolent means.

These adaptations were not haphazard. Al-Qaeda's leadership tried to learn from the past and understand its enemy. For example, Navy SEALs recovered translated sections of Bob Woodward's book *Obama's Wars* from bin Laden's Abbottabad compound, indicating that al-Qaeda's founder was actively trying to understand and counter Obama's approach in Iraq and Afghanistan. That translated copy speaks to al-Qaeda's willingness to learn.

ISIS'S STRATEGIC EVOLUTION

ISIS often eschewed al-Qaeda's more pragmatic approach but still demonstrated a similar capacity for learning. Engaging in direct competition with al-Qaeda for domination over the jihadist movement, ISIS sought to exploit perceived weaknesses, complexities, and nuances in al-Qaeda's efforts. Two examples are ISIS's decision to quickly declare a caliphate and to target Shia communities.

Jihadists have long regarded a caliphate as their goal. Al-Qaeda delayed announcing the formation of a caliphate, and even emirates, because its leaders feared the West would concentrate its power on crushing any jihadist state. Many jihadists, however, did not share this capacity for patience. As ISIS separated from al-Qaeda, it adopted a different approach to the caliphate. While ideology influenced ISIS's decision to declare its reestablishment of the caliphate, this decision also made some strategic sense. The declaration allowed ISIS to distinguish itself as a functioning government rather than a mere band of militants. It also appealed to jihadists frustrated with al-Qaeda's hesitance to stake out more of an overt claim to territory and momentum. The caliphate declaration helped ISIS recruit thousands of foreigners to join its ranks and allowed it to convince jihadist groups around the globe, including some with ties to al-Qaeda, to pledge allegiance to it. Those recruits and *wilayat* bolstered ISIS's manpower. Although bin Laden's concerns that the international community would unite to crush a territorial caliphate seem to have been vindicated, ISIS's divergence from al-Qaeda on this point allowed it to initially outcompete al-Qaeda in Iraq and Syria and helped it grow into an enduring militant group of global reach. ISIS thus successfully engaged in organizational learning designed to help it advance its standing in the intra-jihadist coopetition.

We can see the same dynamic with ISIS's approach to targeting Shia Muslims. Although the Taliban massacred Shia Hazaras in Afghanistan and Sunni jihadists largely loathe the Shia, al-Qaeda adopted a relatively pragmatic approach to Shia groups and was able to forge a relationship with Iran that ran both hot and cold. Despite periods of conflict with Iran, al-Qaeda has received money, arms, and training from Iran and its proxies. Al-Qaeda's leniency toward Shia Muslims became a point of attack for ISIS. For example, in its propaganda war with AQAP, ISIS questioned the group's legitimacy due to its reluctance to slaughter Shia. Wilaya Khorasan adopted a similar line of attack against the Taliban and AQIS. ISIS's approach to the Shia may be strategic as well as ideological: ISIS identified an area where al-Qaeda's relative pragmatism was at odds with inflexible jihadist dogma and tried to use it to outcompete its rival militants.

In the prior chapters, we also show how ISIS altered its strategies in response to battlefield developments. For example, ISIS initially called on supporters to emigrate to its territory. It hoped these supporters would provide it not only with raw manpower but also the specialized workforce needed to sustain a functioning state. But as Turkey closed its border crossings with Syria and the global anti-ISIS coalition mobilized, ISIS's supporters struggled to reach the caliphate. ISIS began calling on its supporters abroad to carry out attacks in their home countries rather than emigrating. This strategic shift helped to produce a wave of attacks in Western countries from 2015 to 2018.

We have also seen a strategic shift over time in ISIS's messaging. As ISIS seized territory, the group's propaganda came to link its legitimacy to its control of territory. Its slogan of *baqiya wa tatamadad* (remaining and expanding) referred to the group's control of territory and was the cornerstone of the caliphate's online narrative of strength. But ISIS's later territorial losses forced it to alter that message. ISIS's propaganda thus pivoted from showcasing its strength and momentum to three different narratives. These were resiliency, the unimportance of territory, and the ISIS's expansion to new areas of the globe:

- The incomplete nature of clearing operations against ISIS's territory allowed the organization to claim resiliency in Homs and Deir Ez-Zor in particular.
- To downplay the importance of territory, ISIS claimed that launching attacks roughly equated to holding territory.[4] Until the Taliban inflicted significant losses upon Wilaya Khorasan, the group's Afghanistan-based province was able to launch a steady stream of attacks that helped ISIS maintain this narrative.[5]
- ISIS's propaganda emphasized the group's new affiliates and territorial expansion in the Philippines, Mozambique, and West Africa.[6]

ISIS's propaganda adaptations have allowed it to endure, keeping together a network of affiliates stretching from Southeast Asia to West Africa.

Thus far, ISIS has been less open to organizational learning on the strategic level than al-Qaeda has been. Al-Qaeda has engaged in more radical, discontinuous learning than ISIS has—although it should be noted that al-Qaeda, as the older organization, has had more time to do so. Al-Qaeda has also executed larger strategic shifts, like its move from a far-enemy strategy to a more localized, low-profile strategy that at least temporarily deprioritizes attacks against the far enemy.

THE FUTURE OF JIHADISTS' STRATEGIC EVOLUTION

Jihadists will continue to adapt their strategies in the years ahead. We must seriously assess ways in which these groups could continue to evolve and the implications for our own counterterrorism efforts. Recent developments raise questions about three particular ways that these organizations could evolve in the near term.

The first development pertains to where jihadists will operate. Bin Laden wrote in 2011 that "chaos and the absence of authority" provided the "best environment" for spreading al-Qaeda's ideology. Events in Syria, Iraq, Afghanistan, Yemen, Libya, Somalia, and West Africa largely support bin Laden's assertion. Al-Qaeda and ISIS have tried to operate in governance vacuums in conflict zones across the globe. The continuation of existing conflicts or outbreak of new conflicts may attract jihadists and shape their strategies. To capitalize on ungoverned or poorly governed spaces, they would likely engage in continuous organizational learning.

The second development relates to how jihadist groups present themselves to the outside world. Bin Laden warned of the dangers of prematurely declaring a caliphate. ISIS's territorial losses in Iraq and Syria may vindicate bin Laden's position. To be clear, outside intervention into the Iraq-Syria theater was driven not just by the caliphate declaration but also by ISIS executing Americans on camera and perpetrating a genocide against the Yazidis. While ISIS maintains an ideological commitment to holding and governing territory, will it reconsider the logic behind bin Laden's warning in light of its territorial losses in Iraq and Syria?

The third development relates to factors that could alter the state of competition between al-Qaeda and ISIS. Abu Bakr al-Baghdadi, a central player in the feud between the two groups, is dead. Further, the inter-jihadist competition in Syria has engendered negative consequences for both al-Qaeda and ISIS. In light of this, it is possible that al-Qaeda and ISIS will tacitly cooperate more often in the future. In 2016 Bruce Hoffman raised the possibility of a merger between the groups due to their relatively similar ideologies, similar strategies, and the rhetorical olive branches that both groups occasionally extend to the other—as well as the central role of individual egos in the initial fissure.[7] While we are far from confident that al-Qaeda and ISIS can overcome their differences, Hoffman's argument should be seriously considered.

Tactical Evolution

Jihadists have demonstrated a greater willingness to assess and adapt their tactics than their strategies. They have demonstrated the ability to learn not just from their own group's tactical successes and failures but also from those of other militant groups.

PLOTS AGAINST AVIATION

Jihadist plots against aviation have epitomized these groups' capacity for tactical innovation. One of the first attempts by jihadists to hijack an airplane failed because they could not fly it on their own. Learning from that error, key members of the 9/11 hijacking group learned to fly before the attacks. Realizing that the United States would bolster its security screenings at airports after the impending 9/11 attacks, Sayf al-Adl and Abu Muhammad al-Masri asked Tariq Mahmoud Ahmed al-Sawah to develop a shoe bomb to circumvent those measures. Richard Reid's resulting plot almost succeeded. Then jihadists turned to liquid explosives, seeking to exploit a remaining loophole in airport security. As passenger screenings became more extensive, AQAP turned to explosive cargo packages, which prompted new countermeasures. ISIS then used insider support from an airport employee to place an explosive on a Russian airliner leaving Egypt.

Jihadists' organizational learning in this context followed a pattern. While plotting to attack planes, their organizational learning was typically reactive. With each new adaption, the militants tried to pinpoint weaknesses in airport security and develop tactics to exploit those weaknesses. Authorities would then enhance security screenings, and jihadists would in turn try to circumvent these new measures. But in some cases, like the shoe-bomb plot, jihadists managed to engage in organizational learning closer to the anticipatory part of the anticipatory–reactive spectrum that we outlined in chapter 2. Jihadists demonstrated a similar willingness to hone their recruitment tactics.

FROM GROUPS TO VIRTUAL PLOTTERS

Until the rise of Anwar al-Awlaki, al-Qaeda's leadership focused on planning and executing professionalized group attacks on the West. During the Awlaki era, the organization's leaders discerned the potential to inspire loosely affiliated supporters around the globe to conduct attacks. To facilitate those attacks, al-Qaeda began publishing attack tips—for example, in the "Open Source Jihad" section of *Inspire*. Although "Open Source Jihad" enjoyed some success, ISIS was able to take this concept to a new level. The tips in its magazine *Rumiyah* helped inform ISIS's supporters planning attacks around the world. But the comparative success of ISIS's model was not its publications but rather the group's new model that allowed individualized coaching for attacks from a distance: the virtual plotter model. ISIS fighters typically located in Iraq and Syria provided encouragement, tactical support, and case-specific guidance to supporters planning attacks around the world. Virtual plotters played an important role in the wave of ISIS attacks that struck Europe from 2015 to 2018.

ASSESSING JIHADISTS' ORGANIZATIONAL LEARNING

Overall, jihadists' organizational learning has been largely reactive and continuous. In some instances, they have engaged in discontinuous learning to take advantage of novel opportunities and have also engaged in more anticipatory learning. Returning to David Nadler and Michael Tushman's organizational learning typologies that we discussed in chapter 2, we can see that jihadists' organizational learning largely fell into the re-creation and adaptation categories. Al-Qaeda's shoe-bomb plot is the primary example discussed in this book that falls into the tuning category. Jihadists' organizational learning did not reach the reorientation category for good

Organization	Change	Key Trigger	Typology
Al-Qaeda	Adopts far-enemy strategy	Failures of country-specific jihads	Re-creation
Al-Qaeda	9/11 attacks: trains pilots before attack	Failed Air France hijacking, 1994	Adaptation
Al-Qaeda	Shoe-bomb plot	Anticipation of new airport security post-9/11	Tuning
Al-Qaeda	Liquid explosive plot	New airport security post-shoe bomb plot	Adaptation
Al-Qaeda (AQAP)	Places explosives in cargo plane	New airport security post–liquid explosive plot	Adaptation
Al-Qaeda	Adopts strategy focused on *dawa* and *hisba*	Revolutions in Egypt and Tunisia	Adaptation
Al-Qaeda	Conceals relationship with affiliates	U.S. military response to al-Qaeda groups	Adaptation

FIG. 11.1 Nadler and Tushman's typologies applied to jihadist organizational learning

reason. Reorientation occurs in low-pressure environments, which the global war on terror largely eliminated for jihadists.

Figure 11.1 summarizes how learning instances discussed in the book align with Nadler and Tushman's typologies. It shows jihadists' penchant for adaptation in response to a triggering event.

In chapter 2, we also outlined alternative frameworks for understanding organizational learning. One framework was the distinction between continuous or discontinuous learning. For continuous organizational learning, jihadist groups adjust their current procedure. For discontinuous organizational learning, these groups adopt more radical changes aimed at upending the status quo. Figure 11.2 shows several examples of how al-Qaeda and ISIS engaged in continuous learning.

This figure highlights the novelty of al-Qaeda's approach in Tunisia and Egypt and further sheds light on why analysts failed to anticipate how al-Qaeda would capitalize on the events of the Arab Spring (see chapters 1 and 6).

Organization	Applying Past Experiences to	Learning from Experiences in	Continuous or Discontinuous
Al-Qaeda	Iraq	Afghanistan	Continuous
Al-Qaeda	Syria	Afghanistan, Iraq	Continuous
Al-Qaeda	Libya	Afghanistan, Iraq	Continuous
Al-Qaeda	Tunisia	—	Discontinuous
Al-Qaeda	Egypt	—	Discontinuous
ISIS	Syria	Iraq	Continuous
ISIS	Afghanistan	Iraq, Syria	Continuous

FIG. 11.2 Continuous and discontinuous learning by AQ and ISIS

Future Evolutions of Jihadist Tactics

While it is hard to predict the tactics that jihadist groups will use in the years to come, the last two decades suggest that they will continue to innovate and adapt. There is some evidence that jihadists will continue to refine their prior tactics used to target aviation and to guide virtual plotters to conduct attacks. For example, U.K. minister of state for security and economic crime Ben Wallace emphasized in December 2018 that al-Qaeda was actively targeting aviation and airports in Europe.[8] Two Shabaab fighters were arrested between the summer of 2019 and spring of 2020 while taking flying lessons in the Philippines and an African country.[9] While jihadists will likely retain this focus on aviation, they will also likely adopt new technologies as they become more widely available.

Jihadists' adoption of new technologies will likely follow the pattern that the violent non-state-actor adoption curve from chapter 2 illuminates: early adoption followed by iteration, then breakthrough, then a phase of competition between jihadists and their foes. While these groups' efforts tend to disproportionately fail in the early stages, jihadists will learn important lessons and refine their techniques. With refinements, they may reach the breakthrough stage, posing a major security challenge. As governments implement countermeasures to counter these breakthroughs, jihadists and their enemies enter the competition stage.

Jihadist groups, of course, will be far from the only violent non-state actors to adopt these emerging technologies. Other extremist groups, drug cartels, transnational gangs, and other violent non-state actors are already experimenting with many technologies. Jihadist groups will likely learn from the successes and failures of these groups' operations and adjust accordingly. And these other violent non-state actors will similarly try to learn what they can from the jihadists' efforts.

Two technologies, drones and artificial intelligence, stand out as potentially salient to jihadists. Jihadists are already using drones to sharpen their propaganda and conduct attacks. While we have not seen evidence to date of jihadists using artificial intelligence, its growing accessibility will likely lead jihadists to begin experimenting with it. The remainder of this section outlines how jihadists could use these technologies in the coming years in light of current trends.

DRONES

Drones' appeal to jihadists is obvious. Drones can allow them to engage in a battlefield domain previously closed off to them: air. Jihadists were relatively absent during the initial adoption and iteration phases of the violent non-state-actor technology adoption curve for drones. Prior to al-Qaeda and ISIS, other militant groups like Hamas and Hizballah had also used drone technology, largely thanks to Iranian support.[10] But since 2013 we have seen jihadists play a key role in the violent non-state-actor breakthrough phase for drones. We discussed in chapter 7 how ISIS used and experimented with drone technology during its territorial conquests. At the same time, the drone workshop described at the outset of this chapter, while showing ISIS's eagerness to experiment with this technology, also demonstrates its limitations. That being said, commercial drone technology is becoming increasingly advanced, cheap, and accessible. This market trend raises the possibility that these groups will incorporate drones into new types of attacks, such as drone swarms.

Drone swarms provide numerous advantages. If jihadists lack drones that can carry heavy weapons, swarms can increase the volume of ordnance. Drone swarms would ideally operate with artificial intelligence (AI) technology that allows the drones to communicate with one another. The AI could enable drones to make specific targeting decisions, such as identifying high-priority over low-priority targets or identifying and disabling enemy communications systems.[11] The development of algorithms to facilitate intelligent drone swarms is being actively pursued by states for military and civilian applications.[12] As has been the case in other areas, commercialization may provide applications that jihadists will be able to acquire, replicate, or adapt.

In addition to new drone tactics, there are several specific technologies we believe jihadists may try to exploit with respect to drones over the next five years. First, jihadists could use heavy-lift drones to carry heavier payloads. The ability to carry heavier loads for longer distances would benefit groups that rely on drones to transport material, whether it is an explosive device or combat resources. These technological improvements will also help jihadists avoid the detection they may risk with human transports and vehicle convoys.

Second, jihadists could use drones for the delivery of chemical, biological, radiological, and nuclear weapons. Although other violent non-state actors have tried to use drones for this purpose, these efforts have so far been stymied by these groups' inability to develop an effective dispersal system. Due to improvements in chemical dispersion technology, however, some state actors have successfully modified commercial drones to deploy chemical, biological, radiological, and nuclear weapons like tear gas.[13] Recently, drones with liquid dispersion capabilities have been developed for agricultural purposes. One early model, released by the company DJI, can carry up to ten kilograms of liquid. Most jihadist groups would consider these models extremely expensive, but the prices are likely to fall.

Third, rapidly developing technology in the quality and diversity of drone sensors will undoubtedly improve jihadists' intelligence, surveillance, and reconnaissance capabilities. Sensors like lidar, forward-looking infrared radar, or true night vision will allow jihadists to improve their imaging. Potential uses include preattack reconnaissance and improving smuggling routes. The price of advanced sensors is falling rapidly at present.

Fourth, while jihadists have historically made some use of remote-controlled vehicles, limits in maneuverability and complicated controls have impeded their adoption. Some companies have recently shown significant progress on heavier remote-controlled commercial vehicles, advances that could potentially be applied to passenger vehicles as well.[14] Developments in this technology present possibilities for jihadists, who may use remote-controlled cars for vehicle-borne improvised explosive device attacks, car ramming attacks, or resource transportation. Parallel to this innovation is the developing industry of self-driving cars.

Fifth, while quadcopter drones have been the primary design used by most jihadist groups, fixed-wing drones can fly farther and faster. Fixed-wing drones have generally remained in a higher-end commercial market: They are more expensive and require professional operability as well as long runways for takeoff. Additionally, prohibitions on operating drones beyond visual line of sight in many countries could inhibit fixed-wing drones from expanding into the hobbyist market. However, both ISIS and also some cartels have shown evidence of researching and developing their own fixed-wing drone technology.[15] The drones used by jihadists to attack the Khmeimim Air Base in Syria in January 2018 were rudimentary fixed-wing models.[16]

Sixth, jihadists will likely exploit the proliferation of simpler and higher-quality components for constructing custom devices.[17] Although many parts of the Khmeimim attack drones were jerry-rigged and built by hand, they also incorporated customizable components, including a bomblet release mechanism.[18] Rather than purchasing expensive models, some jihadists will opt for in-house manufacturing by using relatively cheap and accessible components.

ARTIFICIAL INTELLIGENCE

Many of the AI systems that jihadist groups could deploy already exist, but these systems are not yet widely available to consumers. But, similar to drones, AI systems are likely to become adopted by jihadists as they become more widely accessible. AI has the potential to augment all aspects of jihadist activity, including recruitment; fundraising; intelligence, surveillance, and reconnaissance; and attacks.

We have identified two primary criteria likely to have an impact on whether jihadist groups will adopt different AI systems in the near term. First, is the AI system commercially available, cheap, and easy to use, or will it be in the next five years? Second, will it fit into strategies, planning structures, and recruitment tactics currently employed by jihadists? AI systems that we evaluate to be *likely* to be adopted by jihadist groups in the next five years will be accessible to general audiences and fit into these groups' current strategies. To be clear, likely adoption does not mean likely success: Per the violent non-state-actor technology adoption curve, initial uses may look like failures, and jihadist groups may never succeed in reaching the breakthrough phase. With those criteria in mind, we believe that jihadists will likely adopt two AI systems: deep fakes and virtual agents.

Deep fake technology can alter videos, images, or voice recordings to create fake content that appears strikingly real. This is achieved by providing photographs, videos, and audio recordings of a specific person to an advanced machine-learning algorithm, which in turn generates a nearly identical appearance and voice. Typically this algorithm will refine its creation by checking it against another algorithm intended to detect fraudulent videos or recordings. Once the fraud checker no longer indicates the content is fake, the original algorithm concludes that it has successfully created a functioning deep fake.[19] This means that, to the human eye, it will often be nearly impossible to detect a deep fake.[20] Deep fakes prey on the notion that seeing—or hearing—is believing, as they are designed to trick individuals into believing that their fabricated content is legitimate. Thus far, deep fakes have been used in contexts that include pornography and political mudslinging.

Deep faking apps are readily available today. They are typically cheap or even free. FakeApp, the most popular deep fake app for Windows operating systems, is free to download and free to use. Users may buy hardware to improve FakeApp's functionality, but it appears that standard computer components will support the program. There are also numerous online tutorials for FakeApp. Aspiring deep fakers can watch YouTube videos or find written guides explaining how to create a fabricated image from start to finish.

It is easy to imagine how jihadists could leverage deep fakes. For example, they could create fabricated videos depicting Western forces desecrating the Qur'an. Such videos have a history of inciting violence in certain locations. Notably, a March 2011 video of a Florida pastor burning a Qur'an led to riots in Afghanistan, including riots in Mazar-i-Sharif that killed seven UN staff members. Jihadists could also use deep fakes to produce videos exaggerating the degree of support they enjoy.

Jihadists could also use virtual agents, which are also referred to as "chatbots," for recruiting. Virtual agents are AI programs that mimic human interactions over text. They have been used in various ways, perhaps most commonly as a mechanism to answer questions or provide information to someone viewing a website. For example, a user who sends an instant message to a company offering 24/7 chat-based customer support may be interacting with a chatbot. Virtual agent technology is already widely available. For example, people can now create chatbots in "a few minutes" through a company called Dexter.[21] The company allows people to build the bots for free: Users only pay if the bots are able to attract users. Even then, the bots are not expensive: A bot able to accommodate simultaneous chats with five thousand users costs only eighty dollars per month.[22] Jihadists could weaponize this technology—for example, by using virtual agents to post high volumes of propaganda on websites, chat boards, and social media platforms.

Outside of deep fakes and virtual agents, jihadists may also adapt AI-facilitated social network mapping for their purposes. Social network mapping software allows users to analyze social networks to identify distinct communities, influencers, and demographics of users in online networks. Even for individuals who attempt to extricate themselves from web-based social networks, "data inference" can provide insights into one's interests, habits, and social circles.[23] Coupled with machine-learning algorithms that can identify trends and linkages within and between one's social networks, collecting information on users is becoming increasingly effective, efficient, and accurate. In chapter 7, we mention how ISIS used human intelligence to map the social networks of cities it wanted to capture. AI-facilitated social network mapping may allow jihadists to enhance their targeting capabilities and attack planning in areas where it is hard to collect human intelligence. Jihadists could also use this technology to microtarget their online recruitment efforts.

The Path Forward

This book demonstrates that jihadist organizations are strategically and tactically adaptable, and it sheds insight into their organizational learning in practice. This oft-underappreciated adaptability has several key implications for the strategies and tactics that governments should use to defeat jihadist organizations. This section outlines those implications and discusses the role of organizational learning in developing countermeasures.

TACTICS

To counter jihadist organizations' existing tactics and innovative uses of emerging technologies, governments must first internalize the dynamism of jihadist organizations and appreciate their capacity for adaptation. Governments also need to focus on disrupting jihadists' organizational learning and facilitating organizational learning in their own departments and agencies.

As discussed in chapter 4, governments' responses to jihadist plots are usually reactive. After governments respond to a particular type of plot, jihadists seek out ways to circumvent that specific countermeasure. As a result, government countermeasures must become harder for jihadists to predict. While governments should retain some standardized security checks and procedures, like those established for aviation, they should heed the advice of former Transportation Security Administration chief Kip Hawley: Governments should add an element of unpredictability to measures such as airport screening procedures. That increased unpredictability will, in turn, prevent jihadists from focusing their efforts on circumventing a rigid set of security checks.

This focus on organizational learning must also apply to government efforts to counter jihadists' messaging. Jihadists have proven to be innovative online communicators. Awlaki's effective use of the internet, ISIS's propaganda machine, and the success of virtual plotters have demonstrated that jihadists can use a variety of techniques and platforms to spread their message. The most promising route to counter jihadist groups that are adept at messaging is for governments to create de-bureaucratized cells composed of strategic communications professionals and intelligence analysts. Those cells can monitor jihadist groups' communications and develop campaigns to counter jihadist disinformation and undermine these groups' core narratives. These de-bureaucratized cells need to embrace the fact that some messaging campaigns will succeed while others will fail. Jihadists' messaging is tricky to counter. Their messaging model focuses on building a dedicating fan base while assuming that most viewers will despise and reject them. Confronted with this messaging model, these de-bureaucratized cells must internalize the lessons of each success or failure and constantly refine their work. They must work with private sector partners.

Rather than waiting for jihadists to achieve the same breakthrough with emerging technologies that they have already achieved in other technological spheres, security and law enforcement agencies need to actively prepare and train for jihadists integrating new technologies into their attacks, recruitment, and financing efforts. Governments should consider the feasibility of limiting the distribution of technologies that could substantially improve jihadists' military capabilities. When it is difficult to limit the spread of those technologies, governments must preemptively implement strategies and develop tools to counter jihadists' (and other violent non-state actors') potential use of these technologies.

When developing tools and strategies focused on emerging technologies, international and cross-sector collaboration are essential to engage in more anticipatory organizational learning. Governments need to develop strong relationships with companies developing key emerging technologies like drones and artificial intelligence. Governments should work with these private sector partners to understand possible modifications that militants might attempt to these technologies.

STRATEGY

The dynamic nature of jihadist groups has two implications for the strategy of countering these organizations. First, jihadists' adaptive nature has allowed them to survive despite the wide-ranging military, political, economic, and social countermeasures against them. That dynamism also facilitated some of their greatest successes: the September 11 attacks, the November 2015 attacks in Paris, the 2019 Easter bombings in Sri Lanka, the military victories in the Iraq–Syria theater that produced ISIS's short-lived caliphate. Governments, therefore, must actively work to undermine jihadists' capacity for organizational learning.

To undermine jihadists' capacity for organizational learning, governments should focus their targeting efforts on innovators and terrorist entrepreneurs like Anwar al-Awlaki, Rachid Kassim, and Ibrahim al-Asiri.

Targeting efforts should also focus on individuals with specialized knowledge that won't be easily replaceable. Conversely, governments should consider leaving in place jihadist personnel who inhibit organizational learning.

Governments should also continue to prioritize eliminating militant safe havens. Safe havens are the ideal environment for these groups to engage in organizational learning.[24] When jihadists operate clandestinely rather than enjoying a safe haven, socialization rarely happens, and internalization requires more time and effort. Easy socialization and internalization of lessons learned allowed for the formation of a global jihadist movement in Afghanistan and for ISIS to develop a highly lethal organization in Iraq and Syria. Preventing these safe havens from emerging is therefore important to handicapping jihadists' organizational learning.[25]

We are ultimately not just fighting a set of groups, like al-Qaeda or ISIS, or a tactic, like terrorism. We are fighting an ideological movement.[26] Although jihadist organizations may change their strategy and tactics, ideology is a relative constant. In jihadists' eyes, there is a good reason for this consistency. In this movement, theological innovation amounts to heresy. This belief is a powerful check on jihadists' ability to change their ideology. This check does not mean that jihadists are exempt from ideological infighting and debates over what counts as a core theological tenet versus what counts as a strategy. This check also does not mean that jihadists never alter their ideology for cynical or pragmatic reasons. That being said, even when there are currents within the jihadist movement that challenge the prevailing ideology, these challengers are frequently more inflexible than are mainstream jihadists. The Hazimis, from chapter 7, illustrate this trend.

The consistency of jihadist ideology allows us to develop a long-term strategy to counter its spread. In particular, we can make investments to counter that ideology that may not pay immediate dividends but that will help in the long run. Preventing radicalization to violent extremism is a good example of this type of investment. Most counterterrorism analysts and policymakers understand that we cannot kill our way out of this problem. If the number of new recruits outpaces the number killed and captured in counterterrorism operations, jihadist organizations will grow stronger over time. Preventing radicalization is thus crucial for defeating the broader movement. However, preventing radicalization is not a precise science, and there is a lot we still do not know about why people radicalize. As part of a long-term strategy, we will need to embrace *our own* organizational learning. As we invest in preventive measures, we should be able to better gauge which ones work and which do not. Investment in effective measures can grow, and ineffective ones can be altered or discarded. The U.S. Department of Homeland Security's Targeted Violence and Terrorism Prevention Grant Program is an example of how these investments might work.[27] By generating a great deal of data, the grant program has helped to illuminate which counter-radicalization pathways hold promise.

Consensus Errors

This book has not only shown that jihadist groups evolve tactically, strategically, and technologically but also that the field of counterterrorism analysis does not always have a strong record of accuracy. As we have illustrated, the main line of the analysis in the field misinterpreted key aspects of al-Qaeda and ISIS's operations over the past two decades. Examples of flawed analysis include estimates of the Arab Spring's impact on al-Qaeda, a misreading of the competition between al-Qaeda and ISIS, and an overestimation of the prevalence of lone-wolf attackers. While everyone makes errors, particularly with respect to anticipatory analysis, the widespread unwillingness to revise certain lines of analysis based on new information is troubling. (To be fair, we do not see this problem as unique to our field. Pride that impels one to never admit error and to groupthink are powerful phenomena that possess a broad reach.)

Many key assessments about jihadist groups endured long after contradictory evidence emerged. These include the assessment that al-Qaeda only had fifty to one hundred fighters in Afghanistan (chapter 9) and confusion about where ISIS and al-Qaeda stood with respect to being near-enemy or far-enemy focused. Many analysts still continue to minimize bin Laden's role in al-Qaeda's operations, a conclusion starkly contradicted by the trove of documents recovered from Abbottabad. While bin Laden's security precautions limited the speed and frequency of his communications with subordinates, he was actively communicating with those subordinates across the globe. And they heeded his advice.

The consensus errors that the field has encountered may make little analytical sense, but there are good reasons they occur. Social psychology has stressed the distorting impact that others' opinions have on our logic. Solomon Asch, a professor at Swarthmore College, conducted a 1951 experiment on how groups influence individual reasoning. He showed participants two cards. One card had a single line and the other had three lines, one of which matched the length of the line on the first card. It was easy to find the matching line. Asch placed participants in groups with others who received prior instructions from Asch without the knowledge of the study's *actual* participants. Asch then asked the individuals in the group, the participants and those working with Asch, which of the three lines on the second card matched the line on the first card. When Asch instructed his collaborators to try to select the right answer, the unwitting participants identified the matching line 99 percent of the time. When Asch instructed his collaborators to give the wrong answer, the unwitting participants—forced to choose between their eyes and the group consensus—picked the group consensus 36.8 percent of the time.[28] While Asch's experiment occurred over fifty years ago, recent psychology textbooks still discuss his findings, and his experiment has become a foundational part of social psychology.

Asch's experiment shows the power of groupthink even when the correct answer is obvious. But what about when both sides of an argument have evidence supporting their conclusions? What happens when you must reach a conclusion based on incomplete information? What about when breaking with the herd means damaging one's professional reputation or standing? And what happens when you have to make that sort of decision in an environment where social media and political polarization magnify groupthink? All of this is the case for counterterrorism analysis today.

Analysts examine organizations that try to conceal much of their activities, and these analysts often must make sense of incomplete information. No one is infallible in this situation, but analysts need to revise their views as new information becomes available and examine dissenting views with curiosity—not with scorn. Ultimately, the prevailing line of analysis about al-Qaeda and the Arab Spring, ISIS's relationship with its *wilayat*, or any other topic *should* outperform the dissenting line of analysis. When that does not happen, analysts inside and outside government need to reassess their assumptions. Given our experiences, we anticipate that creating a results-driven culture that embraces dissent will be a challenge. However, the alternative is financially and morally untenable.

How do we mitigate the possibility of consensus errors? First, we need to incentivize being right, to force analysts to more intensely scrutinize differing sides of arguments. This would also decrease the appetite to double down on clearly wrong conclusions. Governments must also foster cultures that tolerate divergent views by developing procedures that actively solicit those views and consider their merits. Some institutions have developed platforms for dissent or arguing against conventional wisdom, a practice often called red teaming. Red teaming can normalize the presence of dissenting views in an agency. When red teams outperform the main line of analysis, institutions should comprehensively reassess the assumptions in their main line of analysis and perhaps embrace the dissenting line of analysis as a better reflection of reality.

Accomplishing this task outside of government is less straightforward, but there are some good options. Training better counterterrorism analysts must begin at our universities. International relations and security studies programs should focus on teaching rigorous analytic tradecraft. Students must become accustomed to analyzing incomplete information and using new information to update their findings. These programs need to foster a culture that welcomes and honestly reflects upon dissenting ideas. Integrating practices like red teaming into these programs could help create such a culture.

We have no illusions. A paradigmatic shift will not be easy, and many in the field will resist it. But the international community has been fighting jihadists for almost two decades, and there are more jihadists and militant groups now than there were on September 11, 2001.[29] That is a sign that something is wrong. If we are going to defeat the jihadist movement, we need to change how we do business.

Acknowledgments

U nless something goes horribly wrong, this will be the last book
I write about jihadist terrorism. I'm proud of *Enemies Near and
Far* and consider it a worthy swan song.

Enemies almost didn't happen. It featured far more drama than any book
I have worked on before. It wasn't necessarily *interesting* drama, just the
kind of challenges that arise as I am increasingly squeezed for time, as I
worked to stand up and grow my company, Valens Global, even while writing this book.

A lot of people and institutions made *Enemies* possible, and I'll try to
thank them in a roughly chronological order.

At the time I began *Enemies*, I was still a senior fellow at the Foundation
for Defense of Democracies (FDD), a nonpartisan D.C.-based think tank
where Thomas Joscelyn hangs his hat today. FDD generously supported the
beginning of the book, and graciously provided me with grant support that
helped me to continue my work on it. I appreciate FDD and its leadership—
Cliff May, Mark Dubowitz, Bill McCarthy, Toby Dershowitz, and Jonathan
Schanzer—for giving me a home for around a decade where I was able to
think deeply about the complex security challenges the world confronts.
FDD is somewhat unique among think tanks in its willingness to let its fel-
lows reach diametrically opposed conclusions from one another. For an
iconoclast like me, this was essential to allowing me to do my best work.

The process of putting *Enemies* together was supercharged when the Smith Richardson Foundation provided me and a coauthor with a grant to work on it. (Tom, it should be said, was not that initial coauthor; we will get to that.) I would like to thank Smith Richardson and my program manager, Alan Song, for their support. Alan had the patience of Job, as what was supposed to be a relatively quick project ended up extending over the course of years, blowing past multiple self-imposed deadlines. We also received support from Canada's Department of National Defence, which funded a project I led on violent non-state actors' use of technology through its MINDS program. I used that grant to develop the violent non-state-actor technology adoption curve, among other aspects of this book.

One of the fun bits of drama involved in producing *Enemies* was switching coauthors in the middle of the process. That left me scrambling for a while. During the scrambling period, a couple of people made noteworthy contributions. Becca DiLuzio, who was at the time a nineteen-year-old Duke University student, contributed valuable research to the chapter on aviation attacks. Aymenn Jawad Al-Tamimi, a well-known analyst, produced an early draft of the chapter on jihadists' shift toward fighting the far enemy.

But this book really got momentum when I finally settled on bringing on board Thomas Joscelyn as a coauthor. Tom is someone whose work I respect immensely. His grasp of granular details and determination to dig into the evidence and find deeper answers is unparalleled. In addition to Tom serving as a phenomenal coauthor, a number of team members at Valens contributed greatly. Madeleine Blackman was Valens's research manager as work on this book got under way, when I still considered the volume to be an albatross around my neck. Maddie did much to shape the research culture at Valens, and the production process for parts of this book is a testament to the finely oiled machine that she was able to create. Rachel Miller did the bulk of managing work on this book, including helping to make the theoretical chapter more readable and improve its sequencing. As I was putting together the finishing touches on the book, James Ferencsik, an outstanding researcher, played an important role in reviewing the entire manuscript and helping me to plug any remaining research gaps. Mary Bennett Doty did as well.

Others on the Valens team also helped to me to balance all my competing priorities as I moved this book to completion. Matt Shear, my research manager, projects an unflappable aura of calm that makes everyone around him better able to handle the many shocks we encounter in life circa 2021. Matt deserves the credit for originally developing the violent non-state-actor technology adoption curve with me. Derek Jones, Valens's vice president, has been a good friend ever since we first crossed paths at a U.S. Special Operations Command conference in 2008, someone I can always turn to for an outside-the-box perspective that almost unfailingly reveals deeper truths about whatever complex challenge I am contemplating. And I cannot say enough kind things about Carolina "Nina" Ponzeto, Valens's chief operating officer, who is both one of the most brilliant professionals and one of the most truly impressive human beings whom I have ever had the pleasure knowing.

As we moved this book through its two rounds of peer review, two people were especially helpful. One is Bruce Hoffman, whom I regard as one of the few mentors I have had in this field. In addition to being a world-renowned scholar, Bruce is one of the nicest, most genuine, most humane people you will encounter in the field of terrorism studies. He serves as a great role model for all of us in his lack of ego and willingness to selflessly help others, generally expecting nothing in return. Caelyn Cobb, my editor, was also instrumental to the success of this book. Thanks also to all of this book's peer reviewers, including the extremely grouchy anonymous one. All of you genuinely helped to improve the final product.

I would like to thank my family—my wife, Amy Powell, and my daughters, Hope and River—for their unflinching support.

—Daveed Gartenstein-Ross

Unlike my colleague Daveed Gartenstein-Ross, this is the first book I've written on terrorism. That is no accident. Although I'm a prolific writer, I've never found the time to work on a book. The daily demands on my time are not conducive to it. I did so in this instance solely because Daveed asked for my assistance. Daveed is a good friend. I have great respect for his professionalism, intellect, and patience. The last trait was especially valuable as I was tardy in submitting my draft chapters. There are only a few other people I'd even consider coauthoring a book with and I thank Daveed for the opportunity.

I'd like to thank my colleagues at the FDD, especially Cliff May, Mark Dubowitz, and Jonathan Schanzer. Since 2009 they've granted me the intellectual freedom to pursue whatever avenues of research and analysis I found of interest. I can't imagine having that degree of latitude anywhere else. Their generous support has allowed me to survive in a field that often doesn't want to hear what I think.

Several other colleagues have played crucial roles in my career, and I don't know where I'd be without them. As some readers undoubtedly know, I've long been the senior editor of *FDD's Long War Journal*, a widely read website that serves as the minority report in the counterterrorism field. My colleague, Bill Roggio, built the site out of his own personal blog. I first contacted Bill at the email address listed on his blog many years ago. I could not have known at the time that it would lead to a long-term partnership. He and I have gone against the herd together more times than I can remember. I am proud to call him a friend and fellow dissident. There is a fair amount of Bill in this book. Steve Hayes, the editor and chief executive of *The Dispatch*, helped get me started in the counterterrorism field. I can't thank him enough for his friendship and support. Steve has also gone against the herd, often risking his career to do so. Dan Darling is another colleague who has provided countless insights into al-Qaeda and ISIS. Some of Dan's commentary on open-source evidence undoubtedly influenced this book as well.

On a personal note, I'd like to thank my father and mother. My dad, Warren, passed away in 2008. He was my only hero in this crazy world. He thought that facts mattered and that the truth, while elusive, was still knowable. He would not have liked the counterterrorism field. My mother, Marcia, has supported my professional career even as I suddenly changed course from economist to counterterrorism analyst. My wife, Janine, has endured my crazy schedule and work habits. She is my rock. My daughters, Lillian and Amelia, are everything to me. I hope one day, when they are old enough to read this book, they will be proud of their father for coauthoring it.

—Thomas Joscelyn

Abbreviations

ABM	Ansar Bayt al-Maqdis
AGH	Ansar Ghazwat-ul-Hind
AI	artificial intelligence
AQAP	al-Qaeda in the Arabian Peninsula
AQI	al-Qaeda in Iraq
AQIM	al-Qaeda in the Islamic Maghreb
AQIS	al-Qaeda in the Indian Subcontinent
AQSL	al-Qaeda's senior leadership
ASMB	Abu Salim Martyrs Brigade
AST	Ansar al-Sharia in Tunisia
BRSC	Benghazi Revolutionaries Shura Council
CTC	Combating Terrorism Center
DMSC	Derna Mujahedin Shura Council
EIJ	Egyptian Islamic Jihad
ETIM	Eastern Turkistan Islamic Movement
FAA	Federal Aviation Administration
FATA	Federally Administered Tribal Areas (Pakistan)
FDD	Foundation for Defense of Democracies
FSA	Free Syrian Army
GIA	Armed Islamic Group
GSPC	Salafist Group for Preaching and Combat

HTS	Hay'at Tahrir al-Sham
HUJI	Harkat-ul Jihad-al-Islami
HUM	Harkat-ul-Mujahideen
ICE	Islamic Caucasus Emirate
IMU	Islamic Movement of Uzbekistan
ISGS	Islamic State in the Greater Sahara
ISI	Inter-Services Intelligence [agency, Pakistan]
ISI	Islamic State of Iraq
ISIS	Islamic State of Iraq and al-Sham
ISWAP	Islamic State's West Africa Province
IYSC	Islamic Youth Shura Council
JAD	Jamaah Ansharut Daulah
JMWA	Jaysh al-Mujahedin wa-l-Ansar
JNIM	Jama'at Nusrat al-Islam wa-l-Muslimin
JTJ	Jama'at al-Tawhid wal-Jihad
JTTF	Joint Terrorism Task Force
JuA	Jamaat-ul-Ahrar
KSM	Khalid Sheikh Mohammed
LAX	Los Angeles International Airport
LeJ	Lashkar-e-Jhangvi
LeT	Lashkar-e-Taiba
LIFG	Libyan Islamic Fighting Group
LNA	Libyan National Army
MaK	Maktab al-Khidamat
MENA	Middle East and North Africa (region)
MSC	Mujahedin Shura Council
MVP	minimum viable product
PDB	Presidential Daily Brief
PETN	pentaerythritol tetranitrate
SIDE	social identity model of deindividuation effects
TCG	Tunisian Combatant Group
TIP	Turkistan Islamic Party
TSA	Transportation Security Administration
TTP	Tehrik-e Taliban Pakistan
UAS	unmanned aerial system

Notes

1. The Fire Next Time

1. Rukmini Callimachi, "How ISIS Built the Machinery of Terror Under Europe's Gaze," *New York Times*, March 29, 2016.
2. Paul Cruickshank, "Raid on ISIS Suspect in the French Riviera," *CNN*, August 28, 2014.
3. "Jihad: Les services antiterroristes confrontés aux jeunes radicalisés de retour de Syrie," *Le Point* (France), February 12, 2014.
4. "Un supermarché casher attaqué à Sarcelles," *Libération* (France), September 19, 2012.
5. For the claim that Boudina had fought for Nusra, see Patricia Tourancheau, "Attaque de Terrorisme Probable Déchirée," *Libération*, March 27, 2014.
6. Callimachi, "How ISIS Built the Machinery of Terror."
7. Kim Willsher, "French Student Charged with Murder and Links to a Terrorist Organization," *Guardian* (London), April 24, 2015.
8. Greg Botelho, "Man Arrested in France in Plot to Attack Churches," *CNN*, April 22, 2015.
9. Kim Willsher and Tracy McVeigh, "U.S. Student Tells of His Attack on French Train Gunman," *Guardian* (London), August 22, 2015.
10. Katrin Bennhold, Steven Erlanger, and Ceylan Yeginsu, "Terror Alert in Britain Is Raised to Maximum as ISIS Claims Manchester Attack," *New York Times*, May 23, 2017.
11. Callimachi, "How ISIS Built the Machinery of Terror."
12. Quoted in Callimachi, "How ISIS Built the Machinery of Terror."

13. Michael Morell, *The Great War of Our Time: The CIA's Fight Against Terrorism from al Qa'ida to ISIS* (New York: Twelve, 2015), 180.

14. The White House, "Remarks of John O. Brennan, Assistant to the President for Homeland Security and Counterterrorism, on Ensuring al-Qa'ida's Demise—As Prepared for Delivery," June 29, 2011.

15. Fareed Zakaria, "Al-Qaeda Is Irrelevant," *CNN*, March 7, 2011.

16. Ian Black, "Al Qaeda Already Looked Irrelevant After Arab Spring," *Guardian* (London), May 2, 2011.

17. Fawaz Gerges, "The Rise and Fall of al-Qaeda: Debunking the Terrorism Narrative," *Huffington Post*, January 3, 2012.

18. Omar Ashour, "The Arab Spring Is al Qaeda's Winter," *Daily Star* (Lebanon), September 9, 2011.

19. Scott Shane, "As Regimes Fall in Arab World, al-Qaeda Sees History Fly By," *New York Times*, February 27, 2011.

20. Quoted in Daveed Gartenstein-Ross, "Interpreting al-Qaeda," *Foreign Policy*, January 6, 2014.

21. See, for example, Clint Watts, "One Year Later, ISIS Overtakes al-Qaeda: What's Next?," Foreign Policy Research Institute, April 8, 2015; Adam al-Sabiri, "Is an 'Islamic State in the Maghreb' Following in the Footsteps of ISIS?," *Al-Akhbar English*, October 23, 2014; "Al-Qaeda's Next Move: Battling 'the Islamic State' & Irrelevancy," The Soufan Group, July 3, 2014; and Barak Mendelsohn, "Collateral Damage in Iraq: The Rise of ISIS and the Fall of al-Qaeda," *Foreign Affairs*, June 15, 2014.

22. Kurt Eichenwald, "Iraq's ISIS Is Eclipsing al-Qaeda, Especially with Young Jihadists," *Newsweek*, July 7, 2014.

23. See Clint Watts, "Al Qaeda Loses Touch," *Foreign Affairs*, February 4, 2015.

24. See discussion in Daveed Gartenstein-Ross and Nathaniel Barr, "The Myth of Lone-Wolf Terrorism," *Foreign Affairs*, July 26, 2016.

25. See, for example, tweets from Scott Stewart, July 15, 2016, https://twitter.com/stick631/status/753945693010616320.

26. See discussion in Daveed Gartenstein-Ross, "Lone Wolves No More: The Decline of a Myth," *Foreign Affairs*, March 27, 2017; and Bart Schuurman, Lasse Lindekilde, Stefan Malthaner, Francis O'Connor, Paul Gill, and Noémie Bouhana, "End of the Lone Wolf: The Typology That Should Not Have Been," *Studies in Conflict & Terrorism* 42, no. 8 (2019): 771–78.

2. Learning to Win

1. Bruce Hoffman, *Inside Terrorism*, 2nd ed. (New York: Columbia University Press, 2006), 178–79.

2. For discussion of how jihadist groups and other violent non-state actors build resilience, see Derek Jones, *Understanding the Form, Function, and Logic of Clandestine*

Insurgent and Terrorist Networks (MacDill Air Force Base, Fla.: Joint Special Operations University, 2012).

3. Hoffman, *Inside Terrorism*, 178–79.

4. Hoffman, *Inside Terrorism*, 180.

5. Rita Gunther McGrath, "Exploratory Learning, Innovative Capacity and Managerial Oversight," *Academy of Management Journal* 44, no. 1 (2001): 119.

6. Gary Ackerman, "The Theoretical Underpinnings of Terrorist Innovation Decisions," in *Understanding Terrorism Innovation and Learning: Al-Qaeda and Beyond*, ed. Magnus Ranstorp & Magnus Normark (London: Routledge, 2015), 19.

7. Brian Jackson, John C. Baker, Peter Chalk, Kim Cragin, John V. Parachini, and Horacio R. Trujuillo, *Aptitude for Destruction*, Vol. 1: *Organizational Learning in Terrorist Groups and Its Implications for Combating Terrorism* (Santa Monica: RAND, 2005); and Brian Jackson, John C. Baker, Peter Chalk, Kim Cragin, John V. Parachini, and Horacio R. Trujillo, *Aptitude for Destruction*, Vol. 2: *Case Studies of Organizational Learning in Five Terrorist Groups* (Santa Monica: RAND, 2005).

8. Michael Kenney, *From Pablo to Osama: Trafficking and Terrorist Networks, Government Bureaucracies, and Competitive Adaptation* (Philadelphia: University of Pennsylvania Press, 2007).

9. Adam Dolnik, *Understanding Terrorist Innovation* (London: Routledge, 2007).

10. Magnus Ranstorp and Magnus Normark eds., *Understanding Terrorism Innovation and Learning: Al-Qaeda and Beyond* (London: Routledge, 2015).

11. The special issue was titled "How Terrorists Learn: Adaptation and Innovation in Political Violence."

12. Yannick Veilleux-Lepage, *How Terror Evolves* (Lanham, Md.: Rowman and Littlefield, 2020).

13. Charlie Winter, Shiraz Maher, and Aymenn Jawad al-Tamimi, *Understanding Salafi-Jihadist Attitudes Towards Innovation* (London: International Centre for the Study of Radicalisation and Political Violence, 2021); and James Barnett, Shiraz Maher, and Charlie Winter, *Literature Review: Innovation, Creativity and the Interplay Between Far-Right and Islamist Extremism* (London: International Centre for the Study of Radicalisation and Political Violence, 2021).

14. George Romme and Ron Dillen, "Mapping the Landscape of Organizational Learning," *European Management Journal* 15, no. 1 (1997): 69; and Chris Argyris and Donald Schön, *Organizational Learning: A Theory of Action Perspective* (Boston: Addison-Wesley, 1978), 9.

15. Mick Beeby and Charles Booth, "Networks and Inter-Organizational Learning: A Critical Review," *Learning Organization* 7, no. 2 (1994).

16. Jackson et al., *Aptitude for Destruction*, 1:2–3, 9.

17. David O'Sullivan and Lawrence Dooley, *Applying Innovation* (London: Sage, 2009). Their definition is also employed by John Allison in "Innovation and the Improvised Explosive Device (IED)," in Ranstorp and Normark, *Understanding Terrorism Innovation and Learning*, loc. 1779.

18. Louise Kettle and Andrew Mumford, "Terrorist Learning: A New Analytical Framework," *Studies in Conflict & Terrorism* 40, no. 7 (2017): 530.

19. Kettle and Mumford, "Terrorist Learning," 529–30.

20. George P. Huber, "Organizational Learning: The Contributing Processes and the Literatures," *Organization Science* 2, no. 1 (1991): 89.

21. Huber, "Organizational Learning," 89.

22. Huber, "Organizational Learning," 89.

23. Michael Tushman and Charles O'Reilly III, "Ambidextrous Organizations: Managing Evolutionary and Revolutionary Change," *California Management Review* 38, no. 4 (1996): 8–30.

24. For relevant scholarly definitions, see Charles M. Byles, Kenneth E. Aupperle, and Bernard Arogyaswamy, "Organizational Culture and Performance," *Journal of Managerial Issues* 3, no. 4 (1991): 512–27; Jeffrey W. Donnithorne, *Culture Wars: Air Force Culture and Civil-Military Relations* (Maxwell AFB: Air University Press, 2013), 21–38; Julianne Mahler, *Organizational Learning at NASA: The Challenger and Columbia Accidents* (Washington, DC: Georgetown University Press, 2009), 140–60; and Edgar H. Schein, "Culture: The Missing Concept in Organization Studies," *Administrative Science Quarterly* 41, no. 2 (1996): 229–40.

25. Tushman and O'Reilly, "Ambidextrous Organizations," 41.

26. Argyris and Schön, *Organizational Learning*, 3; Mark Dodgson, "Organizational Learning: A Review of Some Literatures," *Organization Studies* 14, no. 3 (1993): 385; and Michael Kenney, *Organizational Learning and Islamic Militancy*, NIJ award no. 2006-IJ-CX-0025 (September 29, 2008), 5.

27. Eric Schmidt and Jonathan Rosenberg, *How Google Works* (New York: Grand Central Publishing, 2014), loc. 2955, Kindle.

28. Kathleen Carley, "Organizational Learning and Personnel Turnover," *Organization Science* 3, no. 1 (1992); Jackson et al., *Aptitude for Destruction*, 1:37–38.

29. Tushman and O'Reilly, "Ambidextrous Organizations," 18.

30. James March, "Exploration and Exploitation in Organizational Learning," *Organization Science* 2, no. 1 (1991): 85.

31. Laurence Weinzimer and Candace Esken, "Learning from Mistakes: How Mistake Tolerance Positively Affects Organizational Learning and Performance," *Journal of Applied Behavioral Science* 53, no. 3 (2017): 323.

32. Clayton Christensen, *The Innovator's Dilemma: When New Technologies Cause Great Firms to Fail* (Boston: Harvard Business Review Press, 2000), xii.

33. Ackerman, "The Theoretical Underpinnings of Terrorist Innovation Decisions," 38.

34. Huber, "Organizational Learning," 88–115.

35. Kettle and Mumford, "Terrorist Learning," 531–32.

36. Huber, "Organizational Learning," 96–97; and Jackson et al., *Aptitude for Destruction*, 1:11.

37. Dodgson, "Organizational Learning," 386.

38. Huber, "Organizational Learning," 97.

39. Kettle and Mumford, "Terrorist Learning," 528; and Kenney, *From Pablo to Osama*, 135–66.

40. Sirous Panahi, Jason Watson, and Helen Partridge, "Information Encountering on Social Media and Tacit Knowledge Sharing," *Journal of Information Science* 42, no. 4 (2016): 539–50; Sirous Panahi, Jason A. Watson, and Helen Partridge, "Social Media and Tacit Knowledge Sharing: Developing a Conceptual Model," *International Journal of Social, Behavioral, Educational, Economic, Business and Industrial Engineering* 6, no. 4 (2012): 653; and Hong-Miao Zhu, Sheng-Tai Zhang, and Zhen Jin, "The Effects of Online Social Networks on Tacit Knowledge Transmission," *Physica A: Statistical Mechanics and its Applications* 441 (2016): 192–98.

41. Huber, "Organizational Learning," 97.

42. Huber, "Organizational Learning," 91.

43. John Meyer and Brian Rowan, "Institutionalized Organizations: Formal Structure as Myth and Ceremony," *American Journal of Sociology* 83, no. 2 (1977): 340.

44. Romme and Dillen, "Mapping the Landscape of Organizational Learning," 71.

45. Jackson et al., *Aptitude for Destruction*, 1:13.

46. Beeby and Booth, "Networks and Inter-Organizational Learning."

47. Beeby and Booth, "Networks and Inter-Organizational Learning," 78.

48. Jackson et al., *Aptitude for Destruction*, 1:16.

49. Argyris and Schön, *Organizational Learning*.

50. David Nadler and Michael Tushman, "Beyond the Charismatic Leader: Leadership and Organizational Change," *California Management Review* 32, no. 2 (1990): 77–97.

51. Carley, "Organizational Learning and Personnel Turnover."

52. Nicolaj Siggelkow and Daniel Levinthal, "Temporarily Divide to Conquer: Centralized, Decentralized, and Reintegrated Organizational Approaches to Exploration and Adaptation," *Organization Science* 14, no. 6 (2003): 655.

53. Calvert Jones, "Al-Qaeda's Innovative Improvisers: Learning in a Diffuse Transnational Network," *Cambridge Review of International Affairs* 19, no. 4 (2006): 563.

54. Jackson et al., *Aptitude for Destruction*, 1:37–39.

55. Christina Fang, Jeho Lee, and Melissa A. Schilling, "Balancing Exploration and Exploitation Through Structural Design: The Isolation of Subgroups and Organizational Learning," *Organization Science* 21, no. 3 (2010): 625–42.

56. Jones, "Al-Qaeda's Innovative Improvisers," 556.

57. Carley, "Organizational Learning and Personnel Turnover."

58. Carley, "Organizational Learning and Personnel Turnover," 22.

59. Daveed Gartenstein-Ross and Nathaniel Barr, "How al-Qaeda Works: The Jihadist Group's Evolving Organizational Design," *Current Trends in Islamist Ideology*, May 30, 2018.

60. Tushman and O'Reilly, "Ambidextrous Organizations."

61. Mary Benner and Michael Tushman explain exploration and exploitation units in ambidextrous organizations, noting that "exploratory units are small and decentralized, with loose cultures and processes, the exploitation units are larger and more centralized, with tight cultures and processes." Mary Benner and Michael

Tushman, "Exploitation, Exploration, and Process Management: The Productivity Dilemma Revisited," *Academy of Management* 28, no. 2 (2003): 238–56.

62. Tushman and O'Reilly, "Ambidextrous Organizations," 26.

63. Assaf Moghadam, "How al Qaeda Innovates," *Security Studies* 22, no. 3 (2013): 466–97.

64. Jackson et al., *Aptitude for Destruction*, 1:41–42.

65. Carley, "Organizational Learning and Personnel Turnover."

66. Fabrizio Perretti and Giacomo Negro, "Filling Empty Seats: How Status and Organizational Hierarchies Affect Exploration Versus Exploitation in Team Design," *Academy of Management Journal* 49, no. 4 (2006): 761.

67. Perretti and Negro, "Filling Empty Seats," 761.

68. Mohammed Hafez and Maria Rasmussen, *Terrorist Innovation in Weapons of Mass Effect: Preconditions, Causes, and Predictive Indicators* (Monterey, Calif.: Naval Postgraduate School, 2010).

69. Weinzimer and Esken, "Learning from Mistakes," 322–48.

70. Leigh Buchanan, "Rethinking Employee Awards," *Inc.*, July 5, 2011.

71. Shiraz Maher, *Salafi-Jihadism: The History of an Idea* (Oxford: Oxford University Press, 2016).

72. Paul Cruickshank, "Learning Terror: The Evolving Threat of Overseas Training to the West," in *Understanding Terrorism Innovation and Learning: Al-Qaeda and Beyond*, ed. Magnus Ranstorp & Magnus Normark (New York: Routledge, 2015), loc. 3838.

73. David Gilbert, "Rovio's 'Overnight' Success with Angry Birds Came After 51 Failed Attempts," *International Business Times*, July 1, 2014.

74. Eric Ries, *The Lean Startup: How Today's Entrepreneurs Use Continuous Innovation to Create Radically Successful Businesses* (New York: Crown Business, 2011).

3. The Far-Enemy Strategy

1. Osama bin Laden, "Declaration of Jihad Against the Americans Occupying the Land of the Two Holy Mosques," September 2, 1996.

2. Sohail H. Hashmi, "Enemies Near and Far: The United States and Its Muslim Allies in Radical Islamist Discourse," in *From Jeremiad to Jihad*, ed. John D. Carlson & Jonathan H. Ebel (Berkeley: University of California Press, 2012), 251. We came up with the title for this book before we encountered Hashmi's book chapter.

3. Steve Coll, *Ghost Wars: The Secret History of the CIA, Afghanistan, and bin Laden, from the Soviet Invasion to September 10, 2001* (New York: Penguin, 2004), 87–88.

4. Bruce Riedel, *The Search for al Qaeda: Its Leadership, Ideology, and Future* (Washington, D.C.: Brookings Institution Press, 2008), 42.

5. However, the CIA did work with some of bin Laden's allies, including Jalaluddin Haqqani.

6. See the founding minutes at http://intelfiles.egoplex.com/1988-08-11-founding-of-al-qaeda.pdf. For an extended discussion of al-Qaeda's organizational structure

at the time of its founding, see Daveed Gartenstein-Ross and Nathaniel Barr, "How al-Qaeda Works: The Jihadist Group's Evolving Organizational Design," *Current Trends in Islamist Ideology*, May 30, 2018.

7. Coll, *Ghost Wars*, 222.
8. Peter Bergen, *The Osama bin Laden I Know: An Oral History of al Qaeda's Leader* (New York: Free Press, 2006), 116.
9. This incident is famously chronicled in Mark Bowden, *Black Hawk Down: A Story of Modern War* (New York: Signet, 2001).
10. Bin Laden, "Declaration of Jihad Against the Americans."
11. Hashmi, "Enemies Near and Far," 260, quoting Osama bin Laden, *Messages to the World: The Statements of Osama bin Laden*, ed. Bruce Lawrence (London: Verso, 2005), 25.
12. Bin Laden, "Declaration of Jihad Against the Americans."
13. Bruce Riedel and Bilal Y. Saab, "Al Qaeda's Third Front: Saudi Arabia," *Washington Quarterly*, Spring 2008.
14. Riedel and Saab, "Al Qaeda's Third Front."
15. The most comprehensive work discussing these three regional jihads is Camille Tawil, *Brothers in Arms: The Story of al-Qa'ida and the Arab Jihadists* (London: Saqi, 2011).
16. Tawil, *Brothers in Arms*, 11.
17. Sayyid Qutb, *Milestones*, A. B. al-Mehri ed. (Birmingham, U.K.: Maktabah, 2006), 25.
18. Qutb. The term *jahiliya* is commonly used to describe Arabia in pre-Islamic times. The idea of *jahiliya* had been revived earlier in the twentieth century by Sayyid Abul A'la Maududi (b. 1903), who believed that Muslim societies had regressed back to this state largely because Western notions of modernity and liberalism had undermined the Muslim population's devotion to Islamic values. Maududi's revival of the term *jahiliya* had a deep impact on Qutb.
19. Qutb, *Milestones*, 93.
20. Qutb, *Milestones*, 93.
21. Qutb, *Milestones*, 27–28.
22. Qutb, *Milestones*, 28.
23. Muhammad Abd al-Salam Faraj, *Jihad: The Neglected Duty* (1980), 5.
24. Faraj, *Jihad*, 28.
25. Faraj, *Jihad*, 28.
26. Hashmi, "Enemies Near and Far," 253.
27. Muhammad Abd al-Salam Faraj, *al-Farida al-gha'iba*, quoted in Hashmi, "Enemies Near and Far," 253.
28. Thomas Hegghammer and Stéphane Lacroix, "Rejectionist Islamism in Saudi Arabia: The Story of Juhayman al-'Utaybi Revisited," *International Journal of Middle East Studies* (2007): 112.
29. The pamphlet is titled "Message on Amirship, Allegiance, Obedience and the Ruling on the Deceit of the Rulers Against the Students of 'Ilm and Populace" (1978).
30. Lawrence Wright, *The Looming Tower: Al-Qaeda and the Road to 9/11* (New York: Knopf, 2006), loc. 1672, Kindle ed.

31. Wright, *The Looming Tower*, loc. 1690.

32. There is little detailed information on the Hama assault. A useful overview of events is offered in Bill Rugh, "Syria: The Hama Massacre," Middle East Policy Council, n.d., available at http://www.mepc.org/commentary/syria-hama-massacre. Rugh, a former U.S. diplomat who was in Syria when the Hama assault occurred, contends that early journalistic accounts of the assault on Hama hyperbolized the scale of destruction. But he still concludes that "a few thousand lives had been lost, perhaps as many as 10,000." Cf. Thomas L. Friedman, *From Beirut to Jerusalem* (New York: Anchor, 1990), which presents a significantly higher estimate of deaths.

33. Abu Musab al-Suri, *The Syrian Experience* (1991), 145.

34. Ayman al-Zawahiri, *Bitter Harvest* (1988), 54.

35. Estimates for the mobilization in Syria (and by extension Iraq) since 2011 stood at some forty thousand fighters as of February 2018. By comparison, one estimate holds that thirty thousand foreign fighters mobilized to fight in Afghanistan. Thomas Johnson, "Financing Afghan Terrorism," in *Terrorism Financing and State Responses: A Comparative Perspective*, ed. Jeanne K. Giraldo & Harold A. Trinkunas (Palo Alto, Calif.: Stanford University Press, 2007), 102. Other estimates of the number of foreign fighters in Afghanistan are generally lower and there is no scholarly consensus on the matter.

36. Gregory Feifer, *The Great Gamble: The Soviet War in Afghanistan* (New York: Harper Perennial, 2009), 9–54.

37. Mohammed M. Hafez, "Jihad After Iraq: Lessons from the Arab Afghans Phenomenon," *CTC Sentinel* 1, no. 4 (March 2008).

38. Steven Brooke, "Strategic Fissures: The Near and Far Enemy Debate," in *Self Inflicted Wounds: Debates and Divisions Within al-Qa'ida and Its Periphery*, ed. Assaf Moghadam and Brian Fishman (New York: Combating Terrorism Center at West Point, 2010), 47.

39. For the definitive study on Azzam, see Thomas Hegghammer, *The Caravan: Abdallah Azzam and the Rise of Global Jihad* (Cambridge: Cambridge University Press, 2020). A well-reasoned guess about who killed Azzam can be found in Peter Bergen and Paul Cruickshank, "Revisiting the Early Al Qaeda: An Updated Account of Its Formative Years," *Studies in Conflict & Terrorism* 35, no. 1 (2012): 9.

40. Vahid Brown and Don Rassler, *Fountainhead of Jihad: The Haqqani Nexus, 1973–2012* (New York: Columbia University Press, 2013), loc. 194, Kindle.

41. Abdullah Azzam, "Defending Muslim Lands: The Most Important of the Obligations on Every Muslim" (1984), 39.

42. Lawrence Wright, "The Rebellion Within," *New Yorker*, June 2, 2008.

43. Sayyid Imam al-Sharif, *The Essential Guide for Preparation* (1988), 314.

44. Fawaz Gerges, *The Far Enemy: Why Jihad Went Global* (Cambridge: Cambridge University Press, 2009), 48.

45. Abdullah Azzam, "Al-Qaeda al-Sulbah," *Al-Jihad*, April 1988.

46. Peter L. Bergen, *The Longest War: The Enduring Conflict Between America and al-Qaeda* (New York: Free Press, 2011), 14.

47. Tawil, *Brothers in Arms*, 19.

48. Bergen, *The Osama bin Laden I Know*, 60.

49. See the founding minutes at http://intelfiles.egoplex.com/1988-08-11-founding-of
    -al-qaeda.pdf. A similar interpretation of these minutes can be found in Bergen
    and Cruickshank, "Revisiting the Early Al Qaeda," 5.

50. See the document at https://ctc.usma.edu/v2/wp-content/uploads/2013/10/Al
    -Qa'ida's-Structure-and-Bylaws-Translation1.pdf.

51. "Al-Qa'ida Goals and Structure," Harmony Document Database, Combating Ter-
    rorism Center at West Point, released February 14, 2006.

52. Jamal al-Fadl's testimony, day 2, *United States v. bin Laden* trial (S.D.N.Y., 2001),
    189–90.

53. Bergen, *The Osama bin Laden I Know*, 83–84.

54. Bergen, *The Osama bin Laden I Know*.

55. Brown and Rassler, *Fountainhead of Jihad*, loc. 688.

56. Brown and Rassler, *Fountainhead of Jihad*, loc. 764.

57. Brown and Rassler, *Fountainhead of Jihad*, loc. 880; and Jeffrey Dressler, *The Haqqani
    Network* (Washington, D.C.: Institute for the Study of War, 2010), 9.

58. Brown and Rassler, *Fountainhead of Jihad*, loc. 886.

59. Coll, *Ghost Wars*, 202.

60. Coll, *Ghost Wars*, 202; and George Crile, *Charlie Wilson's War: The Extraordinary Story
    of How the Wildest Man in Congress and a Rogue CIA Agent Changed the History of Our
    Times* (New York: Grove, 2003), 521. Haqqani openly complained when shipments
    of U.S.-made Stinger missiles were interrupted or seized by the Iranians or Sovi-
    ets. Rawhi Abeidoh, "Afghan Rebels Say Iran, Soviets Captured U.S. Stinger Mis-
    siles," UPI, October 29, 1987.

61. Crile, *Charlie Wilson's War*, 521.

62. Brown and Rassler, *Fountainhead of Jihad*, 78.

63. Brown and Rassler, *Fountainhead of Jihad*, 75–76.

64. Brown and Rassler, *Fountainhead of Jihad*.

65. Brown and Rassler, *Fountainhead of Jihad*, 92.

66. Quoted in Brown and Rassler, *Fountainhead of Jihad*, 93.

67. Brown and Rassler, *Fountainhead of Jihad*, 95.

68. Thomas Barfield, *Afghanistan: A Cultural and Political History* (Princeton, N.J.: Princ-
    eton University Press, 2010).

69. James McDougall, *A History of Algeria* (Cambridge: Cambridge University Press, 2017),
    305.

70. Gilles Kepel, *Jihad: The Trail of Political Islam* (Cambridge, Mass.: Harvard University
    Press, 2002), 174.

71. Abu Musab al-Suri, *Summary of My Testimony on the Jihad in Algeria* (2004), 71.

72. Vahid Brown, "Classical and Global Jihad: Al-Qa'ida's Franchising Frustrations," in
    Fault Lines in Global Jihad: Organizational, Strategic and Ideological Fissures, ed. Assaf
    Moghadam and Brian Fishman (London: Routledge, 2011), 98–99.

73. Quoted in Brown, "Classical and Global Jihad."

74. The crackdown is discussed in Hassanein Tawfik Ibrahim, "The Rise and Fall of Militant Islamic Groups in Egypt," in *Violent Non-State Actors in World Politics*, ed. Klejda Mulaj (New York: Columbia University Press, 2010).

75. Tawil, *Brothers in Arms*, 140.

76. Bureau of Intelligence and Research, U.S. Department of State, "The Wandering Mujahidin: Armed and Dangerous," August 21–23, 1993.

77. Anne Stenersen, *Al-Qaida in Afghanistan* (Cambridge: Cambridge University Press, 2017), loc. 48.

78. *9/11 Commission Report: Final Report of the National Commission on Terrorist Attacks upon the United States* (New York: Norton, 2004), 58.

79. See a confidential informant's account to U.S. authorities at http://intelfiles .egoplex.com/1999-09-16-FBI-FD302-confidential-informant.pdf.

80. "Bin Laden Wanted U.S. to Invade Iraq, Author Says," *ABC News* (Australia), August 24, 2007.

81. Bergen, *The Longest War*, loc. 486.

82. One letter from an unknown individual affiliated with al-Qaeda stressed the need to "expel them from Somalia, even if a semi-Islamic, semi-democratic, semi-etc. government were subsequently to assume power." First Letter of the African Corps Letters, available at https://ctc.usma.edu/app/uploads/2013/10/Five-Letters-to -the-Africa-Corps-Translation.pdf.

83. On al-Qaeda's possible role, see Bergen, *The Longest War*, loc. 486; and Evan F. Kohlmann, *Shabaab al-Mujahideen: Migration and Jihad in the Horn of Africa* (New York: NEFA Foundation, 2009), 4.

84. See Fadl's testimony, Day 2, *United States v. bin Laden*, 304. Numerous open-source accounts corroborated this claim.

85. UN Security Council, press release, "Security Council Demands Sudan Act to Extradite Suspects in Assassination Attempt of Egyptian President by 10 May, or Face Limited Sanctions," April 26, 1996.

86. *9/11 Commission Report*, 65.

87. Fadl's testimony, Day 2, *United States v. bin Laden*, 264–67.

88. Fadl's testimony, Day 2, 268.

89. Fadl's testimony, Day 2, 267.

90. Fadl's testimony, Day 2, 269.

91. CIA report, "Terrorism Fatwa Issued in 1992 by Usama Bin Ladin's Islamic Army to Attack U.S. Military in Saudi Arabia," January 8, 1997.

92. *9/11 Commission Report*, 147.

93. Quoted in Raffaello Pantucci, *We Love Death as You Love Life: Britain's Suburban Terrorists* (New York: Columbia/Hurst, 2013), 133.

94. See Suri, *Summary of My Testimony on the Jihad in Algeria*, 27.

95. Judgment of Mr. Justice Collins on Abu Qatada's Appeal Against His Detention in 2004, 11–12, https://web.archive.org/web/20050406083422/http://www.channel4 .com:80/news/ftp_images2/2004/03/week_4/23_document.pdf.

96. Javier Jordán, "Evolución organizativa de la militancia yihadista en España," Real Instituto, March 5, 2014.

97. "El atentado terrorista más olvidado," *El Pais*, April 18, 2010.

98. Oscar Peréz Ventura, "Mustafa Setmarian, el ideólogo de la yihad moderna," IEEE, March 24, 2014, 7.

99. Ventura, "Mustafa Setmarian."

100. Brynjar Lia, *Architect of Global Jihad: The Life of al-Qaeda Strategist Abu Musab al-Suri* (Oxford: Oxford University Press, 2009), 191.

101. Ahmed Rashid, *Taliban: Militant Islam, Oil and Fundamentalism in Central Asia* (New Haven, Conn.: Yale University Press, 2001), 21.

102. Rashid, *Taliban*, 25.

103. Numerous sources discuss the Inter-Services Intelligence's support for the Taliban. See, for example, Steve Coll, *Directorate S: The CIA and America's Secret Wars in Afghanistan and Pakistan* (New York: Penguin, 2018); and Robert Marquand and Scott Baldauf, "Will Spies Who Know Tell the U.S.?," *Christian Science Monitor*, October 3, 2001.

104. Bin Laden, "Declaration of Jihad Against the Americans."

105. Gerges, *The Far Enemy*, 170.

106. Sajjan M. Gohel, "Deciphering al-Zawahiri and al-Qaeda's Strategic and Ideological Imperatives," *Perspectives on Terrorism* 11, no. 1 (2017): 54–67.

107. Bergen, *The Osama bin Laden I Know*, 204–5.

108. Ali Mohamed plea appearance before Judge Leonard B. Sand, United States District Court for the Southern District of New York, October 24, 2000, 28.

109. *9/11 Commission Report*, 68.

110. *9/11 Commission Report*, 61.

111. Fadl's testimony, Day 2, *United States v. bin Laden* trial, 290.

112. Ali Mohamed plea appearance before Judge Sand, 6–27.

113. Mohamed plea, 30.

114. Gerges, *The Far Enemy*, 156.

115. Brown, "Classical and Global Jihad," 92.

116. Gilles Kepel and Jean-Pierre Milelli, eds., *Al Qaeda in Its Own Words* (Cambridge, Mass.: Harvard University Press, 2008), 201.

4. The Unfriendly Skies

1. The White House, press release, "At O'Hare, President Says 'Get on Board,'" September 27, 2001.

2. *9/11 Commission Report: Final Report of the National Commission on Terrorist Attacks upon the United States* (New York: Norton, 2004), 83.

3. Patt Morrison, "Patt Morrison Asks: Brian Michael Jenkins," *Los Angeles Times*, May 4, 2016.

4. Paul Wilkinson and Brian M. Jenkins, *Aviation Terrorism and Security* (London: Frank Cass, 1999).
5. Quoted in Alex Preston, "Fear of Flying: The Spectre that Haunts Modern Life," *Guardian* (London), December 28, 2014.
6. John Harrison, *International Aviation and Terrorism: Evolving Threats, Evolving Security* (Abingdon, U.K.: Routledge, 2009).
7. Quoted in Edmund L. Andrews and John Kifner, "George Habash, Palestinian Terrorism Tactician," *New York Times*, January 27, 2008.
8. Harrison, *International Aviation and Terrorism*, 50.
9. Yannick Veilleux-Lepage, *How Terror Evolves* (London: Rowman and Littlefield, 2020), 63.
10. Anwar al-Awlaki, "The Objectives of Operation Hemorrhage," *Inspire*, no. 3 (November 2010): 7.
11. Daveed Gartenstein-Ross, *Bin Laden's Legacy: Why We're Still Losing the War on Terror* (New York: Wiley, 2011), 172.
12. International Air Transport Association, "Aviation Benefits," 2017, https://www.icao.int/SAM/Documents/2018-ADPLAN/ICAO%20AVIATION-BENEFITS-2017-web.pdf, 9.
13. Jack Riley, "Terrorism and Rail Security," testimony before the Senate Commerce, Science, and Transportation Committee, March 2004.
14. U.S. Senate Select Committee on Intelligence and U.S. House Permanent Select Committee on Intelligence, *Joint Inquiry into Intelligence Community Activities Before and After the Terrorist Attacks of September 11, 2001* (2002), 212. Hereafter, *Joint Inquiry.*
15. *Joint Inquiry*, 213–14.
16. The August 6, 2001, PDB was prepared by the CIA in response to President Bush asking "his briefers whether any of the [terrorist] threats pointed to the United States." *9/11 Commission Report*, 260.
17. *Joint Inquiry*, 209.
18. *Joint Inquiry*, 211.
19. *Joint Inquiry*, 210.
20. *Joint Inquiry*, 212.
21. By December 1994 GIA had killed around eighty foreigners, including two dozen French citizens. Alan Riding, "The Militant Group Behind the Hijacking," *New York Times*, December 27, 1994.
22. Alan Riding, "Hijacked Airliner Forced to France," *New York Times*, December 26, 1994.
23. Thomas Sancton, "Anatomy of a Hijack," *Time*, June 24, 2001.
24. Tom Secker, "BBC Age of Terror Part 3," 2012, video featured on Vimeo, https://vimeo.com/33348459.
25. Julian Nundy, "Jet Hijackers Die as 170 are Freed," *Independent* (London), December 27, 1994.
26. Secker, "BBC Age of Terror Part 3."
27. Mike Perry, "Flight 8969: GIGN's Greatest Hour," SOFREP, April 26, 2012.

28. Samuel M. Katz, *Against All Odds: Counterterrorist Hostage Rescues* (Minneapolis: Lerner, 2004), 29.

29. Eleanor Hill, "Joint Inquiry Staff Statement, Part 1," testimony before the House and Senate Intelligence Committees, September 18, 2002.

30. Christopher S. Wren, "Plane Bombing Is Described in Terror Trial," *New York Times*, June 4, 1996.

31. *The 9/11 Commission Report*, 148; and Bill Roggio, "Mohammed Jamal Khalifa, Osama bin Laden's Brother-in-Law, Killed in Madagascar," *Long War Journal*, January 31, 2007.

32. Ryan Macasero, "Terror Attack on Cebu Flight to Japan Remembered," *Cebu Daily News* (Philippines), January 22, 2017.

33. Lawrence Wright, *The Looming Tower: Al-Qaeda and the Road to 9/11* (New York: Knopf, 2006), loc. 4338.

34. "Plane Terror Suspects Convicted on All Counts," *CNN*, September 5, 1996.

35. Philip Shenon, "F.B.I. Knew for Years About Terror Pilot Training," *New York Times*, May 18, 2002.

36. Shenon, "F.B.I. Knew for Years."

37. *9/11 Commission Report*, 148.

38. *9/11 Commission Report*, 153.

39. *9/11 Commission Report*, 147, 489.

40. *9/11 Commission Report*, 242.

41. See the discussion of terrorist entrepreneurs in Assaf Moghadam, "How Al Qaeda Innovates," *Security Studies* 22, no. 3 (2013): 466–97.

42. *9/11 Commission Report*, 149.

43. *9/11 Commission Report*, 154.

44. *9/11 Commission Report*, 154–55.

45. *9/11 Commission Report*, 225.

46. *9/11 Commission Report*, 226.

47. *9/11 Commission Report*, 231.

48. *9/11 Commission Report*, 234.

49. *9/11 Commission Report*, 243.

50. *9/11 Commission Report*, 248–50.

51. *9/11 Commission Report*, 249–52.

52. Pam Belluck and Kenneth Chang, "Shoes Were a 'Homemade Bomb,' F.B.I. Agent Says," *New York Times*, December 29, 2001.

53. "Richard Reid Pleads Guilty," *CNN*, January 22, 2003.

54. Thomas Joscelyn, "Egypt Requests Release of al Qaeda Explosives Expert," *Long War Journal*, August 2, 2012.

55. Joint Task Force-Guantanamo (JTF-GTMO) detainee assessment, SECRET/ / NOFORN / / 20330930, September 30, 2008, 7, https://media.miamiherald.com /static/images/escenic-images/gitmopdfs/us9eg-000535dp.pdf.

56. "Richard Reid Fast Facts," *CNN*, n.d., viewed April 3, 2020.

57. See Government Exhibit 450T, *United States v. Medunjanin*, No. 10-CR-019 (E.D.N.Y., 2012).

58. Mark Hughes, "Secret Life of Shoe Bomber Saajid Muhammad Badat Funded by the Taxpayer," *Telegraph* (London), April 23, 2012.

59. Michael Elliot, "The Shoe Bomber's World," *Time*, February 16, 2002.

60. Dan Verton, "Introduction to Improvised Explosive Devices," *Homeland Security Magazine*, October 3, 2017.

61. Philip Baum, *Violence in the Skies: A History of Aircraft Hijacking and Bombing* (West Sussex, U.K.: Summersdale, 2016).

62. C. J. Chivers, "Russians Cite Porous Security in Terror Bombings of 2 Planes," *New York Times*, September 16, 2004.

63. Julius Strauss, "Chechnya 'Black Widows' Linked to Sabotage of Russian Jets," *Telegraph* (London), August 28, 2004.

64. Florence Gaub and Julia Lisiecka, "Women in Daesh: Jihadist 'Cheerleaders,' Active Operatives?" European Institute for Security Studies, October 2016.

65. Valentin Anisimov, "Security Is Strengthened at Most Important Airport in Russia in Wake of Terrorist Attacks," *ICAO Journal* 62, no. 1 (2007): 24–25.

66. Bruce Hoffman, "The Terrorist Threat to Aviation: Back Again," *Cipher Brief*, April 26, 2017.

67. Richard Greenberg, Paul Cruickshank, and Chris Hansen, "Inside the Terror Plot That 'Rivaled 9/11,'" *NBC News*, September 14, 2009.

68. Nic Robertson, Paul Cruickshank, and Tim Lister, "Document Shows Origins of 2006 Plot for Liquid Bombs on Planes," *CNN*, April 30, 2012.

69. Greenberg et al., "Inside the Terror Plot that 'Rivaled 9/11.'"

70. Yochi Dreazen, "Al Qaeda in the Arabian Peninsula's Most Dangerous Man Is Still Alive," *Foreign Policy*, June 16, 2015.

71. "Detroit Bomber: Suspect Started Journey in Ghana, Nigeria Says," *Telegraph* (London), December 31, 2009.

72. Air Documentaries, "How Safe Are Our Skies? Detroit Flight 253," *YouTube*, February 11, 2015, https://www.youtube.com/watch?v=VBYImI4Dtn0.

73. Matthew Dolan, "'Underwear Bomber' Pleads Guilty," *Wall Street Journal*, October 13, 2011. *Mujahideen* is the plural of the term *mujahid*, or holy warrior. It isn't clear if the mistake in Arabic grammar was Abdulmutallab's or the FBI's.

74. Interview Summaries, *United States v. Abdulmutallab*, 1:15-CV-04829 (E.D. Michigan, transcribed December 26, 2009).

75. Government's Sentencing Memorandum, *United States v. Abdulmutallab*, 1:15-CV-04829 (E.D. Michigan, February 10, 2012).

76. Yochi J. Dreazen, "Foiled Bomb Plot Highlights Growing CIA-Saudi Arabian Ties," *National Journal*, May 9, 2012.

77. David Claridge, "Terrorist Act Sheds Light on Security and Intelligence," *World Policy*, November 4, 2010.

78. CNN Wire Staff, "Airports Tighten Security After Bomb Plot," *CNN*, November 1, 2010.

79. Julian Borger, Chris McGreal, and Tom Finn, "Cargo Plane Bomb Plot: Saudi Double Agent 'Gave Crucial Alert,'" *Guardian* (London), November 1, 2010.

80. Dreazen, "Foiled Bomb Plot Highlights Growing CIA-Saudi Arabian Ties."

81. "Bomb Plot Shows Weaknesses," *Airports International* 43, no. 8 (2010).

82. Robert Liscouski and William McGann, *The Evolving Challenges for Explosive Detection in the Aviation Sector and Beyond* (West Point, N.Y.: Combating Terrorism Center at West Point, 2016).

83. Fortunately, they had inadvertently defused the bomb during their earlier search. Paul Cruickshank, Nick Robertson, and Ken Shiffman, "How Safe Is the Cargo on Passenger Flights?," *CNN*, February 19, 2012.

84. Awlaki, "The Objectives of Operation Hemorrhage," 7.

85. "Technical Details: Ikrimah Al-Muhajir Explosives Department," *Inspire*, no. 3 (November 2010): 13.

86. Awlaki, "The Objectives of Operation Hemorrhage," 7.

87. Awlaki, "The Objectives of Operation Hemorrhage," 7.

88. "Letter to Uthman," n.d., Director of National Intelligence website, https://www.dni.gov/files/documents/ubl/english/Letter%20to%20Uthman.pdf.

89. Cruickshank et al., "How Safe Is the Cargo on Passenger Flights?"

90. "Bomb Plot Shows Weaknesses."

91. Michael Crowley, "Beware 'Underwear 2': TSA Chief Offers Rare al Qaeda Bomb Details," *Time*, July 19, 2013.

92. Crowley, "Beware 'Underwear 2.'"

93. There has been a strange inflation in the way public commentary refers to agents. Traditionally, the term *double agent* referred to an individual pretending to serve as a spy for one country or organization while in fact acting on behalf of its foe. Under that definition, the operative in the Underwear Bomb 2 case was simply an *agent* rather than a *double agent*. However, he is commonly referred to as a double agent. Similarly, Humam Khalil al-Balawi, who would be a double agent under traditional parlance, has been frequently called a *triple agent*, with a famous book written about him bearing that title. We employ the terminology of the day, while noting in this perhaps peevish footnote that it is rather ridiculous.

94. Daniel Klaidman, "Al Qaeda's Body Bombs: Al-Asiri's Next Threat," *Newsweek*, May 14, 2012.

95. Owen Matthews, "Metrojet Crash: Why the Insider Threat to Airport Security Isn't Just Egypt's Problem," *Newsweek*, May 24, 2016.

96. Zach Gold, *Salafi Jihadist Violence in Egypt's North Sinai: From Local Insurgency to Islamic State Province* (The Hague: International Centre for Counter-Terrorism—The Hague, 2016).

97. Andrew E. Kramer and Neil MacFarquhar, "Amid Vigils and Debris, Officials Seek Cause of Sinai Peninsula Crash," *New York Times*, November 1, 2015.

98. Quoted in Matthews, "Metrojet Crash."

99. Quoted in Matthews, "Metrojet Crash."

100. Hamza Hendawi, "Egypt Hopes to Revive Russian Tourism with Airport Upgrades," *Skift*, February 27, 2017.

101. Drazen Jorgic, "Somalia Plane Bomber Was Meant to board Turkish Flight: Airline Executive," Reuters, February 8, 2016.

102. Robyn Kriel and Paul Cruickshank, "Source: 'Sophisticated' Laptop Bomb on Somali Plane Got Through X-Ray Machine," *CNN*, February 12, 2016.

103. Harun Maruf, "Mogadishu Flights Safe from Laptop Attacks," *VOA News*, April 25, 2017.

104. Maruf, "Mogadishu Flights Safe from Laptop Attacks."

105. "Bomb Blast Strikes Somalia Airport," *Al Jazeera*, March 7, 2016.

106. Maruf, "Mogadishu Flights Safe from Laptop Attacks."

107. Evan Perez, Jodi Enda, and Barbara Starr, "New Terrorist Laptop Bombs May Evade Airport Security, Intel Sources Say," *CNN*, April 1, 2017.

108. Andrew Zammit, "New Developments in the Islamic State's External Operations: The 2017 Sydney Plane Plot," *CTC Sentinel* 10, no. 9 (October 2017).

109. Sean Rubinsztein-Dunlop and Suzanne Dredge, "Suspected Sydney Plane Bomb Plot Ringleader and Australian IS Terrorist Captured in Iraq," *ABC News* (Australia), April 18, 2018.

110. Rubinsztein-Dunlop and Dredge, "Suspected Sydney Plane Bomb Plot."

111. Jacqueline Williams, "Australia Details 'Sophisticated' Plot by ISIS to Take Down Plane," *New York Times*, August 4, 2017.

112. Paul Cruickshank termed this the IKEA model of terrorism. See transcript at http://www.cnn.com/TRANSCRIPTS/1708/05/cnr.22.html.

113. Rūta Burbaité, "Australian Airports to Undergo Massive Security Upgrade," *Aerotime News Hub*, May 7, 2018.

114. In some countries, particularly in the Middle East and Africa, airport security checkpoints have been moved to the entrances. Terrorists may still be able to target civilians outside these security perimeters, but in airports that have moved the checkpoints in this way, our point about ease of entrance and lack of checks is inapplicable.

115. Testimony of Ahmed Ressam, *United States v. Haouari*, S4-00 (S.D.N.Y., July 3, 2001).

116. Testimony of Ahmed Ressam.

117. The argument that Abu Zubaydah didn't officially join al-Qaeda rests on the claim that he never swore *bayah* to bin Ladin. David Rose, "Tortured Reasoning," *Vanity Fair*, December 2008; and Joby Warrick and Peter Finn, "Interviews Offer Look at Roles of CIA Contractors During Interrogations," *Washington Post*, July 19, 2009. There is no way to verify that this was the case, as *bayah* is a personal oath, given in private, often behind closed doors. Even if Abu Zubaydah didn't personally swear *bayah* to bin Laden, he worked closely with the al-Qaeda founder and his senior lieutenants, thus making claims that he wasn't really a member of the organization beside the point. Moreover, as a review board at Guantanamo has pointed out, Abu Zubaydah personally expressed his loyalty to bin Laden and al-Qaeda's cause in a video recovered in the wake of the 9/11

attacks. "We and the sheikh [bin Ladin] are one. We have been working together for almost 10 years, but we were hoping to keep this work secret . . . hidden. We were forced to make ourselves known because of what took place in Afghanistan and thereafter," Zubaydah said in the video. Periodic Review Secretariat, Department of Defense, "Unclassified Summary of Final Determination," September 22, 2016.

118. Testimony of Ahmed Ressam.

119. Testimony of Ahmed Ressam.

120. *9/11 Commission Report*, 180.

121. *9/11 Commission Report*, 180.

122. Testimony of Ahmed Ressam.

123. Testimony of Ahmed Ressam.

124. Testimony of Ahmed Ressam.

125. *9/11 Commission Report*, 174.

126. *9/11 Commission Report*, 175.

127. *United States v. Ressam*, 593 F.3d 1095, 1111 (9th Cir., 2010).

128. *United States v. Ressam*, 1100.

129. *9/11 Commission Report*, 261.

130. *9/11 Commission Report*, 177.

131. "Swiss Intel Foiled Terror Attack on Israeli Airliner, Prosecutors Say," Associated Press, June 8, 2006.

132. U.S. Department of Homeland Security, Office of Intelligence and Analysis (DHS) and Federal Bureau of Investigation (FBI), "Glasgow Airport Illustrates Varied Terrorist Tactics to Attack Transportation Infrastructure," Joint Homeland Security Assessment, July 2, 2007.

133. "Swiss Intel Foiled Terror Attack."

134. DHS and FBI, "Glasgow Airport Illustrates Varied Terrorist Tactics."

135. "Jordanian Court Sentences Three in Bomb Plot," Agence France-Presse, April 3, 2007.

136. "Jordanian Court Sentences Three."

137. Steven Brocklehurst, "The Day Terror Came to Glasgow Airport," *BBC*, June 30, 2017.

138. Raymond Bonner, Jane Perlez, and Eric Schmitt, "British Inquiry of Failed Plots Points to Iraq's Qaeda Group," *New York Times*, December 14, 2007.

139. Brocklehurst, "The Day Terror Came to Glasgow Airport."

140. Brocklehurst, "The Day Terror Came to Glasgow Airport."

141. Clifford J. Levy, "Moscow Attack a Test for Putin and His Record Against Terror," *New York Times*, March 29, 2010.

142. "Moscow Bombing: Carnage at Russia's Domodedovo Airport," *BBC News*, January 24, 2011.

143. Bill Roggio, " 'Black Widow' Female Suicide Bombers Kill 37 in Moscow Metro Blasts," *Long War Journal*, March 29, 2010.

144. Bill Roggio, "Caucasus Emirate Leader Threatens Russia with 'A Year of Blood and Tears,' " *Long War Journal*, February 6, 2011.

145. See *9/11 Commission Report*, 148, 160; UN Security Council Committee Pursuant to Resolutions 1267 (1999) 1989 (2011) and 2253 (2015) concerning ISIL (Da'esh) Al-Qaida and Associated Individuals Groups Undertakings and Entities, "QDe.100 Riyadus-Salikhin Reconnaissance and Sabotage Battalion of Chechen Martyrs (RSRSBCM)," September 6, 2016; and Andrew E. Kramer, "More of Kremlin's Opponents Are Ending Up Dead," *New York Times*, August 20, 2016.

146. Daren Butler and Margarita Antidze, "Two Suspects in Istanbul Attack Identified as Russian: Turkish Media," Reuters, July 1, 2016.

147. Butler and Antidze, "Two Suspects in Istanbul Attack Identified."

148. U.S. Department of the Treasury, "Treasury Sanctions Individuals Affiliated with Islamic State of Iraq and the Levant, and Caucasus Emirate," October 5, 2015.

149. Morgan Winsor, "Turkey Identifies Two of the Three Suicide Bombers in Istanbul Airport Attack," *ABC News*, July 1, 2016.

150. *Inspire*, November 2010, p. 7.

151. Researcher's interview with Kip Hawley, July 17, 2018.

5. The Early Adopter

1. Report of the DoD Independent Review, "Protecting the Force: Lessons from Fort Hood," January 2010. The review board did mention "self-radicalization" as an issue, but only in a generic sense and often in the context of a litany of other issues, such as suicide prevention, sexual assault, family violence, and workplace violence. See, for example, p. C-2.

2. Dana Priest, "Fort Hood Suspect Warned of Threats Within the Ranks," *Washington Post*, November 10, 2009.

3. "Final Report of the William H. Webster Commission on the Federal Bureau of Investigation, Counterterrorism Intelligence, and the Events at Fort Hood, Texas on November 5, 2009" (hereafter, "Webster Report"), 41. For the full exchange between Hasan and Awlaki, see J. M. Berger, "Anwar Awlaki E-Mail Exchange with Fort Hood Shooter Nidal Hasan," *Intelwire*, July 19, 2012, http://news.intelwire.com/2012/07/the-following-e-mails-between-maj.html.

4. The website (www.anwar-alawlaki.com) is no longer available.

5. Webster Report, 41.

6. Webster Report, 62.

7. FBI National Press Office, "Investigation Continues into Fort Hood Shooting," November 11, 2009.

8. "Yemeni-American Jihadi Cleric Anwar Al-Awlaki in First Interview with Al-Qaeda Media Calls on Muslim U.S. Servicemen to Kill Fellow Soldiers and Says: 'My Message to the Muslims . . . Is That We Should Participate in This Jihad Against America . . . ,'" Middle East Media Research Institute (MEMRI), Special Dispatch 2970, May 23, 2010.

9. Posted to www.anwar-alawlaki.com, December 11, 2008.

10. Webster Report, 67–68.

11. Donald Holbrook, "The Spread of Its Message: Studying the Prominence of al-Qaida Materials in UK Terrorism Investigations," *Perspectives on Terrorism* 11, no. 6 (2017): 90–91; Dana Janbek and Valerie Williams, "The Role of the Internet Post-9/11 in Terrorism and Counterterrorism," *Brown Journal of World Affairs* 20, no. 2 (2014): 297–308; Thérèse Postel, "The Young and the Normless: Al Qaeda's Ideological Recruitment of Western Extremists," *Connections* 12, no. 4 (2013): 9–118; and Anne Speckhard, "The Boston Marathon Bombers: The Lethal Cocktail That Turned Troubled Youth to Terrorism," *Perspectives on Terrorism* 7, no. 3 (2013): 64–78.

12. See, for example, Nicholas Sambanis, "What is Civil War? Conceptual and Empirical Complexities of an Operational Definition," *Journal of Conflict Resolution* 48, no. 6 (2004): 814–58.

13. Peter R. Neumann, "The Trouble with Radicalization," *International Affairs* 89, no. 4 (2013): 875.

14. Neumann, "The Trouble with Radicalization," 874. For other scholarly definitions of *radicalization*, see Clark McCauley and Sophia Moskalenko, "Mechanisms of Political Radicalization: Pathways Toward Terrorism," *Terrorism and Political Violence* 20, no. 3 (2008): 415–31; and David R. Mandel, "Radicalization: What Does It Mean?" in *Homegrown Terrorism: Understanding the Root Causes of Radicalization Among Groups with an Immigrant Heritage in Europe*, ed. Thomas Pick, Anne Speckhard, and Beatrice Jacuch (Brussels: Institute of Physics Press, 2009), 111.

15. Mohammed Hafez and Creighton Mullins, "The Radicalization Puzzle: A Theoretical Synthesis of Empirical Approaches to Homegrown Extremism," *Studies in Conflict & Terrorism* 38 (2015): 959.

16. Hafez and Mullins, "The Radicalization Puzzle," 959.

17. See Stefan Malthaner, "Radicalization: The Evolution of an Analytical Paradigm," *European Journal of Sociology* 58, no. 3 (2017): 382.

18. Malthaner, "Radicalization," 385 (in-text citations removed from quote).

19. Hafez and Mullins, "The Radicalization Puzzle," 959.

20. Eric Schmidt and Jonathan Rosenberg, *How Google Works* (New York: Hachette, 2014), loc. 3235–46.

21. Katelyn Y. A. McKenna and John Bargh, "Coming Out in the Age of the Internet: Identity 'Demarginalization' Through Virtual Group Participation," *Journal of Personality and Social Psychology* 75, no. 3 (1998): 681–94.

22. McKenna and Bargh, "Coming Out in the Age of the Internet."

23. Neil Coulson, "Receiving Social Support Online: An Analysis of a Computer-Mediated Support Group for Individuals Living with Irritable Bowel Syndrome," *Cyberpsychology & Behavior* 8, no. 6 (2005): 580–84.

24. Lynne Hillier, Kimberly J. Mitchell, and Michele L. Ybarra, "The Internet as a Safety Net: Findings from a Series of Online Focus Groups with LGB and Non-LGB Young People in the United States," *Journal of LGBT Youth* 9, no. 1 (2012): 234.

25. Neal Caren, Kay Jowers, and Sarah Gaby, "A Social Movement Online Community: Stormfront and the White Nationalist Movement," *Media, Movements, and Political Change* 33, no. 1 (2012): 163–93.

26. J. M. Berger, "Social Media and Terrorism," testimony before the Senate Homeland Security and Governmental Affairs Committee, May 7, 2015.

27. McKenna and Bargh, "Coming Out in the Age of the Internet"; see also Jeffrey Gavin, Karen Rodham, and Helen Poyer, "The Presentation of 'Pro-Anorexia' in Online Group Interactions," *Qualitative Health Research* 18, no. 3 (2008): 325–33.

28. See, for example, Choon-Ling Sia, Bernard C. Y. Tan, Kwok-Kee Wei, "Group Polarization and Computer-Mediated Communication: Effects of Communication Cues, Social Presence, and Anonymity," *Information Systems Research* 13, no. 1 (2002): 70–90.

29. Sia et al., "Group Polarization and Computer-Mediated Communication," 70.

30. Philip Zimbardo, "The Human Choice: Individuation, Reason, and Order Versus Deindividuation, Impulse, and Chaos," *Nebraska Symposium on Motivation* 1, no. 17 (1969): 237–307.

31. Tom Postmes, Russell Spears, and Martin Lea, "Breaching or Building Social Boundaries? SIDE-Effects of Computer-Mediated Communication," *Communication Research* 25, no. 6 (1998).

32. Tom Postmes, Russell Spears, Khaled Sakhel, and Daphne de Groot, "Social Influence in Computer-Mediated Communication: The Effects of Anonymity in Group Behavior," *Personality and Social Psychology Bulletin* 27, no. 10 (2001).

33. Russell Haines and Joan Ellen Cheney Mann, "A New Perspective on De-Individuation via Computer-Mediated Communication," *European Journal of Information Systems* 20, no. 2 (2011): 156–67.

34. Haines and Mann, "A New Perspective on De-Individuation."

35. Laurie Goodstein, "Influential American Muslims Temper Their Tone," *New York Times*, October 19, 2001.

36. Glenn Greenwald, "The Transformation of Anwar al-Awlaki," *Salon*, July 27, 2011.

37. Bob Orr, "Qaeda-Linked Imam Dined at Pentagon after 9/11," *CBS News*, October 21, 2010.

38. "Obituary: Anwar al-Awlaki," *BBC News*, September 30, 2011.

39. Bobby Ghosh, "How Dangerous Is the Cleric Anwar al-Awlaki?," *Time*, January 13, 2010.

40. Scott Shane and Souad Mekhennet, "Imam's Path from Condemning Terror to Preaching Jihad," *New York Times*, May 8, 2010.

41. Bruce Finley, "Muslim Cleric Targeted by U.S. Made Little Impression During Colorado Years," *Denver Post*, April 10, 2010.

42. Finley, "Muslim Cleric Targeted."

43. Cynthia Ghazali, "Anwar al-Awlaki, Al Qaeda Chief, Killed in Yemen by U.S. Airstrike: Timeline of His Life," *New York Daily News*, September 30, 2011.

44. U.S. Treasury Department Press Center, "United States Designates bin Laden Loyalist," February 24, 2004.

45. Mark Kukis, *"My Heart Became Attached": The Strange Journey of John Walker Lindh* (Washington, D.C.: Potomac Books, 2003); and Andrew Welsh-Huggins, *Hatred at Home: Al-Qaida on Trial in the American Midwest* (Athens, OH: Swallow Press/Ohio University Press, 2011), 73–78.

46. Anwar al-Awlaki, "A Question from a Reader on My Islamic Education," www.anwar-alawlaki.com, December 11, 2008.

47. *Joint Inquiry into Intelligence Community Activities Before and After the Terrorist Attacks of September 11, 2001* (2002), 178–79.

48. *9/11 Commission Report: Final Report of the National Commission on Terrorist Attacks upon the United States* (New York: Norton, 2004), 270–72, 353–55.

49. *9/11 Commission Report*, 215–16.

50. *9/11 Commission Report*, 215–16.

51. *9/11 Commission Report*, 216.

52. *Joint Inquiry into Intelligence Community Activities*, 178.

53. *9/11 Commission Report*, 218.

54. *9/11 Commission Report*, 155, 488.

55. *9/11 Commission Report*, 229–30.

56. *Joint Inquiry into Intelligence Community Activities*, 28.

57. *Joint Inquiry into Intelligence Community Activities*, 178.

58. *9/11 Commission Report*, 221.

59. Webster Report, 50.

60. Susan Schmidt, "Imam from Va. Mosque Now Thought to Have Aided Al-Qaeda," *Washington Post*, February 27, 2008. For background on the case against Timimi, see Indictment, *United States v. Timimi* (E.D. Va., September 2004).

61. Indictment, *United States v. Timimi*, 6.

62. Schmidt, "Imam from Va. Mosque Now Thought to Have Aided Al-Qaeda."

63. Alexander Meleagrou-Hitchens, *As American as Apple Pie: How Anwar al-Awlaki Became the Face of Western Jihad* (London: International Centre for the Study of Radicalisation and Political Violence, 2011). Our account of Awlaki's London years in this chapter draws heavily from Meleagrou-Hitchens's study.

64. For a discussion of Awlaki's early sermons, see Meleagrou-Hitchens, 47, 53.

65. Alex Hern, " 'YouTube Islamist' Anwar al-Awlaki Videos Removed in Extremism Clampdown," *Guardian* (London), November 13, 2017.

66. Indeed, in analyzing this lecture, we relied on a transcription that is easy to find online. See Imam Anwar al-Awlaki, "Constants on the Path of Jihad by Shaykh Yusuf al 'Uyayree," Lecture series, transcribed and edited by Mujahid Fe Sabeelillah.

67. J. M. Berger, "The Enduring Appeal of Al-'Awlaqi's 'Constants on the Path of Jihad,'" *CTC Sentinel* 4, no. 10 (October 2011).

68. Scott Shane, "Born in U.S., a Radical Cleric Inspires Terror," *New York Times*, November 18, 2009.

69. Berger, "The Enduring Appeal of Al-'Awlaqi's 'Constants.'"

70. Government's Sentencing Memorandum, *United States v. Abdulmutallab*, No. 2:10-cr-20005, E.D. Mich., February 10, 2012, 18.

71. Yassin Musharbash, "Jihad 101 for Would-be Terrorists," *Der Spiegel*, August 17, 2006.

72. Scott Shane, "The Enduring Influence of Anwar al-Awlaki in the Age of the Islamic State," *CTC Sentinel* 9, no. 7 (2016): 18.

73. Anwar al-Awlaki, "The Hereafter" lecture series, CD 7, https://archive.org/details/Hreafter/CD_07.mp3.

74. Anwar al-Awlaki, "The Hereafter" lecture series, CD 5, https://archive.org/details/Hreafter/CD_05.mp3.

75. Barbara J. Harner affidavit, *United States v. Daoud*, September 15, 2012, 9.

76. FBI Special Agent Joel T. Anderson, Affidavit in Support of Complaint, *United States v. Marquez* (C.D. Cal., December 17, 2015), 3.

77. Anderson, Affidavit in Support of Complaint, 7.

78. See Daveed Gartenstein-Ross, expert witness report, *United States v. Young*, E.D. Va., November 2017, 41.

79. Christopher Heffelfinger, "Anwar al-'Awlaqi: Profile of a Jihadi Radicalizer," *CTC Sentinel* 3, no. 3 (March 2010). For the copy of *39 Ways to Serve and Participate in Jihād* found in bin Laden's compound, see https://www.cia.gov/library/abbottabad-compound/2D/2D06F676D114500575E4A970D5915C33_39_WAYS_(LAST_PART).pdf.

80. Abdullah Azzam, "Defending Muslim Lands: The Most Important of the Obligations on Every Muslim," self-published, 1984.

81. *Inspire*, no. 4: 14.

82. *Inspire*, no. 13: 49.

83. *Inspire*, no. 2: 8.

84. Samir Khan, "I Am Proud to Be a Traitor," *Inspire* no. 2: 45–49.

85. Khan, "I Am Proud to Be a Traitor," 48.

86. Khan, "I Am Proud to Be a Traitor," 49.

87. Khan, "I Am Proud to Be a Traitor," 49.

88. *Inspire*, no. 1: 14.

89. "Interview with Shaykh Abu Sufyan, the Vice Amir of Al Qaeda in the Arabian Peninsula," *Inspire* no. 2: 43.

90. *Inspire*, no. 1: 17.

91. See Brynjar Lia, *Architect of Global Jihad: The Life of Al-Qaida Strategist Abu Mus'ab al-Suri* (New York: Columbia University Press, 2008).

92. Quoted in *Inspire*, no. 1: 49.

93. *Inspire*, no. 2: 20.

94. In one undated letter to al-Mauritani, for instance, bin Laden discussed at length his reasoning for striking inside the United States and at American targets elsewhere. Bin Laden's long missive was a reply to Mauritani's own correspondence. The letter was released during a Brooklyn terrorism trial in early 2015. See *FDD's Long War Journal*, https://www.longwarjournal.org/wp-content/uploads/2015/03/EXHIBIT-433-ENG-TRANS-EX-432-CB50B16B6-.pdf.

95. *Inspire*, no. 2: 21.

96. *Inspire*, no. 2: 20.

97. *Inspire*, no. 2: 52.

98. Nicole Engard, *Practical Open Source Software for Libraries* (Oxford, U.K.: Chandos, 2010).

99. Ann Larabee, *The Wrong Hands: Popular Weapons Manuals and Their Historic Challenges to a Democratic Society* (Oxford: Oxford University Press, 2015).

100. Emily Langer, "William Powell, the Author Who Later Renounced His Notorious Volume 'The Anarchist Cookbook,' Dies at 66," *Washington Post*, March 30, 2017.

101. *Inspire*, no. 1: 31–44.

102. Richard Valdmanis, "Boston Bomb Suspect Influenced by Al Qaeda: Expert Witness," *Reuters*, March 23, 2015.

103. See https://twitter.com/Al_firdausiA/status/311005838959595520.

104. Pete Williams and Erin McClam, "Search of Tsarnaev's Phones, Computers Finds No Indication of Accomplice, Source Says," *NBC News*, April 23, 2013.

105. U.S. Attorney's Office, Western District of Texas, "Naser Jason Abdo Sentenced to Life in Federal Prison," August 10, 2012.

106. Pierre Thomas, Martha Raddatz, Rhonda Schwartz, and Jason Ryan, "Fort Hood Suspect Yells Nidal Hasan's Name in Court," *ABC News*, July 29, 2011.

107. *Inspire*, no. 9: 30–36.

108. Office of Public Affairs, U.S. Department of Justice, "Faisal Shahzad Indicted for Attempted Car Bombing in Times Square," June 17, 2010.

109. Scott Shane and Mark Mazzetti, "Times Sq. Bomb Suspect Is Linked to Militant Cleric," *New York Times*, May 6, 2010.

110. *Inspire*, no. 1: 4.

111. *Inspire*, no. 6: 39; and *Inspire*, no. 8: 32–39.

112. *Inspire*, no. 4: 42–43; *Inspire*, no. 6: 37; and *Inspire*, no. 8: 29–31.

113. *Inspire*, no. 1: 41–44.

114. Ibrahim al-Rubaish, "Inspire Continues to Inspire," *Inspire*, no. 9: 6.

115. Government's Sentencing Memorandum, *United States v. Abdulmutallab*.

116. Government's Sentencing Memorandum, *United States v. Abdulmutallab*, 13.

117. One image of Abdulmutallab and Awlaki can be seen at *FDD's Long War Journal*, https://www.longwarjournal.org/18-05-01-screen-shot-of-anwar-al-awlaki-and -umar-farouk-abdulmutallab-from-abu-ubaydah-message-on-yemen.

118. Morten Storm with Paul Cruickshank and Tim Lister, *Agent Storm: My Life Inside Al Qaeda and the CIA* (New York: Atlantic Monthly Press, 2014).

119. Steve Swann, "Rajib Karim: The Terrorist Inside British Airways," *BBC News*, February 28, 2011.

120. Vikram Dodd, "British Airways Worker Rajib Karim Convicted of Terrorist Plot," *Guardian* (London), February 28, 2011.

121. Dodd, "British Airways Worker Rajib Karim."

122. Robert Graham, "How Terrorists Use Encryption," *CTC Sentinel* 9, no. 6 (June 2016).

123. "Al Qaeda's Anwar al-Awlaki Killed in Yemen," *CBS News* and Associated Press, September 30, 2011.

124. U.S. Department of Justice, Office of Public Affairs, "Member of Al Qaeda in the Arabian Peninsula Pleads Guilty to Terrorism Charges," January 8, 2016; and U.S. Department of Justice, Office of Public Affairs, "Member of Al Qaeda in the Arabian Peninsula Sentenced to 40 Years in Prison for Terrorism Charges," May 27, 2016.

125. Kim Willsher, "Charlie Hebdo Killings: 'Don't Be Afraid. I Won't Kill You. You're a Woman,'" *Guardian* (London), January 14, 2015.

126. Dan Reed, dir., *Three Days of Terror: The Charlie Hebdo Attacks* (HBO, 2016).

127. Wilson Andrews, Larry Buchanan, David Howley, Haeyoun Park, Sergio Peçanha, Patrick Smith, Archie Tse, Tim Wallace, and Karen Yourish, "Tracking the Aftermath of the Charlie Hebdo Attack," *New York Times*, January 9, 2015.

128. "Charlie Hebdo Shooter Says Financed by Qaeda Preacher in Yemen," Reuters, January 9, 2015.

129. Margaret Coker and Hakim Almasmari, "Paris Attacker Said Kouachi Knew Convicted Nigerian Airline Bomber," *Wall Street Journal*, January 11, 2015.

130. Scott Shane, "In New Era of Terrorism, Voice from Yemen Echoes," *New York Times*, January 10, 2015.

131. "Associate of Charlie Hebdo Attackers Jailed After Seven Years on the Run," *France 24*, December 27, 2018.

132. Sebastian Rotella, "How France Let the Charlie Hebdo Killers Go Free," *ProPublica*, July 12, 2017.

133. "Manhunt After Deadly Attack on Paris Newspaper," *CBS News*, January 7, 2015.

134. Sami Aboudi, "Al Qaeda Claims French Attack, Derides Paris Rally," Reuters, January 14, 2015.

135. Flemming Rose, "Why I Published Those Cartoons," *Washington Post*, February 19, 2006.

136. "Taliban Bounty for Killing Cartoonist," *Al Jazeera*, February 8, 2006.

137. Dan Bilefsky, "3 Arrested in Plot to Kill Cartoonist," *New York Times*, February 13, 2008.

138. Anil Dawar, "Intruder Shot at Home of Danish Cartoonist," *Guardian* (London), January 1, 2010.

139. "Al Qaeda Leader Offers Bounty for Swedish Cartoonist's Death," Associated Press, September 15, 2007.

140. "Transcript: Bin Laden Accuses West," *Al Jazeera*, April 23, 2006.

141. Scott Helfstein, *Deadly Vanguards: A Study of al-Qa'ida's Violence against Muslims* (West Point, N.Y.: Combating Terrorism Center at West Point, 2009).

142. Ayman al-Zawahiri, *The Exoneration: A Treatise Exonerating the Community of the Pen and the Sword from the Debilitating Accusation of Fatigue and Weakness* (Ekhlaas, 2008).

143. Inal Ersan, "Bin Laden Warns EU Over Prophet Cartoons," Reuters, March 19, 2008.

144. Qandeel Siddique, "Danish Embassy Bombing in Islamabad and Pakistan's Security Situation," FFI (Norwegian Defense Research Establishment), June 11, 2008.

145. Kim McLaughlin, "Danish Police Arrest 8 Muslims in Alleged Bomb Plot," Reuters, September 4, 2007.
146. Souad Mekhennet and Alan Cowell, "Qaeda Group Says It Bombed Embassy," *New York Times*, June 6, 2008.
147. John Shiffman, "A Vow Is Confirmed; A Jihad Grows—Jane's Jihad," Reuters, December 8, 2012.
148. John Shiffman, "U.S. Woman Known as Jihad Jane Sentenced to 10 Years in Plot," Reuters, January 6, 2014.
149. Meleagrou-Hitchens, *As American as Apple Pie*, 86.
150. Sebastian Rotella, "American Terrorist," *PBS Frontline*, April 21, 2015.
151. Rotella, "American Terrorist."
152. *Inspire*, no. 1: 21–28.
153. *Inspire*, no. 1: 26–28.
154. Alex Leo, "Matt Stone & Trey Parker Are Not Your Political Allies (No Matter What You Believe)," *Huffington Post*, April 27, 2010.
155. Dave Itzkoff, " 'South Park' Episode Is Altered After Muslim Group's Warning," *New York Times*, April 22, 2010.
156. Anwar al-Awlaki, "May Our Souls be Sacrificed for You," *Inspire*, July 2010, 28.
157. Itzkoff, " 'South Park' Episode Is Altered."
158. U.S. Attorney's Office, Eastern District of Virginia, "Leader of Revolution Muslim Pleads Guilty to Using Internet to Solicit Murder and Encourage Violent Extremism," February 9, 2012.
159. Quoted in U.S. Attorney's Office, Eastern District of Virginia, "Leader of 'Revolution Muslim' Sentenced to 138 Months for Using Internet to Solicit Murder, Encourage Violent Extremism," June 22, 2012, https://www.justice.gov/archive/usao/vae/news/2012/06/20120622mortonnr.html.
160. Muhammad al-Sana'ani, "Roshonara & Taimour: Followers of the Borderless Loyalty," *Inspire*, no. 4 (January 2011): 24.
161. Ibrahim Ibn Hassan al Asiri, "Charlie Hebdo: Military Analysis," *Inspire*, no. 14 (September 2015): 40–42.
162. Asim Umar, "The Dust Will Never Settle Down!," As Sahab Media in the Subcontinent, May 2015.
163. Umar, "The Dust Will Never Settle Down!"
164. Abu Muhammad al-Adnani, "This Is the Promise of Allah," Al-Hayat Media Center, June 29, 2014.
165. Abu Bakr al-Husayni al-Qurashi al-Baghdadi, "A Message to the Mujahidin and the Muslim Ummah in the Month of Ramadan," Al-Hayat Media Center, July 5, 2014.
166. Abu Muhammad al-Adnani, "Indeed, Your Lord Is Ever Watchful," September 21, 2014.
167. Dan Oakes, "Melbourne Shooting: What We Know About Abdul Numan Haidar, Shot Dead After Stabbing Anti-Terrorism Officers at Endeavour Hills," *ABC News* (Australia), September 24, 2014.

168. P. W. Singer and Emerson T. Brooking, *LikeWar: The Weaponization of Social Media* (Boston: Houghton Mifflin Harcourt, 2018).

169. Statista, "Number of Monthly Active Facebook Users Worldwide as of 4th Quarter 2018 (in Millions)," 2019.

170. *Dabiq*, no. 4: 43.

171. 'Isa Ibn Sa'd al-'Ushan, "Advice to the Mujahidin: Listen and Obey," *Dabiq*, no. 12: 9–10.

172. Sean Rubinsztein-Dunlop, "Mohammad Ali Baryalei: Australia's Most Senior Islamic State Member 'Loved Cocaine,' Found Islam After History of Abuse, Mental Illness," *ABC News* (Australia), September 25, 2014.

173. "Authorities Thwart 'Beheading' Plot in Australia's Biggest Ever Counter-Terrorism Raids," *ABC News* (Australia), September 18, 2014.

174. Ian Lloyd Neubauer, "A Teenage Terrorism Suspect Is Shot Dead in Australia After Attacking Police," *Time*, September 24, 2014.

175. Quoted in Thomas Joscelyn, "Islamic State Says Senior Official Killed in Aleppo," *FDD's Long War Journal*, August 30, 2016.

176. Allan Woods, "How Martin Couture-Rouleau Became an Aspiring Islamic State Fighter," *The Star* (Toronto), October 26, 2014.

177. Ian Austen and Rick Gladstone, "Gunman Panics Ottawa, Killing Soldier in Spree at Capital," *New York Times*, October 22, 2014.

178. Michael Schwartz and William K. Rashbaum, "Attacker with Hatchet Is Said to Have Grown Radical on His Own," *New York Times*, October 24, 2014.

179. "Sydney Siege Inquest: Man Haron Monis Was a 'Psychopathic Lone Wolf Terrorist,'" Associated Press, May 2, 2016.

180. "France Dijon: Driver Targets City Pedestrians," *BBC News*, December 22, 2014.

181. Aurelien Breeden and Alan Cowell, "France Puts More Troops on Streets After a String of Attacks," *New York Times*, December 23, 2014.

182. Nigel Duara, "Man Tied to Cartoon Contest Attack Accessed Islamic State List, Authorities Say," *Los Angeles Times*, December 24, 2015.

183. Eyder Peralta, "ISIS Claims Credit for Shooting in Garland, Texas," *NPR*, May 5, 2015.

184. Most of the details on the San Bernardino terrorist attack included here can be found at U.S. Department of Justice, "California Man Charged with Conspiring to Provide Material Support to Terrorism and Being 'Straw Purchaser' of Assault Rifles Ultimately Used in San Bernardino, California Attack," December 7, 2015.

185. U.S. Department of Justice, "California Man Charged with Conspiring."

186. Richard A. Serrano, James Rufus Koren, Richard Winton, and Corina Knoll, "Online Loan May Have Helped Couple Fund Their Terror Arsenal in San Bernardino Attack," *Los Angeles Times*, December 8, 2015.

187. U.S. Department of Justice, "California Man Charged."

188. For a summary of these reports and questions about their validity, see Tim Fitzsimons, "What Really Happened That Night at Pulse," *NBC News*, June 12, 2018.

189. U.S. Department of Justice, "Joint Statement from Justice Department and FBI Regarding Transcript Related to the Orlando Terror Attack," June 20, 2016.

190. "Mateen to News 13 Producer: 'I'm the Shooter. It's Me,'" *News 13 Florida*, June 15, 2016.

191. FBI Director James B. Comey, "Update on Orlando Terrorism Investigation," Press Briefing at FBI Headquarters, Washington, D.C., June 13, 2016.

192. Comey, "Update on Orlando Terrorism Investigation."

193. Comey, "Update on Orlando Terrorism Investigation."

194. The details concerning the attacks in New York and New Jersey recounted here can be found in the complaints filed in this case. See U.S. Department of Justice, "Ahmad Khan Rahami Charged in Manhattan and New Jersey Federal Courts with Executing Bombings in New York City and New Jersey," September 20, 2016.

195. Edgar Sandoval, Nicole Hensley, Ginger Adams Otis, Rocco Parascandola, and Rich Schapiro, "Explosive Fireball Rattles Chelsea Street Injuring 29, Secondary Pressure Cooking Device Found Blocks Away," *New York Daily News*, September 18, 2016.

196. Michael Wilson, "Key Evidence in Chelsea Bombing Trial: Articles on Building Bombs," *New York Times*, October 3, 2017.

197. Stephen Montemayor, "Before '60 Minutes' Interview, ISIL Defendant Abdirizak Warsame Detailed His Story in Unfinished Book," *Star Tribune*, October 29, 2016.

198. Mitch Smith and Richard Pérez-Peña, "Ohio State Attacker May Have Been 'Inspired' by Al Qaeda, F.B.I. Says," *New York Times*, November 30, 2016.

199. U.S. Department of Justice, "New York Man Pleads Guilty to Attempting to Provide Material Support to ISIS and Passport Fraud," February 21, 2018.

200. Marc Santora and Benjamin Weiser, "Bronx Man Accused of Trying to Join ISIS Is Arrested," *New York Times*, May 24, 2016.

201. U.S. Department of Justice, "Ohio Man Arrested on Terrorism Charge After Planning Attack on Jewish Synagogue," December 10, 2018.

202. Europol, "European Union Terrorism Situation and Trend Report 2019 (TE-SAT)," June 27, 2019, 29.

203. Europol, "European Union Terrorism Situation," 8.

204. Europol, "European Union Terrorism Situation," 30.

205. Europol, "European Union Terrorism Situation," 31–32.

206. Thomas Joscelyn, "AQAP Leader Calls for 'Simple' Attacks in the West," *FDD's Long War Journal*, May 8, 2017.

207. Joscelyn, "AQAP Leader Calls for 'Simple' Attacks in the West."

6. Strategic Learning

1. Rania Abouzeid, "Bouazizi: The Man Who Set Himself and Tunisia on Fire," *Time*, January 21, 2011.

2. Karem Yehia, "Q&A: Tunisian Policewoman Who 'Slapped' Bouazizi Says 'I Was Scapegoated by Ben Ali,'" *Ahram Online*, December 16, 2014.

3. The best account of the beginnings of the Syrian insurgency can be found in Emile Hokayem, *Syria's Uprising and the Fracturing of the Levant* (London: IISS/Routledge, 2013).

4. Michael Morell, *The Great War of Our Time: The CIA's Fight Against Terrorism from al Qa'ida to ISIS* (New York: Twelve, 2015), 186.

5. See page 153 of Osama bin Laden's personal diary, which was released by the CIA on November 1, 2017. The original diary, in Arabic, can be found at https://www .longwarjournal.org/archives/2017/11/read-osama-bin-ladens-handwritten -journal.php. For a comprehensive treatment of the public writings of salafi jihad-ist figures concerning the implications of the Arab Spring revolutions, see Daveed Gartenstein-Ross and Tara Vassefi, "Perceptions of the 'Arab Spring' Within the Salafi-Jihadi Movement," *Studies in Conflict & Terrorism* 35, no. 12 (2012): 831–48.

6. Letter from Osama bin Laden to Atiyah Abd al-Rahman, April 26, 2011.

7. "Zawahiri Praises Libyan Rebels, Eilat Attackers; Urges Algerians to Revolt," SITE Intelligence Group, October 11, 2011.

8. "Zawahiri Rallies for Jihad; Calls for Intellectual Debate, Advocacy," SITE Intelli-gence Group, August 15, 2011.

9. Ayman al-Zawahiri, "General Guidelines for Jihad," As Sahab Media, dated 1434 (2012–13).

10. Zawahiri sent a letter to al-Qaeda's wayward branch, ISIS, on September 4, 2013. It indicates that Zawahiri shared the guidelines with al-Qaeda's regional branches before publishing. The letter was originally published online at https://justpaste .it/asrarwkk.

11. Zawahiri, "General Guidelines for Jihad," 1.

12. Zawahiri, "General Guidelines for Jihad," 2.

13. Zawahiri, "General Guidelines for Jihad," 2.

14. Zawahiri, "General Guidelines for Jihad," 2.

15. See, for example, Steven Brooke, "Strategic Fissures: The Near and Far Enemy Debate," in *Self Inflicted Wounds: Debates and Divisions Within al-Qa'ida and Its Periph-ery*, ed. Assaf Moghadam & Brian Fishman (New York: Combating Terrorism Cen-ter at West Point, 2010), 48; Sajjan M. Gohel, "Deciphering al-Zawahiri and al-Qaeda's Strategic and Ideological Imperatives," *Perspectives on Terrorism* 11, no. 1 (2017): 56; and Sohail H. Hashmi, "Enemies Near and Far: The United States and Its Muslim Allies in Radical Islamist Discourse," in *From Jeremiad to Jihad*, ed. John D. Carlson & Jonathan H. Ebel (Berkeley: University of California Press, 2012), 262.

16. Zawahiri, "General Guidelines for Jihad," 2.

17. Zawahiri, "General Guidelines for Jihad," 2, 3.

18. Other al-Qaeda-connected organizations calling themselves Ansar al-Sharia were also eventually established in Pakistan and Syria, though they are less consequential.

19. Lawrence Wright, "The Man Behind bin Laden," *New Yorker*, September 8, 2002.

20. Wright, "The Man Behind bin Laden."

21. Wright, "The Man Behind bin Laden."

22. *Black Hole: The Fate of Islamists Rendered to Egypt* (Washington, DC: Human Rights Watch, 2005), 24.

23. Wright, "The Man Behind bin Laden."

24. See, for example, *Black Hole*, 24–25.

25. Lawrence Wright, *The Looming Tower: Al-Qaeda and the Road to 9/11* (New York: Knopf, 2006), 268.

26. Thomas Joscelyn, "Ansar al Sharia Egypt Founder 'Honored to be an Extension of al-Qaeda," *FDD's Long War Journal*, November 27, 2012. See also Jean-Pierre Filiu, "The Fractured Jihadi Movement in the Sahara," *Current Trends in Islamist Ideology*, January 10, 2014.

27. Islamic State, "The Murtadd Brotherhood," *Dabiq*, no. 14: 42.

28. As Sahab Foundation for Media Production, "Carry the Martyr's Weapon, Part 4," February 18, 2017.

29. "Westerners 'Will Burn First' Over Mali," *Euronews*, January 22, 2013, https://www.youtube.com/watch?v=ks1tJxZZySU.

30. "Mysterious Anti-Muslim Movie Prompts Protest in Egypt," Associated Press, September 11, 2012.

31. Matt Bradley and Dion Nissenbaum, "U.S. Missions Stormed in Libya, Egypt," *Wall Street Journal*, September 12, 2012.

32. "Protesters Attack U.S. Diplomatic Compounds in Egypt, Libya," *CNN*, September 12, 2012.

33. SITE Intelligence Group, "Ayman al-Zawahiri Gives Eulogy for Abu Yahya al-Libi," September 10, 2012. Just after Zawahiri boasted that al-Qaeda's message had "spread," the video cut to footage of Mohammed al-Zawahiri and Ahmed Ashush proselytizing in Egypt. See also Ayman al-Zawahiri, "A Lion of Knowledge and Jihad," As Sahab Media, September 10, 2012.

34. Helene Cooper and Robert F. Worth, "In Arab Spring, Obama Finds a Sharp Test," *New York Times*, September 24, 2012.

35. Donovan Slack, "Obama Warns Egypt, Thanks Libya," *Politico*, September 13, 2012.

36. Josh Rogin, "White House Clarifies Obama's Statement That Egypt is not an 'Ally,'" Foreign Policy, September 13, 2012.

37. Thomas Joscelyn, "Old School Egyptian Jihadists Linked to 9/11 Cairo Protest, Benghazi Suspect," *FDD's Long War Journal*, November 1, 2012.

38. Thomas Joscelyn, "US Strikes al-Qaeda's 'Khorasan Group' in Syria," *FDD's Long War Journal*, April 8, 2016.

39. See the tweet at https://twitter.com/CENTCOM/status/718465997011881985.

40. As Sahab Foundation, "Carry the Martyr's Weapon, Part 4."

41. U.S. Department of State, "Terrorist Designations of the Muhammad Jamal Network and Muhammad Jamal," October 7, 2013.

42. UN Security Council, "Security Council Al-Qaida Sanctions Committee Adds Two Entries to Its Sanctions List," October 21, 2013.

43. UN Security Council, "Security Council Al-Qaida Sanctions Committee."

44. Siobhan Gorman and Matt Bradley, "Militant Link to Libya Attack," *Wall Street Journal*, October 1, 2012.

45. Thomas Joscelyn, "Communications with Ayman al Zawahiri Highlighted in 'Nasr City Cell' Case," *FDD's Long War Journal*, February 10, 2013.

46. UN Security Council, "Security Council Al-Qaida Sanctions Committee."

47. Joscelyn, "Communications with Ayman al Zawahiri."

48. See the Arabic-language reporting at https://www.vetogate.com/871342.

49. David Barnett, "Former bin Laden Doctor Reportedly Heads al-Qaeda in the Sinai Peninsula," *FDD's Long War Journal*, July 17, 2013.

50. SITE Intelligence Group, "Zawahiri Praises Libyan Rebels, Eilat Attackers; Urges Algerians to Revolt," October 11, 2011.

51. Daveed Gartenstein-Ross, *Ansar Bayt Al-Maqdis's Oath of Allegiance to the Islamic State* (Wikistrat, 2015), 8.

52. "Ansar Beit Al-Maqdis Denies Pledging Allegiance to ISIS," *Daily News Egypt*, November 4, 2014.

53. Mustafa Basyouni, "Ansar Bayt al-Maqdis Tabaayi'e Daesh," *Al-Safir* (Lebanon), November 11, 2014.

54. Declan Walsh and Nour Youssef, "Militants Kill 305 at Sufi Mosque in Egypt's Deadliest Terrorist Attack," *New York Times*, November 24, 2017.

55. Tim Lister, "Why the Massacre of Muslims in Sinai Was Too Extreme for al-Qaeda," *CNN*, November 28, 2017.

56. "Deadly Fighting as Gadhafi Tries to Retake Rebel-Held Town," *CNN*, March 3, 2011.

57. Christopher S. Chivvis, *Toppling Qaddafi: Libya and the Limits of Liberal Intervention* (Cambridge: Cambridge University Press, 2013), loc. 1143, Kindle ed.

58. Chivvis, *Toppling Qaddafi*, loc. 1198.

59. Chivvis, *Toppling Qaddafi*, loc. 1223.

60. Chivvis, *Toppling Qaddafi*, loc. 1233.

61. Ivo H. Daalder and James G. Stavridis, "NATO's Victory in Libya: The Right Way to Run an Intervention," *Foreign Affairs*, March/April 2012.

62. "NATO's Intervention in Libya Deemed a Success," *NPR*, October 21, 2011.

63. Ken Dilanian, "U.S. Finds No Organized al-Qaeda Presence in Libya Opposition, Officials Say," *Los Angeles Times*, March 23, 2011.

64. Missy Ryan and Susan Cornwell, "Intelligence on Libya Rebels Shows 'Flickers' of Qaeda," Reuters, March 29, 2011.

65. Ryan and Cornwell, "Intelligence on Libya Rebels." Similarly, Robert Pape of the University of Chicago claimed: "There's no evidence that any of the leaders are extremists, and to the extent that we know anything, they seem to be secular professionals." Dilanian, "U.S. Finds No Organized Al Qaeda Presence."

66. Letter from Atiyah Abd al-Rahman to Osama bin Laden, April 5, 2011.

67. Thomas Joscelyn, "Osama bin Laden's Files: The Arab Revolutions," *FDD's Long War Journal*, March 3, 2015.

68. Joscelyn, "Osama bin Laden's Files."

69. Paul Cruickshank, "LIFG Revisions Posing Critical Challenge to Al-Qa'ida," *CTC Sentinel* 2, no. 12 (December 2009).

70. Charles Levinson, "Ex-Mujahedeen Help Lead Libyan Rebels," *Wall Street Journal*, April 2, 2011.

71. Ian Black, "Libya Rebels Reject Gaddafi's al-Qaida Spin," *Guardian* (London), March 1, 2011. Black reported that Qaddafi had accused Ben Qumu of seeking to establish an emirate in Derna. Noman Benotman, the former LIFG commander, noted that Qaddafi was warning the West that al-Qaeda could gain a "safe haven in Libya" without him in power. Benotman dismissed Qaddafi's claims regarding Ben Qumu and al-Qaeda as "just not credible." Qaddafi was a mass murderer but his allegations concerning Ben Qumu were legitimate. Ben Qumu and his men were key power brokers in the city for more than seven years after his role was initially reported. And yes, it served as a safe haven for jihadists during that time.

72. Frederic Wehrey, *The Struggle for Security in Eastern Libya* (Washington, D.C.: Carnegie Endowment for International Peace, 2012), 10.

73. "Al-Qaeda Backs Libyan Protesters and Condemns Gaddafi," Reuters, February 24, 2011.

74. *Al-Masra* newsletter, March 14, 2016, 4–5. Although *al-Masra* claimed to be an independent publication, it was actually produced by AQAP on behalf of al-Qaeda's senior leadership. *Al-Masra* acted as a clearinghouse for information on al-Qaeda's global efforts.

75. Combating Terrorism Technical Support Office's Irregular Warfare Support Program, *Al-Qaeda in Libya: A Profile* (Washington, DC: Library of Congress, 2012), 1.

76. Combating Terrorism Technical Support Office, *Al-Qaeda in Libya*, 1.

77. Combating Terrorism Technical Support Office, *Al-Qaeda in Libya*, 43.

78. Combating Terrorism Technical Support Office, *Al-Qaeda in Libya*, 11–12.

79. U.S. Department of State, "Designations of Foreign Terrorist Fighters," September 24, 2014, https://www.state.gov/j/ct/rls/other/des/266548.htm.

80. Combating Terrorism Technical Support Office, *Al-Qaeda in Libya*, 2.

81. Michael Morell, "The Real Story of Benghazi," *Politico*, May 11, 2015.

82. David Sanger, "Ex-C.I.A. Official Rebuts Republican Claims on Benghazi Attack in 'The Great War of Our Time,'" *New York Times*, May 3, 2015.

83. Ahmed Maher, "Meeting Mohammad Ali al-Zahawi of Libyan Ansar al-Sharia," *BBC*, September 18, 2012.

84. SITE Intelligence Group, "AQAP Senior Cleric Gives Eulogy for Leader of Ansar al-Shariah in Libya in Posthumous Audio," February 11, 2015.

85. Thomas Joscelyn, "Ansar al Sharia Libya Relaunches Social Media Sites," *FDD's Long War Journal*, April 9, 2015.

86. Thomas Joscelyn, "Ansar al Sharia Libya Relies on al-Qaeda Ideologues to Guide Followers," *FDD's Long War Journal*, February 2, 2016.

87. Report of the U.S. Senate Select Committee on Intelligence, *Review of the Terrorist Attacks on U.S. Facilities in Benghazi, Libya, September 11–12, 2012, Together with Additional Views* (2014), 40.

88. Report of the U.S. Senate Select Committee on Intelligence, *Review of the Terrorist Attacks*, 10–11.

89. UN Security Council Press Release, "Security Council Al-Qaida Sanctions Committee Adds Two Entities to Its Sanctions List," November 19, 2014, https://www.un.org/press/en/2014/sc11659.doc.htm.

90. UN Security Council, "Ansar Al Charia Benghazi" (QDe.146), November 19, 2014 (updated February 3, 2016), https://www.un.org/securitycouncil/sanctions/1267/aq_sanctions_list/summaries/entity/ansar-al-charia-benghazi.

91. Barak Barfi, *Khalifa Haftar: Rebuilding Libya from the Top Down* (Washington, DC: Washington Institute for Near East Policy, 2014), 3.

92. Sharif Abdel Kouddous, "A Q&A with Khalifa Hifter, the Mastermind behind Libya's New Revolt," *Washington Post*, May 20, 2014.

93. Aaron Y. Zelin, "The Rise and Decline of Ansar al-Sharia in Libya," *Current Trends in Islamist Ideology*, April 6, 2015.

94. U.S. Department of State, *Country Reports on Terrorism 2016*, chap. 2, "Country Reports: Middle East and North Africa," https://www.state.gov/reports/country-reports-on-terrorism-2016/.

95. Kevin Truitte, "The Derna Mujahideen Shura Council: A Revolutionary Islamist Coalition in Libya," *Perspectives on Terrorism* 12, no. 5 (2018): 10.

96. *Al-Masra* newsletter, March 14, 2016, 4–5.

97. Tarek Amara, "Two Dead as Protesters Attack U.S. Embassy in Tunisia," Reuters, September 14, 2012.

98. The State Department said that AST's leader, Abu Iyadh al-Tunisi, "was implicated as the mastermind behind the September 14 attack on the U.S. Embassy" in Tunis. U.S. Department of State, *Country Reports on Terrorism 2012*, chap. 2, "Country Reports: Middle East and North Africa Overview," https://2009-2017.state.gov/j/ct/rls/crt/2012/209982.htm.

99. Fabio Merone, "Salafism in Tunisia: An Interview with a Member of Ansar al-Sharia," *Jadaliyya*, April 11, 2013.

100. UN Security Council, "Tunisian Combatant Group" QDe.090, April 7, 2011 (updated February 3, 2016, and January 18, 2018).

101. UN Security Council.

102. John Tagliabue and Susan Sachs, "European Cell of al-Qaeda Cited in Killing of Massoud," *New York Times*, December 8, 2001.

103. U.S. Department of State, *Patterns of Global Terrorism 2001* (May 2002), 38.

104. Leo Sisti and Maud S. Beelman, "Arrested Italian Cell Sheds Light on Bin Laden's European Network," The Center for Public Integrity, October 3, 2001.

105. Sergio Galasso, "Intervista ad Hassan Ben Brik: 'Non crediamo nella democrazia, ma senza appoggio del popolo niente jihad,'" *Limes*, October 11, 2012.

106. See, for example, Merone, "Salafism in Tunisia"; and Daniel Nisman, "Tensions with Tunisia's Jihadists: Who Will Blink First?," *Huffington Post*, April 2, 2013.

107. Galasso, "Intervista ad Hassan Ben Brik."

108. For the best explication of the concept of *hisba*, see Michael Cook, *Commanding Right and Forbidding Wrong in Islamic Thought* (Cambridge: Cambridge University Press, 2010).

109. Monica Marks, "Youth Politics and Tunisian Salafism: Understanding the Jihadi Current," *Mediterranean Politics* 18, no. 1 (2013): 110.

110. Ahmed Jdey, "A History of Tunisia, January 14, 2011: The End of a Dictator and the Beginning of Democratic Construction," *boundary 2* 39, no. 1 (2012): 83–84.

111. Alison Pargeter, "Localism and Radicalization in North Africa: Local Factors and the Development of Political Islam in Morocco, Tunisia, and Libya," *International Affairs* 85, no. 5 (2009): 1036.

112. Aaron Y. Zelin, "The Night's Watch: Ansar al-Sharia Tunisia's 'Neighborhood Committees,'" *Al-Wasat*, February 11, 2013.

113. Daveed Gartenstein-Ross and Aaron Y. Zelin, "Uncharitable Organizations," *Foreign Policy*, February 26, 2013.

114. U.S. Department of the Treasury, "Kuwaiti Charity Designated for Bankrolling al Qaeda Network," June 13, 2008.

115. This discussion is adapted in part from Daveed Gartenstein-Ross, "Springtime for Salafists," *Foreign Policy*, March 26, 2013.

116. Nagwa Megahed and Stephen Lack, "Colonial Legacy, Women's Rights and Gender-Educational Inequality in the Arab World with Particular Reference to Egypt and Tunisia," *International Review of Education* 57 (2011): 397–418.

117. Simon Hawkins, "Who Wears *Hijab* with the President: Constructing a Modern Islam in Tunisia," *Journal of Religion in Africa* 41 (2011): 38.

118. Hawkins, "Who Wears *Hijab* with the President," 45–46.

119. Jamie Dettmer, "Tunisia's Dark Turn," *Daily Beast*, March 17, 2013.

120. Alexander Smoltczyk, "Islamist Intimidation: The Battle for the Future of Tunisia," *Der Spiegel*, December 5, 2012.

121. Smoltczyk, "Islamist Intimidation."

122. Sarah Leah Whitson, "Letter to Tunisian Minister of Interior and Minister of Justice," Human Rights Watch, October 14, 2012.

123. Sana Ajmi, "Clashes Between Salafists and Police in Northwestern City of Tunisia," *Tunisia Live*, February 22, 2012.

124. Andrew Gilligan, "Tunisia: Birthplace of the Arab Spring Fears Islamist Resurgence," *Telegraph* (London), May 28, 2011.

125. Smoltczyk, "Islamist Intimidation."

126. "Protesters Attack TV Station over Film Persepolis," *BBC*, October 9, 2011.

127. "Tunisia Salafist Autumn: Extremists Attack Nessma TV Chief's House," *Middle East Online*, October 15, 2011.

128. "Series of Attacks Against Tunisia Shrines Continues: Sufis Accuse Wahhabis," *Middle East Online*, January 23, 2013.

129. "Muslims Bid to Turn Christian Site into Mosque," Agence France-Presse, September 16, 2012.

130. "Tunisie—De nombreuses agressions à Zarzis dont celle de deux Italiens," *Business-news.com.tn*, March 21, 2013.

131. "Salafists Besiege Tunisian University: Dean, Professors Taken Hostage," *Middle East Online*, November 29, 2011.

132. Nura Suleiman, "The Disintegrating Fabric of Tunisian Politics: The Niqab Ban and Tunisian Flag Desecration at Manouba University," *Jadaliyya*, April 13, 2012.

133. Smoltczyk, "Islamist Intimidation."

134. "Sousse University Attack: Armed Group Attacks Tunisian College Because of Face Veils," *Huffington Post*, October 6, 2012.

135. "Tunisie: Lycée de Menzel Bouzelfa—Un directeur agressé par des salafistes," *All Africa*, April 11, 2013.

136. "Islamists Attack Tunisia Hotel Bar," Agence France-Presse, September 4, 2012.

137. Whitson, "Letter to Tunisian Minister of Interior and Minister of Justice."

138. Whitson, "Letter to Tunisian Minister of Interior and Minister of Justice."

139. Daveed Gartenstein-Ross interview with Human Rights Watch Researcher, Tunis, April 3, 2013.

140. "Tunisie: Décès de l'adjudant Anis Jelassi dans des affrontements à Feriana," *Global Net*, December 11, 2012.

141. "Groupes armés, Larayedh sonne l'alerte," *Directinfo*, December 21, 2012.

142. Andrew Lebovich, "Confronting Tunisia's Jihadists," *Foreign Policy*, May 16, 2013.

143. Paul Schemm, "Jihadis Threaten Tunisia's Arab Spring Transition," Associated Press, July 31, 2013.

144. Kareem Fahim, "Syria Blames al-Qaeda After Bombs Kill Dozens in Damascus," *New York Times*, December 23, 2011.

145. Roy Gutman, "How Assad Staged al-Qaeda Bombings," *Daily Beast*, December 2, 2016.

146. Jamie Dettmer, "Jihadists Are Creeping into Syria's Rebel Factions," *Daily Beast*, July 11, 2017.

147. "Unknown Islamist Group Claims Suicide Attacks in Syria," Agence France-Presse, February 29, 2012.

148. Michael R. Gordon and Wesley S. Morgan, "The General's Gambit," *Foreign Policy*, October 1, 2012.

149. Neil MacFarquhar, "Syria Wants U.S. to Lose War, Its Foreign Minister Declares," *New York Times*, March 31, 2003.

150. Ghaith Abdul-Ahad, "Outside of Iraq but Deep in the Fight," *Washington Post*, June 8, 2005.

151. Abdul-Ahad, "Outside of Iraq."

152. Abdul-Ahad, "Outside of Iraq."

153. MacFarquhar, "Syria Wants U.S. to Lose War."

154. *Face the Nation*, April 13, 2003.

155. John R. Bolton, "Syria's Weapons of Mass Destruction and Missile Development Programs," testimony before the House International Relations Committee, Subcommittee on the Middle East and Central Asia, September 16, 2003.

156. Quoted in Pub. Law 108-175, Syria Accountability and Lebanese Sovereignty Restoration Act of 2003, December 12, 2003.

157. Eric Schmitt and Thom Shanker, "Officials Say U.S. Killed an Iraqi in Raid in Syria," *New York Times*, October 27, 2008.

158. U.S. Department of the Treasury, "Treasury Designates Members of Abu Ghadiyah's Network: Facilitates Flow of Terrorists, Weapons, and Money from Syria to al Qaida in Iraq," February 28, 2008.

159. U.S. Department of the Treasury, "Treasury Sanctions Senior Al-Nusrah Front Leaders Concurrently with UN Designations," February 23, 2017.

160. Ragip Soylo, "U.S. Met Ahrar al-Sham, Islamic Front Officials in 2013, Former Ambassador Confirms," *Daily Sabah*, August 28, 2015; Josh Rogin, "Kerry Touts the Russian Line on Syrian Rebel Groups," *Washington Post*, July 12, 2016; and Robert S. Ford and Ali El Yassir, "Yes, Talk with Syria's Ahrar al-Sham," Middle East Institute, July 15, 2015.

161. Labib Al Nahhas, "The Deadly Consequences of Mislabeling Syria's Revolutionaries," *Washington Post*, July 10, 2015; and Labib Al Nahhas, "I'm a Syrian and I Fight Isil Every Day. It Will Take More Than Bombs from the West to Defeat This Menace," *Telegraph* (London), July 21, 2015.

162. Thomas Joscelyn, "Syrian Rebel Leader Was bin Laden's Courier, Now Zawahiri's Representative," *FDD's Long War Journal*, December 17, 2013; and Tim Golden, "Spain Arrests 3 Suspects; Tapes of U.S. Sites Seized," *New York Times*, July 17, 2002.

163. Tim Golden, "Al-Qaeda Money Trail Runs from Saudi Arabia to Spain," *New York Times*, September 21, 2002.

164. Basma Atassi, "Qaeda Chief Annuls Syrian-Iraqi Jihadi Merger," *Al Jazeera*, June 9, 2013.

165. Ayman al-Zawahiri, "We Shall Fight You Until There Is No More Persecution (Inshallah)," As Sahab Media, October 4, 2017.

166. Abu Bakr al-Baghdadi, "And Give Glad Tidings to the Believers," Al-Furqan Media Foundation, April 2013.

167. Abu Muhammad al-Julani, "About the Levantine Front," al-Manara al-Baydha' Media Foundation, April 2013; and SITE Intelligence Group, "Al-Nusra Front Leader Confirms Link to ISI, Pledges to Zawahiri," April 10, 2013.

168. Letter from Ayman al-Zawahiri to Abu Musab al-Zarqawi, July 9, 2005, https://fas .org/irp/news/2005/10/dni101105.html.

169. U.S. Department of the Treasury, "Treasury Designates Additional Supporters of the Al-Nusrah Front and Al-Qaida," August 22, 2014; and U.S. Department of Defense, "Statement on Airstrike in Syria that Killed Sanafi al-Nasr," October 18, 2015.

170. Al-Nusrah Front, "The Heirs of Glory," Al-Manara al-Bayda' for Islamic Media, June 26, 2015. See also Regis Debray, *Revolution in the Revolution? Armed Struggle and Political Struggle in Latin America* (New York: Grove, 1967).

171. UN Security Council, "Jund Al Aqsa" (QDe.156), July 20, 2017, https://www.un.org /securitycouncil/sanctions/1267/aq_sanctions_list/summaries/entity/jund-al

-aqsa; and David A. Weinberg, "Jund al Aqsa's Deep Gulf Roots," *FDD's Long War Journal*, November 18, 2016.

172. A transcript of Julani's speech can be found at https://www.longwarjournal.org/archives/2016/07/transcript-of-abu-muhammad-al-julanis-speech.php.

173. Daveed Gartenstein-Ross and Thomas Joscelyn, "Rebranding Terror: Nusra's Renaming Is Part of al-Qaeda's Plan," *Foreign Affairs*, August 28, 2016.

174. Ahmed Hassan Abu al-Khayr, deputy of Ayman al-Zawahiri, Audio speech, Al-Manara al-Bayda' for Islamic Media, July 28, 2016.

175. "Airstrike Kills al-Qaida-Linked Commander in Syria," Associated Press, October 3, 2016.

176. Thomas Joscelyn, "Analysis: Ayman al Zawahiri Calls for 'Unity' in Syria Amid Leadership Crisis," *FDD's Long War Journal*, December 2, 2017; see also Aymenn Jawad Al-Tamimi, "The Hay'at Tahrir al-Sham-al-Qaeda Dispute: Primary Texts," December 10, 2017.

177. Joscelyn, "Analysis."

178. Joscelyn, "Analysis."

179. Meir Amit Intelligence and Terrorism Information Center, "Fierce Dispute Between the Headquarters for the Liberation of al-Sham and al-Qaeda," December 6, 2017.

180. Thomas Joscelyn, "Hay'at Tahrir al-Sham and Hurras al-Din Reach a New Accord," *FDD's Long War Journal*, February 15, 2019.

181. Part of Ahrar al-Sham, a group known as Jaysh al-Ahrar, did initially joint HTS but eventually left the coalition.

182. Ayman al-Zawahiri, "Sham Will Submit to None Except Allah," As Sahab Media, April 23, 2017.

183. Ayman al-Zawahiri, "Let Us Fight Them as a Solid Structure," As Sahab Media, November 28, 2017.

184. U.S. Department of State, Office of the Spokesperson, "Amendments to the Terrorist Designations of al-Nusrah Front," May 31, 2018; and Ambassador Nathan A. Sales, "Keeping the Pressure on al-Qaida," remarks delivered at International Institute for Counterterrorism World Summit (Herzilya, Israel), September 12, 2019.

185. James Novogrod, "Al-Qaeda in Syria: Our Focus Is Assad, Not West," *NBC News*, May 27, 2015; and "Nusra Leader: Our Mission is to Defeat Syrian Regime," *Al Jazeera*, May 28, 2015.

186. Thomas Joscelyn, "Al Nusrah Front 'Committed' to Ayman al Zawahiri's 'Orders,'" *FDD's Long War Journal*, May 29, 2015.

187. Thomas Joscelyn, "Al Nusrah Front Celebrates 9/11 Attacks in New Video," *FDD's Long War Journal*, June 29, 2015.

188. Authors' conversations with several U.S. intelligence officials, September 2014.

189. Ken Dilanian and Eileen Sullivan, "Al-Qaida's Syrian Cell Alarms U.S.," Associated Press, September 13, 2014; Peter Baker, "In Airstrikes, U.S. Targets Militant Cell Said to Plot an Attack Against the West," *New York Times*, September 23, 2014; and Mark Mazzetti, "A Terror Cell That Avoided the Spotlight," *New York Times*, September 24, 2014.

190. See U.S. Department of the Treasury, "Treasury Takes Action to Stem Funding to the Iraqi Insurgency," February 15, 2005; and U.S. Department of the Treasury, "Treasury Further Exposes Iran-Based Al-Qa'ida Network," October 18, 2012.

191. Thomas Joscelyn, "Former Head of al-Qaeda's Network in Iran Now Operates in Syria," FDD's Long War Journal, March 25, 2014.

192. "Egypt 'al-Qaeda Linked Plot on Western Embassy' Foiled," BBC News, May 11, 2013.

193. Tom Perry and Yasmine Saleh, "Egypt Says Thwarts Suicide Attack on Foreign Embassy," Reuters, May 11, 2013.

194. U.S. Department of Defense, "Pentagon Official Confirms Death of Khorasan Group Leader," July 21, 2015.

195. U.S. Department of the Treasury, "Treasury Designates Additional Supporters of the Al-Nusrah Front and Al-Qaida," August 22, 2014.

196. U.S. Department of Defense, "Transregional Strikes Hit al-Qaida Leaders in Syria, Yemen, Afghanistan," November 2, 2016.

197. Thomas Joscelyn, "Pentagon: Al-Qaeda Veteran in Syria Was Planning Attacks Against the West," FDD's Long War Journal, November 2, 2016.

198. "Mevlut Mert Altintas: Turkish Policeman Who Shot Russia's Envoy," BBC News, December 20, 2016.

199. It is also possible that ISIS dispatched the assassin, although Baghdadi's organization was not part of the jihadist-Islamist coalition opposed to Assad in Aleppo at the time, and the group hasn't claimed responsibility for the slaying. Turkish authorities, including President Recep Tayyip Erdoğan, were quick to blame Fethullah Gülen and his movement. However, Erdoğan has his own domestic political reasons for blaming the U.S.-based Gülen, whom the Turkish president often alleges is behind a bevy of conspiracies in Turkey. The assassin's rhetoric was directly tied to the Syrian jihad, which has not been a Gülenist project, and the Gülenists have denied any ties to him. In sum, it has not yet been proven that any party, beyond the gunman, was responsible.

200. Hamza bin Laden, "Advice for Martyrdom-Seekers in the West," As Sahab Media, May 2017.

201. U.S. Department of State, Bureau of Counterterrorism, Country Reports on Terrorism 2017 (September 2018), 106.

202. Katibat Imam Shamil, "Statement Claiming Credit for the Saint Petersburg Operation," translated by the Global Islamic Media Front (GIMF), April 18, 2017.

203. Ayman al-Zawahiri, "Seven Years Later, Where Is the Salvation?," As Sahab Media, January 26, 2018.

204. Stephen R. Grand, Understanding Tahrir Square: What Transitions Elsewhere Can Teach Us About the Prospects for Arab Democracy (Washington, DC: Brookings Institution Press, 2014), 6.

205. Grand, Understanding Tahrir Square, 6.

206. Portions of Abu Iyadh's correspondence were reproduced in English by Abu Maysarah al-Shami, a top ISIS propagandist. See Abu Maysarah al-Shami, "The Jews of Jihad, Dhawairi's al-Qa'idah," 2016.

207. Thomas Joscelyn, "How a U.S. Citizen Became a Key Player in the Islamic State's Rivalry with al-Qaeda," *FDD's Long War Journal*, April 7, 2017.

208. "Libyan Forces Capture Egyptian Jihadist Hisham Ashmawi," *BBC News*, October 8, 2018.

209. Eli Lake and Josh Rogin, "Al-Qaeda Conference Call Intercepted by U.S. Officials Sparked Alerts," *Daily Beast*, August 7, 2013; and John Reed, "An Enlisted Airman Deciphered al-Qaeda's 'Conference Call' of Doom," *Foreign Policy*, September 18, 2013.

7. The Islamic State's Rise and Rule

1. Abu Bakr al-Husayni al-Qurashi al-Baghdadi, "A Message to the Mujahidin and the Muslim Ummah in the Month of Ramadan," Al Hayat Media Center, July 5, 2014. ISIS released the video of Baghdadi's sermon from Mosul on July 5, 2014, but it was recorded the previous day. Alissa J. Rubin, "Militant Leader in Rare Appearance in Iraq," *New York Times*, July 5, 2014.

2. "Foreign Fighter Fallout: A Conversation with Lt. Gen. Michael K. Nagata," Center for Strategic & International Studies (CSIS), April 5, 2017; UN Security Council, "Twenty-Fourth Report of the Analytical Support and Sanctions Monitoring Team Submitted Pursuant to Resolution 2368 (2017) Concerning ISIL (Da'esh), al-Qaida and Associated Individuals and Entities," June 27, 2019, 19; and Radicalisation Awareness Network (RAN) Manual, "Responses to Returnees: Foreign Terrorist Fighters and Their Families," July 2017, 15.

3. Ellen Francis and Rodi Said, "Hundreds of Islamic State Fighters Surrender in East Syria," Reuters, March 6, 2019.

4. U.S. Central Command (CENTCOM), "Historic Mosque Destroyed by ISIS," June 21, 2017.

5. The White House, Office of the Press Secretary, "Remarks of John O. Brennan, Assistant to the President for Homeland Security and Counterterrorism, on Ensuring al-Qa'ida's Demise—As Prepared for Delivery," June 29, 2011.

6. Sohail H. Hashmi, "Enemies Near and Far: The United States and Its Muslim Allies in Radical Islamist Discourse," in *From Jeremiad to Jihad*, ed. John D. Carlson & Jonathan H. Ebel (Berkeley: University of California Press, 2012), 264.

7. Michael W. S. Ryan, *Decoding Al-Qaeda's Strategy: The Deep Battle Against America* (New York: Columbia University Press, 2013), loc. 3362, Kindle ed.

8. Ryan, *Decoding Al-Qaeda's Strategy*, loc. 3390–91.

9. Ryan, *Decoding Al-Qaeda's Strategy*, loc. 3367–73.

10. Ryan, *Decoding Al-Qaeda's Strategy*, loc. 3405–06.

11. "Bin Laden Tape: Text," *BBC News*, February 12, 2003.

12. Fouad Hussein, *Al-Zarqawi: The Second Generation of al-Qaeda* (London, 2005, translated from Arabic), 7.

13. Mary Anne Weaver, "The Short, Violent Life of Abu Musab Al-Zarqawi," *Atlantic*, July/August 2006.

14. Brian Fishman, *The Master Plan: ISIS, al-Qaeda, and the Jihadi Strategy for Final Victory* (New Haven, Conn.: Yale University Press, 2016), loc. 207, Kindle ed.

15. Weaver, "The Short, Violent Life of Abu Musab Al-Zarqawi."

16. Weaver, "The Short, Violent Life of Abu Musab Al-Zarqawi."

17. Didier Francois, "Top Billing," *Libération* (Paris; original in French), June 13, 2005.

18. Fishman, *The Master Plan*, loc. 257.

19. George Michael, "The Legend and Legacy of Abu Musab Al-Zarqawi," *Defence Studies* 7, no. 3 (2007): 340.

20. *Al-Sharq al-Awsat*, March 8, 2004.

21. *Al-Sharq al-Awsat*, March 8, 2004.

22. *Al-Sharq al-Awsat*, March 8, 2004; and Hazim al-Amin, "Al-Zarqawi's Followers in Jordan Visit Their Shaykhs in Jail and Wait for the Chance to Join Abu Musab in Iraq," *Al-Hayah* (London; original in Arabic), December 14, 2004.

23. Hussein, *Al-Zarqawi*.

24. Jean-Charles Brisard and Damien Martinez, *Zarqawi: The New Face of Al-Qaeda* (New York: Other, 2005), 66.

25. Hussein, *Al-Zarqawi*.

26. Adl has framed himself as central to overcoming the initial skepticism that bin Laden and Zawahiri had toward Zarqawi. But bin Laden disputed this account and pointed to at least one factual error in Adl's recounting. Fishman, *The Master Plan*, loc. 459–63.

27. Hussein, *Al-Zarqawi*; Ari R. Weisfuse, "The Last Hope for the al-Qa'ida Old Guard? A Profile of Saif al-'Adl," *CTC Sentinel* 9, no. 3 (2016); and Brian Fishman, "Revising the History of al-Qa'ida's Original Meeting with Abu Musab al-Zarqawi," *CTC Sentinel* 9, no. 10 (2016).

28. Weaver, "The Short, Violent Life"; and Fawaz Gerges, *ISIS: A History* (Princeton, N.J.: Princeton University Press, 2016), 66.

29. Hussein, *Al-Zarqawi*; and Michael Weiss and Hassan Hassan, *ISIS: Inside the Army of Terror* (New York: Regan Arts, 2015), 13.

30. Weiss and Hassan, *ISIS*, 13.

31. See Saif al-Adl, "Jihadist Biography of the Slaughtering Leader Abu Musab al-Zarqawi," Global Islamic Media Front, 2005 (republished online 2009); and Weaver, "The Short, Violent Life."

32. EDCEF4DCF550215F956BA20DECA75191_003.WAV, released by CIA on November 1, 2017.

33. EDCEF4DCF550215F956BA20DECA75191_003.WAV, released by CIA on November 1, 2017.

34. A similar chart to that used here can be found in Aaron Y. Zelin, "The War Between ISIS and al-Qaeda for Supremacy of the Global Jihadist Movement," *Research Notes*, Washington Institute for Near East Policy, no. 20 (June 2014): 1.

35. CENTCOM Iraq papers, "Insurgent Group Profile: Al Qaeda in Iraq (AQI)," May 2, 2007, 10.
36. CENTCOM Iraq papers, "Insurgent Group Profile," 5.
37. CENTCOM Iraq papers, "Insurgent Group Profile," 3.
38. Ansar al-Mujahideen English Forum, "The English Translation of Biographies of the Prominent Martyrs, from the 46th Issue, Abu Maysara al-Iraqi," August 2010.
39. Ansar al-Mujahideen English Forum, "The English Translation of Biographies."
40. See an October 2005 letter from Zawahiri to Zarqawi, available at the Federation of American Scientists website, https://fas.org/irp/news/2005/10/letter_in _english.pdf.
41. A copy of the Zarqawi letter, February 2004, was translated by the U.S. government and posted on the U.S. State Department's website. See https://2001-2009.state.gov /p/nea/rls/31694.htm. For identification of Zarqawi as its author, see Dexter Filkins, "U.S. Says Files Seek Qaeda Aid in Iraq Conflict," *New York Times*, February 9, 2004.
42. Zarqawi letter, February 2004.
43. Jeffrey Pool, "Zarqawi's Pledge of Allegiance to Al-Qaeda: From Mu'asker Al-Battar, Issue 21," *Terrorism Monitor* (Jamestown Foundation) 2, no. 24 (December 16, 2004).
44. CENTCOM Iraq papers, 3.
45. Christopher M. Blanchard, *Al Qaeda: Statements and Evolving Ideology* (Washington, DC: Congressional Research Service, 2007), 7.
46. Letter from Ayman al-Zawahiri to Abu Musab al-Zarqawi, July 9, 2005, available at the Federation of American Scientists website, https://fas.org/irp/news/2005/10 /letter_in_english.pdf.
47. A copy of Atiyah's letter to Zarqawi (2005) is available at the Combating Terrorism Center at West Point website, https://ctc.usma.edu/harmony-program/atiyahs -letter-to-zarqawi-original-language-2/.
48. Atiyah's letter to Zarqawi.
49. Atiyah's letter to Zarqawi.
50. Muhammad al-'Ubaydi, Nelly Lahoud, Daniel Milton, and Bryan Price, *The Group That Calls Itself a State: Understanding the Evolution and Challengers of the Islamic State* (West Point, N.Y.: Combating Terrorism Center, 2014).
51. Fishman, *The Master Plan*, loc. 151.
52. Fishman, *The Master Plan*, loc. 79.
53. The CIA released the four-page memo on November 1, 2017. It was separated into four different image files.
54. CIA four-page memo, November 1, 2017.
55. Fishman, *The Master Plan*, loc. 1794.
56. Fishman, *The Master Plan*, loc. 1801–08.
57. MEMRI, Islamist Websites Monitor No. 8, "Jihad Groups in Iraq Take an Oath of Allegiance," October 17, 2006.
58. MEMRI, "Jihad Groups in Iraq Take an Oath."
59. CENTCOM Iraq papers, "Insurgent Group Profile," 9.

60. Muhajir went by more than one alias, including Abu Ayyub al-Masri and Yusif al-Dardiri. U.S. officials identified the latter nom de guerre as one of Muhajir's aliases following Zarqawi's death. Ellen Knickmeyer and Jonathan Finer, "Maliki Aide Who Discussed Amnesty Leaves Job," *Washington Post*, June 16, 2006. Former CIA director George Tenet explains that U.S. intelligence officials tracked Dardiri and another veteran al-Qaeda operative, Thirwat Shihata, in Baghdad as of "mid-May of 2002." Tenet wrote that their "activity in sending recruits to train in Zarqawi's camps was compelling enough," but there "was also concern that" Dardiri and Shihata "might be planning operations outside of Iraq." Tenet went on to explain that "credible information" indicated that Shihata "was willing to strike U.S., Israeli, and Egyptian targets sometime in the future." George Tenet, *At the Center of the Storm: My Years at the CIA* (New York: HarperCollins, 2007), 351. Weeks after Muhajir's death in April 2010, his wife confirmed that he arrived in Baghdad in 2002. "Slain Qaeda Commander Arrived in Iraq Under Saddam: Widow," Agence France-Presse, April 28, 2010.

61. CENTCOM Iraq papers, "Insurgent Group Profile: Al Qaeda in Iraq (AQI)," 9.

62. Abu Hamza al-Muhajir, "The Command Is for None but Allah," November 2006.

63. For more on the importance of Qurayshi lineage from the jihadist perspective, see Nibras Kazimi, "The Caliphate Attempted: Zarqawi's Ideological Heirs, Their Choice for a Caliph, and the Collapse of Their Self-Styled Islamic State of Iraq," *Current Trends in Islamist Ideology*, July 1, 2008. For more on Baghdadi's claim of Qurayshi lineage, see Gérard Chaliand, "Jihadism in the Age of ISIS," in *The History of Terrorism: From Antiquity to ISIS*, ed. Gérard Chaliand & Blin Arnaud (Oakland: University of California Press, 2016), 441.

64. On the ISIS side, the group's spokesman, Abu Muhammad al-Adnani, made this claim in 2014. As explained elsewhere in this chapter, Adnani's version of events is riddled with logical inconsistencies. Much of his testimony actually confirmed that ISI continued to operate as part of al-Qaeda's network. As for Western analysts advancing this argument, see Zelin, "The War Between ISIS and al-Qaeda," 3.

65. "Hot Issues Interview with Sheikh Ayman al-Zawahiri," As Sahab Media Production, September 11, 2006. A translation of the interview can be found at https://scholarship.tricolib.brynmawr.edu/bitstream/handle/10066/5094/ZAW20060912.pdf?sequence=3&isAllowed=y.

66. "Hot Issues Interview with Sheikh Ayman al-Zawahiri."

67. Abu Hamza al-Muhajir, "Soon Will Their Multitude be Put to Flight, and They Will Show Their Backs," Media Division of the Mujahidin Shura Council, September 7, 2006.

68. Ayman al-Zawahiri, "The Advice of One Concerned," July 4, 2007, available at the SITE Intelligence Group website, https://ent.siteintelgroup.com/Jihadist-News/site-intel-group-7-4-07-zawahiri-advice-concerned-sahab-video-72007-p.html.

69. Letter to Atiyah Abd-al-Rahman "Senior Shaykhs and Other Issues Pertaining to the Arabian Peninsula," early 2000, SOCOM-2012-0000014, at the Combating

Terrorism Center at West Point website, https://ctc.usma.edu/letters-from
-abbottabad-bin-ladin-sidelined/.

70. U.S. Department of the Treasury, "Treasury Designations Target Terrorist Facilitators," December 7, 2006.

71. "Letter to Shaykh Abu Muhammad 17 August 2007," released by ODNI, https://www
.dni.gov/files/documents/ubl2016/english/Letter%20to%20Shaykh%20Abu%20
Muhammad%2017%20August%202007.pdf.

72. "Letter to Shaykh Abu Muhammad 17 August 2007."

73. Bill Roggio, "Who Is Abu Omar al Baghdadi?," FDD's Long War Journal, September 14, 2008.

74. The biography was authored by a jihadist known as Abu Usama al-Iraqi and posted online by the Global Jihad Network in 2012. Craig Whiteside has posted an English-language translation on his personal website, at https://whitesidenwc.wordpress
.com/2016/05/25/biography-of-abu-omar-al-baghdadi/.

75. Osama bin Laden, "The Way to Contain the Conspiracies," December 29, 2007, available at SITE Intelligence Group website, https://ent.siteintelgroup.com/Jihadist-News
/site-intel-group-12-30-07-sahab-ubl-audio-contain-conspiracies-1207.html.

76. Bin Laden, "The Way to Contain the Conspiracies."

77. The interview appeared online on April 22, 2008.

78. In an August 3, 2009, interview, for example, Zawahiri argued that ISI was built on "proper doctrine and firm methodology."

79. "Letter to Karim," October 18, 2007, https://www.dni.gov/files/documents/ubl2016
/english/Letter%20to%20Karim.pdf.

80. Bill Roggio, Daveed Gartenstein-Ross, and Tony Badran, "Intercepted Letters from al-Qaeda Leaders Shed Light on State of Network in Iraq," Foundation for Defense of Democracies, September 12, 2008.

81. Bill Roggio, "Al Qaeda Operatives Killed in Afghanistan Were Saudis," FDD's Long War Journal, May 13, 2008.

82. For example, "Letter to Ansar Al-Sunnah Group," June 9, 2006, https://www.dni
.gov/files/documents/ubl/english/Letter%20Ansar%20Al-Sunnah%20Group.pdf.

83. Letter from the Special Committee of al-Jihad's Qaeda of the Mujahedin Affairs in Iraq to Ansar al-Sunna, January 29, 2006, https://www.dni.gov/files/documents
/ubl/english/Letter%20to%20Special%20Committee%20of%20al-Jihads%20
Qaida%20of%20the%20Mujahidin%20Affairs%20in%20Iraq%20and%20to%20
the%20Ansar%20al-Sunnah%20Army.pdf.

84. "Letter from Abu Hamza al-Muhajir to Abi 'Abdullah al-Shafi'i," NMEC-2007-636898,
https://ctc.usma.edu/app/uploads/2013/09/Letter-from-Abu-Hamza-al-Mujahir
-to-Abi-Abdullah-al-Shafi%E2%80%99ee-Translation.pdf.

85. Islamic State of Iraq, "Return to the Mountains," released by Al-Furqan Foundation for Media Production, March 14, 2007.

86. U.S. Department of State, "Terrorist Designation of the al-Qaida Kurdish Battalions," January 5, 2012.

87. For instance, Al Furqan's "Rising from the Dead" series included outward expressions of fidelity to al-Qaeda. An ISI martyr said in the first episode of the series: "I pray to God to champion this religion, protect our mujahid shaykh Abu Abdallah Osama bin Laden and our emir Abu Hamza al-Muhajir (may God protect him). I do not forget to pray for our shaykh Mullah Omar. . . . I renew my allegiance to our guardian and imam, the emir of the Islamic State of Iraq, Abu Umar al-Baghdadi. I say to him: We remain true to the pledge." Other Al Furqan Media videos also continued to incorporate references to al-Qaeda and its leadership of the global jihad.

88. "Announcing the Second Cabinet Formation of the Islamic State of Iraq," September 21, 2009. The video was posted online by Al Fajr Media Center, which acted as a clearinghouse for al-Qaeda's messaging.

89. "Announcing the Second Cabinet Formation."

90. *Al-Bayyina al-Jadida* (Arabic), September 20, 2006.

91. Mohammed Abbas, "Al Qaeda's Brutality and Edicts Alienate Iraqis," Reuters, August 8, 2008.

92. Jonathan Karl, "Troop Surge Already Under Way," *ABC News*, January 10, 2007. One of this book's coauthors spent the night in a joint security station in May 2007.

93. Gen. David H. Petraeus, "Report to Congress on the Situation in Iraq," September 10–11, 2007, https://apps.dtic.mil/sti/pdfs/ADA473579.pdf, 5.

94. Gen. David H. Petraeus, "Report to Congress on the Situation in Iraq," April 8–9, 2008, https://media.npr.org/documents/2008/apr/petraeus_as_testimony.pdf, 4.

95. Tim Arango, "Top Qaeda Leaders in Iraq Reported Killed in Raid," *New York Times*, April 19, 2010.

96. Thom Shanker, "Qaeda Leaders in Iraq Neutralized, U.S. Says," *New York Times*, June 4, 2010.

97. Tim Arango and Eric Schmitt, "U.S. Actions in Iraq Fueled Rise of a Rebel," *New York Times*, August 10, 2014.

98. Michael Slackman, "Hussein Putting His Mark on Islamic Faith," *Los Angeles Times*, November 4, 2001. For an overview of the Faith Campaign, see CENTCOM Iraq papers, *History of the Insurgency in Anbar, 2003–2007*, chap. 2, "Iraq and Anbar Between the Wars: Desert Shield to OIF, 1990–2003," 10–13.

99. CENTCOM Iraq papers, *History of the Insurgency in Anbar*, 6–7; Michael R. Gordon, "Fedayeen; New Iraqi Force Emerges," *New York Times*, March 24, 2003; and Sharon Otterman, "Iraq: What is the Fedayeen Saddam?," Council on Foreign Relations, February 3, 2005.

100. Tommy Franks, *American Soldier* (New York: ReganBooks, 2004), 486–87.

101. Joel D. Rayburn and Frank K. Sobchak, eds., *The U.S. Army in the Iraq War*, vol. 1: *Invasion, Insurgency, Civil War* (Carlisle Barracks, PA: Strategic Studies Institute and U.S. Army War College Press, 2019), 176.

102. Aaron Zelin, "Abu Bakr al-Baghdadi: Islamic State's Driving Force," *BBC News*, July 31, 2014.

103. Michael R. Gordon and Bernard E. Trainor, *The Endgame: The Inside Story of the Struggle for Iraq, from George W. Bush to Barack Obama* (New York: Pantheon, 2012), 231.

104. Zelin, "Abu Bakr al-Baghdadi."

105. Letter from UBL to ʿAtiyatullah Al-Libi 4, SOCOM-2012-0000019, available at https://ctc.usma.edu/letters-from-abbottabad-bin-ladin-sidelined/.

106. Abu Bakr al-Baghdadi, "Statement on the Martyrdom of Mujahid Shaykh Osama bin Laden," Al-Fajr Media Center, May 9, 2011.

107. Lara Jakes and Qassim Abdul-Zahra, "Al-Qaida Making Comeback in Iraq, Officials Say," Associated Press, October 9, 2012.

108. According to the U.S. government, Baghdadi sent a group of seven men to Syria in 2011 "to establish what would eventually become" Nusra Front. U.S. Department of the Treasury, "Treasury Sanctions Senior Al-Nusrah Front Leaders Concurrently with UN Designations," February 23, 2017.

109. U.S. Department of the Treasury, "Treasury Sanctions Senior Al-Nusrah Front Leaders."

110. Ruth Sherlock, "Syrian Rebels Defy U.S. and Pledge Allegiance to Jihadi Group," *The Telegraph* (London), December 10, 2012; and "Syria Opposition Urges U.S. to Reconsider al-Nusra Move," Agence France-Presse, December 12, 2012.

111. Abu Bakr al-Baghdadi, "Give Good News to the Believers: The Declaration of the Islamic State in Iraq and al-Sham," April 8, 2013.

112. Thomas Joscelyn, "Analysis: Zawahiri's Letter to al Qaeda Branches in Syria, Iraq," *FDD's Long War Journal*, June 10, 2013.

113. Thomas Joscelyn, "Al Qaeda Head Addresses Infighting in Syria," *FDD's Long War Journal*, January 23, 2014.

114. Thomas Joscelyn, "Saudi Cleric's Reconciliation Initiative for Jihadists Draws Wide Support, Then a Rejection," *FDD's Long War Journal*, January 27, 2014.

115. Thomas Joscelyn, "Al Qaeda's General Command Disowns the Islamic State of Iraq and the Sham," *FDD's Long War Journal*, February 3, 2014; and Aaron Zelin, "Al-Qaeda Disaffiliates with the Islamic State of Iraq and al-Sham," The Washington Institute for Near East Policy, February 3, 2014.

116. Ayman al-Zawahiri, "Testimonial to Preserve the Blood of Mujahideen in al Sham," May 3, 2014, available at https://scholarship.tricolib.brynmawr.edu/bitstream/handle/10066/16377/ZAW20140502_3.pdf?sequence=1.

117. Al-Zawahiri, "Testimonial to Preserve the Blood of Mujahideen in al Sham."

118. Abu Muhammad al-Adnani al-Shami, "Apologies, Amir of Al-Qaidah," Al-Furqan Media Foundation, May 11, 2014. Musa Cerantonio, an ISIS supporter living in Australia, translated Adnani's message into English.

119. Adnani added: "Let history record that Iran owes al-Qaeda invaluably."

120. Christopher Reuter, "Secret Files Reveal the Structure of Islamic State," *Spiegel*, April 18, 2015.

121. David K. Kirkpatrick, "Assassination Highlights Rifts Facing Syria Rebels," *New York Times*, September 6, 2012.

122. UN Security Council, "Security Council Al-Qaida Sanctions Committee Adds Names of Four Individuals and Two Entities to Its Sanctions List," September 29, 2015.

123. U.S. Treasury Department, "Treasury Designates Twelve Foreign Terrorist Fighter Facilitators," September 24, 2014.

124. U.S. Treasury Department, "Treasury Designates Twelve Foreign Terrorist Fighter Facilitators"; and Bill Roggio, "State Department Adds Chechen, Moroccan-Led Jihadist Groups to Terrorist List," *FDD's Long War Journal*, September 24, 2014.

125. UN Security Council, "Turki Mubarak Abdullah Ahmad al-Binali," April 20, 2016.

126. UN Security Council, "Turki Mubarak Abdullah Ahmad al-Binali."

127. Peter Bergen and Emily Schneider, "Now ISIS Has Drones?," *CNN*, August 25, 2014.

128. Michael S. Schmidt and Eric Schmitt, "Pentagon Confronts a New Threat From ISIS: Exploding Drones," *New York Times*, October 11, 2016.

129. Conflict Armament Research, *Frontline Perspective: Islamic State's Weaponised Drones* (London: Conflict Armament Research, October 2016).

130. Nick Waters, "Death from Above: The Drone Bombs of the Caliphate," Bellingcat, February 10, 2017.

131. Aaron Zelin, "The Islamic State of Iraq and Syria Has a Consumer Protection Office," *Atlantic*, June 13, 2014; and Rukmini Callimachi, "The ISIS Files," *New York Times*, April 4, 2018.

132. Zelin, "The Islamic State of Iraq and Syria."

133. Callimachi, "The ISIS Files."

134. Letter Regarding Al-Qaʾida Strategy, SOCOM-2012-0000017, available at https://ctc .usma.edu/letters-from-abbottabad-bin-ladin-sidelined/.

8. The *Fitna*

1. "In the Company of the Emir of the Believers, Caliph Ibrahim Ibn 'Awad al-Badri al-Husayni al-Qurashi al-Baghdadi, May Allah Almighty Protect Him," Al-Furqan Media Establishment, April 29, 2019.

2. Graeme Wood, "What ISIS's Leader Really Wants," *New Republic*, September 1, 2014.

3. "In the Company of the Emir of the Believers."

4. Abu Muhammad al-Adnani, "This Is the Promise of Allah," Al Furqan Media Foundation, June 29, 2014.

5. Abu Yaman al-Wazzani's comment was shared on a Telegram channel associated with Sheikh Abu Muhammad al-Maqdisi (@ShMaqdisi06), May 13, 2019.

6. Mostafa Mahamed, a U.S.-designated terrorist who goes by the nom de guerre Abu Sulayman al-Muhajir, praised Shishani's death on his Twitter feed (@AbuSulaymanMM) on July 13, 2016. Although Mahamed later claimed to be independent from al-Qaeda, he initially trumpeted his loyalty to al-Qaeda on social media.

7. Abu Bakr al-Baghdadi, "Even Though the Disbelievers Despise Such," Al-Furqan Media, November 13, 2014.

8. The difference between a two-player and three-player game is the *simplest* way to understand this competition. One could add Iran, Syria, and the Gulf Cooperation Council states as players in their own right, among others.

9. John Shy and Thomas Collier, "Revolutionary War," in *Makers of Modern Strategy: From Machiavelli to the Nuclear Age*, ed. Peter Paret (Princeton, N.J.: Princeton University Press, 1986), 817.

10. David Kilcullen, *The Accidental Guerrilla: Fighting Small Wars in the Midst of a Big One* (Oxford: Oxford University Press, 2009); and Michael Vlahos, *Terror's Mask: Insurgency Within Islam* (Laurel, MD: Johns Hopkins University Applied Physics Laboratory, 2002).

11. Stathis Kalyvas, "Is ISIS a Revolutionary Group and if Yes, What Are the Implications?," *Perspectives on Terrorism* 9, no. 4 (2015).

12. Michael W. S. Ryan, *Decoding al-Qaeda's Strategy: The Deep Battle Against America* (New York: Columbia University Press, 2013), loc. 1057, Kindle ed.

13. Mao Tse-tung, *On Guerrilla Warfare*, Samuel B. Griffith trans. (Royal Oak, NZ: Pickle Partners, 2014), loc. 474, Kindle ed.

14. Lawrence Freedman, *Strategy: A History* (Oxford: Oxford University Press, 2013), 186.

15. Henry Butterfield Ryan, *The Fall of Che Guevara: A Story of Soldiers, Spies, and Diplomats* (New York: Oxford University Press, 1998).

16. Illustrating the two groups' lack of complete adherence to either a Maoist or Focoist framework, Abu Firas al-Suri, the spokesman for al-Qaeda-aligned Jabhat al-Nusra, referred explicitly to the Focoist theoretician Régis Debray in one of his statements. Thomas Joscelyn, "Al Nusrah Front Celebrates 9/11 Attacks in New Video," *FDD's Long War Journal*, June 29, 2015.

17. Derek Jones, *Understanding the Form, Function, and Logic of Clandestine Insurgent and Terrorist Networks* (MacDill Air Force Base, FL: Joint Special Operations University, 2012), 64.

18. Thomas Joscelyn, "Ayman al-Zawahiri Defends 9/11 Hijackings in Anniversary Address," *FDD's Long War Journal*, September 11, 2019.

19. Gilles Kepel and Jean-Pierre Milelli, eds., *Al Qaeda in Its Own Words* (Cambridge, Mass.: Belknap Press of Harvard University Press, 2008), 199.

20. Abu Bakr al-Husayni al-Qurashi al-Baghdadi, "A Message to the Mujahidin and the Muslim Ummah in the Month of Ramadan," Al-Hayat Media Center, July 5, 2014.

21. Leah Farrall, "How al-Qaeda Works," *Foreign Affairs*, March/April 2011.

22. Al-Qaeda has praised Azzam for awakening "the ummah to defend Afghanistan" and declared "most unequivocally that jihad has been a *fard ayn* since the fall of al-Andalus." Ayman al-Zawahiri, "Brief Messages to a Victorious Nation, Part 7: One Ummah, One War on Multiple Fronts," As Sahab Media, June 9, 2017.

23. U.S. Department of the Treasury, "Treasury Designates AQIM Emir," December 4, 2007.

24. Salafist Group for Preaching and Combat (GSPC), Charter, n.d., p. 14, available at http://somalimidnimo.com/audio/balantii_jamaacada_salafiyiinta_ee_dacwada_iyo_jihaadka_ay_ku_galeen1.pdf.

25. See document posted at the DNI website, https://www.dni.gov/files/documents/ubl2017/english/Addendum%20to%20the%20report%20of%20the%20Islamic%20Maghreb.pdf.

26. U.S. Department of the Treasury, "Treasury Targets Three Senior Al-Qa'ida Leaders," September 7, 2011.

27. See document posted at the DNI website, https://www.dni.gov/files/documents/ubl2017/english/Addendum%20to%20the%20report%20of%20the%20Islamic%20Maghreb.pdf.

28. "An Interview with Abdelmalek Droukdal," *New York Times*, July 1, 2008.

29. "From Here We Begin . . . and at Al-Aqsa We Meet," Al-Malahem Media Foundation, January 23, 2009.

30. "From Here We Begin."

31. Bill Roggio, "AQAP Confirms Deputy Emir Killed in U.S. Drone Strike," *FDD's Long War Journal*, July 17, 2013.

32. Nelly Lahoud, Stuart Caudill, Don Rassler, Liam Collins, Gabriel Koehler-Derrick, and Muhammad al-ᶜUbaydi, *Letters from Abbottabad: Bin Ladin Sidelined?* (West Point, N.Y.: Combating Terrorism Center at West Point, 2012), 12.

33. Lahoud et al., *Letters from Abbottabad*, 38.

34. Lahoud et al., *Letters from Abbottabad*, 40.

35. This document can be found at https://www.longwarjournal.org/multimedia/SOCOM-2012-0000005%20Trans.pdf.

36. See https://www.longwarjournal.org/wp-content/uploads/2015/03/EXHIBIT-425-ENG-TRANS-EX-424-AC52C7B7-.pdf.

37. Al-Qaeda in the Indian Subcontinent, "Code of Conduct," As-Sahab Media, June 2017, 2.

38. Abu Muhammad al-Adnani al-Shami, "Apologies, Emir of al-Qaeda," Al Furqan Media Foundation, May 2014.

39. Ayman al-Zawahiri, "Testimonial to Preserve the Blood of Mujahedin in al-Sham," As Sahab Media, May 2014.

40. ISIS's English-language *Rumiyah* magazine published a glowing biography of Abu Maysara after his death. The biography trumpeted his decision to label al-Qaeda's top leaders and the scholars who defended them as the "Jews of Jihad." See "Among the Believers Are Men: Shaykh Abu Sulayman Ash-Shami," *Rumiyah*, no. 8 (April 2017): 40–45.

41. Federal Bureau of Investigation, Boston Field Office, "Wanted Fugitive Ahmad Abousamra Added to the FBI's Most Wanted Terrorists List," December 18, 2013.

42. "IS Confirms Death of Propaganda Chief Abu Mohammed al-Furqan," *BBC*, October 11, 2016.

43. U.S. Department of Defense, "Statement from Pentagon Press Secretary Peter Cook on Airstrike Against ISIL Senior Leader," September 16, 2016.

44. U.S. Department of Defense, "Statement from Pentagon Press Secretary Peter Cook."

45. Abū Jarīr ash-Shamālī, "Al Qa'idah of Waziristan: A Testimony from Within," *Dabiq*, no. 6 (December 2014): 40–55.

46. "They Fight the People of Islam and Support Idolaters," *al-Naba*, no. 182 (May 16, 2019): 3.

47. Abu Muhammad al-Adnani, "Say, Die in Your Rage!," Al-Furqan Media Foundation, January 26, 2015.

48. Kenneth J. Cooper, "Taliban Massacre Based on Ethnicity," *Washington Post*, November 28, 1998; and Barbara Crossette, "Rights Group Tells of Taliban Massacres," *New York Times*, February 19, 2001.

49. Mullah Akhtar Mohammad Mansour, "Letter of Islamic Emirate's Leadership Commission to the Distinguished Abu Bakr al Baghdadi," June 16, 2015.

50. Dawood Azami, "Why Taliban Special Forces Are Fighting Islamic State," *BBC*, December 18, 2015; and Joseph Goldstein, "In ISIS, the Taliban Face an Insurgent Threat of Their Own," *New York Times*, June 4, 2015.

51. Rod Norland and Fahim Abed, "ISIS Captures Tora Bora, Once Bin Laden's Afghan Fortress," *New York Times*, June 14, 2017.

52. Najim Rahim and Rod Nordland, "Taliban Surge Routs ISIS in Northern Afghanistan," *New York Times*, August 1, 2018.

53. "Apostate Taliban Movement Follows in Footsteps of Syria's and Iraq's Awakenings," *al-Naba*, no. 79 (May 4, 2017).

54. "The Rafidah: From Ibn Saba' to the Dajjal," *Dabiq*, no. 13 (January 2016): 32–45.

55. For example, in 2019 AQIS released a series of videos titled "Is Pakistan . . . an Islamic State?" in which the group argued that Pakistan is not governed according to sharia. See also Ayman al-Zawahiri, "Don't Forget Kashmir," As Sahab Media, July 2019.

56. See U.S. Department of State, *Country Reports on Terrorism 2017*, September 2018, 166.

57. On Iran and Russia, see Sami Yousafzai, "Iran and the Afghan Taliban Teaming Up Against ISIS," *Daily Beast*, June 17, 2015; and Brian Todd and Steve Almasy, "Russia, Taliban Share Intelligence in Fight Against ISIS," *CNN*, December 25, 2015. On assurance to American diplomats, see Thomas Joscelyn and Bill Roggio, "Trump's Bad Deal with the Taliban," *Politico*, March 18, 2019.

58. Adnani recognized this pair as the leaders of Wilayah Khorasan in his January 2015 speech, "Say, Die in Your Rage!" See also U.S. Department of the Treasury, "Treasury Sanctions Major Islamic State of Iraq and the Levant Leaders, Financial Figures, Facilitators, and Supporters," September 29, 2015.

59. SITE Intelligence Group, "Al-Qaeda Faction Allegedly Pledges to ISIL in Unauthenticated Statement," April 1, 2014.

60. SITE Intelligence Group, "Al-Qaeda Faction Allegedly Pledges to ISIL."

61. Thomas Joscelyn, "Previously Obscure al Qaeda Leader Responds to Dissenters," *FDD's Long War Journal*, May 30, 2014.

62. Zahir Shah Sherazi, "Islamic State Footprints Surface in Parts of Bannu," *Dawn* (Pakistan), November 13, 2014.

63. Sherazi, "Islamic State Footprints Surface."

64. "Daesh's Cruelty in Kot District Unjustifiable: Muslim Dost," Pajhwok Afghan News, July 9, 2016.

65. "Daesh's Cruelty in Kot District Unjustifiable."

66. SITE Intelligence Group, "TTP Spokesman Shahidullah, Five Officials Allegedly Pledge to IS," October 13, 2014.

67. SITE Intelligence Group, "IS Releases Video of Former TTP Spokesman Announcing Pledges to IS from Group Leaders in Afghanistan, Pakistan," January 11, 2015.

68. Pakistani Taliban, "Statement of Pakistani Taliban (TTP Central) About Their 'Former' Spokesman Who Has Allegedly Given *Baya* to Jama'at al-Dawla (ISIS)," October 18, 2014.

69. Thomas Joscelyn, "Pakistani Taliban Rejects Islamic State's 'Self-Professed Caliphate,'" *FDD's Long War Journal*, May 27, 2015.

70. UN Security Council, "Tenth Report of the Analytical Support and Sanctions Monitoring Team Submitted Pursuant to Resolution 2255 (2015) Concerning the Taliban and Other Associated Individuals and Entities Constituting a Threat to the Peace, Stability and Security of Afghanistan," April 30, 2019, 18.

71. Amira Jadoon, Nakissa Jahanbani, and Charmaine Willis, "Challenging the ISK Brand in Afghanistan-Pakistan: Rivalries and Divided Loyalties," *CTC Sentinel* 11, no. 4 (April 2018).

72. Amira Jadoon, *Allied & Lethal: Islamic State Khorasan's Network and Organizational Capacity in Afghanistan and Pakistan* (West Point, N.Y.: Combating Terrorism Center at West Point, 2018).

73. Office of the Director of National Intelligence, Counterterrorism Guide, "Lashkar-e-Jhangvi (LJ)," https://www.dni.gov/nctc/groups/lj.html.

74. UN Security Council, "Jamaat-ul-Ahrar (JuA)" (QDe.152), July 6, 2017.

75. One such figure was Juma Namangani, a former Soviet soldier who operated at the nexus of the Taliban and al-Qaeda in pre-9/11 Afghanistan. Ahmed Rashid, "They're Only Sleeping: Why Militant Islamicists in Central Asia Aren't Going to Go Away," *New Yorker*, January 6, 2002.

76. Jacob Zenn, "The IMU Is Extinct: What Next for Central Asia's Jihadis?," *Central Asia-Caucasus Analyst*, May 3, 2016.

77. Bill Roggio and Caleb Weiss, "Islamic Movement of Uzbekistan Faction Emerges After Group's Collapse," *FDD's Long War Journal*, June 14, 2016.

78. Andrew E. Kramer and Rukmini Callimachi, "ISIS Says It Killed 4 Cyclists in Tajikistan," *New York Times*, July 30, 2018.

79. "IS Members Kill Dozens in Tajikistan Prison Riot," *BBC*, May 20, 2019.

80. UN Security Council, "Twenty-Fourth Report of the Analytical Support and Sanctions Monitoring Team Submitted Pursuant to Resolution 2368 (2017) Concerning ISIL (Da'esh), Al-Qaida and Associated Individuals and Entities," June 27, 2019, 15.

81. U.S. Department of Defense, "Statement by Chief Pentagon Spokesperson Dana W. White on Death of ISIS-K Leader in Afghanistan," July 14, 2017.

82. NATO Resolute Support, "U.S. Forces in Afghanistan Strike Islamic State Leader; Maintain Pressure on Terror Network," September 2, 2018.

83. U.S. Department of Defense, "Department of Defense Press Briefing by General Nicholson in the Pentagon Briefing Room," December 2, 2016.

84. UN Security Council, "Twenty-Fourth Report of the Analytical Support and Sanctions Monitoring Team," 15.

85. Mujib Mashal and Zahra Nader, "ISIS Claims Deadly Bombing at Demonstration in Kabul, Afghanistan," *New York Times*, July 23, 2016.

86. Jeff Seldin, "Islamic State Poised for Possible Resurgence in Afghanistan, US Officials Warn," Voice of America, February 9, 2021.

87. "The Taliban Say They Control Panjshir, The Last Holdout Afghan Province," Associated Press, September 6, 2021; and "Mapping the Advance of the Taliban in Afghanistan," *BBC News*, August 16, 2021.

88. Thomas Gibbons-Neff, "U.S. Special Forces Battle Against ISIS Turns to Containment, and Concern," *New York Times*, June 14, 2019.

89. UN Security Council, "Twentieth Report of the Analytical Support and Sanctions Monitoring Team Submitted Pursuant to Resolution 2253 (2015) Concerning ISIL (Da'esh), Al-Qaida and Associated Individuals and Entities," June 30, 2017, 14–15.

90. UN Security Council, "Twentieth Report of the Analytical Support and Sanctions Monitoring Team," 15.

91. UN Security Council, "Twenty-First Report of the Analytical Support and Sanctions Monitoring Team Submitted Pursuant to Resolution 2253 (2015) Concerning ISIL (Da'esh), Al-Qaida and Associated Individuals and Entities," December 29, 2017, 16; UN Security Council, "Twenty-Second Report of the Analytical Support and Sanctions Monitoring Team Submitted Pursuant to Resolution 2253 (2015) Concerning ISIL (Da'esh), Al-Qaida and Associated Individuals and Entities," June 27, 2018, 3, 15; and UN Security Council, "Twenty-Third Report of the Analytical Support and Sanctions Monitoring Team Submitted Pursuant to Resolution 2253 (2015) Concerning ISIL (Da'esh), Al-Qaida and Associated Individuals and Entities," December 27, 2018, 16.

92. "Tenth Report of the Analytical Support and Sanctions Monitoring Team," 9.

93. Federal Bureau of Investigation, *Terrorism 2000/2001* (2001), https://www.fbi.gov/stats-services/publications/resolveuid/4167460530e11fcf4fa7d0c8c6918672.

94. Christopher Boucek, *Yemen: Avoiding a Downward Spiral* (Washington, DC: Carnegie Endowment for International Peace, 2009).

95. "Time Running Out for Solution to Yemen's Water Crisis," *Guardian* (London), August 27, 2012.

96. Boucek, *Yemen*.

97. U.S. Department of the Treasury, "Treasury Sanctions Political Spoilers Threatening the Peace, Security and Stability of Yemen," November 11, 2014; and U.S. Department of the Treasury, "Treasury Sanctions Instigators of the Violent Takeover of Yemen," April 14, 2015.

98. Dina al-Shibeeb, "Your Guide to 'Operation Decisive Storm,' " *Al Arabiya*, March 26, 2015.

99. Abu Bakr al-Baghdadi, "Even if the Disbelievers Despise Such," Al-Furqan Media Foundation, November 13, 2014.
100. SITE Intelligence Group, "AQAP Denies Connection to Bombings at Houthi Mosques in Sana'a," March 20, 2015.
101. Thomas Joscelyn and Bill Roggio, "U.S. Reportedly Kills Ansar al Sharia Official in Drone Strike in Yemen," *FDD's Long War Journal*, May 12, 2015.
102. Harith bin Ghazi al-Nadhari, "A Statement on the Issue of What Was Stated in Sheikh Abu Bakr al-Baghdadi's Speech Titled, 'Even if the Disbelievers Dislike It,'" Al-Malahem Media, November 2014.
103. Harith bin Ghazi al-Nadhari, "A Statement on the Issue of What Was Stated."
104. Abū Maysarah ash-Shāmī, "The Qa'idah of Adh-Dhawahiri, Al-Harari, and An-Nadhari, and the Absent Yemeni Wisdom," *Dabiq*, no. 6 (December 2014), 18.
105. Scott Shane, "U.S. Drone Kills a Top Figure in Al Qaeda's Yemen Branch," *New York Times*, April 14, 2015; "Top al-Qaeda Militant Nasser al-Ansi 'Killed' in Yemen," BBC, May 7, 2015; and Jethro Mullen, "Al Qaeda's Second in Command Killed in Yemen Strike; Successor Named," *CNN*, June 16, 2015.
106. Thomas Joscelyn, "Dagestani Jihadist Swears Allegiance to Islamic State, Invoking Backlash," *FDD's Long War Journal*, December 31, 2014.
107. The original fatwa endorsing the emir of the Islamic Caucasus Emirate and denouncing those who defected to ISIS can be found at justpaste.it/Kavkazz.
108. Andrew Roth, "Leader of Militant Group in Russia Is Killed, Reports Say," *New York Times*, April 20, 2015.
109. Abu Muhammad al-Adnani, "Say to Those Who Disbelieve, 'You Will Be Overcome,'" Al-Hayat Media Center, October 2015.
110. Khalid Batarfi, "Statement Regarding the Address Titled 'Say to Those Who Disbelieve,' Given by the Official Spokesman of Baghdadi's Group," Al-Malahem Media, October 2015. The video bore the logos of both AQAP's Al Malahem Media and AQIM's Al Andalus Media. Batarfi explicitly stated that his address was given on behalf of both al-Qaeda branches.
111. Asa Fitch and Mohammed al-Kibsi, "As Yemen's Civil War Rages, Al Qaeda Gains," *Wall Street Journal*, December 3, 2015.
112. U.S. Department of State, "Terrorist Designations of Ansar al-Sharia as an Alias for Al-Qaida in the Arabian Peninsula," October 4, 2012.
113. Bruce Riedel, "Al-Qaida's Hadramawt Emirate," Brookings Institution, July 12, 2015.
114. Thomas Joscelyn, "AQAP Hosts Large Rally in Mukallah," *FDD's Long War Journal*, March 4, 2016.
115. SITE Intelligence Group, "AQAP Claims al-Mukalla Withdrawal a Strategic Move to Protect Civilians, Denies High Number of Reported Casualties," April 30, 2016.
116. Quoted in SITE Intelligence Group, "IS Criticizes AQAP for Failing to Implement Shariah, Losing Territories in Yemen in al-Naba," May 11, 2016.
117. SITE Intelligence Group, "IS Claims Suicide Bombing at Yemeni Base in Hadramawt," May 12, 2016.
118. "Deadly Bombing Targets Police in Yemen's Mukalla," *Al Jazeera*, May 15, 2016.

119. "Yemen Attacks Kill 43 as Government and Houthis Move to Break Off Talks," Associated Press, June 27, 2016.
120. The document is available at https://www.longwarjournal.org/wp-content/uploads/2015/05/Letter-Addressed-to-Atiyah.pdf.
121. Rukmini Callimachi, "In Timbuktu, al-Qaida Left Behind a Manifesto," Associated Press, February 14, 2013. A copy of the letters can be found at https://www.longwarjournal.org/images/al-qaida-papers-how-to-run-a-state.pdf.
122. Images from AQAP's execution of one alleged adulterer are included in Thomas Joscelyn, "AQAP Provides Social Services, Implements Sharia While Advancing in Southern Yemen," *FDD's Long War Journal*, February 3, 2016.
123. "New Video Message from al-Qā'idah in the Arabian Peninsula's Shaykh Abū Basīr Nāsir al-Wūhayshī: 'About Understanding the Implementation of Sharī'ah,'" *Jihadology*, July 20, 2015.
124. "Exclusive Interview with Sheikh Qasim al-Raymi," Al-Malahem Media, April 2017.
125. *Al-Masra*, no. 25 (October 3, 2016): 1–2. The letter, dated August 8, 2016, had been shared on Twitter.
126. *Al-Masra*, no. 25: 6.
127. Suhayb Rami, "The Sheikhs in the Prisons of al-Saud and Their Positions Regarding the State Organization," *al-Masra*, no. 37 (January 24, 2017): 5.
128. Abd-al-Aziz al-Tarifi has had a noteworthy social media presence in Arabic, English and Turkish. For instance, his Arabic-language Twitter feed, @abdulaziztarefe, had over 1 million followers as of mid-2019.
129. Cole Bunzel, "Caliphate in Disarray: Theological Turmoil in the Islamic State," *Jihadica*, October 3, 2017.
130. "Symbols or Idols?!," *Al-Naba*, June 15, 2017, 12.
131. Zawahiri has even praised al-Banna even though Zawahiri frequently criticizes the current Brotherhood's practices. Al-Zawahiri, "Brief Messages to a Victorious Nation, Part 7. A still image of al-Banna was shown on screen as one of his messages was read aloud. The photo of al-Banna was part of a set that included bin Laden and other al-Qaeda and Taliban figures.
132. "Symbols or Idols?!," 12.
133. R. Green, "Dispute Over Takfir Rocks Islamic State," Middle East Media Research Institute (MEMRI), August 4, 2017.
134. There is no evidence that the Hazimi trend self-identifies by this name. Rather, the term *Hazimis* is used to describe them by observers within the jihadist community.
135. Vera Mironova, Ekaterina Sergtskova, and Karam Alhamad, "The Bloody Split Within ISIS: Inside the Group's Crackdown on Ultra-Extremists," *Foreign Affairs*, December 8, 2017.
136. "ISIS Executes One of Its Sharia Judges," *Middle East Monitor*, March 10, 2015.
137. Abdallah Suleiman Ali, "IS Disciplines Some Emirs to Avoid Losing Base," *Al-Monitor*, September 2, 2014.
138. Green, "Dispute Over Takfir Rocks Islamic State."

139. Thomas Joscelyn, "Islamic State Rescinds One of Its Most Problematic Religious Rulings," *FDD's Long War Journal*, September 20, 2017.

140. Joscelyn, "Islamic State Rescinds"; and Bunzel, "Caliphate in Disarray."

141. Joscelyn, "Islamic State Rescinds One of Its Most Problematic Religious Rulings."

142. "Khabib al-Jazrawi: Declaring Ibn-Taymiyah and al-Tabari Infidels Has Become Common Among Organization [ISIS] Members," *al-Masra*, July 26, 2017, 4.

143. UN Security Council, "Twenty-Third Report of the Analytical Support and Sanctions Monitoring Team Submitted Pursuant to Resolution 2368 (2017) Concerning ISIL (Da'esh), Al-Qaida and Associated Individuals and Entities," December 27, 2018, 9.

144. Thomas Joscelyn and Bill Roggio, "Divisions Emerge Within the Islamic State's Yemen 'Province,'" *FDD's Long War Journal*, December 23, 2015.

145. Sudarsan Raghaven, "With the ISIS Caliphate Defeated in Syria, an Islamist Militant Rivalry Takes Root in Yemen," *Washington Post*, April 14, 2019.

146. Thomas Joscelyn, "Islamic State Defector in Yemen Apologizes to al-Qaeda," *FDD's Long War Journal*, January 23, 2016.

147. Josie Ensor, "Al Qaeda Releases 'Blooper Reel' of Islamic State Videos Amid Jihadi Spat," *Telegraph* (London), August 15, 2019.

148. UN Security Council, "Twenty-Second Report of the Analytical Support and Sanctions Monitoring Team," 9–10.

149. Virgil, *Aeneid, Book IV*, line 41.

150. Dirk Vandewalle, *A History of Modern Libya*, 2nd ed. (Cambridge: Cambridge University Press, 2012), 11.

151. Vincent O'Hara, *Struggle for the Middle Sea: The Great Navies at War in the Mediterranean Theater, 1940-1945* (Annapolis, Md.: Naval Institute Press, 2009), viii.

152. "Libya," in *Europa World Year 2004*, Vol. 2 (London: Europa Publications, 2004), 2651.

153. United States Africa Command, "AFRICOM Concludes Operation Odyssey Lightning," December 20, 2016.

154. U.S. Department of Defense, "Statement from Pentagon Press Secretary Peter Cook on U.S. Strike in Libya," November 14, 2015.

155. Frederic Wehrey and Ala' Alrababa'h, "Rising Out of Chaos: The Islamic State in Libya," *Diwan*, Carnegie Middle East Center, March 5, 2015.

156. For analysis of how this erroneous claim spread, see Daveed Gartenstein-Ross, Nathaniel Barr, and Bridget Moreng, "How the Islamic State's Propaganda Feeds into Its Global Expansion Efforts," *War on the Rocks*, April 28, 2016.

157. Facebook page of Majlis Shura Shabab al-Islam fi Madinat Darnah, April 4, 2014.

158. See, for example, Twitter account of Shabab al-Islam Shura Council, July 3–4, 2014.

159. See "Libya's Islamist Militants Parade with ISIS Flags," *Al-Arabiya*, October 6, 2014.

160. Tweets from Prophet's Khilafah, @PKH1974, October 31, 2014.

161. Maggie Michael, "How a Libyan City Joined the Islamic State Group," Associated Press, November 9, 2014; and Paul Cruickshank, Nic Robertson, Tim Lister, and Jomana Karadsheh, "ISIS Comes to Libya," *CNN*, November 18, 2014.

162. U.S. Department of Defense, "Statement from Pentagon Press Secretary Peter Cook on U.S. Strike in Libya," November 14, 2015.

163. Thomas Joscelyn, "AQIM Rejects Islamic State's Caliphate, Reaffirms Allegiance to Zawahiri," *FDD's Long War Journal*, July 14, 2014. AQIM's statement was translated by the SITE Intelligence Group.

164. Letter from Atiyah Abd al-Rahman to Osama bin Laden, April 5, 2011; and Atiyah Abu Abd al-Rahman, "Taheya le-āhlna fī Lībyā," As Sahab Media, March 18, 2011.

165. Hamzah bin Muhammad al-Bassam, "Heeding the Advantages and Lessons of the Two Uprisings in Egypt and Tunisia," Ansar Dawlat al-Iraq al-Islamiyah, February 11, 2011.

166. Interview with Abu Abd-al-Iylah Ahmad, *al-Masra*, March 14, 2016, 4–5.

167. Atiyah Abd al-Rahman, "The People's Revolt . . . The Fall of Corrupt Arab Regimes . . . The Demolition of the Idol of Stability . . . and the New Beginning," distributed by the Global Islamic Media Front, February 16, 2011.

168. SITE Intelligence Group, "Zawahiri Rallies for Jihad; Calls for Intellectual Debate, Advocacy," August 15, 2011.

169. Aaron Zelin, "The Rise and Decline of Ansar al-Sharia in Libya," *Current Trends in Islamist Ideology*, April 6, 2015.

170. Joscelyn, "AQIM Rejects Islamic State's Caliphate."

171. Abu Iyadh al-Tunisi's offer is recounted in Abu Maysara al-Shami's anti-al Qaeda screed "The Jews of Jihad."

172. Interview with Abu Abd-al-Iylah Ahmad, 4–5.

173. "ISIS Executes One of Its Sharia Judges."

174. U.S. Department of Defense, "Statement by Pentagon Press Secretary Peter Cook on Coalition Strike Against Boubaker al-Hakim," December 10, 2016.

175. Thomas Joscelyn, "Veteran Jihadists Killed by Islamic State's 'Province' in Derna, Libya," *FDD's Long War Journal*, June 12, 2015.

176. Thomas Joscelyn, "Al Qaeda in the Islamic Maghreb Backs Jihadists Fighting Islamic State in Derna, Libya," *FDD's Long War Journal*, July 9, 2015.

177. "Libya's Derna Is Now Free of ISIS," *Libya Observer*, April 20, 2016.

178. "Interview with Abul-Mughīrah al-Qahtānī," *Dabiq*, September 2015, 60–63.

179. Abdallah bin Muhammad, "Hurub al-asabat a-sīyasīya," March 2015.

180. "Libya's Ansar al-Sharia Announces Dissolution," *Al Jazeera*, May 28, 2017.

181. Interview with Muhammad al-Darsi, *Al-Masra*, November 18, 2016, 4–5.

182. Abdulkader Assad, "Libyan Revolutionary Factions Form Defend Benghazi Brigades," *Libya Observer*, June 2, 2016.

183. Ayman al-Warfalli, "Haftar's Forces Say They Have Captured Libyan City of Derna," Reuters, June 28, 2018.

184. "Libyan Forces Capture Egyptian Jihadist Hisham Ashmawi," *BBC*, October 8, 2018.

185. SITE Intelligence Group, "Exclusive in IS' Naba 120 Reports Resumption of 'War of Attrition' in Libya, Attacks in Sirte, Including Suicide Bombing," February 22, 2018.

186. UN Security Council, "Twenty-Fourth Report of the Analytical Support and Sanctions Monitoring Team," 9.

187. UN Security Council, "Twenty-Fourth Report of the Analytical Support and Sanctions Monitoring Team," 9.

188. U.S. Department of State, "State Department Terrorist Designations of ISIS Affiliates and Senior Leaders," February 27, 2018.

189. Carlotta Gall, "Group Linked to Islamic State Claims Responsibility for Tunisia Attack," *New York Times*, March 31, 2015.

190. Abu Muhammad al-Adnani, "So They Kill and Are Killed," Al-Furqan Media, March 12, 2015.

191. Letter written by Abu Muhammad Abu Bakr bin Muhammad al-Shakwi al-Muslimi Bishku, available at https://www.dni.gov/files/documents/ubl2016/english/Praise%20 be%20to%20God%20the%20Lord%20of%20all%20worlds.pdf.

192. Letter from Abdallah Abu Zayd Abd-al-Hamid to AQIM emir Abdul Musab Abdel Wadoud, August 2009, https://www.longwarjournal.org/wp-content/uploads/2017 /02/Letter-from-Abdallah-Abu-Zayd-Abd-al-Hamid-to-Abu-Mus-ab-Abd-al -Wadud.pdf.

193. U.S. Department of State, Rewards for Justice, "Abubakar Shekau," n.d.

194. For a discussion of Ansaru's formation and the controversies surrounding Shekau's management of Boko Haram, see Jacob Zenn, "Boko Haram's Factional Feuds: Internal Extremism and External Interventions," *Terrorism and Political Violence*, March 13, 2019.

195. Zenn, "Boko Haram's Factional Feuds," 13.

196. Thomas Joscelyn, "Jihadist Divisions Grow in Nigeria," *FDD's Long War Journal*, February 23, 2015.

197. SITE Intelligence Group, "IS' al-Naba Newspaper Interviews West Africa 'Governor' Abu Musab al-Barnawi," August 3, 2016.

198. UN Security Council, "Twenty-Fourth Report of the Analytical Support and Sanctions Monitoring Team," 11.

199. Jason Warner and Charlotte Hume, "The Islamic State in Africa: Estimating Fighter Numbers in Cells Across the Continent," *CTC Sentinel* 11, no. 7 (2018).

200. Paul Carsten, Ahmed Kingimi, and Ola Lanre, "Islamic State Insurgents Overrun Northeast Nigerian Town: Security Sources," Reuters, January 14, 2019.

201. Thomas Joscelyn and Caleb Weiss, "Islamic State Recognizes Oath of Allegiance from Jihadists in Mali," *FDD's Long War Journal*, October 31, 2016.

202. Caleb Weiss, "Alleged Statement from Mokhtar Belmokhtar Denies His Group Swore Allegiance to the Islamic State," *FDD's Long War Journal*, May 15, 2015.

203. Rukmini Callimachi, "ISIS Affiliate Claims October Attack on U.S. Troops in Niger," *New York Times*, January 13, 2018.

204. Thomas Joscelyn, "Analysis: Al Qaeda Groups Reorganize in West Africa," *FDD's Long War Journal*, March 13, 2017.

205. UN Security Council, "Twenty-Fourth Report of the Analytical Support and Sanctions Monitoring Team," 10.

206. UN Security Council, "Twenty-Third Report of the Analytical Support and Sanctions Monitoring Team Submitted Pursuant to Resolution 2368 (2017)," 11.

207. Ayman al-Zawahiri, "Islamic Spring" episode 1, As Sahab Media, 2015.

208. Godane's statement to Zawahiri in 2013, as reported in the first episode of the "Islamic Spring" series, is consistent with the former's public rhetoric. See Thomas Joscelyn and Bill Roggio, "Shabaab Leader Calls for Mediation in Syria, Says Zawahiri Is 'Our Shaikh and Emir,'" *FDD's Long War Journal*, May 17, 2014.

209. Thomas Joscelyn, "Shabaab's Leadership Fights Islamic State's Attempted Expansion in East Africa," *FDD's Long War Journal*, October 26, 2015.

210. Harun Maruf and Dan Joseph, *Inside al-Shabaab: The Secret History of al-Qaeda's Most Powerful Ally* (Bloomington: Indiana University Press, 2018), 259.

211. Abdi Sheikh, "Small Group of Somali al Shabaab Swear Allegiance to Islamic State," Reuters, October 23, 2015.

212. Al-Muhajiroun, "Hold Fast, Altogether," October 24, 2015.

213. The best public description of how Shabaab's *amniyat* works can be found in a UN report published in 2013. See "Report of the Monitoring Group on Somalia and Eritrea Pursuant to Security Council Resolution 2060 (2012): Somalia," June 19, 2013, 7, 13–14, 50, 56–59. The Monitoring Group described the *amniyat* as Shabaab's "secret service." The *amniyat* "integrates the functions of a secret police, responsible for counter-intelligence and political control, and a clandestine special operations unit conducting assassinations and suicide attacks."

214. A former *amniyat* operative told the UN Monitoring Group that a Sudanese national known as Hassan had been "specifically tasked by Ayman al-Zawahiri" to train jihadists in Somalia who were "unable to travel to Afghanistan and Pakistan." Hassan reportedly worked with Ahmed Godane and other al-Qaeda operatives "to plan training strategies" for Shabaab and other al-Qaeda affiliates in Africa. "Report of the Monitoring Group on Somalia and Eritrea," 66.

215. La Wadaag, "Al-Shabab Oo Xirtay 30 Ajaaniib & Soomaali ah," *VOA Soomaaliya*, October 14, 2015.

216. Maruf and Joseph, *Inside al-Shabaab*, 260.

217. "Suspected Leader of Pro-IS al-Shabaab Faction Reported Killed," *VOA News*, November 22, 2015.

218. Maruf and Joseph, *Inside al-Shabaab*, 256, 261.

219. Ian Duncan, "Accused al-Shabaab Fighter Came from Heart of Baltimore's African-American Muslim Community," *Baltimore Sun*, January 17, 2016.

220. "U.S. Fighter Flees al-Shabab After ISIL Allegiance Row," *Al Jazeera*, December 7, 2015.

221. "Report of the Monitoring Group on Somalia and Eritrea Pursuant to Security Council Resolution 2244 (2015): Somalia," September 28, 2016, 15–16, 61–69.

222. "Report of the Monitoring Group on Somalia and Eritrea Pursuant to Security Council Resolution 2244 (2015)," 3.

223. "Report of the Monitoring Group on Somalia and Eritrea Pursuant to Security Council Resolution 2244 (2015)," 16.

224. Colin Freeman, "British Extremist Preacher Linked to Lee Rigby Killer Emerges as Head of Islamic State in Somalia," *Telegraph* (London), April 29, 2016; and Duncan

Gardham and John Simpson, "Jihadist Attended Same Mosque as Lee Rigby Killer," *The Times* (London), February 28, 2015.

225. U.S. Department of State, "Terrorist Designations of ISIS Affiliates and Senior Leaders," February 27, 2018; and "Officials: Deputy Chief of IS-Linked Group in Somalia Killed," VOA News, October 23, 2018.

226. UN Security Council, "Twentieth Report of the Analytical Support and Sanctions Monitoring Team Submitted Pursuant to Resolution 2253 (2015) Concerning ISIL (Da'esh), Al-Qaida and Associated Individuals and Entities," August 7, 2017, 14.

227. Nimo-ilhan Ali, "Going on Tahriib: The Causes and Consequences of Somali Youth Migration to Europe," Rift Valley Institute Research Paper 5, 2016.

228. UN Security Council Counter-Terrorism Committee Executive Directorate, "Identifying and Exploring the Nexus Between Human Trafficking, Terrorism, and Terrorism Financing," 2019, 13.

229. U.S. Department of the Treasury, "Counter Terrorism Designations; Cuba Designations Update," February 9, 2018.

230. Caleb Weiss has tracked this increasing operational tempo. See his interactive map: "Claimed Islamic State Attacks in Somalia," https://public.tableau.com/profile /fddmaps#!/vizhome/SomaliaClaims/Dashboard1.

9. How al-Qaeda Survived the War in Afghanistan

1. U.S. Department of Defense, "Statement by Pentagon Press Secretary Peter Cook Confirming Death of al-Qaeda Leader," November 2016.

2. In an interview published in *CTC Sentinel*, Gen. John Nicholson, commander of NATO's Resolute Support and U.S. Forces–Afghanistan, explained: "There's active plotting against our homeland going on in Afghanistan." General Nicholson made this comment after describing Qahtani as al-Qaeda's "external operations director," and saying that he "was actively involved in the last year in plotting attacks against the United States." Brian Dodwell and Don Rassler, "A View from the CT Foxhole: General John W. Nicholson, Commander, Resolute Support and U.S. Forces—Afghanistan," *CTC Sentinel* 10, no. 2 (2017).

3. The handwritten letter was accessed at https://www.cia.gov, file name 58DC907C 4E083D258161FB44F3B4ECB2_msoCF341.jpg.

4. "Mullah Omar—In His Own words," *Voice of America*, September 26, 2001. The original interview was taken down at the request of the Bush administration, but a transcript can be found at https://www.theguardian.com/world/2001/sep/26 /afghanistan.features11.

5. *9/11 Commission Report: Final Report of the National Commission on Terrorist Attacks upon the United States* (New York: Norton, 2004), 206.

6. *9/11 Commission Report*, 111.

7. *9/11 Commission Report*, 125.

8. *9/11 Commission Report*, 125.

9. *9/11 Commission Report*, 125.

10. *9/11 Commission Report*, 121–22.

11. *9/11 Commission Report*, 183.

12. *9/11 Commission Report*, 171.

13. At one point the successor organization to the Arab 055 Brigade was known as Lashkar al-Zil, or the Shadow Army. Its name spoke to al-Qaeda's desire to hide in the shadows and avoid international attention when possible.

14. *9/11 Commission Report*, 252.

15. Khalid Sheikh Mohammed told American officials that there was dissent within al-Qaeda's elite Shura Council regarding the 9/11 hijackings. The dissent apparently centered on the need to obtain Mullah Omar's permission before such an attack could be carried out. According to KSM, bin Laden "countered that Mullah Omar lacked authority to prevent al-Qaeda from conducting jihad outside Afghanistan." *9/11 Commission Report*, 252. This interpretation of bin Laden's oath to Mullah Omar is consistent with what one al-Qaeda insider reported many years later. Thomas Joscelyn, "Well-Connected Jihadist Tweets, Then Deletes, Explanation of al-Qaeda's Oath to Mullah Omar," *FDD's Long War Journal*, July 30, 2014.

16. Thomas Joscelyn, "Analysis: Al Qaeda Attempts to Undermine New Islamic State with Old Video of Osama bin Laden," *FDD's Long War Journal*, July 15, 2014, https://www.longwarjournal.org/archives/2014/07/osama_bin_laden_disc.php.

17. Thomas Joscelyn, "Ayman al Zawahiri Pledges Allegiance to the Taliban's New Emir," *FDD's Long War Journal*, August 13, 2015.

18. Only Hayat Tahrir al-Sham, once an overt arm of al-Qaeda, failed to publicly rehearse its own *bayah* to Zawahiri and the Taliban's leader.

19. Vahid Brown and Don Rassler, *Fountainhead of Jihad: The Haqqani Nexus, 1973–2012* (New York: Oxford University Press, 2013), 228–33.

20. U.S. Department of Defense, "Department of Defense Press Briefing by General Nicholson via Teleconference from Kabul, Afghanistan," November 28, 2017.

21. The video was released by Manba al-Jihad media unit, which was originally the Haqqanis' propaganda outfit but has been integrated into the Taliban's propaganda machine.

22. During an interview with ABC's *This Week* in June 2010, Leon Panetta, who was then the CIA's director, claimed the number of al-Qaeda fighters in Afghanistan was "relatively small." He said, "At most, we're looking at 50 to 100, maybe less. It's in that vicinity. There's no question that the main location of al-Qaeda is in the tribal areas of Pakistan." Jack Date, "CIA Director Leon Panetta: Serious Problems with Afghanistan War but Progress Being Made," *This Week*, ABC News, June 27, 2010.

23. Letter from Atiyah Abd al-Rahman to Osama bin Laden, June 19, 2010.

24. Letter from Atiyah to bin Laden.

25. See Letter Regarding Al-Qaʾida Strategy, SOCOM-2012-0000017, available at https://ctc.usma.edu/letters-from-abbottabad-bin-ladin-sidelined/.

26. Letter from Atiyah to bin Laden.

27. Letter from Zamray (Osama bin Laden) to Shaykh Mahmud (Atiyah), dated October 21, 2010.

28. Letter to "Shaykh Mahmud" (Atiyah), dated December 3, 2010.

29. The Taliban's eulogy for Yazid was recovered in bin Laden's compound. See Islamic Emirate of Afghanistan, "Condolences on the Occasion of the Martyrdom of Shaykh Abu Yazid al-Mustafa, May Allah Bestow His Soul," https://www.dni.gov/files /documents/ubl/english2/Letter%20to%20Islamic%20Emirate%20of%20 Afghanistan.pdf.

30. Letter from Mahmud (Atiyah) to Sheikh Abu Abdallah (bin Laden), July 17, 2010.

31. U.S. Department of the Treasury, "Treasury Designates Senior al-Qaida Leader in Afghanistan," February 10, 2016.

32. Thomas Joscelyn, "Al-Qaeda's General Command Comments on 'Martyrdom' of Senior Figure in Afghanistan," *FDD's Long War Journal*, November 23, 2016.

33. U.S. Department of Defense, "Department of Defense Press Briefing by General Nicholson via Teleconference from Afghanistan," September 23, 2016.

34. Bill Roggio, "Afghan Intelligence Service Destroys al-Qaeda Base in Zabul," *FDD's Long War Journal*, September 19, 2016.

35. U.S. Department of Defense, "Department of Defense Press Briefing by General Nicholson in the Pentagon Briefing Room," December 2, 2016.

36. Letter from "Mahmud" (Atiyah) to Sheikh Abu Abdallah (bin Laden), November 23, 2010.

37. U.S. Department of the Treasury, "Treasury Designates Three Senior Al-Qaida Members," July 20, 2016.

38. Assaf Moghadam, "Marriage of Convenience: The Evolution of Iran and al-Qa'ida's Tactical Cooperation," *CTC Sentinel* 10, no. 4 (April 2017).

39. "Terrorism Establishment of a Tripartite Agreement Among Usama Bin Laden, Iran and the NIF," CIA report, January 31, 1997, 3, available at https://www .documentcloud.org/documents/368918-1997-01-31-terrorism-establishment-of -a.html.

40. For details on the meeting between bin Laden and Mughniyeh, see *Flanagan v. Iran*, No. 10-1643 (D.D.C., March 31, 2015), 14.

41. *9/11 Commission Report*, 68; Moghadam, "Marriage of Convenience"; and *Flanagan v. Iran*, 14.

42. *Mwila v. Islamic Republic of Iran*, No. 08-1377 (D.D.C., November 28, 2011), 7.

43. *9/11 Commission Report*, 68.

44. *Mwila v. Iran*, 7.

45. Transcript, Day 2, *United States v. Bin Laden*, No. S7 98 Cr. 1023 (S.D.N.Y, February 6, 2001).

46. Peter L. Bergen, *The Osama bin Laden I Know* (New York: Free Press, 2006), 108–9; and Nasser al-Bahri, *Guarding Bin Laden: My Life in al-Qaeda*, trans. Susan de Muth (London: Thin Man Press, 2013), 22.

47. U.S. Department of the Treasury, "Treasury Targets al Qaeda Operatives in Iraq," January 16, 2009.

48. *Flanagan v. Iran*, 20.

49. Bergen, *The Osama bin Laden I Know*, 354.

50. Brian Fishman, *The Master Plan: ISIS, al-Qaeda, and the Jihadi Strategy for Final Victory* (New Haven, Conn.: Yale University Press, 2016), loc. 472, Kindle ed.

51. Fishman, *The Master Plan*, loc. 509.

52. "Statement by Sulayman Abu Ghayth to the Federal Bureau of Investigation," document no. 415-A-NY-307616, March 1, 2013, 7; and Cathy Scott-Clark and Adrian Levy, *The Exile: The Stunning Inside Story of Osama Bin Laden and Al Qaeda in Flight* (New York: Bloomsbury, 2017), 146.

53. "Letter Dated 13 Oct 2010," released in Bin Laden's Bookshelf, Office of the Director of National Intelligence, https://www.dni.gov/files/documents/ubl/english/Letter%20dtd%2013%20Oct%202010.pdf; and Scott-Clark and Levy, *The Exile*, 146.

54. Scott-Clark and Levy, *The Exile*, 520.

55. Adrian Levy and Cathy Scott-Clark, "Al Qaeda Has Rebuilt Itself—with Iran's Help," *Atlantic*, November 11, 2017.

56. See "Letter Dated 13 Oct 2010"; "Letter Dated 5 April 2011," released in Bin Laden's Bookshelf, Office of the Director of National Intelligence, https://www.dni.gov/files/documents/ubl/english/Letter%20dtd%205%20April%202011.pdf; U.S. Department of the Treasury, "Treasury Targets Key Al-Qa'ida Funding and Support Network Using Iran as a Critical Transit Point," July 28, 2011; and Adam Goldman, "Senior al-Qaeda Figure Leaves Iran Amid a Series of Departures by Terrorist Suspects," *Washington Post*, February 14, 2014.

57. al-Bahri, *Guarding Bin Laden*, 209; and "Letter Dated 13 Oct 2010."

58. Fishman, *The Master Plan*, loc. 679–86.

59. Levy and Scott-Levy, "Al-Qaeda Has Rebuilt Itself"; Daniel Byman, "Unlikely Alliance: Iran's Secretive Relationship with Al-Qaeda," IHS Defense, Risk and Security Consulting (July 2012), 31; Moghadam, "Marriage of Convenience"; Toby Dershowitz, "Iran's Support for al-Qaeda Is Incompatible with FATF Standards," Foundation for Defense of Democracies, February 6, 2019; and Seth Jones, "Al Qaeda in Iran," *Foreign Affairs*, January 29, 2012.

60. This point was referenced by ISIS spokesman Abu Muhammad al-Adnani in his May 2014 denunciation of Zawahiri. Abu Muhammad al-Adnani, "Pardon, Emir of al-Qaeda," al-Furqan Media Foundation, May 11, 2014.

61. Thomas Joscelyn, "Al Qaeda's Interim Emir and Iran," *FDD's Long War Journal*, May 18, 2011.

62. Tim Lister, "Military Documents Reveal Details About Guantanamo Detainees, al Qaeda," *CNN*, April 25, 2011; and Clemmie Douchez, "Ex-Guantanamo Detainee Allegedly Led Recruiting Cell for the Islamic State," *FDD's Long War Journal*, March 1, 2016.

63. U.S. Department of the Treasury, "Treasury Targets Key Al-Qa'ida Funding and Support Network."

64. Thomas Joscelyn, "5 Transferred GITMO Detainees Served al Qaeda, Leaked Files Allege," *FDD's Long War Journal*, November 21, 2014.

65. U.S. Department of the Treasury, "Treasury Takes Action to Stem Funding to the Iraqi Insurgency," February 15, 2005.

66. U.S. Department of the Treasury, "Treasury Targets al Qaeda Operatives in Iraq"; and Ari R. Weisfuse, "The Last Hope for the al-Qa'ida Old Guard? A Profile of Saif al-'Adl," *CTC Sentinel* 9, no. 3 (March 2016): 24.

67. U.S. Department of State, "Rewards for Justice—Ezedin Abdel Aziz Khalil (aka Yasin al-Suri) Reward Offer," December 22, 2011.

68. U.S. Department of the Treasury, "Treasury Further Exposes Iran-Based Al-Qa'ida Network," October 18, 2012.

69. "Letter to Karim," released in Bin Laden's Bookshelf, Office of the Director of National Intelligence, https://www.dni.gov/files/documents/ubl2016/english /Letter%20to%20Karim.pdf.

70. U.S. Department of the Treasury, "Treasury Further Exposes Iran-Based Al-Qa'ida Network."

71. Moghadam, "Marriage of Convenience"; and Byman, "Unlikely Alliance," 33.

72. U.S. Department of the Treasury, "Treasury Designates Three Senior Al-Qaida Members."

73. U.S. Department of State, *Country Reports on Terrorism, 2017* (2018), 218.

74. UN Security Council, "Letter Dated 16 July 2018 from the Chair of the Security Council Committee Pursuant to Resolutions 1276 (1999), 1989 (2011), 2253 (2015) Concerning Islamic State in Iraq and the Levant (Da'esh), Al-Qaida and Associated Individuals, Groups, Undertakings and Entities Addressed to the President of the Security Council," July 27, 2018, 6.

75. UN Security Council, "Letter Dated 16 July 2018," 8.

76. U.S. Department of State, Rewards for Justice, "Wanted: Information That Brings to Justice Muhammad Abbatay ('Abd al-Rahman al-Maghrebi)," n.d., https:// rewardsforjustice.net/english/muhammad_abbatay.html.

77. Tim Craig, "An Offshoot of al-Qaeda Is Regrouping in Pakistan," *Washington Post*, June 3, 2016.

78. Security Council Committee Pursuant to Resolutions 1267 (1999) and 1989 (2011) Concerning Al-Qaida and Associated Individuals and Entities, "Narrative Summaries of Reasons for Listing, QE.I.10.01. Islamic Movement of Uzbekistan," April 7, 2011.

79. Some jihadists maintained a dual affiliation with the IMU and al-Qaeda, training in camps that provided instruction for both groups. U.S. intelligence analysts found this was the case for Ravil Mingazov. See Joint Task Force—Guantanamo (JTF-GTMO), Detainee Assessment for Ravil Mingazov, March 14, 2008.

80. Letter from Ahmad Hasan Abu al-Khayr to Mustafa Hamid, August 22, 2009, https://www.dni.gov/files/documents/ubl2016/english/Letter%20to%20Professor%20Mustafa%20Hamid.pdf.

81. Roman Kozhevnikov, "Tajik Court Jails 53 for Terrorism," Reuters, December 26, 2011.

82. Igor Rotar, "Islamic Extremist Group Jamaat Ansarullah Overcomes Tajikistan's Inter-Tribal Conflicts," *Eurasia Daily Monitor*, September 25, 2012.

83. U.S. Department of the Treasury, "Treasury Targets Leader of Group Tied to Al Qaida," April 20, 2009.

84. Bill Roggio, "Turkistan Islamic Party Emir Thought Killed in 2010 Reemerged to Lead Group in 2014," *FDD's Long War Journal*, June 11, 2015.

85. For AQIS's description of the plot, see Thomas Joscelyn, "Al-Qaeda in the Indian Subcontinent Claims Attacks on Pakistani Ships Were More Audacious than Reported," *FDD's Long War Journal*, September 29, 2014. See also Steve Coll, *Directorate S: The C.I.A. and America's Secret Wars in Afghanistan and Pakistan* (New York: Penguin, 2018), 657–59.

86. Joscelyn, "Al-Qaeda in the Indian Subcontinent."

87. Coll, *Directorate S*, 659.

88. Office of the Director of National Intelligence, "Worldwide Threat Assessment of the U.S. Intelligence Community," Senate Select Committee on Intelligence, as delivered by DNI Daniel R. Coats, May 11, 2017, 25.

89. Ali Zain, "5 Pakistan Navy Officers to be Hanged for Conspiring to Hijack Naval Ship," *Daily Pakistan*, May 24, 2016.

90. Shuja Nawaz, *Crossed Swords: Pakistan, Its Army, and the Wars Within* (Oxford: Oxford University Press, 2008), xxvii.

91. Zahid Hussain, *Frontline Pakistan: The Struggle with Militant Islam* (New York: Columbia University Press, 2007), 14.

92. Hussain, *Frontline Pakistan*, 13.

93. Author telephone interview with Stephen P. Cohen, November 24, 2008.

94. Husain Haqqani, *Pakistan: Between Mosque and Military* (Washington, D.C.: Carnegie Endowment for International Peace, 2005), 132.

95. Ahmed Rashid, *Descent into Chaos: The United States and the Failure of Nation Building in Pakistan, Afghanistan, and Central Asia* (New York: Viking/Penguin, 2008), 38.

96. W. Eric Gustafson, "Pakistan 1978: At the Brink Again?," *Asian Survey*, February 1979, 161–62.

97. Stephen Cohen, *The Pakistan Army* (Pakistan: Oxford University Press, 1984), 95; and Hussain, *Frontline Pakistan*, 19.

98. Hussain, *Frontline Pakistan*, 20.

99. Hussain, *Frontline Pakistan*, 20.

100. Robert Marquand and Scott Baldauf, "Will Spies Who Know Tell the U.S.?," *Christian Science Monitor*, October 3, 2001.

101. Haqqani, *Pakistan*, 292.

102. Bill Roggio, "Al-Qaeda in the Indian Subcontinent Incorporates Regional Jihadist Groups," *FDD's Long War Journal*, September 5, 2014.

103. Raffaello Pantucci, "A Biography of Rashid Rauf: Al-Qa'ida's British Operative," *CTC Sentinel* 5, no. 7 (July 2012).

104. U.S. Department of State, "Designations of Harakat-ul Jihad Islami (HUJI) and Its Leader Mohammed Ilyas Kashmiri," August 6, 2010.

105. Letter from Muhammad Ilyas al-Kashmiri to Osama bin Laden, May 31, 2010, https://www.dni.gov/files/documents/ubl2017/english/Letter%20to%20 Usama%20Bin%20Muhammad%20Bin%20Ladin.pdf.

106. Letter from Osama bin Laden to Atiyah Abd al-Rahman, SOCOM-2012-0000019, available at https://ctc.usma.edu/letters-from-abbottabad-bin-ladin-sidelined/.

107. Office of Public Affairs, U.S. Department of Justice, "Tahawwur Rana and David Headley Indicted for Alleged Roles in India and Denmark Terrorism Conspiracies, Ilyas Kashmiri & Retired Pakistan Major Charged in Denmark Plot," January 14, 2010.

108. For instance, the United States killed Hazrat Abbas, a "senior AQIS" and Pakistani Taliban commander, in an April 2018 airstrike in Nangarhar province. Resolute Support Headquarters, "U.S. Forces Strike AQIS Leader in Nangarhar," April 23, 2018.

109. U.S. Department of State, "Designations of Tehrik-e Taliban Pakistan and Two Senior Leaders," September 1, 2010.

110. A copy of the Pakistani Taliban's charter, with comments by two senior al-Qaeda ideologues, was recovered from bin Laden's compound. See https://www.dni.gov /files/documents/ubl2016/english/TEHRIK-E%20TALIBAN%20PAKISTAN%20 (TPP)%20CHARTER.pdf.

111. Bill Roggio, "3 Jihadist Groups Merge with Movement of the Taliban in Pakistan," *FDD's Long War Journal*, May 6, 2015.

112. U.S. Department of State, "State Department Terrorist Designations," June 30, 2016.

113. Carlotta Gall, Pir Zubair Shah, and Eric Schmitt, "Seized Phone Offers Clues to Bin Laden's Pakistani Links," *New York Times*, June 23, 2011.

114. Al-Qaeda in the Indian Subcontinent, "Code of Conduct," As-Sahab Media Subcontinent, June 2017, 1.

115. Al-Qaeda in the Indian Subcontinent, "Code of Conduct," 5.

116. Dan Lamothe, " 'Probably the Largest' al-Qaeda Training Camp Ever Destroyed in Afghanistan," *Washington Post*, October 30, 2015.

117. Josh Smith, "Joint U.S.-Afghan Operation Targets al-Qaida in Southern Afghanistan," *Stars and Stripes*, October 13, 2015.

118. Nick Paton Walsh, Jason Hanna, and Mark Morgenstein, "Al-Qaeda Sites in Afghanistan Dismantled in Joint Operation, U.S. Military Says," *CNN*, October 13, 2015.

119. Bill Roggio, "Afghanistan's Terrorist Resurgence: Al Qaeda, ISIS, and Beyond," *FDD's Long War Journal*, April 27, 2017.

120. Dodwell and Rassler, "A View from the CT Foxhole."

121. U.S. Department of Defense, "Statement by Secretary of Defense Ash Carter on Hostage Rescue in Afghanistan," May 10, 2016.

122. Letter from Atiyah Abd al-Rahman to Osama bin Laden, April 2011, available at https://www.longwarjournal.org/wp-content/uploads/2015/03/EXHIBIT-431 -ENG-TRANS-EX-430-2F2C1C9A-.pdf.

123. NATO Resolute Support, "Afghan and U.S. Forces—Afghanistan Kill Top Terrorist Leaders," December 5, 2017.

124. "Senior al-Qaeda Member Killed in Joint Military Operation," *TOLONews*, December 5, 2017.

125. UN Security Council, "Twenty-First Report of the Analytical Support and Sanctions Monitoring Team Submitted Pursuant to Resolution 2368 (2017) Concerning ISIL (Da'esh), Al-Qaida and Associated Individuals and Entities," January 26, 2018, 15.

126. UN Security Council, "Twenty-First Report of the Analytical Support and Sanctions Monitoring Team," 15.

127. Dodwell and Rassler, "A View from the CT Foxhole."

128. Al-Qaeda in the Indian Subcontinent, "Code of Conduct," 1.

129. Jason Burke and Saad Hammadi, "Abdul Quader Mollah Execution Leads to Violence in Bangladesh," *Guardian* (London), December 13, 2013.

130. "Hanging of Top Islamist Leader Abdul Quader Mollah Triggers Bangladesh Violence," Agence France-Presse, December 13, 2013.

131. Burke and Hammadi, "Abdul Quader Mollah Execution Leads to Violence in Bangladesh."

132. "Two Sentenced to Death for Bangladesh Blogger Murder," Agence France-Presse, December 31, 2015.

133. Asim Umar, "The Dust Will Never Settle Down!," As Sahab Media, May 3, 2015.

134. Umar, "The Dust Will Never Settle Down!"

135. Ansar al-Islam released the statement, attributed to its spokesman Mufti Abdullah Ashraf, via social media on April 25, 2016.

136. U.S. Department of State, "Terrorist Designations of the Indian Mujahideen," September 15, 2011.

137. Bruce Riedel has discussed this possibility on several occasions. See Bruce Riedel, "Mumbai Attacks: Four Years Later," Brookings Institution, November 26, 2012. Riedel argues that in addition to LeT and Pakistani intelligence, "there was a third party behind the scenes in the Mumbai plot: al-Qaeda," which he claims "deliberately kept a very low profile, but helped the LeT plan and select the targets." See also Bruce Riedel, *Avoiding Armageddon: America, India, and Pakistan to the Brink and Back* (Washington, D.C.: Brookings Institution Press, 2013), 19–20. Syed Saleem Shahzad, a Pakistani journalist who was well-connected in jihadist circles, claimed that Ilyas Kashmiri "hijacked" the plot, which was conceived by Pakistani intelligence, and "turned it into the devastating attacks" that unfolded. Syed Saleem Shahzad, *Inside Al-Qaeda and the Taliban: Beyond Bin Laden and 9/11* (New York: Palgrave Macmillan, 2011), 69 and 96. Shahzad personally interviewed Kashmiri, making his theory of the plot quite interesting.

138. Ginger Thompson, "Terror Trial Witness Ties Pakistan to 2008 Attacks," *New York Times*, May 23, 2011.

139. Riedel, *Avoiding Armageddon*, 19–20.

140. *9/11 Commission Report*, 64–65, 67.

141. Letter from Muhammad Ilyas al-Kashmiri to Osama bin Laden, May 31, 2010.

142. "No Place for ISIS in Kashmir: Hizb," *Kashmir Observer*, May 13, 2017.

143. Thomas Joscelyn, "Al-Qaeda-Linked Jihadist in Kashmir Criticizes Pakistani Army," *FDD's Long War Journal*, September 2, 2017.

144. Al-Qaeda in the Indian Subcontinent, "Code of Conduct," 15–16.

145. "Zakir Musa's Call Redrawing Militant Alliances," *Kashmir Today*, June 27, 2017.

146. Ayman al-Zawahiri, "Don't Forget Kashmir," As Sahab Media, July 9, 2019.

147. Khalid al-Batarfi, "Burma: The Forgotten Word," Al Malahem Media, September 2017.

148. General Leadership of al-Qaeda, "Burma Calling," As Sahab Media, September 2017.

149. "Agreement for Bringing Peace to Afghanistan Between the Islamic Emirate of Afghanistan Which Is Not Recognized by the United States as a State and Is Known as the Taliban and the United States of America," February 29, 2020.

150. Mujib Mashal and Eric Schmitt, "White House Orders Direct Taliban Talks to Jump-Start Afghan Negotiations," *New York Times*, July 15, 2018.

151. Bill Roggio, "Taliban's Prime Objectives: U.S. Withdrawal, 'Establishment of an Islamic Government,'" *FDD's Long War Journal*, September 24, 2019.

152. "Agreement for Bringing Peace to Afghanistan between the Islamic Emirate of Afghanistan which is not recognized by the United States as a state and is known as the Taliban and the United States of America," February 29, 2020, part 1, para. C. A copy of the agreement is found on the *Washington Post* website: https://www.washingtonpost.com/context/u-s-taliban-peace-deal/7aab0f58-dd5c-430d-9557-1b6672d889c3/?itid=lk_inline_manual_3.

153. Humeyra Pamuk, Hamid Shalizi, and Charlotte Greenfield, "U.S. to Reduce Afghan Aid by $1 Billion After Pompeo Fails to Break Impasse," Reuters, March 23, 2020.

154. "Agreement for Bringing Peace to Afghanistan," part 1, paras. D and E.

155. "Transcript: Mike Pompeo on 'Face the Nation,'" *CBS News*, March 1, 2020.

156. "Agreement for Bringing Peace to Afghanistan," part 2, III.

157. Thomas Joscelyn and Bill Roggio, "Taliban Continues to Host Foreign Terrorist Groups, Despite Assurances to the Contrary," *FDD's Long War Journal*, February 7, 2019.

158. Joscelyn and Roggio, "Taliban Continues to Host Foreign Terrorist Groups."

159. "Agreement for Bringing Peace to Afghanistan," part 2, paras 2, 3, and 5.

160. Bill Roggio, "Afghan Intelligence Confirms Death of AQIS Emir," *FDD's Long War Journal*, October 8, 2019.

161. "Afghan Security Forces Kill Senior al Qaeda Leader al-Masri," Reuters, October 24, 2020.

162. "Agreement for Bringing Peace to Afghanistan," part 2, para. 2.

163. Thomas Joscelyn and Bill Roggio, "Taliban Leader Declares Victory After U.S. Agrees to Withdrawal Deal," *FDD's Long War Journal*, March 3, 2020.

164. Thomas Joscelyn, "Al-Qaeda Lauds Taliban's Great 'Victory' over America and Allies," *FDD's Long War Journal*, March 13, 2020.

165. "11 Days in August: How Afghanistan Fell," CBS News, August 22, 2021.

166. For example, Bill Roggio of *FDD's Long War Journal* warned throughout 2021 that the Afghan government was at risk of collapsing. On July 5, 2021, one month before the final eleven days cited by General Milley, Roggio assessed that the entire government could quickly collapse. See Bill Roggio, "Afghanistan at Risk of Collapse as Taliban Storms North," *FDD's Long War Journal*, July 5, 2021.

167. Susannah George, "Afghanistan's Military Collapse: Illicit Deals and Mass Desertions," *Washington Post*, August 15, 2021.

168. "Taliban Launches Major Afghan Offensive after Deadline for U.S. Pullout," Reuters, May 4, 2021.

169. "Remarks by President Biden on the Way Forward in Afghanistan," The White House, April 14, 2021.

170. UN Security Council, "Twenty-Second Report of the Analytical Support and Sanctions Monitoring Team Submitted Pursuant to Resolution 2368 (2017) Concerning ISIL (Da'esh), Al-Qaida and Associated Individuals and Entities," July 27, 2018, 3 and 15.

171. UN Security Council, "Twenty-Second Report of the Analytical Support and Sanctions Monitoring Team," 16.

172. UN Security Council, "Twenty-Second Report of the Analytical Support and Sanctions Monitoring Team," 9.

173. Thomas Joscelyn, "Al Qaeda Praises Taliban's 'Historic Victory' in Afghanistan," *FDD's Long War Journal*, August 31, 2021.

10. ISIS's External Operations

1. "Hong Kong Family Reveals Terror of German Train Attack," Agence France-Presse, July 20, 2016.

2. Thomas Joscelyn, "Teenager Who Terrorized German Train Appears in Islamic State Video," *FDD's Long War Journal*, July 19, 2016.

3. Elizabeth Roberts, "Germany Train Attack: ISIS Inspired Teen, Official Says," *CNN*, July 20, 2016.

4. Von Hans Leyendecker and Georg Mascolo, "Die Chats der Attentäter von Würzburg und Ansbach mit dem IS," *Süddeutsche Zeitung*, September 14, 2016.

5. Christoph Reuter, "Secret Files Reveal the Structure of the Islamic State," *Spiegel*, April 18, 2015.

6. Rukmini Callimachi, "How a Secretive Branch of ISIS Built a Global Network of Killers," *New York Times*, August 3, 2016.

7. U.S. Department of Defense, "Statement by Pentagon Press Secretary Peter Cook on Precision Airstrike Targeting Abu Muhammad Al-Adnani," August 30, 2016.

8. Daveed Gartenstein-Ross and Nathaniel Barr, "Bloody Ramadan: How the Islamic State Coordinated a Global Terrorist Campaign," *War on the Rocks*, July 20, 2016.

9. Rukmini Callimachi, "How ISIS Built the Machinery of Terror Under Europe's Gaze," *New York Times*, March 29, 2016.

10. Callimachi, "How a Secretive Branch of ISIS Built a Global Network of Killers."

11. "Interview with Abū 'Umar al-Baljīkī," *Dabiq* 7, February 12, 2015, 72–75.

12. Mariano Castillo and Paul Cruickshank, "Who Was Abdelhamid Abaaoud, Suspected Ringleader of Paris Attack?," *CNN*, November 19, 2015.

13. David Remnick, "Going the Distance: On and Off the Road with Barack Obama," *New Yorker*, January 19, 2014.

14. Ben Rhodes, "Airstrikes in Iraq: What You Need to Know," White House blog, August 11, 2014, https://obamawhitehouse.archives.gov/blog/2014/08/11/air strikes-iraq-what-you-need-to-know.

15. Abu Muhammad al-Adnani, "Indeed, Your Lord is Ever Watchful," al-Furqan Media, September 21, 2014.

16. Thomas Joscelyn, "Why the U.K. Launched Its First Targeted Drone Strike Ever," *FDD's Long War Journal*, April 26, 2017.

17. Intelligence and Security Committee of Parliament, "U.K. Lethal Drone Strikes in Syria," April 26, 2017, 1.

18. Adam Goldman and Eric Schmitt, "One by One, ISIS Social Media Experts Are Killed as Result of F.B.I. Program," *New York Times*, November 24, 2016.

19. David Cameron, "Syria: Refugees and Counter-terrorism—Prime Minister's Statement," September 7, 2015, https://www.gov.uk/government/speeches/syria -refugees-and-counter-terrorism-prime-ministers-statement.

20. Intelligence and Security Committee of Parliament, "U.K. Lethal Drone Strikes in Syria," 7.

21. Intelligence and Security Committee of Parliament, "U.K. Lethal Drone Strikes in Syria," 7.

22. Intelligence and Security Committee of Parliament, "U.K. Lethal Drone Strikes in Syria," 7.

23. Intelligence and Security Committee of Parliament, "U.K. Lethal Drone Strikes in Syria," 10.

24. Lorenzo Franceschi-Bicchierai, "How a Teenage Hacker Became the Target of a U.S. Drone Strike," *Vice*, August 28, 2015.

25. Intelligence and Security Committee of Parliament, "U.K. Lethal Drone Strikes in Syria," 13.

26. Intelligence and Security Committee of Parliament, "U.K. Lethal Drone Strikes in Syria," 13.

27. Intelligence and Security Committee of Parliament, "U.K. Lethal Drone Strikes in Syria," 10.

28. Intelligence and Security Committee of Parliament, "U.K. Lethal Drone Strikes in Syria," 14–15.

29. Intelligence and Security Committee of Parliament, "U.K. Lethal Drone Strikes in Syria," 13.

30. Intelligence and Security Committee of Parliament, "U.K. Lethal Drone Strikes in Syria," 9.

31. U.S. Department of Justice, "Acting Assistant Attorney General Mary B. McCord for National Security Delivers Keynote Remarks at Second Annual Billington International Cybersecurity Dinner," March 29, 2017.

32. Criminal Complaint, *United States v. Ferizi*, No. 1:15-MJ-515 (E.D. Va., October 6, 2015), 10.

33. Criminal Complaint, *United States v. Ferizi*, 11.

34. Criminal Complaint, *United States v. Ferizi*, 12.

35. U.S. Department of Justice, "ISIL-Linked Hacker Arrested in Malaysia on U.S. Charges," October 15, 2015; and U.S. Attorney's Office, Eastern District of Virginia, "ISIL-Linked Hacker Pleads Guilty to Providing Material Support," June 15, 2016.

36. Callum Paton, "ISIS 'White Widow' Recruiter Sally Jones Killed with Child in U.S. Airstrike: Reports," *Newsweek*, October 12, 2017.

37. Del Quentin Wilber, "Here's How the FBI Tracked Down a Tech-Savvy Terrorist Recruiter for the Islamic State," *Los Angeles Times*, April 13, 2017.

38. GW Extremism Tracker, "The Islamic State in America, Numbers by State," November 2019 Update, https://extremism.gwu.edu/sites/g/files/zaxdzs2191/f/Nov19%20Update.pdf.

39. GW Extremism Tracker, "The Islamic State in America, Numbers by State," December 2015 Update, https://extremism.gwu.edu/sites/g/files/zaxdzs2191/f/downloads/Dec.%202015%20Snapshot.pdf.

40. Wilber, "Here's How the FBI Tracked Down a Tech-Savvy Terrorist Recruiter."

41. U.S. Department of Justice, "Cincinnati-Area Man Pleads Guilty to Plot to Attack U.S. Government Officers," July 7, 2016.

42. Goldman and Schmitt, "One by One, ISIS Social Media Experts Are Killed."

43. "Local Man Had Direct Contact with an ISIS Terrorist, Prosecutors Say," *WCVB 5 ABC* (Boston), April 21, 2016.

44. Wilber, "Here's How the FBI Tracked Down a Tech-Savvy Terrorist Recruiter."

45. Pete Williams and Alex Johnson, "Usaamah Rahim, Killed by Boston Police, Was Plotting to Behead Activist: Sources," *NBC News*, June 4, 2015.

46. U.S. Attorney's Office, District of Massachusetts, "Everett Man Alleged to Support ISIL Charged with Additional Charge of Obstructing Justice," February 15, 2017.

47. U.S. Department of Justice, "Massachusetts Man Convicted of Supporting ISIS and Conspiring to Murder U.S. Citizens," October 18, 2017.

48. U.S. Department of Justice, "Two New York City Residents Pleaded Guilty to All Charges in Terrorism Case," February 10, 2017.

49. "New York Man Munther Omar Saleh Admits Plotting to Help ISIS," *CBS News*, February 10, 2017.

50. U.S. Department of Justice, "New York Man Sentenced to 17 Years in Prison for Attempted Murder of a Federal Officer," April 26, 2018.

51. U.S. Department of Justice, "Two New York City Residents Pleaded Guilty."

52. Jack Moore, "ISIS in America: North Carolina Jihadi Pleads Guilty to Murdering Elderly Neighbor," *Newsweek*, July 19, 2017.

53. U.S. Department of Justice, "North Carolina Man Pleads Guilty to Attempting to Commit an Act of Terrorism Transcending National Boundaries," November 29, 2016.

54. U.S. Attorney's Office, Western District of New York, "New York Man Sentenced for Conspiracy to Provide Material Support to ISIL in Connection with Planned New Year's Eve Attack," January 26, 2017; and U.S. Department of Justice, "New York Man Pleads Guilty to Conspiracy to Provide Material Support to ISIL in Connection with Planned New Year's Eve Attack," August 11, 2016.

55. U.S. Department of Justice, "New York Man Pleads Guilty."

56. U.S. Department of Justice, "Former Army National Guardsman Sentenced to 11 Years for Attempting to Provide Material Support to ISIL," February 10, 2017.

57. Alexander Meleagrou-Hitchens and Seamus Hughes, "The Threat to the United States from the Islamic State's Virtual Entrepreneurs," *CTC Sentinel* 10, no. 3 (March 2017).

58. U.S. Department of Justice, "Former Army National Guardsman Sentenced."

59. U.S. Department of Justice, "Ohio Man Arrested for Attempting to Provide Material Support to ISIL," November 7, 2016.

60. U.S. Department of Justice, "Columbus Man Sentenced to 80 Months in Prison for Attempting to Provide Material Support to ISIS," July 6, 2018.

61. Ashish Pandey, "Islamic State Module in Hyderabad: Spit on Their Faces If You Can't Kill Them, Handlers Told Operatives," *India Today*, December 26, 2016.

62. Rukmini Callimachi, "Not 'Lone Wolves' After All: How ISIS Guides World's Terror Plots from Afar," *New York Times*, February 4, 2017.

63. U.S. Department of Defense, "Department of Defense Press Briefing by Pentagon Press Secretary Peter Cook in the Pentagon Briefing Room," May 5, 2016.

64. U.S. Department of Defense, "Department of Defense Press Briefing."

65. For a profile of Kassim's role as a virtual plotter, see Bridget Moreng, "ISIS' Virtual Puppeteers: How They Recruit and Train 'Lone Wolves,'" *Foreign Affairs*, September 21, 2016.

66. "Nice: La conférence de presse de François Molins en intégralité," *CNews*, July 18, 2016, https://www.youtube.com/watch?v=fapoL8A0zkY.

67. William Horobin and Stacy Meichtry, "Attacker in Nice Showed Online Fascination with Islamic State," *Wall Street Journal*, July 18, 2016.

68. Horobin and Meichtry, "Attacker in Nice Showed Online Fascination with Islamic State."

69. "Nice: la conférence de presse de François Molins en intégralité."

70. Alissa J. Rubin and Aurelien Breeden, "ISIS Claims Truck Attacker in France Was Its 'Soldier,'" *New York Times*, July 16, 2016 (quoting le Drian); and Marie-Caroline Meijer, "Attentat à Nice: Comment Hollande muscle sa riposte contre Daesh," *RTL*, July 21, 2016 (quoting Hollande).

71. "The Latest: Did Nice Attacker Have Contacts in Italy?," Associated Press, July 18, 2016.

72. Bethan McKernan, "France's Most Wanted Isis Fighter Killed in Iraq Leaves Final Message Accusing His Leaders of Hypocrisy," *Independent* (U.K.), February 16, 2017.

73. Moreng, "ISIS' Virtual Puppeteers."

74. Moreng, "ISIS' Virtual Puppeteers"; and Stacy Meichtry and Sam Schechner, "How Islamic State Weaponized the Chat App to Direct Attacks in the West," *Wall Street Journal*, October 20, 2016.

75. Thomas Joscelyn, "The Islamic State's Allegiance Videos," *FDD's Long War Journal*, April 23, 2019.

76. Leyendecker and Mascolo, "Die Chats der Attentäter."

77. Ryan Browne and Paul Cruickshank, "U.S.-Led Coalition Targets Top ISIS Figure in Iraq Strike," *CNN*, February 10, 2017.

78. U.S. Department of Treasury, "Treasury Designates Indonesian and Malaysian ISIS Operatives and Leaders," March 30, 2017.

79. "8 Things to Know About Muhammad Bahrun Naim, Alleged Mastermind of Jakarta Attack," *Straits Times*, January 15, 2016.

80. Brian Padden, "Indonesians Struggle to Combat Extremist Ideologies," *Voice of America*, January 22, 2016.

81. Wahyudi Soeriaatmadja, "Militant Bahrun Naim Used PayPal, Bitcoin to Transfer Funds for Terror Attacks in Indonesia," *Straits Times*, January 9, 2017.

82. U.S. Department of the Treasury, "Treasury Designates Australian and Southeast Asian ISIL Operatives and Leaders," January 10, 2017.

83. Rendi A. Witular, "The Rise of Aman Abdurrahman, IS Master Ideologue," *Jakarta Post*, January 25, 2016.

84. Randy Fabi and Kanupriya Kapoor, "Jail to Jihad: Indonesian Prisons a Breeding Ground for Militancy," Reuters, January 18, 2016.

85. U.S. Department of the Treasury, "Treasury Designates Australian and Southeast Asian ISIL Operatives."

86. U.S. Department of State, "State Department Terrorist Designation of Jamaah Ansharut Daulah," January 10, 2017.

87. Tom Allard and Kanupriya Kapoor, "Fighting Back: How Indonesia's Elite Police Turned the Tide on Militants," Reuters, December 23, 2016.

88. Kanupriya Kapoor, "Police Find Bomb-Making Materials for Alleged Singapore Attack," Reuters, August 6, 2016.

89. Francis Chan, "Indonesia Terror Cell was Planning Dec Holiday Strike," *Straits Times*, December 1, 2016.

90. Francis Chan, "Bomb Plot by Indonesian Terrorists Targeted at Jakarta Presidential Palace: Police," *Straits Times*, December 11, 2016 (parentheses in original).

91. Chan, "Bomb Plot by Indonesian Terrorists."

92. Charlie Campbell, "ISIS Unveiled: The Story Behind Indonesia's First Female Suicide Bomber," *Time*, March 3, 2017.

93. Ali Kotarumalos, "Arrested Indonesian Woman Says IS Militant Ordered Bombing," Associated Press, December 14, 2016.

94. Adam Harvey, "Indonesia Not Prepared to Deal with Female Extremist Threat, Expert Says," *ABC News* (Australia), January 13, 2017.

95. U.S. Department of the Treasury, "Treasury Designates Australian and Southeast Asian ISIL Operatives and Leaders."

96. Thomas Joscelyn, "Indonesia Authorities Hunt Islamic State Operative's Cyber Recruits," *FDD's Long War Journal*, April 18, 2017.

97. Roni Toldanes, "Pentagon: No Confirmation on Indonesian IS Leader's Purported Death," *Benar News*, April 20, 2018.

98. "Malacca Man Behind Terror Plots in Malaysia," *Straits Times*, August 15, 2016.

99. M. Kumar, "Cops Confirm Movida Bombing First Ever IS Attack in Malaysia," *The Star*, July 4, 2016.

100. U.S. Department of Treasury, "Treasury Designates Indonesian and Malaysian ISIS Operatives and Leaders."

101. Jacqueline Williams, "Australia Details 'Sophisticated' Plot by ISIS to Take Down Plane," *New York Times*, August 4, 2017.

102. "Israel Foiled 'Plane Terror Plot' in Australia," *BBC*, February 22, 2018; and "IDF Unit 8200 Thwarted ISIS Terror Attack on Australian Flight," *Israel Defense*, February 22, 2018.

103. Paul Maley, "From Syria to Sydney: How the Airport Terror Plot Unfolded," *The Australian*, August 5, 2017.

104. Ellen Whinnett, "Evil Engineer: Basil Hassan Behind Passenger Bomb Plot," *Herald Sun*, September 21, 2019.

105. Bill Roggio, "U.S. Adds Islamic State Leader, External Operations Planners to Global Terrorist List," *FDD's Long War Journal*, November 22, 2016.

106. U.S. Department of State, "State Department Terrorist Designations of Abdullah Ahmed al-Meshedani, Basil Hassan, and Abdelilah Himich," November 22, 2016.

107. Andrew Zammit, "Operation Silves: Inside the 2017 Islamic State Sydney Plane Plot," *CTC Sentinel* 13, no. 4 (April 2020).

108. Whinnett, "Evil Engineer."

109. Zammit, "Operation Silves."

110. "Australian Brothers Guilty of IS Plane Bomb Plot," *BBC*, September 20, 2019.

111. Andrew Zammit, "New Developments in the Islamic State's External Operations: The 2017 Sydney Plane Plot," *CTC Sentinel* 10, no. 9 (October 2017).

112. Zammit, "New Developments."

113. Thomas Joscelyn, "Australia Disrupts 'Sophisticated' Plot Directed by the Islamic State," *FDD's Long War Journal*, August 4, 2017.

114. Whinnett, "Evil Engineer."

115. Mette Mayli Albaek, Jens Vithner, and Troels Kingo, "Dømt australsk terrorist: Basil Hassan bag bombe på russisk fly: En australier sætter Basil Hassan i forbindelse med et terrorangreb i 2015," *Drone-sagen*, November 6, 2019, https://www.dr.dk/nyheder/indland/doemt-australsk-terrorist-basil-hassan-bag-bombe-paa-russisk-fly.

11. The Past and Future of Jihadist Organizational Learning

1. Matt Novak, "This Is What an ISIS Drone Workshop Looks Like," *Gizmodo*, June 29, 2017.
2. Joby Warrick, "Use of Weaponized Drones by ISIS Spurs Terrorism Fears," *Washington Post*, February 21, 2017.
3. Novak, "This Is What an ISIS Drone Workshop Looks Like."
4. Michael Munoz, "Selling the Long War: Islamic State Propaganda After the Caliphate," *CTC Sentinel* 11, no. 10 (November 2018).
5. Munoz, "Selling the Long War."
6. See, for example, Amaq News Agency releases on April 10, 2020, and April 20, 2020.
7. Bruce Hoffman, "The Coming ISIS-al Qaeda Merger" *Foreign Affairs*, March 29, 2016.
8. Rob Merrick, "Al-Qaeda Plotting New Plane Attacks in Europe after 'Resurgence' of Terror Group, Security Minister Warns," *Independent*, December 23, 2018.
9. Eric Schmitt and Abdi Latif Dahir, "Al Qaeda Branch in Somalia Threatens Americans in East Africa—and Even the U.S.," *New York Times*, March 21, 2020.
10. Michael Shkolnik, "The Drone Threat to Israeli National Security," *War on the Rocks*, January 10, 2017.
11. Kyle Mizokami, "The U.K. Promises to Develop Drome Swarms, But on an Unrealistic Timetable," *Popular Mechanics*, February 12, 2019.
12. Clayton Schuety and Lucas Will, "An Air Force 'Way of the Swarm:' Using Wargaming and Artificial Intelligence to Train Drones," *War on the Rocks*, September 21, 2018; and Randy Rieland, "Teaching Drones to Sniff Out Toxic Air," *Smithsonian Magazine*, September 11, 2018.
13. Nick Waters describes Israel's dispersal of tear gas against protesters as "by far the most prominent and controversial IDF use of commercial drones." Nick Waters, "First ISIS, Then Iraq, Now Israel: IDF Use of Commercial Drones," *Bellingcat*, June 18, 2018.
14. Ira Boudway, "With Driverless Cars Running Late, a Startup Tries Remote-Control Trucks," *Bloomberg*, April 18, 2019.
15. Don Rassler, Muhammad Al-'Ubaydi, and Vera Mironova, "The Islamic State's Drone Documents: Management, Acquisitions, and DIY Tradecraft," Combating Terrorism Center at West Point, January 31, 2017; and "Descubren un 'Narcodron' en Colombia; Enviaba Cocaína a Panamá," *Excelsior* (Mexico), November 16, 2016.
16. Nick Waters, "The Poor Man's Air Force? Rebel Drones Attack Russia's Airbase in Syria," *Bellingcat*, January 12, 2018.
17. Mark Jacobsen, "Why the Flying IED Threat Has Barely Started," *War on the Rocks*, October 19, 2016.
18. Waters, "The Poor Man's Air Force?"
19. J. M. Porup, "How and Why Deepfake Videos Work—and What Is at Risk," *CSO Online*, April 10, 2019.
20. Here is a video demonstrating the versatility, verisimilitude, and potential of deep fakes: NOVA, "Deepfake Videos Are Getting Terrifyingly Real," April 2, 2019, YouTube, https://www.youtube.com/watch?v=T76bK2t2r8g.

21. Todd Wasserman, "Chatbots Are All the Rage—and Something of a Risk," *Security Roundtable*, March 21, 2018.
22. Dexter, "Pricing," n.d., accessed July 5, 2019, https://rundexter.com/pricing/.
23. Zeynep Tufekci, "Think You're Discreet Online? Think Again," *New York Times*, April 21, 2019.
24. Risa Brooks, "Territorial Havens and the Risk of Complex Terrorist Attacks in the United States," in *The Future of ISIS*, ed. Faisal al-Istrabadi & Sumit Ganguly (Washington, D.C.: Brookings Institution Press, 2018), 206–7.
25. Lisa Monaco, "Preventing the Next Attack: A Strategy for the War on Terrorism," *Foreign Affairs*, November/December 2017.
26. Lorne Dawson and Amarnath Amarasingam, "Talking to Foreign Fighters: Insights into Motivations for *Hijrah* to Syria and Iraq," *Studies in Conflict and Terrorism* 40, no. 3 (2017): 191; Simon Cottee, " 'What ISIS Really Wants' Revisited: Religion Matters in Jihadist Violence, But How?," *Studies in Conflict and Terrorism* 40, no. 6 (May 2016): 439; and Graeme Wood, "What ISIS Really Wants," *Atlantic*, March 2015.
27. Office for Targeted Violence and Terrorism Prevention, *Fiscal Year 2016 Countering Violent Extremism Grant Program: Preliminary Report on Programmatic Performance*, March 26, 2020.
28. Solomon Asch, "Opinions and Social Pressure," *Scientific American* 193, no. 5 (November 1955). For a worthwhile discussion of the relationship between Asch's work and politics today, see Ezra Klein, *Why We're Polarized* (New York: Avid Reader Press, 2020).
29. Seth G. Jones, Charles Vallee, Danika Newlee, Nicholas Harrington, Clayton Sharb, and Hannah Byrne, *The Evolution of the Salafi-Jihadist Threat* (Washington, D.C.: Center for Strategic and International Studies, 2018).

Index

Abaaoud, Abdelhamid, 5, 358–59
Abbas, Hazrat, 469n108
Abbottabad raid, 91, 133, 168, 224, 264–66, 315–17, 323–24, 330, 340, 382
Abdaly, Taimour Abdulwahab al-, 148
Abdo, Naser Jason, 136
Abdulkader, Munir, 365–66
Abdulla, Bilal, 102–3
Abdullah II (King), 223
Abdulmutallab, Umar Farouk, 87–88, 125; Awlaki and, 137–38
ABM. See Ansar Bayt al-Maqdis
Absi brothers, 249
Abu Dahdah, 65
Abu Doha, 100–101
Abu Ghadiya, 200
Abu Hoshar, Khadr, 100
Abu Ibrahim, 199
Abu Jaffar, 100–101
Abu Maysara, 269–70
Abu Muhammad, 224
Abu Muntasir, 122
Abu Qaqaa, 199
Abu Qatada, 64

Abu Rumman, Abdallah, 223
Abu Salha, Moner Mohammad, 159
Abu Salim Martyrs Brigade, 300
Abu Yazid, Mustafa, 323–24
Abu Zubaydah, 99–101, 422n117
Ackerman, Gary, 18, 25
Adl, Sayf al-, 82, 223, 328, 386, 445n26
Adnani, Abu Muhammad al-, 151–52, 161, 247–48, 256–57, 284–85, 360–61, 447n64; Khorasan region and, 271–73, 278; media and, 269
Aeneid (Virgil), 295
Afghanistan, 393; collapse of, 352–53; Hazaras in, 272, 278; Islamic Emirate of, 268, 316–25, 340–43, 349–50; Kabul in, 278, 315, 337, 340–41, 349–50, 352–53; al-Qaeda in, 14, 61, 66–67, 227–29, 253, 272–74; Taliban in, 221, 227–29, 272–74, 315–34, 339, 349–54; Zarqawi in, 222–24, 228–30
Afghanistan war: "Agreement for Bringing Peace to Afghanistan" peace deal and, 349–53, 471n152; AQIS and, 334–49, 352; bin Laden and, 314–15;

Afghanistan war (*continued*)
how al-Qaeda survived, 314–16, 332, 353–54; Iran and, 325–31; ISIS, Wilayah Khorasan and, 277–78; Islamic Emirate of Afghanistan and, 316–25; Nicholson on, 463n2; Pakistan and, 325, 331, 335–38; al-Qaeda and, 273–74, 314–54; al-Qaeda's ethnic fighting groups and, 332–34; United States and, 273–74, 314–16, 349–53, 464n22, 471n152

Afghan jihad: A. Azzam and, 51–52; far-enemy strategy and, 51–54; ideology of, 52–54

Afghan-Soviet war, 42–43, 51, 52, 53–59, 65, 337–38

Africa: Boko Haram in, 303–7; *fitna* in, 294–312; Horn of Africa al-Qaeda-ISIS relations, 307–12; North African al-Qaeda-ISIS relations, 295–303; al-Qaeda-ISIS relations in, 294–312; West African al-Qaeda-ISIS relations, 303–7. *See also specific countries*

African aviation: Daallo Airlines flight 159 and, 95–96; Metrojet flight 9268 and, 93–95; post-Arab Spring attacks on, 93–96

afterlife, 126–27

"Agreement for Bringing Peace to Afghanistan" peace deal, 349–53, 471n152

Ahmad, Abu Abd-al-Iylah, 183–84, 299

Ahmed, Kafeel, 102–3

AI. *See* artificial intelligence

AIDS epidemic, 126–27

Air France flight 8969, 76–77

Akbar, Hasan, 109

Akhundzada, Hibatullah, 269; Taliban and, 320–21, 352

Algeria, 44, 76–77, 186, 196–97, 306; GSPC and, 101–2, 264–65

Ali, Ali Hussein, 311–12

Ali, Hamid al-, 234–36

Almani, Abu Talha al-, 322

Almeida Santos, Paulo Jose de, 43

alNeda, 125

ambidextrous organizations, 33

America, Egypt, and the Islamist Movement (EIJ document), 53–54

American embassy bombings, 45, 188

Amman hotel attacks, 102

amn al-kharji, 357–58; Amriki and, 367–69; Hussain and, 361–67; Kassim and, 369–71; virtual plotters of, 360–71

amniyat: ISIS, 356–60; al-Shabaab, 310, 357, 462nn213–14

Amriki, Abu Issa al-, 367–69

Anarchist Cookbook, The (Powell), 135

Anbari, Abu Ali al-, 246

Anbari, Abu Nabil al-, 296, 300–301

Ansar al-Sharia chapters, 299

Ansar al-Sharia in Tunisia (AST), 173, 185–86, 187, 299, 438n98; banning of, 196–97; *dawa, hisba,* and, 189–96; roots and background on, 188–89; social media and, 190–91

Ansar al-Sharia Libya, 299, 301

Ansar Bayt al-Maqdis (ABM), 177–79, 215–16

Ansar Ghazwat-ul-Hind (AGH), 347–48

anticipatory/reactive spectrum, 31, 31

Aptitude for Destruction (RAND Corporation report), 18

AQAP. *See* al-Qaeda in Arabian Peninsula

AQI. *See* al-Qaeda in Iraq

AQIM. *See* al-Qaeda in Islamic Maghreb

AQIS. *See* al-Qaeda in Indian Subcontinent

al-Aqsa Mosque, 66–67

AQSL. *See* al-Qaeda senior leadership

Arab 055 Brigade, 318–19, 464n13

Arabian Peninsula: AQAP's gradualism in, 285–90; *fitna* in, 280–94; future of *fitna* in, 293–94; Hazimi trend in, 290–93; al-Qaeda-ISIS relations in,

280–94; "war of words" in, 282–87. *See also* al-Qaeda in Arabian Peninsula; *specific countries*

Arab Spring: bin Laden and, 167; consensus errors on, 6–8; *dawa* and, 167, 188–96; events leading to, 165–67; jihadism and, 6–8, 13, 165–215, 382; overview of, 6–8, 13; post-Arab Spring attacks on African aviation, 93–96; post-Arab Spring Libya, 179–87; post-Arab Spring al-Qaeda guidelines, 168–70; post-Mubarak Egypt and, 171–79; al-Qaeda and, 7–8, 11, 165–216; in Syria, 165–66, 197–209; in Tunisia, 165–66, 188–97; in Yemen, 280–81

Argyris, Chris, 30

Ariana Grande concert attack, 4

Armed Islamic Group (GIA), 44–45, 59–60; in Air France Flight 8969, 76–77

artificial intelligence (AI), 390–94

Asch, Solomon, 399

Ashour, Omar, 7

Asiri, Ibrahim al-, 86–93

Asrar al-Mujahideen, 136–37

Assad, Bashar al-, 166, 197–200, 250; al-Qaeda and, 204–5

Assad, Hafez al-, 49–50

AST. *See* Ansar al-Sharia in Tunisia

Atatürk Airport attack, 104–5

Atef, Mohammed. *See* Masri, Abu Hafs al-

Atta, Mohammed, 80–81

Atwan, Abdel Bari, 61–62

Australia, 152; ISIS in, 155; "Sydney" plot and aviation in, 96–98, 376–77

aviation: aircraft hijacking history in, 73–76; Air France flight 8969 and, 76–77; airline hijackings, 19; airport attacks and, 98–105; al-Asiri and bomb designs for, 86–93; Atatürk Airport attack and, 104–5; Awlaki and, 89–91, 137–39; Bagram Air Base attack and, 322; "Bojinka" plot and, 63–64, 77–79; Brussels Airport attack

and, 104; Chechen female suicide attackers and, 83–85, 94; Daallo Airlines flight 159 and, 95–96; Domodedovo International Airport attack and, 103–4; economics and, 72–73; FAA and, 74, 83; flag carriers in, 72; Glasgow International Airport attack and, 102–3; Indian Airlines Flight 814 and, 74–75; ISIS and, 93–94, 96–98, 104–5, 376–78; jihadism in, 12–13, 19, 63–64, 70–106, 386–87; law in, 70–71, 83–85, 86; "LAX" plot and, 99–101; "liquid bomb" plot on, 85–86; Metrojet flight 9268 and, 93–95; beyond 9/11, the early years of, 79–81; organizational learning and, 79–81, 84, 89–91, 105–6; "parcels" plot on, 88–91, 105; Philippine Airlines Flight 434 and, 77–78; post-Arab Spring attacks on African aviation, 93–96; al-Qaeda and, 70–93, 99–106; "Queen Alia International Airport" plot and, 102; security checkpoints and, 94–96, 422n114; September 11, 2001 and, 70–71, 73–76, 80–81; "shoe bomber" and, 81–83, 386–88; strategies for attacking, 71–73; "Swiss Airport" plot and, 101; "Sydney" plot and, 96–98, 376–77; tactical evolution in, 386–87; threat reporting in, 75–76; TSA and, 71, 83, 86, 92–96, 106; underwear bomber and, 87–88, 137–38; underwear bomber 2.0 and, 92–93, 421n93; virtual plotters and, 96–98, 376–78. *See also* September 11, 2001

Aviation and Transportation Act (2001), 70–71

Awakening (Sahwa), 236, 240–41

Awfi, Abu al-Harith Muhammad, 265

Awlaki, Anwar al-, 13–14, 72, 88, 363, 387; Abdulmutallab and, 137–38; aviation and, 89–91, 137–39; blogging by, 110–11, 127–29, 145–46; cartoon

Awlaki, Anwar al- (*continued*)
   controversies and, 139–51; *Charlie
   Hebdo* attack and, 139–41, 148–49;
   Comedy Central and, 146–48;
   "Constants on the Path of Jihad"
   lectures by, 123–26; *Dabiq* magazine
   and, 153–55; death of, 122; as "early
   adopter," 123–29; early life of, 117–19;
   evolution of jihadism and terrorism
   relating to, 162–64; Fort Hood attack
   and, 108–11; "The Hereafter" lecture
   series by, 126–27; ideology and
   portrait of, 117–22; *Inspire* magazine
   and, 129–37, 148–51; ISIS's call to
   attack and, 151–62; ISIS's success and,
   152–53; "Jihad Jane" and, 144;
   Jyllands-Posten controversy and,
   141–45; London years of, 121–22; on
   martyrdom, 124; messages by, 123–29;
   operational planning by, 137–39; as
   preacher, 118; radicalization and,
   111–17; as radicalizer, 111–13;
   September 11, 2001, and, 117, 119–21;
   in United States, 118–19; "Why
   Muslims Love Death" by, 121; Yemen
   and, 117–18, 122
Ayeri, Yusuf al-, 123–26
Azari, Omarjan, 155–56
Azhar, Maulana Masood, 74–75
Azzam, Abdullah, 118, 127–28, 131,
   452n22; Afghan jihad and, 51–54; bin
   Laden and, 52, 54; "Defending Muslim
   Lands" by, 51–52, 129–30; *Inspire*
   magazine and, 129–30
Azzam, Omar, 172
Azzouz, Abd al-Baset, 184–85

Badat, Saajid Mohammed, 82–83
Baghdadi, Abu Bakr al-, 104–5, 140, 142,
   151, 178, 202, 444n1; AQAP and,
   282–84, 294; Boko Haram and, 303–4;
   as caliphate, 217–20; ISI and, 242–46,
   269–71; ISIS and, 218–20, 242–46,

248–49, 254–57, 261–63, 269, 272–84,
   288–311; leadership under, 217–19,
   242–44; MSC and, 229–31, 243–44;
   al-Shabaab and, 307–9
Baghdadi, Abu Umar: background and
   biography on, 235–36; bin Laden and,
   235–37, 254; death of, 242–43; ISI and
   Muhajir's *bayah* to, 232–39; al-Qaeda
   and, 232, 235–39, 254
Bagram Air Base attack, 322
Balawi, Humam Khalil al-, 421n93
Bali bombings, 125, 374
Bangladesh, 343, 344–46
Banshiri, Abu Obaida al-, 56, 61–62
Bardo National Museum attack, 197
Bargh, John, 114–15
Barnawi, Abu Musab al-, 305
Baryalei, Mohammad Ali, 155–56
Basha, Abu Dujana al-, 334
Bastille Day attack, 3–4, 10, 163, 369–70
Bataclan theater, 3
Batarfi, Khalid, 284–85, 321, 348–49
Battar Brigade, 296
Battle of Jaji, 54–56
bayah, 227–28, 232–39, 261, 422n117
Beeby, Mick, 29
beheadings, 155, 253–54
Beirut attacks, 68–69, 326, 381–82
Belaïd, Chokri, 191, 196
Belgium, 104, 358
beliefs, 112. *See also* ideology
Belmokhtar, Mokhtar, 186, 305–6
Ben Ali, Zine El Abidine, 6, 189
Ben Brik, Hassan, 189–90
Benevolence International Foundation,
   55, 61
Benghazi attacks, 174–77, 185–87
Benghazi Revolutionaries Shura Council
   (BRSC), 301
Benner, Mary, 411n61
Benotman, Noman, 181, 437n71
Ben Qumu, 183, 437n71
Bergen, Peter, 62

Berlin Christmas market attack, 4, 156
Beugnet, Yannick, 76
Bhutto, Zulfikar Ali, 336
Biden, Joe, 353
Binali, Turki al-, 249–50
Binalshibh, Ramzi, 80
bin Baz, Abdul Aziz, 49
bin Laden, Osama, 7, 36, 125, 262, 294, 329, 385, 428n94; Abbottabad raid and, 91, 133, 168, 224, 264–66, 315–17, 323–24, 330, 340, 382; Afghanistan war and, 314–15; AQAP and, 287; AQIM and, 298–99; AQIS and, 340–41; Arab Spring and, 167; A. Azzam and, 52, 54; background on, 41–43; Abu Umar Baghdadi and, 235–37, 254; Battle of Jaji and, 54–56; on cartoonists, 143; death of, 168; declaration of war against America by, 41–42, 43–44; EIJ and, 67; Global Islamic Front and, 66–68; Hizballah and, 68–69, 326; Iraq and, 221, 253; ISI and, 233–39; ISIS and, 203, 253–54; KSM and, 80; "LAX" plot and, 101; Libya and, 181–82; Muhajir and, 233–35; in Pakistan, 42; Saudi Arabia and, 42–44; September 11, 2001, and, 316–18; Taliban and, 316–20, 322; Zarqawi and, 226–31, 445n26; A. Zawahiri and, 171–72, 203; Zubayr and, 266–67
bin Muhammad, Abdallah, 300–301
Bitter Harvest (Zawahiri), 50, 53, 171–72
Black, Ian, 7, 437n71
"Black Hawk Down" incident, 43
"black widows," 83–85
blasphemers, 150, 344–46
blogging: by Awlaki, 110–11, 127–29, 145–46; murders of bloggers, 150, 345
"Bojinka" plot, 63–64, 77–79
Boko Haram, 302–7
Bolton, John, 200, 440n155
bomb-making guides, 135–36
Booth, Charles, 29

Bor, Robert, 71
Borleh, Abdullahi Abdisalam, 95–96
Boston Marathon bombing, 135–36, 159–60, 366, 373
Bouazizi, Mohamed, 165–66
Boudina, Ibrahim, 1–2, 16, 358
Bouyali, Mustafa, 59
Bouzid, Nouri, 193
Brahmi, Mohammed, 196
Breivik, Anders, 15
Bremer, L. Paul, 200
Brennan, John, 7, 219
Brooke, Steven, 51, 61
Brown, Vahid, 57
BRSC. See Benghazi Revolutionaries Shura Council
Brussels Airport attack, 104
Brussels suicide bombings, 3, 14, 358
Bulgarov, Rahim, 104
Bush, George W., 70, 74, 220, 350–51
business: innovation and, 24–25, 37, 39–40; risk tolerance in, 37; technology and, 18

caliphate, 163–64; amniyat and, 357; Abu Bakr al-Baghdadi as, 217–20; Inspire magazine and, 130–34, 161; ISIS and, 217–20, 248–54, 256–57, 275–76, 305–6, 311; learning from past caliphate failures, 252–54
Callimachi, Rukmini, 252
Cameron, David, 361
Campbell, John F., 342
Canada, 156; "Toronto 18" in, 125
Cannes-Torcy cell, 2
Capitol insurrection, 15
cartels, 15
cartoon controversies: Awlaki and, 139–51; Charlie Hebdo attack and, 139–41, 148–49; Comedy Central and, 146–48; at Inspire magazine, 148–51; "Jihad Jane" and, 144; Jyllands-Posten controversy, 141–45

Cayat, Elsa, 140
Central Intelligence Agency (CIA), 7, 166, 211, 447n60, 464n22
centralized organizations, 33–34
Charbonnier, Stéphane, 139–40
Charitable Society for Social Welfare, 118–19
Charlie Hebdo attack, 139–41, 148–49
Chatayev, Akhmed, 104–5
Châtelain, Aurélie, 3
Chechen female suicide attackers, 83–85, 94
chemical weapons, 377, 391, 478n13
Chertoff, Michael, 86
Chesser, Zachary, 147
China, 332–33; Tiananmen Square massacre in, 179–80
Chivvis, Christopher, 180
Christensen, Clayton, 24–25
CIA. *See* Central Intelligence Agency
Clausewitz, Carl von, 129
Clinton, William J., ("Bill"), 78, 134
Cohen, Stephen P., 336
Coll, Steve, 335
Collier, Thomas, 258–59
Combating Terrorism Center (CTC), 266, 343
Comedy Central, 146–48
Comey, James, 159–60
communication: encryption software and, 136–38, 153, 378–79; intragroup, 34–35
consensus errors, 5; on Arab Spring, 6–8; competition between al-Qaeda and ISIS, 8–10; in counterterrorism, 6–15, 398–400; lone-wolf terrorism label as, 10; organizational learning and antidote to, 10–15
"Constants on the Path of Jihad" lectures (Awlaki), 123–26
continuous learning, 30, 387, *388*
Coulibaly, Amedy, 160
counterterrorism, 219, 313, 358–59; consensus errors in, 6–15, 398–400; by

CTC, 266, 343; errors in, 6–15, 398–400; in France, 1–2; future measures for, 14–15, 389–94, 396–400; JTTF and, 109–11. *See also* United States
Couture-Rouleau, Martine, 156
Crocker, Ryan, 241
CTC. *See* Combating Terrorism Center
cultural inertia, 23–24
culture, organizational, 23–24, *31*, 36–37
cyber hackers, 125, 362, 364

Daalder, Ivo, 181
Daallo Airlines flight 159, 95–96
Dabiq magazine: Awlaki and, 153–55; ISIS and, 153–55, 270–71, 283–84, 300; Maysara and, 270–71
Dadullah, Mullah, 142
Daleel, Mohammad, 371
Daniels, Aaron Travis, 368
Daoud, Adel, 127
dawa: Arab Spring and, 167, 188–96; *hisba*, jihadism, and, 189–96; al-Qaeda and, 167, 188–96
Debray, Régis, 205
decentralized organizations, 33–34
deep fake technology, 393–94
"Defending Muslim Lands" (Azzam, A.), 51–52, 129–30
demarginalization theory, identity, 114–16
democracy, 124–25, 128
Derna, Libya, 9, 13
Derna Mujahedin Shura Council (DMSC), 214–15, 299–300
deutero-learning, 30
discontinuous learning, 387, *388*
disruptive innovation, 24–25
DMSC. *See* Derna Mujahedin Shura Council
Dolnik, Adam, 18
Domodedovo International Airport attack, 103–4
Dooley, Lawrence, 21

Dost, Abdul Rahim Muslim, 275
double agents, 92, 421n93
double-loop learning, 30
drones: AI and, 390–91; drone campaign, United States, 14; jihadism and, 14, 380, 390–92
Duka, Shain, 125
"Dust Will Never Settle Down, The" speech (Umar, Asim), 149–50
Dzhbirkhanova, Satsita, 83–85

Eastern Turkistan Islamic Movement (ETIM), 333
economics, 22–23, 90–91, 191, 294; aviation and, 72–73; ISIS's finances and, 312, 372
education, 345; Salafi jihadism and, 194–95; women and, 194–95
Egypt, 47, 130; ABM and, 177–79, 215–16; American embassy riot in, 174–76; military in, 176–79; Morsi and, 173–74, 177; Mubarak and, 44–45, 60, 166, 171; post-Mubarak Egypt and Arab Spring, 171–79; al-Qaeda and, 171–79, 215–16; Al-Rawda mosque attack in, 179; A. Zawahiri and, 171–72
Egyptian Islamic Jihad (EIJ) (Tanzim al-Jihad), 44–45, 47–48, 53–54, 59, 61; bin Laden and, 67; Muhammad Jamal Network and, 176–77, 186; A. Zawahiri and, 171–72, 325–26
Elhuzayel, Nader, 365
Emanuel African Methodist Episcopal Church, 15
Emwazi, Mohammed, 155, 311
encryption software, 136–38, 153, 378–79; virtual plotters and, 355–56
Encyclopedia of Jihad, 126
"End of Sykes-Picot, The" (video), 257
endogenous factors, 23–25
environment: organizational learning and, 37–38; technology and, 18
Erdoğan, Tayyip, 443n199

Essential Guide for Preparation, The (Sharif), 52–53
ethnic fighting groups, 332–34
ETIM. See Eastern Turkistan Islamic Movement
Europol, 162–63
exogenous factors, 22–23
experiential learning, 28
exploration/exploratory units, 37–38, 411n61

FAA. See Federal Aviation Administration
Fadhli, Muhsin al-, 210–11, 329–30
Fadl, Jamal al-, 56, 62–63, 327
Faisal, Turki al-, 49
FakeApp, 393
Faraj, Muhammad Abd al-Salam, 47–48
fard 'ayn (individual obligation), 52
far-enemy strategy: Afghan jihad and, 51–54; Battle of Jaji and birth of, 54–56; declaration of, 41–44; J. Haqqani and, 56–58; of al-Qaeda, 12, 41–45, 51–69, 381–82; religio-nationalist jihads and, 58–60; in Sudan, 60–63; from Syria, 209–13; of A. Zawahiri, 169–70
Farook, Syed, 127, 157–58
Farooqi, Amjad Hussein, 339
FATA. See Federally Administered Tribal Areas
fatwas, 62–63, 66–67; "Defending Muslim Lands," 129–30
Fawwaz, Khalid al-, 64–65
Fayfi, Jabir al-, 88
Fedayeen Saddam, 243
Federal Aviation Administration (FAA), 74, 83
Federally Administered Tribal Areas (FATA), 323
Ferizi, Ardit, 364
Fighting Vanguard, 50
Filistini, Abu Qatada al-, 223
Fishman, Brian, 231, 327–28

fitna: in Africa, 294–312; in Arabian Peninsula, 280–94; defining, 256–57; in Khorasan region, 271–80; origins of Khorasan, 274–77; al-Qaeda-ISIS relations and, 256–58, 271–313
flag carriers, 72
Focoists, 259, 260, 452n16
Foley, James, 155
Foley, Laurence, 223–24
"Fort Dix Six," 125
Fort Hood attack, 13, 107–11
Fountainhead of Jihad (Brown and Rassler), 57
France, 156; Air France flight 8969 and, 76–77; Bastille Day attack in, 4, 10, 163, 369–70; counterterrorism in, 1–2; Grand Mosque takeover and, 49; ISIS Paris attacks, 3, 16; Kassim and, 369–71; Sarcelles grocery attack in, 2; suicide bombings in, 3, 358–59
Free Syrian Army (FSA), 198
From Pablo to Osama (Kenney), 18
FSA. *See* Free Syrian Army
Furqan, Abu Mohammed al-, 270, 449n87

Gama'a al-Islamiyya, 44, 60, 175–76
Garland shooting, 156–57
Gates, Robert, 180
Gedi, Hussein Abdi, 310
Geller, Pamela, 366
"General Guidelines for Jihad" (Zawahiri, A.), 168–70
Gerges, Fawaz, 7, 53–54
Germany: Berlin Christmas market attack, 4, 156; suicide bombings in, 4; train attacks in, 4, 10, 355–56
Ghaly, Iyad Ag, 306–7
Ghlam, Sid Ahmed, 2–3, 16
GIA. *See* Armed Islamic Group
Gilani, Ali Haider, 342
Glasgow International Airport attack, 102–3

Global Call to Islamic Resistance, The (Suri, A.M.), 132–34
Global Islamic Front, 66–68
Godane, Ahmed Abdi, 266, 307–8
Grande, Ariana, 4
Grand Mosque takeover, 49
Great War of Our Time, The (Morell), 6–7
Greece, 1–2
group polarization, 114–16
groupthink, 8
GSPC. *See* Salafist Group for Preaching and Combat
Guantánamo Bay, 265, 274, 329
Guevara, Che, 260
Gülen, Fethullah, 443n199
Gulf War, 43

Hadi, Abd Rabbuh Mansour, 281
Hafez, Mohammed, 112–13
Haftar, Khalifa, 186–87, 214–15, 301
Haider, Abdul Numan, 152, 155–56
Haider, Rajib, 344–45
Haines, David, 155
Haines, Russell, 116
Hamdy, Fayda, 165
Hamid, Mustafa, 332
Hamza, Mir, 66
Hanjour, Hani, 120–21
Haq, Muhammad Zia ul-, 336–37
Haqqani, Husain, 338
Haqqani, Jalaluddin, 56–58
Haqqanis, 273–74, 322
Al Haramain Islamic Foundation, 61
Harkat-ul Jihad-al-Islami (HUJI), 338–39
Hasan, Nidal Malik, 13, 107–12, 121
Hashmi, Sohail H., 41, 48, 220
Hasib, Abdul, 277
Hassan, Basil, 376–77
Hatem, Ma'moun Abdulhamid, 282–83
Hattab, Abu Jaffar al-, 291–92
Hawley, Kip, 106, 395
Hay'at Tahrir al-Sham (HTS), 207–8

Hazaras, 272, 278

Hazimi, Ahmad al-, 290–93

Hazimi trend, 290–93, 458n134

Hazmi, Nawaf al-, 81, 119–21

Headley, David Coleman, 144, 339–40, 346–47

"Heirs of Glory, The" (video), 210

Hekmatyar, Gulbuddin, 57

Henning, Alan, 155

Herat camp, 223–24, 327

Hereafter, The, lecture series (Awlaki), 126–27

hisba, 189–96

Hizballah, 209; bin Laden and, 68–69, 326; al-Qaeda and, 326–27

Hizbul Mujahideen, 347

Hoffman, Bruce, 8, 17–18, 85, 386

homosexuality, 345–46

Horn of Africa: al-Qaeda in, 61–62, 307–12; al-Qaeda-ISIS relations in, 307–12

Houthi family, 281

How Terror Evolves (Veilleux-Lepage), 19

HTS. See Hay'at Tahrir al-Sham

Huber, George P., 22, 26–27

HUJI. See Harkat-ul Jihad-al-Islami

Human Rights Watch, 195

Hussain, Junaid, 361–67, 379

Hussein, Saddam, 43, 66, 220, 221, 225–26, 243

"I Am Proud to Be A Traitor" (Khan, S.), 130–31

Ibn Taymiyya, 62–63

ICE. See Islamic Caucasus Emirate

identity: anonymity and, 114–16; demarginalization theory, 114–16; group polarization and, 114–16; online identity formation, 114–17; SIDE and, 115–16

ideology: of Afghan jihad, 52–54; of Awlaki, 117–22; of A. Azzam, 51–52;

beliefs and, 112; extremism and, 112, 397–98; of Faraj, 47–48; jihadism and, 37, 46–50; of Muslim Brotherhood, 49–50; of Otaybi, 48–50; of Qutb, 46–47; radicalization and, 112–13, 397–98

Ignorance Is Not an Excuse in Islam (Hazimi, A.), 291

IMU. See Islamic Movement of Uzbekistan

India: Bangladesh, 343–46; Kashmir, 347–49; Mumbai attacks in, 346, 470n137. See also al-Qaeda in Indian Subcontinent

Indian Airlines Flight 814, 74–75

Indian Mujahideen, 346

individual obligation (fard 'ayn), 52

Indonesia, 125, 371–75

infighting, 61, 246, 256, 397

information: distribution, 26, 28–29; interpretation, 26, 28; propaganda and, 261–62, 269–71, 294, 307–10, 383–84, 393–94

"Initiative of Ummah" plan (Muhaysini), 246–47

Innocence of Muslims (film), 174–75

innovation: business and, 24–25, 37, 39–40; disruptive, 24–25; in encryption, 378–79; future of, 394–96; by ISIS, 355–79; organizational learning and, 18–19, 22–25, 37, 39–40, 380–81; virtual plotters and, 360–71, 376–78, 387, 393–94. See also technology

Innovator's Dilemma (Christensen), 24

Inspire magazine: Awlaki and, 129–37, 148–51; A. Azzam and, 129–30; caliphate and, 130–34, 161; cartoon controversies at, 148–51; impact of, 137, 163; "Open Source Jihad" in, 134–37, 387

International Centre for the Study of Radicalisation and Political Violence, 19 internet: cyber hackers and, 125, 362, 364; encryption software and, 136–38, 153, 378–79; evolution of, 113–14; ISIS and, 152–53; ISIS virtual plotters and, 5, 96–98, 360–71, 376–78, 387; online identity formation, 114–17; online radicalization and, 113–17

Inter-Services Intelligence agency (ISI), 335–38

intragroup communication, 34–35

Iran: Afghanistan war and, 325–31; post-9/11, 327–31; pre-9/11, 325–27; al-Qaeda and, 325–31

Iraq: AQI and, 198, 228–31; bin Laden and, 221, 253; Fedayeen Saddam and, 243; Hussein and, 43, 66, 220–21, 225–26, 243; ISI and, 231–41, 244–48, 269–71; ISIS and war in, 220–28; al-Qaeda and, 13, 220–28, 242; Syria and, 244–45; war, 13, 220–28, 243, 261; Zarqawi and, 222–28, 243. See also al-Qaeda in Iraq

Iraqi, Abu Maysara al-, 226

ISGS. See Islamic State in Greater Sahara

ISI. See Inter-Services Intelligence agency; Islamic State of Iraq

ISIS. See Islamic State

Islamic Army Shura, 61

Islamic Caucasus Emirate (ICE), 284

Islamic Emirate of Afghanistan: Afghanistan war and, 316–25; AQIS and, 340–43; al-Qaeda and, 316–25, 340–43; restoration of, 349–50; September 11, 2001, and, 316–18; Taliban and, 268, 316–25, 340–43

Islamic Movement of Uzbekistan (IMU), 276–77, 332–34, 467n79

Islamic reform movement, 43–44

Islamic Salvation Front, 59, 76

"Islamic Spring" series (al-Qaeda), 307–9

Islamic State (ISIS): ABM and, 177–79, 215–16; amn al-kharji and, 357–58, 360–71; amniyat, 356–60; Amriki and,
367–69; AQI and, 228–331; AQIM and, 297–302; Ariana Grande concert attack and, 4; in Australia, 155; authority of, 248–49; aviation and, 93–94, 96–98, 104–5, 376–78; Awlaki and attack style of, 155–62; Awlaki and call to attack by, 151–62; Abu Bakr al-Baghdadi and, 218–20, 242–46, 248–49, 254, 255–57, 261–63, 269, 272–84, 288–311, 297–98; bin Laden and, 203, 253–54; Boko Haram and, 302–7; Boudina and, 1–2, 16, 358; caliphate and, 217–20, 248–54, 256–57, 275–76, 305–6, 311; central leadership of, 277–78; contextualizing success of, 152–53; Dabiq magazine and, 153–55, 270–71, 283–84, 300; Derna, Libya, and, 9, 13; early origins of, 220–28; encryption and, 378–79; expansion of, 256–58, 294–95, 384; external operations of, 355–79; failed attacks by, 2–3, 5, 16; financial operatives of, 312, 372; founding of, 222–28; governance structure of, 251–52; growth strategy of, 9, 13; Hazimi trend and, 290–93; in Horn of Africa, 307–12; Hussain and, 361–67; IMU and, 276–77, 467n79; innovation by, 355–79; internet and, 152–53; Iraq war and, 220–28; ISI and, 231–41; Istanbul nightclub attack and, 4; IYSC and, 296–97, 300; Kassim and, 369–71; in Khorasan region, 210–11, 271–80; in Libya, 214–15, 295–97, 299–300; London Bridge attack by, 4; al-Naba newsletter by, 271, 286, 291; Nice's Bastille Day celebration attack by, 3–4, 10, 163, 369–70; in North Africa, 295–303; organizational learning by, 251–52; overview of attacks by, 3–5; Paris attacks by, 3, 16; propaganda by, 261–62, 269–71, 383–84; provinces of, 262–71; al-Qaeda's competition with,

8–10, 11, 13–14, 202–6, 215, 258–62;
al-Qaeda's differences from, 258–61;
rebranding of, 202–3; recruitment by,
296, 361–63, 368; remote-controlled
terrorism and, 5, 356–57, 371–75, 380;
rise of, 13, 217–20, 242–54; *Rumiyah*
magazine and, 154, 292, 387, 453n40;
Russia and, 274; al-Shabaab and,
308–11, 357; slogan of, 384; social
media and, 4–5, 9, 153, 158–59, 258,
296, 355–56, 364–65; in Somalia,
307–11; strategic evolution of, 383–85;
suicide bombings by, 3–4, 14; Syria
and, 154, 159, 200–204, 219, 246–52,
255–56, 383–85; Syrian Democratic
Forces and, 252; Taliban and, 272–80;
technology and, 250–51, 258;
tradecraft by, 4–5; in Tunisia, 302;
virtual plotters, 5, 96–98, 355–56,
360–71, 376–78, 387; West African,
303–7; Wilayah Khorasan and, 272–74,
277–80; Würzburg train attack by, 4,
10, 355–56; in Yemen, 281–87, 311;
Zarqawi and, 222–28; A. Zawahiri and,
233, 434n10. *See also* Awlaki, Anwar
al-; al-Qaeda-ISIS relations
Islamic State in Greater Sahara (ISGS),
306
Islamic State of Iraq (ISI): H. Ali on,
234–36; Abu Bakr al-Baghdadi and,
242–46, 269–71; Abu Umar Baghdadi
and, 232–39; bin Laden and, 233–39;
formation of, 231–34; ISIS and,
231–41; MSC and, 243–44; Muhajir's
bayah and, 232–39; al-Qaeda-ISIS
relations and, 227–28, 232–39; Sahwa
and, 236, 240–41; setbacks of, 240–41;
Syria and, 231, 240, 244–46; United
States and, 242; Zarqawi's *bayah* and,
227–28; A. Zawahiri and, 232–39,
246–48
Islamic State's West Africa Province
(ISWAP), 305

Islamic Youth Shura Council (IYSC),
296–97, 300
Istanbul nightclub attack, 4
ISWAP. *See* Islamic State's West Africa
Province
Italy, 188–89
IYSC. *See* Islamic Youth Shura Council

Jabhat al-Nusra, 2, 65
Jabhat Fatah al-Sham, 206–7
Jackson, Brian, et al., 18, 21, 30
JAD. *See* Jamaah Ansharut Daulah
jahiliya, 46, 413n18
Jaish-e-Mohammed, 275–76
Jalloh, Mohamed Bailor, 368
Jamaah Ansharut Daulah (JAD), 373
Jama'at al-Tawhid wal-Jihad (JTJ),
225–26
Jama'at Nusrat al-Islam wa-l-Muslimin
(JNIM), 306–7
Jamaat-ul-Ahrar (JuA), 276
Jarrah, Ziad, 80
Jaysh al-Fatah, 205–6
Jaysh al-Muhajireen wa-l- Ansar (JMWA),
249
Jazrawi, Khabib al-, 292–93
Jedi, Muhammad Wanndy bin Mohamed
("Wanndy"), 375
Jelassi, Anis, 196
Jenkins, Brian Michael, 71
Jihad (Faraj), 47–48
jihadism: Afghan, 51–54; AI and,
390–94; Arab Spring and, 6–8, 13,
165–215, 382; in aviation, 12–13, 19,
63–64, 70–106, 386–87; Awlaki and
evolution of, 162–64; consensus
errors on, 6–15, 398–400;
"Constraints on the Path of Jihad"
lecture on, 123–26; *dawa, hisba*, and,
189–96; defining, 1–2; drones and,
14, 380, 390–92; exploration/
exploratory units, 37–38, 411n61;
future counterterrorism measures

jihadism (*continued*)
for, 14–15, 389–94, 396–400; ideology
and, 37, 46–50; individual, 13;
membership and, 35–36;
organizational learning and, 5–6,
10–15, 17–40, 380–400; religion and,
37; religio-nationalist, 58–60; rivalry
and, 17–18; Salafi, 37, 50, 191–96, 258;
in Spain, 64–65; state actors and, 17;
technology and, 17–18, 38–40, 226,
378–79, 389–96; transnationalism and,
60–61; in Tunisia, 191–97;
understanding, 10–15; in United
Kingdom, 4, 64, 162–63, 339, 361–67,
378–79. *See also* Islamic State; Muslim
Brotherhood; al-Qaeda; *specific topics*
"Jihad Jane," 144
JMWA. *See* Jaysh al-Muhajireen wa-l- Ansar
JNIM. *See* Jama'at Nusrat al-Islam
wa-l-Muslimin
Johansson, Ulf, 142
John Paul II (Pope), 78
Joint Terrorism Task Force (JTTF), 109–11
Jones, Calvert, 33
Jones, Sally, 364–65
Jordan, 99, 102, 222–23
Joseph, Damon M., 161–62
JTJ. *See* Jama'at al-Tawhid wal-Jihad
JTTF. *See* Joint Terrorism Task Force
JuA. *See* Jamaat-ul-Ahrar
Julani, Abu Muhammad al-, 200–202, 204,
206–10, 245–46
Jund al-Islam, 179
Jund al-Sham (Soldiers of the Levant),
223–24
Jyllands-Posten controversy, 141–44, 145

Kabul, 278, 315, 337, 340–41, 349–50, 352–53
Kahane, Meir, 134
Karim, Rajib, 138
Karlov, Andrei, 212
Karoui, Nabil, 193–94
Kashif, Muhammad Jamal Abd al-Rahim
Ahmad al-, 176–77

Kashmir, India, 347–49
Kashmiri, Ilyas, 144, 339–40, 347
Kassim, Rachid, 369–71
Katibat Imam Shamil, 213
Katibat Uqba ibn Nafi, 196
Kazdaghli, Habib, 194–95
Kenney, Michael, 18
Kermiche, Adel, 370
Kettle, Louise, 21, 26
Khadim, Abdul Rauf, 277
Khalidi, Abu Hamzah al-, 325
Khalilzad, Zalmay, 350–51
Khalis, Muhammad, 57
Khan, Hafiz Saeed, 277
Khan, Reyaad, 361–63, 379
Khan, Riaz, 355–56, 371
Khan, Samir, 122, 129, 132; "I Am Proud to
Be A Traitor" by, 130–31
Khashoggi, Jamal, 56
Khayat brothers, 96–98, 376–77
Khazzani, Ayoub El, 3, 5
Khetab, Omar, 343
Khorasan region: *fitna* in, 271–80; ISIS In,
210–11, 271–80; origins of Khorasan
fitna, 274–77; al-Qaeda-ISIS relations
in, 271–80; Wilayah Khorasan and ISIS
in, 272–74, 277–80
Kilcullen, David, 259
Kirkan, Haydar, 211–12
Knights Under the Prophet's Banner
(Zawahiri, A.), 203, 204–5
knowledge: acquisition, 26, 27–28;
conversion, 29–30
Kouachi brothers, 139–41, 149, 160
KSM. *See* Mohammed, Khalid Sheikh
Kurds, 226–27, 238–39, 251–52
Kuwait, 43, 210
Kuwaiti, Abu Umar al-, 291–92

Lahouaiej-Bouhlel, Mohamed, 3–4, 10,
369–70
LaRose, Colleen ("Jihad Jane"), 144
Lashkar al-Zil (Shadow Army), 318–19,
464n13

Lashkar-e-Jhangvi (LeJ), 276
Lashkar-e-Taiba (LeT), 275–76, 338, 347–48
law: in aviation, 70–71, 83–86; Muslim, 48–49; sharia, 43–44, 131
"LAX" plot, 99–101
learning. See organizational learning
Lebanon, 68–69, 326, 381–82
LeJ. See Lashkar-e-Jhangvi
LeT. See Lashkar-e-Taiba
LGBT activists, 345–46
Libi, Abu Anas al-, 182, 184
Libi, Abu Yahya al-, 175, 267
Libi, 'Urwah al-, 182
Libya: Ansar al-Sharia Libya in, 299, 301; AQIM in, 183–87, 264–65, 297–302; Benghazi attacks in, 174–77, 185–87; bin Laden and, 181–82; DMSC and, 214–15, 299–300; Haftar and, 186–87, 214–15; ISIS in, 214–15, 295–97, 299–300; Operation Odyssey Lightning in, 295–96; post-Arab Spring, 179–87; post-Qaddafi, 298; Qaddafi and, 44–45, 60, 166, 179–87, 295–97; al-Qaeda in, 179–87, 203, 215; Sirte, 295–97; United States and, 179–81, 185–87, 295–96
Libyan Islamic Fighting Group (LIFG), 44–45, 60–61, 67, 182–83, 300–301, 437n71
Libyan National Army (LNA), 301
LIFG. See Libyan Islamic Fighting Group
"liquid bomb" plot, 85–86
LNA. See Libyan National Army
London Bridge attack, 4
lone-wolf terrorism: evolution of individual terrorism and, 162–64; individual jihadism and, 13; mislabeling ISIS attacks as, 5, 10, 11, 355–56; in United States, 15
Lutchman, Emanuel, 367–68

Mabrouk, Ahmed Salama, 172–73, 204, 207
Maghrebi, 'Abd al-Rahman al-, 330–31

Magri, Rajab, 195
Mahsum, Hassan, 333
Maizière, Thomas de, 355
Majlis Shura Mujahedin, 249
Makers of Modern Strategy (Shy and Collier), 258–59
Maktab al-Khidamat (Services Bureau) (MaK), 51–52, 54–55
Mali, 306–7
Malik, Tashfeen, 157–58
Management of Savagery (Naji), 220
Mann, Joan Ellen Cheney, 116
Mannan, Xulhaz, 345–46
Mansour, Mullah, 269, 272, 277, 320–21
Maoists, 259–60, 452n16
Maow, Abdiweli, 95
Maples, Michael D., 85
March, James, 24
Marks, Monica, 191
Marquez, Enrique, Jr., 127, 157–58
martyrdom, 81, 109–10, 240, 344, 356; Awlaki on, 124; Zarqawi and, 225–26
Marxism, 205
al-Masada, 54
Masood, Khalid, 4
al-Masra (magazine), 289–90, 292–93
Masri, Abu al-Khayr al-, 206, 332–33
Masri, Abu Ayyub al-, 330
Masri, Abu Hafs al- ("Mohammed Atef"), 79
Masri, Abu Muhammad al-, 82, 386
Massoud, Ahmad Shah, 188
Mateen, Omar, 158–60, 163, 369–70
Maududi, Sayyid Abul A'la, 413n18
Mauritani, Abu Hafs al-, 327–28
Mauritani, Younis al-, 264–65
McKenna, Katelyn, 114–15
media, 238–39; media war and propaganda, 269–71; propaganda and, 261–62, 269–71, 294, 307–10, 383–84, 393–94; al-Qaeda-ISIS relations and, 269–71. See also social media
Mehsood, Haji Mansoor, 347
Meleagrou-Hitchens, Alexander, 122

MENA region. *See* Middle East and North
    Africa region
Metrojet flight 9268, 93–95
Middle East and North Africa (MENA)
    region, 6–9, 12, 44–45. *See also specific
    countries*
Mihdhar, Khalid al-, 81, 119–20
Miles, Oliver, 181
Milestones (Qutb), 47
Milley, Mark, 352–53
Mingazov, Ravil, 467n79
minimum viable product (MVP), 39–40
Al-Misri Al-Yawm (newspaper), 178
Mohamed, Ali, 68–69
Mohammed, Khalid Sheikh (KSM), 25,
    63–64, 78–79, 80, 120; on
    September 11, 2001, 464n15
Mollah, Abdul Quader, 344–45
Morell, Michael, 6–7, 166, 185
Morsi, Mohamed, 172–74, 177
Morton, Jesse, 147
Mowafi, Ramzi, 177
MSC. *See* Mujahedin Shura Council
Mubarak, Hosni, 44–45, 60, 166, 173; fall
    of, 171
Muhajir, Abu Hamza al-: aliases of,
    447n60; bin Laden and, 233–35; death
    of, 242–43; ISI and *bayah* of, 232–39;
    al-Qaeda-ISIS relations and, 232–39,
    248; A. Zawahiri and, 232–35
Muhammad Jamal Network, 176–77, 186
Muhaysini, Abdullah Muhammad al-,
    246–47
Mujahedin Shura Council (MSC), 229–31,
    243–44
Mukalla attacks, 286–87
al-Mulathameen Brigade, 305–6
Mullins, Creighton, 112
Mumbai attacks, 346, 470n137
Mumford, Andrew, 21, 26
Mumin, Abdiqadir, 309–12
Mumuni, Fareed, 366–67
Murad, Abdul Hakim, 78–79

Musa, Zakir, 347–48
Muslim Brotherhood, 167, 173–74, 214,
    291; ideology of, 49–50; Syrian revolt
    and, 49–50; A. Zawahiri on, 171
MVP. *See* minimum viable product
Myanmar, 348–49

al-Naba (newsletter), 271, 286, 291
Nadhari, Harith al-, 185–86, 283–84
Nadler, David, *31*, 32, 387, *388*
Nagayeva, Amanat, 83–85
Naim, Bahrun, 371–75
Nairobi attack, 67–68, 326–27
Naji, Abu Bakr, 220–21
Najibullah, Mohammad, 59, 337–38
Napoule, Mandelieu-la, 1
Nasr, Sanafi al-, 211
Nasser, Gamal Abdel, 47
National Commanders Shura, 58
National Transitional Council, 187
NATO. *See* North Atlantic Treaty
    Organization
near-enemy strategy: Faraj and, 47–48;
    ideological antecedents and early
    fights in, 45–50; Otaybi and, 48–50; of
    al-Qaeda, 45–50, 61–62; Qutb and,
    46–47; religio-nationalist jihads and,
    58–60
Nemmouche, Mehdi, 358
Neumann, Peter, 112
New Zealand mosque attack, 15
Nice's Bastille Day celebrations, 3–4, 10,
    163, 369–70
Nicholson, John, 324–25, 343, 463n2
Nigeria, 305
nightclub attacks, 4, 158–59
Normark, Magnus, 19
Norris, Molly, 146–47
North African al-Qaeda-ISIS relations,
    295–303
North Atlantic Treaty Organization
    (NATO), 180–81, 277, 313, 322,
    342–43, 349

Northern Alliance, 318–19
Norway attack, 15
Nosair, El Sayyid, 134
Novi, Dian Yulia, 374
al-Nusra Front, 198, 200–210, 245

Obama, Barack, 175, 210, 349–51,
  359–60
Obama's Wars (Woodward), 382
Odierno, Ray, 242
Omar, Mullah Mohammed, 65–67, 125,
  268–69, 284–85; death of, 320;
  al-Qaeda and, 317–20
online identity formation, 114–17
online radicalization, 113–17
"Open Source Jihad" (*Inspire* magazine),
  134–37, 387
operational planning, 137–39
Operation Odyssey Lightning, 295–96
Operation Restore Hope, 43
Orakzai, Abu Saad, 277
O'Reilly, Charles, 24, 34
organizational culture, 23–24, 36–37;
  anticipatory/reactive spectrum
  of, *31*
organizational learning, 315; assessment
  of, 387, *388–89*; aviation and, 79–81, 84,
  89–91, 105–6; continuous learning
  and, 30, 387, *388*; defining, 20–22;
  discontinuous, 387, *388*; endogenous
  factors of, 23–25; exogenous factors
  of, 22–23; experiential learning and,
  28; external environment and, 37–38;
  factors influencing outcome of, 32–38;
  future of, 394–98; information
  distribution and, 26, 28–29;
  information interpretation and, 26,
  28; innovation and, 18–19, 22–25, 37,
  39–40, 380–81; intragroup
  communication and, 34–35; by ISIS,
  251–52; jihadism and, 5–6, 10–15,
  17–40, 380–400; knowledge
  acquisition and, *26*, 27–28;

membership relating to, 35–36;
  obstacles and drivers of, 22–25;
  organizational centralization and,
  33–34; organizational culture and
  learning mechanisms, 23–24, 36–37;
  organizational memory and, 29–30;
  organizational size and, 24;
  organizational structure of, 32–34;
  paradigm, 10–15; processes of, 25 *26*,
  27–30; risk tolerance and, 36–37;
  rival organizations and, 17–18; state
  actors and, 17; strategic/incremental
  spectrum of, *31*; strategic learning
  and, 165–67, 381–86; tactical
  evolution and, 386–94; technology
  and, 17, 18, 23, 38 *39*, 40, 378–79,
  380–81; types of, 30, *31*, 32, 387, *388*;
  vicarious learning and, 27; violent
  non-state actors and, 17–20, 32–40,
  250–51
Orlando, Florida nightclub attack, 4,
  158–59
Osmanov, Vadim, 104
O'Sullivan, David, 21
Otaybi, Juhayman al-, 48–50

Pakistan: Afghanistan war and, 325, 331,
  335–38; AQIS and, 334–38; bin Laden
  in, 42; FATA in, 323; Inter-Services
  Intelligence agency of, 335–38;
  Pakistani military, 335–38; al-Qaeda
  in, 14, 61, 184–85, 273–76, 316, 323–25,
  331, 335–38; Saudi-Pakistani war and,
  42; Taliban in, 330, 337–38, 340; United
  States and, 330–31
Panetta, Leon, 464n22
"parcels" plot, 88–91, 105
Paris attacks, 3, 16
Parker, Trey, 16–148
PDB. *See* Presidential Daily Brief
Pearl, Daniel, 75
Persepolis (film), 193–94
Petitjean, Abdel Malik Nabil, 370

Petraeus, David, 198–99, 241

Pham, Minh Quang, 138–39

Philippine Airlines Flight 434, 77–78

Pistole, John, 92

Pompeo, Mike, 350–51

post-Arab Spring Libya, 179–87

post-Mubarak Egypt: Arab Spring and, 171–79; "bitter harvest" and, 171–72; military in, 176–79; Morsi years in, 173–74

post-Qaddafi Libya, 298

Powell, William, 135

Presidential Daily Brief (PDB), 74, 75

propaganda: deep fake technology and, 393–94; by ISIS, 261–62, 269–71, 383–84; media war and, 269–71; by al-Qaeda, 261–62, 294, 307–10

prostitution, 192–93

Qaddafi, Muammar al-, 44–45, 60, 166, 179–87, 295–97

al-Qaeda: affiliates and branches of, 263–67, 268, 269; in Afghanistan, 14, 61, 66–67, 227–29, 253, 272–74; Afghanistan war and, 273–74, 314–54; American embassy bombings by, 45; Amman hotel attacks and, 102; Arab Spring and, 7–8, 11, 165–216; al-Asiri and, 86–93; B. Assad and, 204–5; aviation and, 70–93, 99–106; Ayeri and, 123–26; Abu Umar Baghdadi and, 232, 235–39, 254; Battle of Jaji and birth of, 54–56; Benghazi attacks and, 174–77, 185–87; Boko Haram and, 304; bylaws of, 55; cartoon controversies and, 139–51; challenges ahead for, 212–16; dawa and, 167, 188–96; drone campaign and, 14; Egypt and, 171–79, 215–16; ethnic fighting groups of, 332–34; far-enemy strategy of, 12, 41–45, 51–69, 381–82; first United States attacks by, 62–65; founding of, 42–45, 54–56; goals and mission of,

55–56; growth of, 61–63; J. Haqqani and, 56–58; hierarchy within, 55; Hizballah and, 326–27; in Horn of Africa, 61–62, 307–12; HTS and, 207–8; IMU and, 332–34; infighting within, 61; Iran and, 325–31; Iraq and, 13, 220–28, 242; ISIS's competition with, 8–11, 13–14, 202–6, 215, 258–62; ISIS's differences from, 258–61; Islamic Emirate of Afghanistan and, 316–25, 340–43; "Islamic Spring" series by, 307–9; in Italy, 188–89; Jabhat al-Nusra and, 2; leadership, before bin Laden, 46–50; learning from failures of, 252–54; in Libya, 179–87, 203, 214–15; MSC and, 229–31, 243–44; near-enemy strategy of, 45–50, 61–62; North African, 295–303; "not standing out" policy of, 14; Omar and, 317–20; in Pakistan, 14, 61, 184–85, 273–76, 316, 323–25, 331, 335–38; post-9/11 Iranian support for, 327–31; post-Arab Spring guidelines by, 168–70; pre-9/11 Iranian support for, 325–27; propaganda by, 261–62, 294, 307–10; Qutb and, 46–47; recruitment, 335–38, 382; regional branches of, 262–71; religio-nationalist jihads and, 58–60; Russia and, 212–13, 274; Salafi jihadism and, 37, 50, 191–96, 258; in Saudi Arabia, 44, 265, 289–90; Shorabak camps and, 341–44; in Somalia, 266–68, 294, 307–11; strategic evolution of, 381–82; in Sudan, 60–63, 294; in Syria, 197–215, 244–48; Taliban and, 65–66, 221, 227–29, 253, 268, 272–75, 279–80, 315–34, 339–43, 349–53; TCG and, 188–89; TIP and, 333–34; in Tunisia, 188–97; Uighurs and, 332–34; West African, 303–7; Western attacks and, 41–42, 45, 53–54, 63–69; Zarqawi and, 226–31, 253, 327; A. Zawahiri and, 168–71, 173–75,

177–78, 203, 228–39, 246–48, 268–69,
298–99, 321. *See also* bin Laden, Osama;
September 11, 2001

al-Qaeda in Arabian Peninsula (AQAP),
72, 79, 86–93, 123, 126–28, 163–64, 213;
Abu Bakr al-Baghdadi and, 282–84,
294; Benghazi attack and, 186; bin
Laden and, 287; *Charlie Hebdo* attack
and, 139–41, 148–49; future of, 293–94;
gradualism in, 285–90; *Inspire*
magazine, Awlaki, and, 129–37,
148–51; objectives and growth of,
265–66; *Sawt al-Jihad* by, 154; "war of
words" and, 282–87; in Yemen, 280–94

al-Qaeda in Indian Subcontinent (AQIS),
268–69, 469n108; Afghanistan war
and, 334–49, 352; beyond Bangladesh,
346–49; in Bangladesh, 344–46; code
of conduct, 341; Islamic Emirate of
Afghanistan and, 340–43; JNIM and,
306–7; militants of, 338–40;
operations of, 343–49; Pakistan and,
334–38; Pakistani military and
recruitment for, 335–38; United States
and, 341–42, 352; A. Zawahiri and,
334–41, 345, 348–49

al-Qaeda in Iraq (AQI), 198; ISIS and,
228–331

al-Qaeda in Islamic Maghreb (AQIM): ISIS
and, 297–302; in Libya, 183–87, 264–65,
297–302; Sahara branch of, 306–7

al-Qaeda-ISIS relations: in Africa,
294–312; AQI, Zarqawi, and, 228–331;
in Arabian Peninsula, 280–94;
competition between groups and,
8–11, 13–14, 202–6, 215, 258–62;
"divorce" of al-Qaeda and ISIS, 233,
246–48; *fitna* and, 256–58, 271–313; in
Horn of Africa, 307–12; ISI and,
227–28, 232–39; ISIS's provinces *versus*
al-Qaeda's regional branches, 262–71;
in Khorasan region, 271–80; media
and, 269–71; Muhajir's *bayah* and,

232–39, 248; North African, 295–303;
two competing jihadist models and,
258–62; West African, 303–7;
Zarqawi's *bayah* and, 227–28

al-Qaeda's Brigades of Kurdistan,
238–39

al-Qaeda senior leadership (AQSL),
184–85, 202, 238–39, 268

Qahtani, Abul Mughirah ("Abu Nabil
al-Anbari"), 296, 300–301

Qahtani, Faruq al-, 314, 316, 324

Qahtani, Muhammad al-, 49

Al-Quds Al-Arabi (newspaper), 41

Quds Force, 327–28

"Queen Alia International Airport" plot,
102

Qutb, Sayyid, 46–47

radicalization, 107–10; Awlaki and,
111–17; definition of, 112; ideology
and, 112–13, 397–98; online, 113–17;
social media and, 114–15

Rage, Ali Mahmud, 309–10

Rahami, Ahmad Khan, 160–61

Rahim, Usaamah, 366–67

Rahman, Atiyah Abd al-, 181–83, 229, 291,
322–25, 328–29

Rahman, Fazlur, 66

Rahman, Omar Abdel, 63–64, 74, 174–75

Rahmani, Jashim Uddin, 345

Ramda, Rachid, 64

Rami, Suhayb, 290

RAND Corporation, 18, 19

Ranstorp, Magnus, 19

Rassler, Don, 57

Rauf, Rashid, 85–86, 338–39

Al-Rawda mosque attack, 179

Raymi, Qasim al-, 265, 289

Reagan, Ronald, 68, 326

recruitment: AQIS, from Pakistani
military, 335–38; ISIS, 296, 361–63, 368;
al-Qaeda, 335–38, 382

Reid, Richard, 81–83

religion: afterlife and, 126–27; Islamic
    reform movement and, 43–44;
    jihadism and, 37; violence and, 49–50.
    See also ideology
religio-nationalist jihads and, 58–60
remote-controlled terrorism: drones
    and, 14, 380, 390–92; ISIS and, 5,
    356–57, 371–75, 380; in Southeast Asia,
    371–75
Ressam, Ahmed, 99–101
Revival of Islamic Heritage Society,
    191–92
Rezgui, Rezgui, 195
Rhodes, Ben, 359–60
Richardson, Bill, 318
Riedel, Bruce, 470n137
"Rising from the Dead" (video), 449n87
risk tolerance, 36–37
Riyad-us Saliheen Martyrs' Brigade,
    103–4
Rochman, Oman, 372–75
Roggio, Bill, 472n166
Roof, Dylann, 15
Rose, Flemming, 141–42
Rovio Entertainment Corporation, 39
Rumiyah magazine, 154, 292, 387, 453n40
Rumsfeld, Donald, 199–200
Russia, 83–84; Domodedovo International
    Airport attack in, 103–4; ISIS and, 274;
    al-Qaeda and, 212–13, 274; Saint
    Petersburg train attack in, 212–13;
    Syria and, 211–13
Ryan, Michael W. S., 220–21

Sadat, Anwar, 48, 171
Sahrawi, Adnan Abu Walid al-, 305–6
Sahwa (Awakening), 236, 240–41
Saint Petersburg train attack, 212–13
Salafi jihadism, 37, 50, 258; education
    and, 194–95; in Tunisia, 191–96
Salafist Group for Preaching and Combat
    (GSPC), 101–2, 264–65
Salahuddin, Syed, 347

Saleh, Ali Abdullah, 166, 281
Saleh, Munther Omar, 366–67
San Bernardino County shooting, 157–58
Sarcelles grocery attack, 2
Saud, Fahd bin Abdul Aziz al-, 42
Saudi Arabia, 65; bin Laden and, 42–44;
    al-Qaeda in, 44, 265, 289–90; Soviet
    Union and, 42
Saudi-Pakistani war, 42
Sawah, Tariq Mahmoud Ahmed al-, 82,
    386
Sawt al-Jihad (AQAP publication), 154
scanning, 27
Schön, Donald, 30
Schuringa, Jasper, 87
September 11, 2001, 12, 42, 45, 69;
    aviation and, 70–71, 73–76, 80–81;
    Awlaki and, 117, 119–21; bin Laden
    and, 316–18; Commission Report on,
    61, 68, 318, 464n15; early years of
    aviation and, 79–81; Islamic Emirate
    of Afghanistan and, 316–18; Joint
    Congressional Inquiry into, 2002,
    74–75, 119–20; KSM on, 464n15; PDB
    and, 74–75; staffing attack, 80–81
September 11, 2012, 174–77, 185–87
Services Bureau. *See* Maktab
    al-Khidamat
sexual assault, 65–66
al-Shabaab, 95–96, 266–68, 307–11, 357,
    462nn213–14
Shadow Army, 318–19, 464n13
Shafi'i, Abu Abdullah al-, 224
Shah, Mohammed Zahir, 43
Shahzad, Faisal, 136
Shahzad, Syed Saleem, 470n137
Shami, Abu Abdullah al-, 207
Shami, Abu Hammam al-, 204
Shami, Abu Maysarah al-, 154
Shane, Scott, 7
Sharaa, Farouq al-, 199
sharia law, 43–44, 131
Sharif, Sayyid Imam al-, 52–53

Shehhi, Marwan al-, 80

Sheikh, Omar Saeed, 75

Shekau, Abubakar, 303–5

Shias, 226–27, 231–32, 240, 254, 272, 278, 281–82, 383–84

Shihri, Said al-, 131–32, 265–66

ship attacks, 334–35

Shishani, Abu Umar al-, 249, 256–57

"shoe bomber," 81–83, 386, 387–88

Shoffner, Wilson, 342

Shorabak camps, 341–44

Shy, John, 258–59

Sibai, Hani al-, 64

SIDE. See social identity model of deindividuation effects

Simpson, Elton, 156–57

Sinai, Wilayat, 93–94

single-loop learning, 30

Sirte, Libya, 295–97

Sisi, Abdel Fattah el-, 178–79

social identity model of deindividuation effects (SIDE), 115–16

social media: AST and, 190–91; ISIS and, 4–5, 9, 153, 158–59, 258, 296, 355–56, 364–65; radicalization and, 114–15; Twitter and, 114, 156–57, 178, 282, 364–65; virtual plotters and, 355–56; white nationalism and, 115

social science, 113–17

Soldiers of God (Soldados de Alá), 65

Soldiers of the Levant (Jund al-Sham), 223–24

Somalia: ISIS in, 307–11; al-Qaeda in, 266–68, 294, 307–11; al-Shabaab and, 95–96, 266–68, 307–11, 357, 462nn213–14; United States and, 63

Soofi, Nadir, 156

Sotloff, Steven, 155

Southeast Asia, 371–75

South Park (television show), 146–48

Soviet Union: Afghan-Soviet war and, 42–43, 51–59, 65, 337–38; Battle of Jaji and, 54–56; Maktab al-Khidamat and

anti-Soviet mobilization, 51–52, 54–55; Saudi Arabia and, 42

Spain, 64–65

Sri Lanka, 4

Stavridis, James, 181

Stone, Matt, 146–47

Stormfront, 115

strategic/incremental spectrum, 31

strategic learning: future of evolution and, 385–86; ISIS's strategic evolution and, 383–85; organizational learning and, 165–67, 381–86; al-Qaeda's strategic evolution and, 381–82

Studies in Conflict & Terrorism (journal), 19

Sudan, 60–63, 294

Sudani, Abu Khalil al-, 342

Sufis, 194

suicide bombings: in Brussels, 3, 14, 358; in France, 3, 358–59; in Germany, 4; by Global Islamic Front, 67–68; by ISIS, 3–4, 14; by Riyad-us Saliheen Martyrs' Brigade, 103–4; Zarqawi and, 225–26. See also aviation; September 11, 2001; specific attacks

Sullivan, Justin Nojan, 367

Sunnis, 226–27, 231–32, 236, 240–41, 263

SurePayroll, 37

Suri, Abu Firas al-, 204–5

Suri, Abu Khalid al-, 65, 201–2

Suri, Abu Musab al-, 50, 64, 132–34

Suri, Yasin al-, 329

"Swiss Airport" plot, 101

"Sydney" plot, 96–98, 376–77

Syria, 65, 414n32, 414n35; Aleppo military and, 50; al-Nusra Front in, 198, 200–210, 245; Arab Spring in, 165–66, 197–209; B. Assad and, 166, 197–200, 204–5, 250; bombings and blowback in, 198–200; far-enemy strategy from, 209–13; Fighting Vanguard in, 50; fragmentation in, 206–9; FSA in, 198; HTS and, 207–8; Iraq and, 244–45; ISI and, 231, 240, 244–46; ISIS and, 154,

Syria (*continued*)
159, 200–204, 219, 246–52, 255–56, 383–85; Jaysh al-Fatah in, 205–6; Julani and, 200–202, 204, 206–10, 245–46; Khorasan group in, 210–11; Muslim Brotherhood and revolt in, 49–50; Otaybi and, 48–50; al-Qaeda in, 197–215, 244–48; al-Qaeda's Syria strategy, 204–6; Russia and, 212–13; TIP and, 205–6; United States and, 198–200; A. Zawahiri and, 203–10, 213–14, 245–47
Syrian Democratic Forces, 252
Syrian Experience, The (al-Suri, A.M.), 50

tactical evolution: in aviation, 386–87; organizational learning and, 386–94; of virtual plotters, 387, 393–94
Taha, Rifa'i Ahmad, 66, 175–76
Tajikistan, 277, 332–33
takfir, 290–92
Taliban, 124–25; in Afghanistan, 221, 227–29, 272–74, 315–34, 339, 349–54; Akhundzada and, 320–21, 352; Arab 055 Brigade and, 318–19, 464n13; background on, 65–66; bin Laden and, 316–20, 322; current allies of, 353–54; ISIS and, 272–80; Islamic Emirate of Afghanistan and, 268, 316–25, 340–43; Mansour and, 320–21; in Pakistan, 330, 337–38, 340; al-Qaeda and, 65–66, 221, 227–29, 253, 268, 272–75, 279–80, 315–34, 339–43, 349–53; United States and, 316–25, 349–54
Tanzim al-Jihad. *See* Egyptian Islamic Jihad
Tarifi, Abd-al-Aziz al-, 290, 458n128
Tartars, 62–63
Tawhid wa-l-Jihad, 222–23
Tawil, Camille, 45
TCG. *See* Tunisian Combatant Group
technology: adoption curve, 38, *39*, 40, 226, 250–51; AI and, 390–94; business

and, 18; deep fake, 393–94; drones and, 14, 380, 390–92; environment and, 18; innovation and technology "treadmill," 18–19; ISIS and, 250–51, 258; jihadism and, 17–18, 38–40, 226, 378–79, 389–96; organizational learning and, 17–18, 23, 38, *39*, 40, 378–79, 380–81; UAS, 250–51. *See also* internet
Tehran, 329–30
Tehrik-e Taliban Pakistan (TTP), 330, 340
Tenet, George, 447n60
terrorism. *See specific topics*
threat reporting, 75–76
Three Days of Terror (documentary), 140
Tiananmen Square massacre, 179–80
TIP. *See* Turkistan Islamic Party
"Toronto 18," 125
tradecraft, 4–5
train attacks, 3; in Germany, 4, 10, 355–56; Saint Petersburg train attack, 212–13
Transportation Security Administration (TSA), 71, 83, 86, 92–96, 106
transportation terrorism, 73, 311, 328, 339; ship attacks, 334–35; train attacks, 3–4, 10, 212–13, 355–56. *See also* aviation
Treasury Department, U.S., 329–30, 372–73, 375
Tree of Life synagogue, 15
triple agents, 421n93
Trump, Donald, 349–50
TSA. *See* Transportation Security Administration
Tsarnaev brothers, 135–36, 159–60, 373
TTP. *See* Tehrik-e Taliban Pakistan
Tunisi, Abu Iyadh al-, 188–89, 299
Tunisi, Abu Musab al-, 292
Tunisia, 125, 296; American embassy attack in, 188; Arab Spring in, 165–66, 188–97; AST and, 173, 185–97, 299, 438n98; Bardo National Museum

attack in, 197; Ben Ali and, 6, 189; economy in, 191; Human Rights Watch and, 195; ISIS in, 302; jihadism in, 191–97; al-Qaeda in, 188–97; Revival of Islamic Heritage Society in, 191–92; Salafi jihadism in, 191–96; turn to jihad in, 196–97; women in, 192–93

Tunisian Combatant Group (TCG), 188–89

Turkey, 212, 443n199; Atatürk Airport attack in, 104–5; Istanbul nightclub attack in, 4

Turkistani, Abdul Haq al-, 333

Turkistan Islamic Party (TIP), 205–6, 333–34

Tushman, Michael, *31*, 32, 34, 387, *388*, 411n61

Twitter, 114, 156–57, 178, 282, 364–65

UAS. *See* unmanned aerial systems

Uighurs, 332–34

Umar, Asim, 149–50, 345

Umarov, Doku, 103–4

Understanding Terrorism Innovation and Learning (Ranstorp and Normark), 19

Understanding Terrorist Innovation (Dolnik), 18

underwear bomber, 87–88, 137–38

underwear bomber 2.0, 92–93, 421n93

United Kingdom: Ariana Grande concert attack, 4; Awlaki's London years in, 121–22; Glasgow International Airport attack in, 102–3; jihadism in, 4, 64, 162–63, 339, 361–67, 378–79; "liquid bomb" plot and, 85–86; London Bridge attack in, 4; Pham and, 138–39; Westminster Bridge attack in, 4, 10

United States: Afghanistan war and, 273–74, 314–16, 349–53, 464n22, 471n152; American embassy attack in Tunisia, 188; American embassy bombings and, 45, 188; American embassy riot in Egypt, 174–76; Amriki and, 367–69; AQIS and, 341–42, 352; Awlaki in, 118–19; Benghazi attacks and, 174–77, 185–87; Biden and, 353; "Black Hawk Down" incident and, 43; Boston Marathon bombing in, 135–36, 159–60, 366, 373; Bush and, 70, 74, 220, 350–51; Capitol insurrection in, 15; CIA of, 7, 166, 211, 447n60, 464n22; drone campaign by, 14; Emanuel African Methodist Episcopal Church in, 15; Fort Hood attack in, 13, 107–11; Garland shooting in, 156–57; Global Islamic Front against, 66–68; Hussain and, 364–66; Iraq war and, 13, 220–28, 243, 261; ISI and, 242; JTTF and, 109–11; "LAX" plot and, 99–101; Libya and, 179–81, 185–87, 295–96; lone-wolf terrorism in, 15; Obama and, 175, 349–51, 359–60; Operation Restore Hope and, 43; Orlando, Florida nightclub attack in, 4, 158–59; Pakistan and, 330–31; al-Qaeda's first attacks on, 62–65; Rahami's bombs in, 160–61; Reagan and, 68, 326; San Bernardino County shooting in, 157–58; Somalia and, 63; Syria and, 198–200; Taliban and, 316–25, 349–54; Treasury Department of, 329–30, 372–73, 375; Trump and, 349–50; World Trade Center bombing in, 63–64, 134; Yemen and, 63; Zarqawi and, 227; A. Zawahiri and, 168–70. *See also* September 11, 2001

unmanned aerial systems (UAS), 250–51

Usman, Bachrumsyah Mennor, 374–75

Uzbekistan, 276–77, 332–34

Veilleux-Lepage, Yannick, 19, 72

vicarious learning, 27

Vilks, Lars, 142, 145

violent non-state actors: organizational
learning and, 17–20, 32–40, 250–51;
technology adoption curve of, 38, *39*,
40, 226, 250–51
Virgil, 295
virtual plotters, 13; of *amn al-kharji*,
360–71; Amriki, 367–69; aviation and,
96–98, 376–78; encryption software
and, 355–56; Hussain, 361–67; ISIS, 5,
96–98, 355–56, 360–71, 376–78, 387;
Kassim and, 369–71; social media and,
355–56; tactical evolution of, 387,
393–94
Vivian, Mike, 94–95
Vlahos, Michael, 259

Wadoud, Abu Musab Abdel, 287–89, 306
warships, 334–35
Waters, Nick, 478n13
Wazzani, Abu Yaman al-, 256
Weaver, Mary Anne, 222
West African al-Qaeda-ISIS relations,
303–7
Westergaard, Kurt, 142
Western attacks, 41–42, 45, 53–54, 63–69.
See also specific attacks
Westminster Bridge attack, 4, 10
white nationalism, 115
white supremacy, 15
"Why Muslims Love Death" (Awlaki),
121
Wilayah Khorasan: evaluating, 279–80;
ISIS and, 272–74, 277–80
Wilayat Sinai, 177–79
Wilson, Charlie, 57
women, 139–40; Chechen female suicide
attackers, 83–85, 94; education and,
194–95; sexual assault and, 65–66;
Tunisian, 192–93
Woodward, Bob, 382
World Trade Center: bombing, 63–64, 134;
in September 11, 2001, 73–74
Wright, David Daoud, 366

Wuhayshi, Nasir al-, 131–32, 265, 287–89
Würzburg train attack, 4, 10, 355–56

Yazdani, Mohammed Ibrahim, 369
Yemen, 86, 88, 265; AQAP in, 280–94; Arab
Spring in, 280–81; Awlaki and, 117–18,
122; civil war in, 280–81; hotel
bombings in, 43; ISIS in, 281–87, 311;
leadership in, 281; Mukalla attacks in,
286–87; A. A. Saleh and, 166, 281;
United States and, 63
Young, Nicholas, 127
Yousef, Ramzi, 63–64, 78–79, 134
Yusuf, Mohamed Mire Ali, 312

Zakaria, Fareed, 7
Zargar, Mushtaq Ahmed, 75
Zarqawi, Abu Musab al-: in Afghanistan,
222–24, 228–30; AQI and, 228–331; bin
Laden and, 226–31, 445n26; death of,
231; early life of, 222–23; Herat camp
and, 223–24; Iraq and, 222–28, 243;
ISIS and, 222–28; in Jordan, 222–23; JTJ
and, 225–26; martyrdom and, 225–26;
MSC and, 229–31; Abu Muhammad's
testimony on, 224; name changes for
network of, *225*; overview of, 222–28;
al-Qaeda and, 226–31, 253, 327; rise of,
225–28; suicide bombings and, 225–26;
United States and, 227; A. Zawahiri
and, 228–31
Zawahiri, Ayman al-, 7, 52–53, 59–60,
66–69, 143, 458n131; AQI and,
228–331; AQIM and, 298–99; AQIS and,
334–41, 345, 348–49; bin Laden and,
171–72, 203; *Bitter Harvest* by, 50, 53,
171–72; EIJ and, 171–72, 325–26;
far-enemy strategy of, 169–70;
"General Guidelines for Jihad" by,
168–70; ISI and, 232–39, 246–48; ISIS
and, 233, 434n10; "Islamic Spring"
series and, 307–9; *Knights Under the
Prophet's Banner* by, 203–5; Muhajir

and, 232–35; al-Qaeda and, 168–71, 173–75, 177–78, 203, 228–39, 246–48, 268–69, 298–99, 321; speeches by, 213–14; A. K. Suri and, 65, 201–2; Syria and, 203–10, 213–14, 245–47; Zarqawi and, 228–31

Zawahiri, Mohammed, 172, 175, 185–86
Zindani, Shaykh Abd al-Majid al-, 118–19
Zitouni, Djamel, 59–60
Zubayr, Abu al-, 266–67
Zulfiqar attack, 334–35

Columbia Studies in Terrorism and Irregular Warfare

BRUCE HOFFMAN, SERIES EDITOR

Ami Pedahzur, *The Israeli Secret Services and the Struggle Against Terrorism*

Ami Pedahzur and Arie Perliger, *Jewish Terrorism in Israel*

Lorenzo Vidino, *The New Muslim Brotherhood in the West*

Erica Chenoweth and Maria J. Stephan, *Why Civil Resistance Works: The Strategic Logic of Nonviolent Conflict*

William C. Banks, editor, *New Battlefields/Old Laws: Critical Debates on Asymmetric Warfare*

Blake W. Mobley, *Terrorism and Counterintelligence: How Terrorist Groups Elude Detection*

Jennifer Morrison Taw, *Mission Revolution: The U.S. Military and Stability Operations*

Guido W. Steinberg, *German Jihad: On the Internationalization of Islamist Terrorism*

Michael W. S. Ryan, *Decoding Al-Qaeda's Strategy: The Deep Battle Against America*

David H. Ucko and Robert Egnell, *Counterinsurgency in Crisis: Britain and the Challenges of Modern Warfare*

Bruce Hoffman and Fernando Reinares, editors, *The Evolution of the Global Terrorist Threat: From 9/11 to Osama bin Laden's Death*

Boaz Ganor, *Global Alert: The Rationality of Modern Islamist Terrorism and the Challenge to the Liberal Democratic World*

M. L. R. Smith and David Martin Jones, *The Political Impossibility of Modern Counterinsurgency: Strategic Problems, Puzzles, and Paradoxes*

Elizabeth Grimm Arsenault, *How the Gloves Came Off: Lawyers, Policy Makers, and Norms in the Debate on Torture*

Assaf Moghadam, *Nexus of Global Jihad: Understanding Cooperation Among Terrorist Actors*

Bruce Hoffman, *Inside Terrorism*, 3rd edition

Stephen Tankel, *With Us and Against Us: How America's Partners Help and Hinder the War on Terror*

Wendy Pearlman and Boaz Atzili, *Triadic Coercion: Israel's Targeting of States That Host Nonstate Actors*

Bryan C. Price, *Targeting Top Terrorists: Understanding Leadership Removal in Counterterrorism Strategy*

Mariya Y. Omelicheva and Lawrence P. Markowitz, *Webs of Corruption: Trafficking and Terrorism in Central Asia*

Aaron Y. Zelin, *Your Sons Are at Your Service: Tunisia's Missionaries of Jihad*

Lorenzo Vidino, *The Closed Circle: Joining and Leaving the Muslim Brotherhood in the West*

Erin M. Kearns and Joseph K. Young, *Tortured Logic: Why Some Americans Support the Use of Torture in Counterterrorism*

Arie Perliger, *American Zealots: Inside Right-Wing Domestic Terrorism*

Boaz Ganor, *Israel's Counterterrorism Strategy: Origins to the Present*